# Oh! 1001 Homemade Greek Recipes

*(Oh! 1001 Homemade Greek Recipes - Volume 1)*

Lisa Morales

Copyright: Published in the United States by Lisa Morales/ © LISA MORALES

Published on October, 13 2020

All rights reserved. No part of this publication may be reproduced, stored in retrieval system, copied in any form or by any means, electronic, mechanical, photocopying, recording or otherwise transmitted without written permission from the publisher. Please do not participate in or encourage piracy of this material in any way. You must not circulate this book in any format. LISA MORALES does not control or direct users' actions and is not responsible for the information or content shared, harm and/or actions of the book readers.

In accordance with the U.S. Copyright Act of 1976, the scanning, uploading and electronic sharing of any part of this book without the permission of the publisher constitute unlawful piracy and theft of the author's intellectual property. If you would like to use material from the book (other than just simply for reviewing the book), prior permission must be obtained by contacting the author at author@parsniprecipes.com

Thank you for your support of the author's rights.

# Content

## CHAPTER 1: GREEK APPETIZER RECIPES ............................................. 15

1. 7 Layer Greek Dip ................................. 15
2. Basic Hummus ....................................... 15
3. Black Bean Hummus ............................... 15
4. Creamy Yogurt Hummus ......................... 16
5. Dolmathes ............................................... 16
6. Duke ....................................................... 17
7. Easy Greek Yogurt Cucumber Sauce ...... 17
8. Easy Hummus ........................................ 18
9. Easy Roasted Red Pepper Hummus ........ 18
10. Extra Easy Hummus ............................... 18
11. Feta And Roasted Red Pepper Dip ......... 19
12. Figs Oozing With Goat Cheese ............... 19
13. Garlic Feta Dip ........................................ 19
14. Gorgonzola And Olive Stuffed Grape Leaves ............................................................. 20
15. Grape Leaves Aleppo .............................. 20
16. Grecian Cherries .................................... 21
17. Greek Dip ............................................... 21
18. Greek Feta And Olive Spread ................. 21
19. Greek Feta Hot Spread (Tyrokafteri) ..... 22
20. Greek Salad On A Stick .......................... 22
21. Greek Style Cheese Ball ......................... 22
22. Hummus I ............................................... 23
23. Hummus II .............................................. 23
24. Hummus III ............................................. 24
25. Hummus IV ............................................. 24
26. Lamb And Rice Stuffed Grape Leaves ...... 24
27. My Own Famous Stuffed Grape Leaves ... 25
28. Olivada ................................................... 26
29. Pickled Cheese ....................................... 26
30. Prawn Saganaki ..................................... 27
31. Roasted Garlic Tyrokavteri .................... 27
32. Robin's Best Ever Hummus .................... 28
33. Root Veggie Crisps With Greek Yogurt Dip 28
34. Sheila's Greek Style Avocado Dip ........... 29
35. Shrimps Saganaki (Greek Recipe) .......... 29
36. Spanakopita II ........................................ 30
37. Spiced Sweet Roasted Red Pepper Hummus 30
38. Spicy Baked Feta (Feta Psiti) ................. 31
39. Spicy Feta Dip ........................................ 31
40. Spinach Strudels .................................... 31
41. Stuffed Grape Leaves (Dolmades) ......... 32
42. Tiropetes ................................................ 33
43. Tiropitas ................................................. 33
44. Two Layer Greek Dip ............................. 34
45. Tyrokavteri ............................................. 34
46. Wendy Jae's Hummus ............................ 35
47. Zucchini Balls (Kolokythokeftedes) ....... 35
48. Zucchini And Feta Cheese Fritters (Kolokithokeftedes) .............................................. 35

## CHAPTER 2: GREEK SIDE DISH RECIPES ............................................. 36

49. Arakas Latheros (Greek Peas With Tomato And Dill) ............................................................ 36
50. Arica's Green Beans And Feta ............... 36
51. Baked Greek Fries .................................. 37
52. Briam (Greek Mixed Vegetables In Tomato Sauce) ............................................................. 37
53. Burnt Butter Rice ................................... 38
54. Classic Greek Spinach ............................ 38
55. Delicious Spinach Rice With Feta .......... 39
56. Dolmas (Stuffed Grape Leaves) ............. 39
57. Easy Marinated Vegetables .................... 40
58. Eggplant With Almonds ......................... 40
59. Gigantes (Greek Lima Beans) ................ 41
60. Grecian Green Beans In Tomato Sauce ... 41
61. Greek Garlic Lemon Potatoes ................ 42
62. Greek Potato Stew .................................. 42
63. Greek Spaghetti I ................................... 43
64. Greek Style Potatoes .............................. 43
65. Greek Vegetables ................................... 44
66. Greek Style Lemon Roasted Potatoes ..... 44
67. Greek Style Potatoes .............................. 44
68. Greeked Zucchini ................................... 45
69. Hariton's 'Famous' Vegetarian Casserole .. 45
70. Herbed Greek Roasted Potatoes With Feta Cheese ............................................................. 46
71. Melitzanes Imam .................................... 47
72. Oven Roasted Greek Potatoes ............... 47
73. Paleo Greek 'Rice' .................................. 48
74. Penne With Yogurt Tahini Sauce ........... 48
75. Sarah's Feta Rice Pilaf ............................ 49
76. Spaghetti Squash With Fire Roasted Tomatoes .......................................................... 49
77. Spinach And Rice (Spanakorizo) ........... 50

78. Yia Yia's Tzatziki Sauce .................................. 50

## CHAPTER 3: GREEK MAIN DISH RECIPES ............................................................. 51

79. A Lot More Than Plain Spinach Pie (Greek Batsaria) .................................................................. 51
80. Amazing Greek Chicken Casserole ............ 51
81. American Gyros ........................................... 52
82. Best Greek Stuffed Turkey .......................... 52
83. Big Ray's Greek Grilled Catfish Recipe ..... 53
84. Bourtheto ...................................................... 53
85. Branzino Mediterranean ............................. 54
86. Briam (Greek Baked Zucchini And Potatoes) ............................................................. 55
87. Brown Sugar Glazed Pork Chops ............... 55
88. Calamari Macaronatha ................................ 56
89. Chef John's Lamb Moussaka Burger ......... 56
90. Chef John's Spinach And Feta Pie ............. 57
91. Chicken Kokkinisto With Orzo .................. 58
92. Chicken Souvlaki Gyro Style ...................... 58
93. Chicken Souvlaki With Tzatziki Sauce ...... 59
94. Chicken With Greek Style Vegetables ....... 60
95. Chicken With Rice Pilaffe ........................... 60
96. Clams Kokkinisto ......................................... 61
97. Cousin Cosmo's Greek Chicken ................. 61
98. Easy Greek Skillet Dinner ........................... 62
99. Easy Mediterranean Fish ............................. 62
100. Feta Cheese Turkey Burgers ...................... 63
101. Garithes Yiouvetsi ....................................... 63
102. George's Greek Fried Chicken ................... 64
103. Glasser's Greek Marlin ............................... 64
104. Grecian Pork Tenderloin ............................ 65
105. Greek Burgers .............................................. 65
106. Greek Chicken (Maybe) .............................. 66
107. Greek Chicken Burgers With Feta ............ 66
108. Greek Chicken Couscous Bowl .................. 67
109. Greek Chicken Kozani ................................ 67
110. Greek Couscous ........................................... 68
111. Greek Cowboy Hash And Eggs .................. 68
112. Greek God Pasta .......................................... 69
113. Greek Grilled Cheese .................................. 70
114. Greek Island Chicken Shish Kebabs ......... 70
115. Greek Lamb Kabobs With Yogurt Mint Salsa Verde ............................................................. 71
116. Greek Lasagna .............................................. 71
117. Greek Lazy Lasagna .................................... 72
118. Greek Lemon Chicken And Potato Bake . 72
119. Greek Lemon Chicken And Potatoes ........ 73
120. Greek Meat Pasta (Makaronia Me Kima) .. 74
121. Greek Omelet With Asparagus And Feta Cheese ................................................................. 74
122. Greek Orzo With Feta ................................. 75
123. Greek Pasta With Tomatoes And White Beans ................................................................... 75
124. Greek Penne And Chicken ......................... 76
125. Greek Pizza With Spinach, Feta And Olives 76
126. Greek Pulled Pork ....................................... 77
127. Greek Ribs .................................................... 77
128. Greek Scrambled Eggs ................................ 78
129. Greek Slow Cooker Chicken ...................... 78
130. Greek Souzoukaklia ..................................... 79
131. Greek Stuffed Burgers ................................. 79
132. Greek Stuffed Peppers ................................ 80
133. Greek Stuffed Tomatoes And Peppers (Yemista) ............................................................. 80
134. Greek Stuffed Zucchini ............................... 81
135. Greek Style Garlic Chicken Breast ............ 82
136. Greek Traditional Turkey With Chestnut And Pine Nut Stuffing ....................................... 82
137. Greek Turkey Burgers ................................. 83
138. Greek Inspired Skillet Lasagna ................... 83
139. Greek Italian Fusion Beef Souvlaki Pizza . 84
140. Greek Stuffed Chicken Breasts .................. 84
141. Greek Style Stuffed Peppers ....................... 85
142. Grilled Eggplant Moussaka ........................ 86
143. Grilled Greek Chicken ................................ 86
144. Gyros Burgers .............................................. 87
145. High Seas Chicken Souvlaki ....................... 87
146. Jeanie's Falafel ............................................. 88
147. Kalamata Pork Tenderloin With Rosemary 89
148. Kefta .............................................................. 89
149. LIZZY217's Lamb Gyros ........................... 90
150. Lamb Feta Peppers ...................................... 91
151. Lamb Lover's Pilaf ...................................... 91
152. Lamb Spaghetti ............................................ 92
153. Loaded Greek Burgers ................................ 92
154. Low Carb Lamb Burgers ............................ 93
155. Margaret's Keftedes (Greek Meatballs) ..... 94
156. Maria Athans' Spinach Pie ......................... 94
157. Mediterranean Chicken With Pepperoncini And Kalamatas ................................................... 95
158. Mediterranean Roast Chicken ................... 95

159. Mediterranean Stuffed Swordfish ............... 96
160. Methi Murgh (Fenugreek Chicken) ........... 96
161. My Big Fat Greek Omelet .......................... 97
162. Octapodi Kokkinisto (Greek Octopus In Tomato Sauce) ................................................... 98
163. Pasta With Veggies In A Tahini And Yogurt Sauce ............................................................... 98
164. Pastitsio I .................................................. 99
165. Pastitsio IV ............................................... 99
166. Poulet A La Grecque ................................ 100
167. Quick And Easy Greek Spaghetti ........... 100
168. R. B. Miller's Gyro Meat .......................... 101
169. Rabbit Greek Recipe ................................ 102
170. Roasted Eggplant Pastitsio ...................... 102
171. Sharon's Scrumptious Souvlaki ............... 103
172. Spanakopita (Greek Spinach Pie) ........... 104
173. Spinach And Tomato Filo Pastry Parcels 104
174. Spinach Casserole .................................... 105
175. Spinach Pie ............................................... 105
176. Spinach Pie V ........................................... 106
177. Spinach And Cheese Pie .......................... 106
178. Spinach And Feta Pita Bake .................... 107
179. Steamed Mussels With Fennel, Tomatoes, Ouzo, And Cream ........................................... 107
180. Stuffed Bell Peppers, Greek Style ........... 108
181. Tempeh Gyros .......................................... 108
182. Traditional Gyros .................................... 109
183. Turkey Zucchini Meatballs With Roasted Pepper Dipping Sauce ................................... 110
184. Tzatziki Chicken ...................................... 110
185. Vegan Gyro Sandwich ............................. 111
186. Vegetarian Moussaka ............................... 111
187. Venison Gyros ......................................... 112

## CHAPTER 4: GREEK DESSERT RECIPES ................................................................. 113

188. Baked Halva ............................................. 113
189. Baklava I .................................................. 113
190. Christmas Baklava ................................... 114
191. Easy Baklava ............................................ 115
192. Fanouropita (Vegan Greek Raisin, Walnut, And Olive Oil Cake) ........................................ 115
193. Finikia ...................................................... 116
194. Fran's Greek Butter Cookies ................... 116
195. Frozen Greek Yogurt ............................... 117
196. Galaktoboureko ....................................... 117
197. Grecian Baklava ....................................... 118

198. Greek Baklava .......................................... 119
199. Greek Butter Cookies .............................. 119
200. Greek Egg Biscuits ................................... 120
201. Greek Lemon Cake .................................. 120
202. Greek Pumpkin Pie .................................. 121
203. Honey Pie From Sifnos ............................ 121
204. Incredible Watermelon Pie ...................... 122
205. Karithopita ............................................... 122
206. Koulourakia I ........................................... 123
207. Koulourakia II .......................................... 124
208. Kourabiedes I ........................................... 124
209. Kourabiedes II .......................................... 125
210. Kourambiathes (Greek Cookies) ............. 125
211. Kourambiedes III ..................................... 125
212. Kritika Patouthia ...................................... 126
213. Loukoumades ........................................... 126
214. Paximade .................................................. 127
215. Pistachio Hazelnut Baklava ..................... 128
216. Portokalopita (Greek Orange Phyllo Cake) 128
217. Serano Chocolate Cake ............................ 129
218. Traditional Galaktoboureko .................... 130
219. Vaselopita Greek New Years Cake ......... 131
220. Vasilopita ................................................. 131
221. Yia Yia's Baklava ..................................... 132

## CHAPTER 5: GREEK SALAD RECIPES. 133

222. Absolutely Fabulous Greek/House Dressing ......................................................... 133
223. Beet And Arugula Salad .......................... 133
224. Best Greek Quinoa Salad ........................ 134
225. Broiled Shrimp And Veggie Salad .......... 134
226. Chef Bevski's Greek Salad ...................... 135
227. Couscous Feta Salad ................................ 135
228. Darla's Italian, Greek, And Spanish Fusion Pasta Salad ..................................................... 136
229. Dianne's Lemon Feta Quinoa Salad ........ 136
230. Good For You Greek Salad ..................... 137
231. Greek Cucumber Salad ............................ 137
232. Greek Farro Salad .................................... 138
233. Greek Garbanzo Bean Salad .................... 138
234. Greek Goddess Pasta Salad ..................... 139
235. Greek Green Bean Salad With Feta And Tomatoes ........................................................ 140
236. Greek Kale Tomato Salad ........................ 140
237. Greek Lentil Salad ................................... 140
238. Greek Pasta Salad I .................................. 141

239. Greek Pasta Salad II .................................141
240. Greek Pasta Salad III ................................142
241. Greek Pasta Salad With Roasted Vegetables And Feta .................................................142
242. Greek Pasta Salad With Shrimp, Tomatoes, Zucchini, Peppers, And Feta .......................143
243. Greek Quinoa ..........................................144
244. Greek Quinoa Salad .................................144
245. Greek Rice Salad .....................................145
246. Greek Salad I ...........................................145
247. Greek Salad II ..........................................146
248. Greek Salad III .........................................146
249. Greek Salad IV .........................................146
250. Greek Salad V ..........................................147
251. Greek Salad, The Best! .............................147
252. Greek Veggie Salad ..................................148
253. Greek Veggie Salad II ...............................148
254. Greek Inspired Chicken Salad ...................149
255. Greek Style Shrimp Salad On A Bed Of Baby Spinach .................................................149
256. Greek Style Tuna Salad .............................150
257. Greek Alicious Pasta Salad .......................150
258. Heirloom Tomato Salad With Pearl Couscous .......................................................151
259. Hot Greek Salad .......................................151
260. Jen's Greek Couscous Salad .....................152
261. Light And Easy Greek Potato Salad ..........152
262. Mediterranean Greek Salad ......................153
263. Mediterranean Potato Salad .....................153
264. Melitzanosalata Agioritiki (Athenian Eggplant Salad) .............................................154
265. Oia Greek Salad .......................................154
266. Orzo With Feta, Cucumber And Tomato 154
267. Party Size Greek Couscous Salad .............155
268. Quick Greek Pasta Salad With Steak .......155
269. Quinoa Crab Salad ...................................156
270. Quinoa Greek Inspired Salad ....................157
271. Quinoa With Feta, Walnuts, And Dried Cranberries ...................................................157
272. Salad Taverna .........................................157
273. Sandy's Greek Pasta Salad ......................158
274. Stacy's Greek Inspired Tuna Salad ..........158
275. Standard Greek Salad .............................159
276. Sylvia's Easy Greek Salad ........................159
277. Tuna Souvlaki Pasta Salad .......................159

## CHAPTER 6: GREEK DINNER RECIPES ...................................................... 160

278. Andalusian Pork Tenderloin For Two .... 160
279. Apple Halibut Kabobs ............................... 161
280. Apricot Turkey Stir Fry ............................. 161
281. Artichoke & Lemon Pasta ......................... 162
282. Baked Tilapia ............................................ 162
283. Balsamic Beef Kabob Sandwiches ........... 163
284. Barbecued Lamb Chops ........................... 164
285. Barbecued Lamb Kabobs ......................... 164
286. Barley Lentil Stew .................................... 165
287. Basic Braised Lamb Shanks ..................... 165
288. Basil Marinated Fish ................................ 166
289. Beef Cabbage Rolls .................................. 166
290. Beef Squash Shish Kabobs ...................... 167
291. Beef And Potato Moussaka ..................... 167
292. Bell Peppers And Pasta ............................ 168
293. Best Leg Of Lamb .................................... 169
294. Best Paella ............................................... 169
295. Best Rosemary Chicken ........................... 170
296. Braised Lamb Shanks ............................... 170
297. Breaded Pork Chops For Two ................. 171
298. Broiled Beef Kabobs ................................ 171
299. Broiled Sirloin .......................................... 172
300. Caesar Chicken With Feta ....................... 172
301. Caesar Salmon With Roasted Tomatoes & Artichokes ................................................ 173
302. California Quinoa .................................... 173
303. Caribbean Chutney Crusted Chops ......... 174
304. Casablanca Chicken Couscous ................ 174
305. Catfish With Pecan Butter ....................... 175
306. Champion Lamb Burgers ......................... 175
307. Champion Lamb Burgers For Two ......... 176
308. Cheesy Lamb Cups .................................. 177
309. Cheesy Summer Squash Flatbreads ........ 177
310. Chicken Athena ....................................... 178
311. Chicken Sausage Gyros ........................... 178
312. Chicken Sweet Potato Stew .................... 179
313. Chicken With Couscous ........................... 179
314. Chicken With Garlic Caper Sauce ........... 180
315. Chicken With Sugar Pumpkins & Apricots 180
316. Chicken Feta Phyllo Bundles ................... 181
317. Chickpea Mint Tabbouleh ....................... 181
318. Contest Winning Greek Pizza ................. 182
319. Corsican Chicken ..................................... 182

| # | Recipe | Page |
|---|---|---|
| 320. | Couscous Chicken Supper | 183 |
| 321. | Cranberry Salsa Chicken | 183 |
| 322. | Crescent Beef Casserole | 184 |
| 323. | Curried Lamb Chops | 184 |
| 324. | Curried Lamb Stew | 185 |
| 325. | Curried Lamb Stir Fry | 186 |
| 326. | Curried Lamb And Barley Grain | 186 |
| 327. | Curried Meat Loaf | 187 |
| 328. | Curry Lamb Stir Fry | 187 |
| 329. | Dijon Leg Of Lamb | 188 |
| 330. | Easy Greek Pizza | 188 |
| 331. | Feta Shrimp With Linguine | 189 |
| 332. | Feta Steak Tacos | 189 |
| 333. | Feta Tomato Basil Fish | 190 |
| 334. | Feta Dill Chicken Burgers | 190 |
| 335. | Feta Stuffed Chicken | 191 |
| 336. | Fig & Wine Sauced Chicken Kabobs | 192 |
| 337. | Flavorful Chicken Pasta | 192 |
| 338. | Glazed Pork With Strawberry Couscous | 193 |
| 339. | Greek Chicken | 193 |
| 340. | Greek Chicken Bake | 194 |
| 341. | Greek Chicken Pasta | 195 |
| 342. | Greek Chicken Penne | 195 |
| 343. | Greek Feta Casserole | 196 |
| 344. | Greek Feta Chicken | 196 |
| 345. | Greek Flatbread Pizzas | 197 |
| 346. | Greek Garlic Chicken | 197 |
| 347. | Greek Grilled Catfish | 198 |
| 348. | Greek Isle Pizza | 198 |
| 349. | Greek Lamb Kabobs | 199 |
| 350. | Greek Lemon Chicken | 199 |
| 351. | Greek Lemon Turkey | 200 |
| 352. | Greek Meat Loaves | 200 |
| 353. | Greek Orzo Chicken | 201 |
| 354. | Greek Pasta Toss | 201 |
| 355. | Greek Pasta And Beef | 202 |
| 356. | Greek Pita Pizzas | 203 |
| 357. | Greek Pita Veggie Pizzas | 203 |
| 358. | Greek Pizza | 203 |
| 359. | Greek Pizzas | 204 |
| 360. | Greek Pizzas For Two | 205 |
| 361. | Greek Ravioli Skillet | 205 |
| 362. | Greek Salad Ravioli | 206 |
| 363. | Greek Sausage Pita Pizzas | 206 |
| 364. | Greek Shepherd's Pie | 207 |
| 365. | Greek Shrimp Orzo | 208 |
| 366. | Greek Spaghetti | 208 |
| 367. | Greek Spaghetti Squash | 209 |
| 368. | Greek Spaghetti With Chicken | 209 |
| 369. | Greek Spinach Bake | 210 |
| 370. | Greek Spinach Pizza | 210 |
| 371. | Greek Tacos | 211 |
| 372. | Greek Turkey Burgers With Spicy Yogurt Sauce | 211 |
| 373. | Greek Zucchini & Feta Bake | 212 |
| 374. | Greek Style Chicken Skewers | 212 |
| 375. | Greek Style Lemon Garlic Chicken | 213 |
| 376. | Greek Style Ravioli | 213 |
| 377. | Greek Style Ribeye Steaks | 214 |
| 378. | Grilled Artichoke Mushroom Pizza | 214 |
| 379. | Grilled Eggplant Pita Pizzas | 215 |
| 380. | Grilled Greek Fish | 215 |
| 381. | Grilled Greek Pita Pizzas | 216 |
| 382. | Grilled Halibut With Mustard Dill Sauce | 216 |
| 383. | Grilled Herbed Salmon | 217 |
| 384. | Grilled Lamb Chops | 217 |
| 385. | Grilled Lamb Kabobs | 218 |
| 386. | Grilled Peppered Ribeye Steaks | 218 |
| 387. | Grilled Rack Of Lamb | 219 |
| 388. | Grilled Ribeyes With Greek Relish | 220 |
| 389. | Grilled Salmon With Cheese Sauce | 220 |
| 390. | Grilled Salmon With Chorizo Olive Sauce | 221 |
| 391. | Grilled Salmon With Creamy Tarragon Sauce | 221 |
| 392. | Grilled Salmon With Dill Sauce | 222 |
| 393. | Grilled Steaks With Greek Relish | 222 |
| 394. | Halibut Steaks | 222 |
| 395. | Halibut With Citrus Olive Sauce | 223 |
| 396. | Hearty Paella | 223 |
| 397. | Heavenly Greek Tacos | 224 |
| 398. | Herb Marinated Lamb Chops | 225 |
| 399. | Herbed Lamb Chops | 225 |
| 400. | Herbed Lamb Kabobs | 226 |
| 401. | Herbed Portobello Pasta | 226 |
| 402. | Herbed Seafood Skewers | 227 |
| 403. | Herbed Spareribs | 228 |
| 404. | Honey Barbecued Spareribs | 228 |
| 405. | Howard's Sauerbraten | 229 |
| 406. | Individual Greek Pizzas | 229 |
| 407. | Individual Tuna Casseroles | 230 |
| 408. | Irish Stew | 230 |
| 409. | Italian Leg Of Lamb With Lemon Sauce | 231 |
| 410. | Juicy & Delicious Mixed Spice Burgers | 232 |

411. Kathy's Smoked Salmon Pizza..................232
412. Lamb Chops With Mint Stuffing.............232
413. Lamb Fajitas......................................233
414. Lamb Kabobs With Bulgur Pilaf.............233
415. Lamb Kabobs With Yogurt Sauce ..........234
416. Lamb Ratatouille ................................235
417. Lamb And Beef Kabobs .......................235
418. Lamb And Potato Stew ........................236
419. Lamb With Apricots ...........................236
420. Lamb With Raspberry Sauce .................237
421. Lamb With Spinach And Onions............237
422. Leg Of Lamb Dinner............................238
423. Lemon Chicken Skewers......................239
424. Lemon Chicken With Oregano .............240
425. Lemon Feta Chicken ..........................240
426. Lemon Garlic Chicken ........................240
427. Lemon Herb Lamb Chops ....................241
428. Lemon Turkey With Couscous Stuffing .241
429. Lemon Caper Baked Cod ....................242
430. Lemon Garlic Pork Tenderloin .............242
431. Lemon Herb Leg Of Lamb ...................243
432. Lemony Spinach Stuffed Chicken Breasts For Two .................................................243
433. Lentil Vegetable Stew ........................244
434. Linguine With Seafood Sauce .............244
435. Makeover Greek Chicken Penne...........245
436. Makeover Greek Spaghetti .................246
437. Makeover Mediterranean Chicken & Beans 246
438. Maple Salmon With Mushroom Couscous 247
439. Marinated Chicken Breasts .................247
440. Marinated Grilled Lamb......................248
441. Marinated Lamb Chops ......................248
442. Marinated Pork Loin Roast .................249
443. Marinated Pork With Caramelized Fennel 249
444. Marrakesh Chicken & Couscous .............250
445. Mediterranean Beef Toss ....................251
446. Mediterranean Chicken Bake ...............251
447. Mediterranean Chicken Orzo................252
448. Mediterranean Chicken Pasta...............252
449. Mediterranean Chicken Stew................253
450. Mediterranean Chicken Stir Fry.............253
451. Mediterranean Chicken In Creamy Herb Sauce ....................................................254
452. Mediterranean Chicken In Eggplant Sauce 255
453. Mediterranean Chicken With Spaghetti Squash .................................................. 255
454. Mediterranean Chickpeas .......................... 256
455. Mediterranean Cod................................... 256
456. Mediterranean Fettuccine.......................... 257
457. Mediterranean Fish Skillet........................ 258
458. Mediterranean One Dish Meal.................. 258
459. Mediterranean Pizza.................................. 259
460. Mediterranean Pizzas ................................ 259
461. Mediterranean Pork And Orzo ................. 259
462. Mediterranean Rack Of Lamb................... 260
463. Mediterranean Roasted Salmon ............... 260
464. Mediterranean Seafood Stew .................... 261
465. Mediterranean Shrimp 'n' Pasta............... 261
466. Mediterranean Shrimp Linguine .............. 262
467. Mediterranean Shrimp And Linguine ..... 263
468. Mediterranean Shrimp And Pasta........... 263
469. Mediterranean Tilapia ............................... 264
470. Mediterranean Turkey Potpies ................. 264
471. Mediterranean Vegetable Casserole......... 265
472. Mediterranean Style Chicken .................... 265
473. Mediterranean Style Red Snapper............ 266
474. Minted Lamb 'n' Veggie Kabobs .............. 267
475. Minted Meatballs ....................................... 267
476. Moroccan Apple Beef Stew ....................... 268
477. Moroccan Beef Kabobs.............................. 268
478. Moroccan Chicken ..................................... 269
479. Mustard Herb Grilled Tenderloin ........... 270
480. Nikki's Perfect Pastitsio............................. 270
481. North African Chicken And Rice............. 271
482. Orange Blossom Lamb............................... 271
483. Oregano Olive Chicken.............................. 272
484. Oregano Lemon Chicken........................... 272
485. Pan Fried Chicken Athena........................ 273
486. Parmesan Chicken Couscous .................... 273
487. Parmesan Chicken With Artichoke Hearts 274
488. Pasta Lamb Skillet ..................................... 274
489. Pastry Topped Salmon Casserole ............. 275
490. Pesto Veggie Pizza...................................... 276
491. Phyllo Chicken........................................... 276
492. Phyllo Chicken Potpie ............................... 277
493. Phyllo Wrapped Halibut............................ 277
494. Pineapple Beef Kabobs .............................. 278
495. Pineapple Pork Kabobs.............................. 279
496. Plum Glazed Lamb .................................... 279

497. Pork Kabobs ...................................280
498. Portobello Lamb Chops ....................280
499. Pressure Cooker Mediterranean Chicken Orzo 281
500. Pronto Pita Pizzas ...........................282
501. Quick Marinated Flank Steak ...........282
502. Rack Of Lamb ..................................282
503. Rack Of Lamb With Figs ..................283
504. Roast Lamb With Plum Sauce ..........284
505. Roast Leg Of Lamb ..........................284
506. Roast Leg Of Lamb With Rosemary ...285
507. Roast Pork With Currant Sauce .......285
508. Roast Rack Of Lamb With Herb Sauce ..286
509. Rocky Mountain Grill .......................286
510. Rosemary Leg Of Lamb ....................287
511. Rosemary Seasoned Lamb ...............287
512. Rosemary Rubbed Lamb Chops .......288
513. Rosemary Skewered Artichoke Chicken .288
514. Rosemary Thyme Lamb Chops ........289
515. Rubbed Sage Lamb Chops ...............289
516. Rustic Phyllo Vegetable Pie .............290
517. Salmon Couscous Supper .................291
518. Salmon Spirals With Cucumber Sauce ....291
519. Salmon And Asparagus In Phyllo .....292
520. Salmon With Cucumber Dill Sauce ..292
521. Sausage & Feta Stuffed Tomatoes ....293
522. Sausage Florentine Potpie ...............294
523. Sausage Marinara Over Pasta ..........294
524. Savory Marinated Flank Steak .........295
525. Sea Bass With Shrimp And Tomatoes ....295
526. Shrimp Orzo With Feta ...................296
527. Shrimp Scampi With Lemon Couscous ..296
528. Shrimp Stew ....................................297
529. Shrimp And Feta Linguine ...............297
530. Simple Mediterranean Chicken ........298
531. Sirloin Squash Shish Kabobs ...........298
532. Skewered Lamb With Blackberry Balsamic Glaze ................................................299
533. Skillet Lamb Chops ..........................299
534. Slow Cook Lamb Chops ...................300
535. Slow Cooked Chicken Marbella ........300
536. Slow Cooked Lamb Chops ...............301
537. Slow Cooked Lemon Chicken ..........301
538. Slow Cooked Moroccan Chicken ......302
539. Southwestern Lamb Chops ..............303
540. Spaghetti Squash With Balsamic Vegetables And Toasted Pine Nuts ...........................303
541. Spanako Pasta .................................304
542. Speedy Hummus Pizza .....................304
543. Spiced Lamb Stew With Apricots ...........305
544. Spicy Chicken Breasts .....................305
545. Spicy Lamb Kabobs .........................306
546. Spicy Shrimp Fettuccine ..................307
547. Spiedis .............................................307
548. Spinach & Chicken Phyllo Pie ..........308
549. Spinach Beef Biscuit Bake ...............308
550. Spinach Cheese Phyllo Squares .......309
551. Spinach Feta Turnovers ...................310
552. Spinach Ricotta Tart ........................310
553. Spinach Tomato Linguine ................311
554. Spinach And Feta Flank Steak .........311
555. Spinach Stuffed Lamb .....................312
556. Spinach Tomato Phyllo Bake ...........312
557. Spit Roasted Lemon Rosemary Chicken 313
558. Spring Lamb Supper ........................314
559. Stuffed Sweet Peppers .....................314
560. Stuffed Olive Cod ............................315
561. Sun Dried Tomato Chicken ..............315
562. Sunday Paella ..................................316
563. Supreme Kabobs .............................316
564. Sweet 'n' Zesty Chicken Breasts ......317
565. Swordfish Shrimp Kabobs ...............317
566. Swordfish With Fennel And Tomatoes ..318
567. Swordfish With Sauteed Vegetables ...319
568. Tangy Lamb Tagine .........................319
569. Tangy Lemon Catfish ......................320
570. Tapenade Stuffed Chicken Breasts ........320
571. Tarragon Chicken Kiev ....................321
572. Tasty Shrimp Penne ........................322
573. Tender Lamb With Mint Salsa .........322
574. Tex Mex Chicken Starter .................323
575. Thick Beef Stew ..............................323
576. Tomato Dill Shrimp Stew ................324
577. Tomato Poached Halibut .................324
578. Traditional Lamb Stew ....................325
579. Tropical Lime Chicken ....................325
580. Tuna With Tuscan White Bean Salad ....326
581. Turkey Gyro Pizza ...........................327
582. Turkey Spinach Meat Loaf ...............327
583. Tuscan Roast Pork Tenderloin .........328
584. Vegetable Stew ................................328
585. Wyoming Lamb Stew ......................329

## CHAPTER 7: GREEK VEGETARIAN

# RECIPES .................................................. 329

586. A Touch Of Greek Dip ......................... 329
587. Almond "Feta" With Herb Oil ............... 330
588. Anytime Frittata .................................. 330
589. Apple Goat Cheese Bruschetta ............ 331
590. Around The World Tapenade ............... 331
591. Artichoke Tomato Salad ...................... 332
592. Artichokes With Lemon Mint Dressing .. 332
593. Asparagus Cheese Bundles ................. 333
594. Asparagus Phyllo Bake ........................ 333
595. Asparagus Spanakopita ....................... 334
596. Asparagus Fennel Pasta Salad ............ 334
597. Balsamic Cucumber Salad ................... 335
598. Bean Spread On Pita Crackers ............ 335
599. Berries In A Nest ................................. 336
600. Black Bean Pineapple Salad ................ 337
601. Blarney Stone Appetizer ...................... 337
602. Bow Tie & Spinach Salad ..................... 338
603. Brown Rice, Tomato & Basil Salad ....... 338
604. Bulgur Salad In Lemon Baskets ........... 339
605. Bulgur Wheat Salad ............................. 339
606. Buttercup Squash Coffee Cake ............ 340
607. Calico Cranberry Couscous Salad ........ 341
608. Cashew & Olive Feta Cheese Dip ........ 341
609. Cheese Boereg ................................... 342
610. Cheese Spread Pinecone .................... 342
611. Cheese Tortellini Salad ....................... 343
612. Cheese Stuffed Cherry Tomatoes ........ 343
613. Cheese Stuffed Sweet Onions ............. 343
614. Cheesy Chive Potatoes ....................... 344
615. Cheesy Herbed Eggs ........................... 344
616. Chickpea & Feta Salad ........................ 345
617. Chickpea Cucumber Salad ................... 345
618. Chickpea Patties With Yogurt Sauce .... 346
619. Cilantro Couscous Salad ..................... 346
620. Citrus Spiced Olives ............................ 347
621. Classic Hummus .................................. 347
622. Cold Bean Salad .................................. 348
623. Colorful Garbanzo Bean Salad ............. 348
624. Colorful Greek Orzo Salad ................... 349
625. Confetti Couscous ............................... 349
626. Cool Couscous Salad .......................... 350
627. Cool Tomato Soup ............................... 350
628. Couscous Salad .................................. 351
629. Couscous Salad With Olives & Raisins .. 351
630. Couscous Tabbouleh With Fresh Mint &

Feta 352
631. Couscous With Feta 'n' Tomatoes ........... 352
632. Couscous With Grilled Vegetables ......... 353
633. Couscous Stuffed Mushrooms ................ 353
634. Cranberry Couscous Salad .................... 354
635. Cranberry Feta Cheesecake .................. 355
636. Cranberry Brie Phyllo Triangles .............. 355
637. Creamy Basil Feta Spread ..................... 356
638. Creamy Feta Spinach Dip ...................... 356
639. Cucumber Couscous Salad ................... 357
640. Curried Couscous ................................. 357
641. Dad's Greek Salad ................................ 358
642. Dilled Potatoes With Feta ...................... 358
643. Dilled Potatoes With Feta For Two ........ 359
644. Easy Colorful Bean Salad ...................... 359
645. Easy Garden Tomatoes ......................... 359
646. Eggplant Dip ......................................... 360
647. Fast Marinated Tomatoes ...................... 360
648. Favorite Mediterranean Salad ................ 361
649. Favorite Raspberry Tossed Salad .......... 361
650. Feta 'n' Chive Muffins ............................ 362
651. Feta Artichoke Bites .............................. 362
652. Feta Bruschetta .................................... 363
653. Feta Cheese Mashed Potatoes .............. 363
654. Feta Cucumber Salad ............................ 363
655. Feta Frittata ......................................... 364
656. Feta Olive Dip ...................................... 364
657. Feta Pitas ............................................ 365
658. Feta Romaine Salad .............................. 365
659. Feta Scrambled Egg Wraps ................... 365
660. Feta Spinach Pizza ............................... 366
661. Feta Olive Romaine Salad ..................... 366
662. Feta Spinach Melts ............................... 367
663. Feta Topped Asparagus ......................... 367
664. Flavorful Rice Salad .............................. 368
665. Fresh Greek Garden Salad .................... 368
666. Fresh Tomato & Cucumber Salad ........... 369
667. Fresh As Summer Salad ........................ 369
668. Fruit 'N' Feta Tossed Salad ................... 370
669. Fruited Feta Spread .............................. 370
670. Fruity Greek Salad ................................ 370
671. Garbanzo Bean Pitas ............................ 371
672. Garbanzo Bean Salad With Citrusy
Dressing ................................................... 371
673. Garbanzo Beans 'N' Rice ...................... 372
674. Garden Barley Salad ............................. 372
675. Garden Cucumber Salad ....................... 373

| # | Entry | Page |
|---|---|---|
| 676. | Garden Herb Rice Salad | 373 |
| 677. | Garden Vegetable Pasta Salad | 374 |
| 678. | Garlic Artichoke Dip | 374 |
| 679. | Garlic Cucumber Dip | 375 |
| 680. | Garlic Feta Spread | 375 |
| 681. | Garlic Garbanzo Bean Spread | 375 |
| 682. | Garlic Lemon Dip | 376 |
| 683. | Garlic And Artichoke Roasted Potatoes | 376 |
| 684. | Garlic Herb Bagel Spread | 377 |
| 685. | Garlic Kissed Tomatoes | 377 |
| 686. | Garlic Sesame Pita Chips | 378 |
| 687. | Garlicky Kale | 378 |
| 688. | Goat Cheese 'n' Veggie Quesadillas | 378 |
| 689. | Goat Cheese Wontons | 379 |
| 690. | Goat Cheese, Pear & Onion Pizza | 379 |
| 691. | Golden Greek Lemon Potatoes | 380 |
| 692. | Gourmet Garden Tomato Salad | 381 |
| 693. | Gourmet Grilled Cheese Sandwich | 381 |
| 694. | Grecian Garden Salad | 381 |
| 695. | Grecian Potato Cups | 382 |
| 696. | Greek Bruschetta | 383 |
| 697. | Greek Cheese Balls | 383 |
| 698. | Greek Chickpea & Walnut Burgers | 383 |
| 699. | Greek Country Salad | 384 |
| 700. | Greek Couscous Salad | 385 |
| 701. | Greek Crostini | 385 |
| 702. | Greek Deviled Eggs | 386 |
| 703. | Greek Feta Salad | 386 |
| 704. | Greek Garden Salad | 386 |
| 705. | Greek Garden Salad With Dressing | 387 |
| 706. | Greek Green Beans | 387 |
| 707. | Greek Hero | 388 |
| 708. | Greek Lettuce Salad | 388 |
| 709. | Greek Loaf | 389 |
| 710. | Greek Macaroni Salad | 389 |
| 711. | Greek Olive Bread | 390 |
| 712. | Greek Orzo Salad | 390 |
| 713. | Greek Orzo And Broccoli | 391 |
| 714. | Greek Pasta | 391 |
| 715. | Greek Pasta Salad | 392 |
| 716. | Greek Pinwheels | 392 |
| 717. | Greek Potato Salad | 393 |
| 718. | Greek Romaine Salad | 393 |
| 719. | Greek Salad | 394 |
| 720. | Greek Salad Pitas | 394 |
| 721. | Greek Salad With Bean Spread Pitas | 395 |
| 722. | Greek Salad With Greek Artisan's Olives | 395 |
| 723. | Greek Salad With Green Grapes | 396 |
| 724. | Greek Salad With Lemon Dressing | 396 |
| 725. | Greek Salad With Orzo | 397 |
| 726. | Greek Salsa | 397 |
| 727. | Greek Sandwich Bites | 397 |
| 728. | Greek Side Salad | 398 |
| 729. | Greek Stuffed Mini Potatoes | 398 |
| 730. | Greek Three Bean Salad | 399 |
| 731. | Greek Tomato Salad | 399 |
| 732. | Greek Tomatoes | 400 |
| 733. | Greek Tortellini Salad | 400 |
| 734. | Greek Tossed Salad | 401 |
| 735. | Greek Vegetable Salad | 401 |
| 736. | Greek Veggie Omelet | 401 |
| 737. | Greek Veggie Tartlets | 402 |
| 738. | Greek Inspired Quinoa Salad | 402 |
| 739. | Greek Style Green Beans | 403 |
| 740. | Greek Style Pizza | 403 |
| 741. | Greek Style Squash | 404 |
| 742. | Green Garden Salad | 405 |
| 743. | Grilled Dijon Summer Squash | 405 |
| 744. | Grilled Eggplant Sandwiches | 406 |
| 745. | Grilled Eggplant With Feta Relish | 406 |
| 746. | Grilled Feta Quesadillas | 407 |
| 747. | Grilled Greek Crostini Topping | 407 |
| 748. | Grilled Greek Potato Salad | 408 |
| 749. | Grilled Greek Style Zucchini | 408 |
| 750. | Grilled Lebanese Salad | 409 |
| 751. | Grilled Mediterranean Eggplant & Tomato Salad | 409 |
| 752. | Grilled Pizza With Greens & Tomatoes | 410 |
| 753. | Grilled Vegetable Orzo Salad | 411 |
| 754. | Grilled Veggie Sandwiches | 411 |
| 755. | Grilled Veggie Wraps | 412 |
| 756. | Healthy Zucchini Pancakes | 413 |
| 757. | Hearty Tabbouleh | 413 |
| 758. | Herbed Feta Dip | 414 |
| 759. | Herbed Tomato Cucumber Salad | 414 |
| 760. | Italian Tomato Cucumber Salad | 414 |
| 761. | Jalapeno Hummus | 415 |
| 762. | Kalamata Cheesecake Appetizer | 415 |
| 763. | Lavender & Olive Focaccia | 416 |
| 764. | Layered Artichoke Cheese Spread | 417 |
| 765. | Layered Mediterranean Dip | 417 |
| 766. | Layered Mediterranean Dip With Pita Chips | 418 |

767. Leeks In Mustard Sauce ..........................418
768. Lemon Dill Couscous................................419
769. Lemon Mint Beans..................................419
770. Lemon Parmesan Orzo ............................419
771. Lemon Feta Angel Hair ...........................420
772. Lemon Garlic Spread................................420
773. Lemon Herb Olives With Goat Cheese..421
774. Lemony Almond Feta Green Beans ........421
775. Lemony Fennel Olives .............................422
776. Lemony Tossed Salad...............................422
777. Lentil Bulgur Salad..................................422
778. Lick The Bowl Clean Hummus ................423
779. Lime Cilantro Hummus ...........................424
780. Mandarin Couscous Salad........................424
781. Marinated Cheese Topped Salad .............424
782. Marinated Cucumbers .............................425
783. Marvelous Mediterranean Vegetables......426
784. Mediterranean Apricot Phyllo Bites.........426
785. Mediterranean Artichoke And Red Pepper Roll Ups .........................................................427
786. Mediterranean Broccoli Slaw....................427
787. Mediterranean Bulgur Bowl ....................428
788. Mediterranean Bulgur Salad ....................428
789. Mediterranean Dip With Garlic Pita Chips 429
790. Mediterranean Dip With Pita Chips ........429
791. Mediterranean Green Salad .....................430
792. Mediterranean Layered Dip.....................430
793. Mediterranean Lentil Salad .....................431
794. Mediterranean Mashed Potatoes .............431
795. Mediterranean Omelet.............................432
796. Mediterranean Orange Salad ...................432
797. Mediterranean Palmiers...........................433
798. Mediterranean Pasta Salad ......................433
799. Mediterranean Pastry Pinwheels...............434
800. Mediterranean Polenta Cups ...................434
801. Mediterranean Romaine Salad ................435
802. Mediterranean Salad Sandwiches.............435
803. Mediterranean Salsa ................................436
804. Mediterranean Vegetable Pitas...436
805. Mexican Salsa Dip ...................................437
806. Millet Stuffed Red Peppers......................437
807. Mimi's Lentil Medley ..............................438
808. Mini Feta Pizzas......................................438
809. Mint Dressing For Fruit...........................439
810. Minted Cucumber Salad ..........................439
811. Minted Potato Salad................................440

812. Minty Beet Carrot Salad ..........................440
813. Minty Orzo And Peas...............................441
814. Minty Rice Salad .....................................441
815. Mixed Greens And Apple Salad .............442
816. Moroccan Chickpea Stew.........................442
817. Moroccan Stuffed Mushrooms ...............443
818. Moroccan Tapenade.................................443
819. Mushroom Caponata ...............................444
820. Mushroom Polenta Appetizers ...............444
821. Navy Bean Tossed Salad .........................445
822. Onion Bulgur Salad .................................445
823. Onion Tart...............................................446
824. Onion Trio Salad .....................................446
825. Onions And Spice, Parsley And Rice......447
826. Orange 'n' Red Onion Salad ....................447
827. Orange Couscous .....................................448
828. Orange Streusel Muffins..........................448
829. Orzo Vegetable Salad...............................449
830. Orzo With Feta And Almonds ...............449
831. Orzo With Spinach And Pine Nuts ........450
832. Orzo With Zucchini And Feta................450
833. Oven Roasted Veggies..............................451
834. Parsley Tabbouleh ...................................451
835. Pasta With Tomatoes And White Beans 452
836. Peachy Tossed Salad With Poppy Seed Dressing...........................................................452
837. Pecan Pear Tossed Salad .........................453
838. Penne From Heaven ................................453
839. Penne With Caramelized Onions ............454
840. Pepperoncini Pasta Salad.........................454
841. Persimmon Breakfast Parfaits .................455
842. Pesto Buttermilk Dressing .......................455
843. Pesto Egg Wraps .....................................455
844. Pesto Pita Appetizers ...............................456
845. Picnic Salad Skewers ...............................456
846. Picnic Vegetable Salad .............................457
847. Portobello Pockets ...................................457
848. Potato Tossed Salad .................................458
849. Pressure Cooker Frittata Provencal.........458
850. Pumpkin Hummus ...................................459
851. Quick Colorful Tossed Salad....................460
852. Quick Couscous Salad .............................460
853. Quick Garlic Bean Dip ............................461
854. Quick Greek Pasta Salad .........................461
855. Quinoa Tabbouleh ...................................461
856. Quinoa Tabbouleh Salad .........................462
857. Red Pepper & Feta Dip............................462

858. Red Potato Salad With Lemony Vinaigrette 463
859. Rice And Mushrooms .................................463
860. Rice With Lemon And Spinach .................464
861. Roasted Asparagus With Feta ...................464
862. Roasted Garlic White Bean Dip ................465
863. Roasted Goat Cheese With Garlic ............465
864. Roasted Parmesan Green Beans................466
865. Roasted Potato Salad With Feta ...............466
866. Roasted Red Pepper Bread.........................467
867. Roasted Red Pepper Hummus ..................467
868. Roasted Red Pepper Spread ......................468
869. Roasted Sweet Potato & Chickpea Pitas. 468
870. Roasted Veggie Orzo ..................................469
871. Rosemary Beet Phyllo Bites......................469
872. Rosemary Goat Cheese Bites ....................470
873. Salsa Bean Dip ............................................470
874. Saucy Portobello Pitas ...............................471
875. Savory Marinated Mushroom Salad .........471
876. Savory Omelet Cups ..................................472
877. Seasoned Asparagus...................................473
878. Seasoned Couscous ....................................473
879. Seven Layer Mediterranean Dip ...............473
880. Slim Greek Deviled Eggs..........................474
881. Smoky Cauliflower ....................................474
882. Spanakopita Bites .......................................475
883. Spanakopita Pinwheels ..............................475
884. Spicy Hummus............................................476
885. Spinach Feta Croissants .............................476
886. Spinach Feta Croissants For 2 ..................476
887. Spinach Flatbreads .....................................477
888. Spinach Mushroom Salad ..........................477
889. Spinach Orzo Salad....................................478
890. Spinach Penne Salad ..................................478
891. Spinach Phyllo Bundles .............................479
892. Spinach Phyllo Triangles...........................479
893. Spring Greek Pasta Salad ..........................480
894. Stovetop Orzo Medley ...............................480
895. Strawberry Orange Phyllo Cups ...............481
896. Stuffed Phyllo Pastries...............................481
897. Stuffed Red Peppers ..................................482
898. Summer Garden Couscous Salad .............483
899. Summer Garden Salad ...............................483
900. Summer Orzo ..............................................484
901. Summer Squash & Tomato Medley..........484
902. Summer Squash And Tomato Side Dish With Feta.............................................................485
903. Summer Fresh Quinoa Salad....................486
904. Sun Dried Tomato Goat Cheese Spread 486
905. Sun Dried Tomato Hummus ....................486
906. Sweet Onion, Tomato & Cuke Salad ......487
907. Sweet Potato Hummus..............................487
908. Tabbouleh Salad.........................................488
909. Tabouli Primavera .....................................488
910. Tahini Roasted Vegetables .......................489
911. Tangerine Tabbouleh ................................489
912. Tangy Caesar Salad ...................................490
913. Tangy Feta Herb Dip .................................490
914. Tangy Marinated Vegetables....................491
915. Terrific Tomato Tart..................................491
916. Three Cheese Tomato Garlic Bread........492
917. Thyme 'n' Thyme Again Salad Dressing. 492
918. Tomato Artichoke Salad ...........................493
919. Tomato Couscous Soup ............................493
920. Tomato Feta Salad.....................................494
921. Tomato Pea Couscous...............................494
922. Tomato Rosemary Hummus ....................495
923. Tomato Zucchini Platter ...........................495
924. Tomato Green Bean Salad .......................496
925. Tomatoes With Feta Cheese.....................496
926. Tossed Greek Salad ...................................496
927. Traditional Greek Salad ............................497
928. Tuscan Bean And Olive Spread ...............497
929. Tzatziki Potato Salad.................................498
930. Vegetarian Spinach Curry.........................498
931. Veggie Couscous Quiche ..........................499
932. Viva Panzanella..........................................499
933. Walnut Balls................................................500
934. Walnut Cheese Spinach Salad..................501
935. Warm Feta Cheese Dip .............................501
936. Warm Mushroom Salad.............................501
937. Watermelon Cups.......................................502
938. White Bean 'n' Olive Toasts .....................502
939. Whole Wheat Orzo Salad .........................503
940. Whole Wheat Pita Bread ..........................503
941. Witch's Caviar............................................504
942. Witches' Hats..............................................504
943. Zesty Greek Salad......................................505
944. Zesty Veggie Pitas .....................................505
945. Zucchini & Cheese Roulades ...................506
946. Zucchini Carrot Couscous .......................506

**CHAPTER 8: AWESOME GREEK CUISINE RECIPES .................................................507**

947. Ali's Greek Tortellini Salad .......................... 507
948. Amazing Greek Pasta .................................. 507
949. Avgolemono Soup ....................................... 508
950. Avocado Tzatziki ......................................... 508
951. Cephalonian Meat Pie ................................. 509
952. Chef John's Tzatziki Sauce ......................... 510
953. Cucumber Gyro Sauce ................................ 510
954. Fasolatha .................................................... 511
955. Fijian Dhal Soup ......................................... 511
956. French Greek Salad Dressing .................... 512
957. Greek Avgolemono Chicken Soup ............ 512
958. Greek Brown Rice Salad ............................. 513
959. Greek Chicken Stew (Stifado) ................... 513
960. Greek Cream Cheese Stuffed Chicken .... 514
961. Greek Lamb Stew ....................................... 514
962. Greek Lamb Feta Burgers With Cucumber Sauce .......................................................... 515
963. Greek Lemon Chicken Soup ..................... 516
964. Greek Lentil Soup (Fakes) ......................... 516
965. Greek Saganaki ........................................... 517
966. Greek Sausage: Sheftalia ............................ 517
967. Greek Seasoning ......................................... 518
968. Greek Seasoning Blend .............................. 518
969. Greek Shrimp Dish From Santorini ......... 519
970. Greek Spice Rub ......................................... 519
971. Greek Squid (Soupies) ............................... 519
972. Greek Stew .................................................. 520
973. Greek Style Beef Stew ................................ 520
974. Greek Tzatziki ............................................. 521
975. Greek Inspired Lemon Chicken Soup ..... 522
976. Homemade Spanakopita ........................... 522
977. Instant Pot® Greek Chicken ..................... 523
978. Kagianas (Greek Eggs And Tomato) ....... 523
979. Kreatopita Argostoli .................................. 524
980. Lamb Stew With Green Beans ................. 525
981. Lemon Chicken Orzo Soup ...................... 525
982. Lemon And Potato Soup .......................... 526
983. Mediterranean Orzo Spinach Salad ......... 526
984. Molly's Mouthwatering Tzatziki Cucumber Sauce .......................................................... 527
985. Orzo Pasta Salad ........................................ 527
986. Orzo And Tomato Salad With Feta Cheese 528
987. Peppy's Pita Bread ..................................... 528
988. Raw Hummus ............................................. 529
989. Real Hummus ............................................ 529
990. Roasted Garlic Tzatziki ............................. 529
991. Saffron Mussel Bisque ............................... 530
992. Traditional Pita Breads ............................. 530
993. Tzatziki A Greek Mother's Sauce ............. 531
994. Tzatziki II .................................................... 531
995. Tzatziki Sauce ............................................. 532
996. Tzatziki Sauce (Yogurt And Cucumber Dip) 532
997. Tzatziki Sauce I .......................................... 533
998. Tzatziki Sauce II ......................................... 533
999. Tzatziki VII ................................................. 533
1000. Vasilopita (Orange Sweet Bread) ............ 534
1001. Whole Wheat Rigatoni And Cauliflower, Wilted Arugula, Feta & Olives ........................... 535

**INDEX** .................................................. **536**
**CONCLUSION** ................................... **543**

# Chapter 1: Greek Appetizer Recipes

***

## 1. 7 Layer Greek Dip

*Serving: 12 | Prep: 15mins | Cook: | Ready in:*

### Ingredients

- 1 (10 ounce) container hummus spread
- 1 teaspoon Greek seasoning
- 5 ounces feta cheese
- 3 ounces Kalamata olives, pitted and sliced
- 1 large English cucumber, diced
- 1 pound tzatziki sauce
- 1 pint grape tomatoes, diced
- 3 green onions, chopped
- 2 (8 ounce) packages pita chips

### Direction

- Prepare a pie dish then scatter the hummus in it and dash with Greek seasoning. Put feta cheese on top of hummus then scatter, making it into small portions. Then scatter the diced cucumber and Kalamata olives on top. Next is put the tzatziki sauce on top and gently spread. Put green onions and tomatoes on top. Lastly, let it chill until serving time.

### Nutrition Information

- Calories: 314 calories;
- Total Fat: 43.7
- Sodium: 599
- Total Carbohydrate: 33.7
- Cholesterol: 11
- Protein: 9.4

## 2. Basic Hummus

*Serving: 12 | Prep: 15mins | Cook: 5mins | Ready in:*

### Ingredients

- 2 cloves garlic, peeled and crushed
- 2 tablespoons olive oil
- 1 (15 ounce) can garbanzo beans, drained, liquid reserved
- 1 tablespoon sesame seeds
- salt and pepper to taste

### Direction

- On medium heat, cook and stir the garlic in olive oil for about 3 minutes in a medium pan, until it becomes soft.
- In a food processor or blender, put the garbanzo beans and around 1 teaspoon of reserved liquid, then blend until it becomes smooth. Stir in the pepper, salt, sesame seeds and garlic and blend to your preferred consistency, putting more reserved garbanzo bean liquid as desired. Put in the refrigerator to chill until ready to serve.

### Nutrition Information

- Calories: 53 calories;
- Total Fat: 2.9
- Sodium: 70
- Total Carbohydrate: 5.6
- Cholesterol: 0
- Protein: 1.3

## 3. Black Bean Hummus

*Serving: 8 | Prep: 5mins | Cook: | Ready in:*

### Ingredients

- 1 clove garlic
- 1 (15 ounce) can black beans; drain and reserve liquid
- 2 tablespoons lemon juice
- 1 1/2 tablespoons tahini
- 3/4 teaspoon ground cumin
- 1/2 teaspoon salt
- 1/4 teaspoon cayenne pepper
- 1/4 teaspoon paprika
- 10 Greek olives

### Direction

- In the bowl of a food processor, mince the garlic. Stir in the 1/8 teaspoon of cayenne pepper, 1/2 teaspoon of salt, 1/2 teaspoon of cumin, tahini, 2 tablespoons of lemon juice, 2 tablespoons of reserved liquid and black beans, then blend until it become smooth. Scrape down the sides as needed. Stir in additional liquid and seasoning to taste. Decorate with Greek olives and paprika.

### Nutrition Information

- Calories: 81 calories;
- Total Fat: 3.1
- Sodium: 427
- Total Carbohydrate: 10.3
- Cholesterol: 0
- Protein: 3.9

## 4. Creamy Yogurt Hummus

*Serving: 24 | Prep: 5mins | Cook: | Ready in:*

### Ingredients

- 1 (15.5 ounce) can garbanzo beans, drained
- 1 clove garlic, peeled
- 1 teaspoon salt
- 1/2 cup fresh lemon juice
- 2/3 cup plain non-fat yogurt

### Direction

- Process the garbanzo beans in a food processor or a blender until it becomes smooth, then stir in the yogurt, lemon juice, salt and garlic; process until the preferred consistency is achieved.

### Nutrition Information

- Calories: 26 calories;
- Total Fat: 0.2
- Sodium: 156
- Total Carbohydrate: 5.2
- Cholesterol: < 1
- Protein: 1.2

## 5. Dolmathes

*Serving: 7 | Prep: 45mins | Cook: 45mins | Ready in:*

### Ingredients

- 1 cup olive oil, divided
- 1 1/2 pounds onions, chopped
- 1 3/4 cups uncooked white rice
- 2 lemons, juiced
- 2 tablespoons chopped fresh dill
- 1/2 cup chopped fresh parsley
- 2 tablespoons pine nuts
- 1 (8 ounce) jar grape leaves, drained and rinsed

### Direction

- Set an oven to preheat to 190°C (375°F).
- In a big saucepan, heat the 2 tbsp. of oil on medium heat. Sauté the onions until it becomes tender. Mix in the rice and cook until it browns slightly. Add 1/2 of the lemon juice and 3 1/2 cups of water. Lower the heat, put on the cover and let it simmer for 20 minutes or until the rice becomes tender and all the liquid has been absorbed. Stir in pine nuts, parsley and dill.

- Take off the stems from the grape leaves and put 1 tbsp. of the rice mixture in the middle. Fold in the sides and roll it tightly. Put it in a baking dish, folded side facing down, and cover it using the leftover lemon juice, olive oil and enough water to cover half of the dolmathas.
- Use aluminum foil to cover and let it bake for 45 minutes in the preheated oven.

## Nutrition Information

- Calories: 535 calories;
- Sodium: 935
- Total Carbohydrate: 55.3
- Cholesterol: 0
- Protein: 7.4
- Total Fat: 33.4

## 6. Duke

*Serving: 5 | Prep: 5mins | Cook: | Ready in:*

### Ingredients

- 32 ounces plain yogurt
- 2 large cucumbers, chopped
- 1 tablespoon chopped fresh dill weed
- 1 bunch green onions, chopped
- salt to taste

### Direction

- Mix salt, green onion, dill, cucumbers, and yogurt together in a medium-sized mixing bowl. Enjoy chilled.

### Nutrition Information

- Calories: 144 calories;
- Total Carbohydrate: 20.1
- Cholesterol: 11
- Protein: 11
- Total Fat: 3

- Sodium: 135

## 7. Easy Greek Yogurt Cucumber Sauce

*Serving: 16 | Prep: 25mins | Cook: | Ready in:*

### Ingredients

- 1 cup plain yogurt
- 1 cup sour cream
- 1 teaspoon white vinegar
- 1/2 teaspoon lemon juice
- 1 small cucumber - peeled, seeded, and finely chopped
- 1 green onion
- 1 garlic clove, minced
- 1/4 cup crumbled feta cheese
- 1/2 teaspoon oregano
- 1/4 teaspoon lemon zest
- salt and pepper to taste

### Direction

- In a bowl, stir pepper, salt, lemon zest, oregano, feta cheese, garlic, green onion, cucumber, lemon juice, vinegar, sour cream and yogurt together. Put a cover on and refrigerate about 8 hours to overnight before serving.

### Nutrition Information

- Calories: 53 calories;
- Sodium: 63
- Total Carbohydrate: 2.3
- Cholesterol: 11
- Protein: 1.9
- Total Fat: 4.1

## 8. Easy Hummus

*Serving: 16 | Prep: 5mins | Cook: |Ready in:*

### Ingredients

- 1 (15 ounce) can garbanzo beans, drained, liquid reserved
- 2 ounces fresh jalapeno pepper, sliced
- 1/2 teaspoon ground cumin
- 2 tablespoons lemon juice
- 3 cloves garlic, minced

### Direction

- Blend 1 tablespoon of the reserved bean liquid, garlic, lemon juice, cumin, jalapeño and garbanzo beans in a blender or a food processor until it becomes smooth.

### Nutrition Information

- Calories: 23 calories;
- Total Fat: 0.2
- Sodium: 53
- Total Carbohydrate: 4.5
- Cholesterol: 0
- Protein: 1

## 9. Easy Roasted Red Pepper Hummus

*Serving: 2 | Prep: | Cook: |Ready in:*

### Ingredients

- 2 cloves garlic, minced
- 1 (15 ounce) can garbanzo beans, drained
- 1/3 cup tahini
- 1/3 cup lemon juice
- 1/2 cup roasted red peppers
- 1/4 teaspoon dried basil

### Direction

- Process the lemon juice, tahini, garbanzo beans and garlic in an electric food processor until the mixture becomes smooth. Stir in basil and roasted peppers then blend until the peppers are chopped finely. Sprinkle pepper and salt to season, then move it into a small bowl, cover, and let it chill in the fridge until it's time to serve.

### Nutrition Information

- Calories: 445 calories;
- Cholesterol: 0
- Protein: 15.9
- Total Fat: 26.9
- Sodium: 908
- Total Carbohydrate: 44.1

## 10. Extra Easy Hummus

*Serving: 4 | Prep: 5mins | Cook: |Ready in:*

### Ingredients

- 1 (15 ounce) can garbanzo beans, drained, liquid reserved
- 1 clove garlic, crushed
- 2 teaspoons ground cumin
- 1/2 teaspoon salt
- 1 tablespoon olive oil

### Direction

- Mix olive oil, salt, garlic, cumin, and garbanzo beans in a food processor or blender. Then blend on low speed while slowly adding the reserved bean liquid until the consistency desired is achieved.

### Nutrition Information

- Calories: 118 calories;
- Sodium: 502
- Total Carbohydrate: 16.5

- Cholesterol: 0
- Protein: 3.7
- Total Fat: 4.4

## 11. Feta And Roasted Red Pepper Dip

*Serving: 7 | Prep: 5mins | Cook: | Ready in:*

### Ingredients

- 1 roasted red bell pepper
- 1 clove garlic, minced
- 8 ounces feta cheese
- 1/4 cup plain yogurt
- 1 pinch cayenne pepper, or to taste

### Direction

- Blend cayenne pepper, yogurt, feta cheese, garlic and roasted pepper, covered, till smooth in blender.

### Nutrition Information

- Calories: 96 calories;
- Protein: 5.3
- Total Fat: 7.1
- Sodium: 415
- Total Carbohydrate: 2.8
- Cholesterol: 29

## 12. Figs Oozing With Goat Cheese

*Serving: 4 | Prep: 15mins | Cook: 3mins | Ready in:*

### Ingredients

- 8 fresh figs
- 1/2 cup goat cheese, softened
- 8 grape leaves, drained and rinsed
- 1/2 cup honey
- skewers

### Direction

- Preheat the grill to medium heat.
- At the bottom of every fig create a small incision big enough to hold a pastry bag tip. Put goat cheese into a pastry bag with a plain tip. Fill goat cheese into figs by squeezing a bit of cheese into every fig's bottom. The figs plump up when you fill them. Wrap a grape leaf on every fig. On each skewer, skewer 2-3 figs.
- Oil the grate lightly. Put fig skewers onto hot grill. Cook, turning once for 2-3 minutes. Drizzle honey on. Serve.

### Nutrition Information

- Calories: 272 calories;
- Total Fat: 5.7
- Sodium: 321
- Total Carbohydrate: 55.5
- Cholesterol: 14
- Protein: 5

## 13. Garlic Feta Dip

*Serving: 8 | Prep: 5mins | Cook: | Ready in:*

### Ingredients

- 1 cup crumbled feta cheese
- 1/2 cup sour cream
- 1/2 cup plain yogurt
- 2 cloves garlic, peeled
- 1/4 teaspoon salt
- 1/4 teaspoon freshly ground black pepper

### Direction

- In the container of a blender or food processor, combine garlic, yogurt, sour cream and feta cheese. Briefly pulse to mince the garlic.

Transfer into a serving dish and add salt and pepper to taste.

## Nutrition Information

- Calories: 125 calories;
- Sodium: 443
- Total Carbohydrate: 3.3
- Cholesterol: 35
- Protein: 5.8
- Total Fat: 10

## 14. Gorgonzola And Olive Stuffed Grape Leaves

*Serving: 20 | Prep: 45mins | Cook: | Ready in:*

### Ingredients

- 3/4 cup chopped green olives
- 3/4 cup chopped kalamata olives
- 1/2 cup crumbled Gorgonzola cheese
- 3/4 cup chopped macadamia nuts
- 5 tablespoons chopped fresh basil leaves
- 4 roma (plum) tomatoes, seeded and chopped
- 1 red bell pepper, chopped
- 3 1/2 tablespoons chopped fresh garlic
- 2 tablespoons brown sugar
- salt to taste
- ground black pepper to taste
- 1 (8 ounce) jar grape leaves packed in brine

### Direction

- Combine brown sugar, garlic, bell pepper, tomatoes, basil, macadamia nuts, Gorgonzola cheese, kalamata olives and green olives in a bowl. Add pepper and salt for seasoning.
- Arrange each grape leaf flat, then generously place a heaped tablespoonful of the Gorgonzola and olive mixture in the middle. Roll or fold the leaves around the mixture. Chill before serving.

## Nutrition Information

- Calories: 91 calories;
- Total Carbohydrate: 5.3
- Cholesterol: 4
- Protein: 2.2
- Total Fat: 7.3
- Sodium: 605

## 15. Grape Leaves Aleppo

*Serving: 32 | Prep: 45mins | Cook: 1hours15mins | Ready in:*

### Ingredients

- 1 cup uncooked white rice
- 2 pounds ground lamb
- 2 (16 ounce) jars grape leaves, drained and rinsed
- 1 teaspoon salt
- 1 teaspoon ground black pepper
- 1 tablespoon ground allspice
- 6 cloves garlic, sliced
- 1 cup lemon juice
- 2 kalamata olives (optional)

### Direction

- Soak the rice in cold water, then drain. Combine the pepper, salt, allspice, rice and ground lamb in a big bowl until well combined. Put approximately 1 tbsp. of the meat mixture onto the middle of each leaf. Fold the leaf over once, then flip in the edges on each side and roll the leaf to close.
- In a big pot, stack the leaf-rolls, then use garlic slices to cover each layer. Pour just enough water to cover the rolls, then pour lemon juice. Add olives into the pot for the flavoring, if preferred. Put a plate over the rolls to help them remain under water.
- Let it boil, then lower the heat, put on cover and let it simmer for 1 hour and 15 minutes. Taste the rice if it's done. The grape leaves

taste even better after letting it sit for a couple of hours. Serve.

### Nutrition Information

- Calories: 101 calories;
- Total Fat: 4.5
- Sodium: 902
- Total Carbohydrate: 9.2
- Cholesterol: 19
- Protein: 6.5

## 16. Grecian Cherries

*Serving: 8 | Prep: 10mins | Cook: | Ready in:*

### Ingredients

- 2 cups cherries, pitted and coarsely chopped
- 1 cup whole-milk ricotta cheese
- 1/2 cup crumbled feta cheese
- 4 teaspoons ground coriander
- 4 teaspoons white sugar
- 1 tablespoon lemon juice

### Direction

- In a large bowl, mix lemon juice, sugar, coriander, feta cheese, ricotta cheese, and accumulated juices with chopped cherries. Before serving time, let sit in the refrigerator.

### Nutrition Information

- Calories: 106 calories;
- Cholesterol: 18
- Protein: 5.4
- Total Fat: 5
- Sodium: 143
- Total Carbohydrate: 10.8

## 17. Greek Dip

*Serving: 14 | Prep: 5mins | Cook: | Ready in:*

### Ingredients

- 1/3 cup crumbled feta cheese
- 1/3 cup grated Parmesan cheese
- 1 (8 ounce) package cream cheese, softened
- 1 tablespoon sun-dried tomato pesto

### Direction

- In a food processor, blend sun-dried tomato pesto, cream cheese, Parmesan cheese and feta cheese to mix completely. Let the dip chill overnight or serve right away.

### Nutrition Information

- Calories: 76 calories;
- Cholesterol: 22
- Protein: 2.5
- Total Fat: 7.1
- Sodium: 118
- Total Carbohydrate: 0.7

## 18. Greek Feta And Olive Spread

*Serving: 12 | Prep: 10mins | Cook: | Ready in:*

### Ingredients

- 1 (6 ounce) package feta cheese, crumbled
- 2 tablespoons olive oil
- 1 teaspoon lemon juice
- 1/2 teaspoon minced garlic
- 2 ounces sun-dried tomatoes, softened
- 1/2 teaspoon dried oregano
- 1 tablespoon chopped black olives, drained

### Direction

- Put oregano, feta cheese, sun-dried tomatoes, olive oil, garlic, and lemon juice in a food processor then pulse the mixture until smooth; move to a medium bowl. Mix in olives using a spoon or your hands. Chill until serving.

## Nutrition Information

- Calories: 70 calories;
- Sodium: 260
- Total Carbohydrate: 3.3
- Cholesterol: 12
- Protein: 2.7
- Total Fat: 5.4

## 19. Greek Feta Hot Spread (Tyrokafteri)

*Serving: 20 | Prep: 15mins | Cook: |Ready in:*

## Ingredients

- 1 (8 ounce) package feta cheese, crumbled well
- 3 hot green peppers, stemmed, or more to taste
- 1 cup full-fat Greek yogurt
- 1/3 cup olive oil
- 2 tablespoons sweet red pepper paste (optional)
- 1 tablespoon white vinegar
- 1 clove garlic, mashed (optional)
- 1 pinch cayenne pepper

## Direction

- In a large glass bowl, put feta cheese. In a food processor, put green peppers; blend into a paste; move into the bowl with feta. Put in cayenne pepper, garlic, vinegar, red pepper paste, olive oil and Greek yogurt. Combine properly.

## Nutrition Information

- Calories: 78 calories;
- Total Carbohydrate: 1.5
- Cholesterol: 12
- Protein: 2.3
- Total Fat: 7
- Sodium: 282

## 20. Greek Salad On A Stick

*Serving: 8 | Prep: 15mins | Cook: |Ready in:*

## Ingredients

- 2 tablespoons dried oregano, or to taste
- 8 (1/2 inch) cubes feta cheese
- 8 1/2-inch cucumber slices
- 8 grape tomatoes
- 8 Kalamata olives, pitted
- 8 bamboo toothpicks

## Direction

- Put oregano in a shallow bowl. Coat feta cheese cubes in the oregano.
- Insert a toothpick into the feta cube. Thread a cucumber, an olive, a tomato into the skewer. Repeat with the rest of the toothpicks.

## Nutrition Information

- Calories: 53 calories;
- Total Fat: 3.7
- Sodium: 202
- Total Carbohydrate: 3.1
- Cholesterol: 12
- Protein: 2.4

## 21. Greek Style Cheese Ball

*Serving: 10 | Prep: 25mins | Cook: |Ready in:*

## Ingredients

- 1 (8 ounce) package cream cheese, softened
- 1/4 cup mayonnaise

- 2 tablespoons balsamic vinegar
- 10 ounces shredded Cheddar cheese
- 1 (8 ounce) package crumbled feta cheese
- 1/4 cup grated Parmesan cheese
- 1 tablespoon dried oregano
- 2 teaspoons onion powder
- 1 teaspoon garlic powder
- 1/4 cup pecan halves
- 3/4 cup pine nuts, divided

### Direction

- Mix balsamic vinegar, mayonnaise and cream cheese till smooth in a bowl.
- Mix garlic powder, onion powder, oregano, parmesan cheese, cheddar cheese and feta cheese in another bowl. Mix cheddar cheese mixture into the cream cheese mixture.
- Pulse 1/4 cup pine nuts and pecans till crumbly in a blender/food processor. Mix leftover 1/2 cup pine nuts into the pecan mixture; spread 1/4 pecan mixture on plate.
- Shape cheese mixture to 2 5-in. balls. In pecan mixture, roll each ball till coated fully; as needed, add more pecan mixture.

### Nutrition Information

- Calories: 383 calories;
- Sodium: 559
- Total Carbohydrate: 5.3
- Cholesterol: 78
- Protein: 15.6
- Total Fat: 34.1

## 22. Hummus I

*Serving: 24 | Prep: 10mins | Cook: | Ready in:*

### Ingredients

- 2 (15 ounce) cans garbanzo beans, drained
- 1/2 cup roasted tahini
- 1/4 cup lemon juice
- 1 teaspoon grated lemon zest, minced
- 2 cloves garlic
- 1/4 cup packed flat leaf parsley
- 1/4 cup chopped green onions
- salt to taste
- ground black pepper to taste

### Direction

- In the bowl of a food processor, put the green onion, parsley, garlic, lemon zest, lemon juice, tahini and garbanzo beans. Blend until it becomes smooth, then add water if the mixture seems too thick. Season pepper and salt to taste.

### Nutrition Information

- Calories: 62 calories;
- Total Fat: 3.4
- Sodium: 72
- Total Carbohydrate: 6.5
- Cholesterol: 0
- Protein: 2.3

## 23. Hummus II

*Serving: 40 | Prep: 10mins | Cook: | Ready in:*

### Ingredients

- 2 cloves garlic
- 2 (15 ounce) cans garbanzo beans, drained
- 8 ounces tofu
- 3 lemons, juiced
- 1/4 cup parsley
- 3/4 cup tahini
- 1 teaspoon ground ginger
- 1 pinch ground cayenne pepper
- 1 tablespoon tamari
- salt to taste
- ground black pepper to taste

### Direction

- In a big bowl of a food processor, mince the garlic. Stir in the tahini, parsley, lemon juice, tofu and garbanzo beans then process until it becomes smooth. Stir in tamari, cayenne pepper and ginger then blend. Put black pepper and salt to season. If the hummus is too thick, add in water then blend.

## Nutrition Information

- Calories: 52 calories;
- Total Fat: 3.3
- Sodium: 69
- Total Carbohydrate: 5
- Cholesterol: 0
- Protein: 2.2

## 24. Hummus III

*Serving: 16 | Prep: 10mins | Cook: |Ready in:*

## Ingredients

- 2 cups canned garbanzo beans, drained
- 1/3 cup tahini
- 1/4 cup lemon juice
- 1 teaspoon salt
- 2 cloves garlic, halved
- 1 tablespoon olive oil
- 1 pinch paprika
- 1 teaspoon minced fresh parsley

## Direction

- In a food processor or blender, process the garlic, salt, lemon juice, tahini, and garbanzo beans until it becomes smooth, then move to a serving bowl.
- Trickle olive oil on top and sprinkle it with parsley and paprika.

## Nutrition Information

- Calories: 77 calories;
- Sodium: 236
- Total Carbohydrate: 8.1
- Cholesterol: 0
- Protein: 2.6
- Total Fat: 4.3

## 25. Hummus IV

*Serving: 40 | Prep: 20mins | Cook: |Ready in:*

## Ingredients

- 2 (15.5 ounce) cans garbanzo beans, drained
- 4 tablespoons lemon juice
- 6 cloves garlic, peeled and crushed
- 3 tablespoons tahini
- 1/4 teaspoon crushed red pepper

## Direction

- In a food processor, process the garbanzo beans until it becomes a spreadable paste. Stir in crushed red pepper, tahini, garlic and lemon juice, the process until it becomes smooth. If the consistency appears too thick, use more lemon juice.

## Nutrition Information

- Calories: 34 calories;
- Cholesterol: 0
- Protein: 1.3
- Total Fat: 0.9
- Sodium: 67
- Total Carbohydrate: 5.5

## 26. Lamb And Rice Stuffed Grape Leaves

*Serving: 8 | Prep: 45mins | Cook: 45mins |Ready in:*

## Ingredients

- 1/2 pound ground lamb
- 1/2 cup uncooked long grain rice
- 1/4 cup olive oil
- 2 tablespoons chopped fresh mint
- 1 tablespoon dried currants
- 1 tablespoon pine nuts
- 1 1/2 teaspoons kosher salt
- 1 teaspoon ground black pepper
- 1/2 teaspoon ground cumin
- 1/4 teaspoon ground cinnamon
- 1/4 teaspoon dried oregano
- 1 large egg
- 1 (16 ounce) jar grape leaves
- 1 tablespoon olive oil
- juice of one lemon
- 4 cups hot chicken broth
- 2 teaspoons olive oil, or as desired

## Direction

- In a bowl, place the egg, oregano, cinnamon, cumin, pepper, salt, pine nuts, currants, mint, 1/4 cups olive oil, rice, and ground lamb. Use a fork to mix thoroughly. Cover and chill until ready to use.
- Unroll and separate grape leaves gently. Wash in cold water to remove the saline. Let drain. Store the less-than-perfect or broken leaves to line the pot.
- Put grape leaves on the work surface with rib side up (smooth side down). Place a rounded tablespoon of the lamb-rice filling close to the bottom-center of the grape leaf. Next, fold the bottom part of the leaf over the filling, fold over sides and roll toward the top of leaf to make a firm cylinder. Do not roll too tightly or these leaves may be torn when cooking.
- In the pot, drizzle a tablespoon olive oil; apply 1 or 2 layers of the reserved grape leaves to line the bottom of pot. Put in the dolmas by placing them along the sides, then moving toward the center to cover the bottom. To allow for expansion, set enough space between dolmas, but close enough to keep their shapes when cooking. Stack another layer on top of the first so that they're all fit, if necessary.

Then pour in 2 teaspoons olive oil and lemon juice.
- Overturn a small dish and then a larger one over the dolmas to weigh them down while cooking and to prevent them from slipping. Then add the hot chicken broth. Simmer over medium-high heat, uncovered. Reduce the heat to low as soon as the liquid is heated through and starting to bubble (about 2-4 minutes), cover the pot, and keep cooking for about 35 minutes. Next, take away the dishes and check for doneness. A completely one should be pierced easily with a fork, and a little puffed up. Keep cooking without the weights if they're not done yet: cover the pot and simmer for 10 to 15 minutes longer, or until the rice is softened.
- Serve chilled or warm. If desired, garnish with curls of lemon zest.

## Nutrition Information

- Calories: 250 calories;
- Protein: 9.8
- Total Fat: 16.1
- Sodium: 2485
- Total Carbohydrate: 18.1
- Cholesterol: 45

## 27. My Own Famous Stuffed Grape Leaves

*Serving: 12 | Prep: 40mins | Cook: 1hours | Ready in:*

## Ingredients

- 2 cups uncooked long-grain white rice
- 1 large onion, chopped
- 1/2 cup chopped fresh dill
- 1/2 cup chopped fresh mint leaves
- 2 quarts chicken broth
- 3/4 cup fresh lemon juice, divided
- 60 grape leaves, drained and rinsed
- hot water as needed

- 1 cup olive oil

### Direction

- Sauté mint, dill, onion and rice in a big saucepan on medium high heat until onion is softened, for 5 minutes. Add in 1-qt. broth and lower heat to low, then simmer for another 10-15 minutes, until rice is nearly cooked. Stir in half of the lemon juice and take away from the heat.
- Take one leaf with shiny side down and put 1 tsp. rice mixture at the bottom (stem) end of the leaf. Fold both sides of the leaf towards the center and roll up from the broad bottom to the top, then put into a 4-qt. pot. Repeat the process with all leaves, leaving no gaps as leaves are put in pot (to avoid opening while cooking). Sprinkle over with olive oil and leftover lemon juice.
- Pour over all with chicken broth to cover grape leaves. Cover pot and simmer for an hour without boiling to avoid making the stuffing burst out of the leaves. Take away from the heat, then remove cover and allow to cool about a half hour. Turn to a serving dish and serve.

### Nutrition Information

- Calories: 303 calories;
- Total Fat: 18.7
- Sodium: 573
- Total Carbohydrate: 30.9
- Cholesterol: 0
- Protein: 3.6

## 28. Olivada

*Serving: 14 | Prep: 5mins | Cook: | Ready in:*

### Ingredients

- 3 cups whole, pitted kalamata olives
- 1/3 cup olive oil
- 2 cloves garlic

### Direction

- In an electric blender, puree garlic and olives while streaming in olive oil; process until the mixture turns to a thick yet unsmooth paste.

### Nutrition Information

- Calories: 127 calories;
- Sodium: 472
- Total Carbohydrate: 2.8
- Cholesterol: 0
- Protein: 0.5
- Total Fat: 12.8

## 29. Pickled Cheese

*Serving: 7 | Prep: 20mins | Cook: | Ready in:*

### Ingredients

- 7 ounces feta cheese
- 4 sprigs fresh thyme
- 7 fluid ounces white wine vinegar
- 1 teaspoon honey

### Direction

- Rinse and pat the feta cheese dry using paper towels; slice into 1/2-inch cubes. Put cheese cubes in a layer in a one-pint glass jar then add a thyme layer; repeat layers until the jar is almost full. Combine honey and white wine vinegar; put in the jar until full. Secure lid then refrigerate for at least a day to marinate.

### Nutrition Information

- Calories: 79 calories;
- Total Carbohydrate: 2.1
- Cholesterol: 25
- Protein: 4.1

- Total Fat: 6
- Sodium: 320

## 30. Prawn Saganaki

*Serving: 4 | Prep: 15mins | Cook: 35mins | Ready in:*

### Ingredients

- 1 tablespoon olive oil
- 1 red onion, halved and thinly sliced
- 3 cloves garlic, thinly sliced
- 2 tablespoons tomato paste
- 1/2 cup white wine
- 1 (13.5 ounce) jar tomato and olive pasta sauce (such as Papayiannides® Tomato & Olive & Ouzo Sauce)
- 1 1/2 pounds prawns, peeled and deveined, tail on
- 1/2 cup crumbled Greek feta cheese
- 2 tablespoons chopped fresh flat-leaf parsley

### Direction

- Preheat oven to 400°F (200°C).
- Heat olive oil over medium heat in a big skillet; cook and stir onion for about 5 minutes, until tender. Mix in garlic and cook for about a minute until fragrant. Blend into onion mixture with tomato paste; cook and mix for a minute.
- Put wine into tomato blend; simmer for about 5 minutes, until about half of the liquid is reduced. Mix the wine blend with tomato sauce and simmer for about 10 minutes until the blend is thick.
- Distribute tomato blend into the base of a 6-cup baking dish; put prawns on top and sprinkle with feta cheese evenly.
- Bake in the preheated oven for about 10 minutes, until the outsides of prawns are bright pink and the meat is no longer transparent in the middle; add parsley on top.

### Nutrition Information

- Calories: 341 calories;
- Total Fat: 11.5
- Sodium: 968
- Total Carbohydrate: 19.7
- Cholesterol: 277
- Protein: 33

## 31. Roasted Garlic Tyrokavteri

*Serving: 24 | Prep: 15mins | Cook: | Ready in:*

### Ingredients

- 1 (6 ounce) jar roasted red peppers, drained and coarsely chopped
- 1/4 cup roasted garlic
- 1 teaspoon hot pepper sauce, or to taste
- 1/2 cup freshly squeezed lemon juice
- 1/4 teaspoon dried oregano
- 1/8 teaspoon ground white pepper
- 8 ounces crumbled feta
- 4 ounces cream cheese, softened
- 1/4 cup extra-virgin olive oil
- 1/4 cup half-and-half (optional)

### Direction

- In a blender, add white pepper, oregano, lemon juice, hot pepper sauce, roasted garlic and roasted red peppers, then process until smooth. Put in cream cheese and feta cheese; puree until smooth.
- Add in olive oil gradually while processor is running until thickened and blended. Stir in half-and-half, if necessary, to get a dip consistency. Cover and keep in the fridge until serving.

### Nutrition Information

- Calories: 71 calories;
- Total Fat: 6.3
- Sodium: 151

- Total Carbohydrate: 1.9
- Cholesterol: 15
- Protein: 2

## 32. Robin's Best Ever Hummus

*Serving: 8 | Prep: 10mins | Cook: 5mins | Ready in:*

### Ingredients

- 3 cloves garlic
- 2 teaspoons coarse salt
- 1 (19 ounce) can garbanzo beans, drained
- 3 tablespoons tahini (sesame-seed paste)
- 3 tablespoons lemon juice
- 1 tablespoon honey
- 2 tablespoons water, or as needed
- 1/4 cup olive oil, divided
- 6 pita bread rounds
- salt to taste
- 1 tablespoon chopped fresh rosemary

### Direction

- In a small bowl, crush the garlic with salt, and put it in a food processor or a blender together with honey, lemon juice, tahini, garbanzo beans and enough water to cover the beans, then blend it until it becomes smooth. Scoop it onto a serving dish and top it with a trickle of 2 tablespoons of olive oil.
- Set an oven to preheat at 200°C (400°F). Use the leftover olive oil to brush the pita breads and slice it into wedges. Sprinkle with fresh rosemary and salt to season, then bake in the preheated oven for 5 minutes. Let it cool and serve alongside hummus.

### Nutrition Information

- Calories: 308 calories;
- Cholesterol: 0
- Protein: 8.5
- Total Fat: 11.1

- Sodium: 930
- Total Carbohydrate: 44.6

## 33. Root Veggie Crisps With Greek Yogurt Dip

*Serving: 6 | Prep: 30mins | Cook: 15mins | Ready in:*

### Ingredients

- 1 quart peanut oil for frying, or as needed
- 1 large beet, peeled and sliced paper-thin
- 1 large sweet potato, peeled and sliced paper-thin
- 1 turnip, peeled and sliced paper-thin
- 1 parsnip, peeled and sliced paper-thin
- 1 golden beet, peeled and sliced paper-thin
- sea salt to taste
- freshly cracked black pepper to taste
- 1 tablespoon malt vinegar, or to taste
- 1 cup plain Greek yogurt
- 1/4 cup chopped fresh parsley
- 1 tablespoon chopped fresh mint
- 1 clove garlic, finely minced
- 4 green onions, finely chopped
- 2 tablespoons lemon juice, or to taste
- salt and ground white pepper to taste

### Direction

- Put oil in a large saucepan or deep-fryer and heat it to 360°F (182°C).
- Fry the golden beet slices, parsnip, turnip, sweet potato and beet carefully in hot oil, in batches, for 2-4 minutes until golden brown.
- Use a slotted spoon to transfer the vegetable chips into the paper towels; drain. Let them dry and cool.
- Season the chips with malt vinegar, cracked black pepper and sea salt to taste.
- In a bowl, mix the green onions, garlic, mint, parsley and yogurt; stir in white pepper, salt and lemon juice according to your taste.

## Nutrition Information

- Calories: 275 calories;
- Cholesterol: 8
- Protein: 4.6
- Total Fat: 18.2
- Sodium: 124
- Total Carbohydrate: 25

## 34. Sheila's Greek Style Avocado Dip

*Serving: 5 | Prep: 20mins | Cook: | Ready in:*

### Ingredients

- 1 avocado - peeled, pitted and diced
- 1 clove garlic, minced
- 2 tablespoons lime juice
- 1 roma (plum) tomato, seeded and diced
- 1/4 cup crumbled feta cheese

### Direction

- Crush together in a bowl the lime juice, garlic and avocado until almost smooth. Gently mix the feta cheese and diced tomato.

### Nutrition Information

- Calories: 102 calories;
- Sodium: 144
- Total Carbohydrate: 5.1
- Cholesterol: 11
- Protein: 2.8
- Total Fat: 8.6

## 35. Shrimps Saganaki (Greek Recipe)

*Serving: 4 | Prep: 5mins | Cook: 35mins | Ready in:*

### Ingredients

- 1 pound medium shrimp, with shells
- 1 onion, chopped
- 2 tablespoons chopped fresh parsley
- 1 cup white wine
- 1 (14.5 ounce) can diced tomatoes, drained
- 1/4 teaspoon garlic powder (optional)
- 1/4 cup olive oil
- 1 (8 ounce) package feta cheese, cubed
- salt and pepper to taste (optional)

### Direction

- In a big saucepan, boil approximately 2-inch water. Put in shrimp and the water should cover them. Boil for 5 minutes, and then strain, saving the water and put aside.
- In a saucepan, heat approximately 2 tablespoons of oil. Put in onions, stir and cook until the onions are tender. Stir in the leftover olive oil, garlic powder, tomatoes, wine, and parsley. Simmer until the sauce is thick, about 30 minutes, stirring sometime.
- As the sauce simmers, the shrimps should be cool enough to touch. First, pinch the legs to remove, and then pull off the shells, keeping the tail and head intact.
- Once the sauce is thick, mix in shrimp and shrimp stock. Simmer for 5 minutes. Add feta cheese and take away from the heat. Allow to sit until the cheese begins to melt. Serve warm.

### Nutrition Information

- Calories: 441 calories;
- Protein: 27.8
- Total Fat: 26.6
- Sodium: 1035
- Total Carbohydrate: 10.1
- Cholesterol: 223

## 36. Spanakopita II

*Serving: 27 | Prep: 30mins | Cook: 1hours5mins | Ready in:*

### Ingredients

- 1/2 cup vegetable oil
- 2 large onions, chopped
- 2 (10 ounce) packages frozen chopped spinach - thawed, drained and squeezed dry
- 2 tablespoons chopped fresh dill
- 2 tablespoons all-purpose flour
- 2 (4 ounce) packages feta cheese, crumbled
- 4 eggs, lightly beaten
- salt and pepper to taste
- 1 1/2 (16 ounce) packages phyllo dough
- 3/4 pound butter, melted

### Direction

- Preheat the oven to 175°C or 350°Fahrenheit.
- On medium heat, heat vegetable oil in a big pot. Cook and stir onions slowly until soft. Stir in flour, dill and spinach. Cook for about 10 minutes until nearly all the moisture is absorbed. Take off from the heat; mix in pepper, salt, eggs and feta cheese.
- Separate one phyllo sheet from the stack and brush evenly with a thin coat of butter. Put another phyllo sheet on top of the butter then press the 2 phyllo sheets together. Make 3-in wide long strips from the layered phyllo dough. Keep the rest of the phyllo sheets covered in plastic wrap to avoid drying out.
- On a work surface, place one phyllo strip at a time with one of the slender ends near you. Put a heaping tablespoonful of filling an inch from the end nearest to you. Fold the lower right corner over the filling then to the left corner to make a triangle. Fold it up joining the point at the lower left up to lay along the left corner. Turn the bottom left edge to touch the right corner. Continue to fold the triangle over in this way until you reach the phyllo's end.
- Repeat with the rest of the phyllo dough and filling. Arrange the filled phyllo dough triangles on a big baking sheet then slather with the rest of the butter. You can freeze the pastries at this point.
- Bake the phyllo in the preheated oven for 45 minutes to an hour until golden brown.

### Nutrition Information

- Calories: 246 calories;
- Sodium: 313
- Total Carbohydrate: 15.9
- Cholesterol: 62
- Protein: 5
- Total Fat: 18.4

## 37. Spiced Sweet Roasted Red Pepper Hummus

*Serving: 8 | Prep: 15mins | Cook: | Ready in:*

### Ingredients

- 1 (15 ounce) can garbanzo beans, drained
- 1 (4 ounce) jar roasted red peppers
- 3 tablespoons lemon juice
- 1 1/2 tablespoons tahini
- 1 clove garlic, minced
- 1/2 teaspoon ground cumin
- 1/2 teaspoon cayenne pepper
- 1/4 teaspoon salt
- 1 tablespoon chopped fresh parsley

### Direction

- Puree the salt, cayenne, cumin, garlic, tahini, lemon juice, red peppers and chickpeas in a food processor or an electric blender. Using long pulses, blend the mixture until it becomes a bit fluffy and fairly smooth. In between pulses, scrape off the mixture from the blender or food processor's sides. Move the mixture to a serving bowl and let it chill in the fridge for a minimum of 1 hour. This can be made up to 3

days in advance, chilled. When serving, bring to room temperature.
- Sprinkle chopped parsley on top then serve.

## Nutrition Information

- Calories: 64 calories;
- Cholesterol: 0
- Protein: 2.5
- Total Fat: 2.2
- Sodium: 370
- Total Carbohydrate: 9.6

## 38. Spicy Baked Feta (Feta Psiti)

*Serving: 4 | Prep: 5mins | Cook: 10mins | Ready in:*

## Ingredients

- 1 (8 ounce) slice feta cheese
- 2 teaspoons olive oil (optional)
- 2 tablespoons crushed red pepper flakes, or as needed
- 1 pinch dried oregano

## Direction

- Set an oven to preheat to 200°C (400°F).
- In an ovenproof baking dish, put the feta, then drizzle olive oil on top. Liberally cover with pepper flakes and sprinkle oregano on top.
- Let it bake for about 10 minutes in the preheated oven without a cover, until the feta becomes soft.

## Nutrition Information

- Calories: 186 calories;
- Sodium: 635
- Total Carbohydrate: 5
- Cholesterol: 51
- Protein: 8.6
- Total Fat: 15.3

## 39. Spicy Feta Dip

*Serving: 8 | Prep: 15mins | Cook: | Ready in:*

## Ingredients

- 1 cup crumbled feta cheese
- 1/2 cup chopped roasted red peppers
- 4 pepperoncini peppers, drained and stemmed
- 1 teaspoon cayenne pepper, or more to taste
- 1 cup ricotta cheese
- 1 teaspoon lemon juice

## Direction

- In a food processor, pulse the feta cheese just enough to get uniformly small crumbles, then remove to a bowl.
- In the food processor, puree together cayenne pepper, pepperoncini peppers and red peppers until smooth. Combine into the feta cheese with lemon juice, ricotta cheese and pepper puree until the dip has an even texture and color. Remove to a sealed container and chill for 2 hours or overnight.

## Nutrition Information

- Calories: 134 calories;
- Protein: 8.3
- Total Fat: 9.3
- Sodium: 734
- Total Carbohydrate: 4.2
- Cholesterol: 38

## 40. Spinach Strudels

*Serving: 40 | Prep: 30mins | Cook: 18mins | Ready in:*

## Ingredients

- 1/2 cup olive oil
- 1 bunch green onions, chopped

- 2 (10 ounce) packages frozen chopped spinach, thawed, well drained
- 2 tablespoons chopped fresh dill
- 3 extra large eggs, lightly beaten
- 7 ounces feta cheese, crumbled
- 1/4 teaspoon salt
- 1/4 teaspoon freshly ground black pepper
- 40 sheets frozen phyllo pastry, thawed in refrigerator
- 1 cup unsalted butter, melted
- 1/2 cup plain bread crumbs

## Direction

- Preheat oven to 200°C/400°F.
- Place a medium skillet over medium heat and heat the olive oil. Stir and cook green onions in the hot oil for 5 minutes, or until soft. Set aside.
- Combine pepper, salt, feta, eggs, dill, and spinach in a large bowl. Add the cooked green onions and mix thoroughly.
- Unfold a sheet of phyllo pastry and brush melted butter over it. Lightly sprinkle breadcrumb. Layer with another sheet of phyllo pastry, brush butter and sprinkle breadcrumbs again. Repeat process until there are 10 layers of pastry.
- Along the long side of the top layer, spoon 3/4 cup of the spinach mixture in a line. Roll up the pastry and place it on a baking sheet. Lightly brush with butter. Use a knife to score 1-inch rounds of the rolls for cutting easier later. Repeat process with the rest of the pastry sheets. There should be 4 rolls in total.
- Bake until edges are lightly browned, about 12 minutes. Slice servings following the scores. Serve right away.

## Nutrition Information

- Calories: 152 calories;
- Total Fat: 10.1
- Sodium: 190
- Total Carbohydrate: 12.2
- Cholesterol: 33
- Protein: 3.5

## 41. Stuffed Grape Leaves (Dolmades)

*Serving: 8 | Prep: 35mins | Cook: 55mins | Ready in:*

### Ingredients

- 1 1/2 pounds ground lamb
- 2 medium onions, finely chopped
- 2/3 cup long grain white rice
- 2/3 cup pine nuts
- 1 teaspoon salt
- 1/4 teaspoon pepper
- 1 teaspoon chopped fresh mint
- 1 (8 ounce) jar grape leaves, drained and rinsed
- 1 1/2 cups water

### Direction

- In a mixing bowl, combine lamb with mint, pepper, salt, pine nuts, rice, and onions until evenly incorporated. Open up a grape leaf gently; arrange grape leaf onto a work surface, rib-side down. In the center of the grape leaf, place a rounded tablespoon of the meat mixture. Fold the leaf's bottom over the meat mixture, fold in the sides, and roll tightly into cylinder. Arrange the rolled grape leaf, seam side down, in a large skillet. Repeat the steps with the rest of the grape leaves, pressing them in a tight, single layer.
- Bring water in a skillet to a simmer. Turn heat to medium-low; simmer, covered, for 50 to 55 minutes until rice is tender. Check once in a while; pour in more water if needed. Remove water before serving.

### Nutrition Information

- Calories: 321 calories;
- Protein: 20

- Total Fat: 18
- Sodium: 1152
- Total Carbohydrate: 20.6
- Cholesterol: 57

## 42. Tiropetes

*Serving: 100 | Prep: 45mins | Cook: 15mins | Ready in:*

### Ingredients

- 1/4 cup butter, melted
- 3 tablespoons all-purpose flour
- 2 cups hot milk
- salt and white pepper to taste
- 1 (16 ounce) package frozen phyllo dough, thawed
- 1 pound feta cheese, crumbled
- 3 egg yolks
- 1 cup shredded Monterey Jack cheese
- 1 cup butter, melted and divided
- 2 tablespoons chopped Italian flat leaf parsley

### Direction

- In a saucepan, melt the butter over medium heat. Beat in flour till smooth. Slowly mix in hot milk to prevent lumps from forming. Allow to cook, mixing continuously, till sauce thick enough to coat a metal spoon. Put white pepper and salt to season, take off from heat and reserve to cool.
- Once sauce is cooled, mix in parsley, 3 tablespoons melted butter, Monterey jack cheese, egg yolks and feta cheese.
- Preheat an oven to 190 °C or 375 °F. Slice phyllo dough sheets into strips approximately 3-inches wide. Use a stack at a time, covering the remaining using a damp towel to prevent from drying out.
- Lay out a phyllo piece at a time. Glaze with butter, and put approximately a teaspoon of cheese mixture on an end. Fold up a corner to meet the other edge. Keep folding in triangle form till you come to the end of strip. Put on baking sheet, and proceed with the rest of dough strips.
- In the prepped oven, bake till golden brown for 15 to 20 minutes. These can be made in advance, freeze after folding. Bake once set to serve.

### Nutrition Information

- Calories: 55 calories;
- Total Fat: 4.1
- Sodium: 97
- Total Carbohydrate: 3
- Cholesterol: 18
- Protein: 1.5

## 43. Tiropitas

*Serving: 16 | Prep: 20mins | Cook: 30mins | Ready in:*

### Ingredients

- 1 (16 ounce) container small curd cottage cheese
- 5 eggs, beaten
- 8 ounces feta cheese, crumbled
- 1 cup butter, melted
- 1 (16 ounce) package frozen phyllo pastry, thawed in refrigerator

### Direction

- Preheat an oven to 220 °C or 425 °F.
- Combine together the feta cheese, eggs and cottage cheese in a big bowl till well mixed. Onto sheets of phyllo dough, brush melted butter one at a time, and layer them in the base of a baking dish, 9x13 inch in size, till you got 7 sheets. Allow the sheets to rest also up sides of the dish. Scatter cheese mixture on the phyllo layers, then redo the process with 7 other sheets, tucking sides in surrounding edges.

- In the prepped oven, bake for approximately half an hour, till crisp and golden brown. Slice into squares and serve while warm.

## Nutrition Information

- Calories: 274 calories;
- Total Fat: 19
- Sodium: 510
- Total Carbohydrate: 16.2
- Cholesterol: 105
- Protein: 9.6

## 44. Two Layer Greek Dip

*Serving: 10 | Prep: 20mins | Cook: | Ready in:*

### Ingredients

- 2 (8 ounce) containers plain yogurt
- 1 (8 ounce) package cream cheese, softened
- 1 (8 ounce) package feta cheese, drained and crumbled
- 3 cloves garlic, crushed
- salt and pepper to taste
- 1 English cucumber, peeled and diced
- 5 roma (plum) tomatoes, seeded and chopped
- 5 green onions, chopped
- 1 (4 ounce) can sliced black olives
- black pepper to taste
- pita bread rounds, cut into triangles

### Direction

- Stir pepper and salt to taste, garlic, feta cheese, softened cream cheese and yogurt together in a bowl. Mix till smooth.
- In a baking dish or a shallow serving dish, spread the mixture. Store, covered, for 3 hours to overnight in the fridge.
- Top the mixture with green onion, tomatoes, cucumber and sliced olives; add pepper to taste if preferred. Place into pita wedges and serve.

## Nutrition Information

- Calories: 269 calories;
- Total Fat: 15
- Sodium: 719
- Total Carbohydrate: 23.9
- Cholesterol: 48
- Protein: 10.6

## 45. Tyrokavteri

*Serving: 24 | Prep: 15mins | Cook: | Ready in:*

### Ingredients

- 1 (8 ounce) package cream cheese, softened
- 1 pound crumbled feta
- 2 teaspoons hot pepper sauce, or to taste
- 1 cup lemon juice
- 1/4 teaspoon ground white pepper
- 1/2 cup olive oil
- 1 cup half-and-half (optional)
- 4 roasted red peppers, drained and chopped

### Direction

- Mix together lemon juice, white pepper, hot pepper sauce, feta cheese and cream cheese in the bowl of a stand mixer or a big bowl. Mix until combined on low speed. Blend in the olive oil gradually until it is blended completely. Stir in half-and-half until the mixture is soft and smooth. Stir in roasted red peppers if you want. Cover and store in the fridge until serving.

## Nutrition Information

- Calories: 144 calories;
- Sodium: 319
- Total Carbohydrate: 3.3
- Cholesterol: 31
- Protein: 4

- Total Fat: 13

## 46. Wendy Jae's Hummus

*Serving: 8 | Prep: 15mins | Cook: | Ready in:*

### Ingredients

- 3 tablespoons chopped roasted garlic
- 1/4 cup chopped red onion
- 2 (15 ounce) cans garbanzo beans, drained
- 1 1/2 teaspoons dried sage
- 1 1/2 teaspoons dried basil
- 1 1/2 teaspoons dried oregano
- 1 1/2 teaspoons dried parsley
- 1 tablespoon lemon juice
- 1 tablespoon olive oil

### Direction

- Process the onions and garlic in a blender or food processor, until chopped finely. Stir in garbanzo beans one can at a time, then process until pureed. Stir in oil, lemon juice, parsley, oregano, basil and sage then puree until it becomes smooth.

### Nutrition Information

- Calories: 108 calories;
- Cholesterol: 0
- Protein: 3.8
- Total Fat: 2.6
- Sodium: 211
- Total Carbohydrate: 17.9

## 47. Zucchini Balls (Kolokythokeftedes)

*Serving: 2 | Prep: 35mins | Cook: 5mins | Ready in:*

### Ingredients

- 1 zucchini, grated
- 1 onion, grated
- 1/2 carrot, grated
- 1 clove garlic, minced
- 1/2 celery root (celeriac), peeled and grated
- 3/4 tablespoon anise seed, crushed
- 1/2 tablespoon celery seed
- 1 teaspoon salt
- 1 pinch ground black pepper
- 1/2 cup all-purpose flour, or as needed
- oil for frying

### Direction

- In a bowl, combine pepper, salt, celery seed, anise seed, celery root, garlic, carrot, onion and zucchini. Slowly stir in flour until the dough turns soft and wet to stick to hands.
- In a deep-fryer, heat oil to 375°F (190°C). Drop in tablespoons of dough, and fry until both sides turn light brown.

### Nutrition Information

- Calories: 644 calories;
- Cholesterol: 0
- Protein: 8.6
- Total Fat: 45.9
- Sodium: 1387
- Total Carbohydrate: 53.8

## 48. Zucchini And Feta Cheese Fritters (Kolokithokeftedes)

*Serving: 15 | Prep: 30mins | Cook: 30mins | Ready in:*

### Ingredients

- 1 potato
- 3 zucchini, shredded
- 1 egg, beaten
- 1/2 sweet onion, finely chopped
- 10 fresh mint leaves, finely chopped
- 1 (8 ounce) package feta cheese, crumbled

- 1/4 cup dry bread crumbs
- 6 tablespoons all-purpose flour
- 1/2 cup olive oil, or as needed
- salt and ground black pepper to taste

### Direction

- Pour lightly salted water into a saucepan and bring to a boil. Put in the potato. Boil for about 20 minutes until tender; take out and allow it to cool enough to handle. Dice well.
- Combine bread crumbs, feta cheese, mint leaves, onion, egg, zucchini, and cooked potato in a bowl until the mixture holds together when lightly pressed.
- In another shallow dish, put flour. Shape the zucchini mixture into small patties, then dredge both sides of patties with flour.
- In a skillet, heat the olive oil over medium heat. Pan-fry zucchini patties for 3-5 minutes on each side until both sides turn golden brown. Place on the paper towels for draining; serve hot.

### Nutrition Information

- Calories: 112 calories;
- Protein: 3.8
- Total Fat: 7.3
- Sodium: 201
- Total Carbohydrate: 8.1
- Cholesterol: 26

# Chapter 2: Greek Side Dish Recipes

***

## 49. Arakas Latheros (Greek Peas With Tomato And Dill)

*Serving: 4 | Prep: 10mins | Cook: 40mins | Ready in:*

### Ingredients

- 3 tablespoons olive oil
- 6 green onions, chopped
- 1 (16 ounce) package frozen peas
- 1 cup crushed tomatoes
- 1 potato, peeled and cut into wedges
- 1/2 cup chopped fresh dill
- 1/2 cup water (optional)
- salt and ground black pepper to taste

### Direction

- In a saucepan, heat olive oil over medium heat and sauté onion for about 5 minutes until soft yet not browned. Add potato, tomatoes, peas, and dill; sprinkle with pepper and salt for seasoning. If there is not enough liquid from the tomatoes, add more water.
- Mix well and bring to a boil. Reduce heat and cook, partly covered for about 30 minutes until potato and peas are tender. Make sure that all the liquid from the tomatoes has vaporized before serving.

### Nutrition Information

- Calories: 245 calories;
- Total Carbohydrate: 31
- Cholesterol: 0
- Protein: 8.5
- Total Fat: 10.8
- Sodium: 255

## 50. Arica's Green Beans And Feta

*Serving: 4 | Prep: 10mins | Cook: 20mins | Ready in:*

### Ingredients

- 2 teaspoons olive oil, or as needed
- 1 red bell pepper, chopped
- 1 tablespoon minced garlic, or to taste
- salt and ground black pepper to taste
- 1 pound green beans, cut into 1-inch pieces
- 1/4 cup white wine
- 1/4 cup crumbled feta cheese

## Direction

- Heat the olive oil on medium heat in a skillet. Whisk the garlic and red bell pepper into the hot oil; use the black pepper and salt to season. Cook and whisk for 5-7 minutes till bell pepper softens.
- Mix the green beans with red bell pepper. Add the white wine onto the green bean mixture. Put the cover on skillet and cook for roughly 10 minutes till green beans soften.
- Stir the green bean mixture. Drizzle the feta cheese on the mixture. Replace the cover and keep cooking for roughly 3 minutes till feta is tender.

## Nutrition Information

- Calories: 106 calories;
- Total Fat: 4.6
- Sodium: 153
- Total Carbohydrate: 11.4
- Cholesterol: 8
- Protein: 3.8

## 51. Baked Greek Fries

*Serving: 4 | Prep: 10mins | Cook: 20mins | Ready in:*

## Ingredients

- 2 large potatoes, cut into wedges
- 2 tablespoons olive oil
- 1 tablespoon Greek seasoning
- 1 teaspoon grated lemon zest
- salt and ground black pepper to taste
- 2 ounces feta cheese
- 2 tablespoons chopped fresh mint

## Direction

- Preheat the oven to 200°C or 400°Fahrenheit.
- On a baking sheet, scatter the potatoes then sprinkle with olive oil and mix to coat. In a small bowl, combine pepper, Greek seasoning, salt, and lemon zest; evenly sprinkle mixture of seasoning over the potatoes.
- Bake for 20 minutes in the preheated oven until fork-tender.
- Break the feta cheese into pieces then scatter over the potatoes; scatter with mint.

## Nutrition Information

- Calories: 244 calories;
- Total Fat: 10
- Sodium: 564
- Total Carbohydrate: 33.8
- Cholesterol: 13
- Protein: 5.9

## 52. Briam (Greek Mixed Vegetables In Tomato Sauce)

*Serving: 12 | Prep: 30mins | Cook: 1hours10mins | Ready in:*

## Ingredients

- 4 tomatoes
- 1/2 cup olive oil
- 2 tablespoons red wine vinegar
- 2 tablespoons white sugar
- 1/3 cup chopped fresh parsley
- 1/3 cup chopped fresh mint
- 1/3 cup chopped fresh basil
- 2 tablespoons fresh oregano
- 1/4 cup capers
- 2 cloves garlic
- salt and ground black pepper to taste

- 2 tablespoons olive oil
- 2 onions, sliced
- 2 potatoes, sliced
- 2 eggplant, sliced
- 3 zucchini, sliced
- 3 green bell peppers, sliced
- 2 cups okra

### Direction

- Set the oven at 350°F (175°C) and start preheating. In a food processor's bowl, put garlic, capers, oregano, basil, mint, parsley, sugar, red wine vinegar, 1/2 cup of olive oil and three of the tomatoes; process to form a fresh tomato sauce. Season with black pepper and salt; set aside. Chop the remaining tomatoes and set aside.
- Place a skillet on medium heat and heat 2 tablespoons of olive oil, cook onions while stirring for around 10 minutes till slightly golden.
- Combine together the fresh tomato sauce, the reserved chopped tomato, okra, bell peppers, zucchini, eggplant, potatoes and onions; arrange the mixture on a large baking pan. Mix in a little water if necessary so the sauce just covers the vegetables.
- Bake for around 1 hour in the preheated oven or till all the vegetables turn tender.

### Nutrition Information

- Calories: 177 calories;
- Total Fat: 11.6
- Sodium: 97
- Total Carbohydrate: 17.7
- Cholesterol: 0
- Protein: 2.7

## 53. Burnt Butter Rice

*Serving: 8 | Prep: 5mins | Cook: 40mins | Ready in:*

### Ingredients

- 4 cups chicken broth
- 2 cups long grain white rice
- 1/2 cup butter
- salt to taste

### Direction

- In a big pot, add rice and chicken broth, then bring the mixture to a boil. Lower heat to low and simmer with a cover about 15 minutes.
- During the final 5 minutes of the rice cooking process, in a small skillet, melt butter on moderately high heat until foam begins to clear and butter is browned. Butter will have dark brown color, the same as chocolate.
- Take the rice away from the heat after rice has simmered about 15 minutes. Add over rice with burnt butter, being careful not to spatter. Avoid stirring into the rice. Replace the lid and allow to stand about 15 minutes. Stir and use salt to season to taste before serving.

### Nutrition Information

- Calories: 271 calories;
- Protein: 3.4
- Total Fat: 11.8
- Sodium: 84
- Total Carbohydrate: 37
- Cholesterol: 31

## 54. Classic Greek Spinach

*Serving: 6 | Prep: 30mins | Cook: 40mins | Ready in:*

### Ingredients

- 1 cup olive oil
- 2 onions, chopped
- 1 (10 ounce) package frozen chopped spinach, thawed and drained
- 2 large tomatoes, coarsely chopped
- 3 cups water

- 1 clove garlic, minced
- 1 tablespoon tomato paste
- 1 cube beef bouillon
- salt and pepper to taste
- 1/2 cup uncooked long-grain white rice

## Direction

- On medium heat, heat olive oil in a medium saucepan. Cook and stir onions in hot oil until tender; stir in spinach and tomatoes. Let it simmer for 5 minutes.
- Add two cups of water in the saucepan; boil. Stir in pepper, garlic, salt, bouillon cube, and tomato paste. Lower heat; cook for 15 minutes at a low boil until the water reduces by half.
- Mix the remaining water and rice into the spinach mixture; boil. Lower heat; let it simmer for 20 minutes with cover until the rice is fluffy and tender.

## Nutrition Information

- Calories: 418 calories;
- Sodium: 206
- Total Carbohydrate: 20.9
- Cholesterol: < 1
- Protein: 4
- Total Fat: 36.6

## 55. Delicious Spinach Rice With Feta

*Serving: 6 | Prep: 15mins | Cook: 36mins | Ready in:*

## Ingredients

- 2 1/4 cups water
- 1 1/2 cups long-grain white rice
- 1 tablespoon olive oil
- 4 green onions, chopped
- 2 cloves garlic, crushed
- 1 (10 ounce) bag fresh spinach
- 1/3 cup chopped fresh dill
- 2 tablespoons pine nuts
- 1 (4 ounce) package crumbled feta cheese
- 2 tablespoons chopped fresh mint, or to taste
- 1 lemon, zested and juiced
- 1 teaspoon sumac

## Direction

- In a saucepan, bring rice and water to a boil. Lower heat to moderately low, then place on a cover and simmer rice for 20-25 minutes, until liquid is absorbed and rice is softened.
- In a big skillet, heat oil on moderate heat. Put in garlic and green onions, then cook for 5 minutes, stirring, until tender. Stir in dill and spinach for 3-5 minutes, until wilted. Stir in cooked rice, then remove to a big serving dish.
- Heat a small skillet on moderate heat. Put in pine nuts, then cook for 3-5 minutes while stirring, until toasted.
- Place sumac, lemon juice, lemon zest, mint, feta cheese and toasted pine nuts on top of rice.

## Nutrition Information

- Calories: 276 calories;
- Total Carbohydrate: 43.2
- Cholesterol: 17
- Protein: 8.6
- Total Fat: 8.3
- Sodium: 256

## 56. Dolmas (Stuffed Grape Leaves)

*Serving: 8 | Prep: 30mins | Cook: 45mins | Ready in:*

## Ingredients

- 1 tablespoon olive oil
- 2 onions, minced
- 1 1/2 cups uncooked white rice
- 2 tablespoons tomato paste
- 2 tablespoons dried currants

- 2 tablespoons pine nuts
- 1 tablespoon ground cinnamon
- 1 tablespoon dried mint
- 1 tablespoon dried dill weed
- 1 teaspoon ground allspice
- 1 teaspoon ground cumin
- 1 (8 ounce) jar grape leaves, drained and rinsed

## Direction

- In a medium saucepan, heat oil over medium heat. Sauté onions till tender. Mix in rice and hot water to cover. Put on a cover and simmer for 10 minutes till rice is half cooked.
- Take away from heat and mix in cumin, allspice, dill weed, mint leaves, cinnamon, pine nuts, currants and tomato paste. Allow the mixture to cool.
- Put an inverted plate on the bottom of a big pot; this protects dolmas from direct heat once steaming.
- Use warm water to wash grape leaves; drain and chop off any stems. In the middle of a leaf, put approximately a teaspoon of cooled rice mixture. Fold in sides and roll into a cigar shape. Put in prepped pot. Redo with the rest of the ingredients.
- Put in just sufficient warm water to reach the bottom of first layer of the dolmas. Put on a cover and simmer for 30 to 45 minutes over low heat, till rice is completely cooked. Check water level frequently and put in additional water as needed.

## Nutrition Information

- Calories: 207 calories;
- Total Carbohydrate: 39.1
- Cholesterol: 0
- Protein: 5.3
- Total Fat: 3.8
- Sodium: 847

## 57. Easy Marinated Vegetables

*Serving: 4 | Prep: | Cook: | Ready in:*

## Ingredients

- 1 1/2 cups broccoli florets
- 1 1/2 cups cauliflower florets
- 1 green bell pepper, cut into 1 inch pieces
- 1 cucumber - peeled, seeded and chopped
- 1 carrot, coarsely chopped
- 1/4 cup Italian-style salad dressing

## Direction

- Boil salted water in a large pot. Add cauliflower florets and broccoli into the boiling water for one minute. Remove from water and rinse florets.
- In a medium size mixing bowl, combine Italian salad dressing, carrots, cucumber, bell pepper, cauliflower, and broccoli. Refrigerate the bowl of vegetables with a cover, 1 hour.

## Nutrition Information

- Calories: 82 calories;
- Sodium: 278
- Total Carbohydrate: 9.9
- Cholesterol: 0
- Protein: 2.5
- Total Fat: 4.5

## 58. Eggplant With Almonds

*Serving: 4 | Prep: 40mins | Cook: 35mins | Ready in:*

## Ingredients

- 2 large eggplants, cut into cubes
- salt
- 1/4 cup olive oil
- 1 large onion, minced
- 2 cloves garlic, minced
- 1 cup whole almonds, skin removed

- 2 cups cherry tomatoes, halved and seeded
- 4 mint leaves, sliced
- 2 tablespoons white wine
- 2 tablespoons white sugar
- 1 pinch salt
- 1/2 teaspoon chili powder
- 1/2 cup chopped fresh parsley

### Direction

- In a colander, put the eggplant and sprinkle salt on top. Put the colander in the sink and drain off the liquid, approximately 20 minutes. Use paper towel to pat the cubes to remove extra salt.
- In a big frying pan, heat the olive oil on medium-high heat. Cook the onion in the oil until it turns translucent. Add the garlic and let it cook and stir for 2 minutes more. Stir in the almonds and eggplant, then cook and stir for about 20 minutes, until the eggplant becomes soft, yet not mushy.
- Mix in the chili powder, salt, sugar, white wine, mint and tomatoes, once the eggplant is cooked through. Cook the mixture for 10 minutes, stirring from time to time, then take it out of the heat and put parsley on top to garnish.

### Nutrition Information

- Calories: 458 calories;
- Total Carbohydrate: 37.2
- Cholesterol: 0
- Protein: 11.7
- Total Fat: 32.4
- Sodium: 22

## 59. Gigantes (Greek Lima Beans)

*Serving: 8 | Prep: 10mins | Cook: 1hours50mins | Ready in:*

### Ingredients

- 1 (16 ounce) package dried lima beans
- 2 (16 ounce) cans chopped tomatoes with juice
- 1 cup olive oil
- 3 cloves garlic, chopped
- sea salt to taste
- 1 teaspoon chopped fresh dill

### Direction

- Put lima beans into a large saucepan. Pour in water just enough to cover by 2 inches above the beans. Let steep overnight.
- Turn oven to 375°F (190°C) to preheat.
- Bring the pan containing lima beans to a boil over medium heat; turn heat to medium-low and simmer for 20 minutes; drain well. Transfer beans to a 9x13-inch baking dish. Stir in dill, salt, garlic, olive oil, and tomatoes.
- Bake for 1 1/2 to 2 hours in the preheated oven until done, stirring sometimes and pouring in more water if the mixture seems dry.

### Nutrition Information

- Calories: 449 calories;
- Total Carbohydrate: 40.4
- Cholesterol: 0
- Protein: 13
- Total Fat: 27.5
- Sodium: 171

## 60. Grecian Green Beans In Tomato Sauce

*Serving: 8 | Prep: 15mins | Cook: 45mins | Ready in:*

### Ingredients

- 2 pounds fresh green beans, trimmed
- 6 tablespoons lemon juice
- 1 medium onion, chopped
- 3/4 cup olive oil
- 1 (16 ounce) can diced tomatoes

- 1 (8 ounce) can tomato sauce
- 2 tablespoons dried parsley
- 1 cup water
- salt and pepper to taste
- 1 bay leaf

## Direction

- In a pot, put the green beans, then combine in bay leaf, pepper, salt, water, parsley, tomato sauce, tomatoes, olive oil, onion, and lemon juice. Cook and stir from time to time until the sauce thickens, for 45 minutes on moderate heat. Before serving, retrieve the bay leaf.

## Nutrition Information

- Calories: 242 calories;
- Sodium: 245
- Total Carbohydrate: 13.9
- Cholesterol: 0
- Protein: 3.2
- Total Fat: 20.5

## 61. Greek Garlic Lemon Potatoes

*Serving: 12 | Prep: 25mins | Cook: 1hours30mins | Ready in:*

## Ingredients

- 3 pounds potatoes, peeled and cubed
- 3 cups hot water
- 1/2 cup fresh lemon juice
- 1/3 cup vegetable oil
- 1 tablespoon olive oil
- 1 1/2 teaspoons dried oregano
- 2 teaspoons salt
- 1/2 teaspoon ground black pepper
- 2 cloves garlic, minced
- 1/4 cup chopped fresh parsley

## Direction

- Preheat the oven to 245°C or 475°Fahrenheit.
- In a 12-in by 18-in roasting pan or baking dish, put olive oil, cubed potatoes, vegetable oil, lemon juice, and water. Scatter garlic, oregano, pepper, and salt to season.
- Roast for approximately 1 1/2 hrs. In the preheated oven without a cover until the water evaporates and the potatoes are golden and tender. Mix the potatoes every 20 mins of baking. If needed, pour in more water to avoid sticking. Let the water evaporate on the last 15-20mins of cooking but be careful to prevent the potatoes from burning. Mix in chopped fresh parsley. Serve.

## Nutrition Information

- Calories: 156 calories;
- Cholesterol: 0
- Protein: 2.4
- Total Fat: 7.4
- Sodium: 397
- Total Carbohydrate: 21.1

## 62. Greek Potato Stew

*Serving: 6 | Prep: 25mins | Cook: 30mins | Ready in:*

## Ingredients

- 2 1/2 pounds potatoes, peeled and cubed
- 1/3 cup olive oil
- 2 cloves garlic, minced
- 3/4 cup whole, pitted kalamata olives
- 1 1/3 cups chopped tomatoes
- 1 teaspoon dried oregano
- salt and pepper to taste

## Direction

- Heat the oil in a big sauté pan over medium heat. Put in the potatoes then stir. Mix in garlic then put in the olives and cook and stir for several minutes. Mix in oregano and tomatoes.

- Decrease the heat then cover. Allow to simmer until potatoes become tender, about 30 minutes. Use pepper and salt to season.

## Nutrition Information

- Calories: 309 calories;
- Total Fat: 16.7
- Sodium: 289
- Total Carbohydrate: 36.7
- Cholesterol: 0
- Protein: 4.5

## 63. Greek Spaghetti I

*Serving: 8 | Prep: 20mins | Cook: 40mins | Ready in:*

## Ingredients

- 1 pound spaghetti
- 1/4 pound Romano cheese, grated
- 1/4 pound shredded mozzarella cheese
- 1/4 pound shredded provolone cheese
- 1/2 cup margarine, melted
- 1 pinch garlic powder

## Direction

- Cook spaghetti in a big pot of boiling and lightly salted water for 8-10 minutes until al dente; drain the spaghetti.
- Preheat the oven to 175°C or 350°Fahrenheit. Oil a medium casserole dish lightly. Combine provolone cheese, mozzarella cheese, and Romano cheese in a bowl. Combine garlic powder and melted margarine in another bowl.
- Put 1/3 of cooked spaghetti at the bottom of the greased dish to cover; add 1/3 of cheese mixture on top and sprinkle with 1/3 margarine mixture. Repeat the layer ending with cheese on top. You can also sprinkle garlic in each layer if you want.
- Bake in the preheated oven for half an hour until the cheese is pale brown and bubbly.

## Nutrition Information

- Calories: 441 calories;
- Cholesterol: 34
- Protein: 18.5
- Total Fat: 22
- Sodium: 515
- Total Carbohydrate: 41.6

## 64. Greek Style Potatoes

*Serving: 4 | Prep: 20mins | Cook: 2hours | Ready in:*

## Ingredients

- 1/3 cup olive oil
- 1 1/2 cups water
- 2 cloves garlic, finely chopped
- 1/4 cup fresh lemon juice
- 1 teaspoon dried thyme
- 1 teaspoon dried rosemary
- 2 cubes chicken bouillon
- ground black pepper to taste
- 6 potatoes, peeled and quartered

## Direction

- Preheat the oven to 175°C or 350°Fahrenheit.
- Combine pepper, olive oil, bouillon cubes, water, rosemary, garlic, thyme, and lemon juice in a small bowl.
- Evenly place the potatoes in the base of a medium baking dish; drizzle olive oil mixture all over the potatoes then cover. Bake in the preheated oven for 1 1/2-2 hours, flipping from time to time until the potatoes are tender yet firm.

## Nutrition Information

- Calories: 418 calories;

- Total Fat: 18.5
- Sodium: 596
- Total Carbohydrate: 58.6
- Cholesterol: < 1
- Protein: 7

## 65. Greek Vegetables

*Serving: 6 | Prep: 20mins | Cook: 25mins | Ready in:*

### Ingredients

- 1 clove garlic, minced
- 1 teaspoon dried oregano
- salt and ground black pepper to taste
- 6 tablespoons extra-virgin olive oil
- 8 red potatoes, cut into quarters
- 10 crimini mushrooms, quartered
- 1 large zucchini cut in half lengthwise, then cut into 1-inch moons

### Direction

- In a big skillet, cook and stir together olive oil, pepper, salt, oregano and garlic on moderate heat for a minute, until tangy. Put in zucchini, mushrooms and potatoes, then cover the skillet and cook the vegetables on high heat for 5 minutes. Stir, replace the lid and lower heat to moderate. Cook for 15 minutes while stirring sometimes, until the potatoes are softened.

### Nutrition Information

- Calories: 340 calories;
- Total Carbohydrate: 48.3
- Cholesterol: 0
- Protein: 7.4
- Total Fat: 14
- Sodium: 34

## 66. Greek Style Lemon Roasted Potatoes

*Serving: 6 | Prep: 15mins | Cook: 1hours | Ready in:*

### Ingredients

- 3 pounds potatoes, peeled and cut into thick wedges
- 1/3 cup olive oil
- 2 lemons, juiced
- 2 teaspoons salt
- 1 teaspoon oregano
- 1/2 teaspoon ground black pepper
- 3 cups chicken broth

### Direction

- Preheat the oven to 200 degrees C (400 degrees F).
- Place the potato wedges to the big bowl. Drizzle the lemon juice and olive oil on top of wedges and coat by tossing. Use the black pepper, oregano and salt to season the potatoes; coat by tossing one more time.
- Spread the potato wedges in one layer in the 2 in. deep pan. Add the chicken broth on top of potatoes.
- Roast the potatoes in the preheated oven for roughly 60 minutes till soft and golden brown.

### Nutrition Information

- Calories: 282 calories;
- Cholesterol: 0
- Protein: 4.6
- Total Fat: 12.2
- Sodium: 789
- Total Carbohydrate: 39.9

## 67. Greek Style Potatoes

*Serving: 6 | Prep: 15mins | Cook: 1hours30mins | Ready in:*

## Ingredients

- 1 1/2 cups water
- 1/3 cup olive oil
- 1/4 cup fresh lemon juice
- 1/4 cup chopped fresh dill
- 2 cubes chicken bouillon, crushed
- 2 cloves garlic, finely chopped
- 1 teaspoon dried thyme
- 1 teaspoon dried rosemary
- 1 teaspoon dried oregano
- salt and ground black pepper to taste
- 6 potatoes, peeled and cut into inch-thick wedges

## Direction

- Turn oven to 350°F (175°C) to preheat.
- In a mixing bowl, combine pepper, salt, oregano, rosemary, thyme, garlic, chicken bouillon, dill, lemon juice, olive oil, and water until no lumps remain.
- Arrange potato wedges all over the bottom of a baking dish. Drizzle seasoning mixture over the potatoes. Cover the dish with aluminum foil.
- Bake for 90 to 120 minutes in the preheated oven, flipping occasionally, until potatoes are tender in the middle.

## Nutrition Information

- Calories: 280 calories;
- Cholesterol: < 1
- Protein: 4.7
- Total Fat: 12.4
- Sodium: 426
- Total Carbohydrate: 39.3

### 68. Greeked Zucchini

*Serving: 4 | Prep: 20mins | Cook: 35mins | Ready in:*

## Ingredients

- 1 medium zucchini, halved and sliced
- 1/4 cup diced red onion
- 1/4 cup diced green bell pepper
- 2 (4 ounce) cans sliced black olives, drained
- 1/4 cup crumbled feta cheese
- 2 tablespoons Greek vinaigrette salad dressing
- 1/4 cup grape or cherry tomatoes, halved

## Direction

- Set an oven to 175°C (350°F) and start preheating.
- Use non-stick cooking spray to grease a large piece of aluminum foil. Layer on the center with the olives, pepper, onion, and zucchini. Use feta cheese to drizzle, and vinaigrette to sprinkle. Let fold into a packet and seal its edges.
- Bake in the preheated oven for 30 minutes until the veggies become tender. Unseal the foil packet, place the oven on Broil, and broil until the feta browns lightly. Put in the grape tomatoes; serve.

## Nutrition Information

- Calories: 143 calories;
- Total Fat: 11.6
- Sodium: 792
- Total Carbohydrate: 8.4
- Cholesterol: 14
- Protein: 3.6

### 69. Hariton's 'Famous' Vegetarian Casserole

*Serving: 36 | Prep: 30mins | Cook: 2hours30mins | Ready in:*

## Ingredients

- 8 large eggplants
- 8 large potatoes
- 8 green bell peppers

- 8 large onions
- 8 summer squash
- 6 tomatoes
- 1 pound fresh green beans
- 1 pound whole fresh mushrooms
- 2 bulbs garlic, cloves separated and peeled
- 1/4 cup chopped fresh dill weed
- 1/4 cup chopped fresh oregano
- 1/4 cup chopped fresh basil
- 1 (15 ounce) can tomato sauce
- 3/4 cup olive oil
- salt and pepper to taste

## Direction

- Prep eggplant before assembling ingredients; cut to 2-in. chunks. Put into extra big bowl; add salted water to cover. This draws out bitterness from eggplant and let sit for 3 hours.
- Preheat an oven to 190°C/375°F.
- Cut tomatoes, squash, onion, green bell peppers and potatoes to 2-in. chunks. Cut mushrooms and green beans in half; peel garlic cloves.
- Drain then rinse eggplant; mix with other chopped veggies, basil, oregano and dill. Put into 3x13x18-in. roasting pan. Put olive oil and tomato sauce on all.
- Bake for 2 1/2 hours at 190°C/375°F, adding a bit of water halfway through cooking time to keep moist.

## Nutrition Information

- Calories: 176 calories;
- Sodium: 75
- Total Carbohydrate: 30.9
- Cholesterol: 0
- Protein: 5.2
- Total Fat: 5.1

# 70. Herbed Greek Roasted Potatoes With Feta Cheese

*Serving: 10 | Prep: 20mins | Cook: 1hours20mins | Ready in:*

## Ingredients

- 5 pounds potatoes, cut into wedges
- 6 cloves garlic, minced
- 3/4 cup olive oil
- 1 cup water
- 1/4 cup fresh lemon juice
- sea salt to taste
- ground black pepper to taste
- 1 1/2 tablespoons dried oregano
- 1 teaspoon chopped fresh mint
- 1 (8 ounce) package crumbled feta cheese

## Direction

- Preheat an oven to 450 degrees F (230 degrees C). Prepare a large lightly oiled baking dish.
- In a bowl, combine the pepper, salt, lemon juice, water, olive oil, garlic, and potatoes together until the potatoes become equally coated; pour to the prepared baking dish.
- In the preheated oven, roast for around 40 minutes, until the potatoes start browning. Flavor the potatoes with the mint and oregano. Pour in another half cup of water if the dish appears dry. Transfer back to the oven and bake for around 40 more minutes. To serve, top with the crumbled feta cheese.

## Nutrition Information

- Calories: 379 calories;
- Total Fat: 21.3
- Sodium: 305
- Total Carbohydrate: 41
- Cholesterol: 20
- Protein: 8

## 71. Melitzanes Imam

*Serving: 2 | Prep: 30mins | Cook: 45mins | Ready in:*

### Ingredients

- 1 eggplant
- 1 (14.5 ounce) can diced tomatoes, drained
- 1 tablespoon tomato paste
- 1 medium onion, chopped
- 1 tablespoon minced garlic, or to taste
- 1 teaspoon ground cinnamon, or to taste
- 3 tablespoons olive oil
- salt and pepper to taste

### Direction

- Set the oven to 175°C or 350°F.
- Halve the eggplant lengthways and hollow out the halves to leave approximately a 1 cm. shell. Set aside the flesh from the insides for later use. Put the shells on a baking tray and drizzle a little olive oil over.
- In the preheated oven, bake for about half an hour until softened.
- While those are baking, chop the remaining eggplant into small pieces. In a big skillet, heat approximately 2 tbsp. olive oil on medium heat, then add garlic and onion. Cook and stir for several minutes. Put in the chopped eggplant, then cook and stir until softened. Stir in tomato paste and tomatoes until well blended, then simmer on low heat until the halves in the oven are ready.
- Take the baked eggplant shells out of the oven, then scoop in the eggplant and tomato mixture. Sprinkle on top of each one with a little cinnamon and take them back to the oven. Bake for 30 minutes more or so.

### Nutrition Information

- Calories: 314 calories;
- Sodium: 391
- Total Carbohydrate: 28.7
- Cholesterol: 0
- Protein: 5.3
- Total Fat: 20.8

## 72. Oven Roasted Greek Potatoes

*Serving: 6 | Prep: 25mins | Cook: 1hours15mins | Ready in:*

### Ingredients

- 2 teaspoons lemon pepper
- 1/2 teaspoon dried marjoram
- 1 teaspoon dried basil
- 1/8 teaspoon dried thyme
- 1 teaspoon dried rosemary
- 1/4 cup white wine
- 1 cup water
- 2 tablespoons olive oil
- 2 tablespoons Italian salad dressing
- 2 cloves garlic, minced
- 1 lemon, juiced
- 1 tablespoon lemon zest
- 6 medium potatoes, peeled and quartered

### Direction

- Combine rosemary, thyme, basil, marjoram and lemon pepper in a small bowl. In another bowl, combine 1/2 seasoning mixture, lemon zest, lemon juice, garlic, dressing, olive oil, water and wine. Add mixture to a medium glass baking dish. Arrange potatoes in the dish and coat well with the mixture, sprinkle over coated potatoes with remaining seasonings. Keep in refrigerator, covered, for 8 hours or overnight.
- Set the oven to 350°F (175°C) and start preheating.
- In the preheated oven, bake potatoes for 75 minutes, remember to baste one time half way through the bake time.

### Nutrition Information

- Calories: 234 calories;

- Sodium: 249
- Total Carbohydrate: 40.8
- Cholesterol: 0
- Protein: 4.7
- Total Fat: 6.2

## 73. Paleo Greek 'Rice'

*Serving: 6 | Prep: 15mins | Cook: 15mins | Ready in:*

### Ingredients

- 1/2 yellow onion, diced small
- 1/4 cup fresh lemon juice
- 1 head cauliflower, cut into large florets
- 1/2 red bell pepper, diced small
- 1/2 cup grape tomatoes, halved
- 3 tablespoons chopped fresh mint
- 1/4 cup extra virgin olive oil
- salt and ground black pepper to taste

### Direction

- In a bowl, mix lemon juice and onion together. Leave to stand for about 30 minutes until the onion flavor mellows. Drain the onion and save lemon juice.
- In a food processor, shred the cauliflower until it's the size of small rice grains.
- Over medium heat, put the cauliflower in a skillet, cover and then cook while stirring once in a while, for 8 to 10 minutes until the cauliflower is steamed. Take out the lid and mix grape tomatoes and red bell pepper into the cauliflower. Cook while stirring occasionally for about 3 minutes until heated through. Add mint and onion to the cauliflower mixture. Cook while stirring for about 3 minutes until heated through.
- In a bowl, whisk olive oil, pepper, salt, and three tablespoons of reserved lemon juice together. Pour lemon juice mixture atop the cauliflower mixture and stir to coat. Season to taste with black pepper and salt.

### Nutrition Information

- Calories: 120 calories;
- Total Fat: 9.5
- Sodium: 57
- Total Carbohydrate: 8
- Cholesterol: 0
- Protein: 2.3

## 74. Penne With Yogurt Tahini Sauce

*Serving: 8 | Prep: 20mins | Cook: 20mins | Ready in:*

### Ingredients

- 3 tablespoons tahini
- 1/8 cup lemon juice
- 1 cup plain yogurt
- 3/4 cup water
- 3 cloves garlic
- 1/4 cup olive oil
- 1 onion, chopped
- 2 large portobello mushrooms, sliced
- 1/2 red bell pepper, diced
- 1 (16 ounce) package penne pasta
- 1/2 cup chopped parsley
- ground black pepper to taste

### Direction

- Cook the pasta in a big pot with lightly salted boiling water for 10-12 minutes or until it becomes al dente.
- As the pasta cooks, mix together the lemon juice and tahini. Put it in a food processor together with garlic cloves, water and yogurt, then process until it becomes smooth.
- In a sauté pan, heat the oil on medium heat. Put in the onion and let it cook until it becomes soft. Put in mushrooms and let it cook until it becomes soft. During the last several minutes of cooking, put in the bell pepper (the pepper must be still crispish).

- Let the pasta drain, then toss it together with freshly ground black pepper, chopped parsley and yogurt-tahini sauce. Serve the veggie sauté on top of the noodles.

## Nutrition Information

- Calories: 332 calories;
- Cholesterol: 2
- Protein: 11.1
- Total Fat: 11.7
- Sodium: 36
- Total Carbohydrate: 48.2

## 75. Sarah's Feta Rice Pilaf

*Serving: 4 | Prep: 10mins | Cook: 30mins | Ready in:*

## Ingredients

- 2 tablespoons butter
- 1/2 cup orzo pasta
- 1/2 cup diced onion
- 2 cloves garlic, minced
- 1/2 cup white rice
- 2 cups chicken broth
- 1 cup chopped spinach
- 1/2 cup chopped Bulgarian feta cheese

## Direction

- Melt the butter in a pan on medium-low heat. Cook and stir the orzo in the melted butter for 3-5 minutes, until it turns golden brown in color. Mix the onion into the orzo and let it cook for 5-10 minutes, until it turns translucent. Cook and stir the garlic into the onion-orzo mixture for around 1 minute, until it becomes aromatic.
- Stir the chicken broth and rice into the onion-orzo mixture; boil. Lower the heat to medium-low, cover the pan, and let it simmer for 20-25 minutes, until the liquid has been absorbed and the rice is tender. Take off from the heat,

then mix in feta and spinach; cover. Allow to stand for about 5 minutes, until the feta melts and the spinach wilts. Fluff it using a fork.

## Nutrition Information

- Calories: 295 calories;
- Protein: 8.8
- Total Fat: 10.6
- Sodium: 739
- Total Carbohydrate: 41
- Cholesterol: 34

## 76. Spaghetti Squash With Fire Roasted Tomatoes

*Serving: 6 | Prep: 25mins | Cook: 1hours | Ready in:*

## Ingredients

- 1 spaghetti squash, halved lengthwise and seeded
- 2 tablespoons vegetable oil
- 1 cup chopped asparagus
- 1 cup chopped onion
- 1 tablespoon minced garlic
- 2 (14.5 ounce) cans fire-roasted tomatoes with garlic (such as Hunt's®), drained
- 1 cup crumbled feta cheese
- 12 pitted kalamata olives, halved
- salt and ground black pepper to taste

## Direction

- Preheat an oven to 190 °C or 375 °F.
- Onto a baking sheet, place halves of spaghetti squash with cut sides facing down.
- In the prepped oven, bake squash for 45 minutes till a knife can easily cuts skin. Take off from the oven and scrape and part squash strands from skin use a fork; in a big bowl, reserve spaghetti squash and retain warmth.
- In a skillet over medium heat, heat the vegetable oil; let cook and mix garlic, onion

and asparagus for 10 minutes till soft. Mix in olives, feta cheese and fire-roasted tomatoes; allow to cook for 3 to 5 minutes till warmed through. Toss spaghetti squash and tomato mixture to combine till well mixed; put salt and pepper to season prior serving.

## Nutrition Information

- Calories: 220 calories;
- Total Fat: 12.6
- Sodium: 790
- Total Carbohydrate: 21.4
- Cholesterol: 22
- Protein: 6.4

## 77. Spinach And Rice (Spanakorizo)

*Serving: 4 | Prep: 5mins | Cook: 45mins | Ready in:*

### Ingredients

- 1/3 cup olive oil
- 2 onions, chopped
- 2 pounds fresh spinach, rinsed and stemmed
- 1 (8 ounce) can tomato sauce
- 2 cups water
- 1 teaspoon dried dill weed
- 1 teaspoon dried parsley
- salt and pepper to taste
- 1/2 cup uncooked white rice

### Direction

- On medium-high heat, heat olive oil in a big pan; sauté onions in oil until translucent and soft. Put in spinach; cook and stir for a couple of minutes then add water and tomato sauce. Boil then sprinkle pepper, parsley, salt, and dill; mix in rice. Turn to low heat; let it simmer for 20-25 minutes without cover until the rice is tender. If needed, pour in more water.

### Nutrition Information

- Calories: 337 calories;
- Total Fat: 19.3
- Sodium: 553
- Total Carbohydrate: 35.7
- Cholesterol: 0
- Protein: 9.8

## 78. Yia Yia's Tzatziki Sauce

*Serving: 25 | Prep: 10mins | Cook: | Ready in:*

### Ingredients

- 2 English cucumbers
- 2 (16 ounce) containers sour cream
- 1 (16 ounce) container Greek yogurt
- 2 tablespoons minced garlic
- 1 tablespoon extra virgin olive oil

### Direction

- Peel cucumbers and grate into a colander to squeeze out excess water.
- In a big bowl, combine olive oil, garlic, yogurt and sour cream together, then stir in cucumbers. Refrigerate for a minimum of a half hour and maximum of 2 hours before serving.

### Nutrition Information

- Calories: 108 calories;
- Sodium: 31
- Total Carbohydrate: 2.6
- Cholesterol: 20
- Protein: 2.3
- Total Fat: 10

# Chapter 3: Greek Main Dish Recipes

***

## 79. A Lot More Than Plain Spinach Pie (Greek Batsaria)

*Serving: 9 | Prep: 50mins | Cook: 1hours | Ready in:*

### Ingredients

- 3 eggs
- 1 pound chopped fresh spinach
- 3 leeks, chopped
- 5 green onions, chopped
- 2 1/3 cups crumbled feta cheese
- 1 bunch parsley, chopped
- 1 bunch dill, chopped
- 1 bunch spearmint, chopped
- 1 teaspoon white sugar
- 1 cup milk
- 3/4 cup olive oil
- 1 pinch salt and ground black pepper to taste
- 2 1/2 cups all-purpose flour
- 1/2 cup semolina flour
- 1 pinch salt
- 1/4 cup olive oil
- 2 cups water
- 1 1/4 cups grated Parmesan cheese (optional)
- 2 tablespoons cold butter, cut into pieces
- 2 tablespoons olive oil

### Direction

- Turn oven to 350°F (175°C to preheat). Lightly oil a deep 9x9-inch baking dish.
- In a mixing bowl, beat eggs, then mix in 3/4 cup olive oil, milk, sugar, spearmint, dill, parsley, feta cheese, green onions, leeks, and spinach until well combined. Add pepper and salt to taste; put to one side. In another mixing bowl, combine 1 pinch of salt, semolina flour, and all-purpose flour. Mix in water and 1/4 cup olive oil until smooth. Transfer two-thirds of the batter into the greased 9x9-inch baking dish, distribute evenly. Ladle spinach filling over the cake batter, then pour the rest of the batter over the top of the whole thing. Add 2 tablespoons of olive oil, butter pieces, and Parmesan cheese on top.
- Bake for about 1 hour in the preheated oven until the bottom crust and the surface has set and beautifully browned.

### Nutrition Information

- Calories: 650 calories;
- Total Fat: 44.1
- Sodium: 714
- Total Carbohydrate: 45
- Cholesterol: 115
- Protein: 20.1

## 80. Amazing Greek Chicken Casserole

*Serving: 3 | Prep: 10mins | Cook: 45mins | Ready in:*

### Ingredients

- 1 skinless, boneless chicken breast
- 1 (10.75 ounce) can cream of mushroom soup
- 2 teaspoons Greek seasoning, or to taste
- 1 cup brown rice
- 2 cups water

### Direction

- Preheat an oven to 175°C/350°F. Grease the 9x9-in. casserole dish.
- In prepped baking dish, put chicken breast. Evenly spread cream of mushroom soup on chicken. Sprinkle with Greek seasoning generously. Use aluminum foil to cover the dish.

- In preheated oven, bake for about 45 minutes till juices are clear and chicken isn't pink the middle. An inserted instant-read thermometer in the middle should register at least 74°C/165°F.
- In a saucepan, boil water and brown rice. Lower heat to medium low. Simmer, covered, for 45-50 minutes till liquid is absorbed and rice is tender.
- Cut chicken into bite-sized pieces. Mix rice into the chicken mixture. Before serving, put aside for 5 minutes to cool.

## Nutrition Information

- Calories: 358 calories;
- Sodium: 995
- Total Carbohydrate: 55.8
- Cholesterol: 20
- Protein: 13.9
- Total Fat: 8.5

## 81. American Gyros

*Serving: 8 | Prep: 15mins | Cook: 40mins | Ready in:*

### Ingredients

- 1 pound ground lamb
- 1 pound ground beef
- 1/2 cup finely diced yellow onion
- 4 cloves garlic, crushed
- 1 tablespoon minced fresh rosemary
- 2 teaspoons dried oregano
- 2 teaspoons kosher salt, or to taste
- 1 teaspoon fresh ground black pepper
- 1 teaspoon cumin
- 1 teaspoon paprika
- 1/8 teaspoon ground cinnamon
- 1/8 teaspoon cayenne pepper
- 2 tablespoons dry bread crumbs
- 1 tablespoon olive oil

### Direction

- Preheat the oven to 175°C or 350°F. Grease a 9-inch by 13-inch baking dish. Place parchment paper up to the sides of the dish. Flip the parchment paper until the greased side is up.
- In a mixing bowl, put the ground beef and lamb; mix in bread crumbs, onions, cayenne pepper, garlic, cinnamon, rosemary, paprika, oregano, cumin, pepper, and salt until well blended. Press the meat mixture on the prepared baking dish firmly in an even layer that reaches the edges. It should be fairly dense and packed.
- Bake for 40-45 minutes in the preheated oven at 350°F until nicely brown. An instant-read thermometer inserted in the middle should register at least 70°C or 160°F. Let it cool down to room temperature then move to a plate. Use a sheet of plastic wrap to cover then place in the refrigerator for 1-2 hours.
- Slice the meat crosswise into 3 portions on a cutting board. Cut each portion into 1/8-in pieces as desired.
- On medium-high heat, heat oil in a pan; cook meat slices for 2 minutes on each side until brown.

## Nutrition Information

- Calories: 255 calories;
- Total Fat: 17.8
- Sodium: 549
- Total Carbohydrate: 3.4
- Cholesterol: 72
- Protein: 19.3

## 82. Best Greek Stuffed Turkey

*Serving: 18 | Prep: 30mins | Cook: 4hours | Ready in:*

### Ingredients

- 1 (12 pound) whole turkey, thawed
- 3 lemons, juiced
- 1/4 cup butter

- 4 medium onions, chopped
- 2 turkey livers, finely chopped
- 1 pound ground lamb
- 2 1/2 cups long grain white rice
- 1 tablespoon ground cinnamon
- 1/4 cup chopped fresh mint leaves
- 2 tablespoons tomato paste
- 3 cups water
- salt and pepper to taste
- 1/2 cup butter, melted

## Direction

- Preheat an oven to 230°C or 450°F. Wash turkey inside and out, and pat it dry using paper towels. Massage lemon juice on the entire outer part of turkey and inside the cavity. Reserve.
- In a big skillet, liquify a quarter cup of butter over moderate heat. Put in onion, and cook for 5 minutes, till soft. Put in ground lamb and chopped livers. Cook, mixing to break up, till equally browned. Mix in tomato paste, mint, cinnamon and rice. Stir in 1 cup water, and add pepper and salt to season. Allow to cook for 10 minutes over low heat, mixing continuously.
- Stuff the turkey with filling mixture, and truss. In shallow roasting pan, put on a rack, and add the leftover 2 cups water into pan. Combine together the melted butter and the rest of the lemon juice. It will be the basting sauce.
- In the prepped oven, bake for an hour, then lower oven temperature to 175°C or 350°F and keep roasting for 2 hours longer, or till the inner temperature of chunkiest part of the thigh reads 80°C or 180°F. Baste from time to time with lemon juice and liquified butter.

## Nutrition Information

- Calories: 703 calories;
- Total Fat: 33.7
- Sodium: 240
- Total Carbohydrate: 26.7
- Cholesterol: 246
- Protein: 69.8

## 83. Big Ray's Greek Grilled Catfish Recipe

*Serving: 6 | Prep: 15mins | Cook: 20mins | Ready in:*

### Ingredients

- 6 (8 ounce) fillets catfish
- Greek seasoning, or to taste
- 4 ounces crumbled feta cheese
- 6 toothpicks
- 1 tablespoon dried mint
- 2 tablespoons olive oil

### Direction

- Set the grill to medium heat to preheat and lightly grease the grate.
- Dust Greek seasoning to season both sides of each catfish fillet. Next, sprinkle 1 side of each fillet with mint and feta cheese; pour olive oil over the mint and cheese. Tightly roll the fish around the filling, starting with the narrower end, then use a toothpick to secure.
- On the preheated grill, cook for 20-25 minutes or until the fish easily flakes with a fork.

### Nutrition Information

- Calories: 359 calories;
- Protein: 35.6
- Total Fat: 22.6
- Sodium: 589
- Total Carbohydrate: 1.5
- Cholesterol: 129

## 84. Bourtheto

*Serving: 4 | Prep: 20mins | Cook: 35mins | Ready in:*

### Ingredients

- 6 tablespoons olive oil
- 1 large onion, grated
- 1 pound tomatoes, grated
- 1 1/2 tablespoons tomato paste
- 1 teaspoon ground cayenne pepper
- 8 potatoes, peeled
- 1 teaspoon salt
- 4 (6 ounce) fillets cod
- 1 pint water

### Direction

- In a wide shallow casserole, heat 1/2 of olive oil and cook the tomatoes and the onion for roughly 10 minutes till tender and reduced to form a thick paste. Mix in the cayenne and the tomato puree.
- Chop the potatoes lengthwise into 4-6 wedges and arrange over the tomato mixture. Drizzle with salt and put fish fillets on top. Add in the cold water, be sure to cover potatoes barely. Boil then lower to a simmer.
- Keep it covered and simmered for 20 minutes till the potatoes are soft—in that amount of time, the fish will be cooked.
- Take out the lid and bubble the mixture quickly to reduce it if you want. But leaving a large amount of juice when making this dish to smash the potatoes in is the best.

### Nutrition Information

- Calories: 687 calories;
- Total Carbohydrate: 83.8
- Cholesterol: 72
- Protein: 40.3
- Total Fat: 22.1
- Sodium: 757

## 85. Branzino Mediterranean

*Serving: 4 | Prep: 15mins | Cook: 25mins | Ready in:*

### Ingredients

- 2 tablespoons olive oil, divided
- 1 red onion, chopped
- salt and ground black pepper to taste
- 2 whole Branzino (sea bass) fish, cleaned
- 2 wedges fresh lemon
- 2 sprigs fresh rosemary
- 1/2 cup white wine
- 1/4 cup lemon juice
- 1 tablespoon fresh oregano leaves
- 1/4 cup chopped Italian flat-leaf parsley
- 2 lemon wedges

### Direction

- Preheat the oven to 165°C or 325°Fahrenheit.
- In a big baking pan, sprinkle 1tbsp olive oil then put onion. Sprinkle pepper and salt to season.
- In the baking pan, put two cleaned dish then stuff each cavity with some of the red onion, a sprig of rosemary, and one lemon wedge. Pour lemon juice and white wine over the fish then top with sprinkled oregano. Dribble the remaining 1tbsp olive oil all over the fish.
- Bake for approximately 25 mins in the preheated oven until the fish easily flakes using a fork and is opaque. Separate the fish by sliding gently between the bones. Put fish on a platter then serve with lemon wedges and parsley on top.

### Nutrition Information

- Calories: 380 calories;
- Total Fat: 12.6
- Sodium: 237
- Total Carbohydrate: 6.6
- Cholesterol: 117
- Protein: 53

## 86. Briam (Greek Baked Zucchini And Potatoes)

*Serving: 4 | Prep: 30mins | Cook: 1hours30mins | Ready in:*

### Ingredients

- 2 pounds potatoes, peeled and thinly sliced
- 4 large zucchini, thinly sliced
- 4 small red onions, thinly sliced
- 6 ripe tomatoes, pureed
- 1/2 cup olive oil
- 2 tablespoons chopped fresh parsley (optional)
- sea salt and freshly ground black pepper to taste

### Direction

- Set oven to 400 0 F (200 0 C) and preheat.
- In a 9x13-inch baking dish or preferably a larger one, spread red onions, zucchini and potatoes. If needed, use two baking dishes. Spread parsley, olive oil and pureed tomatoes on top. Add freshly ground pepper and salt to season. Mix all ingredients together until the vegetables are evenly coated.
- Put in the prepared oven and bake for about 90 minutes, stirring after an hour, until vegetables get tender and moisture has evaporated. Before serving, let it cool slightly, or serve at room temperature.

### Nutrition Information

- Calories: 534 calories;
- Cholesterol: 0
- Protein: 11.3
- Total Fat: 28.3
- Sodium: 141
- Total Carbohydrate: 65.8

## 87. Brown Sugar Glazed Pork Chops

*Serving: 6 | Prep: | Cook: | Ready in:*

### Ingredients

- 1/2 cup chopped celery
- 1/2 cup chopped onion
- 1/2 tablespoon butter
- 15 slices day-old bread, torn into small pieces
- 1/2 tablespoon Greek-style seasoning
- 1 (14 ounce) can chicken broth
- 6 pork chops
- 1 cup packed brown sugar
- 1/2 cup butter, melted

### Direction

- Melt half tablespoon margarine or butter in a small pan; put and sauté celery and onion until translucent. In a big bowl, mix the sauté mixture, broth, Greek seasoning, and bread to evenly coat the bread yet not too soggy.
- Preheat the oven to 175°C or 350°Fahrenheit.
- In a lightly greased 9-in by 13-in baking dish, scatter the stuffing/bread mixture in the base then put the pork chops on top. Scatter chops with more Greek seasoning if desired. Mix melted butter or margarine and brown sugar in a medium bowl; slather over the pork chops tops then drizzle on the toppings and chops. Let some of the mixture soak through the stuffing.
- Bake for half an hour in the preheated oven until the pork's internal temperature reads 63°C or 145°Fahrenheit. The time of baking will vary a bit based on the chops' thickness. Baste it with more butter/sugar mixture as you bake if desired. Put the chops and stuffing on a dish to serve.

### Nutrition Information

- Calories: 584 calories;
- Total Fat: 22.4
- Sodium: 1047

- Total Carbohydrate: 69.8
- Cholesterol: 110
- Protein: 25.9

## 88. Calamari Macaronatha

*Serving: 4 | Prep: 15mins | Cook: 40mins | Ready in:*

### Ingredients

- 2 1/2 cups elbow macaroni
- 1 pound squid, cleaned
- 1/4 cup red wine vinegar
- 6 tablespoons extra virgin olive oil
- 4 cloves garlic, minced
- 1 large onion, chopped
- 1 1/2 cups crushed tomatoes
- 1/4 cup dry white wine
- 1/2 lemon, juiced
- 1 cinnamon stick, broken in half
- 2 bay leaves
- 1/4 teaspoon dried basil leaves
- 1/2 teaspoon dried oregano
- salt and ground black pepper to taste
- 1/2 cup grated Mizithra cheese

### Direction

- Boil a big pot of lightly salted water. Add pasta then cook until al dente or for about 8-10 minutes. Drain.
- Boil squid in 3 cups of water mixed with red wine vinegar in a small saucepan for 8-10 minutes. Drain. Slice to bite-sized rings/pieces. Put aside.
- In a big heavy skillet, heat olive oil. Sauté garlic and onion until onion is soft yet not brown. Mix in squid. Sauté for 2 minutes. Pour in lemon juice, white wine, and crushed tomatoes. Season with pepper, salt, oregano, basil, bay leaves, and cinnamon stick. Boil, lower heat, and simmer for 15-20 minutes, occasionally stirring, partially covered.
- Take off from heat. Mix in cooked pasta. Serve with grated cheese on top.

### Nutrition Information

- Calories: 679 calories;
- Total Fat: 25.1
- Sodium: 537
- Total Carbohydrate: 86.7
- Cholesterol: 275
- Protein: 36.8

## 89. Chef John's Lamb Moussaka Burger

*Serving: 4 | Prep: 40mins | Cook: 25mins | Ready in:*

### Ingredients

- 2 tablespoons olive oil
- 1 yellow onion, diced
- 1 teaspoon salt
- 2 cups diced eggplant
- 3 cloves garlic, crushed
- 1 teaspoon freshly ground black pepper
- 1/2 teaspoon cumin
- 1/4 teaspoon ground cinnamon
- 1/4 teaspoon dried oregano
- 2 teaspoons tomato paste
- 1 1/2 tablespoons olive oil
- 2 tablespoons flour
- 1 cup cold milk
- 1 pinch ground nutmeg
- 1 pinch cayenne pepper
- 1 pinch freshly ground black pepper
- 1/2 cup grated Parmesan cheese
- 1 pound ground lamb
- salt to taste
- 8 slices tomato
- 1 tablespoon chopped fresh mint
- 1 tablespoon rice vinegar
- 1 tablespoon olive oil, or as needed
- 4 hamburger buns, split and toasted

### Direction

- On medium-high heat, heat 2tbsp olive oil in a pan; add diced onion and a teaspoon of salt. Cook and stir for 5mins until the onion is a bit translucent; put in eggplant. Turn to medium heat, cook and stir for another 3-5mins until the eggplant is soft and opaque.
- Mix oregano, garlic, cinnamon, cumin, and a teaspoon of black pepper into the eggplant mixture. Cook while stirring regularly for a minute until aromatic; put tomato paste. Cook and stir for 2mins until completely heated. Move to a plate then cool through; use a plastic wrap to cover. Place in the refrigerator for at least 15mins until chilled.
- On medium-high heat, mix flour and 1 1/2tbsp olive oil together in a pot for 2-3mins until bubbling and golden; add milk. Let it simmer while stirring constantly for 3-5mins until it forms into a thick and smooth sauce. Add nutmeg and a pinch each of cayenne and black pepper to season; take off heat. Mix in Parmesan cheese until it melts.
- In a bowl, mix a pinch of salt, chilled eggplant mixture, and lamb together; shape into 4 patties then put on a plate. Use a plastic wrap to cover then place in the refrigerator until ready to cook.
- In a shallow bowl, put tomato slices then season with chopped mint and a pinch each of black pepper and salt; toss in rice vinegar to coat.
- On medium-high heat, heat a tablespoon of olive oil in a big pan. Cook burgers for 4mins on each side until the center is a bit pink. An inserted instant-read thermometer in the middle should register 60°C or 140°Fahrenheit for medium.
- Slather the preferred amount of cheese sauce on each side of the hamburger buns; put burgers on the bottom bun. Add two slices of tomato on top then put the top bun.

## Nutrition Information

- Calories: 620 calories;
- Cholesterol: 90
- Protein: 31.2
- Total Fat: 37.3
- Sodium: 1133
- Total Carbohydrate: 39.9

## 90. Chef John's Spinach And Feta Pie

*Serving: 6 | Prep: 15mins | Cook: 30mins | Ready in:*

### Ingredients

- 1 tablespoon butter
- 1 pound fresh spinach
- 12 eggs
- salt and freshly ground black pepper to taste
- 1 pinch cayenne pepper
- 6 slices bacon, chopped
- 1/2 onion, diced
- 1 pinch salt
- 3 ounces crumbled feta cheese

### Direction

- Preheat oven to 350°F (175°C).
- In a large oven-proof skillet, heat butter over high heat. Stir spinach in heated butter for about 30 seconds until wilted. Drain well and squeeze out as much liquid as possible from the spinach. Remove spinach to a cutting board and chop.
- In a bowl, beat eggs with cayenne pepper, black pepper, and salt until well blended.
- Put bacon in the same skillet used for spinach and cook, stirring sometimes, for about 5 to 8 minutes over medium-high heat until fat renders and bacon is nearly crisp. Remove bacon drippings with paper towels held in tongs. Lower heat to medium; sauté onion and bacon with a pinch of salt for seasoning, about 5 more minutes, until onion is translucent.
- Sauté in chopped spinach until heated; stream in eggs. Spread spinach to combine evenly with the eggs using a wooden spoon. Sprinkle over the mixture with feta cheese.

- Bake for 10 to 15 minutes in the preheated oven until eggs are firm. The surface may remain a little wet.
- Turn the broiler of the oven on. Broil quiche for 2 to 3 minutes until the top is lightly golden brown.

### Nutrition Information

- Calories: 268 calories;
- Sodium: 584
- Total Carbohydrate: 5.1
- Cholesterol: 400
- Protein: 20.3
- Total Fat: 19

## 91. Chicken Kokkinisto With Orzo

*Serving: 4 | Prep: 10mins | Cook: 1hours15mins | Ready in:*

### Ingredients

- 2 tablespoons olive oil
- 1 onion, chopped
- 4 chicken legs, rinsed and patted dry
- 4 cloves garlic, pressed
- 1 (15 ounce) can tomato sauce
- 15 fluid ounces water
- 2 bay leaves
- 1 pinch ground cloves
- salt and ground black pepper to taste
- 1/2 (16 ounce) package uncooked orzo pasta

### Direction

- Heat the oil in a big, wide pot on medium heat. Add the onion and let it cook in the hot oil for 5-7 minutes until tender. Cook the chicken legs in the pot until all sides turn brown. Add the garlic and let it cook and stir for about a minute. Pour the water and tomato sauce on top of the chicken. Add bay leaves into the pot. Put in pepper, salt and cloves to season. Lower the heat to medium-low and let the mixture simmer for about 45 minutes, until the chicken meat falls off the bone and becomes really tender.
- Mix the orzo into the liquid in the pot and let it cook for 15-25 minutes more, until the orzo is soft. Take off the bay leaves. Serve.

### Nutrition Information

- Calories: 586 calories;
- Total Fat: 20.1
- Sodium: 674
- Total Carbohydrate: 51.1
- Cholesterol: 135
- Protein: 49.4

## 92. Chicken Souvlaki Gyro Style

*Serving: 4 | Prep: 30mins | Cook: 20mins | Ready in:*

### Ingredients

- Souvlaki Marinade:
- 3/4 cup balsamic vinaigrette salad dressing
- 3 tablespoons lemon juice
- 1 tablespoon dried oregano
- 1/2 teaspoon freshly ground black pepper
- 4 skinless, boneless chicken breast halves
- Tzatziki Sauce (cucumber sauce):
- 1/2 cup seeded, shredded cucumber
- 1 teaspoon kosher salt
- 1 cup plain yogurt
- 1/4 cup sour cream
- 1 tablespoon lemon juice
- 1/2 tablespoon rice vinegar
- 1 teaspoon olive oil
- 1 clove garlic, minced
- 1 tablespoon chopped fresh dill
- 1/2 teaspoon Greek seasoning
- kosher salt to taste
- freshly ground black pepper to taste
- 4 large pita bread rounds

- 1 heart of romaine lettuce, cut into 1/4 inch slices
- 1 red onion, thinly sliced
- 1 tomato, halved and sliced
- 1/2 cup kalamata olives
- 1/2 cup pepperoncini
- 1 cup crumbled feta cheese

## Direction

- Combine half a teaspoon of black pepper, oregano, juice from half a lemon and balsamic vinaigrette in a small bowl. Transfer chicken into a big resealable plastic bag. Pour marinade onto the chicken, seal, and leave in the fridge for 60 minutes minimum.
- Set an outdoor grill to high heat and start preheating.
- Mix 1 teaspoon of kosher salt with shredded cucumber and let it rest for a minimum of 5 minutes. Combine olive oil, rice vinegar, 1 tablespoon of lemon juice, sour cream and yogurt in a medium bowl. Add Greek seasoning, fresh dill and garlic to season. Squeeze out any excess water in the cucumber, then mix into the sauce. Add pepper and kosher salt to taste. Leave in the fridge until ready to serve.
- Take chicken out of the marinade and transfer to preheated grill. Remove the leftover marinade. Cook chicken for about 8 minutes for each side until juices run clear. Take chicken away from the heat, allow to stand for about 10 minutes, then slice into thin strips.
- Arrange pita rounds on the grill, and cook, while flipping often to prevent burning until warm, for about 2 minutes. Lay pepperoncini, olives, tomato, onion, lettuce, sliced chicken and warmed pita on a serving platter. Place feta cheese and tzatziki sauce in different bowls to serve on the side. Stuff chicken and toppings into pita pockets, then serve.

## Nutrition Information

- Calories: 764 calories;
- Sodium: 3170
- Total Carbohydrate: 55.9
- Cholesterol: 133
- Protein: 44.4
- Total Fat: 40.5

## 93. Chicken Souvlaki With Tzatziki Sauce

*Serving: 6 | Prep: 15mins | Cook: 15mins | Ready in:*

### Ingredients

- 1/4 cup olive oil
- 2 tablespoons lemon juice
- 2 cloves garlic, minced
- 1 teaspoon dried oregano
- 1/2 teaspoon salt
- 1 1/2 pounds skinless, boneless chicken breast halves - cut into bite-sized pieces
- Sauce:
- 1 (6 ounce) container plain Greek-style yogurt
- 1/2 cucumber - peeled, seeded, and grated
- 1 tablespoon olive oil
- 2 teaspoons white vinegar
- 1 clove garlic, minced
- 1 pinch salt
- 6 wooden skewers, or as needed

## Direction

- Take a large re-sealable plastic bag and add in it lemon juice, 1/4 cup olive oil, oregano, 2 cloves minced garlic, 1/2 teaspoon salt, and the chicken. Seal the air out of the bag and squeeze the bag to distribute the marinade. Keep in the refrigerator for 2 hours.
- In a bowl, mix together 1 tablespoon olive oil, yogurt, vinegar, cucumber, 1 clove minced garlic, and 1 pinch salt. This is the tzatziki. Let the flavors meld in the fridge for 1-2 hours.
- Set an outdoor grill on medium-high to preheat. Lightly oil the grates. Immerse wooden skewers in a water for a quarter of an hour.
- Take chicken out of the bag, discarding its marinade. Thread chicken onto skewers.

- Grill the skewers, turning often to cook and evenly brown all sides until chicken is no longer pink in the center, 8 minutes each side. Serve with tzatziki.

## Nutrition Information

- Calories: 268 calories;
- Sodium: 295
- Total Carbohydrate: 2.6
- Cholesterol: 71
- Protein: 25.5
- Total Fat: 16.8

## 94. Chicken With Greek Style Vegetables

*Serving: 4 | Prep: 30mins | Cook: 14mins | Ready in:*

## Ingredients

- 2/3 cup olive oil
- 3 tablespoons lemon juice, divided
- 3 tablespoons water
- 2 teaspoons Italian seasoning
- 4 teaspoons lemon zest, divided
- 1/2 teaspoon oregano
- salt and ground black pepper to taste
- 3 large tomatoes, seeded and thinly sliced
- 1 large English cucumber, thinly sliced
- 2 green bell pepper, cut into rings
- 1/2 small red onion, thinly sliced
- 1/4 cup artichoke hearts, drained and chopped
- 2 cloves garlic, pressed
- 4 pita bread rounds
- 4 chicken breasts, cut into bite-size pieces

## Direction

- Set the grill on medium heat, start preheating, and coat the grate lightly with oil.
- In a bowl, mix pepper, salt, oregano, a teaspoon of lemon zest, 2 teaspoons of Italian seasoning, water, 2 tablespoons of lemon juice, and olive oil.
- In a large bowl, arrange garlic, artichoke hearts, red onion, green pepper, and cucumber. Toss the salad to evenly mix. Slice each pita bread round into 4-5 slices.
- On the prepared grill, toast the pita bread for 4 minutes until slight grill marks form.
- In a grill pan, arrange the chicken, add the pepper, salt, a tablespoon of lemon zest, and remaining 1 tablespoon of lemon juice to coat. Place the pan onto the grill.
- Grill the chicken for 5-10 minutes on each side, until the juices run clear and the center of chicken is not pink anymore. An instant-read thermometer should register at least 74°C (165°F) when pierced into the center.
- On a serving plate, place pita bread, salad, and chicken; serve as separate components or in sandwich-style.

## Nutrition Information

- Calories: 641 calories;
- Total Carbohydrate: 41.9
- Cholesterol: 65
- Protein: 30.7
- Total Fat: 39.9
- Sodium: 386

## 95. Chicken With Rice Pilaffe

*Serving: 6 | Prep: 10mins | Cook: 2hours | Ready in:*

## Ingredients

- 1 (4 pound) whole chicken, cut into pieces
- 3 cups uncooked white rice, rinsed
- 1/2 cup butter
- 1 teaspoon salt
- 1 teaspoon black pepper
- 1/2 teaspoon poultry seasoning

## Direction

- In a big soup pot, put the chicken and add water to cover. Boil it. Mix in poultry seasoning, pepper and salt; boil for 60 minutes, sometimes skim off the fat from the water.
- Turn the oven to 350°F (175°C) to preheat.
- In a big skillet, melt butter over low heat. Add rice and cook for 10 minutes, tossing. Remove the rice into a big roasting pan. Pour into the roasting pan with the broth from the chicken; put the chicken on top.
- Put in the preheated oven and bake for 30 minutes until the rice has cooked.

## Nutrition Information

- Calories: 1115 calories;
- Sodium: 595
- Total Carbohydrate: 78.5
- Cholesterol: 148
- Protein: 33.6
- Total Fat: 72.4

## 96. Clams Kokkinisto

*Serving: 6 | Prep: 15mins | Cook: 1hours |Ready in:*

### Ingredients

- 1/2 cup chopped onion
- 2 large stalks celery, chopped
- 4 cloves garlic, minced
- 2 tablespoons olive oil
- 1 (28 ounce) can canned peeled and diced tomatoes
- 1 (6 ounce) can tomato paste
- 2 (7 ounce) cans whole baby clams, undrained
- 4 bay leaves
- 1/2 teaspoon chili pepper flakes
- 2 teaspoons dried oregano
- salt and pepper to taste
- 2 tablespoons olive oil

### Direction

- Sauté garlic, celery and onion in 2 tablespoons of the olive oil in large saucepan, until tender. Mix in clams, tomato paste and tomatoes. Season to taste with pepper, salt, oregano, chili pepper flakes and bay leaves. Simmer, covered, until sauce thickens and tomatoes' color start to turn deep red, about 60 mins. Stir in the remaining two tablespoons of the olive oil near the end of cooking time.

## Nutrition Information

- Calories: 210 calories;
- Protein: 13.4
- Total Fat: 11.3
- Sodium: 984
- Total Carbohydrate: 15.4
- Cholesterol: 53

## 97. Cousin Cosmo's Greek Chicken

*Serving: 6 | Prep: 20mins | Cook: 20mins |Ready in:*

### Ingredients

- 2 tablespoons all-purpose flour, divided
- 1/2 teaspoon salt
- 1/4 teaspoon black pepper
- 1/4 pound feta cheese, crumbled
- 1 tablespoon fresh lemon juice
- 1 teaspoon dried oregano
- 6 boneless, skinless chicken breast halves
- 2 tablespoons olive oil
- 1 1/2 cups water
- 1 cube chicken bouillon, crumbled
- 2 cups loosely packed torn fresh spinach leaves
- 1 ripe tomato, chopped

### Direction

- Mix pepper, salt and 1 tbsp. flour on big plate; put aside. Mix oregano, lemon juice and cheese in a small bowl; put aside.

- Pound every chicken breast using meat mallet to 1/2-in. thick. On each chicken breast, spread cheese mixture; leave 1/2-in. border. Fold the chicken breasts in half; use toothpick to secure each. Use flour mixture to coat chicken breasts.
- Heat oil on medium heat in a big skillet; cook chicken breasts till golden for 1-2 minutes per side. Whisk leftover flour, chicken bouillon cube and 1 1/2 cups water in a small bowl; put on chicken breasts in the pan. Put tomato and spinach in skillet; boil. Cover; lower heat to low. Simmer till chicken isn't pink inside for 8-10 minutes. Before serving, discard toothpicks.

## Nutrition Information

- Calories: 239 calories;
- Protein: 31
- Total Fat: 10.2
- Sodium: 686
- Total Carbohydrate: 4.8
- Cholesterol: 85

## 98. Easy Greek Skillet Dinner

*Serving: 6 | Prep: 10mins | Cook: 30mins | Ready in:*

## Ingredients

- 1/2 pound dried elbow macaroni
- 1 pound lean ground beef
- 2 cloves garlic, pressed or minced
- 2 medium carrots, quartered lengthwise and sliced
- 1 large zucchini, quartered lengthwise and sliced
- 1 1/2 tablespoons dried oregano leaves
- salt and pepper
- 1 (10.75 ounce) can condensed tomato soup, plus
- 1 (10.75 ounce) can water
- crumbled feta cheese (optional)

## Direction

- Add the lightly salted water in a large pot and let it boil. Add elbow macaroni and cook for 8-10 minutes until al dente; strain and reserve.
- In a large skillet over medium heat, sear ground beef with garlic. Remove fat, if needed. Once the meat is lightly browned, put the carrots and cook for about 5 minutes until soft. Mix in oregano and zucchini and keep on cooking for 5 more minutes. Add pepper and salt to taste.
- Once vegetables are softened, mix in prepared elbow macaroni, water and tomato soup and cook for another 5-10 minutes. Add crumbled feta cheese on top, if wished, then serve.

## Nutrition Information

- Calories: 354 calories;
- Total Fat: 13.3
- Sodium: 787
- Total Carbohydrate: 39.3
- Cholesterol: 50
- Protein: 20.8

## 99. Easy Mediterranean Fish

*Serving: 4 | Prep: 15mins | Cook: 30mins | Ready in:*

## Ingredients

- 4 (6 ounce) fillets halibut
- 1 tablespoon Greek seasoning (such as Cavender's®)
- 1 large tomato, chopped
- 1 onion, chopped
- 1 (5 ounce) jar pitted kalamata olives
- 1/4 cup capers
- 1/4 cup olive oil
- 1 tablespoon lemon juice
- salt and pepper to taste

## Direction

- Preheat oven to 175°C/350°F.
- On a big sheet of aluminum foil, put halibut fillets. Season using Greek seasoning. In a bowl, mix pepper, salt, lemon juice, olive oil, capers, olives, onion and tomato. Over halibut, spoon tomato mixture. Seal all foil edges carefully to make a big packet. Put packet onto baking sheet.
- In preheated oven, bake for 30-40 minutes till fish easily flakes with a fork.

## Nutrition Information

- Calories: 429 calories;
- Cholesterol: 54
- Protein: 36.6
- Total Fat: 26.8
- Sodium: 1275
- Total Carbohydrate: 9.2

## 100. Feta Cheese Turkey Burgers

Serving: 4 | Prep: | Cook: |Ready in:

### Ingredients

- 1 pound ground turkey
- 1 cup crumbled feta cheese
- 1/2 cup kalamata olives, pitted and sliced
- 2 teaspoons dried oregano
- ground black pepper to taste

### Direction

- Preheat the outdoor grill, lightly brush the grate with oil or spray with cooking spray. Prepare the patties, combine ground turkey, olives, feta cheese, oregano and pepper in a big bowl. Mix well and divide into equal patties. Grill the patties, 6 minutes per side or 10-12 minutes.

## Nutrition Information

- Calories: 318 calories;
- Sodium: 800
- Total Carbohydrate: 3.6
- Cholesterol: 123
- Protein: 25.5
- Total Fat: 21.9

## 101. Garithes Yiouvetsi

Serving: 8 | Prep: 30mins | Cook: 15mins |Ready in:

### Ingredients

- 4 tablespoons extra virgin olive oil
- 1 medium onion, finely chopped
- 3/4 cup chopped green onion
- 2 cloves garlic, crushed
- 2 cups chopped, peeled tomatoes
- 1/2 cup dry white wine
- 1/4 cup chopped fresh parsley
- 1 tablespoon chopped fresh oregano
- salt and pepper to taste
- 2 pounds large uncooked shrimp, peeled
- 4 ounces crumbled feta cheese

### Direction

- In a skillet, heat the oil over medium heat. In the oil, sauté the onion until it turns transparent. Stir in garlic and green onions; cook and stir often for 2 minutes more. Stir in pepper and salt to taste, oregano, most of the parsley, wine, and tomatoes. Put on a cover and gently simmer for half an hour.
- Set an oven to 260°C (500°F) and start preheating.
- On the bottom of a large oven dish, place 1/2 of the sauce. Evenly spread the shrimp on the sauce and top with the rest of the sauce. Dust with the feta cheese.
- In the prepared oven, cook until the feta is browned lightly and melted and the shrimp

turns pink, about 10-15 minutes. Dust with the rest of the parsley and serve right away.

## Nutrition Information

- Calories: 218 calories;
- Total Carbohydrate: 5.2
- Cholesterol: 185
- Protein: 21.4
- Total Fat: 10.9
- Sodium: 436

## 102. George's Greek Fried Chicken

*Serving: 4 | Prep: 10mins | Cook: 20mins | Ready in:*

## Ingredients

- 4 skinless chicken pieces
- 1/2 cup Greek olive oil
- 1 lemon, juiced
- 1 1/2 tablespoons freshly ground black pepper
- 1 teaspoon salt
- 1 1/2 tablespoons dried oregano
- 1 dash cinnamon
- 1 dash poultry seasoning
- 1/2 cup olive oil for frying
- 1 lemon, cut into wedges

## Direction

- Mix poultry seasoning, cinnamon, oregano, salt, pepper, lemon juice, 1/2 cup olive oil and chicken pieces in medium bowl; soak chicken for 5 minutes in seasonings and oil. Rub marinate in chicken with hands.
- Heat 1/2 cup olive oil in 1 1/2-in. deep frying pan with lid to keep juices in chicken on low heat; lay chicken pieces carefully into frying pan. Put lid on pan; cook for 20 minutes till chicken is done, occasionally flipping pieces. Put heat on medium high; cook till outside of chicken browns.

- Serve hot; use lemon wedges to garnish. For extra flavor, squeeze some lemon on chicken for delicious taste.

## Nutrition Information

- Calories: 428 calories;
- Cholesterol: 61
- Protein: 20.9
- Total Fat: 36.1
- Sodium: 644
- Total Carbohydrate: 9.9

## 103. Glasser's Greek Marlin

*Serving: 4 | Prep: 10mins | Cook: 25mins | Ready in:*

## Ingredients

- 1/2 cup butter, divided
- 2 teaspoons minced garlic, divided
- 3 tomatoes, cubed
- 4 ounces fresh basil, chopped
- 2 tablespoons fresh lime juice
- 2 (6 ounce) swordfish steaks

## Direction

- Set an oven to preheat to 175°C (350°F).
- In a medium pot, put 1 tsp. garlic and 1/4 cup butter on medium-low heat. Stir in the lime juice, basil and tomatoes once the butter is melted. Lower the heat to low just before the mixture boils.
- Melt the leftover butter in a small pot and stir in the leftover garlic.
- In a baking pan, lay out the swordfish and drizzle it with the garlic and butter mixture from the small pot.
- Let the fish bake in the preheated oven for 7 minutes. Flip the fish and keep on baking for 7 minutes or until it flakes easily using a fork. To serve, scoop the tomato mixture on top of

the fish, then top it with the leftover garlic and butter sauce from the baking pan.

## Nutrition Information

- Calories: 332 calories;
- Sodium: 237
- Total Carbohydrate: 5.6
- Cholesterol: 93
- Protein: 18.6
- Total Fat: 26.7

## 104. Grecian Pork Tenderloin

*Serving: 6 | Prep: 15mins | Cook: 30mins | Ready in:*

### Ingredients

- 1 1/2 cups fresh lime juice
- 3/4 cup olive oil
- 6 cloves garlic, sliced
- 2 teaspoons salt
- 6 tablespoons dried oregano
- 2 (1 pound) pork tenderloins

### Direction

- In a large resealable plastic bag, combine the oregano, salt, olive oil, lime juice, and garlic. Seal the bag and shake it until the ingredients are well-combined. Taste the mixture for tartness. Add more oil if the mixture is too tart and add more lime if the mixture has not enough zing. Also, the flavors of garlic and salt should be upfront, and not overpowering. Add the tenderloins into the bag with marinade. Seal the bag and flip it until coated. Marinate it inside the fridge for 2-5 hours.
- Set the grill to medium heat for preheating.
- Oil the grill grate lightly. Discard the marinade and grill the tenderloins for 20-30 minutes, flipping only once until the desired doneness is reached.

## Nutrition Information

- Calories: 404 calories;
- Cholesterol: 65
- Protein: 24.3
- Total Fat: 31.1
- Sodium: 829
- Total Carbohydrate: 9.1

## 105. Greek Burgers

*Serving: 8 | Prep: 25mins | Cook: 10mins | Ready in:*

### Ingredients

- 1/2 cup mayonnaise
- 1 teaspoon minced garlic
- 2 pounds ground lamb
- 1/4 cup breadcrumbs
- 1 cup trimmed, diced fennel bulb
- 3 tablespoons shallots, minced
- 1 teaspoon dried oregano
- 1/2 teaspoon salt
- ground black pepper to taste
- 1 tablespoon olive oil
- 8 hamburger buns

### Direction

- Blend together minced garlic and mayonnaise in a small bowl. Cover; put in the fridge for at least 1 hour.
- Set grill to high heat and start preheating.
- Combine together salt, oregano, shallot, fennel, breadcrumbs, and lamb. Shape into 3/4-in.-thick patties; sprinkle black pepper on top of each.
- Use olive oil to brush grate; put the burgers on grill. Cook until done, about 3-5 minutes on each side, turning once. Place onto buns and serve with garlic mayonnaise.

## Nutrition Information

- Calories: 479 calories;

- Total Fat: 30.4
- Sodium: 559
- Total Carbohydrate: 26.2
- Cholesterol: 81
- Protein: 23.9

## 106. Greek Chicken (Maybe)

*Serving: 2 | Prep: 10mins | Cook: 15mins | Ready in:*

### Ingredients

- 2 skinless, boneless chicken breast halves
- salt and ground black pepper to taste
- 1 tablespoon olive oil
- 1 clove garlic, minced
- 20 pitted kalamata olives
- 20 red seedless grapes
- 1/2 cup crumbled feta cheese
- 1 cup orange muscat wine

### Direction

- Sprinkle chicken breasts with salt and pepper to season. In a skillet over medium-high heat, heat oil. Place chicken breasts in hot oil and cook for about 5 minutes total until both sides have golden brown color. Stir in grapes, olives and garlic; cook for 1 minute, remember to stir while cooking. Add feta cheese on top of chicken. Add in wine and bring to a boil. Cook, covered for about another 5 minutes until cheese is fully melted and the amount of sauce is reduced by half.

### Nutrition Information

- Calories: 627 calories;
- Total Fat: 26.3
- Sodium: 1116
- Total Carbohydrate: 31.6
- Cholesterol: 99
- Protein: 32.8

## 107. Greek Chicken Burgers With Feta

*Serving: 5 | Prep: 15mins | Cook: 10mins | Ready in:*

### Ingredients

- 1 pound ground chicken
- 1/2 cup dry bread crumbs
- 1 egg
- 1 tablespoon lemon juice
- 2 tablespoons chopped sun-dried tomatoes
- 1 tablespoon chopped fresh basil
- 3 teaspoons chopped fresh oregano
- salt and pepper to taste
- 2 ounces crumbled feta cheese

### Direction

- Preheat an outdoor grill to medium high heat; oil the grate lightly.
- Mix pepper, salt, oregano, basil, sun-dried tomatoes, lemon juice, egg, breadcrumbs and chicken in a bowl; shape mixture to 5 patties. Divide feta cheese to 5 patties; put a feta cheese portion on each patty. Fold chicken mixture around cheese so cheese is in the middle.
- On the preheated grill, cook, 5-7 minutes per side, till not pink in the inside and juices are clear. An instant-read thermometer inserted in the middle should read 75°C/165°F.

### Nutrition Information

- Calories: 192 calories;
- Cholesterol: 100
- Protein: 25.5
- Total Fat: 5.2
- Sodium: 307
- Total Carbohydrate: 9.5

## 108. Greek Chicken Couscous Bowl

*Serving: 4 | Prep: 35mins | Cook: 15mins | Ready in:*

### Ingredients

- Chicken:
- ½ teaspoon dried rosemary
- ½ teaspoon ground black pepper
- ½ teaspoon salt
- ½ teaspoon dried oregano
- ½ teaspoon garlic powder
- ½ teaspoon onion powder
- ⅛ teaspoon ground cardamom
- ¼ teaspoon ground coriander
- 2 skinless, boneless chicken breasts
- 2 tablespoons vegetable oil
- ½ lemon, juiced
- Couscous:
- 1 ½ cups water
- 1 cup dry couscous
- Tzatziki Sauce:
- ½ cucumber, peeled and shredded
- ½ cup sour cream
- ½ cup Greek yogurt
- ½ lemon, juiced
- 1 tablespoon olive oil
- 1 clove garlic, minced
- 1 teaspoon chopped fresh mint
- 1 teaspoon chopped fresh dill
- ½ teaspoon salt
- ½ teaspoon black pepper
- Toppings:
- 1 broccoli crown, cut into florets
- 1 medium red onion, diced
- ½ cucumber, peeled and diced
- 2 roma tomatoes, diced
- ½ cup chopped Kalamata olives, or to taste
- ½ cup chopped fresh parsley
- 1 (4 ounce) package crumbled feta cheese, or to taste
- 

### Direction

- In a small bowl, mix the salt, garlic powder, cardamom, coriander, rosemary, oregano, black pepper, and onion powder. Lay the chicken on a plate and season it with the spice mixture. Put vegetable oil in a saucepan and heat it over medium heat for 2-3 minutes until it starts to shimmer. Add the seasoned chicken into the pan. Cook the chicken while covered for 4-5 minutes. Flip the chicken over and cook the other side for 5-6 minutes, uncovered until browned on the outside and its inside is no longer pink. To check, see if the inserted instant-read thermometer in its center registers at least 165°F or 74°C. Squeeze the lemon juice all over the chicken. Let it cool for 5 minutes before slicing it into strips.
- Meanwhile, boil water in a saucepan. Add the salt according to your taste. Add the couscous, stirring only once and cover the pan. Remove the pan from the heat. Allow the couscous to steam for 5 minutes. Use a fork to fluff it.
- In a bowl, mix the olive oil, salt, black pepper, mint, yogurt, sour cream, cucumber, lemon juice, dill, and garlic until the tzatziki sauce is just mixed.
- Divide the couscous among the 4 bowls. Place the cooked chicken, tzatziki sauce, onion, tomatoes, cucumber, broccoli, feta cheese, parsley, and olives on top of the couscous. Serve it right away. You can also store it in a sealed container and reheat it before using it.

### Nutrition Information

- Calories: 622 calories;
- Sodium: 1334
- Total Carbohydrate: 55.5
- Cholesterol: 76
- Total Fat: 35
- Protein: 24.6

## 109. Greek Chicken Kozani

*Serving: 4 | Prep: 10mins | Cook: 35mins | Ready in:*

### Ingredients

- 4 skinless chicken thighs
- 4 cups water
- 3 tablespoons olive oil
- 3 large red onions, halved, then sliced lengthwise
- 20 pitted prunes
- 1 1/2 tablespoons sweet paprika
- 2 bay leaves
- 1 tablespoon salt, or to taste
- ground black pepper to taste

### Direction

- Into saucepan, put water and chicken thighs. Boil on high heat, then lower the heat to medium-low, and let simmer for 10 to 15 minutes. Scoop off any froth that rise on top.
- Meantime, in big skillet, heat olive oil on low heat. Mix in onions, and cook with cover for 10 minutes till translucent and soft. Prevent onions form browning. To onions, put the chicken including 3 cups cooking liquid. Mix in pepper, salt, bay leaves, paprika and prunes. Bring back to a simmer, put cover, and let cook for 15 to 25 minutes till prunes are soft and flavors have incorporated.

### Nutrition Information

- Calories: 393 calories;
- Total Fat: 18.3
- Sodium: 1816
- Total Carbohydrate: 38.5
- Cholesterol: 69
- Protein: 22

---

## 110.    Greek Couscous

*Serving: 3 | Prep: 20mins | Cook: 5mins | Ready in:*

### Ingredients

- 1/4 cup chicken broth
- 1/2 cup water
- 1 teaspoon minced garlic
- 1/2 cup pearl (Israeli) couscous
- 1/4 cup chopped sun-dried tomatoes
- 1/4 cup sliced Kalamata olives
- 2 tablespoons crumbled feta cheese
- 1 cup canned garbanzo beans, rinsed and drained
- 1 teaspoon dried oregano
- 1/2 teaspoon ground black pepper
- 1 tablespoon white wine vinegar
- 1 1/2 teaspoons lemon juice

### Direction

- In a saucepan, put water, chicken broth and garlic; let it boil. Add in the couscous then cover and remove the pan from heat. Let the couscous soak in the water mixture for about 5 minutes until the liquid is completely absorbed. Use a fork to fluff the couscous. Let the couscous cool down until warm in temperature.
- In a big serving bowl, lightly mix the garbanzo beans, couscous, olives, sun-dried tomatoes and feta cheese. In a small bowl, combine white wine vinegar, lemon juice, oregano and black pepper and put it on top of the couscous mixture. Mix everything then serve.

### Nutrition Information

- Calories: 254 calories;
- Total Fat: 5.6
- Sodium: 592
- Total Carbohydrate: 42.4
- Cholesterol: 6
- Protein: 9

---

## 111.    Greek Cowboy Hash And Eggs

*Serving: 2 | Prep: 20mins | Cook: 15mins | Ready in:*

## Ingredients

- 2 tablespoons olive oil
- 1 large sweet potato, peeled and cut into 1/4-inch cubes
- 1 red onion, chopped
- 4 cloves garlic, minced
- 1 tablespoon chipotle chile powder
- 1 teaspoon ground cumin
- 1 teaspoon ground coriander
- salt and ground black pepper to taste
- 2 tablespoons olive oil
- 4 eggs
- 1/4 cup fresh cilantro, chopped
- 1/2 cup crumbled feta cheese
- 1/2 avocado, sliced

## Direction

- On medium heat, heat 2 tbsp. olive oil in a skillet. Cook potatoes for approximately 5 mins in hot oil until they start to turn soft. Put in garlic and onion; keep cooking until the onions start to caramelize and sweat. Stir in pepper, chipotle chile powder, salt, coriander, and cumin. Move to a bowl then use a plate to cover and keep the heat.
- Add 2 tbsp. olive oil in the skillet then set back to medium heat. Crack in eggs then cook until they start to become opaque; turn over then keep cooking until there are no remaining clear whites. Avoid overcooking the eggs to achieve the smoothness of the yolks so as to put in the dish for the best result. Add the cooked eggs over the potato mixture. Put avocado, feta cheese, and cilantro on top. Serve.

## Nutrition Information

- Calories: 769 calories;
- Protein: 24.6
- Total Fat: 51.6
- Sodium: 777
- Total Carbohydrate: 56.1
- Cholesterol: 434

## 112. Greek God Pasta

*Serving: 6 | Prep: 20mins | Cook: 30mins | Ready in:*

## Ingredients

- 1 (16 ounce) package whole wheat rotini pasta
- 1 (16 ounce) can peeled and diced tomatoes, drained
- 2 tablespoons chopped green bell pepper
- 1/4 cup chopped green onion
- 3 cups tomato sauce
- 1 teaspoon dried basil
- 1 teaspoon dried oregano
- 1 cup sliced black olives
- 1/2 cup shredded mozzarella cheese
- 2 tablespoons crumbled feta cheese

## Direction

- Preheat oven to 200 degrees C/400 degrees F.
- Boil a big pot of lightly salted water. Add the rotini pasta. Cook for 8 minutes until al dente. Drain then pour in a deep casserole dish.
- Mix tomato sauce, olives, green onion, green pepper, and tomatoes in pasta. Season oregano and basil, mixing until blended evenly. Sprinkle feta cheese and mozzarella on top.
- Bake in preheated oven for 30 minutes until cheese is bubbly and has melted. Let stand for several minutes then serve.

## Nutrition Information

- Calories: 371 calories;
- Total Fat: 6
- Sodium: 1068
- Total Carbohydrate: 68.5
- Cholesterol: 9
- Protein: 16.4

## 113. Greek Grilled Cheese

*Serving: 1 | Prep: 5mins | Cook: 5mins | Ready in:*

### Ingredients

- 1 1/2 teaspoons butter, softened
- 2 slices whole wheat bread, or your favorite bread
- 2 tablespoons crumbled feta cheese
- 2 slices Cheddar cheese
- 1 tablespoon chopped red onion
- 1/4 tomato, thinly sliced

### Direction

- Place a skillet over medium heat. Spread butter on 1 side of each bread slice. Layer feta cheese, Cheddar cheese, red onion, and tomato on the unbuttered side of 1 bread slice. Place the other bread slice atop the filling, buttered side out.
- Fry sandwich, approximately 2 minutes on each side, until golden brown. (The second side takes a shorter time to cook).

### Nutrition Information

- Calories: 482 calories;
- Sodium: 876
- Total Carbohydrate: 27.1
- Cholesterol: 92
- Protein: 24.6
- Total Fat: 30.9

## 114. Greek Island Chicken Shish Kebabs

*Serving: 6 | Prep: 20mins | Cook: 10mins | Ready in:*

### Ingredients

- 1/4 cup olive oil
- 1/4 cup lemon juice
- 1/4 cup white vinegar
- 2 cloves garlic, minced
- 1 teaspoon ground cumin
- 1 teaspoon dried oregano
- 1/2 teaspoon dried thyme
- 1/4 teaspoon salt
- 1/4 teaspoon ground black pepper
- 2 pounds skinless, boneless chicken breast, cut into 1 1/2-inch pieces
- 6 wooden skewers
- 2 large green or red bell peppers, cut into 1-inch pieces
- 1 large onion, quartered and separated into pieces
- 12 cherry tomatoes
- 12 fresh mushrooms

### Direction

- In a large glass or ceramic bowl, whisk together vinegar, olive oil, lemon juice, salt, black pepper, thyme, garlic, oregano, and cumin. Toss in the chicken to coat. Cover with plastic wrap and keep in the refrigerator for 2 hours.
- Immerse wooden skewers in water for about 30 minutes.
- Set an outdoor grill on medium-high heat to preheat. Lightly grease the grate.
- Take the chicken pieces and shake off excess marinade. Discard the marinade. Skewer the chicken, onions, bell peppers, mushrooms, and cherry tomatoes alternately.
- Grill and turn often for 10 minutes, or until brown on all sides and chicken is cooked and no longer pink in the center.

### Nutrition Information

- Calories: 290 calories;
- Total Fat: 13.1
- Sodium: 181
- Total Carbohydrate: 9.3
- Cholesterol: 86
- Protein: 33.8

## 115. Greek Lamb Kabobs With Yogurt Mint Salsa Verde

*Serving: 4 | Prep: 25mins | Cook: 8mins | Ready in:*

### Ingredients

- Lamb Skewers:
- 8 6-inch rosemary sprigs
- 1 tablespoon minced garlic
- 1 tablespoon chopped fresh thyme
- 1/3 cup extra virgin olive oil
- 1/4 cup sherry vinegar
- 1 teaspoon sea salt
- 1 teaspoon ground white pepper
- 1 1/2 pounds lamb tenderloin, cut into 2-inch pieces
- Salsa Verde:
- 1/4 cup fresh lemon juice
- 1/2 cup extra virgin olive oil
- 1/3 cup Greek yogurt
- 1 crushed garlic clove
- 1/4 teaspoon sea salt
- 2 teaspoons chopped fresh mint
- 1 teaspoon chopped fresh oregano
- 1 teaspoon chopped fresh parsley
- 1 teaspoon small capers
- 1 anchovy filet

### Direction

- Immerse the rosemary sprigs in water for half an hour. Whisk together olive oil, garlic, sherry vinegar, thyme, salt, and pepper in a glass bowl. Toss the lamb in the marinade and soak for 30 minutes at room temperature. Skewer onto rosemary sprigs.
- Make the salsa verde: Blend yogurt, lemon juice, olive oil, garlic, mint, oregano, parsley, salt, capers, and anchovy fillet until smooth. Transfer to a serving dish and put aside until serving time.
- Set an outdoor grill on medium to pre-heat.
- Grill the lamb, turning from time to time, until the meat is not pink anymore, about 8 minutes. Serve with salsa verde.

### Nutrition Information

- Calories: 688 calories;
- Total Fat: 57.6
- Sodium: 908
- Total Carbohydrate: 4
- Cholesterol: 115
- Protein: 36.1

## 116. Greek Lasagna

*Serving: 12 | Prep: 30mins | Cook: 1hours | Ready in:*

### Ingredients

- 2 pounds uncooked elbow macaroni
- 2 pounds ground beef
- 1 medium onion, chopped
- 1 cup grated Parmesan cheese
- 1 (4 ounce) package feta cheese
- 2 (8 ounce) cans diced tomatoes
- 2 teaspoons ground cinnamon
- salt and pepper to taste
- 3 cups milk
- 3 tablespoons cornstarch
- 1/4 cup butter

### Direction

- Put slight salt in water using a large pot and let it boil. Put in macaroni pasta, cook until tender about 8 min. Strain pasta and set aside.
- Preheat oven to 175° C (350° F). Cook onion and ground beef in a large skillet with medium-high heat until the beef is browned evenly. Take out from the heat and drain the grease. Add in the tomatoes, parmesan cheese, feta cheese and cinnamon. Add the pasta and transfer to a large baking dish.

- In a saucepan over medium heat, blend the milk and cornstarch until there's no more lumps. Put butter and let it boil for a minute. Remove from the heat and place the sauce over the mixture in the baking dish.
- Bake in preheated oven until the top turns golden brown for 1 hour. Let it set 10 minutes before serving.

### Nutrition Information

- Calories: 601 calories;
- Sodium: 568
- Total Carbohydrate: 65
- Cholesterol: 91
- Protein: 31.8
- Total Fat: 22.8

## 117. Greek Lazy Lasagna

*Serving: 8 | Prep: 20mins | Cook: 1hours | Ready in:*

### Ingredients

- 1 (16 ounce) package uncooked mafalda pasta (mini lasagne noodles)
- 2 tablespoons extra-virgin olive oil
- 1/4 cup chopped onion
- 3 cloves garlic, chopped
- 2 (6 ounce) boneless, skinless chicken breasts, thinly sliced
- 1 (10 ounce) bag chopped fresh spinach
- 1 (8 ounce) can sliced black olives
- 1 1/2 tablespoons fresh lemon juice
- 2 cups crumbled feta cheese

### Direction

- Pour lightly salted water into a large pot; over high heat, bring to a rolling boil. When the water boils, mix in malfada pasta and bring back to a boil. Cook pasta for about 10 minutes, occasionally stirring until the pasta is firm to the bite but well-cooked. Drain pasta; transfer it back to the pot.
- Turn on the oven to 350°F (175°C) to preheat. Prepare a 9x13-inch baking dish by greasing.
- In a large skillet, mix together garlic, onion and olive oil. Cook on medium heat for 3 minutes while stirring until soft. Put in sliced chicken; cook and stir for about 5 minutes until the center is no longer pink and the chicken is lightly browned. Stir in lemon juice, black olives and spinach. Cook for another 1-2 minutes until heated through. Mix the chicken mixture into pasta, put in feta cheese and stir well. Transfer into the prepared baking dish and use aluminum foil to cover.
- Put into the prepped oven to bake for 30 minutes until the cheese melts and the pasta is hot.

### Nutrition Information

- Calories: 489 calories;
- Total Carbohydrate: 47.5
- Cholesterol: 81
- Protein: 27.6
- Total Fat: 21.8
- Sodium: 1009

## 118. Greek Lemon Chicken And Potato Bake

*Serving: 4 | Prep: 10mins | Cook: 1hours | Ready in:*

### Ingredients

- 4 chicken leg quarters
- 1 (24 ounce) bag small potatoes
- 1/2 cup olive oil
- 2 lemons, juiced, divided
- 2 tablespoons dried basil
- 2 tablespoons dried oregano
- 1 tablespoon salt
- 1 tablespoon ground black pepper
- 2 tablespoons lemon and herb seasoning

- 1 (12 ounce) package fresh green beans

### Direction

- Preheat the oven to 220°C or 425°Fahrenheit. Oil a big baking sheet with sides.
- Arrange the chicken quarters on the greased baking sheet. In a big bowl, combine lemon herb seasoning, potatoes, pepper, olive oil, salt, juice of one lemon, oregano, and basil until the potatoes are coated. Put the potatoes on the baking sheet surrounding the chicken. Drizzle 3/4 oil mixture all over the chicken; set the remaining oil aside. Pour the remaining lemon juice all over the potatoes and chicken.
- Bake for half an hour in the preheated oven; quiver the baking sheet to loosen the potatoes. Bake for another 15 minutes. Toss the green beans in the reserved oil mixture to coat. Take the chicken mixture out of the oven; put the green bean mixture over the potatoes and chicken.
- Place the pan back in the oven; bake for another 15 minutes until the chicken is not pink at the bone and the juices are clear, and the green beans are tender yet firm to bite. An inserted instant-read thermometer close to the bone should register 74°C or 165°Fahrenheit.

### Nutrition Information

- Calories: 551 calories;
- Protein: 34.8
- Total Fat: 29.1
- Sodium: 1859
- Total Carbohydrate: 41.9
- Cholesterol: 103

## 119. Greek Lemon Chicken And Potatoes

*Serving: 4 | Prep: 10mins | Cook: 50mins | Ready in:*

### Ingredients

- 4 pounds skin-on, bone-in chicken thighs
- 1 tablespoon kosher salt
- 1 tablespoon dried oregano
- 1 teaspoon freshly ground black pepper
- 1 teaspoon dried rosemary
- 1 pinch cayenne pepper
- 1/2 cup fresh lemon juice
- 1/2 cup olive oil
- 6 cloves garlic, minced
- 3 russet potatoes, peeled and quartered
- 2/3 cup chicken broth, plus splash to deglaze pan
- chopped fresh oregano for garnish

### Direction

- Preheat the oven to 220°C or 425°Fahrenheit. Grease a big roasting pan lightly.
- In a big bowl, put the chicken pieces then sprinkle cayenne pepper, salt, rosemary, pepper, and oregano. Put in garlic, olive oil, and fresh lemon juice. Stir potatoes on a bowl of chicken until the potatoes and chicken are coated in marinade evenly.
- Move the chicken pieces on the greased roasting pan with the skin-side up; set the marinade aside. Divide the potato pieces between the chicken thighs; sprinkle 2/3 cup chicken broth. Scoop the rest of the marinade over the potatoes and chicken.
- Put in prepped oven. Bake for 20 minutes in the preheated oven. Mix the potatoes and chicken; keep the chicken skin-side up. Bake for another 25 minutes until the chicken is completely cooked and brown. An inserted instant-read thermometer close to the bone should register 74°C or 165°Fahrenheit. Move chicken to a serving platter; keep warm.
- Set the oven on highest setting or broil. Mix the potatoes once more in pan juices; put the pan beneath the broiler. Broil for 3 minutes until the potatoes caramelize. Move to the chicken in a serving platter.
- On medium heat, put the roasting pan on a stove; mix in a splash of broth to loosen the brown bits in the bottom of pan. Filter then

drizzle the juices over the potatoes and chicken. Add chopped oregano on top.

## Nutrition Information

- Calories: 1139 calories;
- Sodium: 1866
- Total Carbohydrate: 34.5
- Cholesterol: 284
- Protein: 80.4
- Total Fat: 74.5

## 120. Greek Meat Pasta (Makaronia Me Kima)

*Serving: 10 | Prep: 15mins | Cook: 1hours10mins | Ready in:*

## Ingredients

- 1 (16 ounce) package rotini pasta
- 3 tablespoons olive oil, divided
- 1 pound ground beef
- 6 tomatoes, grated
- 1 sweet yellow onion, grated
- 1/2 cup water
- 3 tablespoons tomato paste
- 1 tablespoon ground cinnamon
- 1/2 teaspoon white sugar
- 1/2 teaspoon cayenne pepper
- salt and ground black pepper to taste
- 4 cups shredded Mizithra cheese
- 1 cup shredded mozzarella cheese

## Direction

- Cook rotini for around 8 mins in a big pot with boiling lightly salted water until tender yet firm to the bite. Move to a big bowl then mix with 2 tbsp. olive oil.
- On medium heat, heat 1 tbsp. olive oil in a big skillet. Cook and stir the ground beef for approximately 10 mins until brown. Mix in pepper, tomatoes, salt, onion, cayenne, water, sugar, cinnamon, and tomato paste to blend. On medium-low heat, let it simmer for 20 mins until the flavors combine.
- Preheat the oven to 175°C or 350°Fahrenheit.
- Put meat sauce on top of rotini. Mix the rotini and meat sauce thoroughly. In a casserole dish, pour 1/2 of the pasta mixture then top with scattered 1/2 each of mozzarella cheese and Mizithra cheese.
- Bake for around 40 mins in the preheated oven until the cheese is bubbling and melted.

## Nutrition Information

- Calories: 516 calories;
- Total Fat: 21.9
- Sodium: 1278
- Total Carbohydrate: 95.3
- Cholesterol: 69
- Protein: 23.9

## 121. Greek Omelet With Asparagus And Feta Cheese

*Serving: 4 | Prep: 20mins | Cook: 10mins | Ready in:*

## Ingredients

- 2 tablespoons olive oil
- 6 spears fresh asparagus, trimmed and chopped
- 1/2 red bell pepper, chopped
- 1/2 cup cherry tomatoes, halved
- 1/2 cup chopped fresh spinach
- 1/2 teaspoon minced garlic
- 1/2 teaspoon dried oregano
- 1/2 teaspoon dried basil
- salt to taste
- 2 tablespoons butter
- 6 large eggs
- 1/4 cup whole milk
- 1/2 cup crumbled feta cheese
- 1/4 cup shredded Cheddar cheese

### Direction

- In a big frying pan, heat olive oil on medium heat, stir and cook red bell pepper and asparagus for 3 minutes until the vegetables are tender. Mix in salt, basil, oregano, garlic, spinach, and cherry tomatoes and keep cooking for addition of 3-5 minutes until the spinach is cooked down and the tomatoes are tender. Take away from heat and move the vegetables to a dish.
- In a clean frying pan, heat butter over medium heat. In a bowl, beat milk and eggs and put in the hot butter, twirl the frying pan so that the egg mixture fully covers the bottom. Use a spatula to lift 1 edge of the omelet and tip the pan to let the raw egg flow underneath and cook; keep going around the pan, raising the edge of the omelet and tip the pan, until the entire mixture sets. Use salt to drizzle over the omelet.
- Put on one side of the omelet with the cooked asparagus mixture and use Cheddar and Feta cheese to drizzle. Carefully fold half of the omelet over the cheese and vegetables and gently press the edges to close in the filling. Cook for another 1-2 minutes until the Cheddar cheese melts and the filling is hot. Slice into slices to enjoy.

### Nutrition Information

- Calories: 321 calories;
- Total Fat: 27
- Sodium: 413
- Total Carbohydrate: 5.3
- Cholesterol: 320
- Protein: 15.5

### 122. Greek Orzo With Feta

*Serving: 6 | Prep: 30mins | Cook: 10mins | Ready in:*

### Ingredients

- 1/4 cup olive oil
- 1/2 cup fresh lemon juice
- 1/2 cup pitted kalamata olives, chopped
- 2 ripe tomatoes, seeded and diced
- 1 red bell pepper, chopped
- 1 red onion, chopped
- 2 cloves garlic, minced
- 1 teaspoon finely chopped fresh oregano
- 1 (8 ounce) package crumbled feta cheese
- 1/2 pound dried orzo pasta
- 1 cup chopped fresh parsley

### Direction

- In a big bowl, combine the feta cheese, oregano, garlic, red onion, red pepper, tomatoes, olives, lemon juice and olive oil. Let it stand for an hour at room temperature.
- Boil a big pot of lightly salted water. Cook orzo in boiling water for 8-10mins or until al dente; drain the orzo. Toss the orzo with the tomato mixture, then sprinkle with chopped parsley. Serve.

### Nutrition Information

- Calories: 381 calories;
- Total Fat: 20.8
- Sodium: 618
- Total Carbohydrate: 38.4
- Cholesterol: 34
- Protein: 12

### 123. Greek Pasta With Tomatoes And White Beans

*Serving: 4 | Prep: 10mins | Cook: 15mins | Ready in:*

### Ingredients

- 2 (14.5 ounce) cans Italian-style diced tomatoes
- 1 (19 ounce) can cannellini beans, drained and rinsed
- 10 ounces fresh spinach, washed and chopped

- 8 ounces penne pasta
- 1/2 cup crumbled feta cheese

### Direction

- In a big pot, cook pasta in boiling salted water till al dente.
- Meanwhile in a big nonstick skillet, boil beans and tomatoes on medium high heat. Lower heat. Simmer for 10 minutes.
- Put spinach into sauce. Cook till spinach wilts for 2 minutes, constantly mixing.
- Serve sauce on pasta. Sprinkle feta on top.

### Nutrition Information

- Calories: 460 calories;
- Total Fat: 5.9
- Sodium: 593
- Total Carbohydrate: 79
- Cholesterol: 17
- Protein: 23.4

## 124. Greek Penne And Chicken

*Serving: 4 | Prep: 20mins | Cook: 30mins | Ready in:*

### Ingredients

- 1 (16 ounce) package penne pasta
- 1 1/2 tablespoons butter
- 1/2 cup chopped red onion
- 2 cloves garlic, minced
- 1 pound skinless, boneless chicken breast halves - cut into bite-size pieces
- 1 (14 ounce) can artichoke hearts in water
- 1 tomato, chopped
- 1/2 cup crumbled feta cheese
- 3 tablespoons chopped fresh parsley
- 2 tablespoons lemon juice
- 1 teaspoon dried oregano
- salt to taste
- ground black pepper to taste

### Direction

- In a big pot, cook penne pasta in boiling salted water until al dente; drain.
- In the meantime, on medium-high heat, melt butter in a big skillet; add and cook garlic and onion for 2 mins. Put in chopped chicken; keep cooking for around 5-6 mins while mixing from time to time until golden brown.
- Turn to medium-low heat. Drain the artichoke hearts then chop. Put the chopped artichoke hearts, drained penne pasta, chopped tomato, dried oregano, feta cheese, lemon juice, and fresh parsley into the big skillet. Cook for approximately 2-3 mins until thoroughly heated.
- Sprinkle ground black pepper and salt to season. Serve warm.

### Nutrition Information

- Calories: 685 calories;
- Sodium: 826
- Total Carbohydrate: 96.2
- Cholesterol: 94
- Protein: 47
- Total Fat: 13.2

## 125. Greek Pizza With Spinach, Feta And Olives

*Serving: 6 | Prep: 30mins | Cook: 12mins | Ready in:*

### Ingredients

- 1/2 cup mayonnaise
- 4 cloves garlic, minced
- 1 cup crumbled feta cheese, divided
- 1 (12 inch) pre-baked Italian pizza crust
- 1/2 cup oil-packed sun-dried tomatoes, coarsely chopped
- 1 tablespoon oil from the sun-dried tomatoes
- 1/4 cup pitted kalamata olives, coarsely chopped

- 1 teaspoon dried oregano
- 2 cups baby spinach leaves
- 1/2 small red onion, halved and thinly sliced

### Direction

- To lowest position, adjust oven rack; heat oven to 450°. In a small bowl, mix 1/2 cup feta, garlic and mayonnaise. Put pizza crust onto cookie sheet; spread the mayonnaise mixture on pizza. Put oregano, olives and tomatoes over; bake for 10 minutes till crisp and heated through.
- Toss 1 tbsp. sun-dried tomato oil, onion and spinach; put spinach mixture and leftover 1/2 cup feta cheese over hot pizza. Put in oven; bake for 2 minutes till cheese melts. Cut to 6 slices; serve.

### Nutrition Information

- Calories: 461 calories;
- Protein: 14.1
- Total Fat: 29
- Sodium: 894
- Total Carbohydrate: 39.3
- Cholesterol: 36

## 126. Greek Pulled Pork

*Serving: 8 | Prep: 10mins | Cook: 4hours | Ready in:*

### Ingredients

- 1 (2 pound) pork tenderloin, fat trimmed
- 2 tablespoons Greek seasoning (such as Cavender's®), or more to taste
- 1 (16 ounce) jar sliced pepperoncini peppers (such as Mezzetta®)

### Direction

- Put pork tenderloin into a slow cooker, generously dust meat with Greek seasoning, and then pour the peperoncini peppers jar with their juice over the pork. Cook on High for 4 hours.
- Shred the pork with 2 forks, let cook for another 10 to 15 more minutes.

### Nutrition Information

- Calories: 146 calories;
- Protein: 21
- Total Fat: 4.6
- Sodium: 1135
- Total Carbohydrate: 3.7
- Cholesterol: 63

## 127. Greek Ribs

*Serving: 6 | Prep: 30mins | Cook: 1hours10mins | Ready in:*

### Ingredients

- 3 pounds baby back ribs, membranes removed
- 1/2 cup finely chopped onion
- 1/4 cup olive oil
- 1/4 cup fresh lemon juice
- 1/4 cup chopped fresh oregano
- 1 tablespoon liquid honey
- 5 cloves garlic, minced
- 1 teaspoon kosher salt
- 1 teaspoon freshly ground black pepper
- cooking spray

### Direction

- In a big resealable plastic bag, mix pepper, salt, garlic, honey, oregano, lemon juice, olive oil, onion and baby back ribs. Flip to guarantee ribs are nicely coated.
- Refrigerate to marinate for 4 to 8 hours, flipping from time to time.
- Preheat an oven to 200 °C or 400 °F. With aluminum foil, line a baking sheet; coat with cooking spray.

- On the prepped baking sheet, set the ribs, retaining gap among them.
- In the prepped oven, let bake for 10 minutes till browned. Lower the oven temperature to 150 °C or 300 °F. Continue to bake for an hour till ribs are soft.

## Nutrition Information

- Calories: 473 calories;
- Cholesterol: 117
- Protein: 24.5
- Total Fat: 38.5
- Sodium: 422
- Total Carbohydrate: 6.4

## 128. Greek Scrambled Eggs

*Serving: 2 | Prep: 10mins | Cook: 5mins | Ready in:*

## Ingredients

- 1 tablespoon butter
- 3 eggs
- 1 teaspoon water
- 1/2 cup crumbled feta cheese
- salt and pepper to taste

## Direction

- On medium-high heat, heat butter in a pan. Whip water and eggs; pour into a pan then put in feta cheese; cook while mixing from time to time to scramble. Sprinkle pepper and salt to season.

## Nutrition Information

- Calories: 257 calories;
- Protein: 14.8
- Total Fat: 21.2
- Sodium: 710
- Total Carbohydrate: 2.1
- Cholesterol: 328

## 129. Greek Slow Cooker Chicken

*Serving: 6 | Prep: 20mins | Cook: 4hours | Ready in:*

## Ingredients

- 1 (3 pound) whole chicken, skin removed
- 1 lemon, cut in half
- 6 cloves peeled garlic, or more to taste (divided)
- 6 red potatoes, sliced into 1-inch thick rounds
- 1 large onion, roughly chopped
- 1/4 cup white wine
- 1/4 cup olive oil
- 1 teaspoon chicken bouillon granules
- 1/4 cup boiling water
- 2 teaspoons dried oregano
- salt and pepper to taste

## Direction

- Wash the inside and out of the chicken. Insert 3 garlic cloves and a lemon half in chicken cavity. Put the other lemon half aside.
- Into a slow cooker crock, arrange the onions and sliced potatoes in layer. Scatter around the inside of cooker with the leftover three cloves of garlic then put chicken on vegetables. Add olive oil and wine. In boiling water, dissolve bouillon, and pour into the cooker.
- Squeeze juice from the leftover half of lemon on top of chicken (drain out the seeds); scatter oregano over. Add black pepper and salt to season the chicken.
- Cook for 4-6 hours on High setting or for about 8-10 hours on Low setting with a cover. An inserted meat thermometer in the thickest portion of a thigh, without touching the bone, must register no less than 70 ° C or 160 ° F.

## Nutrition Information

- Calories: 471 calories;
- Total Fat: 17.9
- Sodium: 173
- Total Carbohydrate: 39.8
- Cholesterol: 96
- Protein: 36.7

## 130. Greek Souzoukaklia

*Serving: 6 | Prep: 30mins | Cook: 15mins | Ready in:*

### Ingredients

- 1 1/2 pounds ground beef
- 1 onion, chopped
- 3/8 cup raisins, chopped
- 1 1/2 teaspoons chopped flat leaf parsley
- 1/2 teaspoon cayenne pepper
- 1/2 teaspoon ground cinnamon
- 1/2 teaspoon ground coriander
- 1 pinch ground nutmeg
- 1/2 teaspoon white sugar
- salt and pepper to taste
- skewers
- 1 tablespoon vegetable oil

### Direction

- Preheat grill on high.
- Stir together ground beef, onion, parsley, raisins, cinnamon, nutmeg, coriander, cayenne pepper, sugar, salt, and pepper in a large bowl. Form around skewers and flatten; brush with oil to prevent sticking on grates.
- Grill for about 15 minutes, turning from time to time until evenly browned and cooked through.

### Nutrition Information

- Calories: 289 calories;
- Sodium: 261
- Total Carbohydrate: 10.8
- Cholesterol: 70
- Protein: 19.5
- Total Fat: 18.7

## 131. Greek Stuffed Burgers

*Serving: 6 | Prep: 25mins | Cook: 14mins | Ready in:*

### Ingredients

- 2 pounds lean ground beef (90%)
- 2 tablespoons minced garlic
- 1 teaspoon Italian seasoning, or to taste
- 1 teaspoon dried dill, or to taste
- salt and ground black pepper to taste
- 1 (4 ounce) package feta cheese
- 1 (4 ounce) container Gorgonzola cheese

### Direction

- Place plastic wrap over the baking sheet. In a bowl, combine pepper, salt, dill, Italian seasoning, garlic and beef. Mix until fully incorporated and sticky using your hand. Shape beef mixture into balls; splash with some water to tighten. Press balls into large, thin patties.
- In a bowl, combine Gorgonzola cheese and feta cheese. Spread cheese mixture over the patties. Use your wet hands to fold the edges of the patties to seal the cheese. Arrange on the baking sheet and chill for about half an hour until firmed.
- Bring a large skillet to medium heat. Cook patties, about 7 to 8 minutes on each side, until the center is no longer pink or when an instant read thermometer inserted into the middle reaches at least 160°F (70°C)

### Nutrition Information

- Calories: 449 calories;
- Cholesterol: 141
- Protein: 39
- Total Fat: 30.5

- Sodium: 513
- Total Carbohydrate: 1.9

## 132. Greek Stuffed Peppers

*Serving: 8 | Prep: 15mins | Cook: 20mins | Ready in:*

### Ingredients

- 1 (8 ounce) package crumbled feta cheese
- 1 (2 ounce) jar chopped pimento peppers
- 1 teaspoon Greek seasoning
- ground black pepper, to taste
- 1/4 cup olive oil
- 2 green bell peppers, cored and cut into quarters
- 8 slices bacon

### Direction

- Set the oven at 400°F (200°C) and start preheating.
- In a bowl, mix together olive oil, black pepper, Greek seasoning, pimiento peppers and feta cheese; on each of the 8 bell pepper segments, put 2 tablespoons of the mixture. Use a slice of bacon to wrap each segment; secure with toothpicks; distribute on a baking dish.
- Bake for around 20 minutes in the preheated oven, till the bacon begins to crisp and is browned. Serve hot.

### Nutrition Information

- Calories: 193 calories;
- Total Carbohydrate: 3.3
- Cholesterol: 35
- Protein: 7.8
- Total Fat: 16.7
- Sodium: 589

## 133. Greek Stuffed Tomatoes And Peppers (Yemista)

*Serving: 12 | Prep: 20mins | Cook: 1hours25mins | Ready in:*

### Ingredients

- 8 large ripe tomatoes
- 4 large green bell peppers
- 1/4 cup butter
- 1 onion, diced
- 1 clove garlic, minced, or to taste
- 2 pounds ground beef chuck
- 2 tablespoons soy sauce
- 1 tablespoon seasoned salt
- 1 tablespoon ground black pepper
- 1/2 cup water
- 1 1/2 cups converted (parboiled) rice (such as Uncle Ben's®)
- 1/2 cup olive oil

### Direction

- Slice the tops off the tomatoes and keep one corner attached to make a lid. Remove the insides of the tomatoes and put the 'meat' into a large bowl; squeeze the juices from the tomatoes. Slice off the tops of the green peppers and retain to use later; remove the membranes and seeds. In an 11x17-inch baking dish, place bell peppers and tomatoes.
- Set an oven to 190°C (375°F) and start preheating.
- In a large skillet, heat the butter on medium; stir and cook garlic and onion in the melted butter for 5-10 minutes until they soften. Add black pepper, seasoned salt, soy sauce, and ground chuck into the onion mixture; cook for 5-10 minutes until the ground chuck becomes crumbly and browned.
- Combine the water and the squeezed tomato meat into the browned chuck; simmer for about 15 minutes. Add rice and boil; take the skillet away from the heat. Put the rice-beef mixture into the tomatoes; arrange the tops on

the filled tomatoes and put them to the baking dish, lid-sides down.
- Put the rice-beef mixture into the bell peppers and place the retained lids on top; in the baking dish, place the bell peppers sideways. Pour the olive oil on the bell peppers and stuffed tomatoes; flavor with pepper and salt.
- In the prepared oven, bake for half an hour. Flip the bell peppers and keep on baking for half an hour longer until tomatoes and bell peppers soften.

## Nutrition Information

- Calories: 348 calories;
- Total Fat: 20.6
- Sodium: 412
- Total Carbohydrate: 28.5
- Cholesterol: 44
- Protein: 13

## 134. Greek Stuffed Zucchini

*Serving: 4 | Prep: 30mins | Cook: 45mins | Ready in:*

### Ingredients

- 1/4 cup uncooked white rice
- 8 zucchini, ends trimmed
- 1 pound ground beef
- 4 shallots, chopped
- 2 cloves garlic, finely chopped
- 1/4 cup chopped fresh mint
- 1/4 cup chopped fresh parsley
- 2 tablespoons olive oil
- salt and ground black pepper to taste
- 3 tablespoons water
- Avgolemono Sauce:
- 2 eggs, separated
- 4 lemons, juiced

### Direction

- In a bowl, arrange the rice and add water to cover, then let it soak for an hour.
- Cut a long slice with 1/2 inch in thickness from the side of each zucchini to serve as a lid; use a spoon to hollow out seeds and flesh from the inside of the zucchini and leave a thick shell with 1/2 inch in thickness. Reserve the flesh for other uses or discard. Drain the soaked rice and arrange into a bowl. Combine in parsley, mint, garlic, shallots, and ground beef. Stuff the mixture in the zucchini boats to 3/4 full; the filling will expand when cooking. Use the cut-off lid slices to cover the zucchini.
- In a large skillet, heat olive oil on medium heat and scatter pepper and salt over the pan. Arrange the stuffed zucchini in the pan, then pour around the zucchini with water and turn down the heat to medium-low. Use a lid to cover and cook for 35-40 minutes until the meat is not pink anymore and the zucchini becomes tender.
- In a bowl, whisk the egg whites using an electric mixture roughly 10 minutes before the zucchini are finished until stiff peaks formed. Beat in lemon juice and yolks until mixed thoroughly. Take the zucchini out of the skillet and leave the juices, then put aside the zucchini in a warm place. Beat half the liquid from the skillet by tablespoons into the egg mixture, then pour the egg mixture to the skillet with the rest of the liquid. Rotate gently the skillet to combine the contents in order to mix the sauce together with the pan liquid on low heat; heat the sauce until it thickens enough to coat the back of the spoon, for a minute. Don't boil. Serve zucchini alongside the lemon sauce.

## Nutrition Information

- Calories: 592 calories;
- Total Fat: 40.2
- Sodium: 161
- Total Carbohydrate: 31.8
- Cholesterol: 189
- Protein: 29.1

## 135. Greek Style Garlic Chicken Breast

*Serving: 4 | Prep: 10mins | Cook: 25mins | Ready in:*

### Ingredients

- 4 skinless, boneless chicken breast halves
- 1 cup extra virgin olive oil
- 1 lemon, juiced
- 2 teaspoons crushed garlic
- 1 teaspoon salt
- 1 1/2 teaspoons black pepper
- 1/3 teaspoon paprika

### Direction

- Make three gashes in each chicken breast to let the marinade soak in. Whisk paprika, olive oil, pepper, lemon juice, salt, and garlic in a small bowl for half a minute. In a big bowl, put the chicken then add the marinade over; massage the marinade in chicken with your hands. Cover then chill overnight.
- Prepare the grill on medium heat then greased the grate lightly.
- Grill the chicken until the juices run clear and the meat is not pink.

### Nutrition Information

- Calories: 644 calories;
- Total Carbohydrate: 4
- Cholesterol: 68
- Protein: 27.8
- Total Fat: 57.6
- Sodium: 660

## 136. Greek Traditional Turkey With Chestnut And Pine Nut Stuffing

*Serving: 12 | Prep: 30mins | Cook: 4hours15mins | Ready in:*

### Ingredients

- 1 cup chestnuts
- 2/3 cup butter
- 1/4 cup orange juice
- 1/4 cup tangerine juice
- 2/3 cup lemon juice
- 1 (10 pound) whole turkey
- salt and ground black pepper to taste
- 1/2 pound ground beef
- 1/2 pound ground pork
- 1/4 cup chopped onion
- 1/2 cup uncooked instant rice
- 1/4 cup pine nuts
- 1/4 cup raisins (optional)
- 1/3 cup butter
- 1/2 cup chicken broth
- 2 tablespoons brandy
- 1 teaspoon salt
- 1/2 teaspoon ground black pepper

### Direction

- Preheat the oven to 165°C or 325°F.
- Create a small cut on sides of every chestnut, and put in a skillet over moderate heat. Cook till toasted, mixing frequently. Take off heat, skin, and cut.
- In a saucepan, liquify 2/3 cup of butter, and stir in lemon juice, tangerine juice and orange juice. Massage the mixture on the inside and outside of turkey, setting aside some for basting. Put pepper and salt to season the turkey.
- Cook onion, ground pork, and ground beef in a big skillet over moderate heat till pork and beef are equally brown and onion is soft. Drain oil. Stir in rice. Mix in brandy, broth, 1/3 cup butter, raisins, pine nuts and chestnuts. Add 1/2 teaspoon pepper and 1 teaspoon salt to

season. Keep cooking till all liquid has been soaked up. Fill every turkey cavity with the mixture, and use kitchen twine to tie in place.
- On a rack in roasting pan, put the turkey, and cover thighs and breast loosely using aluminum foil. Into the base of pan, add approximately a quarter inch of water. Keep this water level throughout the cook time. In the prepped oven, let turkey roast for 3 to 4 hours, brushing from time to time with the rest of the juice and butter mixture. Raise the oven temperature to 200°C or 400°F on the last hour of roasting, and take off foil. Let the turkey cook to a minimum internal temperature of 82°C or 180°F.

### Nutrition Information

- Calories: 930 calories;
- Total Carbohydrate: 22.3
- Cholesterol: 322
- Protein: 86.1
- Total Fat: 52.2
- Sodium: 572

### 137. Greek Turkey Burgers

*Serving: 8 | Prep: 15mins | Cook: 10mins | Ready in:*

### Ingredients

- 2 pounds ground turkey
- 1 1/2 cups fresh bread crumbs
- 1 1/2 cups chopped baby spinach
- 1/2 cup light Greek dressing
- 5 ounces feta cheese, cubed
- 1/4 large onion, finely chopped
- 1 egg
- salt and ground black pepper to taste

### Direction

- Preheat outdoor grill to medium high heat; oil grate lightly.
- Mix black pepper, salt, egg, onion, feta cheese, Greek dressing, spinach, breadcrumbs and turkey in a bowl; shape to patties.
- On preheated grill, cook turkey burgers, 5-10 minutes per side, till juices are clear and not pink anymore in the center. An inserted instant-read thermometer in middle should read at least 74°C/165°F.

### Nutrition Information

- Calories: 331 calories;
- Protein: 28.7
- Total Fat: 16.3
- Sodium: 583
- Total Carbohydrate: 17
- Cholesterol: 123

### 138. Greek Inspired Skillet Lasagna

*Serving: 4 | Prep: 20mins | Cook: 20mins | Ready in:*

### Ingredients

- 1 pound ground lamb
- 1 onion, chopped
- 2 cloves garlic, minced
- 1/2 cup tomato paste
- 1 tablespoon ground cinnamon
- 1/2 teaspoon cayenne pepper
- salt and ground black pepper to taste
- 4 cups water
- 6 lasagna noodles, broken into 2-inch pieces
- 2 tablespoons balsamic vinegar
- 1 1/2 cups plain Greek yogurt
- 1 tablespoon chopped fresh mint
- 1/4 cup crumbled feta cheese
- 5 fresh mint leaves, chopped, or to taste

### Direction

- Put a skillet on medium-high heat. Stir and cook ground lamb in skillet until crumbly and

brown, 5-7 minutes. Drain excess fat. Add in garlic and onion; stir and cook until onion becomes translucent, 3-6 minutes.
- To the lamb mixture, mix in cayenne pepper, black pepper, tomato paste, salt, and cinnamon. Continue cooking for 2-3 minutes until spice are aromatic. Put the lasagna pasta, water, and balsamic vinegar to the lamb mixture and let it boil. Lower down the heat and cover. Let it simmer 5 minutes. Remove the cover and let it simmer until pasta is al dente and sauce is thick, 5-7 minutes.
- Mix 1 tbsp. mint, salt and Greek yogurt in a bowl. Scoop yogurt mixture with a tablespoon and spread across lasagna top 2 tablespoons at a time Drizzle feta cheese and chopped mint leaves on top.

## Nutrition Information

- Calories: 523 calories;
- Total Carbohydrate: 41.5
- Cholesterol: 101
- Protein: 31.9
- Total Fat: 26
- Sodium: 488

### 139. Greek Italian Fusion Beef Souvlaki Pizza

*Serving: 4 | Prep: 15mins | Cook: 15mins | Ready in:*

## Ingredients

- 1 (12 inch) pre-baked pizza crust
- 1 cup tzatziki sauce
- 1/2 cup sliced, cooked beef, or to taste
- 1 cup sliced and quartered cucumber
- 1 cup pitted and diced kalamata olives
- 1 cup crumbled feta cheese
- 1 cup shredded mozzarella cheese
- 1 egg yolk

## Direction

- Set the oven at 220° C (425° F) to preheat.
- Arrange the pizza crust on a pizza pan or a baking sheet. Spread tzatziki sauce over the crust and put beef, olives, cucumber, feta cheese and mozzarella cheese on top following the order. Brush over the exposed pizza crust with egg yolk.
- Bake the pizza in the preheated oven until the cheese melts and the crust has a shiny golden-brown color, approximately 15 minutes.

## Nutrition Information

- Calories: 693 calories;
- Total Fat: 80.7
- Sodium: 1790
- Total Carbohydrate: 61
- Cholesterol: 129
- Protein: 36.3

### 140. Greek Stuffed Chicken Breasts

*Serving: 2 | Prep: 20mins | Cook: 55mins | Ready in:*

## Ingredients

- 1 lemon
- 2 tablespoons extra-virgin olive oil
- ⅓ cup finely chopped onion
- 1 clove garlic, minced
- ⅓ cup chopped cooked spinach
- ⅓ cup crumbled feta cheese
- 3 tablespoons finely chopped Kalamata olives
- salt and ground black pepper to taste
- 2 boneless, skinless chicken breasts
- 2 teaspoons all-purpose flour, or as needed
- toothpicks
- 2 tablespoons extra-virgin olive oil

## Direction

- Zest the lemon. Use a sharp knife to take off the pith and cut the flesh horizontally. Set aside the slices.
- In an oven-safe nonstick frying pan, heat 2 tbsp. of olive oil on medium heat for 2-3 minutes, until it shimmers. Add onion and let it cook for 3-5 minutes, until it turns translucent. Add the garlic and lemon zest and heat it for around 1 minute, until it becomes aromatic.
- Add the spinach to the onion mixture and let it cook and stir for around 3 minutes, until heated through. Transfer the spinach-onion mixture to a bowl. Wipe the frying pan clean, then put aside. Mix the olives and feta cheese into the spinach mixture, then sprinkle pepper and salt to season.
- Set an oven to preheat to 175°C (350°F).
- Cut a 2-inch slit along the edges of the thick side of each chicken breast. Slice it lengthwise and be careful not to cut through the opposite edge or the bottom to create a pocket. Sprinkle pepper and salt to season the pocket.
- Stuff 1/2 the spinach and onion mixture on each chicken breast, then use toothpicks to close the slits. Lightly dust the chicken with pepper, salt and flour.
- In the same frying pan, heat 2 tbsp. olive oil on medium-high heat for about 2 minutes, until it shimmers. Put the chicken in the hot oil, rib side up. Let it cook for 3-5 minutes on each side, until it turns brown. Flip the chicken rib side down and put the slices of lemon on top.
- Let it bake for about 35 minutes in the preheated oven, until an inserted instant-read thermometer in the middle reads 74°C (165°F).

## Nutrition Information

- Calories: 595 calories;
- Total Fat: 46.5
- Protein: 30.1
- Sodium: 1130
- Total Carbohydrate: 17.2
- Cholesterol: 87

## 141. Greek Style Stuffed Peppers

*Serving: 8 | Prep: 20mins | Cook: 1hours | Ready in:*

### Ingredients

- 4 large green bell peppers, tops removed, seeded
- 4 large red bell peppers, tops removed, seeded
- 1 tablespoon olive oil
- 1/2 pound ground pork
- 2 onions, chopped
- salt and pepper to taste
- 1/4 cup dry white wine
- 1 (10.75 ounce) can tomato puree
- 1 (4 ounce) package feta cheese
- 1/2 cup cooked white rice
- 1/2 cup raisins
- 1/2 cup pine nuts
- 2 tablespoons chopped fresh parsley

### Direction

- Set the oven to 350°F (175°C) and start preheating. In a bowl, put red and green bell peppers with enough warm water to cover; soak for 5 minutes.
- In a skillet, over medium heat, heat olive oil. Put onions and pork in the skillet, sprinkle with pepper and salt; cook until pork turns brown evenly. Drain grease; mix in tomato puree and wine. Keep cooking for 10 minutes.
- Place skillet mixture in a large bowl; mix in parsley, pine nuts, raisins, cooked rice and feta cheese. Stuffed peppers with the mixture; place in a baking dish. Use aluminum foil to cover.
- Bake in the prepared oven for half an hour. Get rid of the foil; keep baking for 10 minutes until stuffing turns brown lightly. Can be served hot or cold.

### Nutrition Information

- Calories: 355 calories;
- Total Fat: 20.6
- Sodium: 595
- Total Carbohydrate: 28.7
- Cholesterol: 54
- Protein: 15.2

## 142. Grilled Eggplant Moussaka

*Serving: 8 | Prep: 50mins | Cook: 50mins | Ready in:*

### Ingredients

- 3 large eggplant, sliced into 1/4 inch rounds
- 3 large potatoes, thinly sliced
- 3 large zucchini, cut lengthwise into 1/4 inch slices
- 1/2 cup extra-virgin olive oil
- 5 tablespoons butter
- 7 tablespoons all-purpose flour
- 5 cups milk
- 1 pinch ground nutmeg
- salt to taste
- 1 egg yolk, beaten
- 1 tablespoon olive oil
- 1 1/2 pounds ground beef
- 1 onion, chopped
- 1 teaspoon oregano
- salt and pepper to taste
- 1/2 cup chopped fresh parsley
- 5 ripe tomatoes, chopped
- 1 cup crumbled feta cheese

### Direction

- Set the outdoor grill over medium-high heat for preheating. Put oil onto the grate lightly.
- Coat the zucchini, eggplant, and potatoes with extra-virgin olive oil lightly. Grill the vegetables until golden brown and tender. Place the potatoes into the bottom of the 9x13-inches glass baking dish. Layer it with eggplant, and then with zucchini; put aside.
- Set the oven to 375°F or 190°C for preheating.
- Put butter in a large saucepan and melt it over medium heat. Mix in the flour. Cook for 5 minutes until the flour already smells slightly toasted. Mix in nutmeg, milk, and salt. Bring the mixture to a bare simmer over medium-high heat. Adjust the heat to medium-low. Simmer the mixture for 10 minutes. In a bowl, place the egg yolk and whisk in quickly 1/4 cup of the thickened milk, adding it 1 tbsp. at a time. Mix the egg yolk mixture into the thickened milk quickly until smooth; put aside.
- In the meantime, put 1 tbsp. of olive oil into the large skillet and heat it over medium-high. Mix in onion and ground beef. Cook until the beef is no longer pink and turns crumbly. Drain any excess grease off. Mix in pepper, oregano, tomatoes, salt, and parsley. Adjust the heat to medium-low. Cover the skillet and simmer the mixture for 10 minutes while occasionally stirring it.
- For assembly: Spread the meat mixture all over the vegetables. Sprinkle the mixture with feta cheese. Top the mixture with white sauce and use a spatula to smoothen it.
- Bake the moussaka inside the preheated oven and bake for 30 minutes until golden brown and bubbly.

### Nutrition Information

- Calories: 722 calories;
- Sodium: 405
- Total Carbohydrate: 60.7
- Cholesterol: 125
- Protein: 30.9
- Total Fat: 41.6

## 143. Grilled Greek Chicken

*Serving: 6 | Prep: 15mins | Cook: 20mins | Ready in:*

### Ingredients

- 6 cloves garlic (or more to taste), crushed or very finely minced
- 2 tablespoons dried oregano
- 1 teaspoon red pepper flakes, or to taste
- 1 teaspoon freshly ground black pepper
- 1/2 cup lemon juice
- 1/4 cup olive oil
- 1 tablespoon distilled white vinegar
- 6 chicken leg quarters
- 1 lemon, cut into wedges

### Direction

- In a large mixing bowl, combine vinegar, olive oil, lemon juice, black pepper, red pepper flakes, oregano, and garlic.
- Cut 1 slash in the leg part of each leg quarter and 2 on the skin side down to the bone in the thigh part. This helps chicken pieces absorb marinade better and shorten cooking time. Sprinkle kosher salt liberally over both sides of chicken. Put chicken into the bowl along with marinade and turn until all sides are coated. Marinate, covered, for 4 to 12 hours in the fridge.
- Remove chicken to a sheet pan lined with paper towels to drain slightly.
- Arrange leg quarter on the grill over semi-direct heat, skin side down (intense direct heat will burn chicken). Grill chicken for 6 to 7 minutes. Flip over; cook for 6 to 7 minutes longer. Keep cooking and turning, about 8 to 10 minutes longer, until internal temperature of chicken achieves 165°F (74°C). Serve warm with lemon wedges on the side.

### Nutrition Information

- Calories: 449 calories;
- Cholesterol: 140
- Protein: 40
- Total Fat: 29.7
- Sodium: 134
- Total Carbohydrate: 4.5

## 144. Gyros Burgers

*Serving: 4 | Prep: 10mins | Cook: 15mins | Ready in:*

### Ingredients

- 1/2 pound lean ground beef
- 1/2 pound lean ground lamb
- 1/2 onion, grated
- 2 cloves garlic, pressed
- 1 slice bread, toasted and crumbled
- 1/2 teaspoon dried savory
- 1/2 teaspoon ground allspice
- 1/2 teaspoon ground coriander
- 1/2 teaspoon salt
- 1/2 teaspoon ground black pepper
- 1 dash ground cumin

### Direction

- Set the outdoor grill on medium heat; preheat and oil lightly the grill grate.
- Mix together the ground lamb, garlic, ground beef, bread crumbs, and onion in a big bowl. Sprinkle on allspice, salt, cumin, pepper, savory, and coriander. Massage mixture until stiff. Mold mixture in 4 thin patties about 1/8-1/4 inch in thickness.
- For 5-7 minutes per side, cook the patties until thoroughly cooked.

### Nutrition Information

- Calories: 338 calories;
- Sodium: 408
- Total Carbohydrate: 5.7
- Cholesterol: 84
- Protein: 20.3
- Total Fat: 25.4

## 145. High Seas Chicken Souvlaki

*Serving: 4 | Prep: 20mins | Cook: 15mins | Ready in:*

### Ingredients

- 8 bamboo skewers
- 1 cucumber - peeled, seeded, and shredded
- 1 (12 ounce) container Greek-style yogurt
- 2 cloves garlic, minced
- 2 sprigs fresh dill, chopped
- salt and freshly ground black pepper to taste
- 2 skinless, boneless chicken breasts, cut into 1/2-inch strips
- 2 sprigs fresh oregano, chopped
- 2 cloves garlic, minced
- 1 lemon, juiced
- 2 tablespoons extra-virgin olive oil
- salt and freshly ground black pepper to taste
- 3 Roma tomatoes, diced
- 1 cucumber - peeled, seeded, and diced
- 1/2 red onion, cut into thin 1-inch-long strips
- 2 tablespoons extra-virgin olive oil
- 1/2 lemon, juiced
- 8 pita bread rounds
- 4 ounces feta cheese, cut into 1/4-inch slices

### Direction

- Steep bamboo skewers for 30-40 minutes in water.
- Place shredded cucumber in a fine mesh strainer and press to remove excess liquid; let drain for 15 minutes.
- In a small mixing bowl, combine pepper, salt, dill, shredded cucumber, 2 cloves minced garlic, and yogurt. Chill in the fridge.
- Place chicken in a bowl and add pepper salt, 2 tablespoons olive oil, lemon juice, 2 cloves minced garlic, and oregano; stir well to combine and chill for 20 minutes in the fridge.
- Set an outdoor grill to medium-high heat and grease the grate lightly with oil.
- In a mixing bowl, combine pepper, salt, 2 tablespoons olive oil, onion, diced cucumber, and tomatoes. Stir until well combined.
- Skewer the marinated chilled chicken.
- Grill the chicken, about 5 minutes per side until no longer pink inside and browned outside, add juice squeezed from 1/2 a lemon while cooking.
- Heat pita bread, 1 to 2 minutes per side on the grill until heated through. Top each pita bread round with tomato salad, 1 to 2 spoonfuls of yogurt sauce, and chicken from a skewer. Add feta cheese slices on top and serve.

### Nutrition Information

- Calories: 688 calories;
- Total Fat: 31
- Sodium: 944
- Total Carbohydrate: 70.1
- Cholesterol: 77
- Protein: 31.9

### 146.     Jeanie's Falafel

*Serving: 6 | Prep: 25mins | Cook: 7mins | Ready in:*

### Ingredients

- 1 (19 ounce) can garbanzo beans, rinsed and drained
- 1 small onion, finely chopped
- 2 cloves garlic, minced
- 1 1/2 tablespoons chopped fresh cilantro
- 1 teaspoon dried parsley
- 2 teaspoons ground cumin
- 1/8 teaspoon ground turmeric
- 1/2 teaspoon baking powder
- 1 cup fine dry bread crumbs
- 3/4 teaspoon salt
- 1/4 teaspoon cracked black peppercorns
- 1 quart vegetable oil for frying

### Direction

- Mash garbanzo beans in big bowl; mix pepper, salt, breadcrumbs, baking powder, turmeric, cumin, parsley, cilantro, garlic and onion in with your hands. Form mixture to get 18-24 1 1/2-inch balls; add little water if mixture doesn't hold together.

- Heat oil to 190°C/375°F in deep fryer. Drop balls into hot oil carefully; fry till brown. If you don't own a deep fryer, heat oil in heavy deep skillet on medium high heat; after the first few falafels, you might have to adjust heat slightly. Frequently turn to evenly brown.

## Nutrition Information

- Calories: 317 calories;
- Cholesterol: 0
- Protein: 7.2
- Total Fat: 16.8
- Sodium: 724
- Total Carbohydrate: 35.2

## 147. Kalamata Pork Tenderloin With Rosemary

*Serving: 4 | Prep: 20mins | Cook: 15mins | Ready in:*

## Ingredients

- 1 pound pork tenderloin medallions
- 1/4 cup all-purpose flour
- 1/2 teaspoon salt
- 1/4 teaspoon pepper
- 1 tablespoon olive oil
- 1 tablespoon chopped fresh rosemary
- 1 clove garlic, minced
- 1/2 cup dry red wine
- 1/2 cup chicken stock
- 1/8 cup sliced kalamata olives
- 1 tablespoon minced lemon zest

## Direction

- Flatten the meat until a quarter-inch thick. Mix pepper, salt, and flour in a shallow bowl; dredge pork into flour to coat.
- On medium-high heat, heat 1 tablespoon olive oil in a pan; cook pork in olive oil until brown, flip once. Move pork to a heated plate.
- Turn to low heat; put garlic and rosemary in the pan. Add wine then boil; keep on boiling until the mixture is thick. Add chicken stock then boil until the mixture reduces by half. Mix in lemon zest and olives. Pour the sauce all over the pork then serve.

## Nutrition Information

- Calories: 233 calories;
- Cholesterol: 63
- Protein: 21.1
- Total Fat: 10.1
- Sodium: 404
- Total Carbohydrate: 7.8

## 148. Kefta

*Serving: 10 | Prep: 20mins | Cook: 50mins | Ready in:*

## Ingredients

- 1 bunch fresh parsley, chopped
- 3 medium onions, finely chopped
- 1 1/2 pounds ground lamb
- 2 teaspoons ground allspice
- 1 1/2 teaspoons grated lemon zest
- 2 teaspoons salt
- 1/4 cup butter, softened
- 1 medium tomato, sliced

## Direction

- Preheat an oven to 175°C/350°F.
- Mix butter, salt, lemon zest, allspice, lamb, onions and parsley till well blended in a big bowl; for best results, use your hands. Pat into 2-in. tall round on baking sheets with sides/put in baking dish. Put tomato slices over.
- In the preheated oven, bake with no cover, till internal temperature is 72°C/160°F and not pink for 50 minutes; serve with rice or pita bread.

## Nutrition Information

- Calories: 192 calories;
- Total Fat: 14
- Sodium: 541
- Total Carbohydrate: 4.3
- Cholesterol: 58
- Protein: 12.4

## 149. LIZZY217's Lamb Gyros

*Serving: 4 | Prep: 30mins | Cook: 10mins | Ready in:*

### Ingredients

- 1/4 cup vegetable oil
- 2 tablespoons lemon juice
- 2 tablespoons brandy
- 1 clove garlic, crushed
- 1 teaspoon salt
- 1/2 teaspoon ground black pepper
- 1/2 teaspoon dried marjoram
- 1/8 teaspoon ground dried thyme
- 1/8 teaspoon ground dried rosemary
- 1/8 teaspoon dried oregano
- 1 pound boneless lamb shoulder, cut into 1-inch cubes
- 1 cup plain yogurt
- 1/2 cucumber, shredded
- 1 clove garlic, minced
- 1 tablespoon lemon juice
- 1 teaspoon salt
- 1/4 teaspoon ground black pepper
- 4 (10 inch) bamboo skewers, soaked in water for 20 minutes
- 8 pocket bread rounds
- 1 tomato, sliced
- 1/2 red onion, thinly sliced
- 1 cup shredded lettuce
- 1/2 cup crumbled feta cheese (optional)

### Direction

- In a bowl, whisk oregano, rosemary, thyme, marjoram, half teaspoon of black pepper, one teaspoon of salt, crushed garlic, brandy, 2 tablespoons of lemon juice and vegetable oil together. Transfer to a resealable plastic bag. Put in cubed lamb, coat marinade over. Then squeeze any excess air out. Seal the bag. Marinate in fridge for about 12 hours to 1 day.
- Discard the meat from fridge when it has completed marinating. Let stand for 60 mins at room temperature. In a mixing bowl, whisk cucumber and yogurt together along with a quarter teaspoon pepper, one teaspoon of salt, one tablespoon of lemon juice and one clove of minced garlic while meat is warming up to prepare tzatziki sauce. Cover sauce in the plastic wrap. Place in the refrigerator till ready to use.
- Start preheating oven's broiler, place oven rack about 4-inch from heat source. Take out lamb cubes from marinade, then squeeze any excess off. Dispose remaining marinade. Spray the cooking spray over the broiling pan, thread meat into skewers, then arrange them into prepared pan.
- Broil under prepared broiler to the preferred degree of doneness, flipping every few minutes so the meat cooks equally. This will take about 10 minutes to cook meat to medium-well.
- To assemble sandwiches, in a microwave, cook every pocket bread for 20-30 seconds each on high, until they are hot. Split every piece in 1/2. Open pockets up. Portion onion and tomato slices among each half of pocket bread. Fill with the shredded lettuce, then stuff with broiled lamb. Dust with the crumbled feta cheese. Drizzle with tzatziki sauce. Enjoy!

## Nutrition Information

- Calories: 698 calories;
- Total Fat: 32.1
- Sodium: 2131
- Total Carbohydrate: 67.6
- Cholesterol: 77

- Protein: 29.1

## 150. Lamb Feta Peppers

*Serving: 6 | Prep: 15mins | Cook: 1hours | Ready in:*

### Ingredients

- 1 tablespoon olive oil
- 1 medium onion, chopped
- 1 clove garlic, minced
- 6 medium green bell peppers
- 2 tablespoons chopped fresh dill
- 3/4 teaspoon salt
- 1/2 teaspoon ground allspice
- 1/2 teaspoon ground black pepper
- 1 cup cooked rice
- 8 ounces ground lamb
- 1 cup crumbled feta cheese
- 1 cup tomato sauce
- 1 cup cold water
- 1 tablespoon fresh lemon juice
- 1 teaspoon white sugar

### Direction

- Preheat the oven to 190°C or 375°Fahrenheit.
- On medium heat, heat oil in a medium pan; add and cook onion for 4 minutes until soft. Mix in garlic then cook for a minute.
- Cut off the tops of peppers then take the seeds out. Place the peppers straight up in a 9-in by 12-in baking dish.
- Combine pepper, onion mixture, allspice, salt, and dill in a big bowl; mix in lamb and rice, then fold feta cheese in. Stuff the mixture into peppers.
- Combine sugar, tomato sauce, lemon juice, and water; drizzle 1/2 on top of the peppers and the other half on the bottom of the dish. Use foil to cover.
- Bake for 45 minutes in the preheated oven; remove the cover. Bake for another 15 minutes until an inserted meat thermometer in the middle of the filling registers 70°C or 160°Fahrenheit, occasionally baste with sauce.

### Nutrition Information

- Calories: 273 calories;
- Total Fat: 16.8
- Sodium: 912
- Total Carbohydrate: 19.3
- Cholesterol: 50
- Protein: 12.4

## 151. Lamb Lover's Pilaf

*Serving: 6 | Prep: 10mins | Cook: 20mins | Ready in:*

### Ingredients

- 2 tablespoons vegetable oil, divided
- 1 1/2 pounds boneless lamb stew meat cut into 1/2 inch strips
- 1/2 teaspoon Greek-style seasoning
- 1 onion, chopped
- 2 stalks celery, minced
- 1 cup dry bulgur wheat
- 1 1/2 cups chicken broth
- 1 pinch ground cinnamon
- 1 pinch ground allspice
- 1/4 cup raisins
- 1/4 cup slivered almonds

### Direction

- In a big skillet, heat 1 tbsp. of oil over moderately high heat. Use Greek seasoning to season the lamb strips and sauté them in the hot oil until browned. Take out of the skillet and put aside.
- Lower heat to moderate and heat leftover tablespoon of oil. Sauté celery and onion until soft, then put in bulgur wheat and keep on cooking for 5 more minutes, while stirring frequently.

- Stir in allspice, cinnamon, broth and reserved lamb. Lower heat to low and simmer with a cover until liquid is absorbed, about 15-20 minutes. Use raisins and almonds to decorate and serve.

## Nutrition Information

- Calories: 297 calories;
- Total Fat: 12.4
- Sodium: 89
- Total Carbohydrate: 26.6
- Cholesterol: 54
- Protein: 21.4

## 152. Lamb Spaghetti

*Serving: 10 | Prep: 25mins | Cook: 1hours | Ready in:*

### Ingredients

- 2 tablespoons olive oil
- 4 pounds ground lamb
- 1 whole head garlic, peeled and crushed
- 1 tablespoon onion powder
- 3 tablespoons lemon juice
- 1/2 teaspoon ground cinnamon
- 1/2 teaspoon dried oregano
- 1 1/2 cups water
- 4 small potatoes, peeled and cut into 1/2-inch dice
- salt and pepper to taste
- 1 (16 ounce) package linguine pasta

### Direction

- Heat olive oil in a large skillet; cook ground lamb, onion powder, and garlic, stirring and crumbling meat while cooking, until no pink remains in the lamb. Whisk in oregano, cinnamon, and lemon juice; keep cooking for about 20 minutes, stirring from time to time, until all the liquid in the skillet vaporizes and garlic and lamb turn brown nicely.
- Add potatoes and water; bring to a boil; turn heat to medium-low. Simmer for about 20 minutes or until potatoes are very soft and starting to break apart. Mash potatoes against the side of the skillet using a spoon to thicken the sauce. Season with pepper and salt. Simmer for 10 minutes longer (and up to 1 hour) until flavors have combined and gravy is thickened. Stir from time to time while cooking.
- Bring lightly salted water in a large pot to a rolling boil; add linguine and cook, about 11 minutes, until al dente. Drain off water. Remove cooked pasta to serving plates; spoon lamb gravy over pasta to serve.

## Nutrition Information

- Calories: 604 calories;
- Cholesterol: 122
- Protein: 38.8
- Total Fat: 28.5
- Sodium: 110
- Total Carbohydrate: 47.4

## 153. Loaded Greek Burgers

*Serving: 4 | Prep: 25mins | Cook: 15mins | Ready in:*

### Ingredients

- 1 red bell pepper
- Spread:
- 2 ounces crumbled feta cheese
- 2 tablespoons mayonnaise
- 2 teaspoons lime juice
- 1 sprig fresh mint, chopped
- 1 sprig fresh parsley, chopped
- Burgers:
- 1 pound lean ground beef
- 6 ounces crumbled feta cheese
- 8 ounces fresh spinach - rinsed, drained and coarsely chopped
- 1/4 cup bread crumbs

- 1 egg
- 1 clove garlic, minced
- 1/4 cup chopped onion
- 2 sprigs fresh basil, coarsely chopped
- 3 sprigs fresh mint, coarsely chopped
- 2 sprigs fresh parsley, coarsely chopped
- salt and ground black pepper to taste
- 4 Kaiser rolls, split and toasted
- 1 tomato, sliced
- 4 leaves lettuce

### Direction

- Preheat the oven's broiler; put oven rack 6-inches away from the heat source. Line aluminum foil on a baking sheet. Cut red bell peppers, from top to bottom, in half; remove ribs, seeds and stem. Put pepper on the prepared baking sheet, cut side down.
- Cook under the preheated broiler for 5 minutes till pepper skin is blistered and blackened. Cool and steam blackened pepper for 5 minutes in a paper bag; peel then dice. Put aside.
- Mix 1 sprig chopped parsley, 1 sprig chopped mint, lime juice, mayonnaise and 2-ounces of feta cheese in a small bowl; put aside.
- Preheat an outdoor grill to medium heat; oil the grate lightly.
- Put leftover parsley, leftover mint, basil, onion, garlic, egg, breadcrumbs, spinach, feta cheese, ground beef and roasted red pepper in a bowl. Sprinkle pepper and salt; gently mixing till evenly combined with your hands. Divide the meat mixture to make 4 equal 4 1/2-inch patties.
- On the preheated grill, cook, 4 minutes per side for medium/ or to the desired degree of doneness. An instant-read thermometer inserted in middle should read 70°C/160°F. Serve burgers over warm toasted Kaiser Roll with lettuce, fresh tomatoes and feta cheese spread.

### Nutrition Information

- Calories: 634 calories;
- Total Carbohydrate: 36.5
- Cholesterol: 174
- Protein: 38.7
- Total Fat: 37.1
- Sodium: 1082

## 154. Low Carb Lamb Burgers

*Serving: 4 | Prep: 5mins | Cook: 10mins | Ready in:*

### Ingredients

- 1 pound ground lamb
- 1 tablespoon soy sauce
- 1/3 cup chopped onion
- salt and ground black pepper to taste
- 1/8 cup avocado oil
- 1/3 cup crumbled feta cheese (optional)

### Direction

- In a bowl, put onion, soy sauce, and lamb. Use pepper and salt to season to taste. Combine using your hands to blend. Shape the lamb mixture into 4 patties.
- In a skillet, heat avocado oil over medium heat. Cook the lamb patties for 5-8 minutes per side until turning brown. An instant-read meat thermometer should display a minimum of 145°F (65°C) when you insert it into the middle of a patty. Sprinkle feta cheese over and enjoy.

### Nutrition Information

- Calories: 296 calories;
- Total Fat: 20.9
- Sodium: 524
- Total Carbohydrate: 3.1
- Cholesterol: 95
- Protein: 22.9

## 155. Margaret's Keftedes (Greek Meatballs)

*Serving: 4 | Prep: 25mins | Cook: 30mins | Ready in:*

### Ingredients

- 4 slices white bread, torn into pieces
- 2 tablespoons milk
- 1 clove garlic
- 1 onion, quartered
- 4 teaspoons dried mint
- 1 teaspoon salt
- ground black pepper to taste
- 1/2 pound ground beef
- 1/2 pound ground lamb
- 4 eggs
- 1/2 cup all-purpose flour for dredging
- vegetable oil for frying

### Direction

- In a large bowl, moisten bread pieces with milk. Put aside. In a food processor, mince garlic. Put in pepper, salt, mint and onion. Process until onion is chopped finely. Put onion mixture into the moist bread in the bowl, along with eggs, lamb and beef. Using your hands, mix until they are blended thoroughly.
- Roll to form mixture into the balls measuring 1 1/2-2-inch in diameter. In a shallow pan, put flour, then coat the balls by rolling in the flour. Shake off all the excess flour. Arrange meatballs onto a baking sheet or plate, slightly flatten by pressing. It will prevent the meatballs from rolling away.
- In a large skillet, heat 1-in. oil over medium heat. Put in meatballs, 8 or 10 at a time; cook for 10 mins until no longer pink in the middle and browned nicely outside; drain on the paper towel-lined plate. Repeat with the remaining meatballs.

### Nutrition Information

- Calories: 522 calories;
- Total Fat: 31.5
- Sodium: 893
- Total Carbohydrate: 28.6
- Cholesterol: 259
- Protein: 29.7

## 156. Maria Athans' Spinach Pie

*Serving: 15 | Prep: 1hours | Cook: 55mins | Ready in:*

### Ingredients

- 1/4 cup butter
- 4 (10 ounce) packages frozen chopped spinach, thawed and well drained
- 18 green onions, chopped
- 4 eggs, slightly beaten
- 1 (16 ounce) package small curd cottage cheese
- 1/2 pound feta cheese, crumbled
- 1 tablespoon dried dill weed
- 3/4 cup butter
- 1 (16 ounce) package phyllo dough, thawed

### Direction

- Preheat an oven to 175 °C or 350 °F. With cooking spray, coat bottom and sides of a square baking dish, 9x13-inch in size.
- In a big skillet, melt a quarter cup butter, and cook green onions and spinach for approximately 8 minutes, mixing from time to time, till white areas of onions are clear. Take off the heat, and let it cool for approximately 10 minutes; stir in dill, feta cheese, cottage cheese and eggs till well incorporated.
- In a saucepan, melt the leftover 3/4 cup butter. Into the prepped baking dish, put a phyllo dough sheet, and brush with melted butter. Redo by laying down and greasing the sheets with butter till 1/2 of the sheets are used. Spread the filling in an even layer on top of the sheets. Over the filling, put the rest of phyllo sheets, greasing every sheet with butter as earlier. Brush butter over the top sheet.

- In the prepped oven, bake for 45 to 50 minutes till golden brown.

### Nutrition Information

- Calories: 315 calories;
- Protein: 12.9
- Total Fat: 20.4
- Sodium: 598
- Total Carbohydrate: 21.9
- Cholesterol: 100

## 157. Mediterranean Chicken With Pepperoncini And Kalamatas

*Serving: 4 | Prep: 20mins | Cook: 6hours30mins | Ready in:*

### Ingredients

- 12 pepperoncini peppers, rinsed and drained
- 1 cup sliced pitted kalamata olives
- 8 cloves minced garlic
- 3 1/2 pounds chicken leg quarters
- 1 1/2 teaspoons paprika
- 1/4 teaspoon salt
- 1/4 teaspoon fresh ground pepper
- 1/2 teaspoon grated lemon zest
- 1/2 cup fresh-squeezed lemon juice
- 1 cup sour cream
- 1/2 teaspoon paprika

### Direction

- On bottom of a slow cooker, layer whole pepperoncini. Sprinkle garlic and olive slices over peppers.
- Rinse chicken; pat dry. Put over pepperoncini mixture. Sprinkle 1 1/2 tsp. paprika, lemon zest, pepper and salt on chicken. Put lemon juice in slowly.
- Cover. Cook till meat pulls away easily from bone, about 6 – 6 1/2 hours on low. Put chicken on a warm plate. Cover; keep warm.
- Put slow cooker onto high. Skim fat from the cooking liquid. Whisk sour cream in till blended; cover. Depending on your cooker, simmer for 8-10 minutes on high till heated through. Mix paprika and pepper in.

### Nutrition Information

- Calories: 841 calories;
- Total Fat: 55.9
- Sodium: 2694
- Total Carbohydrate: 13.8
- Cholesterol: 249
- Protein: 68.1

## 158. Mediterranean Roast Chicken

*Serving: 6 | Prep: 30mins | Cook: 1hours | Ready in:*

### Ingredients

- 1 large orange, juiced
- 1/4 cup Dijon mustard
- 1/4 cup olive oil
- 4 teaspoons dried Greek oregano
- salt and freshly ground black pepper to taste
- 12 potatoes, peeled and cubed
- 5 cloves garlic, minced
- 1 whole chicken

### Direction

- Preheat the oven to 190°C or 375°Fahrenheit.
- In a big bowl, beat pepper, orange juice, salt, Dijon mustard, Greek oregano, and olive oil; toss in potatoes to coat well in mixture. Move potatoes to a big baking dish.
- Push garlic cloves beneath the chicken skin. Put the chicken in the bowl with the rest of the orange juice mixture then coat well. Move

chicken over the potatoes in the baking dish. Drizzle the remaining orange juice mixture over the potatoes and chicken.
- Bake for 60-90 minutes in the preheated oven without cover until the juices are clear and the meat is not pink at the bone. An inserted instant-read thermometer in the thickest thigh part close to the bone should register 74°C or 165°Fahrenheit. Check every half hour of roasting, pour in a bit of hot water if the potatoes look too dry.
- Take the chicken out of the oven then cover with two aluminum foil sheets; let it sit for 10 minutes in a warm place before carving.

## Nutrition Information

- Calories: 724 calories;
- Sodium: 395
- Total Carbohydrate: 81.6
- Cholesterol: 97
- Protein: 39.8
- Total Fat: 26.6

## 159. Mediterranean Stuffed Swordfish

*Serving: 2 | Prep: 15mins | Cook: 20mins | Ready in:*

## Ingredients

- 1 (8 ounce) swordfish steak (about 2 inches thick)
- 1 tablespoon olive oil
- 1 tablespoon fresh lemon juice
- 2 cups fresh spinach - rinsed, dried and torn into bite size pieces
- 1 teaspoon olive oil
- 1 clove garlic, minced
- 1/4 cup crumbled feta

## Direction

- On high heat, preheat the outdoor grill then grease the grate lightly.
- Make a gash in steak to make a pocket that is open just on a side. Combine lemon juice and 1 tablespoon olive oil in a cup; slather on each side of the fish. Set it aside.
- On medium heat, heat garlic and a tablespoon of olive oil in a small pan; cook spinach in oil until it wilts. Take off heat then stuff the mixture in the pocket. Put feta over the spinach in the pocket.
- Put the fish on the grill then grill for 8 minutes; flip then grill until completely cooked.

## Nutrition Information

- Calories: 310 calories;
- Cholesterol: 72
- Protein: 27.5
- Total Fat: 20.4
- Sodium: 476
- Total Carbohydrate: 3.5

## 160. Methi Murgh (Fenugreek Chicken)

*Serving: 6 | Prep: 10mins | Cook: 45mins | Ready in:*

## Ingredients

- 1/4 cup cooking oil
- 1 (4 to 6 pound) whole chicken, cut into 8 pieces (skin removed and discarded)
- 1 teaspoon cumin seeds
- 1 cinnamon stick
- 1 black cardamom pod
- 4 whole cloves
- 1 large onion, sliced thin
- 1 tablespoon ginger-garlic paste
- 4 green chile peppers, halved lengthwise
- 1/2 cup chopped fresh spinach
- 1/2 cup chopped fresh fenugreek leaves
- 1 tablespoon dried fenugreek leaves
- 1/2 teaspoon ground turmeric

- 1/2 teaspoon ground red pepper
- salt to taste
- 1 cup water
- 1/2 teaspoon garam masala

## Direction

- In a pressure cooker, heat oil on medium heat; add chicken slices. Cook for about 5 minutes until all sides are brown. Take the chicken out and put aside. In the same pressure cooker, combine green chili peppers, cumin seeds, ginger-garlic paste, cinnamon stick, onion slices, cardamom pod, and cloves. Cook for 5 to 7 minutes until the onions are golden. Mix in salt, spinach, red pepper, fresh fenugreek leaves, turmeric, and dried fenugreek leaves. Cook for 5 minutes until the fenugreek leaves and spinach darkens and wilts. Pour in water and place the chicken pieces back in the cooker, boil for 2-3 minutes.
- Secure the lid and cook chicken for half hour until tender. Relieve the pressure completely, uncover. Add garam masala on top. Cook while continuously stirring for 3-5 minutes until thick. Serve while hot.

## Nutrition Information

- Calories: 493 calories;
- Cholesterol: 103
- Protein: 36.7
- Total Fat: 34
- Sodium: 195
- Total Carbohydrate: 8

## 161. My Big Fat Greek Omelet

Serving: 4 | Prep: | Cook: | Ready in:

## Ingredients

- 1 cup halved grape tomatoes
- 1 teaspoon dried oregano, divided
- 1/2 teaspoon salt, divided
- Black pepper, to taste
- 1/2 cup crumbled feta cheese (can use reduced-fat)
- 8 large eggs
- 1 (10 ounce) package chopped frozen spinach, thawed and squeezed dry
- 1 tablespoon olive oil

## Direction

- Heat over low heat a non-stick frying pan, 12-inch large. (Or 10-inch if you make 1/2 of the recipe for 2 servings instead of 4.) In the meantime, mix in a small bowl tomatoes, half teaspoon oregano, 1/4 teaspoon salt and pepper to taste. Add feta and stir.
- Whisk together eggs in a medium bowl; stir in pepper, 1/4 tsp. salt, 1/2 tsp. oregano and spinach. Several minutes prior to cooking, pour oil in the pan, turn up heat to medium-high. Cook until wisps of smoke from the pan begin to rise. Pour in the egg mixture. Push back with a wooden or plastic spatula the eggs that already set, tilt the pan and let the runny egg mixture flow to the empty area of the pan. Continue the pushing cooked eggs back, tilting pan to let runny egg flow to the empty are for about 3 minutes until omelette is fully cooked but still moist. Lower heat to low. Over half of the omelette, pour in the tomato mixture. Carefully fold the untopped half with a flat, slotted spatula or turner over the filling. Slide the omelette using the turner onto a cutting board. For the filling to warm, let stand for 1-2 minutes.
- Cut the omelette into 4 wedges and serve immediately.

## Nutrition Information

- Calories: 253 calories;
- Sodium: 696
- Total Carbohydrate: 6.7
- Cholesterol: 389
- Protein: 18.2
- Total Fat: 17.9

## 162. Octapodi Kokkinisto (Greek Octopus In Tomato Sauce)

*Serving: 6 | Prep: 20mins | Cook: 1hours10mins | Ready in:*

### Ingredients

- 2 pounds octopus, cut into 3-inch pieces
- 3/4 cup olive oil
- 8 small red onions, cut into thin wedges
- 3 bay leaves
- 2 cups crushed tomatoes
- 1/2 teaspoon sea salt
- freshly ground black pepper to taste

### Direction

- In a big saucepan, put octopus pieces. Cover then cook for 10-15 minutes on medium-high heat until the octopus releases its juices. Take out cover; keep simmering for 20-25 minutes until liquid reduces to 3-4 tablespoons.
- Drizzle olive oil on octopus. Mix in bay leaves and onions. Sauté for about 10 minutes until onions are soft. Add pepper, salt, and tomatoes. Lower heat to medium-low. Cover then simmer for about 25 minutes until sauce is thick and octopus is tender. Cook uncovered in the final 10 minutes if sauce is thin.

### Nutrition Information

- Calories: 412 calories;
- Total Fat: 28.8
- Sodium: 502
- Total Carbohydrate: 14.6
- Cholesterol: 73
- Protein: 24.2

## 163. Pasta With Veggies In A Tahini And Yogurt Sauce

*Serving: 6 | Prep: 15mins | Cook: 10mins | Ready in:*

### Ingredients

- 1 (16 ounce) package wide egg noodles
- 3 tablespoons tahini
- 1 lemon, juiced
- 1 1/4 cups water
- 3 cloves garlic, minced
- 1 cup yogurt, drained
- 1/4 teaspoon hot pepper sauce
- 1/4 cup olive oil
- 1 large red bell pepper, thinly sliced
- 1 zucchini, thinly sliced
- salt to taste
- ground black pepper to taste

### Direction

- In a big pot of boiling water, cook noodles until al dente; drain.
- In the meantime, combine water, lemon juice, and tahini until smooth; put in pepper sauce, yogurt, and garlic.
- On medium-high heat, heat oil in a medium pan; sauté zucchini and red pepper in oil for 2-3 minutes until crisp-tender. Put it tahini sauce then heat completely. Sprinkle pepper and salt to taste. Avoid overcooking or boiling since the sauce easily curdles. Mix sauce with noodles.

### Nutrition Information

- Calories: 456 calories;
- Sodium: 47
- Total Carbohydrate: 61.4
- Cholesterol: 68
- Protein: 14.4
- Total Fat: 18.3

## 164. Pastitsio I

*Serving: 6 | Prep: 45mins | Cook: 1hours | Ready in:*

### Ingredients

- 1 pound lean ground beef
- 1 onion, chopped
- 3/4 teaspoon salt
- 1 pinch ground black pepper
- 4 ounces tomato sauce
- 1/4 teaspoon ground cinnamon
- 3 1/2 cups macaroni
- 1/4 cup butter
- 5 tablespoons all-purpose flour
- 3 1/2 cups milk
- 3/4 cup grated Parmesan cheese
- 1/4 teaspoon salt
- 3 eggs
- 6 thick slices white bread, toasted and cut into cubes
- 1/4 cup melted butter

### Direction

- Cook onion and beef in a big skillet on medium heat, until meat turns brown. Mix in the cinnamon, tomato sauce, a pinch of pepper and 3/4 teaspoon salt and cook for 1-2 more minutes. Reserve.
- Place lightly salted water in a big pot and make it boil. Put in the pasta and cook for 8-10 minutes or until al dente; strain. Reserve.
- Dissolve 1/4 cup butter in a medium saucepan on medium heat. Throw in flour, all at once, and stir until formed a smooth roux. Mix in 2 1/2 cups milk gradually, whisking until it turns smooth. Mix in 1/4 cup Parmesan, pepper and 1/4 teaspoon salt; make it boil, and whisk until thickened. Separate from heat.
- Whisk 1 cup milk and eggs in a small bowl. Reserve.
- Prepare the oven by preheating to 375°F (190°C). Prepare a 9x13 inch baking dish with grease. Put half of the cooked macaroni inside the baking dish and place all the beef mixture on top. Dust the leftover 1/2 cup grated Parmesan on the meat. Put the leftover macaroni on the cheese. Then place the egg mixture on the macaroni. Pour white sauce to cover everything.
- Mix dissolved butter and bread cubes in a medium bowl, until bread is well covered. Put bread cubes equally over macaroni.
- Bake in the preheated oven for 50-60 minutes or until topping becomes golden brown.

### Nutrition Information

- Calories: 847 calories;
- Total Carbohydrate: 77.7
- Cholesterol: 427
- Protein: 38.4
- Total Fat: 41.7
- Sodium: 1065

## 165. Pastitsio IV

*Serving: 5 | Prep: 30mins | Cook: 30mins | Ready in:*

### Ingredients

- 1 (16 ounce) package elbow macaroni
- 1 tablespoon extra virgin olive oil
- 1 clove garlic, minced
- 1/2 large onion, diced
- 1 pound lean ground beef
- 1 (14.5 ounce) can peeled and diced tomatoes
- ground black pepper to taste
- 1 teaspoon dried oregano
- 6 ounces grated Parmesan cheese, divided
- 1 tablespoon butter
- 1 tablespoon all-purpose flour
- 1 cup milk
- 1 egg yolk

### Direction

- Set the oven to 190°C (375°F) to preheat.

- Boil a large pot of lightly salted water. Put in macaroni paste, cook until al dente, about 8-10 minutes; drain.
- In a skillet, heat olive oil and cook beef, onions, and garlic until beef is browned; drain the fat. Put in oregano, pepper, and tomatoes. Cook and stir for 5 minutes. Add 1/2 Parmesan cheese.
- Lightly coat olive oil in a baking dish or a casserole and spread in 1/2 cooked paste. Pour in meat sauce and add the rest of pasta to cover.
- In a saucepan, melt butter and mix in flour. Gradually pour in milk while stirring almost to boiling. Mix egg yolk, and the rest of parmesan cheese in a bowl and gradually add to milk sauce while stirring constantly.
- Pour over macaroni with sauce and bake for half an hour. The top should be a little crispy and golden.

## Nutrition Information

- Calories: 851 calories;
- Sodium: 751
- Total Carbohydrate: 78.7
- Cholesterol: 149
- Protein: 45.4
- Total Fat: 37.5

## 166. Poulet A La Grecque

*Serving: 6 | Prep: 20mins | Cook: 30mins | Ready in:*

## Ingredients

- 1/2 cup all-purpose flour for coating
- 1 pinch salt and pepper
- 1 1/2 pounds bone-in chicken parts
- 2 tablespoons butter
- 1 tablespoon olive oil
- 2 shallots, chopped
- 1 onion, chopped
- 2 cloves garlic, chopped
- 3 medium fresh tomatoes, chopped
- 2 cups white wine
- 2 pinches saffron threads
- 1/2 teaspoon curry powder
- 1 teaspoon white sugar
- 3/4 cup raisins
- salt and black pepper to taste

## Direction

- Season flour with pepper and salt; use it to coat chicken pieces.
- Heat olive oil and butter in big skillet on medium high heat. Add chicken pieces; cook for 6 minutes to brown both sides, turning once.
- Mix in garlic, onions and shallots; cook for 3 minutes till soft. Mix in wine and tomatoes; boil. Mix in salt, pepper, raisins, sugar, curry powder and saffron. Cover, cook for 12-15 minutes on medium heat.

## Nutrition Information

- Calories: 502 calories;
- Total Carbohydrate: 34.7
- Cholesterol: 95
- Protein: 24.2
- Total Fat: 23.6
- Sodium: 120

## 167. Quick And Easy Greek Spaghetti

*Serving: 4 | Prep: 15mins | Cook: 40mins | Ready in:*

## Ingredients

- 1 (8 ounce) package spaghetti
- extra-virgin olive oil, or as needed
- 1 (10 ounce) bag fresh spinach
- 1 (8 ounce) package sliced fresh mushrooms
- 1/4 cup red wine vinegar
- 1/4 cup balsamic vinegar

- 2 (14.5 ounce) cans diced tomatoes
- 1/4 cup chopped fresh basil
- 1 tablespoon chopped fresh parsley
- 1 (6 ounce) can sliced black olives, drained (optional)
- 2 ounces crumbled feta cheese, or to taste

### Direction

- Allow lightly salted water in a big pot to come to a rolling boil. At a boil, cook spaghetti for 12 minutes until soft yet firm to the bite, tossing sometimes. Strain and put aside.
- In a big saucepan, heat olive oil over medium heat. In the hot oil, stir and cook mushrooms and spinach for 10 minutes until they release their liquid. Add balsamic vinegar and red wine vinegar, boil it. Mix black olives, parsley, basil and tomatoes into the boiling mixture, keep stirring and cooking for another 10 minutes until the flavors combine.
- Stir into the tomato mixture with the cooked spaghetti and lower the heat to medium-low. Simmer the sauce and pasta for 8-10 minutes until the flavors combine, mix feta cheese into the pasta. Sprinkle additional feta cheese over and enjoy.

### Nutrition Information

- Calories: 413 calories;
- Total Fat: 11.7
- Sodium: 1095
- Total Carbohydrate: 60.7
- Cholesterol: 13
- Protein: 16.1

## 168. R. B. Miller's Gyro Meat

Serving: 8 | Prep: 30mins | Cook: 1hours15mins | Ready in:

### Ingredients

- 1 pound ground beef chuck (80% lean)
- 1 pound boneless lamb chops, cubed
- 1 cup minced onion
- 4 teaspoons minced garlic
- 1 teaspoon ground marjoram
- 1 1/2 teaspoons ground rosemary
- 2 teaspoons sea salt
- 1 teaspoon ground black pepper

### Direction

- Using the meat grinder's coarse plate, grind the lamb cubes and ground chuck twice to combine well. In a food processor, pulse pepper, onion, salt, garlic, rosemary, and marjoram until finely ground. In a bowl, combine the onions mixture and ground meat; use a fine plate to grind again. Press the mixture in a 3-in by 7-in loaf pan; use plastic wrap to tightly wrap. Chill overnight.
- Preheat the oven to 165°C or 325°Fahrenheit.
- Take and discard the plastic wrap from the pan. Bake gyro meat for an hour in the preheated oven until the internal temperature reads 60°C or 140°Fahrenheit. Drain the collected liquid in the pan then take the loaf out of the pan. Put the meat on a rack placed on top of a baking sheet to collect the drips. Bake for another 15-30 minutes until the internal temperature reads 75°C or 165°Fahrenheit. Take it out of the oven. Let it sit for 15 minutes before cutting. The cooked loaf should be quite dry and firm.

### Nutrition Information

- Calories: 226 calories;
- Cholesterol: 71
- Protein: 19.6
- Total Fat: 14.7
- Sodium: 501
- Total Carbohydrate: 2.7

## 169. Rabbit Greek Recipe

*Serving: 4 | Prep: 10mins | Cook: 45mins | Ready in:*

### Ingredients

- 1/4 cup olive oil
- 1 (3 pound) rabbit, cut into pieces
- 2 bay leaves
- 1 teaspoon salt
- 4 whole allspice berries
- 1/2 teaspoon oregano
- 1 lemon, juiced
- 1/2 cup white wine
- warm water, to cover

### Direction

- In a big saucepan, heat 1/4 cup olive oil over medium heat. In the hot oil, fry rabbit pieces until turning brown evenly. Add lemon juice, oregano, allspice berries, salt and bay leaves to the saucepan to season. Pour over the rabbit with white wine. Simmer the mixture, cook for 4-5 minutes. Pour an enough amount of water into the saucepan to fully cover the rabbit.
- Simmer the liquid; cook for 40 minutes until the water has evaporated and the rabbit has thoroughly cooked.

### Nutrition Information

- Calories: 567 calories;
- Sodium: 694
- Total Carbohydrate: 1.3
- Cholesterol: 175
- Protein: 62
- Total Fat: 30.7

## 170. Roasted Eggplant Pastitsio

*Serving: 12 | Prep: 25mins | Cook: 1hours45mins | Ready in:*

### Ingredients

- Meat Sauce:
- 1 large eggplant, halved lengthwise
- 1 tablespoon olive oil
- 1 1/2 cups chopped onions
- 1 pound ground lamb
- 1 clove garlic, minced
- 1 1/2 teaspoons salt
- 1 teaspoon ground cumin
- 1 teaspoon dried oregano
- 1/4 teaspoon freshly ground black pepper
- 1/4 teaspoon ground cinnamon
- 1 (14 ounce) can diced tomatoes
- 1 (14 ounce) can crushed tomatoes
- 1 tablespoon chopped fresh mint
- White Sauce:
- 2 eggs
- 2 tablespoons unsalted butter
- 2 tablespoons all-purpose flour
- 2 cups milk
- 1 clove garlic, lightly crushed
- 1 (8 ounce) package crumbled feta cheese
- 1/2 teaspoon salt
- black pepper to taste
- 1 pinch freshly grated nutmeg
- cooking spray
- 1 (12 ounce) package penne pasta

### Direction

- Place the oven rack 6-inches away from the heat source. Set the oven's broiler to preheating. Use an aluminum foil to line the baking sheet. Arrange eggplant halves onto the foil.
- Broil the eggplant for 15 minutes, checking the eggplant frequently and rotating the baking sheet if necessary until the skin has some chars and turns black. Allow it to cool for 5 minutes until handled easily. Peel the skin off the eggplant. Chop its flesh coarsely.
- Put olive oil in a large skillet and heat it over medium heat. Add the onions. Cook and stir over medium heat for 5 minutes until the onion turns translucent. Add the lamb. Cook for 5 minutes while breaking it into small

pieces until it is no longer pink. Pour the grease off from the skillet.
- Stir the salt, pepper, cinnamon, minced garlic, cumin, and oregano into the skillet. Cook the mixture for 1 minute. Mix in crushed tomatoes, chopped eggplant, and diced tomatoes. Simmer the sauce and cook for 20 minutes until thickened. Remove from the heat. Mix in chopped mint.
- Put butter in a saucepan and melt it over medium heat. Mix in flour. Cook and stir constantly for 2 minutes. Pour in milk and stir the mixture until smooth. Add the crushed garlic clove. Adjust the heat to high. Boil the milk. Lower the heat to a simmer and stir frequently for 5 minutes until thickened slightly. Remove from the heat, discarding the garlic clove.
- Beat the eggs in a large heatproof bowl. In a steady stream, pour the hot milk mixture into the beaten eggs while constantly stirring it. Mix in nutmeg, salt, pepper, and feta cheese.
- Set the oven to 425°F (220°C) for preheating. Coat the 9x13-inches baking dish with the cooking spray.
- Boil a large pot of salted water. Add the pasta. Cook for 12 minutes while occasionally stirring it until the pasta is tender yet firm to the bite; drain.
- Divide the pasta between the lamb sauce and white sauce, stirring until well-combined. Add pasta with lamb sauce to the prepared baking dish. Pour white sauce on top of the pasta.
- Let it bake inside the preheated oven for 30 minutes until the pastitsio is bubbling and its top is golden. Allow it to cool for 5 minutes; serve.

## Nutrition Information

- Calories: 330 calories;
- Total Fat: 14.7
- Sodium: 747
- Total Carbohydrate: 33.5
- Cholesterol: 78
- Protein: 17

### 171. Sharon's Scrumptious Souvlaki

*Serving: 8 | Prep: 30mins | Cook: 20mins | Ready in:*

### Ingredients

- 2 pounds lamb, cut into 1 inch square cubes
- 1/2 cup olive oil
- 1 cup red wine
- 1 teaspoon salt
- freshly ground black pepper to taste
- 1 teaspoon dried oregano
- 1 tablespoon dried mint, crushed
- 1 clove garlic, chopped
- 4 cups plain yogurt
- 1 cucumber, shredded
- 4 cloves garlic, minced
- 2 tablespoons olive oil
- 1/2 teaspoon dried dill weed
- salt and pepper to taste
- 8 pita bread rounds
- 2 tablespoons olive oil
- 1 red onion, thinly sliced
- 1 tomato, thinly sliced

### Direction

- In a large bowl, put the lamb, red wine, 1/2 cup olive oil, pepper, 1 teaspoon salt, garlic, mint, and oregano. Toss to coat lamb well. Cover the bowl and keep refrigerated for at least 3 hours, or even overnight.
- Lightly grease the grates of a preheating grill. Prepare the yogurt sauce: take a small bowl and mix together 2 tablespoons olive oil, yogurt, minced garlic, and cucumber. Sprinkle with salt, pepper, and dill weed.
- Skewer the meat and grill for 10 minutes, turning the skewers once. Lightly drizzle some olive oil on the pita and grill for a minute or until warm. Slide the meat off the skewers and arrange on warm pita with some sliced

tomatoes and red onions, and the prepared yogurt sauce.

## Nutrition Information

- Calories: 814 calories;
- Sodium: 766
- Total Carbohydrate: 46.5
- Cholesterol: 91
- Protein: 31.1
- Total Fat: 53.2

## 172. Spanakopita (Greek Spinach Pie)

*Serving: 5 | Prep: 30mins | Cook: 1hours | Ready in:*

## Ingredients

- 3 tablespoons olive oil
- 1 large onion, chopped
- 1 bunch green onions, chopped
- 2 cloves garlic, minced
- 2 pounds spinach, rinsed and chopped
- 1/2 cup chopped fresh parsley
- 2 eggs, lightly beaten
- 1/2 cup ricotta cheese
- 1 cup crumbled feta cheese
- 8 sheets phyllo dough
- 1/4 cup olive oil

## Direction

- Prepare the oven by preheating it to 350° F (175° C). Coat a 9x9 inch square baking pan lightly with oil.
- Place a large pan over medium heat and heat 3 tablespoons of olive oil in it. Sauté the green onions, garlic and onion until they are soft and lightly browned. Add the parsley and spinach, stirring them in and continue to sauté for another 2 minutes until the spinach is limp. Turn the heat off and set it aside to cool.
- Combine the ricotta, eggs, and feta together in a medium bowl. Add the spinach mixture, stirring it in. Lay a sheet of the phyllo dough on the baking pan and brush with olive oil lightly. Lay one more sheet of the phyllo dough on top of it then brush again with olive oil. Do the process again with 2 more phyllo dough sheets. The sheets are supposed to overlap the pan. Put the spinach and cheese mixture into the pan, spreading it and fold the dough that's overhanging over the filling. Brush again with olive oil then add the remaining 4 sheets of dough, layering them in and brushing each sheet with oil. Seal the filling by tucking the overhanging dough into the pan.
- Put the pan in the preheated oven and bake for 30 to 40 minutes until it turns golden brown. Cut the pie into squares and serve it while it's hot.

## Nutrition Information

- Calories: 494 calories;
- Total Fat: 34.7
- Sodium: 894
- Total Carbohydrate: 31.5
- Cholesterol: 100
- Protein: 18.2

## 173. Spinach And Tomato Filo Pastry Parcels

*Serving: 2 | Prep: | Cook: | Ready in:*

## Ingredients

- 4 sheets phyllo dough
- 2 tablespoons melted butter
- 1 bunch fresh spinach
- 1 tablespoon vegetable oil
- 1/2 cup fresh sliced mushrooms
- 1/4 cup tomato sauce
- 3 ounces feta cheese

### Direction

- Preheat the oven to 175°C or 350°Fahrenheit.
- Clean the spinach well; trim the stems then chop. Steam the spinach until it wilts. On high heat, stir-fry mushrooms in oil until brown.
- Slice four phyllo pieces in half; slather melted butter on each sheet then stack into 2 piles. Put half of the spinach in the middle of each stack then half of the feta, tomato sauce, and mushrooms. Take the phyllo sides around to the surface of the bundles; arrange on a baking sheet.
- Bake for 25-30 minutes in a 350 °F or 175°C oven. Let it sit for 5 minutes then serve.

### Nutrition Information

- Calories: 437 calories;
- Protein: 14.5
- Total Fat: 30.4
- Sodium: 1035
- Total Carbohydrate: 30.1
- Cholesterol: 68

## 174. Spinach Casserole

*Serving: 9 | Prep: 15mins | Cook: 20mins | Ready in:*

### Ingredients

- 2 (10 ounce) packages frozen chopped spinach
- 8 ounces crumbled feta cheese
- 2 cups shredded mozzarella cheese
- 1 cup cubed processed cheese food
- 1 cup melted butter, divided
- 2 tablespoons distilled white vinegar
- 1/2 teaspoon garlic powder
- salt and pepper to taste
- 1 (16 ounce) package phyllo dough

### Direction

- Preheat the oven to 220 °C or 425 °F.
- Mix pepper, salt, garlic powder, vinegar, 1/2 the butter, processed cheese food, mozzarella cheese, feta cheese and spinach in a big bowl. Combine thoroughly and reserve.
- In the bottom of a slightly oiled 2-quart casserole dish, put 1 layer of the phyllo dough. In the dish, scatter cheese mixture and spinach and put 4 layers of phyllo dough on top, coating each layer with butter-flavored cooking spray. Over the top, sprinkle the leftover butter.
- Bake for 20 minutes at 220 °C or 425 °F.

### Nutrition Information

- Calories: 548 calories;
- Sodium: 1164
- Total Carbohydrate: 31.8
- Cholesterol: 108
- Protein: 18.6
- Total Fat: 37.7

## 175. Spinach Pie

*Serving: 6 | Prep: 15mins | Cook: 30mins | Ready in:*

### Ingredients

- 2 pounds spinach, rinsed and chopped
- 8 ounces feta cheese, crumbled
- 1 (8 ounce) container cottage cheese
- 1/2 cup chopped onion
- 3/4 teaspoon poultry seasoning
- 2 teaspoons chopped fresh dill
- 1/4 teaspoon ground black pepper
- salt to taste
- 2 cups bread crumbs
- 4 tablespoons butter, melted

### Direction

- Prepare oven for preheating at 350 degrees F (175 degrees C). Prepare a one 9x13 inch casserole dish by lightly greasing.

- Mix feta cheese, onion, dill, cottage cheese, salt, spinach, poultry seasoning and pepper in a large bowl. Combine completely and transfer into the prepared dish.
- Combine together butter and bread crumbs and drizzle into spinach mixture. For 30 minutes, bake at 350 degrees F (175 degrees C).

## Nutrition Information

- Calories: 383 calories;
- Total Carbohydrate: 35.5
- Cholesterol: 57
- Protein: 19.9
- Total Fat: 18.9
- Sodium: 1012

## 176. Spinach Pie V

*Serving: 8 | Prep: 20mins | Cook: 40mins | Ready in:*

## Ingredients

- 1 (10 ounce) package frozen chopped spinach, thawed and squeezed dry
- 1 (12 ounce) container small curd cottage cheese
- 3/4 cup grated Parmesan cheese
- 2 cups shredded Monterey Jack cheese
- 1 egg, lightly beaten
- 1/2 cup chopped onion
- 2 sheets frozen phyllo pastry, thawed

## Direction

- Preheat an oven to 200 °C or 400 °F. Oil a medium baking sheet slightly.
- Combine onion, egg, Monterey Jack cheese, Parmesan cheese, cottage cheese, and spinach in a big bowl. On top of each phyllo pastry sheet, spread 1/2 of the mixture. Roll the pastry sheets of jelly-roll fashion, pinch ends to seal, and set on prepped baking sheet.
- Create several small slits in top of every rolled sheet of pastry. In prepped oven, bake till golden brown for 40 minutes.

## Nutrition Information

- Calories: 227 calories;
- Total Fat: 14.3
- Sodium: 526
- Total Carbohydrate: 6.7
- Cholesterol: 63
- Protein: 18.4

## 177. Spinach And Cheese Pie

*Serving: 10 | Prep: | Cook: | Ready in:*

## Ingredients

- 2 pounds spinach, washed and chopped
- 1 onion, chopped
- 1/2 pound fresh mushrooms, sliced
- 3 tablespoons vegetable oil
- 2 cups ricotta cheese
- 2 tablespoons dried basil
- 2 eggs
- 1 cup feta cheese
- 3/4 cup butter, melted
- 1 (16 ounce) package phyllo dough

## Direction

- Steam the spinach just until wilted.
- Put oil in a medium skillet and heat until hot then add mushrooms and onions and stir-fry. Mix with the spinach.
- Whisk eggs well in a medium bowl. Mix in basil, feta, and ricotta.
- Prepare a deep, buttered dish pie pan. On the bottom of the pan, put a sheet of phyllo then use melted butter to brush over the sheet. Continue until there are 5 or 6 sheets in the pan. Place the ricotta mixture over the phyllo and spread. Layer 5 or 6 more sheets of filo

brushed with butter on top of the cheese. Put spinach mixture over the phyllo and spread. Place 5 or 6 more sheets of phyllo brushed with butter on top of the pie. Cut the dough to the edge of the pie dish.
- Bake it for about 1 hour at 375°F (175°C), or until pie turns golden brown.

## Nutrition Information

- Calories: 406 calories;
- Total Fat: 27.5
- Sodium: 683
- Total Carbohydrate: 30.3
- Cholesterol: 96
- Protein: 11.7

### 178. Spinach And Feta Pita Bake

*Serving: 6 | Prep: 10mins | Cook: 12mins | Ready in:*

## Ingredients

- 1 (6 ounce) tub sun-dried tomato pesto
- 6 (6 inch) whole wheat pita breads
- 2 roma (plum) tomatoes, chopped
- 1 bunch spinach, rinsed and chopped
- 4 fresh mushrooms, sliced
- 1/2 cup crumbled feta cheese
- 2 tablespoons grated Parmesan cheese
- 3 tablespoons olive oil
- ground black pepper to taste

## Direction

- Preheat the oven to 350 degrees F (175 degrees C).
- Use tomato pesto to cover one side of each pita bread then position them pesto-side up on a baking sheet. Top pitas with mushrooms, spinach, tomatoes, feta cheese, and Parmesan cheese; splash with olive oil and flavor with pepper.
- In the preheated oven, bake for around 12 minutes until pita breads turn crisp. Divide pitas into quarters.

## Nutrition Information

- Calories: 350 calories;
- Total Fat: 17.1
- Sodium: 587
- Total Carbohydrate: 41.6
- Cholesterol: 13
- Protein: 11.6

### 179. Steamed Mussels With Fennel, Tomatoes, Ouzo, And Cream

*Serving: 4 | Prep: 15mins | Cook: 5mins | Ready in:*

## Ingredients

- 1 tablespoon olive oil
- 2 shallots, finely chopped
- 4 cloves garlic, finely chopped
- 1 bulb fennel - trimmed, cored and thinly sliced
- 1 large tomato, cubed
- 1/2 cup white wine
- 1/4 cup ouzo
- 1/2 cup heavy cream
- 4 pounds mussels, cleaned and debearded
- 1/3 cup fresh basil leaves, torn
- salt to taste

## Direction

- In a medium saucepan, heat olive oil over medium heat. Mix in garlic and shallots, and allow to cook till soft. Mix in tomato and fennel, and keep cooking for 5 minutes.
- Into the saucepan, combine heavy cream, ouzo and white wine, and boil. Slowly mix in salt, 1/2 the basil and mussels.

- Cover the saucepan, and keep cooking till mussels have opened for 5 minutes. Garnish with leftover basil, serve.

## Nutrition Information

- Calories: 286 calories;
- Sodium: 245
- Total Carbohydrate: 15.7
- Cholesterol: 76
- Protein: 16.3
- Total Fat: 15.7

## 180. Stuffed Bell Peppers, Greek Style

*Serving: 6 | Prep: 20mins | Cook: 1hours | Ready in:*

## Ingredients

- 2 tablespoons extra virgin olive oil
- 1 1/4 cups onion, chopped
- 1 pound ground lamb
- 3/4 cup white rice
- 3/4 teaspoon salt
- 1/2 teaspoon ground black pepper
- 1/2 teaspoon dried mint, crushed
- 1 cup water
- 1/4 cup chopped fresh parsley to taste
- 1 (14.5 ounce) can chicken broth
- 1 (14.5 ounce) can petite diced tomatoes
- 6 green bell pepper, top removed, seeded

## Direction

- Turn the oven to 350°F (175°C) to preheat.
- In a big frying pan, heat olive oil over medium-high heat. Mix in ground lamb and onion; stir and cook for 7 minutes until the meat is not pink anymore and the onion is soft. Mix in mint, black pepper, salt, and rice; cook for another 5 minutes. Add parsley and water. Lower the heat to medium-low and keep stirring and cooking for 15 minutes until the rice has fully absorbed the water. In an oven-proof dish that can just hold the peppers, combine diced tomatoes and chicken broth. In the bell peppers, put the lamb mixture, and put them into the dish.
- Bake for 45 minutes in the preheated oven until the tomatoes are bubbling and the peppers are soft.

## Nutrition Information

- Calories: 325 calories;
- Sodium: 448
- Total Carbohydrate: 29.7
- Cholesterol: 51
- Protein: 16.6
- Total Fat: 15.2

## 181. Tempeh Gyros

*Serving: 4 | Prep: 20mins | Cook: 48mins | Ready in:*

## Ingredients

- 1 cup vegetable broth
- 2 tablespoons soy sauce
- 2 tablespoons lemon juice
- 2 teaspoons dried oregano
- 2 teaspoons ground thyme
- 1 1/2 teaspoons minced garlic
- 1 (8 ounce) package tempeh
- 4 (6 inch) whole-wheat pitas
- 1 dash pink Himalayan salt
- 1 dash ground black pepper
- Tzatziki:
- 2 small cucumbers, peeled and grated
- 1 (12.3 ounce) package silken tofu
- 1 tablespoon (packed) fresh dill
- 1 teaspoon minced fresh garlic
- salt and ground black pepper to taste
- 2 tomatoes, sliced
- 1/2 red onion, thinly sliced

## Direction

- In a big bowl, mix together a dash of pepper, Himalayan salt, 1 1/2 teaspoons garlic, thyme, oregano, lemon juice, soy sauce, and vegetable broth.
- Boil water in a saucepan. Halve tempeh and put into the boiling water. Boil until the tempeh is no longer bitter, about 10 minutes. Transfer the tempeh to a cutting board and let cool slightly.
- Slice tempeh into slices, 1/4-in. each, and put them in vegetable broth marinade. Put on plastic wrap to cover and put in the fridge to marinate for 8 hours to overnight, tossing sometimes to make sure the marinade coat the tempeh.
- Turn the oven to 400°F (200°C) to preheat. Use parchment paper to line a baking sheet.
- Transfer the marinated tempeh slices to the prepared baking sheet.
- Put in the preheated oven and bake for 30-35 minutes until turning golden brown and the edges start to get crispy, flipping halfway through.
- In the hot oven, put pitas for 3-5 minutes until fully warm.
- With a paper towel, force excess liquid out of the cucumbers. In a food processor, put pepper, salt, 1 teaspoon garlic, dill, cucumbers, and tofu. Process until the tzatziki fully combines. Adjust seasonings if you want.
- To assemble the gyro, top a pita with red onions, tomatoes, and 1/4 of tempeh slices. Put on tzatziki to cover. Continue with the rest of the pita, onion, tomatoes, and tempeh.

## Nutrition Information

- Calories: 385 calories;
- Total Fat: 10.6
- Sodium: 1086
- Total Carbohydrate: 53.9
- Cholesterol: 0
- Protein: 25.1

## 182. Traditional Gyros

*Serving: 12 | Prep: 15mins | Cook: 45mins | Ready in:*

### Ingredients

- 1 small onion, cut into chunks
- 1 pound ground lamb
- 1 pound ground beef
- 1 tablespoon minced garlic
- 1 teaspoon dried oregano
- 1 teaspoon ground cumin
- 1 teaspoon dried marjoram
- 1 teaspoon dried thyme
- 1 teaspoon dried rosemary
- 1 teaspoon freshly ground black pepper
- 1/4 teaspoon sea salt
- boiling water as needed
- 12 tablespoons hummus
- 12 pita bread rounds
- 1 small head lettuce, shredded
- 1 large tomato, sliced
- 1 large red onion, sliced
- 6 ounces crumbled feta cheese
- 24 tablespoons tzatziki sauce

### Direction

- In food processor, put onion; blend until chopped finely. Place onion onto a piece of cheese cloth; then squeeze liquid out. Put onion into a large bowl.
- Using hands, mix onion with salt, black pepper, rosemary, thyme, marjoram, cumin, oregano, garlic, beef and lamb until mixed well. Wrap the bowl in plastic wrap. Place in the refrigerator for 120 minutes until the flavors blend.
- Start preheating the oven to 325°F (165°C).
- In food processor, put meat mixture; pulse for one minute, until they are tacky and chopped finely. Pack the meat mixture into a loaf pan (about 7x4 inches), making sure there have no air pockets. Position loaf pan into the roasting pan. Pour around loaf pan with enough of boiling water to reach halfway up sides.

- Bake in prepared oven for 45-60 minutes until middle is no longer pink. The instant-read thermometer should register at least 165°F (74°C) when inserted into middle. Pour off all the accumulated fat. Let cool slightly.
- Slice gyro meat mixture thinly.
- Spread on every pita bread with one tablespoon of the hummus; add tzatziki sauce, feta cheese, red onion, tomato, lettuce and gyro meat mixture over top of each.

## Nutrition Information

- Calories: 425 calories;
- Total Carbohydrate: 42.8
- Cholesterol: 61
- Protein: 22.4
- Total Fat: 40.8
- Sodium: 620

## 183. Turkey Zucchini Meatballs With Roasted Pepper Dipping Sauce

*Serving: 6 | Prep: 20mins | Cook: 25mins | Ready in:*

## Ingredients

- 1 pound ground turkey
- 1 small zucchini, grated and squeezed dry
- 1 large egg, beaten
- 1/2 cup panko bread crumbs
- 10 pitted kalamata olives, diced
- 4 tablespoons crumbled feta cheese
- 1 teaspoon Greek seasoning (such as Cavender's®)
- Dipping Sauce:
- 1 cup Greek yogurt
- 1/4 cup jarred roasted red pepper strips
- 1 teaspoon lemon juice
- 1 teaspoon olive oil
- 1 teaspoon minced garlic
- salt and ground black pepper to taste

## Direction

- Start preheating the oven at 400°F (200°C).
- Mix Greek seasoning, feta cheese, olives, bread crumbs, egg, zucchini, and turkey in a large bowl. Mix until evenly combined.
- Shape meatballs with an ice cream scoop and arrange onto a baking sheet.
- Bake in the prepared oven until not pink in the center anymore, for approximately 25 minutes.
- While baking the meatballs, put garlic, olive oil, lemon juice, red pepper strips, and Greek yogurt in a food processor. Pulse until well-mixed. Flavor with pepper and salt. Serve meatballs along with dipping sauce.

## Nutrition Information

- Calories: 215 calories;
- Protein: 19.4
- Sodium: 387
- Total Carbohydrate: 3.8
- Cholesterol: 100
- Total Fat: 13.7

## 184. Tzatziki Chicken

*Serving: 4 | Prep: 5mins | Cook: 45mins | Ready in:*

## Ingredients

- 4 skinless, boneless chicken breast halves
- 1 cup tzatziki sauce
- 1/2 cup chopped red onion
- 1 tablespoon cumin
- salt and pepper to taste

## Direction

- Place the chicken breast to the base of a baking dish. In a bowl, mix pepper, tzatziki sauce, salt, cumin, and red onion; evenly spread over the chicken. Marinate for half an hour.
- Preheat the oven to 190°C or 375°Fahrenheit.

- Bake chicken for 45 minutes in the preheated oven until the juices run clear and the chicken is not pink in the middle. An inserted instant-read thermometer in the middle should register at least 74°C or 165°Fahrenheit.

## Nutrition Information

- Calories: 189 calories;
- Total Fat: 52.7
- Sodium: 101
- Total Carbohydrate: 6.6
- Cholesterol: 59
- Protein: 24.5

## 185. Vegan Gyro Sandwich

*Serving: 6 | Prep: 20mins | Cook: 10mins | Ready in:*

## Ingredients

- Sauce:
- 1/2 large cucumber, peeled
- 1 cup plain vegan yogurt
- 1 tablespoon lemon juice
- 1 teaspoon dried dill weed
- 1 teaspoon dried chives
- 1 teaspoon sucanat
- 1/2 teaspoon salt
- fresh ground black pepper to taste
- Meat:
- 1 tablespoon olive oil
- 1/2 tablespoon minced garlic
- 1 (16 ounce) package seitan
- 1 teaspoon ground cumin
- 1 teaspoon dried oregano
- 1 teaspoon dried basil
- 1/8 teaspoon ground cinnamon
- 1/8 teaspoon ground nutmeg
- 1/8 teaspoon chili powder
- Sandwich:
- 1 tomato, thinly sliced
- 1 red onion, thinly sliced
- 2 cups shredded lettuce
- 6 pita bread rounds

## Direction

- In a colander over a sink; grate the cucumber then drain for 20 mins. Squeeze out the remaining liquid then move to a small bowl. Stir in black pepper, vegan yogurt, salt, lemon juice, sucanat, chives, and dill, mix thoroughly; cover and chill until needed. Mix thoroughly before use.
- On medium heat, heat olive oil in a sauté pan. Cook garlic gently for around a minute until golden. Put the seitan in one layer if you can; gently brown for approximately 5 mins. While cooking the seitan, combine chili powder, cumin, nutmeg, oregano, cinnamon, and basil in a bowl. Scatter and toss the spice mix onto the browned seitan. Keep on browning for approximately another 5 mins until the seitan is golden brown and thoroughly heated.
- On a sandwich, layer seitan, lettuce, onion, and tomato to assemble; scoop over with sauce. Repeat with the rest of the pita, sauce, and fillings.

## Nutrition Information

- Calories: 328 calories;
- Total Fat: 4.9
- Sodium: 708
- Total Carbohydrate: 43
- Cholesterol: 0
- Protein: 28.7

## 186. Vegetarian Moussaka

*Serving: 7 | Prep: 30mins | Cook: 1hours30mins | Ready in:*

## Ingredients

- 1 eggplant, thinly sliced
- 1 tablespoon olive oil, or more as needed
- 1 large zucchini, thinly sliced

- 2 potatoes, thinly sliced
- 1 onion, sliced
- 1 clove garlic, chopped
- 1 tablespoon white vinegar
- 1 (14.5 ounce) can whole peeled tomatoes, chopped
- 1/2 (14.5 ounce) can lentils, drained with liquid reserved
- 1 teaspoon dried oregano
- 2 tablespoons chopped fresh parsley
- salt and ground black pepper to taste
- 1 cup crumbled feta cheese
- 1 1/2 tablespoons butter
- 2 tablespoons all-purpose flour
- 1 1/4 cups milk
- ground black pepper to taste
- 1 pinch ground nutmeg
- 1 egg, beaten
- 1/4 cup grated Parmesan cheese

## Direction

- Sprinkle salt on the eggplant slices; let it sit for half an hour. Rinse the eggplants then pat dry.
- Preheat the oven to 190°C or 375°Fahrenheit.
- On medium-high heat, heat oil in a big pan. Rinse the eggplant then pat dry. Cook zucchini and eggplant in hot oil for 3 minutes on each side until both sides are light brown. Use a slotted spoon to move the eggplant and zucchini in a plate lined with paper towel to drain. Save as much oil as possible in the pan.
- Pour in more oil in the pan as necessary then heat till hot. Cook potato slices for 3-5 minutes on each side in hot oil until brown. Use a slotted spoon to move the potato slices on a plate lined with paper towel to drain. Save the oil in the pan.
- Sauté garlic and onion for 5-7 minutes in reserved oil until pale brown. Add vinegar then boil. Turn to medium-low heat; cook until the liquid is thick and reduces in volume. Mix in parsley, tomatoes, oregano, half of the lentil juice, and lentils; cover. Turn to medium-low heat; let it simmer for 15 minutes.
- In a 13-in by 9-in baking dish, arrange 1/3 of the eggplant, half the onions, 1/3 of the zucchini, half the potatoes, and half the feta cheese in a layer; pour the tomato mixture all over. Repeat the layers, ending with the zucchini and eggplant layer.
- Cover then bake for 25 minutes in the preheated oven.
- In a small pot, mix and boil milk, flour, and butter; let come to a gentle boil, constantly mix until smooth and thick. Stir in nutmeg and pepper. Take off heat then cool for 5 minutes. Mix in beaten egg.
- Drizzle sauce all over the veggies then scatter Parmesan cheese on top. Bake for another 25-30 minutes without cover.

## Nutrition Information

- Calories: 240 calories;
- Sodium: 426
- Total Carbohydrate: 25.5
- Cholesterol: 58
- Protein: 10.2
- Total Fat: 11.8

## 187. Venison Gyros

*Serving: 6 | Prep: 15mins | Cook: 30mins | Ready in:*

## Ingredients

- 2 tablespoons olive oil
- 1 1/2 tablespoons ground cumin
- 1 tablespoon minced garlic
- 2 teaspoons dried marjoram
- 2 teaspoons ground dried rosemary
- 1 tablespoon dried oregano
- 1 tablespoon red wine vinegar
- salt and pepper to taste
- 3 pounds venison, cut into 1/4 thick strips
- 1 (12 ounce) package pita breads, warmed

## Direction

- Whisk salt, red wine vinegar, oregano, rosemary, marjoram, garlic, cumin and olive oil in big ceramic/glass bowl. Add venison strips; evenly coat by tossing. Use plastic wrap to cover bowl. Marinate for minimum of 2 hours in the fridge.
- Heat a big skillet on medium high heat. 1/2-lb. at a time, cook venison strips for 8 minutes till venison isn't pink inside and browned outside. Pile meet on warmed pitas; serve.

## Nutrition Information

- Calories: 432 calories;
- Protein: 48.4
- Total Fat: 10.2
- Sodium: 384
- Total Carbohydrate: 33.7
- Cholesterol: 159

# Chapter 4: Greek Dessert Recipes

***

### 188. Baked Halva

*Serving: 8 | Prep: 15mins | Cook: 50mins | Ready in:*

## Ingredients

- 1/2 cup all-purpose flour
- 2 teaspoons baking powder
- 1/4 teaspoon salt
- 2 cups semolina flour
- 1 cup finely chopped almonds
- 1 cup white sugar
- 3/4 cup butter
- 3 eggs, beaten well
- 3/4 cup milk
- 1 lemon, zested, or more to taste
- Syrup:
- 3 cups water
- 3 cups white sugar
- 3 whole cloves
- 1 pinch ground cinnamon

## Direction

- Set oven to 175° C (350° F) and start preheating. Lightly coat a 9-in. cake pan with oil.
- In a bowl, sift together salt, baking powder and flour. Blend in almonds and semolina.
- In a big bowl, combine butter with 1 cup sugar. With an electric mixer, beat until fluffy and light. Whisk in eggs. Alternately add flour mixture with milk, whisking the batter shortly between each addition. Mix in lemon zest.
- Transfer batter to the prepared pan.
- Put into the preheated oven and bake 45 minutes, until inserting a toothpick into the center and it comes out clean.
- In a saucepan, combine cinnamon, cloves, 3 cups sugar, and water; boil, mixing until sugar is dissolved into a syrup. Spread syrup over cake right the moment it comes out of the oven. Allow the cake to cool for 30 minutes. Slice into squares.

## Nutrition Information

- Calories: 677 calories;
- Sodium: 357
- Total Carbohydrate: 110.2
- Cholesterol: 117
- Protein: 6.7
- Total Fat: 25.7

### 189. Baklava I

*Serving: 36 | Prep: 15mins | Cook: 30mins | Ready in:*

### Ingredients

- 1 pound walnuts
- 1/2 cup white sugar
- 1 tablespoon ground cinnamon
- 1 (16 ounce) package phyllo dough
- 5 tablespoons margarine
- 5 tablespoons vegetable oil
- 3 1/2 cups white sugar
- 2 cups water
- 2 tablespoons lemon juice

### Direction

- Preheat the oven to 175°C or 350°Fahrenheit. Oil a 9-in by 13-in baking pan.
- Trim the phyllo dough to fit the pan; put 1/2 of the sheets in the base of pan. In a blender or food processor, grind cinnamon, half cup sugar, and walnuts. Evenly scatter the mixture on top of the phyllo. Layer the remaining phyllo sheets over the walnut mixture.
- In a microwave or on low heat, melt margarine with oil in a small pot; slather on top of the phyllo layer. Using a sharp knife, make diamond shapes on the top phyllo layers.
- Place in the oven's middle rack; bake for half hour in the preheated oven until golden brown.
- Prepare the syrup in the meantime. On medium-high heat, mix and boil lemon juice, water, and 3 1/2 cup sugar. Take off heat then slightly cool.
- Take the baklava out of the oven then drizzle with syrup on hot pastry. Completely cool the baklava before serving.

### Nutrition Information

- Calories: 236 calories;
- Protein: 2.8
- Total Fat: 12.4
- Sodium: 78
- Total Carbohydrate: 30.7
- Cholesterol: 0

## 190. Christmas Baklava

*Serving: 45 | Prep: 15mins | Cook: 22mins | Ready in:*

### Ingredients

- 1 pound chopped pecans
- 1 tablespoon ground cinnamon
- 1 teaspoon ground nutmeg
- 1/4 cup honey
- 1 teaspoon vanilla extract
- 2 (1 pound) packages brown sugar substitute (such as Splenda ®)
- 2 cups sugar substitute (such as Splenda)
- 1 cup evaporated milk
- 1/4 cup butter
- 1 (16 ounce) package frozen phyllo dough, thawed
- 1/4 cup all-purpose flour, or as needed
- 2 tablespoons confectioners' sugar for dusting

### Direction

- Preheat an oven to 175°C/350°F; grease jelly roll pan/rimmed baking sheet lightly.
- Mix nutmeg, cinnamon and pecans till evenly blended in bowl; drizzle in vanilla and honey, mixing well.
- Boil butter, evaporated milk, white sugar substitute and brown sugar substitute in a pan. Lower heat; simmer, frequently mixing, for 12-15 minutes till it thickens. Mix in pecan mixture slowly; take off heat.
- Unroll 3 phyllo sheets; put in prepped baking pan. Lightly dust with flour. Put thin pecan-sugar mixture layer on phyllo sheets; cover using 3 extra phyllo sheets and dust with flour then put pecan-sugar mixture on phyllo. Repeat thrice, finishing with phyllo sheets on the top, using all pecan-sugar mixture and phyllo to create a 1-in. high stack.
- In preheated oven, bake for 10-12 minutes till top is golden brown; fully cool. Dust with confectioners' sugar; cut to 2-in. squares.

## Nutrition Information

- Calories: 231 calories;
- Sodium: 61
- Total Carbohydrate: 30.9
- Cholesterol: 4
- Protein: 2.1
- Total Fat: 9.3

## 191. Easy Baklava

*Serving: 36 | Prep: 30mins | Cook: 50mins | Ready in:*

### Ingredients

- 1 pound chopped nuts
- 1 teaspoon ground cinnamon
- 1 (16 ounce) package phyllo dough
- 1 cup butter, melted
- 1 cup white sugar
- 1 cup water
- 1/2 cup honey
- 1 teaspoon vanilla extract
- 1 teaspoon grated lemon zest

### Direction

- Set an oven to 175°C (350°F). Spread butter on a 9x13-inch baking dish.
- Toss nuts and cinnamon together. Unroll the phyllo and slice the entire stack in half so that it fits the dish. While making the baklava, use a damp cloth to cover the phyllo to prevent it from getting dry.
- In the bottom of the prepared dish, arrange 2 sheets of phyllo. Brush over generously with butter. Dust on the top with 2-3 tablespoons of the nut mixture. Repeat with the layers until to use up all ingredients, finish with 6 sheets of phyllo. Slice baklava all the way through the bottom of the dish to have 4 long rows with a sharp knife, then slice 9 times on diagonal into 36 diamond-shapes.
- In the preheated oven, bake for 50 minutes until crisp and golden brown.
- In a small saucepan, mix water and sugar on medium heat while baking the baklava, then boil. Stir in orange zest or lemon, vanilla, and honey; turn down the heat and bring to a simmer for 20 minutes.
- Take the baklava out of the oven and add the syrup on it right away. Before serving, allow to cool completely. Remove the cover and store.

## Nutrition Information

- Calories: 201 calories;
- Protein: 2.9
- Total Fat: 14.1
- Sodium: 97
- Total Carbohydrate: 17.8
- Cholesterol: 14

## 192. Fanouropita (Vegan Greek Raisin, Walnut, And Olive Oil Cake)

*Serving: 12 | Prep: 20mins | Cook: 45mins | Ready in:*

### Ingredients

- 1 3/8 cups olive oil
- 1 1/2 cups freshly squeezed orange juice
- 2 tablespoons brandy
- 1 1/2 cups white sugar
- 5 1/2 cups all-purpose flour
- 1 teaspoon baking soda
- 2 teaspoons baking powder
- 1 1/4 cups chopped walnuts
- 1 cup Thompson seedless raisins
- 1 teaspoon ground cinnamon
- 1/2 teaspoon ground cloves
- 2 tablespoons sesame seeds

### Direction

- Set an oven to preheat to 175°C (350°F), then grease a 12-inch round springform pan.

- In a big bowl, mix together the brandy, orange juice and olive oil, then mix in the sugar. In a separate bowl, mix together the baking powder, baking soda and flour and sift into the oil mixture. Fold in cloves, cinnamon, raisins and walnuts, then stir well. Tip the batter into the prepped springform pan and level the top. Sprinkle sesame seeds on top.
- Let it bake in the preheated oven for 45-60 minutes, until an inserted skewer in the middle exits clean.

## Nutrition Information

- Calories: 678 calories;
- Sodium: 190
- Total Carbohydrate: 85.4
- Cholesterol: 0
- Protein: 8.8
- Total Fat: 34.4

### 193.   Finikia

*Serving: 60 | Prep: 45mins | Cook: 25mins | Ready in:*

## Ingredients

- 1/2 cup butter, softened
- 1/2 cup superfine sugar
- 1 grated zest of one orange
- 1/2 cup corn oil
- 2 1/2 cups all-purpose flour
- 1 1/2 cups semolina
- 4 teaspoons baking powder
- 1 teaspoon ground cinnamon
- 1 teaspoon ground cloves
- 1/2 cup orange juice
- 1 cup water
- 1 cup white sugar
- 1/2 cup honey
- 1 cinnamon stick
- 2 teaspoons lemon juice
- 1/2 cup finely chopped walnuts

## Direction

- Preheat the oven to 175°C or 350°Fahrenheit. Oil cookie sheets.
- Cream orange zest, superfine sugar, and butter in a big bowl; stir in oil gradually then whip until fluffy and light. Mix together cloves, flour, cinnamon, baking powder, and semolina; whip alternately with orange juice in the fluffy mixture. Transfer on a floured board as it thickens and knead until it forms into a firm dough. Tear off dough by tablespoonfuls then shape into ovals or balls; arrange on the greased cookie sheets 2-in apart.
- Bake in the preheated oven until golden for 35 minutes. Cool to room temperature on baking sheets.
- Prepare the syrup. On medium heat, stir lemon juice, water, cinnamon stick, honey, and white sugar in a medium pot and boil; let boil for 10 minutes. Get rid of the cinnamon stick. Submerge a cookie while mixture is boiling hot, at a time, until completely covered. Dry them on a wire rack then scatter top with walnuts. Put paper beneath the rack to collect the drips. Store cookies at room temperature in a sealed container.

## Nutrition Information

- Calories: 100 calories;
- Protein: 1.3
- Total Fat: 4.1
- Sodium: 35
- Total Carbohydrate: 14.9
- Cholesterol: 4

### 194.   Fran's Greek Butter Cookies

*Serving: 12 | Prep: | Cook: | Ready in:*

## Ingredients

- 2 cups sifted all-purpose flour
- 1 cup butter
- 4 tablespoons confectioners' sugar
- 1 cup chopped walnuts
- 2 tablespoons water
- 2 teaspoons vanilla extract
- 1/3 cup confectioners' sugar for decoration
- 30 whole cloves

## Direction

- Cream butter, then gradually add the sugar until it becomes smooth. Blend in the flour, then mix in the vanilla, water and nuts. Stir well.
- Form into small 1-inch balls, then press down while pressing in 1 whole clove on the ungreased baking sheet.
- Let it bake for 20 minutes at 175°C (350°F). Roll it into confectioner's sugar while it is still warm. Roll it again once cooled, if preferred.

## Nutrition Information

- Calories: 308 calories;
- Total Carbohydrate: 24.7
- Cholesterol: 41
- Protein: 4
- Total Fat: 22
- Sodium: 116

### 195. Frozen Greek Yogurt

*Serving: 7 | Prep: 5mins | Cook: | Ready in:*

## Ingredients

- 3 cups plain whole-milk Greek yogurt
- 1 tablespoon lemon juice
- 5 tablespoons honey
- 10 chopped fresh mint leaves

## Direction

- In a freezer-safe metal bowl, combine lemon juice and yogurt until smooth. In a small bowl, mix together mint and honey; pour over the yogurt. Make a few fast stirs until the honey in the yogurt forms ribbons but not completely blended; cover. Place in the freezer for 1-2 hours.

## Nutrition Information

- Calories: 158 calories;
- Cholesterol: 19
- Protein: 5.2
- Total Fat: 8.6
- Sodium: 56
- Total Carbohydrate: 16

### 196. Galaktoboureko

*Serving: 15 | Prep: 1hours | Cook: 45mins | Ready in:*

## Ingredients

- 6 cups whole milk
- 1 cup semolina flour
- 3 1/2 tablespoons cornstarch
- 1 cup white sugar
- 1/4 teaspoon salt
- 6 eggs
- 1/2 cup white sugar
- 1 teaspoon vanilla extract
- 3/4 cup butter, melted
- 12 sheets phyllo dough
- 1 cup water
- 1 cup white sugar

## Direction

- In a large saucepan, add milk and heat up to a boil over medium heat. Blend together the salt, 1 cup sugar, cornstarch and semolina in a medium bowl so there are no cornstarch clumps. Put in the semolina mixture gradually when milk comes to a boil, mixing

continuously with a wooden spoon. Cook, mixing continuously until the mixture becomes thick and fully boiled. Take away from heat and put aside. Keep warm.
- With an electric mixer at high speed, blend eggs in a large bowl. Put in 1/2 cup of sugar and whip about 10 minutes until thick and light in color. Mix in vanilla.
- Fold the whipped eggs into the hot semolina mixture. Cover the pan partly and put aside to cool.
- Heat the oven to 350°F (175°C).
- Grease a 9x13 inch baking dish with butter and put 7 sheets of phyllo into the baking dish, as you lay each one, brush it with butter. Spread the custard into the pan on top of the phyllo and top with the leftover 5 sheets of phyllo, brushing each sheet with butter as you lay it down.
- Bake in the preheated oven for 40 to 45 minutes until the top crust is crispy and the custard filling has set. Mix together water and the remaining cup of sugar in a small saucepan. Heat up to a boil. When Galaktoboureko is taken out of the oven, scoop the hot sugar syrup on top, especially the edges. Let cool completely before slicing and serving. Chill in the refrigerator to store.

## Nutrition Information

- Calories: 391 calories;
- Sodium: 245
- Total Carbohydrate: 55.7
- Cholesterol: 109
- Protein: 8.3
- Total Fat: 15.4

## 197. Grecian Baklava

*Serving: 36 | Prep: 45mins | Cook: 1hours15mins | Ready in:*

## Ingredients

- Syrup:
- 3/4 cup water
- 3/4 cup white sugar
- 1/4 cup orange juice
- 1 1/2 cups honey
- 1 tablespoon ground cinnamon
- Pastry:
- 3/4 cup white sugar
- 1/2 teaspoon ground cinnamon
- 1/8 teaspoon ground nutmeg
- 2 cups ground walnuts
- 1 (16 ounce) package phyllo dough
- 1 1/2 cups melted butter

## Direction

- On medium heat, boil 1 tablespoon cinnamon, water, honey, orange juice, and 3/4 cup sugar in a pot to make the syrup. Turn to medium-low heat then let it simmer for 10 minutes. Take off heat then cool syrup to room temperature.
- Preheat the oven to 165°C or 325°Fahrenheit. Spread butter in a 10-in by 15-in baking dish.
- Combine ground walnuts, 3/4 cup sugar, nutmeg, and half teaspoon cinnamon until blended evenly; set aside.
- In the prepared dish, put two phyllo sheets then slather with melted butter; keep on adding buttered phyllo sheets 2 at a time to make a total of a dozen sheets. Evenly spread 1/3 walnut mixture on top of the phyllo then put another six phyllo sheets, brushing with butter every 2. Evenly spread the half of the remaining walnut mixture over the phyllo then put another 6 buttered sheets of phyllo on top. Lastly scatter the remaining walnut mixture on the phyllo. Top with the remaining phyllo, spreading butter on every 2 sheets. Slather the remaining butter over the baklava.
- Bake for an hour in the preheated oven until crispy and golden brown. Take the baklava out of the oven then drizzle with cooled syrup. Cool the baklava to room temperature then slice into 1-in diamonds or squares. Serve.

## Nutrition Information

- Calories: 211 calories;
- Sodium: 115
- Total Carbohydrate: 27.5
- Cholesterol: 20
- Protein: 1.7
- Total Fat: 11.3

### 198. Greek Baklava

*Serving: 18 | Prep: | Cook: |Ready in:*

## Ingredients

- 1 (16 ounce) package phyllo dough
- 1 pound chopped nuts
- 1 cup butter
- 1 teaspoon ground cinnamon
- 1 cup water
- 1 cup white sugar
- 1 teaspoon vanilla extract
- 1/2 cup honey

## Direction

- Preheat the oven to 175°C or 350°Fahrenheit. Spread butter on the sides and bottom of a 9-in by 13-in pan.
- Chop the nuts then mix with cinnamon; set it aside. Unfurl the phyllo dough then halve the whole stack to fit the pan. Use a damp cloth to cover the phyllo to prevent drying as you proceed. Put two phyllo sheets in the pan then butter well. Repeat to make eight layered phyllo sheets. Scatter 2-3 tablespoons nut mixture over the sheets then place two more phyllo sheets on top, butter then sprinkle with nuts. Layer as you go. The final layer should be six to eight phyllo sheets deep.
- Make square or diamond shapes with a sharp knife up to the bottom of pan. You can slice into four long rows for diagonal shapes. Bake until crisp and golden for 50 minutes.
- Meanwhile, boil water and sugar until the sugar melts to make the sauce; mix in honey and vanilla. Let it simmer for 20 minutes.
- Take the baklava out of the oven then drizzle with sauce right away; cool. Serve the baklava in cupcake papers. You can also freeze them without cover. The baklava will turn soggy when wrapped.

## Nutrition Information

- Calories: 393 calories;
- Total Carbohydrate: 37.5
- Cholesterol: 27
- Protein: 6.1
- Total Fat: 25.9
- Sodium: 196

### 199. Greek Butter Cookies

*Serving: 48 | Prep: 10mins | Cook: 10mins |Ready in:*

## Ingredients

- 1 cup butter, softened
- 3/4 cup white sugar
- 1 egg
- 1/2 teaspoon vanilla extract
- 1/2 teaspoon almond extract
- 2 1/4 cups all-purpose flour
- 1/2 cup confectioners' sugar for rolling

## Direction

- Set oven to 400° F (200° C) to preheat. Coat cookie sheets with grease.
- Cream the egg, sugar, and butter together in a medium bowl until smooth. Stir in the almond extracts and vanilla. Blend in the flour so that a dough forms. At the end, you may need to knead by hand. Take out and roll about a teaspoon of dough at a time to shape into 'S' shapes, logs or balls. On the prepared cookie

sheets, arrange cookies with 1 to 2 inches apart.
- Bake in the preheated oven for 10 minutes, or until firm and slightly brown. Let cookies cool thoroughly before dusting confectioners' sugar over cookies.

## Nutrition Information

- Calories: 74 calories;
- Cholesterol: 14
- Protein: 0.8
- Total Fat: 4
- Sodium: 29
- Total Carbohydrate: 8.9

## 200. Greek Egg Biscuits

*Serving: 96 | Prep: | Cook: | Ready in:*

## Ingredients

- 2 cups unsalted butter
- 1 cup white sugar
- 1 tablespoon vanilla extract
- 5 eggs
- 5 1/2 cups all-purpose flour
- 1/2 teaspoon salt
- 3 tablespoons baking powder
- 1/4 cup sesame seeds

## Direction

- Whip butter in a big mixing bowl until fluffy and light. Beat in sugar on medium speed for 10 minutes. Beat in one egg at a time, mix well before adding another until the four eggs are blended. Stir in vanilla. In another bowl, mix salt, baking powder, and flour; add and combine into the butter mixture until a soft and cohesive dough forms. If the dough is too soft, mix in more flour until you can easily handle it.
- Preheat the oven to 350°Fahrenheit. Oil the cookie sheets.
- Flour a work surface lightly. Pinch an inch of dough lumps off then roll on a floured surface into a 7-in long rope with a quarter-inch diameter. Cross the ends of the rope then twirl in a loop to the opposite way to make a braid. Arrange about an inch apart on cookie sheets.
- Whisk the remaining egg then slather on the braids; scatter sesame seeds on top. Bake for 20-25 minutes. Cool braids for 10 minutes on cookie sheets then move to racks to completely cool.

## Nutrition Information

- Calories: 75 calories;
- Total Fat: 4.4
- Sodium: 62
- Total Carbohydrate: 7.8
- Cholesterol: 20
- Protein: 1.2

## 201. Greek Lemon Cake

*Serving: 12 | Prep: 30mins | Cook: 50mins | Ready in:*

## Ingredients

- 3 cups cake flour
- 1 teaspoon baking soda
- 1/4 teaspoon salt
- 6 eggs, separated
- 2 cups white sugar, divided
- 1 cup butter, softened
- 2 teaspoons grated lemon zest
- 2 tablespoons lemon juice
- 1 cup plain whole-milk yogurt

## Direction

- Preheat the oven to 175°C or 350°Fahrenheit. Oil a ten-inch tube pan.

- Sift together the salt, baking soda, and flour; set aside.
- Whisk egg whites in a big bowl to form soft peaks; beat in half cup sugar gradually until it forms into stiff glossy peaks. Set it aside.
- In a big bowl, whisk the remaining 1 1/2 cup sugar and butter for 3-5 minutes using an electric mixer till fluffy. You should have a light-colored mixture.
- Mix in lemon zest, egg yolks, and lemon juice Mix in flour mixture in turns with the yogurt until blended. Fold in egg whites gently; pour batter into the greased pan.
- Bake for 50-60 minutes in the preheated oven until an inserted tester in the middle comes out without residue. Cool cake for 10 minutes in the pan, then move to rack to completely cool. The cake can serve 12.

## Nutrition Information

- Calories: 443 calories;
- Sodium: 307
- Total Carbohydrate: 62.7
- Cholesterol: 136
- Protein: 7
- Total Fat: 18.8

## 202. Greek Pumpkin Pie

*Serving: 6 | Prep: 30mins | Cook: 30mins | Ready in:*

## Ingredients

- 2 (15 ounce) cans pumpkin puree
- 3/4 cup white sugar
- 1 cup raisins
- 1 cup fine semolina
- 1/2 teaspoon ground cinnamon
- 1/4 teaspoon ground cloves
- 1/8 teaspoon ground nutmeg
- 2 sheets frozen puff pastry, thawed
- 1 egg, slightly beaten

## Direction

- Preheat the oven to 175 °C or 350 °F.
- Oil a rimmed baking sheet.
- In a skillet over medium heat, heat pumpkin puree, mixing from time to time till puree is thick and most of liquid has vaporized. Mix in nutmeg, cloves, cinnamon, semolina, raisins and sugar. Take off from heat.
- Line the prepared baking sheet with one puff pastry sheet. Scatter pumpkin mixture on top of pastry and cover with the rest of the pastry sheet. With beaten egg, brush the top of puff pastry.
- In the prepped oven, bake for 30 to 40 minutes till golden brown.

## Nutrition Information

- Calories: 773 calories;
- Sodium: 557
- Total Carbohydrate: 112.4
- Cholesterol: 31
- Protein: 12.8
- Total Fat: 32.3

## 203. Honey Pie From Sifnos

*Serving: 8 | Prep: 30mins | Cook: 50mins | Ready in:*

## Ingredients

- 1 3/4 cups all-purpose flour
- 2 tablespoons white sugar
- 1/2 cup butter, cut into small pieces
- 1/4 cup cold water
- 4 eggs
- 1/4 cup white sugar
- 1 tablespoon all-purpose flour
- 1/2 teaspoon ground cinnamon, divided
- 1/4 cup thyme honey
- 1 (16 ounce) container ricotta cheese

## Direction

- In a big bowl, combine 2 tbsp. sugar and 1 3/4 cup flour; put in butter until crumbly. Mix in a tablespoon of water at a time just until dough is not dry and forms together. Shape the dough into a ball then use plastic to wrap; chill for half an hour.
- Preheat the oven to 175°C or 350°Fahrenheit.
- On a floured surface, roll out the dough have a 10-in pie pan lined. Cut excess dough on the edges of the pan. Use a fork to prick the bottom for a couple of times; set aside.
- In a big bowl, whisk eggs until it forms into soft peaks. Whisk in 1/2 of the cinnamon, 1 tbsp. flour, and a quarter cup of sugar gradually. Keep on beating until it forms into firm peaks. Whisk in honey then the ricotta cheese until evenly blended. Move the filling into the prepared pie shell using a damp knife to smooth the top.
- Bake for 50-60 mins in the preheated oven until the top is dark golden brown and the middle is set. Take it out of the oven once done then scatter with the rest of the cinnamon.

## Nutrition Information

- Calories: 388 calories;
- Total Fat: 18.8
- Sodium: 189
- Total Carbohydrate: 42.9
- Cholesterol: 141
- Protein: 12.7

### 204. Incredible Watermelon Pie

*Serving: 12 | Prep: 20mins | Cook: 50mins | Ready in:*

## Ingredients

- 1 1/2 cups all-purpose flour
- 4 cups mashed watermelon, seeds removed
- 1/2 cup honey
- 1/2 cup white sugar
- 1/2 teaspoon salt
- 1 teaspoon ground cinnamon
- 1/2 cup sesame seeds

## Direction

- On medium heat, cook flour in a dry pan, stir from time to time, until golden; set aside. Cool.
- Preheat oven to 175°C or 350°Fahrenheit.
- Combine cinnamon, watermelon, salt, flour, sugar, and honey in a big bowl. Oil a nine or ten-inch pie plate; scatter 1/2 of the sesame seeds at the bottom. Top the seeds with watermelon filling, it should be an inch thick. Scatter top with the rest of the sesame seeds.
- Bake in the preheated oven for 40-50 minutes until an inserted knife in the close the middle comes out without residue. Completely cool then slice. Chill any leftovers.

## Nutrition Information

- Calories: 182 calories;
- Cholesterol: 0
- Protein: 3
- Total Fat: 3.2
- Sodium: 99
- Total Carbohydrate: 37.3

### 205. Karithopita

*Serving: 16 | Prep: 15mins | Cook: 40mins | Ready in:*

## Ingredients

- 1 1/4 cups all-purpose flour
- 3/4 cup white sugar
- 1 teaspoon baking powder
- 1/2 teaspoon salt
- 1 teaspoon ground cinnamon
- 1/4 teaspoon ground cloves
- 1/3 cup shortening
- 3/4 cup milk

- 1 egg
- 1 cup finely chopped walnuts
- 1/4 cup white sugar
- 1/4 cup water
- 1/4 cup honey
- 1 teaspoon lemon juice

## Direction

- Preheat the oven to 175°C or 350°Fahrenheit. Grease a 9-inch square baking dish then dust with flour.
- Mix cloves, flour, cinnamon, 3/4 cup sugar, salt, and baking powder in a medium bowl; cut in shortening until it turns to very small portions. With an electric mixer, mix in egg and milk on low speed; mix for a minute. Scrape the bottom of the bowl at least one time to prevent lumps. Use your hands to fold in walnuts; evenly spread the mixture in the prepared pan.
- Bake in the preheated oven for 35-40 minutes until an inserted knife in the middle of the cake comes out without residue. Cool for half an hour in the pan as you make the honey syrup.
- Mix and boil water and quarter cup sugar in a saucepan. Turn to low heat and let it simmer for 5 minutes. Mix in lemon juice and honey; take off heat.
- Make diamond slashes with a knife over the cake; pour hot syrup on top of cake.

## Nutrition Information

- Calories: 198 calories;
- Cholesterol: 13
- Protein: 2.9
- Total Fat: 9.8
- Sodium: 105
- Total Carbohydrate: 26.1

## 206. Koulourakia I

*Serving: 15 | Prep: | Cook: | Ready in:*

## Ingredients

- 1/2 cup butter, softened
- 1/2 cup white sugar
- 3 egg yolks
- 1/4 cup half-and-half cream
- 2 1/4 cups all-purpose flour
- 1 teaspoon baking powder
- 1/4 teaspoon salt
- 3 tablespoons sesame seeds

## Direction

- Preheat the oven to 180°C or 350°Fahrenheit.
- Beat sugar and butter in a big electric mixer bowl until creamy. Whisk in 2 egg yolks, one at a time. Stir in 3 tablespoons of half-and-half.
- Combine salt, baking powder, and flour in a separate bowl; mix into the butter mixture gradually until.
- Tear off an inch of dough balls then roll into 7-in strand to form the cookies. Join the ends together then twist to make a twirled appearance on each.
- Beat the remaining half-and-half with the remaining yolk; gently brush on top of the cookies. Scatter sesame seeds. Bake for 15 minutes until golden.

## Nutrition Information

- Calories: 175 calories;
- Protein: 3
- Total Fat: 8.6
- Sodium: 119
- Total Carbohydrate: 21.8
- Cholesterol: 59

## 207. Koulourakia II

*Serving: 24 | Prep: | Cook: | Ready in:*

### Ingredients

- 1/2 cup butter
- 1/4 cup shortening
- 3 cups all-purpose flour
- 1/2 cup white sugar
- 2 teaspoons baking powder
- 2 eggs
- 1 teaspoon vanilla extract
- 1 teaspoon ground cinnamon
- 1/2 teaspoon ground nutmeg
- 1/2 cup milk
- 3 tablespoons sesame seeds

### Direction

- Prepare the oven by preheating to 350°F (175°C).
- Cream butter and margarine or butter. Put in milk, nutmeg, ground cinnamon, vanilla, 1 egg, baking powder, flour, and sugar.
- Let the dough chill until easy to handle.
- Place tablespoon-size pieces on a floured board and form into ropes. Transfer to cookie sheet in S shapes. Brush with the rest of the egg that is beaten with 1 tablespoon water. Dust with sesame seeds.
- Bake in the preheated oven for 10 to 12 minutes at 350°F (175°C).

### Nutrition Information

- Calories: 142 calories;
- Cholesterol: 26
- Protein: 2.6
- Total Fat: 7.2
- Sodium: 76
- Total Carbohydrate: 16.9

## 208. Kourabiedes I

*Serving: 18 | Prep: | Cook: | Ready in:*

### Ingredients

- 2 cups sifted all-purpose flour
- 1/2 teaspoon baking powder
- 1 cup butter
- 1/4 cup confectioners' sugar
- 1 egg yolk
- 2 tablespoons brandy
- 1/2 teaspoon vanilla extract
- 1/2 cup finely chopped blanched almonds
- 36 whole cloves
- 1/3 cup confectioners' sugar for decoration

### Direction

- Sift together baking powder and flour; set aside.
- Cream the butter then beat in sugar gradually until fluffy; beat in vanilla, brandy, and egg yolk until very light. Fold in almonds.
- Combine with the flour mixture until it forms into a smooth and soft dough. Refrigerate for half an hour until it can be easily handled.
- Preheat the oven to 170°C or 325°Fahrenheit.
- Form dough by even tablespoonfuls to crescent shapes; arrange on an ungreased cookie sheet an inch apart. Push whole cloves in the middle of each crescent. Bake for 25-30 minutes until light but avoid browning. Place on a rack to cool. Generously sprinkle confectioners' sugar.

### Nutrition Information

- Calories: 194 calories;
- Protein: 2.7
- Total Fat: 12.8
- Sodium: 93
- Total Carbohydrate: 16.5
- Cholesterol: 38

## 209. Kourabiedes II

*Serving: 30 | Prep: | Cook: | Ready in:*

### Ingredients

- 2 cups unsalted butter
- 1/3 cup confectioners' sugar
- 2 teaspoons almond extract
- 6 cups all-purpose flour

### Direction

- Preheat the oven to 180°C or 350°Fahrenheit.
- Cream almond extract, powdered sugar, and butter; gradually add flour.
- Use your hand to knead the dough then form into crescents. Bake until light brown for 20 minutes. Roll warm crescents in confectioners' sugar.

### Nutrition Information

- Calories: 206 calories;
- Cholesterol: 33
- Protein: 2.7
- Total Fat: 12.5
- Sodium: 2
- Total Carbohydrate: 20.4

## 210. Kourambiathes (Greek Cookies)

*Serving: 16 | Prep: 30mins | Cook: 15mins | Ready in:*

### Ingredients

- 1 cup butter, room temperature
- 1 egg yolk
- 2 teaspoons anise extract
- 1/4 cup confectioners' sugar
- 2 1/2 cups all-purpose flour
- 1/3 cup confectioners' sugar for dusting

### Direction

- Preheat the oven to 175°C or 350°Fahrenheit. Oil baking sheets.
- Cream anise extract, egg yolk, and butter in a medium bowl until light. Mix in flour and a quarter cup confectioners' sugar until combined.
- Form dough into crescents then arrange on the greased baking sheets two inches apart.
- Bake for 15-20 minutes in the preheated oven until starting to brown on the edges and bottoms. Liberally dust with confectioners' sugar before they cool fully.

### Nutrition Information

- Calories: 194 calories;
- Sodium: 83
- Total Carbohydrate: 19.3
- Cholesterol: 43
- Protein: 2.3
- Total Fat: 12

## 211. Kourambiedes III

*Serving: 18 | Prep: | Cook: | Ready in:*

### Ingredients

- 1 cup unsalted butter
- 4 tablespoons confectioners' sugar
- 1 teaspoon vanilla extract
- 2 cups sifted all-purpose flour
- 1 cup chopped pecans
- 36 whole cloves
- 1/2 cup confectioners' sugar

### Direction

- Start preheating the oven to 350°F (175°C).
- In medium bowl, cream together confectioners' sugar and butter. Stir in vanilla, followed by flour, and the pecans next.
- Form the dough into the walnut sized balls; insert 1 clove into each dough. Arrange on the

unprepared cookie sheet; then bake in prepared oven, about 15-18 mins. While the cookies are still hot, roll them in the powdered sugar. Discard cloves or warn your guests to discard them.

## Nutrition Information

- Calories: 209 calories;
- Sodium: 7
- Total Carbohydrate: 17.7
- Cholesterol: 27
- Protein: 2.2
- Total Fat: 14.8

## 212. Kritika Patouthia

*Serving: 72 | Prep: | Cook: | Ready in:*

## Ingredients

- 1/2 cup olive oil
- 4 tablespoons water
- 4 tablespoons orange juice
- 1 lemon, juiced
- 6 tablespoons white sugar
- 4 cups all-purpose flour
- 1/2 teaspoon baking soda
- 1 teaspoon salt
- 1/3 cup confectioners' sugar for decoration
- 1/2 teaspoon orange flower water
- 1 cup ground walnuts
- 1 cup ground almonds
- 1 cup sesame seeds
- 1 cup honey

## Direction

- Combine sugar, lemon juice, orange juice, water, and olive oil. Reserve. Sift salt, baking soda, and flour together in a large bowl. Add olive oil mixture to flour mixture.
- Work and knead dough on a floured surface until smooth. Cover the dough or you can put the empty bowl on top of it and allow the dough to rest for an hour.
- While resting the dough, prepare the filling. For making the filling: Mix honey, sesame seeds, ground almonds, and ground walnuts together in a bowl. Combine until well coated.
- Prepare the oven by preheating to 350°F (175°C).
- Roll the dough out to a thickness of 1/4-inch. Slice into 3-inch squares. Put 1 heaping teaspoon of filling in the middle of each square. Use orange flower water or orange juice to moisten edges and fold in the four corners and press them firmly together in the middle to cover the filling.
- Bake in the preheated oven for about 25 minutes. While the cookies is still warm, dust lightly with orange flower water or orange juice and sink in a bowl of confectioner's sugar.

## Nutrition Information

- Calories: 90 calories;
- Sodium: 42
- Total Carbohydrate: 12
- Cholesterol: 0
- Protein: 1.7
- Total Fat: 4.3

## 213. Loukoumades

*Serving: 25 | Prep: 10mins | Cook: 15mins | Ready in:*

## Ingredients

- 2 (.25 ounce) packages active dry yeast
- 1 cup warm water
- 1/2 cup warm milk
- 1/4 cup white sugar
- 1 teaspoon salt
- 1/3 cup butter, softened
- 3 eggs
- 4 cups all-purpose flour

- 1/2 cup honey
- 1/2 cup water
- 4 cups vegetable oil, or as needed
- 2 teaspoons ground cinnamon

### Direction

- Scatter yeast in a small bowl with warm water. The water should not exceed 40°C or 100°Fahrenheit. Let it sit for 5 minutes until the yeast is soft and a creamy foam starts to form. Combine salt, sugar, and warm milk in a big bowl and stir until dissolved; add the mixture of yeast into the milk mixture and mix to incorporate.
- Whip in flour, eggs, and butter until a soft and smooth dough forms; cover. Allow to rise for half an hour until it doubles in bulk. Mix dough well then cover again; set aside for another half hour to rise.
- On medium-high heat, mix and boil half cup water and honey in a pot. Take off heat then cool the honey syrup.
- Heat 2-in deep oil to 175°C or 350°Fahrenheit in a big pot or deep-fryer.
- In a glass of water close to the batter, put a soup spoon or a big tablespoon. Using a wet spoon, spoon about 2 tablespoons dough per puff then place in your wet palm; roll the dough back in the spoon to make a circle shape. Avoid overhandling the soft and puffy dough. In batches, place the dough ball in hot oil. Dampen the spoon in each dough ball you make. Fry in hot oil for 2-3 minutes on each batch until the bottom is golden then flip to fry the other side. Slowly put loukoumades aside on paper towels to drain.
- Arrange on a baking sheet then pour honey syrup all over; dust with cinnamon. Serve the loukoumades warm.

### Nutrition Information

- Calories: 167 calories;
- Protein: 3.2
- Total Fat: 6.9
- Sodium: 122
- Total Carbohydrate: 23.5
- Cholesterol: 29

## 214. Paximade

*Serving: 12 | Prep: | Cook: | Ready in:*

### Ingredients

- 2 1/2 cups all-purpose flour
- 2 teaspoons baking powder
- 1/2 teaspoon salt
- 1 teaspoon anise seed
- 1/2 cup unsalted butter, softened
- 1/2 cup white sugar
- 2 eggs
- 1/2 cup milk

### Direction

- Sift together salt, baking powder, and flour; mix in anise seed well.
- Cream sugar and butter in another big bowl until fluffy and light. Whisk in 1 egg then another; whisk for a minute.
- Starting with flour mixture, mix alternating with milk into the big bowl with creamed sugar and butter. Stir until everything is combined.
- Scoop batter in a greased 9-in by 5-in by 3-in loaf pan.
- Bake for 50 minutes in a preheated 175°C or 350°Fahrenheit oven until an inserted toothpick comes out without residue. Cool for 10 minutes in the pan then turn out on a cooling rack. It can last for ten days in the refrigerator.

### Nutrition Information

- Calories: 213 calories;
- Protein: 4.2
- Total Fat: 9
- Sodium: 196

- Total Carbohydrate: 29
- Cholesterol: 52

## 215. Pistachio Hazelnut Baklava

*Serving: 60 | Prep: 1hours | Cook: 1hours25mins | Ready in:*

### Ingredients

- 8 ounces finely chopped pistachio nuts
- 8 ounces finely chopped hazelnuts
- 2 teaspoons ground cinnamon
- 1/2 teaspoon ground cloves
- 1/2 cup white sugar
- 2 cups unsalted butter, melted
- 1 1/2 (16 ounce) packages frozen phyllo pastry, thawed
- 1/4 cup whole cloves (optional)
- 3 cups white sugar
- 2 1/2 cups water
- 2 tablespoons honey
- 1 teaspoon ground cinnamon
- 1/4 teaspoon ground cloves

### Direction

- Preheat the oven to 175°C or 350°Fahrenheit.
- Combine half cup sugar, pistachio nuts, half teaspoon ground cloves, 2 teaspoons cinnamon, and hazelnuts in a big bowl.
- Roll out the thawed phyllo dough, use a damp towel to cover to avoid cracking and drying. Spread melted butter in a 10-inch by 15-inch jellyroll pan using a pastry brush. Put a sheet of phyllo in the pan then spread additional butter. Repeat for another eight sheets of stacked and buttered phyllo dough. Scatter some nut mixture on top of the layer then use three more buttered phyllo sheets to cover. Scatter more nut mixture on top then another three buttered phyllo layers. Repeat until all the nut mixture is used, save eight pastry layers for the top. Spread melted butter on each addition of pastry layer.
- Slice the pastry into strips then cut again to form diamonds; the portions should be a bit small since they are very sweet. You can put a whole clove on each piece at this point. Boil the remaining melted butter then evenly sprinkle over the whole pastry.
- Bake for an hour and 15 minutes until equally golden in the preheated oven.
- Meanwhile, mix a quarter teaspoon ground cloves, remaining three cups sugar, a teaspoon of cinnamon, honey, and water in a big saucepan and boil. Let it simmer for 15 minutes on medium heat; put aside to cool.
- Evenly pour the syrup right away on the freshly baked pastry. The hot syrup might boil and sputter the butter on the pastry so be careful. Cool baklava to room temperature to serve. Discard the whole cloves before eating.

### Nutrition Information

- Calories: 182 calories;
- Total Fat: 10.9
- Sodium: 72
- Total Carbohydrate: 20.1
- Cholesterol: 16
- Protein: 2.3

## 216. Portokalopita (Greek Orange Phyllo Cake)

*Serving: 12 | Prep: 25mins | Cook: 1hours | Ready in:*

### Ingredients

- Syrup:
- 2 cups white sugar
- 1 1/2 cups water
- 1 teaspoon ground cinnamon
- 1 orange, halved
- Cake:
- 1 (16 ounce) package phyllo dough

- 3 oranges
- 5 eggs
- 1 (7 ounce) container Greek yogurt
- 3/4 cup olive oil, divided
- 1/2 cup white sugar
- 1 tablespoon baking powder

## Direction

- On medium-high heat, mix cinnamon, water, and two cups sugar in a saucepan. Press in orange juice and put the squeezed halves; boil. Vigorously boil for 8 minutes; take off heat. Cool as you make the cake.
- Preheat oven to 175°C or 350°Fahrenheit. Use some olive oil to grease a 9-in by 13-in baking pan lightly.
- Unpack the phyllo sheets then roughly tear to shreds; stack in the baking pan. Allow the phyllo shreds to dry slightly as you make the rest of the ingredients. Halve one orange then thinly slice one orange half to half-moons for garnish. Juice and zest the rest of the 2 1/2 oranges.
- In a food processor or blender, blend baking powder, orange juice, half cup sugar, orange zest, olive oil, yogurt, and eggs on high speed for 2 minutes until frothy. Pour egg and orange mixture on top of the phyllo shreds in the pan. Gently mix everything until the egg mixture is blended evenly. Place the orange slices over the cake to garnish.
- Bake for 45 minutes in the preheated oven until golden on top. Take it out of the oven then pour the cooled syrup on top right away. Put aside for at least an hour until the cake absorbs most of the syrup. Cut into squares. Serve.

## Nutrition Information

- Calories: 465 calories;
- Cholesterol: 81
- Protein: 6.7
- Total Fat: 19.5
- Sodium: 305
- Total Carbohydrate: 67.7

## 217. Serano Chocolate Cake

*Serving: 12 | Prep: 1hours | Cook: 30mins | Ready in:*

## Ingredients

- For the Cake:
- 1 cup self-rising flour
- 1/2 cup unsweetened cocoa powder
- 5 eggs
- 3/4 cup white sugar
- For the Simple Syrup:
- 1/2 cup water
- 3/4 cup white sugar
- Italian Meringue-Chocolate Cream Filling:
- 1/4 cup water
- 7/8 cup white sugar
- 3 egg whites
- 6 ounces bittersweet chocolate, chopped
- 1 3/4 cups heavy cream, chilled
- 1/3 cup heavy cream at room temperature

## Direction

- Preheat the oven to 175°C or 350°Fahrenheit. Oil lightly a 9-in cake pan then dust with flour or put parchment paper to line.
- Sift cocoa powder and flour; set aside. In a mixing bowl, beat 3/4 cup sugar and eggs for around 3 mins until very thick. Fold in flour mixture carefully using a spatula. Scoop the batter gently in the prepared pan; bake for 25-30 mins until an inserted toothpick in the middle comes out clean and the tops bounce back when pressed lightly. Cool for 10 mins in the pan then turn out onto a wire rack to completely cool.
- On medium-high heat, boil 3/4 cup sugar and half a cup water in a saucepan to make a simple syrup. Take off the heat; set aside.
- Mix together 7/8 cup sugar and a quarter cup water in a saucepan then boil while mixing until the sugar dissolves for the Italian meringue. Avoid mixing once it starts to boil.

Bring to a soft ball stage with a candy thermometer. It should read 115°C or 240°Fahrenheit. While the sugar boils, use an electric mixer to beat the egg whites on medium-low speed until it forms soft peaks.
- Once the sugar syrup is almost at soft ball stage, put the speed to high to beat the egg whites. Pour the hot sugar syrup carefully into the egg white in the middle of the beaters and at the bowl sides. Keep on beating at high speed until the meringue cools to room temperature.
- Over a double broiler set on top of just-barely simmering water, melt the bittersweet chocolate while frequently mixing and scraping the sides down using a rubber spatula to prevent burning until just melted. Take off the heat then cool the chocolate to room temperature but still fluid.
- Beat 1 3/4 cup of cream until it forms medium-stiff peaks.
- Fold the melted chocolate with the egg white meringue using a rubber spatula. Gently mix in 1/3 cup of room-temperature cream until combined. Lighten the chocolate meringue mixture by folding in 1/3 of the whipped cream. Fold in the remaining 2/3 whipped cream gently.
- Divide the sponge cake into 2 layers to assemble the cake. Place one layer on a plate or turntable; brush with simple syrup well. The cake will absorb the syrup and act as a sponge literally to avoid drying. Spread 1/3 of the chocolate cream over the cake then add the 2nd cake layer on top. Repeat brushing with the syrup and cream. Spread the rest of the chocolate cream on the cake sides. Chill until ready to serve.

## Nutrition Information

- Calories: 378 calories;
- Sodium: 186
- Total Carbohydrate: 59.6
- Cholesterol: 101
- Protein: 6.2

- Total Fat: 15

## 218. Traditional Galaktoboureko

*Serving: 12 | Prep: | Cook: | Ready in:*

### Ingredients

- 6 cups milk
- 7 eggs
- 1 cup semolina
- 3/4 cup white sugar
- 2 tablespoons butter
- 1 teaspoon grated lemon zest
- 1/2 cup butter, melted
- 12 sheets phyllo dough, thawed
- 2 cups white sugar
- 1 cup water
- 1 teaspoon grated lemon zest

### Direction

- In a large saucepan, add milk, and bring to a boil over medium-low heat. Take away from heat. While waiting for the milk to boil, use an electric mixer to beat 3/4 cup sugar, semolina, and the eggs until well incorporated. Stir this into the hot milk using a wooden spoon. Cook over low heat, stirring continuously until it just starts bubbling. Take away from stove, and mix in 1 teaspoon of lemon zest and 2 tablespoons of butter.
- Set the oven to preheat at 175°C (350°F). Grease a 9x13 inch baking dish with butter.
- Brush 6 of the phyllo sheets with butter, and use them to line the baking dish's bottom and sides. Pour the semolina mixture in and evenly spread. Layer the rest of the phyllo dough sheets on top, brush melted butter on each one as you layer them on. Splash a few dashes of water on top. Slice in a diagonal pattern through the top layer of pastry using a knife.
- Bake in the preheated oven for 40 minutes, or until golden brown. While it bakes, put the

remaining lemon zest, water, and 2 cups of sugar in a small saucepan. Bring to a boil, and take away from heat.
- Take the galaktoboureko out of the oven, then immediately pour hot syrup over it. Let cool before serving. After it cools down, refrigerate. It will be kept for 4 to 5 days.

## Nutrition Information

- Calories: 472 calories;
- Total Fat: 16.2
- Sodium: 251
- Total Carbohydrate: 71.9
- Cholesterol: 144
- Protein: 10.9

## 219. Vaselopita Greek New Years Cake

*Serving: 12 | Prep: 30mins | Cook: 1hours | Ready in:*

## Ingredients

- 1 cup butter
- 2 cups white sugar
- 3 cups all-purpose flour
- 6 eggs
- 2 teaspoons baking powder
- 1 cup warm milk (110 degrees F/45 degrees C)
- 1/2 teaspoon baking soda
- 1 tablespoon fresh lemon juice
- 1/4 cup blanched slivered almonds
- 2 tablespoons white sugar

## Direction

- Preheat an oven to 175 degrees C (350 degrees F). Generously coat a 10 inch round cake pan with grease.
- Cream the sugar and butter together in a medium bowl until resulting mix is light. Mix in flour until mixture becomes mealy. Place in eggs one at a time, and combine thoroughly after each addition. Mix the milk and baking powder and then transfer to egg mixture. Combine thoroughly. Mix baking soda and lemon juice and then stir into batter. Transfer to the greased cake pan.
- Bake in prepped oven for 20 minutes. Take out and scatter sugar and nuts on top of the cake. Place it back into the oven to bake for about 20 to 30 more minutes until the cake is able to spring back when touched. Carefully make a small hole in cake and then put a quarter into the hole. Cover the hole with some sugar. Let the cake cool for 10 minutes on a rack prior to inverting on a plate.
- Serve the cake while still warm.

## Nutrition Information

- Calories: 447 calories;
- Total Fat: 19.7
- Sodium: 287
- Total Carbohydrate: 61.2
- Cholesterol: 135
- Protein: 7.7

## 220. Vasilopita

*Serving: 14 | Prep: 30mins | Cook: 1hours | Ready in:*

## Ingredients

- 1 cup butter, softened
- 1 3/4 cups white sugar
- 5 eggs
- 2 tablespoons water
- 2 teaspoons vanilla extract
- 3 cups all-purpose flour
- 1 teaspoon baking powder
- 1/2 cup blanched slivered almonds
- 2 tablespoons sesame seeds

## Direction

- Preheat the oven to 165°C or 325°Fahrenheit.

- Combine sugar and butter or margarine in a big bowl. Split thee of the eggs; put the yolks and the remaining two whole eggs in the butter mixture. Mix in water and vanilla.
- Sift together flour and baking powder in a separate bowl; mix into the creamed mixture.
- Whisk three egg whites until foamy. Put in a tablespoon of sugar. Whisk whites continuously until the mixture is stiff yet not dry; fold whipped whites into the batter.
- Transfer batter in an oiled 10-in by 4-in tube pan. Use foil to wrap a big coin then press it down in the batter to hide completely. Scatter top of batter with seeds and nuts.
- Bake for 70 minutes until done. Place on a wire rack to cool.

## Nutrition Information

- Calories: 372 calories;
- Sodium: 154
- Total Carbohydrate: 47.7
- Cholesterol: 101
- Protein: 6.2
- Total Fat: 17.8

## 221. Yia Yia's Baklava

*Serving: 20 | Prep: 45mins | Cook: 50mins | Ready in:*

## Ingredients

- Syrup:
- 2 cups water
- 2 cups white sugar
- 4 whole cloves
- 1/2 cinnamon stick
- 1 lemon, juiced, divided
- Filling:
- 1 pound finely chopped walnuts
- 1 cup white sugar
- 2 tablespoons ground cinnamon
- 1/2 teaspoon ground nutmeg
- 3/4 cup unsalted butter, melted, or more as needed
- 20 sheets phyllo dough

## Direction

- In a pot, mix and boil half of the lemon juice, water, cinnamon stick, cloves, and two cups sugar. Turn to low heat; let it simmer for 15 minutes until the flavors meld and it reaches the consistency of a syrup. Mix in the remaining half of the lemon juice. Filter then chill for at least half an hour until cool.
- In a bowl, combine nutmeg, walnuts, ground cinnamon, and a cup of sugar.
- Preheat the oven to 175°C or 350°Fahrenheit. Spread butter on the sides and bottom of a 9-in by 13-in glass baking dish.
- On a dry and clean work surface, place the phyllo dough then use a plastic wrap to cover; put a damp towel to cover the plastic wrap.
- Put one phyllo sheet in the buttered baking dish; spread butter lightly. Put another phyllo sheet on top then spread butter. Repeat with four more phyllo sheet layers, slather butter on each.
- Evenly and gently scatter 1/3 of the walnut mixture on top of the phyllo in the baking dish. Put one phyllo sheet on top of the walnut mixture then spread butter. Repeat with three more phyllo sheet layers, buttering each.
- Evenly scatter another 1/3 of the walnut mixture on top of the phyllo in the baking dish. Put one phyllo sheet on top of the walnut mixture then spread butter. Repeat with three more buttered phyllo sheet layers.
- Evenly scatter the remaining 1/3 of the walnut mixture on top of the phyllo in the baking dish. Put one phyllo sheet on top of the walnut mixture then spread butter. Repeat with the remaining five buttered phyllo sheet layers. Slice the baklava into 1-in diamond shapes.
- Bake for 35-45 minutes in the preheated oven until pale golden brown.
- Drizzle the cooled syrup all over the baklava; let it cool for a day to let the baklava absorb the syrup.

Nutrition Information

- Calories: 386 calories;
- Sodium: 95
- Total Carbohydrate: 44
- Cholesterol: 18
- Protein: 4.9
- Total Fat: 22.9

# Chapter 5: Greek Salad Recipes

\*\*\*

### 222. Absolutely Fabulous Greek/House Dressing

*Serving: 120 | Prep: 10mins | Cook: | Ready in:*

### Ingredients

- 1 1/2 quarts olive oil
- 1/3 cup garlic powder
- 1/3 cup dried oregano
- 1/3 cup dried basil
- 1/4 cup pepper
- 1/4 cup salt
- 1/4 cup onion powder
- 1/4 cup Dijon-style mustard
- 2 quarts red wine vinegar

### Direction

- Combine Dijon-style mustard, olive oil, onion powder, garlic powder, salt, oregano, pepper, and basil in a big container. Mix in vinegar forcefully until well combined. Cover tightly and store at room temperature.

Nutrition Information

- Calories: 104 calories;
- Total Fat: 10.8
- Sodium: 13
- Total Carbohydrate: 2.1
- Cholesterol: 0
- Protein: 0.2

### 223. Beet And Arugula Salad

*Serving: 4 | Prep: 15mins | Cook: 15mins | Ready in:*

### Ingredients

- 2 pounds beets, trimmed
- 4 small garlic cloves, minced
- 1 1/2 teaspoons salt
- 5 tablespoons fresh lemon juice, or to taste
- 1/2 pound arugula
- 1 (8 ounce) package feta cheese, thinly sliced
- 16 pitted kalamata olives
- 1/4 cup olive oil, divided

### Direction

- Put beets into a big saucepan and fill in enough water so that the water level is 1 inch higher than the beets. Boil the water then lower the heat to medium-low, use a lid to cover and let simmer for about 15 minutes till you are able to use a fork to pierce the beets easily. Drain and allow them to cool.
- Peel the beets, chop into 1/4-inch thick pieces, then slice in half. Put sliced beets into a bowl.
- In a small bowl, use a spoon to smash garlic with salt to make sure the mixture becomes a paste. Pour lemon juice into the garlic paste then stir. Keep about a tablespoon of lemon dressing in a small bowl. For the remaining lemon dressing, pour over the beets and stir to make sure the beets are coated with dressing.
- Distribute arugula among 4 plates, add olives, feta cheese, beets on top of each plate; pour

drizzles of the lemon dressing you set aside before and olive oil on top of the salad.

## Nutrition Information

- Calories: 432 calories;
- Sodium: 1943
- Total Carbohydrate: 30.1
- Cholesterol: 51
- Protein: 13.7
- Total Fat: 30.3

## 224. Best Greek Quinoa Salad

*Serving: 10 | Prep: 15mins | Cook: 15mins | Ready in:*

## Ingredients

- 3 1/2 cups chicken broth
- 2 cups quinoa
- 1 cup halved grape tomatoes
- 3/4 cup chopped fresh parsley
- 1/2 cup sliced pitted kalamata olives
- 1/2 cup minced red onion
- 4 ounces chopped feta cheese, or more to taste
- 3 tablespoons olive oil
- 3 tablespoons red wine vinegar
- 2 cloves garlic, minced
- 1 lemon, halved
- salt and ground black pepper to taste

## Direction

- Place quinoa and broth in a saucepan and make it boil. Minimize heat to medium low, and simmer for 15 to 20 minutes, covered, until water has been absorbed and quinoa is soft.
- Move quinoa to a large bowl and reserve to cool for about 10 minutes.
- Mix garlic, vinegar, feta cheese, olive oil, onion, Kalamata olives, parsley and tomatoes into quinoa. Then squeeze lemon juice over quinoa salad, add pepper and salt to taste; coat

by tossing. Let it chill inside the refrigerator for 1 to 4 hours.

## Nutrition Information

- Calories: 227 calories;
- Cholesterol: 12
- Protein: 7.4
- Total Fat: 10.6
- Sodium: 666
- Total Carbohydrate: 25.8

## 225. Broiled Shrimp And Veggie Salad

*Serving: 6 | Prep: 25mins | Cook: 17mins | Ready in:*

## Ingredients

- 2 pounds large shrimp, peeled and deveined
- 6 tablespoons extra-virgin olive oil
- 1/4 cup lemon juice
- 2 tablespoons Worcestershire sauce
- 4 cloves garlic, minced
- 2 teaspoons dried oregano
- 1 teaspoon kosher salt
- 1/4 teaspoon ground black pepper
- cooking spray
- 1 (15 ounce) can chickpeas, drained and rinsed
- 1 1/2 cups cherry tomatoes
- 1 English cucumber, chopped
- 1 red onion, chopped
- 8 cups chopped romaine lettuce
- 1 cup crumbled feta cheese
- 1/4 cup chopped fresh parsley

## Direction

- Put shrimp in a large plastic resealable bag. In a small bowl, whisk black pepper, salt, oregano, garlic, Worcestershire sauce, lemon juice and olive oil. Save 1/2 cup of marinade for the vegetables; pour the remaining onto the

shrimp and flip until well coated. Seal the bag and rest for 10 minutes to marinate.
- Set the oven to 450°F (230°C). Place a rack 4 inches from the oven broiler and another in the center. Line aluminium foil on a baking sheet, spray with cooking spray.
- Toss the saved 1/2 cup of marinate with onion, cucumber, tomatoes and chickpeas on the prepared baking sheet and spread in an even layer.
- Roast vegetables in the center rack for 15 to 20 minutes until beginning to brown and pucker.
- Remove the baking sheet from the oven; turn oven to broil setting. Put vegetables to the middle of the pan. Remove the shrimp from the marinade, let the excess liquid drip off, brush off the garlic and place on top of vegetables. Throw away the marinate.
- Broil shrimp on the top rack, turning once, for 1 to 2 minutes on each side until shrimp is cooked through and turn bright pink.
- Place vegetables, shrimp on top of romaine lettuce bed, drizzle with pan juice; add parsley and feta cheese on top and serve.

## Nutrition Information

- Calories: 406 calories;
- Total Carbohydrate: 21.9
- Cholesterol: 253
- Protein: 32.5
- Total Fat: 21.2
- Sodium: 1071

## 226. Chef Bevski's Greek Salad

*Serving: 8 | Prep: 30mins | Cook: | Ready in:*

## Ingredients

- 3/4 cup olive oil
- 1/4 cup red wine vinegar
- 1/4 cup chopped fresh dill
- salt and ground black pepper to taste
- 1 cucumber, peeled and diced
- 1 cup chopped broccoli
- 1 cup chopped cauliflower
- 2 plum tomatoes, diced
- 1/4 head red cabbage, shredded
- 1/4 large red onion, diced
- 1/2 red bell pepper, chopped
- 1/2 green bell pepper, chopped
- 1 (5 ounce) jar pimento-stuffed green olives, sliced
- 1 (4 ounce) package feta cheese, crumbled

## Direction

- In a bowl, whisk together black pepper, salt, dill, vinegar and oil.
- In a large bowl, mix together feta cheese, olives, green bell pepper, red bell pepper, red onion, red cabbage, plum tomatoes, cauliflower, broccoli and cucumber. Add dressing to vegetable mixture and toss until coated. Chill for a minimum of 1 hour until flavors are well marinated.

## Nutrition Information

- Calories: 268 calories;
- Total Fat: 25.4
- Sodium: 538
- Total Carbohydrate: 8.4
- Cholesterol: 13
- Protein: 3.9

## 227. Couscous Feta Salad

*Serving: 8 | Prep: 15mins | Cook: 5mins | Ready in:*

## Ingredients

- 2 cups water
- 1 1/3 cups couscous
- 1 teaspoon salt
- 1/2 teaspoon ground black pepper

- 2 tablespoons red wine vinegar
- 1 1/2 tablespoons Dijon mustard
- 1/2 cup olive oil
- 1 cucumber, seeded and chopped
- 1 (4 ounce) container crumbled feta cheese
- 6 green onions, chopped
- 1/2 cup chopped fresh parsley
- 1/4 cup toasted pine nuts

### Direction

- Boil water in a saucepan over high heat. Remove it from the heat. Mix in couscous. Cover the pan and allow it to stand for 10 minutes. Scrape the couscous into the mixing bowl. Use a fork to fluff the couscous. Refrigerate it for 1 hour until cold.
- Make the dressing once the couscous is cold by mixing the red wine vinegar, Dijon mustard, salt, and black pepper in a small bowl. Drizzle in olive oil slowly while mixing the mixture until the oil has thickened the dressing. Fold in feta cheese, pine nuts, parsley, cucumber, and green onions into the couscous. Pour the dressing all over the top and mix until evenly moistened. Before serving, let the mixture chill first for 30 minutes.

### Nutrition Information

- Calories: 304 calories;
- Total Fat: 18.9
- Sodium: 528
- Total Carbohydrate: 26.8
- Cholesterol: 13
- Protein: 7.3

### 228. Darla's Italian, Greek, And Spanish Fusion Pasta Salad

*Serving: 10 | Prep: 15mins | Cook: 15mins | Ready in:*

### Ingredients

- 4 cups radiatore pasta
- 1/2 pound applewood ham, cut into quarters
- 1 red bell pepper, chopped
- 1 large zucchini, chopped
- 1 (6 ounce) can large black olives, chopped
- 1/2 cup crumbled Cotija cheese
- 1/3 cup Greek salad dressing

### Direction

- Boil a big pot of lightly salted water. Add radiatore to the water and cook, mixing sometimes for 12-15 minutes until cooked through yet firm to chew. Strain and use cold water to rinse. Dip in cold water for 3 minutes. Strain one more time.
- In a big bowl, mix together Greek dressing, Cotija cheese, black olives, zucchini, red bell pepper, ham, and radiatore; toss to coat.

### Nutrition Information

- Calories: 237 calories;
- Sodium: 581
- Total Carbohydrate: 24
- Cholesterol: 20
- Protein: 10
- Total Fat: 11.7

### 229. Dianne's Lemon Feta Quinoa Salad

*Serving: 6 | Prep: 15mins | Cook: 15mins | Ready in:*

### Ingredients

- 2 cups water
- 1 cup quinoa
- 1/2 teaspoon sea salt
- 2/3 cup halved grape tomatoes
- 1/2 cup crumbled feta cheese
- 1/4 cup roasted unsalted sunflower seeds
- 1/4 cup chopped fresh parsley
- 1 (2.25 ounce) can sliced black olives, drained

- 1 tablespoon minced shallot
- 3 tablespoons extra-virgin olive oil
- 3 tablespoons lemon juice
- 1 teaspoon Dijon mustard
- 1 teaspoon minced garlic
- 1/4 teaspoon sea salt
- 1/4 teaspoon fresh ground black pepper

### Direction

- Boil quinoa in water and 1/2 teaspoon of sea salt in a pot. Lower the heat to medium-low. Pop the lid on. Let it simmer for 15-20 minutes, until the water has been absorbed, and the quinoa is softened. Place the quinoa on a baking tray. Let it cool for a half hour.
- Combine quinoa, feta cheese, tomatoes, parsley, sunflower seeds, shallot, and olives in a bowl.
- Stir in a bowl lemon juice, olive oil, garlic, mustard, pepper and 1/4 teaspoon sea salt. Drizzle over the quinoa mix and coat well.

### Nutrition Information

- Calories: 231 calories;
- Total Fat: 13.3
- Sodium: 479
- Total Carbohydrate: 22
- Cholesterol: 11
- Protein: 6.6

## 230. Good For You Greek Salad

*Serving: 6 | Prep: 15mins | Cook: | Ready in:*

### Ingredients

- 3 large ripe tomatoes, chopped
- 2 cucumbers, peeled and chopped
- 1 small red onion, chopped
- 1/4 cup olive oil
- 4 teaspoons lemon juice
- 1 1/2 teaspoons dried oregano
- salt and pepper to taste
- 1 cup crumbled feta cheese
- 6 black Greek olives, pitted and sliced

### Direction

- Mix cucumber, tomatoes, and onion on serving plate or in a shallow salad bowl. Drizzle with lemon juice, oil, oregano, and season with salt and pepper. Sprinkle on olives and feta cheese. Serve.

### Nutrition Information

- Calories: 187 calories;
- Sodium: 347
- Total Carbohydrate: 8.3
- Cholesterol: 22
- Protein: 5
- Total Fat: 15.6

## 231. Greek Cucumber Salad

*Serving: 4 | Prep: 20mins | Cook: | Ready in:*

### Ingredients

- 4 small roma (plum) tomatoes, chopped
- 1 cucumber, chopped
- 1 green bell pepper, chopped
- 1 small yellow onion, chopped
- 5 tablespoons malt vinegar
- 1 1/2 tablespoons white sugar
- 1 tablespoon olive oil
- 1 teaspoon ground black pepper
- 1 teaspoon salt
- 1/2 teaspoon minced garlic
- 1 (12 ounce) jar kalamata olives
- 1 (4 ounce) container crumbled feta cheese

### Direction

- In a large bowl, combine onion, green bell pepper, cucumber and tomatoes. In a small bowl, combine garlic, salt, black pepper, olive oil, sugar and vinegar; whisk well. Drizzle it over the vegetables. Stir in olives so that it is well-coated. Divide salad into 4 plates. Sprinkle feta cheese on top each serving.

## Nutrition Information

- Calories: 400 calories;
- Sodium: 2294
- Total Carbohydrate: 22.9
- Cholesterol: 25
- Protein: 6.7
- Total Fat: 32

## 232. Greek Farro Salad

*Serving: 6 | Prep: 15mins | Cook: 35mins | Ready in:*

## Ingredients

- 1 1/2 cups farro
- 4 cups chicken broth
- 1 teaspoon olive oil
- 1 teaspoon sea salt, or to taste
- 1/4 cup extra-virgin olive oil
- 3 tablespoons fresh lemon juice
- 1 tablespoon Greek seasoning
- 1 clove garlic, minced
- 1 cup seeded, diced tomato
- 1 cup seeded, diced cucumber
- 1 cup chopped red bell pepper
- 3/4 cup thinly sliced red onion
- 1 cup crumbled feta cheese
- salt and ground black pepper to taste

## Direction

- Wash farro with water, allow to drain. Transfer drained farro into a pot. Add chicken broth to at least 1 inch from farro, pour more water if desired. Add sea salt and 1 teaspoon of olive oil into the pot, stir well.
- Boil the liquid mixture; lower heat to medium; simmer without a cover until tender, stirring constantly, about 20 minutes for pearled farro and about 35 minutes for whole grain one.
- Drain off water, wash cooked farro with cold water, and put to one side to cool totally for about 15 minutes. Combine garlic, Greek seasoning, lemon juice, and 1/4 cup extra-virgin olive oil in large bowl. Add feta cheese, red onion, red pepper, cucumber, and tomato, stir well. Add farro into the tomato mixture and stir until evenly combined with dressing. Add pepper and salt to season. Chill salad for about 2 hours in the fridge, then serve.

## Nutrition Information

- Calories: 347 calories;
- Total Fat: 17.3
- Sodium: 1480
- Total Carbohydrate: 42.4
- Cholesterol: 26
- Protein: 10.3

## 233. Greek Garbanzo Bean Salad

*Serving: 8 | Prep: 10mins | Cook: | Ready in:*

## Ingredients

- 2 (15 ounce) cans garbanzo beans, drained
- 2 cucumbers, halved lengthwise and sliced
- 12 cherry tomatoes, halved
- 1/2 red onion, chopped
- 2 cloves garlic, minced
- 1 (15 ounce) can black olives, drained and chopped
- 1 ounce crumbled feta cheese
- 1/2 cup Italian-style salad dressing
- 1/2 lemon, juiced
- 1/2 teaspoon garlic salt
- 1/2 teaspoon ground black pepper

### Direction

- Mix pepper, garlic salt, lemon juice, salad dressing, cheese, olives, garlic, red onion, tomatoes, cucumbers, and beans. Mix and let chill in the fridge for about 2 hours before serving. Serve when it's chilled.

### Nutrition Information

- Calories: 214 calories;
- Sodium: 1067
- Total Carbohydrate: 25.5
- Cholesterol: 3
- Protein: 5.2
- Total Fat: 11.5

## 234. Greek Goddess Pasta Salad

*Serving: 10 | Prep: 40mins | Cook: 10mins | Ready in:*

### Ingredients

- 1 (12 ounce) package tri-colored rotini pasta
- 1 small head broccoli, broken into small florets
- 1/2 teaspoon minced garlic
- 1 small red onion, diced
- 1 (12 ounce) jar marinated artichoke hearts, drained and chopped
- 1 (12 ounce) jar pitted kalamata olives, sliced
- 1 (8 ounce) jar roasted red bell peppers, drained, cut into strips
- 4 Roma tomatoes, diced
- 1 (12 ounce) jar oil-packed sun-dried tomatoes, drained, cut into strips
- 1 small zucchini, chopped
- 1 small cucumber, chopped
- 1 small yellow bell pepper, chopped
- 2 ripe avocados
- 1 (16 ounce) bottle Greek vinaigrette salad dressing

### Direction

- Put water and a little bit of salt in a big pot placed on high heat and let it get to a rolling boil. Add in the pasta once the water has started to boil then bring it back to a boil. Let the pasta cook without cover for 10 minutes while stirring it from time to time until the pasta is cooked thoroughly but still a little bit chewy to the bite. Use a colander set to drain off the water into the sink then wash the cooked pasta in cold water and put it in a big bowl.
- Put a steamer insert on top of the saucepan filled with water up to near the bottom of the steamer. Cover the steamer and let it boil on high heat. Put in the broccoli and put the lid back on the steamer; let the broccoli cook in steam for 2-6 minutes depending on how thick it is until the broccoli is almost soft. Wash the steamed broccoli in cold water and slice it in fine pieces; put it in the cooked pasta.
- Add the kalamata olives, garlic, zucchini, yellow pepper, Roma tomatoes, red onion, sun-dried tomatoes, roasted red peppers, artichoke hearts and cucumber into the pasta mixture and mix everything well until blended.
- Slice the avocado to 2 equal pieces and discard the seed; use a big spoon to scoop out the avocado meat from the skin. Slice the halved avocados to big chunks and put it in a small bowl; use a fork to mash the avocados thoroughly. Gradually mix in the Greek dressing until the mixture is thoroughly blended. Put the prepared avocado dressing on top of the prepared pasta salad and mix everything carefully. Keep the salad in the fridge for not less than 1 hour prior to serving.

### Nutrition Information

- Calories: 478 calories;
- Sodium: 1614
- Total Carbohydrate: 39.9
- Cholesterol: 0
- Protein: 8.4
- Total Fat: 34.7

## 235. Greek Green Bean Salad With Feta And Tomatoes

*Serving: 3 | Prep: 10mins | Cook: 15mins | Ready in:*

### Ingredients

- 1 pound fresh green beans, trimmed
- 3 tomatoes, chopped
- 1/4 cup olive oil
- 2 tablespoons white balsamic vinegar
- salt and freshly ground black pepper to taste
- 1 shallot, minced
- 1/4 cup chopped fresh parsley
- 1 clove garlic, minced
- 2 ounces crumbled feta cheese

### Direction

- Bring lightly salted water to a boil in a pot; add beans and cook for 10 to 15 minutes until tender. Drain properly. Combine tomatoes and green beans in a large bowl.
- In a small bowl, stir together pepper, salt, white balsamic vinegar and olive oil. Add garlic, parsley and shallot. Add dressing to tomatoes and beans; mix well. Mix in crumbled feta cheese. Let sit for 20 minutes before serving.

### Nutrition Information

- Calories: 304 calories;
- Cholesterol: 17
- Protein: 7.4
- Total Fat: 22.6
- Sodium: 287
- Total Carbohydrate: 22.4

## 236. Greek Kale Tomato Salad

*Serving: 2 | Prep: 15mins | Cook: | Ready in:*

### Ingredients

- 1 cup stemmed, chopped kale
- 1/3 cup plain Greek yogurt
- 6 grape tomatoes, halved - or more to taste
- 1/2 cucumber, thinly sliced
- 1 tablespoon crumbled feta cheese
- 1 tablespoon sunflower seeds

### Direction

- In a salad bowl, put kale and add yogurt. To weaken the bitterness, rub yogurt and kale together by your hands for 2-3 minutes. Mix cucumber and grape tomatoes into the kale mixture and put sunflower seeds and crumbled feta cheese on top of the salad.

### Nutrition Information

- Calories: 120 calories;
- Total Fat: 7.1
- Sodium: 95
- Total Carbohydrate: 10.7
- Cholesterol: 12
- Protein: 5.6

## 237. Greek Lentil Salad

*Serving: 6 | Prep: 15mins | Cook: 1hours | Ready in:*

### Ingredients

- 2 (15 ounce) cans brown lentils
- 1 cup crumbled feta cheese
- 1/2 (16 ounce) bottle Greek, or other vinaigrette salad dressing
- 1 English cucumber, peeled and diced
- 1 beefsteak tomato, diced
- 1 large red onion, diced

### Direction

- Train lentils and place in a large bowl. Drizzle with 1/2 of the salad dressing and stir until well coated. Chill in refrigerator while processing with other vegetables. Add red onion, tomato, cucumber, and feta cheese. Cover and keep cold in refrigerator for 1 hour.
- When ready to serve, stir in remaining dressing. Can be kept, covered, in the refrigerator for up to 3 days.

### Nutrition Information

- Calories: 298 calories;
- Total Fat: 15.8
- Sodium: 1054
- Total Carbohydrate: 27.1
- Cholesterol: 22
- Protein: 12.9

## 238. Greek Pasta Salad I

*Serving: 4 | Prep: 15mins | Cook: 10mins | Ready in:*

### Ingredients

- 1/2 cup olive oil
- 1/2 cup red wine vinegar
- 1 1/2 teaspoons garlic powder
- 1 1/2 teaspoons dried basil
- 1 1/2 teaspoons dried oregano
- 3/4 teaspoon ground black pepper
- 3/4 teaspoon white sugar
- 2 1/2 cups cooked elbow macaroni
- 3 cups fresh sliced mushrooms
- 15 cherry tomatoes, halved
- 1 cup sliced red bell peppers
- 3/4 cup crumbled feta cheese
- 1/2 cup chopped green onions
- 1 (4 ounce) can whole black olives
- 3/4 cup sliced pepperoni sausage, cut into strips

### Direction

- Mix sugar, black pepper, oregano, basil, garlic powder, vinegar and olive oil in a big bowl. Put in pepperoni, olives, green onions, feta cheese, red peppers, tomatoes, mushrooms and cooked pasta. Mix till coated evenly. Keep it covered, and chilled for 2 hours or overnight.

### Nutrition Information

- Calories: 746 calories;
- Total Fat: 56.1
- Sodium: 1279
- Total Carbohydrate: 40.4
- Cholesterol: 70
- Protein: 22.1

## 239. Greek Pasta Salad II

*Serving: 6 | Prep: 5mins | Cook: 15mins | Ready in:*

### Ingredients

- 1 (16 ounce) package rotini pasta
- 1 (10 ounce) package frozen chopped spinach
- 3 tablespoons olive oil
- 3 cloves garlic, minced
- 7 ounces crumbled feta cheese
- 1 tablespoon dried dill weed
- salt and pepper to taste

### Direction

- Bring lightly salted water to a boil in a large pot. Add pasta and cook for 8-10 minutes or until al dente; drain and set aside. In the meantime, bring water to a boil in a medium saucepan over medium heat. Add spinach; cook for 5 minutes or until soft; drain and set aside.
- Warm olive oil in a large pot over medium heat; add garlic and sauté until golden; add spinach and pasta, mix well.

- Remove from heat and allow to cool for 10 minutes. Add dill and feta; mix well and serve.

## Nutrition Information

- Calories: 432 calories;
- Cholesterol: 29
- Protein: 16.6
- Total Fat: 15.8
- Sodium: 409
- Total Carbohydrate: 58.5

### 240. Greek Pasta Salad III

*Serving: 10 | Prep: 10mins | Cook: 10mins | Ready in:*

## Ingredients

- 8 ounces rotini pasta
- 1/2 cup olive oil
- 1/2 cup red wine vinegar
- 1 1/2 teaspoons garlic powder
- 1 1/2 teaspoons dried basil leaves
- 1 1/2 teaspoons dried oregano
- 3 cups sliced mushrooms
- 15 halved cherry tomatoes
- 3/4 cup crumbled feta cheese
- 1/2 cup chopped green onions
- 1 (4 ounce) can chopped black olives

## Direction

- Bring lightly salted water to a boil in a large pot. Add rotini pasta and cook for 8 to 10 minutes or until pasta is tender yet firm to the bite; drain.
- Mix together olives, green onions, Feta cheese, tomatoes, mushrooms, oregano, basil, garlic powder, vinegar, olive oil and cooked pasta. Refrigerate, covered, for a minimum of 2 hours, serve cold.

## Nutrition Information

- Calories: 189 calories;
- Sodium: 230
- Total Carbohydrate: 11.7
- Cholesterol: 10
- Protein: 3.9
- Total Fat: 14.7

### 241. Greek Pasta Salad With Roasted Vegetables And Feta

*Serving: 6 | Prep: 20mins | Cook: 40mins | Ready in:*

## Ingredients

- 1 red bell pepper, cut into 1/2 inch pieces
- 1 yellow bell pepper, chopped
- 1 medium eggplant, cubed
- 3 small yellow squash, cut in 1/4 inch slices
- 6 tablespoons extra virgin olive oil
- 1/4 teaspoon salt
- 1/4 teaspoon ground black pepper
- 1 1/2 ounces sun-dried tomatoes, soaked in 1/2 cup boiling water
- 1/2 cup torn arugula leaves
- 1/2 cup chopped fresh basil
- 2 tablespoons balsamic vinegar
- 2 tablespoons minced garlic
- 4 ounces crumbled feta cheese
- 1 (12 ounce) package farfalle pasta

## Direction

- Preheat oven to 230°C/450°F. Line foil on cookie sheet; spray using nonstick cooking spray.
- Toss 2 tbsp. olive oil, pepper, salt, squash, eggplant, and yellow and red bell pepper in medium bowl. Put on prepped cookie sheet.
- In preheated oven, bake veggies for 25 minutes till lightly browned, occasionally tossing.
- Cook pasta in big pot with salted boiling water till al dente for 10-12 minutes; drain.

- Drain softened sun-dried tomatoes; keep water. Toss basil, arugula, sun-drained tomatoes, cooked pasta and roasted veggies in big bowl. Mix feta cheese, garlic, balsamic vinegar, reserved water from tomatoes and leftover olive oil in. Toss till coated. Season to taste with pepper and salt; immediately serve or refrigerate till chilled.

## Nutrition Information

- Calories: 446 calories;
- Protein: 13.8
- Total Fat: 19.5
- Sodium: 324
- Total Carbohydrate: 56.9
- Cholesterol: 17

## 242. Greek Pasta Salad With Shrimp, Tomatoes, Zucchini, Peppers, And Feta

*Serving: 6 | Prep: 35mins | Cook: 17mins | Ready in:*

## Ingredients

- Dijon Vinaigrette
- 1/4 cup rice wine vinegar
- 2 tablespoons Dijon mustard
- 1 large clove garlic, minced
- Big pinch of salt
- Black pepper, to taste
- 2/3 cup extra-virgin olive oil
- Pasta Salad
- 2 medium zucchini, thinly sliced lengthwise
- 1 medium yellow pepper, halved lengthwise, seeded
- 2 tablespoons olive oil
- Ground black pepper and salt, to taste
- 1 gallon water
- 2 tablespoons salt
- 1 pound medium pasta shells
- 1 pound cooked shrimp, halved lengthwise
- 8 ounces cherry tomatoes, halved
- 3/4 cup coarsely chopped, pitted Kalamata olives
- 1 cup crumbled feta cheese
- 1/2 small red onion, cut into small dice
- 2 teaspoons dried oregano

## Direction

- Mix together a pinch of pepper and salt, garlic, mustard and rice wine vinegar to create the vinaigrette; slowly add in 2/3 cup of olive oil while continuing whisking. Transfer the vinaigrette into a jar with a tight-fitting lid for transporting.
- Place the oven rack to the highest position and put the broiler to high. Toss bell pepper and zucchini with 2 tablespoons of olive oil and pepper and salt to taste, transfer the vegetables onto a large baking tray with sides. Let them broil for 8-10 minutes to get brown spots on the vegetables, turning them once. Put into a large bowl to let it cool, then chop them into bite-sized pieces. Get a gallon of water with 2 tbsps. of salt up to a boil. Boil the pasta base on the package to get it tender. Drain well (do not rinse) and place onto the baking tray. Put to one side to cool.
- Add the remaining ingredients (without the dressing), pasta and vegetables into a bowl or a gallon-sized zipper bag (can sit in the fridge for several hours). When it is time to serve, toss with the dressing to coat.

## Nutrition Information

- Calories: 802 calories;
- Sodium: 3398
- Total Carbohydrate: 65.8
- Cholesterol: 185
- Protein: 33.6
- Total Fat: 45.7

## 243. Greek Quinoa

*Serving: 4 | Prep: 15mins | Cook: 15mins | Ready in:*

### Ingredients

- 2 cups water
- 1 cup quinoa, rinsed
- 1/2 cup olive oil
- 1/3 cup sliced Kalamata olives
- 1/3 cup crumbled feta cheese
- 1/3 cup halved cherry tomatoes
- 2 tablespoons shredded fresh basil leaves

### Direction

- Place quinoa and water in a sauce pan then bring to a boil. Minimize the heat to medium low, and simmer for 15 to 20 minutes, covered, until the water has been absorbed and quinoa has softened.
- Move quinoa to a large serving bowl and let it fully cool.
- Trickle olive oil over cooled quinoa and mix. Then add basil, tomatoes, feta cheese and olives by folding through the quinoa.

### Nutrition Information

- Calories: 486 calories;
- Total Fat: 37.1
- Sodium: 425
- Total Carbohydrate: 29.9
- Cholesterol: 19
- Protein: 9.3

## 244. Greek Quinoa Salad

*Serving: 6 | Prep: 20mins | Cook: 15mins | Ready in:*

### Ingredients

- Salad:
- 1/2 cup pine nuts
- 2 cups water
- 1 cup quinoa
- 2 cups chopped fresh spinach
- 1 (15 ounce) can kidney beans, rinsed and drained
- 1 cup halved grape tomatoes
- 1/2 cup halved Kalamata olives
- 1/2 cup crumbled feta cheese
- 1/4 cup minced red onion
- Dressing:
- 1/4 cup olive oil
- 3 tablespoons red wine vinegar
- 1 tablespoon lemon juice
- 1/2 teaspoon dried oregano
- salt and ground black pepper to taste

### Direction

- Place a skillet on medium-high heat; stir and cook pine nuts for about 5 minutes until toasted and aromatic.
- Place quinoa and water in a saucepan then bring to a boil. Minimize heat to medium-low, and simmer for about 15 minutes, covered, occasionally stirring, until water has been absorbed and quinoa is softened. Then separate from heat and for 5 minutes, let it stand; use fork to fluff and let cool to room temperature.
- In a bowl, combine the onion, feta cheese, olives, tomatoes, kidney beans, spinach and quinoa.
- In a bowl, mix together the pepper, salt, oregano, lemon juice, vinegar and olive oil until dressing turns smooth; drizzle over quinoa mixture and coat by tossing.

### Nutrition Information

- Calories: 385 calories;
- Protein: 13
- Total Fat: 22.5
- Sodium: 489
- Total Carbohydrate: 35.1
- Cholesterol: 11

## 245. Greek Rice Salad

*Serving: 8 | Prep: 20mins | Cook: 45mins | Ready in:*

### Ingredients

- 1 cup uncooked long grain brown rice
- 2 1/2 cups water
- 1 avocado - peeled, pitted, and diced
- 1/4 cup lemon juice
- 2 vine-ripened tomatoes, diced
- 1 1/2 cups diced English cucumbers
- 1/3 cup diced red onion
- 1/2 cup crumbled feta cheese
- 1/4 cup sliced Kalamata olives
- 1/4 cup chopped fresh mint
- 3 tablespoons olive oil
- 1 teaspoon lemon zest
- 1/2 teaspoon minced garlic
- 1/2 teaspoon kosher salt
- 1/2 teaspoon ground black pepper

### Direction

- On high heat, boil water and brown rice in a saucepan. Lower the heat to medium-low, cover up, and let it simmer until the rice is soft and the liquid has been absorbed for 45 - 50 minutes; take off heat and allow to cool off, use a fork to fluff once in a while.
- In a big bowl, mix the lemon juice and avocado. Put the pepper, salt, garlic, lemon zest, olive oil, mint, olives, feta, onion, cucumber and tomatoes to the bowl; mixing gently till combined evenly. Fold the cooled rice lightly into the mixture. Serve instantly or keep chilled for the maximum of 1 hour; the salad cannot last well for more than a day as the cucumber and tomatoes start to release their juices and the salad becomes watery.

### Nutrition Information

- Calories: 224 calories;
- Protein: 4.5
- Total Fat: 12.7
- Sodium: 304
- Total Carbohydrate: 24.6
- Cholesterol: 8

## 246. Greek Salad I

*Serving: 6 | Prep: 20mins | Cook: | Ready in:*

### Ingredients

- 1 head romaine lettuce- rinsed, dried and chopped
- 1 red onion, thinly sliced
- 1 (6 ounce) can pitted black olives
- 1 green bell pepper, chopped
- 1 red bell pepper, chopped
- 2 large tomatoes, chopped
- 1 cucumber, sliced
- 1 cup crumbled feta cheese
- 6 tablespoons olive oil
- 1 teaspoon dried oregano
- 1 lemon, juiced
- ground black pepper to taste

### Direction

- Mix cheese, cucumber, tomatoes, bell peppers, olives, onion, and Romaine together in a big salad bowl.
- Mix together black pepper, lemon juice, oregano, and olive oil. Put the dressing on the salad, toss and enjoy.

### Nutrition Information

- Calories: 265 calories;
- Cholesterol: 22
- Protein: 6
- Total Fat: 22.4
- Sodium: 538
- Total Carbohydrate: 14.1

## 247. Greek Salad II

*Serving: 5 | Prep: 20mins | Cook: 20mins |Ready in:*

### Ingredients

- 1 head romaine lettuce- rinsed, dried and chopped
- 4 stalks celery, chopped
- 1 onion, chopped
- 1 (15 ounce) can baby peas
- 2 ripe tomatoes, cut into wedges
- 6 ounces crumbled feta cheese
- 1 1/2 cups mayonnaise
- 1/2 cup vinaigrette salad dressing
- 6 ounces marinated chicken

### Direction

- Start preheating the grill to medium-high heat.
- Take the chicken out from the marinade and strain. Put on the hot grill and cook until juices run clear, or for about 6-8 minutes each side.
- Mix tomatoes, peas, onion, celery, and Romaine together in a big bowl, toss with sufficient vinaigrette to coat.
- Put mayonnaise and crumbled feta in a food processor. Process until smooth.
- On a dinner dish, put the tossed salad; put grilled beef or chicken and the feta mixture on top.

### Nutrition Information

- Calories: 755 calories;
- Cholesterol: 78
- Protein: 16.7
- Total Fat: 68.2
- Sodium: 1181
- Total Carbohydrate: 21.9

## 248. Greek Salad III

*Serving: 4 | Prep: 20mins | Cook: |Ready in:*

### Ingredients

- 3 roma (plum) tomatoes, chopped
- 1 green bell pepper, sliced
- 1 small English cucumber, chopped
- 1 small onion, chopped
- 1/4 cup sliced black olives (optional)
- 2 ounces tomato basil feta cheese, crumbled
- 1/4 cup olive oil
- 1 teaspoon red wine vinegar
- 1 teaspoon lemon juice
- 1 clove garlic, minced
- 1/2 teaspoon dried oregano
- salt and pepper to taste

### Direction

- Combine olives, onion, cucumber, bell pepper, and tomatoes in a salad bowl. Mix pepper, salt, oregano, garlic, lemon juice, vinegar, and oil together. Set aside for 1 hour, stirring sometimes to allow flavors to combine with one another.
- Drizzle dressing over salad, sprinkle feta cheese and mix well. Enjoy!

### Nutrition Information

- Calories: 197 calories;
- Protein: 3.3
- Total Fat: 17.7
- Sodium: 241
- Total Carbohydrate: 8
- Cholesterol: 13

## 249. Greek Salad IV

*Serving: 6 | Prep: 10mins | Cook: |Ready in:*

### Ingredients

- 4 large tomatoes, chopped
- 1 green bell pepper, chopped
- 1 cucumber, peeled and chopped
- 1 red onion, chopped
- 3 ounces crumbled feta cheese
- 1/4 cup olive oil
- 1/8 cup lemon juice

## Direction

- Mix lemon juice, olive oil, red onion, cucumber, green bell pepper, and tomatoes together in a big bowl. Chill thoroughly in the fridge. Use feta cheese to drizzle before eating.

## Nutrition Information

- Calories: 155 calories;
- Sodium: 166
- Total Carbohydrate: 9.2
- Cholesterol: 13
- Protein: 3.7
- Total Fat: 12.4

## 250. Greek Salad V

Serving: 5 | Prep: 5mins | Cook: | Ready in:

## Ingredients

- 1 English cucumber, diced
- 2 large tomatoes, each cut into 8 wedges
- 1/2 cup thinly sliced red onion
- 1/2 cup thinly sliced green bell pepper
- 1/2 cup whole, pitted kalamata olives
- 1 cup crumbled feta cheese
- 2 tablespoons dried oregano
- 2 teaspoons fresh lemon juice
- 2 tablespoons olive oil
- salt and pepper to taste

## Direction

- Layer cucumbers, tomatoes, onion, bell pepper, kalamata olives and feta cheese in a medium bowl. Add oregano on top, then drizzle with olive oil and lemon juice. Add salt and pepper to season to taste.

## Nutrition Information

- Calories: 197 calories;
- Total Fat: 15.7
- Sodium: 677
- Total Carbohydrate: 9.7
- Cholesterol: 27
- Protein: 5.8

## 251. Greek Salad, The Best!

Serving: 8 | Prep: 30mins | Cook: | Ready in:

## Ingredients

- 1 cup olive oil
- 3 tablespoons red wine vinegar
- 3 tablespoons grated Parmesan cheese
- 2 tablespoons lemon juice
- 2 tablespoons finely chopped garlic
- 2 tablespoons dried oregano, or to taste
- 1 1/2 teaspoons dried basil
- 1 teaspoon salt, or to taste
- freshly ground black pepper to taste
- 2 heads romaine lettuce, chopped
- 2 large tomatoes, cut into wedges
- 1 large cucumber, cut into matchsticks
- 1 red onion, sliced
- 1 cup black olives
- 1/2 pound feta cheese, crumbled

## Direction

- In a food processor, combine black pepper, salt, basil, oregano, garlic, lemon juice, Parmesan cheese, vinegar, and olive oil together, process until smooth.
- In a large bowl, mix feta cheese, black olives, red onion, cucumber, tomatoes, and romaine

lettuce together. Pour dressing over vegetable mixture; stir until evenly coated.

## Nutrition Information

- Calories: 385 calories;
- Protein: 7
- Total Fat: 36
- Sodium: 800
- Total Carbohydrate: 11.8
- Cholesterol: 27

## 252. Greek Veggie Salad

*Serving: 8 | Prep: 15mins | Cook: | Ready in:*

## Ingredients

- 1 head cauliflower, chopped
- 1 head broccoli, chopped
- 2 cups cherry tomatoes
- 1 (6 ounce) can small pitted black olives, drained
- 1 (6 ounce) package tomato basil feta cheese, crumbled
- 1 (16 ounce) bottle zesty Italian dressing

## Direction

- Combine cheese, olives, cherry tomatoes, broccoli and cauliflower in a large bowl. Add just the right amount of dressing to coat, toss well and chill overnight.

## Nutrition Information

- Calories: 315 calories;
- Total Fat: 27.2
- Sodium: 1370
- Total Carbohydrate: 13.4
- Cholesterol: 19
- Protein: 6.1

## 253. Greek Veggie Salad II

*Serving: 8 | Prep: 20mins | Cook: | Ready in:*

## Ingredients

- 1 large cucumber, chopped
- 2 roma (plum) tomatoes, chopped
- 1 (5 ounce) jar pitted kalamata olives
- 1 (4 ounce) package feta cheese, crumbled
- 1 red onion, halved and thinly sliced
- 1/2 (10 ounce) package baby greens
- 1/2 (10 ounce) package romaine lettuce leaves
- 6 tablespoons olive oil
- 1 teaspoon garlic powder
- 1 teaspoon dried oregano
- 1 teaspoon dried basil
- 1 teaspoon Dijon mustard
- 1 teaspoon lemon juice
- 1 1/2 cups red wine vinegar

## Direction

- Combine romaine, baby greens, red onion, feta cheese, olives, tomatoes, and cucumber in a big bowl. Combine red wine vinegar, lemon juice, mustard, basil, oregano, garlic powder, and olive oil together in another bowl. Put the dressing on the vegetables and coat by tossing.

## Nutrition Information

- Calories: 211 calories;
- Total Fat: 17.9
- Sodium: 467
- Total Carbohydrate: 10.3
- Cholesterol: 13
- Protein: 3.4

## 254. Greek Inspired Chicken Salad

*Serving: 4 | Prep: 30mins | Cook: |Ready in:*

### Ingredients

- 1 cup diced English cucumbers
- 1 1/4 teaspoons salt, divided
- 2 tablespoons diced red onion
- 1 cup Greek yogurt
- 1/3 cup chopped Kalamata olives
- 1 1/2 tablespoons chopped fresh dill
- 2 teaspoons red wine vinegar
- 2 teaspoons lemon juice
- 1 teaspoon garlic, minced
- 1 teaspoon lemon zest
- 1/2 teaspoon dried oregano
- 1/4 teaspoon ground black pepper
- 3 cups diced cooked chicken
- 3/4 cup crumbled feta cheese
- 1/2 cup diced seeded plum tomatoes
- 1 head Bibb lettuce, or more as needed

### Direction

- In a strainer, put cucumbers; place on a plate. Toss the cucumbers with 1 teaspoon of salt. Let it sit for 30 minutes to draw about any water. Use paper towels to tap dry.
- In a bowl, add 1 cup of cold water and red onion. Let soak for 5-10 minutes to lower the pungency of the onion. Strain and rinse.
- In a bowl, mix together black pepper, oregano, lemon zest, garlic, lemon juice, vinegar, dill, Kalamata olives, Greek yogurt, red onions, and cucumbers. Tuck in tomatoes, feta cheese, and chicken. Use plastic wrap to cover and chill the salad for a minimum of 1 hour.
- Mix the salad and enjoy on lettuce leaves.

### Nutrition Information

- Calories: 385 calories;
- Sodium: 1327
- Total Carbohydrate: 8.7
- Cholesterol: 115
- Protein: 37.1
- Total Fat: 22

## 255. Greek Style Shrimp Salad On A Bed Of Baby Spinach

*Serving: 4 | Prep: | Cook: | Ready in:*

### Ingredients

- 1 pound raw shrimp (26 to 30 count), peeled
- Olive oil to taste
- Salt and pepper to taste
- Sugar to taste
- 2 medium tomatoes, cut into medium dice
- 1/2 cup crumbled feta cheese
- 1/2 cup pitted and coarsely chopped Kalamata or other black olives
- 1 teaspoon dried oregano
- 1/4 cup olive oil
- 4 teaspoons red wine vinegar
- 1 (10 ounce) package factory-washed baby spinach leaves

### Direction

- Thread shrimp onto metal skewers (or bamboo skewers that have been soaked for 15 minutes in water). Glaze both side with oil and sprinkle with a little sugar, pepper and salt to season.
- Fully preheat the gas grill by setting all burners on high for 10 to 15 minutes. Clean grill rack with a wire brush, then lightly glaze the rack with oil. Close the lid and let it return to temperature. Grill shrimp for about 2 minutes each side until spotty brown and completely cooked.
- In the meantime, mix together 2 teaspoons of the vinegar, 2 tablespoons of olive oil, oregano, olives, cheese, and tomatoes in a medium bowl. Remove the shrimp from the skewer and add to bowl. Toss lightly until well coated. Set aside (can be made 1 hour or so in advance)

- When serving, drizzle remaining oil and a generous amount of salt and pepper over spinach in a large bowl. Toss until well coated. Add the remaining 2 teaspoons of vinegar; toss again. Distribute spinach into 4 large plates. Add a portion of shrimp mixture on top of each plate.

## Nutrition Information

- Calories: 423 calories;
- Sodium: 853
- Total Carbohydrate: 12.6
- Cholesterol: 201
- Protein: 30.4
- Total Fat: 28.2

## 256. Greek Style Tuna Salad

*Serving: 1 | Prep: 5mins | Cook: | Ready in:*

## Ingredients

- 1 (5 ounce) can chunk light tuna in water, drained
- 1 tablespoon chopped red onion
- 2 teaspoons prepared Greek vinaigrette salad dressing (such as Kraft®)
- 3 pitted Kalamata olives, chopped
- 1 tablespoon crumbled feta cheese

## Direction

- In a bowl, combine feta cheese, olives, salad dressing, onion and tuna.

## Nutrition Information

- Calories: 240 calories;
- Total Carbohydrate: 2.7
- Cholesterol: 46
- Protein: 33.7
- Total Fat: 9.7
- Sodium: 429

## 257. Greek Alicious Pasta Salad

*Serving: 10 | Prep: 18mins | Cook: 12mins | Ready in:*

## Ingredients

- 2 1/2 cups bow tie (farfalle) pasta
- 1 cup Greek salad dressing
- 2 1/2 tablespoons mayonnaise
- 4 radishes, finely chopped
- 1/2 cucumber, peeled and chopped
- 1 (15 ounce) can garbanzo beans, drained
- 3/4 cup crumbled feta cheese

## Direction

- Fill a big pot with lightly briny water then set over high heat until it comes to a rolling boil. Stir bow tie pasta in the boiling water then bring back to a boil. Cook the pasta without a cover, stirring now and again, for 12 minutes until the pasta is cooked through but still firm to the bite. Use a colander set in the sink to drain the pasta completely.
- In a big salad bowl, whisk together mayonnaise and the Greek dressing until well combined and smooth. Add the cooked pasta, lightly tossing to coat with the dressing. Sprinkle with crumbled feta cheese, garbanzo beans, cucumber, and radishes, carefully fold it all in.
- Cover and refrigerate the salad until able to serve.

## Nutrition Information

- Calories: 207 calories;
- Sodium: 414
- Total Carbohydrate: 15.5
- Cholesterol: 11
- Protein: 4.5
- Total Fat: 14.5

## 258. Heirloom Tomato Salad With Pearl Couscous

*Serving: 10 | Prep: 35mins | Cook: 25mins | Ready in:*

### Ingredients

- 2 cups vegetable stock
- 1 tablespoon extra-virgin olive oil
- 1 cup pearl (Israeli) couscous
- 1/2 cup packed fresh basil leaves
- 1/4 cup flat-leaf parsley leaves
- 1 clove garlic, crushed
- 1 tablespoon chopped fresh oregano
- 1 tablespoon chopped fresh thyme
- 1/2 cup pitted green olives
- 4 heirloom tomatoes, quartered
- 15 cherry tomatoes, quartered
- 1 English cucumber, cubed
- 1/2 small red onion, thinly sliced
- 1 cup crumbled feta cheese
- 1/4 cup white balsamic vinegar
- 1/2 cup extra-virgin olive oil
- 1 lemon, juiced

### Direction

- Simmer the vegetable stock in a saucepan over medium heat. In a skillet, heat 1 tbsp. of olive oil over medium heat. Mix in couscous. Cook and stir the couscous for 10 minutes until golden brown. Pour the toasted couscous into the hot vegetable stock. Simmer the mixture. Cover the pan and cook for 15 minutes until the couscous absorbs all the stock. Scrape the mixture into the mixing bowl. Fluff it using the fork. Let it cool to room temperature.
- In a food processor, pulse the combination of olives, parsley, basil, thyme, oregano, and garlic until they are all coarsely chopped. Mix the herb mixture into the couscous together with the cherry tomatoes, red onion, feta cheese, heirloom tomatoes, and cucumber. Drizzle mixture with 1/2 cup of olive oil, lemon juice, and vinegar. Mix the mixture well until evenly blended.

### Nutrition Information

- Calories: 249 calories;
- Total Carbohydrate: 19.9
- Cholesterol: 13
- Protein: 5.5
- Total Fat: 17.2
- Sodium: 400

## 259. Hot Greek Salad

*Serving: 4 | Prep: 15mins | Cook: 25mins | Ready in:*

### Ingredients

- 1 cup orzo pasta
- 1 1/2 tablespoons olive oil
- 2 skinless, boneless chicken breast halves, cubed
- 4 cloves garlic, crushed
- 1 tablespoon Greek seasoning, or to taste
- 2 cups fresh spinach
- 1 cucumber, cubed
- 1 tomato, cubed
- 1 (15 ounce) can large black olives, drained
- 2 tablespoons sun-dried tomato vinaigrette
- 1/4 cup crumbled feta cheese

### Direction

- Boil a big pot of lightly salted water; add orzo. Cook for about 10mins while mixing from time to time, until the orzo is completely cooked but still firm to chew; drain. Keep the orzo warm.
- On medium heat, heat olive oil in a big pan; add Greek seasoning, garlic and chicken. Cook and stir for about 10mins, until the juices run clear and the chicken is not pink in the middle. Add vinaigrette, olives, tomato, cucumber and spinach. Turn to low heat and let it simmer for

5-10mins, until the spinach starts to wilt. Place it atop the orzo, then put feta cheese on top. Serve.

## Nutrition Information

- Calories: 502 calories;
- Total Carbohydrate: 53.2
- Cholesterol: 46
- Protein: 23.5
- Total Fat: 22.4
- Sodium: 1606

### 260. Jen's Greek Couscous Salad

*Serving: 8 | Prep: 20mins | Cook: 15mins | Ready in:*

## Ingredients

- 2 1/2 cups water
- 2 cups Israeli couscous
- 1 red bell pepper, cut into 1/4-by-2-inch strips
- 1 yellow bell pepper, cut into 1/4-by-2-inch strips
- 1/2 cup olive oil
- lemon, juiced
- salt and ground black pepper to taste
- 1 cup cherry tomatoes, halved
- 1 cup kalamata olives, pitted and halved
- 1/2 cup crumbled feta cheese

## Direction

- Bring the water to a boil in a saucepan. Place the couscous into the water and bring it back to a boil. Cover the pan with its lid. Adjust the heat to low and cook the couscous for 10 minutes until it is tender and the water is absorbed completely. Place the couscous into the bowl.
- Place the skillet over medium heat. Place the yellow bell pepper and red bell pepper strips into the hot skillet and cook them for 5 minutes until slightly charred and softened. Add them into the couscous; stir.
- In a bowl, mix the lemon juice and olive oil. Season the mixture with salt and pepper. Drizzle couscous mixture with the oil mixture, stirring well to coat. Stir in feta cheese, olives, and tomatoes.

## Nutrition Information

- Calories: 365 calories;
- Total Fat: 21.7
- Sodium: 460
- Total Carbohydrate: 35.5
- Cholesterol: 14
- Protein: 7.9

### 261. Light And Easy Greek Potato Salad

*Serving: 8 | Prep: 30mins | Cook: 25mins | Ready in:*

## Ingredients

- 12 red potatoes
- 1/4 cup chopped green onion
- 1/4 cup olive oil
- 1/4 cup red wine vinegar
- 1 1/2 teaspoons fresh lemon juice
- 1/2 teaspoon garlic powder
- 1/2 teaspoon onion powder
- 1/2 teaspoon coarse salt, or to taste
- 1/2 teaspoon ground black pepper, or to taste
- 1/4 teaspoon dried oregano
- 1/4 teaspoon white sugar
- 1/4 teaspoon dried rosemary, crumbled
- 1 pinch ground red pepper

## Direction

- Cover red potatoes with salted water in a large pot then boil. Lower heat to medium-low then simmer for 25 minutes till tender. Let drain

then store in the freezer for 30 minutes to chill till cold.
- In a large salad bowl, slice potatoes and toss with green onion. In a bowl, whisk together red pepper, rosemary, sugar, oregano, black pepper, salt, onion powder, garlic powder, lemon juice, red wine vinegar and olive oil. Spread over the potatoes with the dressing and toss. Chill till serving time or immediately serve.

## Nutrition Information

- Calories: 105 calories;
- Sodium: 150
- Total Carbohydrate: 10.4
- Cholesterol: 0
- Protein: 1.2
- Total Fat: 6.9

### 262. Mediterranean Greek Salad

*Serving: 8 | Prep: 10mins | Cook: | Ready in:*

## Ingredients

- 3 cucumbers, seeded and sliced
- 1 1/2 cups crumbled feta cheese
- 1 cup black olives, pitted and sliced
- 3 cups diced roma tomatoes
- 1/3 cup diced oil packed sun-dried tomatoes, drained, oil reserved
- 1/2 red onion, sliced

## Direction

- Combine red onion, 2 tablespoons reserved sun-dried tomato oil, sun-dried tomatoes, roma tomatoes, olives, feta cheese, and cucumber in a large salad bowl. Refrigerate until chilled before serving.

## Nutrition Information

- Calories: 131 calories;
- Total Fat: 8.8
- Sodium: 486
- Total Carbohydrate: 9.3
- Cholesterol: 25
- Protein: 5.5

### 263. Mediterranean Potato Salad

*Serving: 16 | Prep: 15mins | Cook: 45mins | Ready in:*

## Ingredients

- 2 pounds potatoes
- 1 green bell pepper, minced
- 1 cucumber, sliced and quartered
- 1/2 cup sliced red onion
- 8 ounces crumbled feta cheese
- 1 lemon, juiced
- 1/2 cup Italian-style salad dressing
- salt and pepper to taste
- 3 pita breads, cut into wedges

## Direction

- Boil salted water in a large pot. Add and cook potatoes for 15 minutes till tender but firm. Drain, let the potatoes cool then chop.
- Combine cheese, red onion, cucumbers, green peppers and potatoes in a large bowl.
- Whisk together pepper, salt, salad dressing and lemon juice. Spread over the salad and toss till coated. Serve along with pita bread wedges if preferred.

## Nutrition Information

- Calories: 139 calories;
- Cholesterol: 13
- Protein: 4.5
- Total Fat: 5.3

- Sodium: 344
- Total Carbohydrate: 19.2

## 264. Melitzanosalata Agioritiki (Athenian Eggplant Salad)

*Serving: 8 | Prep: 20mins | Cook: 15mins | Ready in:*

### Ingredients

- 1 large eggplant, washed
- 1 tomato, seeded and chopped
- 1 small onion, diced
- 2 tablespoons chopped fresh parsley
- 2 tablespoons extra-virgin olive oil
- 2 tablespoons distilled white vinegar
- 1/2 cup crumbled feta cheese
- salt to taste

### Direction

- Set an outdoor grill to medium-high heat.
- Use a fork or paring knife to stab the eggplant for a few times. Place eggplant onto the preheated grill, turning frequently and cook for about 15 minutes until the eggplant is soft and the skin is lightly burned. Allow to cool until handleable.
- Peel off the eggplant skin and cube the pulp. Transfer the eggplant cubes into a mixing bowl, add feta cheese, vinegar, olive oil, parsley, onion, and tomato, mix gently. Chill for 1 hour. Add salt to season, and enjoy.

### Nutrition Information

- Calories: 99 calories;
- Total Carbohydrate: 7
- Cholesterol: 14
- Protein: 3.4
- Total Fat: 6.9
- Sodium: 179

## 265. Oia Greek Salad

*Serving: 4 | Prep: 30mins | Cook: | Ready in:*

### Ingredients

- 1 English cucumber, diced
- 2 pints grape tomatoes, halved
- 1 (4 ounce) container crumbled feta cheese
- 1 (4 ounce) jar capers, drained
- 1/2 cup diced red onion
- 1/4 cup Greek salad dressing, such as Yazzo!
- 1/2 cup Greek olives, drained

### Direction

- To keep the onion from overpowering the salad, separate all the ingredients until ready to use. To prepare, combine the salad dressing, cucumber, onion, tomatoes, capers, and feta cheese in a big bowl until coated; add Greek olives. Serve.

### Nutrition Information

- Calories: 229 calories;
- Protein: 6.9
- Total Fat: 16.8
- Sodium: 1563
- Total Carbohydrate: 16
- Cholesterol: 25

## 266. Orzo With Feta, Cucumber And Tomato

*Serving: 10 | Prep: 25mins | Cook: 10mins | Ready in:*

### Ingredients

- 1 1/4 cups orzo pasta
- 1 cup chicken broth
- 1 cup water

- 1 red bell pepper, seeded and chopped - divided
- 2 tablespoons olive oil
- 2 cucumbers, peeled and chopped
- 2 cups crumbled feta cheese
- 2 roma (plum) tomatoes, seeded and chopped
- 1 red onion, very thinly sliced and cut into 1-inch pieces
- 1 cup pitted Kalamata olives, coarsely chopped
- 3 tablespoons fresh lemon juice
- 1 tablespoon white wine vinegar
- 1 teaspoon ground cumin
- 2 tablespoons olive oil
- salt and ground black pepper to taste

### Direction

- In a pot, put 1/2 of the chopped red bell pepper, water, chicken broth and orzo pasta; boil. Lower the heat to low and let it simmer for about 10 minutes, until the liquid is absorbed, and the orzo is tender; drain, then rinse. Let it cool.
- In a big salad bowl with 2 tbsp. olive oil and the remaining red bell pepper, put the orzo, then toss until coated. Stir in cumin, white wine vinegar, lemon juice, Kalamata olives, red onion, roma tomatoes, feta cheese and cucumbers, then toss the salad well. Trickle another 2 tbsp. of olive oil over the salad. Place in the refrigerator for an hour, toss 1-2 times. Sprinkle black pepper and salt to taste prior to serving.

### Nutrition Information

- Calories: 273 calories;
- Total Carbohydrate: 24.8
- Cholesterol: 27
- Protein: 8.5
- Total Fat: 15.9
- Sodium: 560

## 267. Party Size Greek Couscous Salad

*Serving: 20 | Prep: 30mins | Cook: 15mins | Ready in:*

### Ingredients

- 3 (6 ounce) packages garlic and herb couscous mix (or any flavor you prefer)
- 1 pint cherry tomatoes, cut in half
- 1 (5 ounce) jar pitted kalamata olives, halved
- 1 cup mixed bell peppers (green, red, yellow, orange), diced
- 1 cucumber, sliced and then halved
- 1/2 cup parsley, finely chopped
- 1 (8 ounce) package crumbled feta cheese
- 1/2 cup Greek vinaigrette salad dressing

### Direction

- Follow the package directions on how to prepare the couscous. Let it cool in a large serving bowl. Break up the couscous's clusters.
- Once the couscous reached room temperature, stir in olives, cucumber, feta, bell peppers, tomatoes, and parsley. Stir in vinaigrette gradually until the desired moistness is reached.

### Nutrition Information

- Calories: 159 calories;
- Protein: 5.7
- Total Fat: 6.5
- Sodium: 642
- Total Carbohydrate: 21.4
- Cholesterol: 10

## 268. Quick Greek Pasta Salad With Steak

*Serving: 4 | Prep: 15mins | Cook: 20mins | Ready in:*

### Ingredients

- 8 ounces whole wheat penne pasta
- 2 tablespoons extra virgin olive oil
- 1 tablespoon butter
- 1 (1 pound) beef rib eye steak
- 1 tablespoon butter
- 1 teaspoon minced garlic
- 1/4 cup chopped shallots
- 1 tablespoon soy sauce
- 1/2 cup sun-dried tomato pesto
- 1/2 cup sliced black olives
- 1 cup chopped fresh spinach
- 1 teaspoon basil
- 1 tablespoon chopped parsley
- 1/2 cup crumbled feta cheese
- 3 tablespoons sunflower kernels

### Direction

- Bring lightly salted water in a large pot to a boil. Cook pasta in boiling water until al dente, or for 8 - 10 minutes. Once cooked, drain off water, then stir well with olive oil; keep the pasta warm.
- Meanwhile, in a skillet, melt 1 tablespoon butter over medium-high heat. Add the rib-eye and sear both sides for 7 to 10 minutes (basing on thickness) until the center is rosy-pink. Take the steak out of the skillet, and divide into biteable cuts. In the skillet, melt the remaining 1 tablespoon of butter and stir-fry shallots and garlic with melted butter. Cook until aromatic, 5 - 10 seconds; bring the steak back to the pan and cook for another 5 minutes or until reach desired level of doneness. Add soy sauce, and keep cooking for a few seconds longer in order to vaporize.
- Turn off the heat and stir in sunflower kernels, feta cheese, parsley, basil, spinach, olives, and sun-dried tomato pesto. Pour over the pasta in a big bowl and toss to coat. Serve right away.

### Nutrition Information

- Calories: 579 calories;
- Total Fat: 35
- Sodium: 710
- Total Carbohydrate: 44.7
- Cholesterol: 73
- Protein: 24.5

## 269. Quinoa Crab Salad

*Serving: 10 | Prep: 15mins | Cook: 15mins | Ready in:*

### Ingredients

- 1 1/3 cups water
- 2/3 cup quinoa
- 1 pound finely chopped cooked crabmeat
- 1 cup diced cucumber
- 1 cup sliced grape tomatoes
- 1 cup fat-free feta cheese, crumbled
- 1/2 cup Greek salad dressing
- 2 tablespoons lemon juice
- 2 tablespoons balsamic vinegar, or more to taste

### Direction

- Place together in a saucepan the quinoa and water then bring to a boil. Minimize the heat to medium-low, simmer for 15 to 20 minutes, covered, until water has been absorbed and quinoa is softened. Let quinoa cool fully.
- In a large bowl, combine together the feta cheese, tomatoes, cucumber and crabmeat; mix in quinoa. In a separate bowl, combine together the balsamic vinegar, lemon juice, and Greek salad dressing; drizzle over the quinoa mixture then mix to coat.

### Nutrition Information

- Calories: 185 calories;
- Total Fat: 8.4
- Sodium: 597
- Total Carbohydrate: 11
- Cholesterol: 43
- Protein: 17.3

## 270. Quinoa Greek Inspired Salad

*Serving: 4 | Prep: 10mins | Cook: 15mins | Ready in:*

### Ingredients

- 1 cup chicken broth
- 1/2 cup quinoa
- 2 tablespoons pesto
- 1 roma tomatoes, diced
- 2 ounces crumbled feta cheese
- 4 slices cooked bacon, crumbled (optional)

### Direction

- Place quinoa and broth in a saucepan then bring to a boil. Minimize heat to medium-low, and simmer for 15 to 20 minutes, covered, until broth has been absorbed and quinoa has softened.
- Mix bacon, feta cheese, tomatoes and pesto into the quinoa.

### Nutrition Information

- Calories: 210 calories;
- Protein: 10.1
- Total Fat: 11.8
- Sodium: 667
- Total Carbohydrate: 15.7
- Cholesterol: 26

## 271. Quinoa With Feta, Walnuts, And Dried Cranberries

*Serving: 6 | Prep: 15mins | Cook: 15mins | Ready in:*

### Ingredients

- 2 cups low-sodium chicken broth
- 1 cup quinoa
- 1/2 cup chopped walnuts
- 1/2 cup dried cranberries
- 1/3 cup crumbled feta cheese

### Direction

- Boil chicken broth and quinoa in a pot. Lower heat to low. Put the lid on. Let it simmer for 15-20 minutes, until broth has been absorbed and quinoa is tender. Place in a bowl.
- Add cranberries and walnuts. Add feta cheese. Mix gently.

### Nutrition Information

- Calories: 243 calories;
- Total Carbohydrate: 28.6
- Cholesterol: 14
- Protein: 8.6
- Total Fat: 11.4
- Sodium: 195

## 272. Salad Taverna

*Serving: 6 | Prep: 15mins | Cook: 8mins | Ready in:*

### Ingredients

- 8 ounces dry spinach noodles
- 1/3 cup olive oil
- 3 tablespoons lemon juice
- 1 clove garlic, minced
- 1/2 teaspoon green hot pepper sauce
- 1/2 teaspoon anise seed
- 1/2 teaspoon salt
- 1 cup ricotta cheese
- 2 tomatoes, coarsely chopped
- 1/2 cup sliced black olives

### Direction

- Boil a big pot of lightly salted water. Add pasta and cook until al dente, or for about 8-10 minutes. Strain.
- Combine salt, anise seed, hot pepper sauce, garlic, lemon juice, and olive oil in a big bowl.

Stir in olives, tomatoes, ricotta cheese, and cooked pasta. Put a cover on and refrigerate.

## Nutrition Information

- Calories: 273 calories;
- Total Fat: 15.1
- Sodium: 337
- Total Carbohydrate: 29.5
- Cholesterol: 35
- Protein: 6

## 273. Sandy's Greek Pasta Salad

*Serving: 8 | Prep: 30mins | Cook: 10mins | Ready in:*

### Ingredients

- 1 (15.5 ounce) can garbanzo beans, drained
- 1 (10 ounce) container grape tomatoes, halved
- 1 cucumber, peeled and diced
- 1 (4 ounce) can sliced black olives, drained
- 1/4 red onion, finely diced
- 1/4 cup extra-virgin olive oil
- 2 cloves garlic, diced
- 1 tablespoon balsamic vinegar
- 1 tablespoon fresh lemon juice
- 1 tablespoon chopped fresh basil
- salt and ground black pepper to taste
- 1 (12 ounce) package tricolored (rainbow) rotini pasta
- 1/2 cup crumbled feta cheese

### Direction

- In a large salad bowl, combine black pepper, salt, basil, lemon juice, balsamic vinegar, garlic, olive oil, red onion, black olives, cucumber, grape tomatoes, and garbanzo beans.
- In a large pot, bring lightly salted water to a boil; cook rotini for about 10 minutes until tender but still firm to the bite; drain the pasta.

Pour rotini pasta into the salad and fold gently, refrigerate to allow flavors blend for 15 - 20 minutes. Sprinkle feta cheese and mix well with the salad.

## Nutrition Information

- Calories: 337 calories;
- Total Fat: 12.3
- Sodium: 398
- Total Carbohydrate: 48.2
- Cholesterol: 8
- Protein: 10.4

## 274. Stacy's Greek Inspired Tuna Salad

*Serving: 2 | Prep: 20mins | Cook: | Ready in:*

### Ingredients

- 2 (5 ounce) cans solid white albacore tuna in water, drained
- 1/2 cup diced English cucumber
- 1/2 cup seedless red grapes, halved
- 1/4 cup tzatziki sauce, or more to taste
- 1/4 cup slivered or sliced almonds, toasted
- 1/4 cup feta cheese crumbles
- 1 tablespoon finely chopped fresh dill
- salt and ground black pepper to taste
- 1 tablespoon lemon juice
- 2 cups spring mix greens, or as desired
- 1 (6 ounce) package pita chips (optional)

### Direction

- In a medium-sized bowl, add tuna. Put in pepper, salt, dill, feta cheese, almonds, tzatziki sauce, grapes and cucumber. Stir them well. Pour in lemon juice and stir again.
- Serve over a bed of greens and alongside with pita chips.

### Nutrition Information

- Calories: 740 calories;
- Total Fat: 51
- Sodium: 957
- Total Carbohydrate: 63.3
- Cholesterol: 66
- Protein: 50.5

## 275. Standard Greek Salad

*Serving: 12 | Prep: 20mins | Cook: |Ready in:*

### Ingredients

- 5 cucumbers, sliced
- 5 large tomatoes, coarsely chopped
- 1/2 red onion, chopped
- 1 (4 ounce) package feta cheese, crumbled
- 1 (2.25 ounce) can pitted green olives, chopped
- 1/4 cup red wine vinegar

### Direction

- Combine green olives, feta cheese, red onion, tomatoes, and cucumbers in a big bowl; toss. Use red wine vinegar to drizzle. Chill until eating.

### Nutrition Information

- Calories: 102 calories;
- Sodium: 412
- Total Carbohydrate: 8.1
- Cholesterol: 22
- Protein: 4.9
- Total Fat: 6.3

## 276. Sylvia's Easy Greek Salad

*Serving: 4 | Prep: 15mins | Cook: |Ready in:*

### Ingredients

- 3/4 cup red bell pepper, chopped
- 3/4 cup chopped green bell pepper
- 1 cup cucumber - peeled, seeded and chopped
- 1 tomato, chopped
- 1/2 cup diced red onion
- 4 large black olives, quartered
- 1/2 cup crumbled feta cheese
- 1/2 cup vegetable oil
- 2 teaspoons white wine vinegar
- salt to taste

### Direction

- Combine olives, red onion, tomato, cucumber, green bell pepper and red bell pepper in a large bowl.
- Whisk vinegar and oil together. Add salt, feta cheese, vinegar and oil before serving. Toss well and serve.

### Nutrition Information

- Calories: 331 calories;
- Protein: 4
- Total Fat: 32.2
- Sodium: 253
- Total Carbohydrate: 8.2
- Cholesterol: 17

## 277. Tuna Souvlaki Pasta Salad

*Serving: 8 | Prep: 30mins | Cook: 10mins |Ready in:*

### Ingredients

- 1/2 red onion, cut into bite-size pieces
- 4 cups ice water, or as needed
- 1 (8 ounce) package tri-color rotini pasta
- 1 (5 ounce) can light tuna in water, drained and flaked
- 2 stalks celery, cut into bite-size pieces

- 1/2 cup roasted red peppers, drained and chopped
- 1/4 cup smoked sun-dried tomatoes
- 1/4 cup crumbled feta cheese
- 1 sprig parsley, stemmed and leaves minced
- 4 leaves fresh basil, rolled and very thinly sliced
- 2 teaspoons capers
- 1 cup Greek vinaigrette salad dressing

### Direction

- Remove the strong taste of red onion by soaking it in an ice water bowl in a fridge for no less than half an hour. Drain off and wash.
- Boil a big, slightly salted water pot; cook the rotini at a boil for about 8 minutes till soft but firm to the bite; drain and wash in cold water.
- In a big bowl, combine Greek dressing, capers, basil, parsley, feta cheese, sun-dried tomatoes, roasted red peppers, celery, tuna, pasta, and onion. Let it marinate in the fridge for 4 hours to overnight.

### Nutrition Information

- Calories: 248 calories;
- Total Fat: 12.7
- Sodium: 482
- Total Carbohydrate: 24.9
- Cholesterol: 9
- Protein: 9

# Chapter 6: Greek Dinner Recipes

***

## 278. Andalusian Pork Tenderloin For Two

*Serving: 2 servings. | Prep: 20mins | Cook: 20mins | Ready in:*

### Ingredients

- 1 pork tenderloin (3/4 pound)
- 4-1/2 teaspoons olive oil
- 2 garlic cloves, minced
- 1 teaspoon paprika
- 1/4 teaspoon salt
- 1/8 teaspoon ground cinnamon
- 1/8 teaspoon cayenne pepper
- 1/8 teaspoon ground nutmeg
- GREEN OLIVE SALAD:
- 1/3 cup pimiento-stuffed olives, cut in half
- 1/4 cup cherry tomatoes, quartered
- 2 tablespoons chopped red onion
- 1 teaspoon capers, drained
- 1-1/2 teaspoons olive oil
- 1-1/2 teaspoons red wine vinegar
- 1 garlic clove, minced

### Direction

- Use oil to rub tenderloin. Mix together nutmeg, cayenne, cinnamon, salt, paprika and garlic; rub over tenderloin. Refrigerate overnight or for 8 hours.
- In a shallow pan, place the tenderloin. Bake without covering for 20 to 27 minutes at 425 °, or until 145 ° is read by a thermometer. Allow to stand before slicing for 5 minutes.
- Mix the rest of ingredients in a small bowl. Enjoy with pork.

### Nutrition Information

- Calories: 380 calories
- Protein: 35g protein.
- Total Fat: 24g fat (4g saturated fat)
- Sodium: 887mg sodium
- Fiber: 1g fiber)
- Total Carbohydrate: 7g carbohydrate (1g sugars

- Cholesterol: 95mg cholesterol

### 279. Apple Halibut Kabobs

*Serving: 4 servings. | Prep: 20mins | Cook: 10mins | Ready in:*

## Ingredients

- 1/2 cup dry white wine or unsweetened apple juice
- 2 tablespoons lime juice
- 2 tablespoons olive oil
- 2 tablespoons diced onion
- 1 teaspoon salt
- 1/2 teaspoon dried thyme
- 1/4 teaspoon pepper
- 1-1/2 pounds halibut, cut into 1-inch cubes
- 1 small red onion, cut into 1-inch pieces
- 1 medium Golden Delicious apple, cut into 1-inch pieces
- 1 medium sweet red pepper, cut into 1-inch pieces

## Direction

- Combine the first seven ingredients in a large bowl. Transfer half of the mixture into a large re-sealable bag, add in the halibut, seal the bag and turn to coat. Pour the other half of the marinade into another large re-sealable bag, add in the red peppers, onions, and apples; seal the bag and turn to coat. Place both bags in the refrigerator and turn occasionally during the 4-6 hours of refrigeration time. Discard the marinade from the fish, but keep that from the fruit and vegetables, to use for basting. Alternately skewer fish, onion, apple, and red pepper on eight metal or wooden skewers that have been soaked. Grip a piece of paper towel with a pair of long-handled tongs; dip the towel in cooking oil and coat the grille with oil. Place the kabobs on the grill at medium heat, or broil 4 in. from the heat. Cover and cook for 6-10 minutes, turning frequently and basting with marinade, until the fruits and vegetables are tender, and the fish is flaked easily with a fork.

## Nutrition Information

- Calories: 241 calories
- Sodium: 240mg sodium
- Fiber: 1g fiber)
- Total Carbohydrate: 9g carbohydrate (0 sugars
- Cholesterol: 54mg cholesterol
- Protein: 36g protein. Diabetic Exchanges: 5 lean meat
- Total Fat: 6g fat (1g saturated fat)

### 280. Apricot Turkey Stir Fry

*Serving: 4 servings. | Prep: 5mins | Cook: 15mins | Ready in:*

## Ingredients

- 1 tablespoon cornstarch
- 1/2 cup apricot nectar
- 3 tablespoons reduced-sodium soy sauce
- 2 tablespoons white vinegar
- 1/4 teaspoon crushed red pepper flakes
- 1/2 cup dried apricot halves, cut in half lengthwise
- 1 pound turkey breast tenderloin, cut into thin slices
- 1 teaspoon canola oil
- 1 teaspoon sesame oil or additional canola oil
- 2-1/2 cups fresh snow peas
- 1 medium onion, chopped
- 1 medium sweet red or yellow pepper, cut into 1-inch pieces
- Hot cooked couscous, optional

## Direction

- Combine red pepper flakes, vinegar, soy sauce, apricot nectar, and cornstarch in a small mixing bowl until no lumps remain. Add apricots; put aside.

- Sauté turkey in canola and sesame oil in a wok or large skillet until no longer pink inside. Add red pepper, onion, and peas; sauté until vegetables are crisp-tender. Take vegetables and meat out of the pan using a slotted spoon; keep warm.
- Stir cornstarch mixture and slowly pour into the pan. Bring to a boil; cook, stirring, until thickened for 1 to 2 minutes. Add vegetables and meat back into the pan; stir to coat evenly. Cook until thoroughly heated. Serve warm over couscous if desired.

## Nutrition Information

- Calories: 270 calories
- Total Fat: 3g fat (1g saturated fat)
- Sodium: 512mg sodium
- Fiber: 4g fiber)
- Total Carbohydrate: 27g carbohydrate (0 sugars
- Cholesterol: 82mg cholesterol
- Protein: 33g protein. Diabetic Exchanges: 3 lean meat

## 281. Artichoke & Lemon Pasta

*Serving: 6 servings. | Prep: 20mins | Cook: 20mins | Ready in:*

## Ingredients

- 2-1/2 teaspoons salt, divided
- 1/2 pound fresh asparagus, trimmed and cut into 1-1/2-inch pieces
- 4 cups uncooked bow tie pasta (about 12 ounces)
- 3 tablespoons olive oil, divided
- 1 can (14 ounces) water-packed quartered artichoke hearts, well drained
- 2 garlic cloves, minced
- 1 cup crumbled goat cheese
- 2 tablespoons minced fresh parsley
- 1 tablespoon grated lemon peel
- 2 to 3 tablespoons lemon juice
- 1/3 cup grated Parmesan cheese

## Direction

- Add water to a 6-qt. stockpot, 3/4 full; put in 2 teaspoons of salt and bring to a boil. Add asparagus; cook without a cover just until crisp-tender, about 1-2 minutes. Take out the asparagus and drop immediately into ice water. Drain and pat to dry.
- In same water pot, cook pasta following package instructions for al dente. Drain, reserving 1 cup of pasta water. Put the pasta back into pot.
- In the meantime, in a large skillet, heat 1 tablespoon of oil over medium-high heat. Put in artichoke hearts; cook and stir until lightly browned, about 3-4 minutes. Put in garlic; cook for 1 more minute. Add the mixture to pasta.
- Put in oil, the remaining salt, lemon juice, lemon peel, parsley, goat cheese and asparagus; toss to combine, adding enough amount of reserved pasta water to coat. Heat it through. Serve with Parmesan cheese.

## Nutrition Information

- Calories: 343 calories
- Sodium: 919mg sodium
- Fiber: 3g fiber)
- Total Carbohydrate: 43g carbohydrate (2g sugars
- Cholesterol: 27mg cholesterol
- Protein: 14g protein.
- Total Fat: 14g fat (5g saturated fat)

## 282. Baked Tilapia

*Serving: 4 | Prep: 20mins | Cook: 20mins | Ready in:*

### Ingredients

- 3/4 cup extra virgin olive oil
- 4 tablespoons tomato paste
- 1 teaspoon garlic powder
- 1/2 teaspoon dried oregano
- 1/4 teaspoon salt
- 1/8 teaspoon ground black pepper
- 4 (4 ounce) fillets tilapia
- 1 large onion, sliced
- 1 green bell pepper, thinly sliced
- 4 tablespoons butter

### Direction

- Set the oven to 175°C or 350°F to preheat, then coat approximately 1/4 cup of olive oil to the bottom of a medium size baking dish.
- Mix pepper, salt, oregano, garlic powder, tomato paste and the leftover olive oil in a small bowl.
- In the prepared baking dish, place tilapia fillets with skin side up. Spread over the tilapia with tomato paste mixture and olive oil using a spatula, heaping the majority in the middle of the fillets. Put around the fillets with green pepper slices and onion.
- In the preheated oven, bake for 15 minutes until it is easy to use a fork to flake fish. Take away from the heat and put 1 tbsp. of butter on each fillet. Set oven to broil and broil fillets until butter is melted and browned slightly, about 5 to 7 minutes.

### Nutrition Information

- Calories: 629 calories;
- Cholesterol: 72
- Protein: 24.6
- Total Fat: 55.2
- Sodium: 408
- Total Carbohydrate: 8.6

## 283. Balsamic Beef Kabob Sandwiches

*Serving: 8 servings. | Prep: 15mins | Cook: 10mins | Ready in:*

### Ingredients

- 1/4 cup balsamic vinegar
- 1/4 cup olive oil
- 2 garlic cloves, minced
- 1 teaspoon dried rosemary, crushed
- 1/2 teaspoon pepper, divided
- 1/4 teaspoon salt, divided
- 1-1/2 pounds beef top sirloin steak, cut into 1/4-inch-thick strips
- 2 medium onions
- 8 naan flatbreads
- 2 cups chopped heirloom tomatoes

### Direction

- Mix the first four ingredients in the list, then add 1/8 teaspoon salt and 1/4 teaspoon pepper. Stir in the beef and let sit for 20 minutes. Slice each onion into eight wedges and skewer them onto metal skewers or wooden ones that have been soaked. Skewer the beef onto separate skewers, weaving the strips back and forth as you thread them. Grill the onions on a covered medium-heat grille for 5-7 minutes per side, or until they are tender. Grill the beef, also covered and on medium heat, for 3-4 minutes on each side or until done to liking. Lightly brown flatbreads on the grill, about 1-2 minutes per side. Take the beef and the onions off the skewers and arrange on flatbreads. Mix together the tomatoes and the remaining salt and pepper and serve on top of the sandwiches.

### Nutrition Information

- Calories: 353 calories
- Total Carbohydrate: 34g carbohydrate (7g sugars
- Cholesterol: 39mg cholesterol

- Protein: 23g protein. Diabetic Exchanges: 3 lean meat
- Total Fat: 14g fat (3g saturated fat)
- Sodium: 595mg sodium
- Fiber: 2g fiber)

## 284. Barbecued Lamb Chops

*Serving: 9 servings. | Prep: 5mins | Cook: 10mins | Ready in:*

### Ingredients

- 2 to 3 cups olive oil
- 1/4 cup chopped garlic
- 4 teaspoons salt
- 1 teaspoon minced fresh rosemary or 1/2 teaspoon dried rosemary, crushed
- 1 teaspoon salt-free garlic and herb seasoning
- 1 teaspoon pepper
- 18 lamb rib chops (1 inch thick and 4 ounces each)

### Direction

- Mix together in a large resealable plastic bag the seasonings, garlic and oil; put in lamb chops. Secure bag and flip to coat; place inside the refrigerator overnight, flipping occasionally.
- Strain get rid of marinade. Place the chops on the grill over medium heat, uncovered for 5-9 minutes per side or until the meat achieves doneness desired (160°F for medium well and 170°F for well done).

### Nutrition Information

- Calories:
- Protein:
- Total Fat:
- Sodium:
- Fiber:
- Total Carbohydrate:
- Cholesterol:

## 285. Barbecued Lamb Kabobs

*Serving: 8-10 servings. | Prep: 20mins | Cook: 15mins | Ready in:*

### Ingredients

- 2-1/2 pounds boneless leg of lamb, cut into 1-inch cubes
- MARINADE:
- 1/2 tablespoon dried parsley flakes
- 1/2 tablespoon dried minced onion
- 1 teaspoon salt
- 1/2 teaspoon black pepper
- 1/2 cup lemon juice
- 1/2 cup white wine or broth of choice
- 2 tablespoons soy sauce
- DIPPING SAUCE:
- 1/2 cup canola oil
- 1/2 cup lemon juice
- 1 large onion, chopped
- 2 garlic cloves, minced
- Salt to taste
- Pepper to taste
- Hot peppers to taste, chopped

### Direction

- Take a heavy plastic bag and combine all the marinade ingredients with the lamb. Let marinate overnight or at least 5 hours, turning bag from time to time. Drain, discarding marinade. Skewer the lamb and broil or grill on medium-hot for 7-8 minutes per side or until meat is cooked to liking. A thermometer should read 145 degrees for medium-rare; 160 degrees for medium; and 170 degrees for well-done. Make the sauce by blending together all the sauce ingredients. Put the lid on and blend on high until smooth. Serve lamb with dipping sauce.

## Nutrition Information

- Calories:
- Sodium:
- Fiber:
- Total Carbohydrate:
- Cholesterol:
- Protein:
- Total Fat:

### 286. Barley Lentil Stew

*Serving: 9 servings. | Prep: 15mins | Cook: 50mins | Ready in:*

## Ingredients

- 2 large onions, chopped
- 2 cups chopped carrots
- 2 tablespoons olive oil
- 1 tablespoon minced garlic
- 2 teaspoons ground cumin
- 4 cups reduced-sodium chicken broth
- 1 can (28 ounces) diced tomatoes, undrained
- 1 cup lentils, rinsed
- 1 tablespoon brown sugar
- 1 cinnamon stick (3 inches)
- 1/2 cup uncooked medium pearl barley
- 1/2 cup minced fresh parsley
- 1/2 teaspoon salt
- 1/4 teaspoon pepper
- 9 tablespoons fat-free plain yogurt

## Direction

- Sauté carrots and onions with oil in a nonstick skillet until tender-crisp, about 8 minutes. Put in cumin and garlic, then cook and stir about 1 minute more. Put in cinnamon stick, brown sugar, lentils, tomatoes and broth; bring all to a boil. Lower heat, cover and cook about 5 minutes. Put in barley, then cover and cook until barley as well as lentils are softened, while stirring sometimes, about 45 minutes.
- Put in pepper, salt and parsley, then get rid of cinnamon stick. Serve in bowls together with a dollop of yogurt.

## Nutrition Information

- Calories: 189 calories
- Sodium: 440mg sodium
- Fiber: 9g fiber)
- Total Carbohydrate: 31g carbohydrate (0 sugars
- Cholesterol: 1mg cholesterol
- Protein: 10g protein. Diabetic Exchanges: 2 starch
- Total Fat: 4g fat (1g saturated fat)

### 287. Basic Braised Lamb Shanks

*Serving: 2 servings. | Prep: 10mins | Cook: 01hours30mins | Ready in:*

## Ingredients

- 2 lamb shanks (1 pound each)
- 1 cup beef broth
- 1/4 cup soy sauce
- 2 tablespoons brown sugar
- 1 garlic clove, minced
- 2 teaspoons prepared mustard

## Direction

- Arrange lamb in an oiled 2 1/2-quart baking dish. Stir mustard, garlic, brown sugar, soy sauce, and broth together; pour over lamb in the baking dish. Bake, covered, for 90 to 120 minutes at 325° until meat is tender.

## Nutrition Information

- Calories: 451 calories
- Total Fat: 21g fat (9g saturated fat)
- Sodium: 2419mg sodium

- Fiber: 0 fiber)
- Total Carbohydrate: 15g carbohydrate (14g sugars
- Cholesterol: 159mg cholesterol
- Protein: 48g protein.

## 288. Basil Marinated Fish

*Serving: 4 servings. | Prep: 10mins | Cook: 10mins | Ready in:*

### Ingredients

- 1/4 cup Basil Vinegar
- 2 tablespoons olive oil
- 1 tablespoon each chopped, fresh basil, thyme, oregano and parsley or 1 teaspoon each dried basil, thyme, oregano and parsley flakes
- 2 garlic cloves, minced
- 1 teaspoon grated lemon zest
- 1/2 teaspoon salt
- 1/4 teaspoon pepper
- 2 orange roughy fillets or halibut fillets (1 pound)

### Direction

- Combine pepper, salt, lemon zest, garlic, herbs, oil, and vinegar in a large bowl. Lay fillets in; turn to cover. Chill, covered, for 30 minutes, flipping once or twice.
- Strain and discard marinade. Oil the grill rack lightly. Cover and broil fillets 4 inches from the heat or grill over medium-hot heat till fish easily flakes with a fork or for 7-10 minutes.

### Nutrition Information

- Calories: 145 calories
- Sodium: 366mg sodium
- Fiber: 1g fiber)
- Total Carbohydrate: 2g carbohydrate (0 sugars
- Cholesterol: 23mg cholesterol

- Protein: 17g protein. Diabetic Exchanges: 3 lean meat.
- Total Fat: 8g fat (1g saturated fat)

## 289. Beef Cabbage Rolls

*Serving: 4 servings. | Prep: 30mins | Cook: 01hours05mins | Ready in:*

### Ingredients

- 1/3 cup uncooked brown rice
- 1 medium head cabbage
- 1 medium onion, chopped
- 2 egg whites
- 3 tablespoons dried currants
- 2 tablespoons pine nuts
- 2 tablespoons lemon juice
- 1/2 teaspoon dried oregano
- 1/4 teaspoon pepper
- 1/8 teaspoon salt
- 1/8 teaspoon ground cinnamon
- 3/4 pound lean ground beef (90% lean)
- 2 cans (8 ounces each) no-salt-added tomato sauce
- 2 tablespoons brown sugar
- 1/4 teaspoon dried thyme

### Direction

- Based on the instruction on package, cook rice.
- At the same time, cook the cabbage in the boiling water just till the outer leaves can be pulled away easily from the head. Put aside 8 big leaves for rolls. Keep the rest of the cabbage in the refrigerator for future use. Chop out thick vein from bottom of each reserved leaf, shaping one V-shaped cut.
- In the small-sized nonstick skillet that is coated with the cooking spray, sauté the onion till becoming soft. In the big bowl, mix cinnamon, salt, pepper, oregano, lemon juice, pine nuts, currants, egg whites, onion and rice. Break up the beef on the mixture and combine them well.

- Add roughly a third cup of the beef mixture onto each cabbage leaf. Fold in sides, starting from the cut end. Roll them up entirely to enclose the filling. Position with the seam-side facing downward in the greased 13x9-inch baking dish. Mix thyme, brown sugar, and tomato sauce; add on top of the rolls.
- Keep covered and bake at 350 degrees till the thermometer reaches 160 degrees and the cabbage softens or for an hour. Remove the cover; bake till the sauce has the consistency that you want or for 5 to 10 more minutes.

## Nutrition Information

- Calories: 335 calories
- Sodium: 198mg sodium
- Fiber: 4g fiber)
- Total Carbohydrate: 39g carbohydrate (22g sugars
- Cholesterol: 53mg cholesterol
- Protein: 22g protein. Diabetic Exchanges: 2-1/2 starch
- Total Fat: 10g fat (3g saturated fat)

## 290. Beef Squash Shish Kabobs

*Serving: 2 servings. | Prep: 10mins | Cook: 10mins | Ready in:*

## Ingredients

- 1/2 cup packed brown sugar
- 1/2 cup soy sauce
- 1/2 teaspoon each garlic powder, ground mustard and ground ginger
- 1/2 pound beef top sirloin steak, cut into 1-inch pieces
- 1 small zucchini, cut into 1/4-inch slices
- 1 small yellow summer squash, cut into 1/4-inch slices
- 1 small sweet red pepper, cut into 1-inch pieces
- 1/2 medium red onion, cut into four wedges, optional

## Direction

- Mix together soy sauce, brown sugar, mustard, garlic powder, and ginger in a small bowl. Pour half cup of the marinade over the beef in a large re-sealable plastic bag. Close the bag and turn several times to coat. In another re-sealable plastic bag, put in yellow squash, zucchini, red peppers, and onions, if desired. Pour in the remaining marinade. Zip the top and turn the bag to coat. Refrigerate both bags for at least 4 hours, turning occasionally, to let the beef and the vegetables soak in the marinade. Drain, disposing of marinade. Alternately cue beef and vegetables on four metal or water-soaked wooden skewers. Cook in a covered grill at medium heat, or broil 4-6 in. from the heat, turning occasionally during the 8 to 10 minute grilling time, or until beef is cooked to liking.

## Nutrition Information

- Calories: 346 calories
- Cholesterol: 46mg cholesterol
- Protein: 32g protein.
- Total Fat: 5g fat (2g saturated fat)
- Sodium: 2466mg sodium
- Fiber: 3g fiber)
- Total Carbohydrate: 43g carbohydrate (39g sugars

## 291. Beef And Potato Moussaka

*Serving: 8-10 servings. | Prep: 25mins | Cook: 60mins | Ready in:*

## Ingredients

- 1 pound ground beef

- 1 medium onion, chopped
- 1 garlic clove, minced
- 3/4 cup water
- 1 can (6 ounces) tomato paste
- 3 tablespoons minced fresh parsley
- 1 teaspoon salt
- 1/2 teaspoon dried mint, optional
- 1/4 teaspoon ground cinnamon
- 1/4 teaspoon pepper
- PARMESAN SAUCE:
- 1/4 cup butter, cubed
- 1/4 cup all-purpose flour
- 2 cups milk
- 4 eggs, lightly beaten
- 1/2 cup grated Parmesan cheese
- 1/2 teaspoon salt
- 5 medium potatoes, peeled and thinly sliced

### Direction

- Over medium heat, cook onion and beef in a large skillet until the meat is no more pink. Add garlic and continue to cook for 1 minute more. Allow to drain. Stir in the water, pepper, cinnamon, (mint if desired), salt, parsley, and tomato paste. Set aside.
- To make the sauce: Over medium heat, melt butter in a saucepan. Stir in flour until smooth; add milk gradually. Boil; cook while stirring until thickened, for 2 minutes. Remove from the heat. Next, stir a small amount of the hot mixture into the eggs; bring all back to the pan, stirring constantly. Add salt and cheese.
- In a greased shallow 3-qt. baking dish, arrange 1/2 of the potato slices. Lay all of the meat mixture and 1/2 of the cheese sauce on top. Arrange over the meat mixture with the leftover potatoes; put the remaining cheese sauce on top.
- Bake without cover at 350° for 60 minutes, or until a thermometer registers 160°. Allow to sit for 10 minutes before serving.

### Nutrition Information

- Calories: 285 calories
- Sodium: 570mg sodium
- Fiber: 3g fiber)
- Total Carbohydrate: 25g carbohydrate (7g sugars
- Cholesterol: 129mg cholesterol
- Protein: 16g protein.
- Total Fat: 14g fat (7g saturated fat)

## 292. Bell Peppers And Pasta

*Serving: 4 servings. | Prep: 12mins | Cook: 10mins | Ready in:*

### Ingredients

- 2-1/4 cups uncooked penne pasta
- 3/4 cup chopped onion
- 1 tablespoon olive oil
- 3 garlic cloves, minced
- 1 cup chopped sweet red pepper
- 1 cup chopped green pepper
- 1/4 cup sliced ripe olives
- 1 teaspoon dried oregano
- 1/4 teaspoon salt
- 1/8 teaspoon cayenne pepper
- 1/4 cup water
- 1/2 cup crumbled feta cheese

### Direction

- Prepare pasta following the package instructions. Sauté onion for 1 1/2 minutes in a non-stick pan with oil. Put in garlic then cook for another half minute; put in sweet peppers. Cook while stirring for 2-3 minutes until the veggies are tender. Mix in cayenne, olives, salt, and oregano; pour in water. Cook and stir until the mixture boils. Drain and mix pasta into the pan; take off heat. Mix in cheese then serve right away.

### Nutrition Information

- Calories: 274 calories

- Sodium: 434mg sodium
- Fiber: 4g fiber)
- Total Carbohydrate: 40g carbohydrate (0 sugars
- Cholesterol: 17mg cholesterol
- Protein: 9g protein.  Diabetic Exchanges: 2 starch
- Total Fat: 9g fat (4g saturated fat)

## 293. Best Leg Of Lamb

*Serving: 12 servings. | Prep: 15mins | Cook: 02hours30mins |Ready in:*

### Ingredients

- 1/3 cup minced fresh rosemary
- 2 tablespoons Dijon mustard
- 2 tablespoons olive oil
- 8 garlic cloves, minced
- 1 teaspoon reduced-sodium soy sauce
- 1/2 teaspoon salt
- 1/2 teaspoon pepper
- 1 bone-in leg of lamb (7 to 9 pounds), trimmed
- 1 cup chicken broth

### Direction

- Mix the first 7 ingredients in a small bowl; rub over lamb leg. Cover; refrigerate overnight.
- Put lamb onto a rack into a shallow roasting pan, fat side up; bake for 1 1/2 hours at 325°, uncovered.
- Put broth into pan; loosely cover using foil. Bake for 1-1 1/2 hours till meat gets desired doneness (170° for well-done, 160° for medium and 145° for medium-rare on a thermometer); stand for 10-15 minutes then slice.

### Nutrition Information

- Calories:  246 calories
- Sodium: 320mg sodium
- Fiber: 0 fiber)
- Total Carbohydrate: 2g carbohydrate (0 sugars
- Cholesterol: 120mg cholesterol
- Protein: 33g protein.  Diabetic Exchanges: 5 lean meat
- Total Fat: 11g fat (4g saturated fat)

## 294. Best Paella

*Serving: | Prep: 1hours30mins | Cook: 2hours | Ready in:*

### Ingredients

- 1 piece Chicken, whole or 6 thighs deboned
- 1/4 cup olive oil
- 3 pieces Chorizo, spanish, thickly cut
- 1 pinch salt and pepper
- 1  onion, diced
- 4 cloves garlic, crushed
- 1 bunch parsley , flat leaves, chopped
- 1 can tomatoes, 16 oz. fire roasted diced
- 2 cups rice, spanish short grain
- 6 cups chicken broth
- 1 head red bell pepper, roasted, seeded and peeled
- 1/4 pound green beans
- 1 pinch saffron, pinch
- 1/2 cup green peas frozen, thawed
- 1 dash Dry rub for Chicken: 1 Tbsp Smoked Paprika, 2 tsp oregano, salt and pepper

### Direction

- Rub chicken all over with the spice mix; allow to marinate in the refrigerator for 1 hour.
- Place a paella pan on medium-high heat; heat oil. Sauté in the chorizo till browned; take out and reserve. Put in the chicken, skin side down; turn with tongs to brown on all sides.
- Take away from the pan and reserve. Sauté parsley, garlic and onions to make sofrito in the same pan. Cook on medium heat for 2-3 minutes.
- Put in tomatoes; keep cooking till the flavors meld and the mixture caramelizes a bit. Fold in rice; stir-fry to coat the grains. Pour in

water; allow to simmer for 10 minutes; carefully move the pan around so the rice absorbs the liquid and cooks evenly.
- Tuck the mixture of peas, bell pepper, clams, chorizo and chicken into the rice.
- Shake the paella properly; allow to simmer without stirring for around 15 minutes, till the rice is al dente. Put in shrimp during the last 5 minutes of cooking, when the rice is filling the pan.
- When the rice looks moist and fluffy and the paella is cooked, increase the heat for 40 seconds till you can smell the rice toast at the bottom.
- Cook's note: The ideal paella is called socarrat, which has a toasted rice bottom. Take away from the heat; allow to rest for 5 minutes. Garnish with lemon wedges, parsley and peas.

### 295.  Best Rosemary Chicken

*Serving: 2 servings. | Prep: 10mins | Cook: 0mins | Ready in:*

## Ingredients

- 2 boneless skinless chicken breast halves (4 ounces each)
- 2 teaspoons canola oil
- 1 tablespoon lemon juice
- 1 teaspoon dried rosemary, crushed
- 1/2 teaspoon dried oregano
- 1/4 teaspoon pepper

## Direction

- Pound each chicken until a quarter-inch thick. On medium-high heat, cook chicken for 3-4 minutes per side in a non-stick pan with oil until the chicken is not pink. Scatter top with pepper, lemon juice, oregano, and rosemary.

## Nutrition Information

- Calories: 172 calories

- Cholesterol: 66mg cholesterol
- Protein: 26g protein.  Diabetic Exchanges: 3 lean meat
- Total Fat: 6g fat (1g saturated fat)
- Sodium: 74mg sodium
- Fiber: 1g fiber)
- Total Carbohydrate: 1g carbohydrate (0 sugars

### 296.  Braised Lamb Shanks

*Serving: 4 | Prep: 20mins | Cook: 3hours | Ready in:*

## Ingredients

- 2 large white onions, chopped
- 4 lamb shanks
- 2 cups dry red wine
- 1 cup balsamic vinegar
- 1/3 cup olive oil
- 4 cloves garlic, pressed
- 2 lemons, quartered
- 2 (14.5 ounce) cans diced tomatoes
- 1 bunch fresh basil, chopped
- 1 tablespoon kosher salt
- 1 tablespoon cracked black pepper

## Direction

- Set the oven to 350°F (175°C) and start preheating.
- Arrange onions in 1 layer in the bottom of a medium roasting pan with a lid or Dutch oven. Top over onions with lamb shanks. Pour the olive oil, balsamic vinegar and wine over the lamb. Put a clove of pressed garlic next to each shank, and 1/4 of a lemon on each side. Top over everything with tomatoes, season with basil, pepper and salt.
- Cover and transfer into the prepared oven. Cook for 3 hours. Make a nice flavorful gravy with the juices from the pan.

## Nutrition Information

- Calories: 572 calories;
- Total Fat: 25.2
- Sodium: 1851
- Total Carbohydrate: 34.4
- Cholesterol: 86
- Protein: 32.5

## 297.  Breaded Pork Chops For Two

*Serving: 2 servings. | Prep: 10mins | Cook: 60mins | Ready in:*

### Ingredients

- 1 egg
- 1 tablespoon barbecue sauce
- 1/3 cup dry bread crumbs
- 2 teaspoons grated parmesan cheese
- 1/4 teaspoon dried oregano
- 1/8 to 1/4 teaspoon lemon-pepper seasoning
- 1/8 teaspoon onion salt
- 2 bone-in pork chops (3/4 inch thick)

### Direction

- Mix together barbecue sauce and egg in a small shallow bowl. Mix together salt, lemon-pepper, oregano, cheese and bread crumbs in another small shallow bowl. Dip into egg mixture with chops, then coat chops with the crumb mixture.
- Put in a greased 8-inch square baking dish, then cover and chill about 2 hours. Take out of the fridge about a half hour before baking. Bake at 325 degrees without a cover until juices run clear, about an hour.

### Nutrition Information

- Calories: 327 calories
- Protein: 36g protein.
- Total Fat: 13g fat (4g saturated fat)
- Sodium: 486mg sodium

- Fiber: 1g fiber)
- Total Carbohydrate: 15g carbohydrate (2g sugars
- Cholesterol: 193mg cholesterol

## 298.  Broiled Beef Kabobs

*Serving: 4 servings. | Prep: 10mins | Cook: 15mins | Ready in:*

### Ingredients

- 1 tablespoon olive oil
- 1 tablespoon lemon juice
- 1 tablespoon water
- 2 teaspoon Dijon mustard
- 1 teaspoon honey
- 1/2 teaspoon dried oregano
- 1/4 teaspoon pepper
- 1 pound beef top sirloin steak (1 inch thick), cut into 1-inch cubes
- 2 small green and/or sweet red peppers, cut into 1-inch pieces
- 12 large fresh mushrooms
- Hot cooked rice

### Direction

- Combine the first seven ingredients in a large bowl. Add the mushrooms, peppers and beef; toss to cover. On metal or soaked wooden skewers, alternately thread meat and vegetables.
- Broil 3-inch from the heat, turning often, for around 12-16 minutes until vegetables are soften and meat reaches desired doneness. Serve with rice.

### Nutrition Information

- Calories:  209 calories
- Protein: 27g protein.  Diabetic Exchanges: 3 lean meat
- Total Fat: 8g fat (2g saturated fat)

- Sodium: 115mg sodium
- Fiber: 2g fiber)
- Total Carbohydrate: 7g carbohydrate (3g sugars
- Cholesterol: 46mg cholesterol

## 299. Broiled Sirloin

*Serving: 10 servings. | Prep: 10mins | Cook: 15mins | Ready in:*

### Ingredients

- 3 pounds beef top sirloin or round steaks (about 1 inch thick)
- 1 medium onion, chopped
- 1/2 cup lemon juice
- 1/4 cup canola oil
- 1 teaspoon garlic salt
- 1 teaspoon dried thyme
- 1 teaspoon dried oregano
- 1/2 teaspoon celery salt
- 1/2 teaspoon pepper
- 2 tablespoons butter, melted

### Direction

- Pierce holes in both steak's sides with a meat fork. Put into a big resealable bag; add pepper, celery salt, oregano, thyme, garlic salt, oil, lemon juice and onion. Seal bag, turn till coated. Refrigerate it for 6 hours – overnight.
- Drain marinade; discard. Broil steaks for 8 minutes 6-in. from heat. Brush butter; flip. Broil for 6 minutes till meat gets desired doneness; 170° well done, 160° medium and 145° medium-rare on thermometer.

### Nutrition Information

- Calories: 249 calories
- Sodium: 313mg sodium
- Fiber: 0 fiber)

- Total Carbohydrate: 3g carbohydrate (1g sugars
- Cholesterol: 61mg cholesterol
- Protein: 29g protein.
- Total Fat: 13g fat (4g saturated fat)

## 300. Caesar Chicken With Feta

*Serving: 4 servings. | Prep: 5mins | Cook: 5mins | Ready in:*

### Ingredients

- 4 boneless skinless chicken breast halves (4 ounces each)
- 1/2 teaspoon salt
- 1/4 teaspoon pepper
- 2 teaspoons olive oil
- 1 medium tomato, chopped
- 1/4 cup creamy Caesar salad dressing
- 1/2 cup crumbled feta cheese

### Direction

- Sprinkle pepper and salt on chicken. Heat oil in a big skillet on medium high heat. Brown one side of chicken. Flip. Add salad dressing and tomato into skillet. Cook for 6-8 minutes, covered, till an inserted thermometer in chicken registers 165°. Sprinkle cheese over.

### Nutrition Information

- Calories: 262 calories
- Total Carbohydrate: 2g carbohydrate (1g sugars
- Cholesterol: 76mg cholesterol
- Protein: 26g protein.
- Total Fat: 16g fat (4g saturated fat)
- Sodium: 664mg sodium
- Fiber: 1g fiber)

## 301. Caesar Salmon With Roasted Tomatoes & Artichokes

*Serving: 4 servings. | Prep: 10mins | Cook: 15mins | Ready in:*

### Ingredients

- 4 salmon fillets (5 ounces each)
- 5 tablespoons reduced-fat Caesar vinaigrette, divided
- 1/4 teaspoon pepper, divided
- 2 cups grape tomatoes
- 1 can (14 ounces) water-packed artichoke hearts, drained and quartered
- 1 medium sweet orange or yellow pepper, cut into 1-inch pieces

### Direction

- Preheat an oven to 425 degrees F. Put the salmon on one half of a baking pan of 15x10x1-inch that is coated with cooking spray. Coat with two tablespoons of vinaigrette and then drizzle with 1/8 teaspoon of pepper.
- Mix sweet pepper, tomatoes, and artichoke hearts in a large bowl. Place in the remaining pepper and vinaigrette. Stir to coat. Put the tomato mixture onto the remaining half of pan. Then roast for about 12-15 minutes or until the veggies are tender and the fish just starts to flake easily with a fork.

### Nutrition Information

- Calories: 318 calories
- Sodium: 674mg sodium
- Fiber: 2g fiber)
- Total Carbohydrate: 12g carbohydrate (4g sugars
- Cholesterol: 73mg cholesterol
- Protein: 28g protein. Diabetic Exchanges: 4 lean meat
- Total Fat: 16g fat (3g saturated fat)

## 302. California Quinoa

*Serving: 4 servings. | Prep: 15mins | Cook: 15mins | Ready in:*

### Ingredients

- 1 tablespoon olive oil
- 1 cup quinoa, rinsed and well drained
- 2 garlic cloves, minced
- 1 medium zucchini, chopped
- 2 cups water
- 3/4 cup canned garbanzo beans or chickpeas, rinsed and drained
- 1 medium tomato, finely chopped
- 1/2 cup crumbled feta cheese
- 1/4 cup finely chopped Greek olives
- 2 tablespoons minced fresh basil
- 1/4 teaspoon pepper

### Direction

- Heat oil in a big saucepan on medium-high heat. Put in garlic and quinoa, then cook and stir until quinoa is browned slightly, about 2 to 3 minutes. Stir in water and zucchini, then bring to a boil. Lower heat and simmer with a cover until liquid is absorbed, about 12 to 15 minutes. Stir in leftover ingredients and heat through.

### Nutrition Information

- Calories: 310 calories
- Protein: 11g protein. Diabetic Exchanges: 2 starch
- Total Fat: 11g fat (3g saturated fat)
- Sodium: 353mg sodium
- Fiber: 6g fiber)
- Total Carbohydrate: 42g carbohydrate (3g sugars
- Cholesterol: 8mg cholesterol

## 303. Caribbean Chutney Crusted Chops

*Serving: 4 servings. | Prep: 10mins | Cook: 20mins | Ready in:*

### Ingredients

- 1 cup soft bread crumbs
- 1-1/2 teaspoons Caribbean jerk seasoning
- 1/4 cup mango chutney
- 1/2 teaspoon salt
- 1/2 teaspoon pepper
- 4 lamb loin chops (2 inches-thick and 8 ounces each)

### Direction

- Preheat an oven to 450°. Mix jerk seasoning and breadcrumbs in shallow bowl; put aside. Mix pepper, salt and chutney; spread over both sides of the lamb chops. Coat using crumb mixture.
- Put lamb chops onto a rack coated with cooking spray in a shallow baking pan; bake for 20-25 minutes till meat gets desired doneness (thermometer should read 170° for well-done, 160° medium and 145° for medium-rare).

### Nutrition Information

- Calories: 296 calories
- Total Carbohydrate: 20g carbohydrate (9g sugars
- Cholesterol: 91mg cholesterol
- Protein: 30g protein. Diabetic Exchanges: 4 lean meat
- Total Fat: 10g fat (3g saturated fat)
- Sodium: 711mg sodium
- Fiber: 0 fiber)

## 304. Casablanca Chicken Couscous

*Serving: 6 servings. | Prep: 20mins | Cook: 15mins | Ready in:*

### Ingredients

- 1 tablespoon olive oil
- 1 medium onion, chopped
- 1 pound boneless skinless chicken thighs, cut into 1-inch pieces
- 1 package (8.8 ounces) uncooked Israeli couscous
- 1/2 teaspoon salt
- 1/4 teaspoon pepper
- 1/4 teaspoon crushed red pepper flakes
- 2 cans (14-1/2 ounces each ) reduced-sodium chicken broth
- 2/3 cup dried tropical fruit
- 1 can (15 to 15-1/2 ounces) garbanzo beans or chickpeas, rinsed and drained
- 1/2 cup plain yogurt
- 1 small carrot, grated
- 1/4 cup minced fresh parsley
- 1 medium lemon

### Direction

- Heat olive oil on medium high heat in a big skillet. Add onion. Sauté for 3-4 minutes till softened. Add pepper flakes, pepper, salt, couscous and chicken. Stir and cook for 3-5 minutes till chicken starts to brown. Add dried fruit and broth. Cook for 8-10 minutes till fruit is moist and couscous and chicken are tender, uncovered.
- Mix leftover ingredients in; heat through. Take off heat. Let stand for 10 minutes, covered. Meanwhile, zest lemon peel to strips then slice lemon to 6 wedges. Put peel over couscous. Serve it with lemon wedges.

### Nutrition Information

- Calories: 448 calories

- Total Carbohydrate: 63g carbohydrate (17g sugars
- Cholesterol: 53mg cholesterol
- Protein: 25g protein.
- Total Fat: 11g fat (3g saturated fat)
- Sodium: 715mg sodium
- Fiber: 4g fiber)

## 305. Catfish With Pecan Butter

*Serving: 6 servings. | Prep: 15mins | Cook: 10mins | Ready in:*

### Ingredients

- 1 cup butter, softened
- 1/2 cup chopped pecans, toasted
- 1 teaspoon lemon juice
- Dash hot pepper sauce
- 2 eggs, lightly beaten
- 1 cup milk
- 1 cup cornmeal
- 1/2 cup all-purpose flour
- 1 teaspoon garlic powder
- 1 teaspoon paprika
- 1 teaspoon pepper
- 1/2 teaspoon onion powder
- 1/2 teaspoon dried oregano
- 1/2 teaspoon dried thyme
- 1/4 teaspoon salt
- 1/4 teaspoon cayenne pepper
- 6 catfish fillets (6 ounces each)
- Oil for frying
- Lemon wedges

### Direction

- Combine the following ingredients in a food processor - pecans, pepper sauce, butter and lemon juice. Put the cover on and process until smooth. Put to one side.
- Combine milk and eggs in a shallow dish. In a separate shallow dish, put together flour, cornmeal and seasonings. Take the fillets first, dip in egg mixture, and then roll in flour mixture to coat.
- Pour about 1/4 inch of oil in a big skillet and heat on medium temperature. Frying in batches, drop the fillets in oil and cook until using a fork the fish easily flakes, 5 to 6 minutes per side. Transfer the fillets to a serving platter, keep warm, and serve with the pecan butter sauce. Garnish with lemon wedges.

### Nutrition Information

- Calories:
- Fiber:
- Total Carbohydrate:
- Cholesterol:
- Protein:
- Total Fat:
- Sodium:

## 306. Champion Lamb Burgers

*Serving: 6 servings. | Prep: 15mins | Cook: 10mins | Ready in:*

### Ingredients

- 2 large red onions, thinly sliced
- 2 teaspoons olive oil
- 1 tablespoon red wine vinegar
- 2 teaspoons minced fresh rosemary
- 1-1/2 teaspoons sugar
- 1 teaspoon stone-ground mustard
- 1/4 teaspoon salt
- 1/4 teaspoon pepper
- BURGERS:
- 2 pounds ground lamb
- 2 garlic cloves, minced
- 1 teaspoon salt
- 1/4 teaspoon pepper
- 6 pita pocket halves
- 2 tablespoons olive oil
- 1-1/2 cups spring mix salad greens

### Direction

- Sauté the onions in oil in a large skillet until softened. Put in the pepper, salt, mustard, sugar, rosemary and vinegar; then cook for five more minutes. Keep it warm.
- Into A large bowl, crumble the lamb; sprinkle on pepper, salt and garlic and combine well. Form into six patties. Place the burgers on the grill over medium heat, covered, or broil 4 inches from the heat for 4 to 6 minutes per side or until a thermometer says 160°F and the juices run clear.
- Brush with oil the pita pockets; grill both sides lightly. Present burgers in pita pockets with onions and lettuce.

### Nutrition Information

- Calories: 445 calories
- Total Carbohydrate: 23g carbohydrate (4g sugars
- Cholesterol: 100mg cholesterol
- Protein: 29g protein.
- Total Fat: 26g fat (9g saturated fat)
- Sodium: 748mg sodium
- Fiber: 2g fiber)

### 307. Champion Lamb Burgers For Two

*Serving: 2 servings. | Prep: 15mins | Cook: 10mins | Ready in:*

### Ingredients

- 1 medium red onion, thinly sliced
- 1 teaspoon olive oil
- 1-1/2 teaspoons red wine vinegar
- 1 teaspoon minced fresh rosemary
- 1/2 teaspoon sugar
- 1/2 teaspoon stone-ground mustard
- 1/8 teaspoon salt
- 1/8 teaspoon pepper
- BURGERS:
- 12 ounces ground lamb
- 1 garlic cloves, minced
- 1/2 teaspoon salt
- 1/8 teaspoon pepper
- 2 pita pocket halves
- 2 teaspoons olive oil
- 1/2 cup spring mix salad greens

### Direction

- Put the oil and onions in a big skillet and sauté it until the onions have softened. Mix in the rosemary, salt, sugar, pepper, vinegar and mustard and let the mixture cook for 5 more minutes. Make sure to keep the mixture warm.
- In a big bowl, put in the lamb and break it apart then season it with salt, pepper and garlic; mix everything thoroughly. Form the lamb mixture into 2 patties. Put the lamb patties onto the grill over medium heat then cover and let it grill, or put the patties in a broiler and let it broil 4 inches away from the heat for 4 to 6 minutes on every side until the juices are clear and the thermometer inserted on the patties indicate 160°.
- Use a brush to coat the pita pockets with oil then let it grill a little bit on both sides. Put the grilled lamb patties, onions and lettuce inside the pita pockets and serve.

### Nutrition Information

- Calories:
- Protein:
- Total Fat:
- Sodium:
- Fiber:
- Total Carbohydrate:
- Cholesterol:

## 308. Cheesy Lamb Cups

*Serving: 6 servings. | Prep: 15mins | Cook: 20mins | Ready in:*

### Ingredients

- 1 envelope onion soup mix
- 1/3 cup dry bread crumbs
- 1 cup evaporated milk
- 2 pounds ground lamb
- 4 ounces cheddar cheese, cut into 12 cubes
- 1 can (10-3/4 ounces) condensed cheddar cheese soup, undiluted
- 1/2 cup milk
- 1 teaspoon Worcestershire sauce

### Direction

- Whisk together evaporated milk, bread crumbs and soup mix in a small bowl. Crumble lamb over the mixture and stir well.
- Divide the mixture into half and fill 12 greased muffin cups half full with the first portion of the lamb mixture. Insert one cheese cube into the middle of each cup. Layer the remaining portion on top of the cup while mound each lightly. Bake for 20-25 minutes at 375 degrees or until a thermometer registers 160 degrees.
- In the meantime, in a small saucepan, stir Worcestershire sauce, milk and soup together, heat through and stirring until it smooth. Spoon over the lamb cups to serve.

### Nutrition Information

- Calories: 507 calories
- Sodium: 1112mg sodium
- Fiber: 1g fiber)
- Total Carbohydrate: 17g carbohydrate (6g sugars
- Cholesterol: 142mg cholesterol
- Protein: 36g protein.
- Total Fat: 34g fat (16g saturated fat)

## 309. Cheesy Summer Squash Flatbreads

*Serving: 4 servings. | Prep: 15mins | Cook: 15mins | Ready in:*

### Ingredients

- 3 small yellow summer squash, sliced 1/4 inch thick
- 1 tablespoon olive oil
- 1/2 teaspoon salt
- 2 cups fresh baby spinach, coarsely chopped
- 2 naan flatbreads
- 1/3 cup roasted red pepper hummus
- 1 carton (8 ounces) fresh mozzarella cheese pearls
- Pepper

### Direction

- Heat the oven to 425 degrees. Toss squash with salt and oil; scatter evenly in a 15x10x1-inch baking pan. Roast for 8 to 10 minutes or until tender. Place to a bowl; mix in spinach.
- Put naan on a baking sheet; smear hummus on. Place cheese and squash mixture on top. Put on a lower oven rack and bake for 4-6 minutes or just until cheese melts. Dust with pepper.

### Nutrition Information

- Calories: 332 calories
- Sodium: 737mg sodium
- Fiber: 3g fiber)
- Total Carbohydrate: 24g carbohydrate (7g sugars
- Cholesterol: 47mg cholesterol
- Protein: 15g protein.
- Total Fat: 20g fat (9g saturated fat)

## 310. Chicken Athena

*Serving: Serves 4 | Prep: | Cook: |Ready in:*

### Ingredients

- 3 tablespoons olive oil
- 1 3 1/2 pound chicken, cut into 8 pieces
- 6 garlic cloves, chopped
- 1 1/2 teaspoon aniseed, crushed
- 1 28-ounce can Italian plum tomatoes
- 1/2 cup low-salt chicken broth
- 1/4 cup Ouzo, Pernod or Ricard
- 1 tablespoon dried oregano, crumbled
- 12 black brine-cured olives, pitted
- 4 ounces feta cheese, crumbled

### Direction

- Heat olive oil on medium high heat in big heavy skillet. Season chicken with pepper and salt. In batches if needed, sauté chicken for 5 minutes per side till brown; put onto plate.
- Pour all drippings off skillet but 2 tbsp.; add aniseed and garlic. Mix for 30 seconds. Add ouzo, broth, oregano and tomatoes; simmer, using back of spoon to break tomatoes up. Put chicken in skillet; simmer. Cook for 15 minutes, uncovered. Put chicken breasts onto plates. Flip chicken pieces in skillet; simmer for 5 minutes. Put chicken in skillet onto same plate.
- Put heat on high then add olives; cook, occasionally mixing, for 6-8 minutes till liquid reduces to sauce consistency. Use pepper and salt to season to taste. You can make it 1 day ahead. Cover; refrigerate. Gently reheat before continuing. Sprinkle with feta cheese; serve.

### Nutrition Information

- Calories: 842
- Saturated Fat: 18 g(88%)
- Sodium: 540 mg(22%)
- Fiber: 4 g(14%)
- Total Carbohydrate: 13 g(4%)
- Cholesterol: 228 mg(76%)
- Protein: 57 g(114%)
- Total Fat: 59 g(90%)

## 311. Chicken Sausage Gyros

*Serving: 4 servings. | Prep: 10mins | Cook: 10mins | Ready in:*

### Ingredients

- 1 package (12 ounces) fully cooked spinach and feta chicken sausage links or flavor of your choice, cut into 1/4-inch slices
- 1 cup (8 ounces) reduced-fat sour cream
- 1/4 cup finely chopped cucumber
- 1-1/2 teaspoons red wine vinegar
- 1-1/2 teaspoons olive oil
- 1/2 teaspoon garlic powder
- 4 whole wheat pita breads (6 inches)
- 1 plum tomato, sliced
- 1/2 small onion, thinly sliced

### Direction

- Use cooking spray to grease a big pan. On medium heat, cook sausage in the pan until completely heated.
- In the meantime, mix garlic powder, sour cream, oil, vinegar, and cucumber in a small bowl. Top the pita breads with chicken sausage, cucumber sauce, onion, and tomato.

### Nutrition Information

- Calories: 418 calories
- Total Carbohydrate: 42g carbohydrate (6g sugars
- Cholesterol: 75mg cholesterol
- Protein: 27g protein.
- Total Fat: 15g fat (6g saturated fat)
- Sodium: 873mg sodium
- Fiber: 5g fiber)

## 312. Chicken Sweet Potato Stew

*Serving: 6 servings. | Prep: 20mins | Cook: 45mins | Ready in:*

### Ingredients

- 2 pounds boneless skinless chicken thighs, cut into 2-inch pieces
- 2 medium sweet potatoes, peeled and cut into 2-inch pieces
- 1 cup chicken broth
- 1 small onion, coarsely chopped
- 2 tablespoons honey
- 1 tablespoon olive oil
- 1 teaspoon pepper
- 1 teaspoon ground allspice
- 1/4 teaspoon salt
- Dash ground cinnamon
- Dash ground nutmeg
- 1 cup dried cranberries
- 1/4 cup chopped pistachios, toasted
- Hot cooked couscous, optional

### Direction

- Combine the first 11 ingredients in a Dutch oven. Bake, covered, for 30 minutes at 400°.
- Remove cover; drizzle cranberries on top. Bake for another 15 to 20 minutes or until chicken loses its pink color. Add drizzled pistachios on top. Serve with couscous if wanted.

### Nutrition Information

- Calories: 399 calories
- Protein: 30g protein.
- Total Fat: 16g fat (4g saturated fat)
- Sodium: 372mg sodium
- Fiber: 3g fiber)
- Total Carbohydrate: 35g carbohydrate (24g sugars
- Cholesterol: 102mg cholesterol

## 313. Chicken With Couscous

*Serving: 4 | Prep: 20mins | Cook: 25mins | Ready in:*

### Ingredients

- 3 1/4 cups low-sodium chicken broth
- 1 cup quick-cooking couscous
- 2 tablespoons olive oil
- 4 skinless, boneless chicken breast halves - cut into cubes
- 1 pinch ground black pepper
- 1/2 cup finely chopped jalapeno chile peppers
- 1 carrot, thinly sliced
- 1 zucchini, diced
- 3 green onions, thinly sliced
- 1 1/2 teaspoons grated fresh ginger root
- 1 1/2 teaspoons curry powder
- 1/2 teaspoon ground coriander seed
- 1 teaspoon cornstarch

### Direction

- Boil 2 cups of chicken broth in a medium saucepan. Mix 1 1/2 tsp. olive oil and couscous in. Turn heat off. Cover. Let stand for 10 minutes.
- In a medium skillet, heat 1 tbsp. olive oil on medium heat. Mix chicken in. Use pepper to season. Cook till juices are clear and not pink. Take chicken out of skillet. Put aside.
- In skillet, heat leftover olive oil on medium heat. Mix carrot and jalapeno peppers in. Sauté for 2 minutes. Mix 1/4 cup of chicken broth, ginger, green onions and zucchini in. Stir and cook for 5 minutes till tender.
- Blend cornstarch, coriander, curry powder and leftover 1 cup of chicken broth in a small bowl. Pour on veggies. Put chicken into skillet. Cook till chicken is coated and broth mixture starts to thicken for 2 minutes. Serve on top of couscous.

### Nutrition Information

- Calories: 415 calories;
- Cholesterol: 75
- Protein: 35.8
- Total Fat: 11.5
- Sodium: 177
- Total Carbohydrate: 40.6

### 314. Chicken With Garlic Caper Sauce

*Serving: 4 servings. | Prep: 15mins | Cook: 15mins | Ready in:*

## Ingredients

- 4 boneless skinless chicken breast halves (6 ounces each)
- 1/2 teaspoon salt
- 1/2 teaspoon coarsely ground pepper
- 1 tablespoon olive oil
- 5 garlic cloves, minced
- 1/2 cup heavy whipping cream
- 1/3 cup white wine
- 1/4 cup chopped oil-packed sun-dried tomatoes
- 2 tablespoons capers, drained
- Hot cooked bow tie pasta

## Direction

- Lightly flatten the chicken, then use pepper and salt to scatter. Cook chicken in a big skillet with oil on medium heat until juices run clear, or about 5 to 7 minutes per side. Put in garlic and cook for another minute.
- Stir in capers, tomatoes, wine and cream, then cook until sauce is thickened lightly. Serve along with pasta.

## Nutrition Information

- Calories: 351 calories
- Total Carbohydrate: 4g carbohydrate (0 sugars
- Cholesterol: 135mg cholesterol
- Protein: 36g protein.
- Total Fat: 19g fat (9g saturated fat)
- Sodium: 535mg sodium
- Fiber: 1g fiber)

### 315. Chicken With Sugar Pumpkins & Apricots

*Serving: 8 servings. | Prep: 20mins | Cook: 04hours00mins | Ready in:*

## Ingredients

- 3 peeled and cubed fresh Sugar Baby pumpkins (5 to 6 cups each)
- 1 tablespoon canola oil
- 8 boneless skinless chicken thighs (4 ounces each)
- 1 medium red onion, chopped
- 2 garlic cloves, minced
- 3/4 cup dried Turkish apricots, diced
- 1/2 cup apricot nectar
- 1/3 cup apricot preserves
- 2 tablespoons lemon juice
- 1 teaspoon ground ginger
- 1 teaspoon ground cinnamon
- 1 teaspoon salt
- 1/2 teaspoon pepper
- 3 tablespoons minced fresh parsley
- Hot cooked rice
- 1/2 cup pomegranate seeds, optional

## Direction

- In a 5-quart slow cooker that is coated with cooking spray, put pumpkin.
- Heat oil in a big nonstick skillet over medium-high heat; brown all sides of the chicken thighs. Transfer the chicken to the slow cooker. Sauté garlic and onions in the same skillet for 1-2 minutes; transfer to the slow cooker.
- Add the next 8 ingredients to the slow cooker. Put the lid on and cook on low for 4-5 hours until the meat is soft. Put parsley on top. Enjoy

with hot cooked rice and sprinkle pomegranate seeds over if you want.

## Nutrition Information

- Calories: 318 calories
- Protein: 24g protein. Diabetic Exchanges: 2 starch
- Total Fat: 10g fat (3g saturated fat)
- Sodium: 376mg sodium
- Fiber: 3g fiber)
- Total Carbohydrate: 36g carbohydrate (20g sugars
- Cholesterol: 76mg cholesterol

## 316. Chicken Feta Phyllo Bundles

*Serving: 2 servings. | Prep: 20mins | Cook: 30mins | Ready in:*

## Ingredients

- 6 sheets phyllo dough (14 inches x 9 inches)
- 1/4 cup butter, melted
- 2 boneless skinless chicken breast halves
- Lemon-pepper seasoning
- 1/2 cup crumbled feta cheese

## Direction

- Onto work surface, put 1 phyllo dough sheet; brush melted butter over. Repeat using 2 more phyllo sheets, brushing every layer. To avoid leftover phyllo dough from drying out, keep it covered in plastic wrap then a damp towel. Use lemon-pepper to season chicken. Along 1 short pastry edge, put 1 chicken breast. Put 1/4 cup of cheese over. Fold sides over chicken; roll up. Brush melted butter over.
- Put onto ungreased baking sheet and repeat with leftover ingredients; bake at 350°, with no cover, till phyllo dough turns golden brown for 30-35 minutes.

## Nutrition Information

- Calories: 422 calories
- Protein: 20g protein.
- Total Fat: 29g fat (18g saturated fat)
- Sodium: 664mg sodium
- Fiber: 2g fiber)
- Total Carbohydrate: 20g carbohydrate (2g sugars
- Cholesterol: 108mg cholesterol

## 317. Chickpea Mint Tabbouleh

*Serving: 4 servings. | Prep: 10mins | Cook: 20mins | Ready in:*

## Ingredients

- 1 cup bulgur
- 2 cups water
- 1 cup fresh or frozen peas (about 5 ounces), thawed
- 1 can (15 ounces) chickpeas or garbanzo beans, rinsed and drained
- 1/2 cup minced fresh parsley
- 1/4 cup minced fresh mint
- 1/4 cup olive oil
- 2 tablespoons julienned soft sun-dried tomatoes (not packed in oil)
- 2 tablespoons lemon juice
- 1/2 teaspoon salt
- 1/4 teaspoon pepper

## Direction

- Mix together bulgur and water in a big saucepan, then bring to a boil. Lower heat and simmer with a cover for 10 minutes. Stir in frozen or fresh peas, then cook with a cover for about 5 minutes, until peas and bulgur are both softened.

- Turn to a big bowl, then stir in remaining ingredients; serve warm, or leave in the fridge and serve chilled.

## Nutrition Information

- Calories: 380 calories
- Protein: 11g protein. Diabetic Exchanges: 3 starch
- Total Fat: 16g fat (2g saturated fat)
- Sodium: 450mg sodium
- Fiber: 11g fiber)
- Total Carbohydrate: 51g carbohydrate (6g sugars
- Cholesterol: 0 cholesterol

## 318. Contest Winning Greek Pizza

*Serving: 4 servings. | Prep: 15mins | Cook: 15mins | Ready in:*

### Ingredients

- 4 pita breads (6 inches)
- 1 cup reduced-fat ricotta cheese
- 1/2 teaspoon garlic powder
- 1 package (10 ounces) frozen chopped spinach, thawed and squeezed dry
- 3 medium tomatoes, sliced
- 3/4 cup crumbled feta cheese
- 3/4 teaspoon dried basil

### Direction

- On a baking sheet, put pita breads. Mix garlic powder and ricotta cheese; spread over pita. Place basil, feta cheese, tomatoes, and spinach on top.
- Bake for 12 to 15 minutes at 400 degrees or until the bread turns light brown.

## Nutrition Information

- Calories: 320 calories
- Total Carbohydrate: 46g carbohydrate (7g sugars
- Cholesterol: 26mg cholesterol
- Protein: 17g protein. Diabetic Exchanges: 2 starch
- Total Fat: 7g fat (4g saturated fat)
- Sodium: 642mg sodium
- Fiber: 6g fiber)

## 319. Corsican Chicken

*Serving: 8 servings. | Prep: 20mins | Cook: 04hours30mins | Ready in:*

### Ingredients

- 3 tablespoons butter, softened
- 2 tablespoons herbes de Provence
- 1 teaspoon salt
- 2 garlic cloves, minced
- 1/2 teaspoon coarsely ground pepper
- 2 pounds boneless skinless chicken thighs
- 1 large onion, chopped
- 1/2 cup oil-packed sun-dried tomatoes, julienned
- 1 can (10-1/2 ounces) condensed beef consomme, undiluted
- 1/2 cup dry vermouth or orange juice
- 1/2 cup pitted Greek olives, quartered
- 1 teaspoon grated orange zest
- 2 teaspoons cornstarch
- 1 tablespoon cold water
- 2 tablespoons minced fresh parsley or basil, or drained and diced pimientos, optional

### Direction

- In a small bowl, mix pepper, garlic, salt, herbes de Provence, and butter; rub over chicken.
- Put in a 5-qt. slow cooker. Put in vermouth, consomme, tomatoes, and onion. Cook on low, covered, until the chicken is no more pink, for

4-5 hours. Add orange zest and olives. Cover and cook for 30 minutes on high.
- Transfer the chicken to a serving dish and keep warm. Remove the meat and greens to a serving dish; keep warm. Then skim the fat from the cooking juices and transfer to a small saucepan. Boil the liquid.
- Mix water and cornstarch until smooth. Stir gradually into the pan. Boil, cook and stir until thickened, 2 minutes. Pour over the chicken. Sprinkle with basil, parsley, or pimientos if desired.

## Nutrition Information

- Calories: 287 calories
- Fiber: 1g fiber)
- Total Carbohydrate: 8g carbohydrate (4g sugars
- Cholesterol: 89mg cholesterol
- Protein: 23g protein.
- Total Fat: 16g fat (5g saturated fat)
- Sodium: 808mg sodium

## 320. Couscous Chicken Supper

*Serving: 4 servings. | Prep: 10mins | Cook: 30mins | Ready in:*

## Ingredients

- 1 medium yellow summer squash, chopped
- 1 medium sweet red pepper, chopped
- 1 medium green pepper, chopped
- 1 teaspoon dried rosemary, crushed
- 1/2 teaspoon salt
- 1/4 teaspoon pepper
- 4 tablespoons olive oil, divided
- 1 pound boneless skinless chicken breast halves
- 2 garlic cloves, minced
- 1-1/3 cups chicken broth
- 1 tablespoon dried minced onion
- 1 cup uncooked couscous

## Direction

- In a clean and dry 15x10x1-in. baking pan, put peppers and squash. Sprinkle with pepper, salt and rosemary. Drizzle 2 tablespoons oil over; stir gently to coat. Broil 4 in. from the heat, stirring every 5 minutes until tender, or about 10-15 minutes.
- Meanwhile, cook chicken with the remaining oil in a large skillet until a thermometer reads 170°. Put in garlic, cook for 1 more minute. Take out and keep warm.
- Put onion and broth into the skillet; bring to a boil. Mix in couscous. Cover and take away from the heat; allow to stand for 5 minutes. Use a fork to fluff. Cut chicken into several strips. Serve together with vegetables and couscous.

## Nutrition Information

- Calories: 443 calories
- Sodium: 667mg sodium
- Fiber: 4g fiber)
- Total Carbohydrate: 43g carbohydrate (5g sugars
- Cholesterol: 63mg cholesterol
- Protein: 31g protein.
- Total Fat: 17g fat (3g saturated fat)

## 321. Cranberry Salsa Chicken

*Serving: 4 servings. | Prep: 10mins | Cook: 10mins | Ready in:*

## Ingredients

- 4 boneless skinless chicken breast halves (4 ounces each)
- 1 tablespoon olive oil
- 1 jar (16 ounces) chunky salsa
- 1 cup dried cranberries
- 1/4 cup water

- 1 tablespoon honey
- 2 garlic cloves, minced
- 3/4 teaspoon ground cinnamon
- 1/2 teaspoon ground cumin
- 2 cups hot cooked couscous
- 1/4 cup slivered almonds, toasted

### Direction

- Sauté chicken with oil in a big nonstick skillet until both sides are brown.
- Mix cumin, cinnamon, garlic, honey, water, cranberries, and salsa together in a small bowl. Stir thoroughly. Add onto the chicken. Put a cover on and cook over medium-low heat until a thermometer displays 170°, about 10-15 minutes. Enjoy with couscous. Sprinkle almonds over.

### Nutrition Information

- Calories: 428 calories
- Cholesterol: 63mg cholesterol
- Protein: 27g protein.
- Total Fat: 10g fat (1g saturated fat)
- Sodium: 589mg sodium
- Fiber: 8g fiber)
- Total Carbohydrate: 54g carbohydrate (28g sugars

## 322. Crescent Beef Casserole

*Serving: 6 servings. | Prep: 5mins | Cook: 25mins | Ready in:*

### Ingredients

- 1 pound lean ground beef (90% lean)
- 1 cup diced zucchini
- 1/4 cup chopped onion
- 1/4 cup chopped green pepper
- 2 teaspoons olive oil
- 1 cup tomato puree
- 1 teaspoon dried oregano
- 1/4 teaspoon salt
- 1/8 teaspoon pepper
- 1-1/2 cups mashed potatoes
- 1 cup (4 ounces) crumbled feta cheese
- 1 tube (8 ounces) refrigerated crescent rolls

### Direction

- In a large skillet over medium heat, cook beef until not pink anymore; drain and put aside. In the same skillet, sauté green pepper, onion and zucchini in oil until crisp-tender. Mix in pepper, salt, oregano, tomato puree and beef; heat through.
- In an 11x7-in. baking dish greased with cooking spray, spread mashed potatoes. Add beef mixture on top; sprinkle with feta cheese.
- Unroll the crescent dough. Cut into four rectangles; place three rectangles over casserole. Bake at 375° until the top is browned, about 12-15 minutes. Roll the remaining dough into two crescent rolls; bake for later use.

### Nutrition Information

- Calories: 442 calories
- Protein: 26g protein.
- Total Fat: 22g fat (9g saturated fat)
- Sodium: 938mg sodium
- Fiber: 2g fiber)
- Total Carbohydrate: 30g carbohydrate (4g sugars
- Cholesterol: 67mg cholesterol

## 323. Curried Lamb Chops

*Serving: 2 servings. | Prep: 20mins | Cook: 15mins | Ready in:*

### Ingredients

- 4 bone-in loin lamb chops (about 3/4 pound)
- 1 tablespoon vegetable oil

- 1/2 cup chopped onion
- 1/2 cup diced peeled tart apple
- 1/2 teaspoon curry powder
- 4 teaspoons all-purpose flour
- 1/2 teaspoon salt
- 1/2 teaspoon sugar
- 1/4 teaspoon ground mustard
- 1-1/3 cups chicken broth
- 2 tablespoons lemon juice
- Hot cooked rice

### Direction

- Brown both sides of lamb chops in oil in a big skillet. Remove; keep warm. Sauté curry, apple and onion till tender in the same skillet. Mix mustard, sugar, salt and flour; add to pan. Mix in lemon juice and broth slowly till blended; boil on medium heat. Mix and cook for 2 minutes; lower heat.
- Put chops in skillet; cover. Simmer, flipping once, for 15 minutes till meat gets desired doneness; 170° well done, 160° medium and 145° for medium rare on a thermometer. Serve on rice.

### Nutrition Information

- Calories: 345 calories
- Protein: 34g protein.
- Total Fat: 16g fat (4g saturated fat)
- Sodium: 1287mg sodium
- Fiber: 2g fiber)
- Total Carbohydrate: 15g carbohydrate (8g sugars
- Cholesterol: 97mg cholesterol

## 324. Curried Lamb Stew

*Serving: 6 servings. | Prep: 15mins | Cook: 01hours25mins | Ready in:*

### Ingredients

- 2 pounds lean lamb stew meat, cut into 3/4-inch cubes
- 4 teaspoons olive oil
- 1 medium onion, chopped
- 2 garlic cloves, minced
- 1 tablespoon curry powder
- 1 teaspoon salt
- 1/4 teaspoon pepper
- 1/8 teaspoon each ground coriander, cumin and cinnamon
- 1/8 teaspoon cayenne pepper
- 1/4 cup all-purpose flour
- 1-1/4 cups water
- 1 cup unsweetened pineapple juice
- 1 medium tart apple, peeled and chopped
- 1/4 cup tomato sauce
- 1/2 cup sour cream
- Hot cooked noodles or rice, optional

### Direction

- Brown meat, in batches, on all sides with oil in a Dutch oven, then take out of the pan and keep warm. Cook garlic and onion in drippings until onion is softened. Put in cayenne, cinnamon, cumin, coriander, pepper, salt and curry; cook and stir about 2 minutes. Sprinkle over with flour, then cook and stir about 2 to 3 minutes. Stir in tomato sauce, apple, pineapple juice and water.
- Put the meat back to Dutch oven; bring to a boil. Lower heat, then cover and simmer until meat is softened, about an hour. Take away from the heat, stirring in sour cream. Serve together with rice or noodles, if wanted.

### Nutrition Information

- Calories: 310 calories
- Protein: 31g protein. Diabetic Exchanges: 4 lean meat
- Total Fat: 12g fat (4g saturated fat)
- Sodium: 533mg sodium
- Fiber: 2g fiber)
- Total Carbohydrate: 18g carbohydrate (0 sugars

- Cholesterol: 95mg cholesterol

### 325. Curried Lamb Stir Fry

*Serving: 4 servings. | Prep: 15mins | Cook: 0mins | Ready in:*

## Ingredients

- 1 teaspoon cornstarch
- 1/4 cup chicken broth
- 1 tablespoon soy sauce
- 1/4 teaspoon curry powder
- 12 ounces boneless lamb, cut into 1/8-inch strips
- 1 small onion, chopped
- 2 garlic cloves, minced
- 2 tablespoons vegetable oil, divided
- 1 small apple, chopped
- 1/2 cup chopped green pepper
- 1/2 cup sliced celery
- 1 can (8 ounces) sliced water chestnuts, drained
- 6 ounces fresh or frozen snow peas
- 1/4 teaspoon ground ginger
- Hot cooked rice

## Direction

- Combine curry powder, soy sauce, broth, and cornstarch in a mixing bowl until no lumps remain; put to one side. Sauté garlic, onion, and lamb in 1 tablespoon oil in a wok or large skillet until meat turns brown. Take out and keep warm. Sauté ginger, peas, water chestnuts, celery, green pepper, and apple in the remaining oil in the same skillet until crisp-tender. Add cooked lamb mixture. Whisk broth mixture and pour into the skillet. Bring to a boil. Cook, stirring until thickened, about 2 minutes. Serve right away with rice.

## Nutrition Information

- Calories: 264 calories
- Total Fat: 12g fat (0 saturated fat)
- Sodium: 198mg sodium
- Fiber: 0 fiber)
- Total Carbohydrate: 19g carbohydrate (0 sugars
- Cholesterol: 55mg cholesterol
- Protein: 20g protein. Diabetic Exchanges: 2 meat

### 326. Curried Lamb And Barley Grain

*Serving: 4-6 servings. | Prep: 10mins | Cook: 01hours15mins | Ready in:*

## Ingredients

- CURRIED LAMB AND BARLEY:
- 1 pound ground lamb
- 1 large onion, chopped
- 1 cup medium pearl barley
- 1/2 cup sliced celery
- 1 tablespoon canola oil
- 3 cups chicken broth
- 1 to 2 tablespoons curry powder
- CUCUMBER SALSA:
- 1-1/2 cups coarsely chopped seeded cucumber
- 1/2 cup plain yogurt
- 1/4 cup snipped fresh parsley
- 1 tablespoon chopped green onion
- 1 tablespoon snipped fresh mint
- 2 teaspoons lemon juice
- 2 teaspoons olive oil
- 1 garlic clove, minced

## Direction

- In a skillet, sauté onion, lamb, celery and barley in oil till barley is golden and lamb is browned. Add curry powder and broth; set to a boil. Pour into a 2-quart baking dish. Uncover and bake at 350° for approximately 1 and 1/4 to 1 and a half hours till barley is softened.

- In a small bowl, combine the salsa ingredients. Refrigerate, covered, for 1 hour. Serve with lamb.

## Nutrition Information

- Calories: 336 calories
- Total Carbohydrate: 32g carbohydrate (4g sugars
- Cholesterol: 53mg cholesterol
- Protein: 19g protein.
- Total Fat: 15g fat (5g saturated fat)
- Sodium: 531mg sodium
- Fiber: 7g fiber)

### 327. Curried Meat Loaf

*Serving: 6-8 servings. | Prep: 15mins | Cook: 60mins | Ready in:*

## Ingredients

- 1 large egg, beaten
- 1/3 cup milk
- 1/2 cup dry bread crumbs or rolled oats
- 1 garlic clove, minced
- 1 to 2 teaspoons curry powder
- 1 teaspoon ground cumin
- 1/2 teaspoon salt
- 1/2 teaspoon pepper
- 1 cup shredded carrots
- 1 medium onion, chopped
- 1-1/2 pounds lean ground beef

## Direction

- Set oven to 350° and start preheating. Mix the first 10 ingredients. Put in ground beef; combine well. Pat the meat mixture into a 9x5-inch loaf pan. Bake for 60-75 minutes until no longer pink.

## Nutrition Information

- Calories: 188 calories
- Fiber: 1g fiber)
- Total Carbohydrate: 9g carbohydrate (3g sugars
- Cholesterol: 80mg cholesterol
- Protein: 19g protein.
- Total Fat: 8g fat (3g saturated fat)
- Sodium: 262mg sodium

### 328. Curry Lamb Stir Fry

*Serving: 4 servings. | Prep: 15mins | Cook: 0mins | Ready in:*

## Ingredients

- 1 teaspoon cornstarch
- 1/4 teaspoon curry powder
- 1/4 cup chicken broth
- 1 tablespoon soy sauce
- 3/4 pound boneless lamb, cut into 1/8-inch strips
- 1 small onion, chopped
- 2 tablespoons canola oil, divided
- 2 garlic cloves, minced
- 1 small red apple, chopped
- 1/2 cup chopped green pepper
- 1/2 cup sliced celery
- 1 can (8 ounces) sliced water chestnuts, drained
- 6 ounces fresh or frozen snow peas
- 1/4 teaspoon ground ginger
- Hot cooked rice

## Direction

- Combine curry powder and cornstarch in a small mixing bowl. Mix in soy sauce and broth until no lumps remain. Put to one side.
- Sauté onion and lamb in 1 tablespoon oil in a wok or large skillet until lamb turns brown. Add garlic, cook for another 1 minute. Take out and keep warm.
- Sauté ginger, peas, water chestnuts, celery, green pepper, and apple in remainder of oil in

the same skillet until crisp-tender. Put in lamb mixture.
- Stir broth mixture well and pour into the skillet. Bring to a boil. Cook, stirring, until thickened, about 2 minutes. Serve over rice.

## Nutrition Information

- Calories: 250 calories
- Total Fat: 12g fat (3g saturated fat)
- Sodium: 345mg sodium
- Fiber: 4g fiber)
- Total Carbohydrate: 19g carbohydrate (8g sugars
- Cholesterol: 47mg cholesterol
- Protein: 18g protein. Diabetic Exchanges: 2 lean meat

### 329. Dijon Leg Of Lamb

*Serving: 9 servings. | Prep: 10mins | Cook: 01hours30mins | Ready in:*

## Ingredients

- 1 boneless leg of lamb (4 to 5 pounds)
- 1 cup Dijon mustard
- 1/2 cup soy sauce
- 2 tablespoons olive oil
- 1 tablespoon chopped fresh rosemary or 1 teaspoon dried rosemary, crushed
- 1 teaspoon ground ginger
- 1 garlic clove, minced

## Direction

- Slice leg of lamb horizontally from one long side to within 1 inch of the opposite side. To make it lie flat, open meat; take out and get rid of fat. In a large resealable plastic bag, place the lamb. Mix together in a small bowl the seasonings, oil, soy sauce and mustard. Over lamb, Place one cup of marinade. Secure the bag and flip to coat; place inside the refrigerator overnight. Place inside the refrigerator the left marinade, covered.
- Strain and get rid of marinade. Moisten a paper towel with cooking oil and coat the grill's rack lightly using long-handled tongs. Using a drip pan, prepare the grill for indirect heat.
- Put lamb over the drip pan and grill, cover, over medium-low heat for 1 to 1/2 to 2 1/2 hours or until meat achieves the doneness desired (a thermometer should read 145°F for medium rare; 160°F for medium; 170°F for well done). For 10 minutes, let it stand before slicing. Heat reserved mustard sauce; present with lamb.

## Nutrition Information

- Calories:
- Total Carbohydrate:
- Cholesterol:
- Protein:
- Total Fat:
- Sodium:
- Fiber:

### 330. Easy Greek Pizza

*Serving: 6 servings. | Prep: 15mins | Cook: 15mins | Ready in:*

## Ingredients

- 1 prebaked 12-inch pizza crust
- 1/2 cup pizza sauce
- 1 teaspoon lemon-pepper seasoning, divided
- 2 cups shredded cooked chicken breast
- 1-1/2 cups chopped fresh spinach
- 1 small red onion, thinly sliced and separated into rings
- 1/4 cup sliced ripe olives
- 3/4 cup shredded part-skim mozzarella cheese
- 1/2 cup crumbled feta cheese

### Direction

- On an ungreased baking sheet, put the crust; spread with pizza sauce and dust with 1/2 teaspoon of lemon-pepper seasoning. Put chicken, spinach, onion, olives, cheeses, and the rest of lemon-pepper seasoning on top. Bake for 12 to 15 minutes at 450 degrees or until cheese has melted and edges turned light brown.

### Nutrition Information

- Calories: 321 calories
- Protein: 26g protein. Diabetic Exchanges: 3 lean meat
- Total Fat: 9g fat (4g saturated fat)
- Sodium: 719mg sodium
- Fiber: 2g fiber)
- Total Carbohydrate: 32g carbohydrate (3g sugars
- Cholesterol: 49mg cholesterol

## 331. Feta Shrimp With Linguine

*Serving: 4 servings. | Prep: 15mins | Cook: 15mins | Ready in:*

### Ingredients

- 8 ounces uncooked whole wheat linguine
- 4 garlic cloves, minced
- 1 teaspoon olive oil
- 1 can (28 ounces) diced tomatoes, undrained
- 1/4 cup sun-dried tomatoes (not packed in oil), chopped
- 1/4 cup Greek olives, coarsely chopped
- 1/4 teaspoon salt
- 1/4 teaspoon pepper
- 1 pound uncooked medium shrimp, peeled and deveined
- 1/4 cup minced fresh parsley
- 2 tablespoons lemon juice
- 1/4 teaspoon crushed red pepper flakes
- 1/2 cup crumbled feta cheese

### Direction

- Following package directions to cook linguine. In the meantime, sauté garlic in a big skillet with oil about one minute. Put in pepper, salt, olives, sun-dried tomatoes and diced tomatoes. Bring the mixture to a boil. Lower the heat and simmer without a cover until thickened while stirring sometimes, or about 8 to 10 minutes.
- Put shrimp into the tomato mixture, then cook without a cover until shrimp are pink, or about 5 to 6 minutes. Stir in pepper flakes, lemon juice and parsley. Drain pasta and serve together with shrimp mixture. Sprinkle feta cheese on top.

### Nutrition Information

- Calories: 404 calories
- Sodium: 881mg sodium
- Fiber: 10g fiber)
- Total Carbohydrate: 58g carbohydrate (9g sugars
- Cholesterol: 145mg cholesterol
- Protein: 30g protein.
- Total Fat: 8g fat (2g saturated fat)

## 332. Feta Steak Tacos

*Serving: 8 servings. | Prep: 20mins | Cook: 10mins | Ready in:*

### Ingredients

- 1 beef flat iron steak or top sirloin steak (1-1/4 pounds), cut into thin strips
- 1/4 cup Greek vinaigrette
- 1/2 cup fat-free plain Greek yogurt
- 2 teaspoons lime juice
- 1 tablespoon oil from sun-dried tomatoes
- 1 small green pepper, cut into thin strips

- 1 small onion, cut into thin strips
- 1/4 cup chopped oil-packed sun-dried tomatoes
- 1/4 cup sliced Greek olives
- 8 whole wheat tortillas (8 inches), warmed
- 1/4 cup crumbled garlic and herb feta cheese
- Lime wedges

### Direction

- Toss vinaigrette and beef in a big bowl; stand for 15 minutes. Mix lime juice and yogurt in a small bowl.
- Heat oil from the sun-dried tomatoes on medium high heat in a big skillet. Add onion and pepper; mix and cook till crisp tender for 3-4 minutes. Put into a small bowl; mix in olives and sun-dried tomatoes.
- On medium high heat. Arrange same skillet. Put in beef and cook for 2-3 minutes till meat isn't pink, stirring. Take out of pan.
- Serve pepper mixture and steak in tortillas; put cheese over. Serve with lime wedges and yogurt mixture.

### Nutrition Information

- Calories: 317 calories
- Sodium: 372mg sodium
- Fiber: 3g fiber)
- Total Carbohydrate: 25g carbohydrate (2g sugars
- Cholesterol: 48mg cholesterol
- Protein: 20g protein. Diabetic Exchanges: 3 lean meat
- Total Fat: 15g fat (4g saturated fat)

### 333. Feta Tomato Basil Fish

*Serving: 4 servings. | Prep: 10mins | Cook: 10mins | Ready in:*

### Ingredients

- 1/3 cup chopped onion
- 1 garlic clove, minced
- 2 teaspoons olive oil
- 1 can (14-1/2 ounces) Italian diced tomatoes, drained
- 1-1/2 teaspoons minced fresh basil or 1/2 teaspoon dried basil
- 1 pound walleye, bass or other whitefish fillets
- 4 ounces crumbled feta cheese

### Direction

- Sauté garlic and onion together in a saucepan with oil until softened. Put in basil and tomatoes, then bring the mixture to a boil. Lower the heat and simmer without a cover about 5 minutes.
- In the meantime, broil fish away from the heat source about 4 to 6 inches, about 5 to 6 minutes. Put tomato mixture as well as cheese on top of each fillet, then broil until it is easy to make fish flake using a fork, or for another 5 to 7 minutes.

### Nutrition Information

- Calories: 295 calories
- Total Carbohydrate: 11g carbohydrate (0 sugars
- Cholesterol: 172mg cholesterol
- Protein: 38g protein. Diabetic Exchanges: 5 lean meat
- Total Fat: 10g fat (5g saturated fat)
- Sodium: 799mg sodium
- Fiber: 1g fiber)

### 334. Feta Dill Chicken Burgers

*Serving: 4 servings. | Prep: 15mins | Cook: 10mins | Ready in:*

### Ingredients

- 1 large egg, lightly beaten
- 1 large shallot, minced
- 2 tablespoons crushed Ritz crackers
- 2 tablespoons minced fresh dill
- 3 garlic cloves, minced
- 1/4 teaspoon salt
- 1/4 teaspoon pepper
- 1 pound ground chicken
- 1/2 cup finely crumbled feta cheese
- 2 tablespoons canola oil
- 4 hamburger buns, split
- Refrigerated tzatziki sauce and sliced tomato, optional

## Direction

- Mix first 7 ingredients together. Add chicken; lightly toss till thoroughly mixed. Stir cheese in gently.
- Form into 4 patties with 1/2-inch of thickness (mixture should be soft). Use oil to brush patties. Cover and grill over medium heat for 5-6 minutes on each side till a thermometer reads 165 degrees. Place patties on buns and serve. Use tomato and tzatziki sauce for topping if wished.

## Nutrition Information

- Calories: 414 calories
- Total Fat: 22g fat (5g saturated fat)
- Sodium: 608mg sodium
- Fiber: 2g fiber)
- Total Carbohydrate: 27g carbohydrate (4g sugars
- Cholesterol: 129mg cholesterol
- Protein: 27g protein.

### 335. Feta Stuffed Chicken

*Serving: 4 | Prep: 20mins | Cook: | Ready in:*

## Ingredients

- ¼ cup crumbled basil-and-tomato feta cheese (1 ounce) (see Tip)
- 2 tablespoons fat-free cream cheese (1 ounce)
- 4 skinless, boneless chicken breast halves (about 1- ¼ pounds total)
- ¼ to ½ teaspoon black pepper
- Dash salt
- 1 teaspoon olive oil or cooking oil
- ¼ cup chicken broth
- 1 (10 ounce) package prewashed fresh spinach, trimmed (8 cups)
- 2 tablespoons walnut or pecan pieces, toasted
- 1 tablespoon lemon juice
- Lemon slices, halved

## Direction

- Mix cream cheese and feta cheese in a small bowl and reserve. Cut a horizontal slit through the thickest part of every chicken breast half with a sharp knife to create a pocket. Fill the pockets with cheese mixture. You can hold the openings in place with wooden toothpicks if necessary. Drizzle salt and pepper onto the chicken.
- Over medium-high heat, cook the chicken in the hot oil about 12 minutes in a large nonstick skillet, flipping once, or until tender and pink color disappears (decrease the heat to medium if the chicken browns too fast). Take out the chicken from the skillet. Cover the chicken and keep it warm.
- Gently pour chicken broth into the skillet. Heat to boil and place in half of the spinach. Cover the skillet and let it cook for about 3 minutes or until the spinach has wilted. Take out the spinach from the skillet and reserve the liquid in the pan. Repeat this with the remaining spinach. Place all spinach back into the skillet. Mix in lemon juice and nuts.
- To serve, separate the spinach mixture into four dinner plates. Add chicken breasts on top. Stud with slices of lemon if desired.

## Nutrition Information

- Calories: 231 calories;

- Saturated Fat: 2
- Fiber: 6
- Total Carbohydrate: 2
- Total Fat: 8
- Sodium: 334
- Cholesterol: 90
- Sugar: 0
- Protein: 38

## 336. Fig & Wine Sauced Chicken Kabobs

*Serving: 6 servings. | Prep: 60mins | Cook: 15mins | Ready in:*

### Ingredients

- 5 small onions, divided
- 1/2 cup olive oil
- 2 garlic cloves, minced
- 1-1/2 pounds boneless skinless chicken breasts, cut into 1-inch cubes
- 1-1/4 pounds dried figs
- 2-1/2 cups sweet white wine
- 3 tablespoons orange marmalade
- 2 tablespoons fig preserves
- 2 tablespoons lemon juice
- 1/2 teaspoon salt
- 1/4 teaspoon white pepper
- 1/2 pound small fresh portobello mushrooms
- Hot cooked rice
- Fresh mint leaves and lemon wedges, optional

### Direction

- Grate two onions over a large re-sealable plastic bag. Add the oil, garlic, and chicken. Seal the bag and turn several times to coat, refrigerating for 8 hours or overnight to marinate. Meantime, boil a mixture of figs and wine in a large saucepan. Reduce the heat to simmer without cover for 50-60 minutes or until figs are tender. Remove figs from the saucepan but keep them warm. Let the liquid boil and reduce to 2/3 cup. Stir in the preserves, marmalade, lemon juice, salt, and pepper. Stir for 5-6 minutes until consistency is slightly thickened. Slice remaining onions into 1-in. pieces. Drain chicken, disposing of marinade. Alternately cue chicken with mushrooms and onions on six metal or pre-soaked wooden skewers. Use long-handled tongs to moisten a paper towel with cooking oil and to lightly coat the grill rack. Cook kabobs in a covered grill over medium heat, or broil 4 in. from the heat, for 10-15 minutes or until juices are clear, turning from time to time. Plate some rice and reserved figs; serve the kabob over it. Drizzle with sauce and garnish with mint and lemon, if desired.

### Nutrition Information

- Calories: 529 calories
- Total Fat: 9g fat (2g saturated fat)
- Sodium: 273mg sodium
- Fiber: 13g fiber)
- Total Carbohydrate: 80g carbohydrate (59g sugars
- Cholesterol: 63mg cholesterol
- Protein: 28g protein.

## 337. Flavorful Chicken Pasta

*Serving: 2 servings. | Prep: 15mins | Cook: 15mins | Ready in:*

### Ingredients

- 3/4 cup uncooked spiral pasta
- 1/2 pound boneless skinless chicken breasts, cut into 3/4-inch cubes
- 1/8 teaspoon garlic salt
- 1 teaspoon olive oil
- 1 can (14-1/2 ounces) diced tomatoes, drained
- 2 teaspoons dried basil
- 2 teaspoons Italian seasoning
- 1 tablespoon red wine vinegar
- 1/4 cup sliced ripe olives, drained

- 2 tablespoons sour cream
- 1 tablespoon grated Parmesan cheese

## Direction

- Prepare the pasta following the package instructions. In the meantime, sprinkle garlic salt on the chicken. Use cooking spray to grease a big non-stick pan; cook chicken for 5 minutes in oil until the meat is not pink.
- Mix in Italian seasoning, basil, and tomatoes; boil. Mix in vinegar. Lower heat; let it simmer for 5 minutes with cover.
- Put in olives then heat completely. Mix in sour cream until incorporated but avoid boiling. Drain the pasta then toss into the chicken mixture. Scatter with Parmesan cheese.

## Nutrition Information

- Calories: 368 calories
- Fiber: 5g fiber)
- Total Carbohydrate: 36g carbohydrate (9g sugars
- Cholesterol: 75mg cholesterol
- Protein: 31g protein. Diabetic Exchanges: 3 lean meat
- Total Fat: 10g fat (4g saturated fat)
- Sodium: 632mg sodium

## 338. Glazed Pork With Strawberry Couscous

*Serving: 10 servings. | Prep: 15mins | Cook: 01hours20mins | Ready in:*

## Ingredients

- 2 teaspoons dried marjoram
- 1 teaspoon salt
- 1 teaspoon seasoned pepper
- 1 bone-in pork loin roast (5 pounds)
- 1/2 cup seedless strawberry jam
- 1/2 cup orange juice, divided
- 1 can (14-1/2 ounces) chicken broth
- 1 package (10 ounces) plain couscous
- 1 cup fresh strawberries, quartered
- 1/4 cup minced fresh mint
- 2 teaspoons grated orange zest

## Direction

- Line foil over the bottom of a large shallow roasting pan; put aside. Combine pepper, salt, and marjoram. Massage roast with marjoram mixture. Arrange roast in the prepared roasting pan. Bake without covering for 60 minutes at 350°.
- Stir jam and 1/4 cup orange juice together; brush pork with half of the jam mixture. Bake until a thermometer registers 160°, for 20 to 30 minutes, basting with remainder of jam mixture after each 10 minutes. Allow meat to rest for 10 minutes before slicing.
- In the meantime, bring broth in a small saucepan to a boil. Mix in couscous. Put on the lid and turn off the heat; allow to sit until liquid is absorbed, for 5 minutes. Fluff couscous using a fork. Mix in the remaining orange juice, orange zest, mint, and strawberries. Serve couscous with pork.

## Nutrition Information

- Calories: 383 calories
- Cholesterol: 92mg cholesterol
- Protein: 36g protein. Diabetic Exchanges: 4 lean meat
- Total Fat: 11g fat (4g saturated fat)
- Sodium: 493mg sodium
- Fiber: 2g fiber)
- Total Carbohydrate: 35g carbohydrate (12g sugars

## 339. Greek Chicken

*Serving: 8 | Prep: 15mins | Cook: 30mins | Ready in:*

## Ingredients

- 1/2 cup olive oil
- 3 cloves garlic, chopped
- 1 tablespoon chopped fresh rosemary
- 1 tablespoon chopped fresh thyme
- 1 tablespoon chopped fresh oregano
- 2 lemons, juiced
- 1 (4 pound) chicken, cut into pieces

## Direction

- Combine lemon juice, oregano, thyme, rosemary, garlic and olive oil together in a glass dish. Add in chicken pieces; marinate with a cover in the refrigerator for 8 hours or overnight.
- Preheat the grill for high heat.
- Lightly coat the grill grate with oil. Place the chicken in the grill; discard the marinade. Cook the chicken pieces till the juices run clear, up to 15 minutes per side. The smaller pieces will not take as long.

## Nutrition Information

- Calories: 412 calories;
- Cholesterol: 97
- Protein: 31.1
- Total Fat: 30.7
- Sodium: 95
- Total Carbohydrate: 3.5

## 340. Greek Chicken Bake

*Serving: 8 servings. | Prep: 30mins | Cook: 50mins | Ready in:*

## Ingredients

- 3 tablespoons olive oil, divided
- 1 medium onion, chopped
- 7 garlic cloves, minced
- 2 teaspoons minced fresh thyme or 3/4 teaspoon dried thyme
- 2 teaspoons minced fresh rosemary or 3/4 teaspoon dried rosemary, crushed
- 3/4 teaspoon pepper, divided
- 2 pounds red potatoes, cut into 1/2-inch cubes
- 2 cans (14-1/2 ounces each) diced tomatoes, undrained
- 2 cups cut fresh green beans (1-inch pieces)
- 2 tablespoons finely chopped ripe olives
- 8 bone-in chicken thighs (about 3 pounds), skin removed
- 1/2 teaspoon salt
- 1/2 cup crumbled feta cheese
- Minced fresh parsley
- Hot cooked orzo pasta, optional

## Direction

- Set the oven to 375° for preheating. Put 1 tbsp. of oil in a large skillet and heat it over medium heat. Add the onion. Cook and stir it for 3-4 minutes until tender. Add the rosemary, 1/2 tsp. of pepper, thyme, and garlic. Cook the mixture for a minute before removing it from the pan.
- In the used pan, pour in the remaining oil and heat it over medium heat. Add the potatoes. Cook and stir the potatoes until browned lightly. Pour the onion mixture back into the pan. Mix in the olives, tomatoes, and green beans. Cook the mixture for 1 minute.
- Spread the mixture into the greased 13x9-inches baking dish. Sprinkle salt and leftover pepper all over the chicken. Arrange the chicken on top of the potato mixture. Cover and bake the dish for 40 minutes. Remove the cover and bake for 10-15 more minutes until the thermometer registers 170°-175°. Sprinkle the dish with parsley and feta. Serve this dish with orzo if desired. Make-Ahead: This can be prepared several hours ahead. Just cover and refrigerate. Before baking, make sure that the dish is removed from the fridge 30 minutes ahead. Bake the dish as instructed.

## Nutrition Information

- Calories:

- Protein:
- Total Fat:
- Sodium:
- Fiber:
- Total Carbohydrate:
- Cholesterol:

## 341. Greek Chicken Pasta

*Serving: 6 | Prep: 15mins | Cook: 15mins | Ready in:*

### Ingredients

- 1 (16 ounce) package linguine pasta
- 1/2 cup chopped red onion
- 1 tablespoon olive oil
- 2 cloves garlic, crushed
- 1 pound skinless, boneless chicken breast meat - cut into bite-size pieces
- 1 (14 ounce) can marinated artichoke hearts, drained and chopped
- 1 large tomato, chopped
- 1/2 cup crumbled feta cheese
- 3 tablespoons chopped fresh parsley
- 2 tablespoons lemon juice
- 2 teaspoons dried oregano
- salt and pepper to taste
- 2 lemons, wedged, for garnish

### Direction

- Heat a large pot of slightly salted water until it comes to a boil. Put in pasta and cook for 8 - 10 minutes until tender but still firm to the bite; drain the excess water.
- In a large skillet, heat olive oil over medium-high heat. Add in garlic and onion; sauté for about 2 minutes until fragrant. Mix in the chicken; cook for about 5 - 6 minutes, stirring occasionally, until the chicken juices run clear and the middle of chicken is no longer pink.
- Lower heat to medium-low; add in cooked pasta, oregano, lemon juice, parsley, feta cheese, tomato and artichoke hearts. Cook and stir for about 2 - 3 minutes until cooked through. Take away from heat; add in pepper and salt for seasoning, then top with lemon wedges.

### Nutrition Information

- Calories: 488 calories;
- Total Fat: 11.4
- Sodium: 444
- Total Carbohydrate: 70
- Cholesterol: 55
- Protein: 32.6

## 342. Greek Chicken Penne

*Serving: 5 servings. | Prep: 15mins | Cook: 10mins | Ready in:*

### Ingredients

- 2-1/2 cups uncooked penne pasta
- 1 pound boneless skinless chicken breasts, cubed
- 1/2 cup chopped red onion
- 2 garlic cloves, minced
- 1 tablespoon olive oil
- 2 jars (7-1/2 ounces each) marinated quartered artichoke hearts, drained and chopped
- 1 large tomato, chopped
- 1/2 cup crumbled feta cheese
- 3 tablespoons minced fresh parsley
- 2 tablespoons lemon juice
- 2 teaspoons dried oregano
- 1/4 teaspoon salt
- 1/4 teaspoon pepper
- Fresh oregano, optional

### Direction

- Follow the package cooking instructions to cook pasta.
- At the same time, cook garlic, onion, and chicken with oil in a big skillet on medium heat until chicken is not pink anymore; 4 to 5

minutes. Mix in pepper, salt, oregano, lemon juice, parsley, cheese, tomato, and artichokes; heat through.
- Drain pasta; toss with the chicken mixture. Use oregano as a garnish if you wish.

## Nutrition Information

- Calories: 431 calories
- Cholesterol: 56mg cholesterol
- Protein: 26g protein.
- Total Fat: 21g fat (5g saturated fat)
- Sodium: 568mg sodium
- Fiber: 3g fiber)
- Total Carbohydrate: 36g carbohydrate (3g sugars

## 343. Greek Feta Casserole

*Serving: 2 servings. | Prep: 20mins | Cook: 35mins | Ready in:*

### Ingredients

- 1/2 cup uncooked elbow macaroni
- 1 egg, lightly beaten
- 2 tablespoons milk
- 1/2 cup crumbled feta cheese or shredded part-skim mozzarella cheese, divided
- 1/2 pound ground pork
- 2 tablespoons chopped onion
- 1/2 cup tomato sauce
- 1/8 to 1/4 teaspoon ground cinnamon

### Direction

- Follow package instructions to cook macaroni; drain.
- Combine 1/4 cup cheese, milk, and egg in a bowl. Mix in macaroni. Move to an oiled 3-cup baking dish. Cook onion and pork in a skillet on medium heat, until the meat is not pink anymore; drain. Mix in cinnamon and tomatoes sauce.

- Spread over the macaroni mixture. Sprinkle the rest of cheese over top. Put on cover and bake for 20 minutes at 375 degrees. Remove cover and bake for 12-16 minutes more or until heated through and bubbly.

## Nutrition Information

- Calories: 442 calories
- Total Fat: 25g fat (10g saturated fat)
- Sodium: 649mg sodium
- Fiber: 2g fiber)
- Total Carbohydrate: 20g carbohydrate (3g sugars
- Cholesterol: 199mg cholesterol
- Protein: 33g protein.

## 344. Greek Feta Chicken

*Serving: 4 | Prep: | Cook: 10mins | Ready in:*

### Ingredients

- 1 cup plain yogurt
- 2 cloves garlic, minced
- 1/2 teaspoon dried oregano
- 1/4 teaspoon ground black pepper
- 4 skinless, boneless chicken breast halves
- 1/2 cup feta cheese, crumbled
- 1/4 cup chopped fresh parsley, or to taste

### Direction

- In a bowl, combine black pepper, yogurt, oregano, and garlic. Put the chicken into yogurt marinade to coat all sides; cover then chill for 4 hours.
- On medium-high heat, preheat the outdoor grill then grease the grate lightly.
- Take the chicken out of the marinade then arrange on the preheated grill. Grill chicken for 6 minutes then turn; scatter with feta cheese. Grill for another 4-6 minutes until the juices are clear and the chicken is not pink in

the middle. An inserted instant-read thermometer in the middle should register at least 74°C or 165°Fahrenheit. Top chicken with fresh parsley.

## Nutrition Information

- Calories: 252 calories;
- Total Carbohydrate: 6.5
- Cholesterol: 96
- Protein: 31.5
- Total Fat: 10.4
- Sodium: 453

### 345. Greek Flatbread Pizzas

*Serving: 4 servings. | Prep: 10mins | Cook: 10mins | Ready in:*

## Ingredients

- 2 Italian herb flatbread wraps
- 1 tablespoon Greek vinaigrette
- 1/2 cup crumbled feta cheese
- 1/4 cup grated Parmesan cheese
- 1/2 cup pitted Greek olives, sliced
- 1/2 cup water-packed artichoke hearts, rinsed, drained and chopped
- 1/2 cup ready-to-use grilled chicken breast strips, chopped
- 1/8 teaspoon dried oregano
- 1/8 teaspoon dried basil
- Dash pepper
- 1 cup shredded part-skim mozzarella cheese

## Direction

- Put flatbread on an ungreased baking sheet; use vinaigrette to brush it with. Layer with the rest of the ingredients.
- Bake for 8 to 10 minutes at 400 degrees or until cheese melts.

## Nutrition Information

- Calories: 286 calories
- Cholesterol: 39mg cholesterol
- Protein: 19g protein.
- Total Fat: 16g fat (6g saturated fat)
- Sodium: 1035mg sodium
- Fiber: 2g fiber)
- Total Carbohydrate: 17g carbohydrate (2g sugars

### 346. Greek Garlic Chicken

*Serving: 6 servings. | Prep: 20mins | Cook: 03hours30mins | Ready in:*

## Ingredients

- 1/2 cup chopped onion
- 1 tablespoon plus 1 teaspoon olive oil, divided
- 3 tablespoons minced garlic
- 2-1/2 cups chicken broth, divided
- 1/4 cup pitted Greek olives, chopped
- 3 tablespoons chopped sun-dried tomatoes (not packed in oil)
- 1 tablespoon quick-cooking tapioca
- 2 teaspoons grated lemon peel
- 1 teaspoon dried oregano
- 6 boneless skinless chicken breast halves (6 ounces each)
- 1-3/4 cups uncooked couscous
- 1/2 cup crumbled feta cheese

## Direction

- Sauté onion in 1 tablespoon oil in a small skillet until crisp-tender. Put in garlic and continue to cook for 1 minute more.
- Transfer to a 5-qt. slow cooker. Next, stir in oregano, lemon peel, tapioca, tomatoes, olives, and 3/4 cup broth. Add chicken. Cook on low, covered, until the chicken is soft, or for 3-1/2-4 hours.
- Boil the leftover oil and broth in a large saucepan. Stir in couscous. Then cover and remove from the heat; allow to sit until the

broth is absorbed, or for 5 minutes. Serve with the chicken; dust with feta cheese.

### Nutrition Information

- Calories: 318 calories
- Sodium: 625mg sodium
- Fiber: 3g fiber)
- Total Carbohydrate: 47g carbohydrate (3g sugars
- Cholesterol: 21mg cholesterol
- Protein: 16g protein.
- Total Fat: 8g fat (2g saturated fat)

## 347. Greek Grilled Catfish

*Serving: 6 servings. | Prep: 10mins | Cook: 20mins | Ready in:*

### Ingredients

- 6 catfish fillets (8 ounces each)
- Greek seasoning to taste
- 4 ounces feta cheese, crumbled
- 1 tablespoon dried mint
- 2 tablespoons olive oil

### Direction

- Drizzle Greek seasoning on both sides of fillets. Sprinkle each fillet with 1/2 teaspoon mint and 1 rounded tablespoon feta cheese. Drizzle 1 teaspoon oil over each. Roll up fillets and hold in place with toothpicks.
- Over medium heat, grill for 20 to 25 minutes or until fish breaks easily with a fork. You may also grease baking dish, arrange fillets, and bake at 350°F, 30 to 35 minutes or until fish flakes easily with fork.

### Nutrition Information

- Calories: 288 calories
- Cholesterol: 115mg cholesterol
- Protein: 34g protein. Diabetic Exchanges: 4-1/2 lean meat
- Total Fat: 16g fat (0 saturated fat)
- Sodium: 319mg sodium
- Fiber: 0 fiber)
- Total Carbohydrate: 1g carbohydrate (0 sugars

## 348. Greek Isle Pizza

*Serving: 6 slices. | Prep: 20mins | Cook: 10mins | Ready in:*

### Ingredients

- 1 prebaked 12-inch thin pizza crust
- 1/2 cup chopped oil-packed sun-dried tomatoes plus 1 tablespoon of the oil, divided
- 1 small red onion, thinly sliced
- 1 teaspoon olive oil
- 2 garlic cloves, minced
- 1 teaspoon dried rosemary, crushed
- 1/4 teaspoon pepper
- Grated lemon peel, optional
- 2 cups fresh baby spinach, chopped
- 1-1/4 cups crumbled feta cheese
- 1/4 cup Greek olives, pitted and chopped
- 4 slices part-skim mozzarella cheese

### Direction

- On a 12-in. pizza pan without grease place crust; use the oil from sun-dried tomatoes to brush on crust. Set it aside.
- Put olive oil in a small frying pan, sauté onion until tender. Add the garlic and cook for 1 more minute. Take off heat; mix in lemon peel, if desired, pepper, and rosemary. Spread on crust. Put tomatoes and spinach on top.
- Sprinkle on olives and feta cheese, then mozzarella. Bake in a 425-degree oven until cheese melts, 10-12 minutes. Let it cool for 10 minutes before slicing.

### Nutrition Information

- Calories: 328 calories
- Protein: 15g protein. Diabetic Exchanges: 2 starch
- Total Fat: 16g fat (6g saturated fat)
- Sodium: 725mg sodium
- Fiber: 3g fiber)
- Total Carbohydrate: 30g carbohydrate (1g sugars
- Cholesterol: 23mg cholesterol

### 349.     Greek Lamb Kabobs

*Serving: 4 servings. | Prep: 10mins | Cook: 10mins | Ready in:*

## Ingredients

- 1/2 cup lemon juice
- 2 tablespoons dried oregano
- 4 teaspoons olive oil
- 6 garlic cloves, minced
- 1 pound boneless lamb, cut into 1-inch cubes
- 16 cherry tomatoes
- 1 large green pepper, cut into 1-inch pieces
- 1 large onion, cut into 1-inch wedges

## Direction

- Combine garlic, oil, oregano, and lemon juice in a small bowl. Transfer 1/4 cup of the mixture into a covered container and refrigerate for basting later. The remaining marinade goes into a large re-sealable plastic bag with the lamb; zip the top and turn several times to coat the lamb with the mixture. Store in the refrigerator for 8 hours or overnight, turning occasionally in the duration of storage. Drain and discard marinade from bag with the lamb. Thread lamb onions, green peppers, and tomatoes alternately on eight metal or water-soaked wooden skewers. Dab an oil-moistened paper towel on the grates to grease lightly; use a pair of long-handle tongs for safety. Cook on a covered grill at medium heat, or broil 4 in. from heat. Turn and baste occasionally within the grilling time, until lamb is at desired doneness and vegetables are cooked inside but still crisp outside, about 5-6 minutes per side.

## Nutrition Information

- Calories: 226 calories
- Protein: 25g protein. Diabetic Exchanges: 3 lean meat
- Total Fat: 9g fat (3g saturated fat)
- Sodium: 83mg sodium
- Fiber: 2g fiber)
- Total Carbohydrate: 13g carbohydrate (0 sugars
- Cholesterol: 74mg cholesterol

### 350.     Greek Lemon Chicken

*Serving: 6 servings | Prep: 15mins | Cook: | Ready in:*

## Ingredients

- 6 bone-in chicken thighs (1-1/2 lb.)
- 2 lemons, divided
- 1/2 cup KRAFT Greek Vinaigrette Dressing
- 1/2 cup ATHENOS Traditional Crumbled Feta Cheese
- 3 Tbsp. chopped fresh parsley, divided

## Direction

- 1. Put in a 9"x13" baking dish coated with cooking spray with chicken.
- 2. With one lemon, grate zest then squeeze juice. Combine together 2 tbsp. of parsley, cheese, dressing, lemon juice and zest until mixed, then drizzle over chicken.
- 3. Cut remaining lemon into 6 wedges and position around chicken, then chill for a half hour.
- 4. Heat the oven to 375 degrees F. Bake chicken until done (about 165 degrees F), about 30 to 35 minutes, then take chicken out of oven. Turn off oven and heat broiler.

- 5. Broil chicken 6 inches from heat source until turn golden brown, about 4 to 5 minutes. Sprinkle leftover parsley over chicken.

## Nutrition Information

- Calories: 210
- Saturated Fat: 4.5 g
- Fiber: 1 g
- Cholesterol: 95 mg
- Total Carbohydrate: 3 g
- Sugar: 1 g
- Protein: 17 g
- Total Fat: 15 g
- Sodium: 410 mg

## 351. Greek Lemon Turkey

*Serving: 16-20 servings. | Prep: 20mins | Cook: 02hours30mins | Ready in:*

### Ingredients

- 1 turkey (16 to 20 pounds)
- 6 garlic cloves, peeled and quartered
- 1/2 cup dried oregano
- 1/2 cup lemon juice
- 1 tablespoon salt
- 1 tablespoon pepper
- 1 tablespoon all-purpose flour
- 1 turkey-size oven roasting bag
- 5 large onions, quartered
- 6 large potatoes, cut into 2-inch cubes
- 5 medium carrots, quartered

### Direction

- Make a few deep gashes on the turkey then stuff a garlic slice in each. Mix pepper, oregano, salt, and lemon juice; massage over the turkey. In an oven bag, put flour then shake well; put in turkey then close. Chill for 6 hours to overnight.
- In a roasting pan at least two-inch deep, place the oven bag; insert carrots, potatoes, and onions in the bag. Use the provided nylon tie to secure the bag. Do not let the bag hang on top of the pan. Bake for 2 1/2- to 3 hours in 350 degrees oven without cover until a thermometer registers 180 degrees. Take the turkey out of the bag then let it sit for 20 minutes; slice. Keep the veggies warm. Serve the turkey slices with drippings and vegetables.

## Nutrition Information

- Calories: 516 calories
- Cholesterol: 184mg cholesterol
- Protein: 57g protein.
- Total Fat: 19g fat (5g saturated fat)
- Sodium: 498mg sodium
- Fiber: 4g fiber)
- Total Carbohydrate: 27g carbohydrate (5g sugars

## 352. Greek Meat Loaves

*Serving: 2 loaves (6 servings each). | Prep: 20mins | Cook: 50mins | Ready in:*

### Ingredients

- 2 large eggs, lightly beaten
- 1/2 cup ketchup
- 1/4 cup 2% milk
- 1 large red onion, finely chopped
- 3/4 cup quick-cooking oats
- 1/3 cup oil-packed sun-dried tomatoes, patted dry and finely chopped
- 1/3 cup pitted Greek olives, chopped
- 2 garlic cloves, minced
- 1 teaspoon salt
- 1 teaspoon pepper
- 2 pounds lean ground beef (90% lean)
- 1/2 cup crumbled feta cheese

### Direction

- Combine the first 10 ingredients in a large bowl. Put crumbled beef over mixture and mix thoroughly. Pat and shape into two well-greased 8x4-in. loaf pans. Put on a cover and freeze one meat loaf for maximum of 3 months.
- Bake the remaining meat loaf without a cover for 50-60 minutes at 350°, until the meat is no longer pink, and a thermometer reaches 160°. Allow to sit for 5 minutes. Move to a serving plate; top with a sprinkle of cheese.
- To cook the frozen meat loaf: Let thaw overnight in the refrigerator. Bake as instructed; top with a sprinkle of cheese.

### Nutrition Information

- Calories: 254 calories
- Cholesterol: 98mg cholesterol
- Protein: 21g protein.
- Total Fat: 15g fat (7g saturated fat)
- Sodium: 545mg sodium
- Fiber: 1g fiber)
- Total Carbohydrate: 9g carbohydrate (4g sugars

## 353. Greek Orzo Chicken

*Serving: 6 servings. | Prep: 15mins | Cook: 05hours30mins | Ready in:*

### Ingredients

- 6 bone-in chicken thighs, (about 2-1/4 pounds), skin removed
- 1 cup sliced fresh carrots
- 1 cup chicken broth
- 1/4 cup lemon juice
- 1 garlic clove, minced
- 1 teaspoon dried oregano
- 1/2 teaspoon salt
- 1 cup uncooked orzo pasta
- 1/2 cup sliced pitted green olives
- 1/4 cup golden raisins
- 1/2 cup minced fresh parsley
- 1/2 cup crumbled feta cheese

### Direction

- Mix salt, oregano, garlic, lemon juice, broth, carrots and chicken into a 3-quart slow cooker. Cook, covered, chicken for 5 to 6 hours over low heat or until chicken becomes tender.
- Mix in raisins, olives and orzo. Cook, covered, for another 30 minutes or until pasta is soft. Add a sprinkle of feta cheese and parsley.

### Nutrition Information

- Calories: 391 calories
- Total Carbohydrate: 35g carbohydrate (6g sugars
- Cholesterol: 93mg cholesterol
- Protein: 31g protein.
- Total Fat: 14g fat (4g saturated fat)
- Sodium: 783mg sodium
- Fiber: 2g fiber)

## 354. Greek Pasta Toss

*Serving: 4 servings. | Prep: 10mins | Cook: 20mins | Ready in:*

### Ingredients

- 3 cups uncooked whole wheat spiral pasta (about 7 ounces)
- 3/4 pound Italian turkey sausage links, casings removed
- 2 garlic cloves, minced
- 4 ounces fresh baby spinach (about 5 cups)
- 1/2 cup pitted Greek olives, halved
- 1/3 cup julienned oil-packed sun-dried tomatoes, drained and chopped
- 1/4 cup crumbled feta cheese
- Lemon wedges, optional

### Direction

- Following package directions to cook pasta in a 6-quart stockpot, then drain and take pasta back to the pot.
- In the meantime, cook and crumble sausage coarsely in a big skillet on medium high heat for 4 to 6 minutes, until it is not pink anymore. Put in garlic, then cook while mixing for 1 minutes. Put into the pasta.
- Stir in tomatoes, olives and spinach, then heat through, until spinach is wilted slightly. Stir in cheese and serve along with lemon wedges, if wished.

### Nutrition Information

- Calories: 335 calories
- Protein: 19g protein. Diabetic Exchanges: 2 starch
- Total Fat: 13g fat (3g saturated fat)
- Sodium: 742mg sodium
- Fiber: 6g fiber)
- Total Carbohydrate: 36g carbohydrate (1g sugars
- Cholesterol: 35mg cholesterol

## 355. Greek Pasta And Beef

*Serving: 12 servings. | Prep: 30mins | Cook: 45mins | Ready in:*

### Ingredients

- 1 package (16 ounces) elbow macaroni
- 1 pound ground beef
- 1 large onion, chopped
- 1 garlic clove, minced
- 1 can (8 ounces) tomato sauce
- 1/2 cup water
- 1 teaspoon salt
- 1/2 teaspoon ground cinnamon
- 1/4 teaspoon ground nutmeg
- 1/4 teaspoon pepper
- 1 large egg, lightly beaten
- 1/2 cup grated Parmesan cheese
- SAUCE:
- 1/4 cup butter
- 1/4 cup all-purpose flour
- 1/4 teaspoon ground cinnamon
- 3 cups 2% milk
- 2 large eggs, lightly beaten
- 1/3 cup grated Parmesan cheese

### Direction

- Follow the instruction on package to cook the macaroni. In a big skillet, cook the onion and beef on medium heat till the meat is not pink anymore. Put in the garlic; cook for 60 seconds more. Drain off. Whisk in seasonings, water and tomato sauce. Let simmer with cover for 10 minutes, whisk once in a while.
- Drain the macaroni and add into a big bowl. Whisk in the cheese and egg; put aside.
- For the sauce, in a big saucepan, melt the butter; whisk in the cinnamon and flour till smooth. Slowly pour in the milk. Boil on medium heat; cook and whisk till it thickens a bit or for 2 minutes. Take out of heat. Whisk a bit of the hot mixture into the eggs; bring all of them back to the pan, whisk continuously. Whisk in the cheese.
- In the greased 3-quart baking dish, spread 1/2 macaroni mixture. Add the leftover macaroni mixture and beef mixture on top. Add the sauce on top. Bake, with no cover, at 350 degrees till the thermometer reaches 160 degrees or for 45 to 50 minutes. Allow it to rest for 5 minutes prior to serving.

### Nutrition Information

- Calories: 330 calories
- Sodium: 467mg sodium
- Fiber: 2g fiber)
- Total Carbohydrate: 35g carbohydrate (5g sugars
- Cholesterol: 96mg cholesterol
- Protein: 18g protein.
- Total Fat: 13g fat (6g saturated fat)

## 356. Greek Pita Pizzas

*Serving: 2 servings. | Prep: 5mins | Cook: 5mins | Ready in:*

### Ingredients

- 2 whole pita breads
- 2 tablespoons olive oil, divided
- 1/4 cup sliced pimiento-stuffed olives
- 2 teaspoons red wine vinegar
- 1 garlic clove, minced
- 1/2 teaspoon dried oregano
- 1/4 teaspoon dried basil
- Dash pepper
- 1/2 cup torn fresh spinach
- 1/3 cup crumbled feta cheese
- 1 small tomato, seeded and chopped
- 1/4 cup shredded Parmesan cheese

### Direction

- Slather 1 tablespoon oil on pitas then arrange on a baking sheet. Broil for 2 minutes, 4 inches from heat.
- In the meantime, combine the remaining oil, olives, pepper, vinegar, basil, oregano, and garlic in a bowl; slather over the pitas. Add feta cheese, spinach, Parmesan cheese and tomato on top. Broil for another 3 minutes until the cheese melts.

### Nutrition Information

- Calories:
- Protein:
- Total Fat:
- Sodium:
- Fiber:
- Total Carbohydrate:
- Cholesterol:

## 357. Greek Pita Veggie Pizzas

*Serving: 6 servings. | Prep: 15mins | Cook: 10mins | Ready in:*

### Ingredients

- 6 whole wheat pita breads (6 inches)
- 1-1/2 cups meatless spaghetti sauce
- 1 can (14 ounces) water-packed artichoke hearts, rinsed, drained and quartered
- 2 cups fresh baby spinach, chopped
- 1-1/2 cups sliced fresh mushrooms
- 1/2 cup crumbled feta cheese
- 1 small green pepper, thinly sliced
- 1/4 cup thinly sliced red onion
- 1/4 cup sliced ripe olives
- 3 tablespoons grated Parmesan cheese
- 1/4 teaspoon pepper

### Direction

- On an ungreased cookie sheet place pita breads; spread on spaghetti sauce. Put the rest of the ingredients on top. Bake in a 350-degree oven until cheese melts, 8-12 minutes. Eat immediately.

### Nutrition Information

- Calories: 273 calories
- Total Fat: 5g fat (2g saturated fat)
- Sodium: 969mg sodium
- Fiber: 7g fiber)
- Total Carbohydrate: 48g carbohydrate (6g sugars
- Cholesterol: 7mg cholesterol
- Protein: 13g protein. Diabetic Exchanges: 2 starch

## 358. Greek Pizza

*Serving: 4 | Prep: 20mins | Cook: 25mins | Ready in:*

### Ingredients

- 1 tablespoon olive oil
- 1/2 cup diced onion
- 2 cloves garlic, minced
- 1/2 (10 ounce) package frozen chopped spinach, thawed and squeezed dry
- 1/4 cup chopped fresh basil
- 2 1/4 teaspoons lemon juice
- 1 1/2 teaspoons dried oregano
- ground black pepper to taste
- 1 (14 ounce) package refrigerated pizza crust
- 1 tablespoon olive oil
- 1 cup shredded mozzarella cheese
- 1 large tomato, thinly sliced
- 1/3 cup seasoned bread crumbs
- 1 cup shredded mozzarella cheese
- 3/4 cup crumbled feta cheese

### Direction

- Heat the oven to 400°F (200°C). If you are using a pizza stone, put in the oven to preheat.
- Put 1 tablespoon of olive oil in a large skillet and heat; stir and cook garlic and onion for about 5 minutes until tender. Put in spinach and keep on stirring and cooking for 5-7 minutes until all liquid vaporizes. Take away from the heat and season with pepper, oregano, lemon juice, and basil. Let the mixture slightly cool.
- Unfold the pizza dough on a large baking sheet or preheated pizza stone and use the leftover 1 tablespoon olive oil to brush it with. Spread spinach mixture over the dough, keeping a small border at the edge of the pizza crust. Place 1 cup mozzarella cheese on top.
- Put tomato slices into seasoned bread crumbs and press to coat; arrange tomatoes on top of the pizza. Spread the feta cheese and the leftover 1 cup mozzarella cheese on top of tomatoes.
- Place in the preheated oven and bake for about 15 minutes until the cheese melts and pizza crust turn golden brown.

### Nutrition Information

- Calories: 609 calories;
- Total Fat: 26.2
- Sodium: 1531
- Total Carbohydrate: 63.1
- Cholesterol: 61
- Protein: 30

### 359. Greek Pizzas

*Serving: 2 servings. | Prep: 10mins | Cook: 10mins | Ready in:*

### Ingredients

- 2 whole pita breads (6 inches)
- 1 teaspoon olive oil, divided
- 4 cups torn fresh spinach
- 2 tablespoons chopped green onion
- 1 teaspoon minced fresh dill
- 4 tomato slices, halved
- 1/2 cup crumbled feta cheese
- 1/4 to 1/2 cup shredded part-skim mozzarella cheese
- 1/8 teaspoon dried oregano
- 1/8 teaspoon pepper

### Direction

- Put pita breads on a baking sheet. Brush 1/4 teaspoon of oil on each. Broil for 1 to 2 minutes, 6-inches from the heat, or until light brown. Flip pitas over; brush with the leftover oil. Broil for 1 to 2 more minutes.
- Place spinach in a microwave-safe dish and microwave on high for 1 to 1-1/2 minutes or until wilted; strain well. Mix in dill and onion.
- Place cheeses, spinach mixture, and tomatoes on top of pitas. Dust with pepper and oregano. Bake for 7 to 9 minutes at 450 degrees or until cheese is brown lightly.

### Nutrition Information

- Calories: 295 calories
- Cholesterol: 18mg cholesterol
- Protein: 17g protein.
- Total Fat: 9g fat (4g saturated fat)
- Sodium: 810mg sodium
- Fiber: 4g fiber)
- Total Carbohydrate: 39g carbohydrate (3g sugars

### 360. Greek Pizzas For Two

*Serving: 2 servings. | Prep: 10mins | Cook: 10mins | Ready in:*

## Ingredients

- 1 Italian herb flatbread wrap
- 2-1/2 teaspoons Greek vinaigrette
- 1/4 cup crumbled feta cheese
- 2 tablespoons grated Parmesan cheese
- 1/4 cup Greek olives, sliced
- 1/4 cup water-packed artichoke hearts, rinsed, drained and chopped
- 1/4 cup ready-to-use grilled chicken breast strips, chopped
- Dash each dried oregano, dried basil and pepper
- 1/2 cup shredded part-skim mozzarella cheese

## Direction

- On an ungreased baking sheet, put wrap then brush using vinaigrette. Layer it using the rest of the ingredients.
- Bake until cheese is melted or for 8 to 10 minutes at 400 degrees.

## Nutrition Information

- Calories: 295 calories
- Protein: 19g protein.
- Total Fat: 17g fat (6g saturated fat)
- Sodium: 1062mg sodium
- Fiber: 2g fiber)
- Total Carbohydrate: 17g carbohydrate (2g sugars
- Cholesterol: 39mg cholesterol

### 361. Greek Ravioli Skillet

*Serving: 6 servings. | Prep: 15mins | Cook: 15mins | Ready in:*

## Ingredients

- 1 package (20 ounces) refrigerated cheese ravioli
- 1 pound ground beef
- 1 medium zucchini, sliced
- 1 small red onion, chopped
- 3 cups marinara or spaghetti sauce
- 1/2 cup water
- 1/4 teaspoon pepper
- 2 medium tomatoes, chopped
- 1/2 cup cubed feta cheese
- 1/2 cup pitted Greek olives, halved
- 2 tablespoons minced fresh basil, divided

## Direction

- Cook ravioli following package instruction. In the meantime, cook the onion, zucchini and beef in a big skillet over medium heat till meat is not pink anymore; drain.
- Drain the ravioli; put into skillet. Mix in the pepper, water and marinara sauce. Boil. Lower heat; allow to simmer without cover for 5 minutes. Put in a tablespoon basil, olives, cheese, and tomatoes. Scatter leftover basil over.

## Nutrition Information

- Calories: 543 calories
- Total Fat: 20g fat (8g saturated fat)
- Sodium: 917mg sodium
- Fiber: 6g fiber)

- Total Carbohydrate: 58g carbohydrate (13g sugars
- Cholesterol: 89mg cholesterol
- Protein: 32g protein.

### 362. Greek Salad Ravioli

*Serving: 4 dozen. | Prep: 45mins | Cook: 5mins | Ready in:*

## Ingredients

- 10 ounces (about 12 cups) fresh baby spinach
- 1/2 cup finely chopped roasted sweet red peppers
- 1/2 cup pitted and finely chopped ripe olives
- 1/2 cup crumbled feta cheese
- 3 tablespoons snipped fresh dill
- 2 to 3 teaspoons dried oregano
- 2 tablespoons butter
- 3 tablespoons all-purpose flour
- 2 cups whole milk
- 96 pot sticker or gyoza wrappers
- Snipped fresh dill and sauce of choice, optional

## Direction

- In batches, cook and stir spinach for 3-4 mins in a big skillet on medium heat until it wilts. Place on paper towels to drain then mix the next 5 ingredients.
- On medium heat, melt butter in a small saucepan; mix in flour until smooth. Beat in milk gradually; boil for 2-3 mins while constantly mixing until the sauce is thick and coats a spoon. Combine into the spinach mixture.
- In the middle of a potsticker wrapper, put 1tbsp of spinach mixture. Use a damp towel to cover the rest of the wrappers until use. Dampen the edges of the wrapper with water then top with another wrapper; seal by pressing the edges. Repeat with the rest of the wrappers.
- Pour water into a Dutch oven until 2/3 full; boil then lower the heat. In batches, drop the ravioli into the simmering water for 3-4 mins until thoroughly cooked. Scatter more dill if desired then serve with your preferred sauce.
- If freezing: Place the uncooked ravioli on baking sheets lined with waxed paper; cover then place in the freezer until firm. Move to resealable plastic freezer bags then freeze again. Cook as directed to use, add time to 6mins.

## Nutrition Information

- Calories: 47 calories
- Total Fat: 1g fat (1g saturated fat)
- Sodium: 74mg sodium
- Fiber: 0 fiber)
- Total Carbohydrate: 7g carbohydrate (1g sugars
- Cholesterol: 4mg cholesterol
- Protein: 2g protein.

### 363. Greek Sausage Pita Pizzas

*Serving: 4 servings. | Prep: 20mins | Cook: 10mins | Ready in:*

## Ingredients

- 1 package (19 ounces) Johnsonville® Mild Italian Sausage Links, casings removed
- 2 garlic cloves, minced
- 4 whole pita breads
- 2 plum tomatoes, seeded and chopped
- 1 medium ripe avocado, peeled and cubed
- 1/2 cup crumbled feta cheese
- 1 small cucumber, sliced
- 1/2 cup refrigerated tzatziki sauce

## Direction

- Heat the oven to 350 degrees. Place garlic and sausage in a large skillet over medium heat and cook for 6-8 minutes or until not pink anymore, breaking up the sausage into large crumbles; drain.
- In the meantime, on ungreased baking sheets, put pita breads. Bake for 3-4 minutes per side or until almost crisp and brown.
- Place cheese, avocado, tomatoes, and sausage mixture on top of pita breads. Bake for 3 to 4 minutes more or until heated through. Place cucumbers on top; sprinkle with tzatziki sauce.

## Nutrition Information

- Calories: 632 calories
- Total Carbohydrate: 43g carbohydrate (3g sugars
- Cholesterol: 85mg cholesterol
- Protein: 25g protein.
- Total Fat: 40g fat (12g saturated fat)
- Sodium: 1336mg sodium
- Fiber: 5g fiber)

## 364. Greek Shepherd's Pie

*Serving: 6 servings. | Prep: 25mins | Cook: 35mins | Ready in:*

## Ingredients

- 5-1/2 cups cubed eggplant (about 1 large)
- 2 teaspoons salt
- 4 large potatoes, peeled and cubed
- 1/2 cup sour cream
- 1/4 cup butter
- 2 tablespoons all-purpose flour
- 1/4 cup vegetable oil
- 1 pound ground lamb
- 1/2 pound ground turkey
- 1 jar (26 ounces) meatless spaghetti sauce
- 2 tablespoons dried minced onion
- 2 tablespoons minced fresh parsley
- 1 teaspoon garlic powder
- 1/2 teaspoon dried rosemary, crushed
- 1/2 teaspoon dried basil
- 1/2 teaspoon pepper
- 1 cup (4 ounces) crumbled feta cheese

## Direction

- Put eggplant in a strainer over a plate and toss with salt. Let the eggplant sit for 30 minutes. While waiting for eggplant, put potatoes covered with water in a large pot. Bring the potatoes to a boil, then decrease heat, cover, and cook until tender about 10-15 minutes. Drain and mash the potatoes with butter and sour cream. Rinse and drain the eggplant well. Toss the eggplant with flour. In a frying pan on medium heat, cook eggplant in oil until brown and all oil is absorbed. Place eggplant in a 3-qt. baking dish that has been sprayed with cooking spray. Cook turkey and lamb until not pink in the same frying pan on medium heat. Drain excess grease. Mix in seasonings, spaghetti sauce, parsley, and onion. Cook for 5 minutes or so until heated through. Dump mixture over eggplant and evenly spread feta cheese then mashed potatoes on top. Bake in a 350-degree oven, uncovered, until browning begins to appear on top, 35-45 minutes. Remove from oven and let cool for 10-15 minutes.

## Nutrition Information

- Calories: 736 calories
- Protein: 31g protein.
- Total Fat: 39g fat (16g saturated fat)
- Sodium: 1302mg sodium
- Fiber: 9g fiber)
- Total Carbohydrate: 65g carbohydrate (16g sugars
- Cholesterol: 119mg cholesterol

## 365. Greek Shrimp Orzo

*Serving: 6 servings. | Prep: 45mins | Cook: 02hours00mins | Ready in:*

### Ingredients

- 2 cups uncooked orzo pasta
- 2 tablespoons minced fresh basil or 2 teaspoons dried basil
- 3 tablespoons olive oil, divided
- 1-1/2 tablespoons chopped shallot
- 2 tablespoons butter
- 1 can (14-1/2 ounces) diced tomatoes, drained
- 2 tablespoons minced fresh oregano or 2 teaspoons dried oregano
- 3 garlic cloves, minced
- 1 pound uncooked large shrimp, peeled and deveined
- 1 cup oil-packed sun-dried tomatoes, chopped
- 2-1/2 cups (10 ounces) crumbled feta cheese
- 1-1/2 cups pitted Greek olives

### Direction

- Cook orzo as directed on the package; rinse in cold water, drain. Put in a large bowl. Add a tablespoon oil and basil; toss to coat and put aside.
- Sauté shallot in the remaining oil and butter in a large skillet until tender. Add garlic, oregano and diced tomatoes; cook while stirring for 1-2 minutes. Add sun-dried tomatoes and shrimp; cook while stirring until shrimp turns pink or for 2-3 minutes.
- Place in a greased 5-qt. slow cooker. Stir in olives, cheese and orzo mixture. Cook with a cover for 2-3 hours on low or until heated through.

### Nutrition Information

- Calories: 673 calories
- Protein: 31g protein.
- Total Fat: 32g fat (10g saturated fat)
- Sodium: 1262mg sodium
- Fiber: 6g fiber
- Total Carbohydrate: 63g carbohydrate (5g sugars
- Cholesterol: 127mg cholesterol

## 366. Greek Spaghetti

*Serving: 4 servings. | Prep: 10mins | Cook: 20mins | Ready in:*

### Ingredients

- 6 ounces uncooked thin spaghetti
- 1 teaspoon dried oregano
- 1 garlic clove, minced
- 2 teaspoons olive oil
- 3 cups chopped seeded plum tomatoes
- 1/2 cup sliced green onions
- 1/4 cup minced fresh parsley, divided
- 2 tablespoons minced fresh basil
- 2 tablespoons lemon juice
- 1 cup (4 ounces) crumbled feta cheese, divided
- 1/2 teaspoon salt
- 1/8 teaspoon pepper

### Direction

- Follow the package directions to cook pasta. Sauté together garlic and oregano with oil in a nonstick skillet until garlic is softened, 1 minute. Put in lemon juice, basil, 2 tbsp. parsley, green onions and tomatoes, then cook and stir until heated through, 2 minutes. Take away from the heat.
- Drain spaghetti and put into the tomato mixture. Put in pepper, salt and 3/4 cup of feta cheese, then toss to mix. Turn to serving plates, then sprinkle over with parsley and leftover feta. Serve right away.

### Nutrition Information

- Calories: 311 calories
- Total Fat: 10g fat (5g saturated fat)
- Sodium: 628mg sodium

- Fiber: 5g fiber)
- Total Carbohydrate: 50g carbohydrate (0 sugars
- Cholesterol: 25mg cholesterol
- Protein: 12g protein. Diabetic Exchanges: 3 starch

## 367. Greek Spaghetti Squash

*Serving: 2 servings. | Prep: 10mins | Cook: 20mins | Ready in:*

### Ingredients

- 1 medium spaghetti squash (2 pounds)
- 1 boneless skinless chicken breast half (6 ounces), cut into 1/2-inch cubes
- 1/2 cup chopped onion
- 1/2 cup chopped sweet red pepper
- 2 garlic cloves, minced
- 1/4 teaspoon dried oregano
- 1/4 teaspoon dried basil
- 1/8 teaspoon salt
- 1/8 teaspoon pepper
- 1 tablespoon olive oil
- 1 cup fresh baby spinach
- 1/2 cup marinated artichoke hearts, drained
- 1/3 cup chopped pitted Greek olives
- 2 tablespoons crumbled feta cheese

### Direction

- Lengthwise, cut squash in half; throw seeds. Puts quash on microwave-safe plate, cut side down. Microwave on high, uncovered, till tender for 15-18 minutes.
- Meanwhile, sauté pepper, salt, basil, oregano, garlic, red pepper, onion and chicken in oil till chicken isn't pink in a skillet. Mix olives, artichokes and spinach in; cook till spinach wilts.
- Use fork to separate strands when squash is cool to touch. Over 2 cups squash, serve chicken mixture. Sprinkle feta cheese on top; keep leftover squash for another time.

### Nutrition Information

- Calories: 369 calories
- Sodium: 824mg sodium
- Fiber: 4g fiber)
- Total Carbohydrate: 19g carbohydrate (4g sugars
- Cholesterol: 51mg cholesterol
- Protein: 21g protein.
- Total Fat: 24g fat (5g saturated fat)

## 368. Greek Spaghetti With Chicken

*Serving: 10 servings. | Prep: 25mins | Cook: 25mins | Ready in:*

### Ingredients

- 1 package (16 ounces) spaghetti, broken into 2-inch pieces
- 4 cups cubed cooked chicken breast
- 2 packages (10 ounces each) frozen chopped spinach, thawed and squeezed dry
- 2 cans (10-3/4 ounces each) condensed cream of chicken soup, undiluted
- 1 cup mayonnaise
- 1 cup (8 ounces) sour cream
- 3 celery ribs, chopped
- 1 small onion, chopped
- 1/2 cup chopped green pepper
- 1 jar (2 ounces) diced pimientos, drained
- 1/2 teaspoon lemon-pepper seasoning
- 1 cup shredded Monterey Jack cheese
- 1/2 cup soft bread crumbs
- 1/2 cup shredded Parmesan cheese

### Direction

- Cook spaghetti following the instruction of the package; let drain. Place spaghetti back to saucepan. Blend in the spinach, chicken,

mayonnaise, soup, celery, sour cream, green pepper, onion, lemon-pepper and pimientos.
- Place to a greased baking dish of 13x9-inch (dish can be full). Place Parmesan cheese, bread crumbs and Monterey Jack cheese on top. Bake with no cover at 350° for nearly 25 to 30 minutes till heated through.

### Nutrition Information

- Calories: 601 calories
- Sodium: 850mg sodium
- Fiber: 4g fiber)
- Total Carbohydrate: 44g carbohydrate (4g sugars
- Cholesterol: 85mg cholesterol
- Protein: 31g protein.
- Total Fat: 32g fat (10g saturated fat)

## 369. Greek Spinach Bake

*Serving: 6 servings. | Prep: 10mins | Cook: 60mins | Ready in:*

### Ingredients

- 2 cups (16 ounces) 4% cottage cheese
- 1 package (10 ounces) frozen chopped spinach, thawed and squeezed dry
- 8 ounces crumbled feta cheese
- 6 tablespoons all-purpose flour
- 1/2 teaspoon pepper
- 1/4 teaspoon salt
- 4 eggs, lightly beaten

### Direction

- Mix feta cheese, spinach, and cottage cheese in a big bowl. Mix in salt, pepper, and flour. Beat in eggs well.
- Scoop to a greased nine-inch square baking dish. Bake for an hour in 350 degrees oven without cover until a thermometer registers 160 degrees.

### Nutrition Information

- Calories: 262 calories
- Total Carbohydrate: 14g carbohydrate (4g sugars
- Cholesterol: 178mg cholesterol
- Protein: 21g protein.
- Total Fat: 13g fat (7g saturated fat)
- Sodium: 838mg sodium
- Fiber: 3g fiber)

## 370. Greek Spinach Pizza

*Serving: 6-8 slices. | Prep: 10mins | Cook: 10mins | Ready in:*

### Ingredients

- 2 cups fresh baby spinach
- 3 tablespoons olive oil
- 3 teaspoons Italian seasoning
- 1 prebaked 12-inch thin pizza crust
- 2 plum tomatoes, thinly sliced
- 1 cup (4 ounces) crumbled feta cheese
- 1/4 cup shredded part-skim mozzarella cheese
- 1/4 cup chopped pitted Greek olives
- 2 tablespoons chopped sweet onion

### Direction

- Toss Italian seasoning, oil, and spinach in a small bowl. Put the crust on a 12-inch ungreased pizza pan. Place spinach mixture over the crust and arrange to within 1/2-inch of edge. Top with tomatoes; scatter with the onion, olives, and cheeses.
- Bake for 10 to 15 minutes at 450 degrees or until edges turn light brown and cheese melts.

### Nutrition Information

- Calories:
- Total Carbohydrate:
- Cholesterol:
- Protein:

- Total Fat:
- Sodium:
- Fiber:

---

### 371.　　Greek Tacos

*Serving: 12 servings.. | Prep: 10mins | Cook: 20mins | Ready in:*

## Ingredients

- 1 pound lean ground beef (90% lean)
- 1 can (14-1/2 ounces) diced tomatoes, undrained
- 2 teaspoons Greek seasoning
- 1/2 teaspoon minced garlic
- 1/4 teaspoon pepper
- 2 cups fresh baby spinach
- 1 can (2-1/4 ounces) sliced ripe olives, drained
- 1 package (4-1/2 ounces) taco shells
- 1/2 cup crumbled feta cheese
- 1/4 cup chopped red onion

## Direction

- Place a large skillet on medium heat; cook in beef till not pink anymore; strain. Mix in pepper, garlic, Greek seasoning and tomatoes. Boil the mixture. Lower the heat; simmer till thickened, or for 8-10 minutes. Put in olives and spinach; cook while stirring till the spinach is wilted, or for 2-3 minutes.
- Meanwhile, arrange taco shells on an ungreased baking sheet. Bake for 3-5 minutes at 300°, or till heated through. In each shell, spoon around 1/4 cup of the beef mixture. Add onion and feta cheese on top.

## Nutrition Information

- Calories: 130 calories
- Sodium: 386mg sodium
- Fiber: 2g fiber)

---

- Total Carbohydrate: 9g carbohydrate (1g sugars
- Cholesterol: 20mg cholesterol
- Protein: 9g protein. Diabetic Exchanges: 1 lean meat
- Total Fat: 6g fat (2g saturated fat)

---

### 372.　　Greek Turkey Burgers With Spicy Yogurt Sauce

*Serving: 4 servings. | Prep: 15mins | Cook: 10mins | Ready in:*

## Ingredients

- 1 pound ground turkey
- 1/2 cup crumbled reduced-fat feta cheese
- 2 teaspoons McCormick® Oregano Leaves, crushed
- 1/2 teaspoon McCormick® Thyme Leaves
- 1/2 teaspoon McCormick® Ground Black Pepper
- 2 teaspoons olive oil
- 1/4 cup reduced-fat plain yogurt
- McCormick® Ground Cumin
- McCormick® Sea Salt from Sea Salt Grinder
- Additional McCormick® Ground Black Pepper
- 4 whole wheat hamburger buns, split and toasted
- Leaf lettuce, tomato and cucumber slices, optional

## Direction

- Mix together 1/2 tsp. of pepper, thyme, oregano, feta and turkey in a big bowl, then form the mixture into 4 patties.
- Heat oil in a nonstick skillet on moderate heat. Put in patties and cook until not pink anymore and a thermometer reaches 165 degrees, about 4 to 5 minutes per side.
- In a bowl with yogurt, use more pepper, sea salt and cumin to season to taste. Serve burgers on buns and put yogurt mixture on

top of each burger. Use lettuce, tomato and cucumber to decorate, if you want.

## Nutrition Information

- Calories:
- Cholesterol:
- Protein:
- Total Fat:
- Sodium:
- Fiber:
- Total Carbohydrate:

### 373. Greek Zucchini & Feta Bake

*Serving: 12 servings. | Prep: 40mins | Cook: 30mins | Ready in:*

## Ingredients

- 2 tablespoons olive oil, divided
- 5 medium zucchini, cut into 1/2-in. cubes (about 6 cups)
- 2 large onions, chopped (about 4 cups)
- 1 teaspoon dried oregano, divided
- 1/2 teaspoon salt
- 1/4 teaspoon pepper
- 6 large eggs
- 2 teaspoons baking powder
- 1 cup (8 ounces) reduced-fat plain yogurt
- 1 cup all-purpose flour
- 2 packages (8 ounces each) feta cheese, cubed
- 1/4 cup minced fresh parsley
- 1 teaspoon paprika

## Direction

- To preheat: Set oven to 350 degrees. Put a tablespoon oil in a Dutch oven and heat on medium high heat. Put in half a teaspoon of oregano, half of the onions, half of the zucchini and cook for 8 to 10 minutes till zucchini becomes crisp-tender, remember to stir while cooking. Get zucchini out of pan. Repeat the process with the remaining vegetables. Put previously cooked vegetables back to the pan. Add pepper and salt. Allow to cool briefly.
- Put baking powder and egg in a large bowl, whisk till both are blended, add flour, yogurt and whisk till all are blended. Put in zucchini mixture, parsley, cheese and stir. Grease a 13x9 in. baking dish and transfer the mixture into the dish. Use paprika to sprinkle.
- Bake without cover for 30 to 35 minutes till the mixture is set and becomes golden brown. Allow to sit for 10 minutes before cutting.

## Nutrition Information

- Calories: 231 calories
- Sodium: 583mg sodium
- Fiber: 2g fiber)
- Total Carbohydrate: 16g carbohydrate (6g sugars
- Cholesterol: 128mg cholesterol
- Protein: 12g protein.
- Total Fat: 13g fat (7g saturated fat)

### 374. Greek Style Chicken Skewers

*Serving: 4 servings. | Prep: 25mins | Cook: 5mins | Ready in:*

## Ingredients

- 3/4 cup reduced-fat plain yogurt
- 1 tablespoon lemon juice
- 1 tablespoon olive oil
- 1 teaspoon poultry seasoning
- 1 teaspoon dried oregano
- 1/2 teaspoon salt
- 1/2 teaspoon grated lemon peel
- 1/4 teaspoon onion powder
- 1/4 teaspoon pepper
- 1 pound boneless skinless chicken breasts, cut into strips

### Direction

- Lightly toss all ingredients in a large bowl. Place in refrigerator for 10 minutes or up to 8 hours. Take chicken out of the bowl and discard the marinade. Cue chicken onto eight metal or water-soaked wooden skewers. Arrange skewers on an oiled grill rack and cook, covered, at medium heat or broil 4 in. from the heat, for 5-7 minutes or until chicken is cooked through, turning once to grill the other side.

### Nutrition Information

- Calories: 134 calories
- Protein: 23g protein. Diabetic Exchanges: 3 lean meat.
- Total Fat: 3g fat (1g saturated fat)
- Sodium: 120mg sodium
- Fiber: 0 fiber)
- Total Carbohydrate: 1g carbohydrate (1g sugars
- Cholesterol: 63mg cholesterol

## 375. Greek Style Lemon Garlic Chicken

*Serving: 8 servings. | Prep: 15mins | Cook: 60mins | Ready in:*

### Ingredients

- 8 medium Yukon Gold potatoes (about 3 pounds)
- 1 cup pitted Greek olives
- 8 bone-in chicken thighs (about 3 pounds)
- 1/2 cup olive oil
- 3 tablespoons lemon juice
- 6 garlic cloves, minced
- 2 teaspoons salt
- 2 teaspoons dried oregano
- 1/2 teaspoon pepper
- 1-1/2 cups reduced-sodium chicken broth

### Direction

- Preheat an oven to 375°. Scrub potatoes; cut each into 8 wedges. Put into a shallow roasting pan; put chicken and olives over the top. Whisk pepper, oregano, salt, garlic, lemon juice and oil till blended in a small bowl; drizzle over potatoes and chicken. Put chicken broth around the chicken into the pan.
- Bake without cover till potatoes are tender and an inserted thermometer in chicken reads 170-175° for 60-70 minutes; serve with pan juices.

### Nutrition Information

- Calories: 602 calories
- Total Carbohydrate: 48g carbohydrate (4g sugars
- Cholesterol: 81mg cholesterol
- Protein: 29g protein.
- Total Fat: 33g fat (6g saturated fat)
- Sodium: 1071mg sodium
- Fiber: 4g fiber)

## 376. Greek Style Ravioli

*Serving: 2 servings. | Prep: 5mins | Cook: 20mins | Ready in:*

### Ingredients

- 12 frozen cheese ravioli
- 1/3 pound lean ground beef (90% lean)
- 1 cup canned diced tomatoes with basil, oregano and garlic
- 1 cup fresh baby spinach
- 1/4 cup sliced ripe olives
- 1/4 cup crumbled feta cheese

### Direction

- Cook ravioli following package instruction; drain. In the meantime, cook beef in a skillet over medium heat for 4 to 6 minutes till not pink anymore; drain. Mix in tomatoes; boil.

- Lower heat; without cover, allow to simmer for 10 minutes, mixing from time to time.
- Put in olives, spinach and ravioli; heat through, mixing slowly to incorporate. Scatter cheese over.

## Nutrition Information

- Calories: 333 calories
- Sodium: 851mg sodium
- Fiber: 4g fiber)
- Total Carbohydrate: 28g carbohydrate (5g sugars
- Cholesterol: 61mg cholesterol
- Protein: 23g protein. Diabetic Exchanges: 3 lean meat
- Total Fat: 12g fat (5g saturated fat)

## 377. Greek Style Ribeye Steaks

*Serving: 2 servings. | Prep: 5mins | Cook: 20mins | Ready in:*

### Ingredients

- 1-1/2 teaspoons garlic powder
- 1-1/2 teaspoons dried oregano
- 1-1/2 teaspoons dried basil
- 1/2 teaspoon salt
- 1/8 teaspoon pepper
- 2 beef ribeye steaks (1-1/2 inches thick)
- 1 tablespoon olive oil
- 1 tablespoon lemon juice
- 2 tablespoons crumbled feta cheese
- 1 tablespoon sliced ripe olives

### Direction

- Mix together the first 5 ingredients in a small bowl, then rub mixture over steaks, on both sides. Cook steaks in a big skillet with oil until meat achieves desired doneness (for medium-rare, a thermometer should reach 145 degrees, medium, 160 degrees and 170 degrees for well-done), about 7 to 9 minutes per side. Sprinkle olives, cheese and lemon juice on top, then serve instantly.

## Nutrition Information

- Calories:
- Protein:
- Total Fat:
- Sodium:
- Fiber:
- Total Carbohydrate:
- Cholesterol:

## 378. Grilled Artichoke Mushroom Pizza

*Serving: 6 servings. | Prep: 20mins | Cook: 15mins | Ready in:*

### Ingredients

- 1 prebaked 12-inch pizza crust
- 1/2 teaspoon olive oil
- 2/3 cup tomato and basil spaghetti sauce
- 2 plum tomatoes, sliced
- 1/4 cup sliced fresh mushrooms
- 1/4 cup water-packed artichoke hearts, rinsed, drained and chopped
- 2 tablespoons sliced ripe olives, optional
- 1 cup shredded part-skim mozzarella cheese
- 1/2 cup crumbled tomato and basil feta cheese
- 1-1/2 teaspoons minced fresh basil or 1/2 teaspoon dried basil
- 1-1/2 teaspoons minced fresh rosemary or 1/2 teaspoon dried rosemary, crushed
- 1-1/2 teaspoons minced chives

### Direction

- Brush oil over crust. Spread over the crust to within 1 in. of edges with the spaghetti sauce. Put artichokes, mushrooms, tomatoes and olives (if wanted). Sprinkle cheeses over.

- Close the lid and grill the pizza over medium indirect heat until the cheese melts and the crust is slightly brown, about 12-15 minutes. During the final 5 minutes of cooking, sprinkle herbs over. Allow to sit before cutting, about 5 minutes.

## Nutrition Information

- Calories: 283 calories
- Sodium: 712mg sodium
- Fiber: 1g fiber)
- Total Carbohydrate: 34g carbohydrate (3g sugars
- Cholesterol: 17mg cholesterol
- Protein: 14g protein. Diabetic Exchanges: 2 starch
- Total Fat: 10g fat (3g saturated fat)

### 379. Grilled Eggplant Pita Pizzas

*Serving: 4 pizzas. | Prep: 20mins | Cook: 20mins | Ready in:*

## Ingredients

- 2 small eggplants
- 1 teaspoon salt
- 1 large sweet red pepper, halved and sliced
- 1 medium onion, halved and sliced
- 12 garlic cloves, halved
- 3 tablespoons olive oil, divided
- 1/4 teaspoon pepper
- 4 whole pita breads
- 1 large tomato, seeded and chopped
- 3/4 cup shredded fresh mozzarella cheese
- 1/4 cup pitted ripe olives, coarsely chopped
- 1/2 teaspoon crushed red pepper flakes, optional
- 1 cup loosely packed basil leaves, coarsely chopped

## Direction

- Slice eggplants into 3/4-inch pieces. Put in colander on top of a plate; scatter salt over and toss. Allow to sit for half an hour.
- In the meantime, toss garlic, onion and red pepper together with a tablespoon of oil in a bowl. Turn onto an open grill basket or grill wok; put on the grill rack. Grill with no cover for 8 to 12 minutes over moderately-high heat or until vegetables are crisp-tender and lightly blackened, mixing often.
- Wash eggplants and let drain; using paper towels, pat dry. Brush a tablespoon of oil on eggplants; scatter pepper over. Grill with a cover for 4 to 5 minutes per side over moderate heat or until soft. Slice every piece into 4 portions.
- With the rest of the oil, brush each side of pita breads. Grill with a cover for 1 to 2 minutes over moderately-low heat or until the bottoms are slightly browned. Take off from grill.
- Layer grilled vegetables, tomato, cheese and olives on grilled surfaces of pitas. If preferred, scatter with pepper flakes. Put back to grill; cook for 3 to 4 minutes while covering or until cheese melts.
- Scatter basil over.

## Nutrition Information

- Calories: 428 calories
- Protein: 14g protein.
- Total Fat: 17g fat (5g saturated fat)
- Sodium: 721mg sodium
- Fiber: 12g fiber)
- Total Carbohydrate: 59g carbohydrate (12g sugars
- Cholesterol: 17mg cholesterol

### 380. Grilled Greek Fish

*Serving: 4 servings. | Prep: 15mins | Cook: 10mins | Ready in:*

## Ingredients

- 1/3 cup lemon juice
- 3 tablespoons olive oil
- 2 tablespoons minced fresh oregano
- 2 tablespoons minced fresh mint
- 1 garlic clove, minced
- 1/2 teaspoon grated lemon peel
- 1/2 teaspoon Greek seasoning
- 4 tilapia fillets (6 ounces each)

### Direction

- Mix together the first 7 ingredients in a large resealable plastic bag. Place the tilapia in; seal bag and turn to cover. Let sit for 30 minutes in the refrigerator. Strain and discard marinade.
- Grease grill rack and lay tilapia on. Cover and broil 4 inches from the heat or cook over medium heat till fish easily flakes with a fork or for 4-5 minutes on every side.

### Nutrition Information

- Calories: 223 calories
- Sodium: 162mg sodium
- Fiber: 0 fiber)
- Total Carbohydrate: 2g carbohydrate (0 sugars
- Cholesterol: 83mg cholesterol
- Protein: 32g protein. Diabetic Exchanges: 5 lean meat
- Total Fat: 10g fat (2g saturated fat)

## 381. Grilled Greek Pita Pizzas

*Serving: 4 servings. | Prep: 15mins | Cook: 5mins | Ready in:*

### Ingredients

- 1 jar (12 ounces) marinated quartered artichoke hearts, drained and chopped
- 1 cup grape tomatoes, halved
- 1/2 cup pitted Greek olives, halved
- 1/3 cup chopped fresh parsley
- 2 tablespoons olive oil
- 1/4 teaspoon pepper
- 3/4 cup hummus
- 4 whole pita breads
- 1 cup crumbled feta cheese

### Direction

- In a small bowl, toss the first 6 ingredients to combine. Slather hummus on the pita breads then add the artichoke mixture on top; scatter cheese. On medium heat, grill pizza for 4-5 minutes with cover until golden brown on the bottoms.

### Nutrition Information

- Calories: 585 calories
- Protein: 15g protein.
- Total Fat: 34g fat (8g saturated fat)
- Sodium: 1336mg sodium
- Fiber: 6g fiber)
- Total Carbohydrate: 50g carbohydrate (7g sugars
- Cholesterol: 15mg cholesterol

## 382. Grilled Halibut With Mustard Dill Sauce

*Serving: 4 servings. | Prep: 10mins | Cook: 10mins | Ready in:*

### Ingredients

- 1/3 cup fat-free plain yogurt
- 2 tablespoons reduced-fat mayonnaise
- 2 tablespoons snipped fresh dill or 2 teaspoons dill weed
- 2 teaspoons Dijon mustard
- 4 halibut steaks (6 ounces each)
- 1/4 teaspoon salt
- 1/8 teaspoon pepper

### Direction

- Combine mustard, dill, mayonnaise, and yogurt in a small bowl; cover and let sit in the refrigerator. Use pepper and salt to drizzle over halibut.
- Moisten a paper towel with cooking oil and cover the grill rack lightly using long-handled tongs. Cover and broil halibut 4 inches from the heat or grill over medium heat till fish easily flakes with a fork, or for 4-6 minutes per side. Serve halibut with sauce.

## Nutrition Information

- Calories: 224 calories
- Protein: 36g protein. Diabetic Exchanges: 5 lean meat
- Total Fat: 7g fat (1g saturated fat)
- Sodium: 447mg sodium
- Fiber: 0 fiber)
- Total Carbohydrate: 3g carbohydrate (1g sugars
- Cholesterol: 57mg cholesterol

## 383. Grilled Herbed Salmon

*Serving: 6-8 servings. | Prep: 10mins | Cook: 15mins | Ready in:*

## Ingredients

- 1/2 cup butter, cubed
- 1/3 cup lemon juice
- 2 tablespoons minced parsley
- 1-1/2 teaspoons soy sauce
- 1-1/2 teaspoons Worcestershire sauce
- 1 teaspoon dried oregano
- 1/2 teaspoon garlic powder
- 1/4 teaspoon salt
- 1/8 teaspoon pepper
- 1 salmon fillet (2-1/2 to 3 pounds and 3/4 inch thick)

## Direction

- Combine the first nine ingredients together in a small saucepan. Let it cook over low heat until butter if fully melted, stir constantly then set aside.
- Lightly coat the grill rack with cooking oil using moistened paper towel and long handled tongs. Lay salmon on the grill skin-side down. Put the cover on and grill over medium-hot heat. If broiling, set it 4 inches from the heat for 5 minutes. Apply butter sauce over the fish then grill or broil for 10 to 15 minutes longer, baste the fish often. Dish is done when fish separates easily when flaked by a fork.

## Nutrition Information

- Calories: 365 calories
- Protein: 29g protein.
- Total Fat: 27g fat (10g saturated fat)
- Sodium: 342mg sodium
- Fiber: 0 fiber)
- Total Carbohydrate: 1g carbohydrate (0 sugars
- Cholesterol: 114mg cholesterol

## 384. Grilled Lamb Chops

*Serving: 3 servings. | Prep: 15mins | Cook: 15mins | Ready in:*

## Ingredients

- 1/2 cup canola oil
- 1/4 cup finely chopped onion
- 2 tablespoons lemon juice
- 1 teaspoon ground mustard
- 1/2 teaspoon garlic salt
- 1/2 teaspoon dried tarragon
- 1/8 teaspoon pepper
- 6 lamb loin chops (1-1/4 inches thick and 6 ounces each)

## Direction

- Mix together the first seven ingredients in a large resealable plastic bag; put in the lamb chops. Secure the bag and flip the coat; place inside of the refrigerator for 10 to 15 minutes.
- Strain and get rid of marinade. Place the chops on the grill, cover, and cook over medium heat for 7 minutes per side or until meat achieves doneness desired (a thermometer should read 145°F for medium rare; 160°F for medium; and 170°F for well done).

## Nutrition Information

- Calories: 523 calories
- Total Fat: 37g fat (8g saturated fat)
- Sodium: 314mg sodium
- Fiber: 0 fiber)
- Total Carbohydrate: 2g carbohydrate (1g sugars
- Cholesterol: 136mg cholesterol
- Protein: 43g protein.

### 385. Grilled Lamb Kabobs

*Serving: 4 servings. | Prep: 25mins | Cook: 10mins | Ready in:*

## Ingredients

- 1-1/4 cups grapefruit juice
- 1/3 cup honey
- 2 tablespoons minced fresh mint
- 3/4 teaspoon salt
- 3/4 teaspoon ground coriander
- 3/4 teaspoon pepper
- 1 pound lamb stew meat, cut into 1-inch pieces
- CITRUS SALSA:
- 4 medium navel oranges, divided
- 2 medium pink grapefruit
- 1/2 cup mango chutney
- 1 to 2 tablespoons minced fresh mint
- 2 medium onions, cut into wedges
- 1 large sweet red pepper, cut into 1-inch pieces

## Direction

- Combine the first six ingredients in a large bowl. Pour a cup of the marinade into a large re-sealable plastic bag with the lamb. Close the bag, turn to coat, and let marinate in the fridge for 1-4 hours. Keep remaining marinade covered and refrigerated. Make the salsa: peel and separate the sections of 2 oranges and a grapefruit. Chop the sections and combine with mint and chutney in a large bowl. Cling wrap the bowl and refrigerate. Peel the rest of the oranges and slice into eight wedges. Drain the lamb, discarding its marinade. Take eight metal or pre-soaked wooden skewers, and alternately cue the lamb, onions, red peppers, and orange wedges onto them. Cook on an open grill over medium heat, or broil 4 in. from the heat, for 8-10 minutes or until lamb is cooked to preference: a meat thermometer reading of 145 deg is medium-rare, 160 deg is medium, and 170 deg is well-done. Occasionally turn and baste with reserved marinade. Serve warm kabobs with cold salsa.

## Nutrition Information

- Calories: 367 calories
- Total Fat: 7g fat (2g saturated fat)
- Sodium: 282mg sodium
- Fiber: 7g fiber)
- Total Carbohydrate: 56g carbohydrate (0 sugars
- Cholesterol: 65mg cholesterol
- Protein: 24g protein.

### 386. Grilled Peppered Ribeye Steaks

*Serving: 4 servings. | Prep: 5mins | Cook: 15mins | Ready in:*

## Ingredients

- 2 tablespoons canola oil
- 1/2 teaspoon paprika
- 1/2 teaspoon pepper
- 1/4 teaspoon each salt, garlic powder and lemon-pepper seasoning
- 1/8 teaspoon each dried oregano, crushed red pepper flakes, ground cumin and cayenne pepper
- 4 beef ribeye steaks (1 inch thick and about 10 ounces each)

### Direction

- Mix oil and seasonings in a large bowl, and rub the mixture all over the steaks. Cover the steak and grill it over medium heat, about 7-10 minutes per side. You can also cook it inside the broiler, positioning the steak 3-4-inches away from the heat until it reaches its desired doneness. Be sure to baste the steak occasionally with the seasoning mixture while grilling. Allow it to rest for 3-5 minutes before serving it. (Here are the thermometer readings and its desired doneness: for medium-rare, 145°F; medium, 160°F; well-done, 170°F.)

### Nutrition Information

- Calories: 685 calories
- Protein: 51g protein.
- Total Fat: 52g fat (19g saturated fat)
- Sodium: 306mg sodium
- Fiber: 0 fiber)
- Total Carbohydrate: 1g carbohydrate (0 sugars
- Cholesterol: 168mg cholesterol

## 387. Grilled Rack Of Lamb

*Serving: 8 servings. | Prep: 10mins | Cook: 15mins | Ready in:*

### Ingredients

- 2 cups apple cider or juice
- 2/3 cup cider vinegar
- 2/3 cup thinly sliced green onions
- 1/2 cup canola oil
- 1/3 cup honey
- 1/4 cup steak sauce
- 2 teaspoons dried tarragon
- 2 teaspoons salt
- 1/2 teaspoon pepper
- 4 racks of lamb (1-1/2 to 2 pounds each)

### Direction

- Mix first nine ingredients in a big saucepan, allow to boil. Lower heat and simmer for 20 minutes without cover; cool until room temperature. Reserve 1 cup for later basting. Keep in the refrigerator with cover. In a big plastic resealable bag, transfer the rest of the marinade and add the lamb. Seal and turn the bag over to coat. For 2 to 3 hours or overnight, keep in the refrigerator while turning once or twice.
- Drain the marinade; discard. Using foil, cover the ends of the ribs. Use a paper towel to moisten with cooking oil and lightly grease grill rack using tongs with a long handle. On medium heat, grill with a cover or alternatively broil 4 inches from heat, 15 minutes.
- Drizzle the reserved marinade over and broil or grill for an additional of 5 to 10 minutes until meat is cooked to your desired doneness. For doneness of medium rare, the inserted thermometer must register 145 degrees; 160 degrees for medium; 170 degrees for well-done, while occasionally basting.

### Nutrition Information

- Calories:
- Total Fat:
- Sodium:
- Fiber:
- Total Carbohydrate:
- Cholesterol:
- Protein:

### 388. Grilled Ribeyes With Greek Relish

*Serving: 4 servings. | Prep: 20mins | Cook: 10mins | Ready in:*

Ingredients

- 4 plum tomatoes, seeded and chopped
- 1 cup chopped red onion
- 2/3 cup pitted Greek olives
- 1/4 cup minced fresh cilantro
- 1/4 cup lemon juice, divided
- 2 tablespoons olive oil
- 2 garlic cloves, minced
- 2 beef ribeye steaks (3/4 pound each)
- 1 cup crumbled feta cheese

Direction

- Make relish by mixing together garlic, tomatoes, oil, onion, 2 tbsp. lemon juice, olives, and cilantro.
- Pour the leftover lemon juice over the meat. On medium heat, grill steaks while covered or broil four inches from the heat for 5-7mins per side until it reaches the preferred doneness (an inserted thermometer in the steak should register 170° Fahrenheit for well-done, 160 degrees F for medium done, and 145° Fahrenheit for medium rare). Set aside for 5 minutes; halve the steaks. Add cheese and relish on top.

Nutrition Information

- Calories: 597 calories
- Total Carbohydrate: 11g carbohydrate (4g sugars
- Cholesterol: 115mg cholesterol
- Protein: 37g protein.
- Total Fat: 44g fat (16g saturated fat)
- Sodium: 723mg sodium
- Fiber: 3g fiber)

### 389. Grilled Salmon With Cheese Sauce

*Serving: 4 servings. | Prep: 10mins | Cook: 20mins | Ready in:*

Ingredients

- 2 cups cherry tomatoes
- 4 teaspoons Greek seasoning
- 4 salmon fillets (6 ounces each)
- 1 carton (6-1/2 ounces) garden vegetable cheese spread
- 2 tablespoons milk

Direction

- Thread cherry tomatoes atop metal or soaked wooden skewers and reserve. Drizzle Greek seasoning atop salmon. Use cooking oil to moisten a paper towel with long-handled tongs and then coat the grill rack lightly.
- Grill the salmon while covered on medium heat or broil for 5 minutes with 4 inches away from the heat source. Flip and then grill for about 7 to 9 minutes or until the fish easily flakes with a fork. In the meantime, grill the tomatoes for about 5 to 8 minutes while turning often.
- Mix milk and cheese spread in a microwave-safe dish. Cook while uncovered for 1 minute on high. Mix until blended. Serve with tomatoes and salmon.

Nutrition Information

- Calories: 224 calories
- Cholesterol: 89mg cholesterol
- Protein: 11g protein.
- Total Fat: 18g fat (9g saturated fat)
- Sodium: 1272mg sodium
- Fiber: 1g fiber)
- Total Carbohydrate: 6g carbohydrate (5g sugars

## 390. Grilled Salmon With Chorizo Olive Sauce

*Serving: 4 servings. | Prep: 10mins | Cook: 15mins | Ready in:*

### Ingredients

- 3 links (3 to 4 ounces each) fresh chorizo
- 4 green onions, chopped
- 2 garlic cloves, minced
- 1 can (14-1/2 ounces) diced tomatoes, drained
- 1/4 cup chopped pitted green olives
- 1/2 teaspoon grated orange zest
- 1/4 teaspoon salt
- 1/4 teaspoon pepper
- 4 salmon fillets (6 ounces each)

### Direction

- Remove casings from chorizo. Cook and stir garlic, green onions, and chorizo in a large ovenproof skillet set over a stove or grill over medium-high heat; crumble sausage. Allow sausage to cook for 4-6 minutes till it is not pink anymore; strain.
- Lower heat to medium. Add orange zest, olives, and tomatoes in; stir till combined. Use pepper and salt to drizzle on salmon.
- Grill salmon, covered, on a greased grill rack over medium heat till fish just starts to easily flake with a fork, or for 3-4 minutes each side. Place chorizo mixture over top.

### Nutrition Information

- Calories: 545 calories
- Total Carbohydrate: 7g carbohydrate (4g sugars
- Cholesterol: 142mg cholesterol
- Protein: 43g protein.
- Total Fat: 36g fat (10g saturated fat)
- Sodium: 1355mg sodium
- Fiber: 2g fiber)

## 391. Grilled Salmon With Creamy Tarragon Sauce

*Serving: 4 servings. | Prep: 10mins | Cook: 20mins | Ready in:*

### Ingredients

- 1 tablespoon olive oil
- 1 salmon fillet (1 pound)
- 1 cup (8 ounces) plain yogurt
- 1/4 cup chopped green onions
- 1 tablespoon minced fresh tarragon or 1 teaspoon dried tarragon
- 1 tablespoon mayonnaise
- 2 teaspoons lime juice
- 1/2 to 1 teaspoon hot pepper sauce

### Direction

- Ladle oil on each side of salmon. Use cooking oil to moisten a paper towel with the help of long-handled tongs and then coat the grill rack lightly. Transfer the salmon onto the grill rack with the skin side down. Grill while covered on medium heat or broil 4 in. away from heat for approximately 20 to 25 minutes or until the fish easily flakes with a fork.
- For the sauce, in a small bowl, mix the remaining ingredients. You can serve together with salmon.

### Nutrition Information

- Calories: 265 calories
- Cholesterol: 76mg cholesterol
- Protein: 25g protein. Diabetic Exchanges: 4 lean meat
- Total Fat: 15g fat (3g saturated fat)
- Sodium: 130mg sodium
- Fiber: 0 fiber)
- Total Carbohydrate: 6g carbohydrate (0 sugars

## 392. Grilled Salmon With Dill Sauce

*Serving: 2 | Prep: 10mins | Cook: 10mins | Ready in:*

### Ingredients

- 1/4 cup mayonnaise
- 1 tablespoon chopped fresh dill, or to taste
- 2 teaspoons Dijon mustard
- 3 pinches brown sugar, or to taste
- 1 teaspoon vegetable oil
- 1/2 pound salmon fillet, skin on

### Direction

- Preheat the grill over medium heat and coat the grate lightly with oil.
- In a bowl, combine brown sugar, mustard, dill, and mayonnaise. Pour the vegetable oil on top of salmon skin.
- Grill the salmon with the skin-side down on the grill. Pour the mayonnaise mixture atop salmon. Cook the salmon for 6 to 12 minutes until it flakes easily with a fork.

### Nutrition Information

- Calories: 412 calories;
- Cholesterol: 66
- Protein: 19.9
- Total Fat: 35.1
- Sodium: 337
- Total Carbohydrate: 3.5

## 393. Grilled Steaks With Greek Relish

*Serving: 2 servings. | Prep: 20mins | Cook: 10mins | Ready in:*

### Ingredients

- 2 plum tomatoes, seeded and chopped
- 1/2 cup chopped red onion
- 1/3 cup pitted Greek olives
- 2 tablespoons minced fresh cilantro
- 2 tablespoons lemon juice, divided
- 1 tablespoon olive oil
- 1 garlic clove, minced
- 1 beef ribeye steak (3/4 pound)
- 1/2 cup crumbled feta cheese

### Direction

- Combine 1 tablespoon of lemon juice, cilantro, olives, onion, garlic, oil and tomatoes in a small bowl to create the relish.
- Over the steak, drip the rest of the lemon juice. On medium heat broil the steak 4 inches from the heat or grill it with the cover on until desired doneness is achieved. Cook for about 5 to 7 minutes per side. For medium-rare meat, a thermometer should register at 145°F and for medium, it should be 160°F. For well-done meat, it should register at 170°F. Before cutting it in half, leave it for 5 minutes first. Serve with cheese and relish.

### Nutrition Information

- Calories: 562 calories
- Fiber: 2g fiber)
- Total Carbohydrate: 10g carbohydrate (4g sugars
- Cholesterol: 108mg cholesterol
- Protein: 34g protein.
- Total Fat: 42g fat (14g saturated fat)
- Sodium: 587mg sodium

## 394. Halibut Steaks

*Serving: 6 | Prep: 15mins | Cook: 15mins | Ready in:*

### Ingredients

- 1 tablespoon olive oil
- 1 small onion, halved and thinly sliced

- 1/2 bell pepper, sliced thinly
- 8 ounces sliced fresh mushrooms
- 1 clove chopped fresh garlic
- 2 medium zucchini, julienned
- 6 (6 ounce) halibut steaks
- 1/2 teaspoon dried basil
- 1/2 teaspoon salt, or to taste
- 1/2 teaspoon ground black pepper
- 1 medium tomato, thinly sliced

## Direction

- Preheat an oven to 200°C/400°F.
- In a skillet, heat olive oil on medium heat. Add zucchini, garlic, mushrooms, bell pepper and onion. Cook, covered, occasionally mixing, for 5 minutes till onions are translucent.
- In a shallow baking dish, put halibut steaks. Put sautéed veggies over. Season with pepper, salt and basil.
- In preheated oven, bake for 10 minutes. Remove dish. Use a layer of sliced tomatoes to cover fillets. Put into oven. Bake till fish easily flakes with a fork for 10 more minutes.

## Nutrition Information

- Calories: 237 calories;
- Total Fat: 6.5
- Sodium: 296
- Total Carbohydrate: 6.1
- Cholesterol: 54
- Protein: 37.8

## 395. Halibut With Citrus Olive Sauce

*Serving: 4 servings. | Prep: 30mins | Cook: 15mins | Ready in:*

## Ingredients

- 2-1/2 cups orange juice, divided
- 1/3 cup white wine
- 2 tablespoons lime juice
- 2 tablespoons chopped shallot
- 1/4 cup butter, cut into four pieces
- 2 tablespoons chopped sweet red pepper
- 1 tablespoon chopped pitted green olives
- 1 tablespoon chopped Greek olives
- 3 garlic cloves, minced
- 1 teaspoon dried oregano
- 4 halibut fillets (6 ounces each)

## Direction

- Boil shallot, lime juice, wine and 1-1/2 cups of orange juice in a small saucepan; cook until the liquid amount decreases to 1/2 cup, approximately 15 minutes. Reduce heat to low; whip in butter gradually until the butter melts. Take the saucepan away from heat; stir in olives and red pepper. Keep warm.
- Boil remaining orange juice, oregano and garlic in a big skillet. Reduce heat; put in the fillets, steam without a cover for 8 to 10 minutes or until flesh flakes apart easily with a fork. Serve the dish with sauce.

## Nutrition Information

- Calories: 384 calories
- Total Fat: 16g fat (8g saturated fat)
- Sodium: 254mg sodium
- Fiber: 0 fiber)
- Total Carbohydrate: 20g carbohydrate (14g sugars
- Cholesterol: 85mg cholesterol
- Protein: 37g protein.

## 396. Hearty Paella

*Serving: 6 servings. | Prep: 25mins | Cook: 30mins | Ready in:*

## Ingredients

- 1-1/4 pounds boneless skinless chicken breasts, cut into 1-inch cubes
- 1 tablespoon olive oil
- 1 cup uncooked long grain rice
- 1 medium onion, chopped
- 2 garlic cloves, minced
- 2-1/4 cups reduced-sodium chicken broth
- 1 can (14-1/2 ounces) diced tomatoes, undrained
- 1 teaspoon dried oregano
- 1/2 teaspoon paprika
- 1/4 teaspoon salt
- 1/4 teaspoon pepper
- 1/8 teaspoon saffron threads
- 1/8 teaspoon ground turmeric
- 1 pound uncooked medium shrimp, peeled and deveined
- 3/4 cup frozen peas
- 12 pimiento-stuffed olives
- 1 medium lemon, cut into six wedges

### Direction

- On medium heat, cook chicken in a big pan with oil until the chicken is not pink; take it out of the pan then keep warm. Put onion and rice in the pan; cook while frequently mixing until the onion is tender and the rice is pale brown. Put in garlic then cook for another minute.
- Mix in turmeric, broth, saffron, tomatoes, pepper, oregano, salt, and paprika; boil. Turn to low heat; cook for 10 minutes with cover.
- Put in olives, peas, and shrimp; cover. Cook for another 10 minutes until the shrimp is pink, the rice is tender, and the liquid is absorbed. Put in chicken; heat completely. Serve along with lemon wedges.

### Nutrition Information

- Calories: 367 calories
- Total Carbohydrate: 36g carbohydrate (5g sugars
- Cholesterol: 144mg cholesterol
- Protein: 37g protein. Diabetic Exchanges: 5 lean meat
- Total Fat: 8g fat (1g saturated fat)
- Sodium: 778mg sodium
- Fiber: 3g fiber)

## 397. Heavenly Greek Tacos

*Serving: 6 servings. | Prep: 30mins | Cook: 10mins | Ready in:*

### Ingredients

- 1/3 cup lemon juice
- 2 tablespoons olive oil
- 4 teaspoons grated lemon peel
- 3 garlic cloves, minced, divided
- 1 teaspoon dried oregano
- 1/4 teaspoon salt
- 1/4 teaspoon pepper
- 2 pounds mahi mahi
- 1-1/2 cups shredded red cabbage
- 1/2 medium red onion, thinly sliced
- 1/2 medium sweet red pepper, julienned
- 1/2 cup crumbled feta cheese
- 6 tablespoons chopped pitted Greek olives, divided
- 1/4 cup minced fresh parsley
- 1-1/2 cups plain Greek yogurt
- 1/2 medium English cucumber, cut into 1-inch pieces
- 1 teaspoon dill weed
- 1/2 teaspoon ground coriander
- 12 whole wheat tortillas (8 inches), warmed

### Direction

- Mix pepper, salt, oregano, 2 garlic cloves, lemon peel, oil and lemon juice together in a big resealable plastic bag. Insert mahi-mahi before sealing the bag up. Coat them by turning. Keep it in the fridge for up to 1/2 hour. Mix parsley, 3 tablespoons of olives, cheese, red pepper, onion and cabbage together in a big bowl. Put it to one side. In a food processor, blend the rest of the olives and garlic, coriander, dill cucumber and yogurt with the cover on until processed. After draining the fish, get rid of the marinade. Use cooking oil to wet the paper towel a little. Coat the grill rack lightly with long-handled tongs. At medium heat, grill the mahi-mahi with a cover on. Alternately, broil them four inches from heat. Cook for 3 to 4 minutes per side or stop when you can use a fork to peel the fish off easily. On each tortilla, put a portion of the fish. Place the sauce and cabbage mixture over the top.

## Nutrition Information

- Calories: 561 calories
- Fiber: 6g fiber)
- Total Carbohydrate: 52g carbohydrate (7g sugars
- Cholesterol: 130mg cholesterol
- Protein: 41g protein.
- Total Fat: 19g fat (5g saturated fat)
- Sodium: 793mg sodium

## 398. Herb Marinated Lamb Chops

*Serving: 4 servings. | Prep: 10mins | Cook: 15mins | Ready in:*

## Ingredients

- 1/4 cup dry red wine or beef broth
- 2 tablespoons reduced-sodium soy sauce
- 1-1/2 teaspoons minced fresh mint or 1/2 teaspoon dried mint
- 1 teaspoon minced fresh basil or 1/4 teaspoon dried basil
- 1/2 teaspoon pepper
- 1 garlic clove, minced
- 4 bone-in lamb loin chops (1 inch thick and 6 ounces each)

## Direction

- Mix garlic, pepper, basil, mint, soy sauce and broth or wine together in a big resealable plastic bag; put in lamb chops. Enclose the bag and coat by flipping; chill in the fridge for 8 hours or up to overnight.
- Let drain and put away the marinade. Grill lamb without covering on moderate heat or broil for 5 to 7 minutes per side in a 4- to 6-inch distance away from the heat until meat achieves preferred doneness; a thermometer should register 160° for medium and 170° for well-done.

## Nutrition Information

- Calories:
- Sodium:
- Fiber:
- Total Carbohydrate:
- Cholesterol:
- Protein:
- Total Fat:

## 399. Herbed Lamb Chops

*Serving: 4 | Prep: 20mins | Cook: 10mins | Ready in:*

## Ingredients

- 1/2 cup olive oil
- 1/2 cup red wine vinegar
- 1/4 cup white wine
- 2 tablespoons lemon juice
- 2 cloves garlic, peeled and minced
- 1/4 cup minced onion
- 1 teaspoon dried tarragon
- 1 teaspoon chopped fresh parsley
- 1 teaspoon black pepper
- 4 lamb chops

## Direction

- Combine in a large nonreactive container, the onion, garlic, lemon juice, white wine, red wine vinegar and olive oil. Put in pepper, parsley and tarragon the season. Put the lamb chops in mixture. Place inside the refrigerator, covered, to marinate for 2 hours.
- Prepare an outdoor grill by preheating to high heat and put oil on the grate lightly.
- Place the lamb chops on the grill and cook for 5 minutes each side, inside temperature should be 145°F (63°C). Get rid of any left marinade.

### Nutrition Information

- Calories: 566 calories;
- Total Fat: 52.4
- Sodium: 56
- Total Carbohydrate: 5.2
- Cholesterol: 70
- Protein: 15.9

### 400. Herbed Lamb Kabobs

*Serving: 8 servings. | Prep: 15mins | Cook: 20mins | Ready in:*

### Ingredients

- 1 cup canola oil
- 1 medium onion, chopped
- 1/2 cup lemon juice
- 1/2 cup minced fresh parsley
- 3 to 4 garlic cloves, minced
- 2 teaspoons salt
- 2 teaspoons dried marjoram
- 2 teaspoons dried thyme
- 1/2 teaspoon pepper
- 2 pounds boneless lamb
- 1 medium red onion, cut into wedges
- 1 large green pepper, cut into 1-inch pieces
- 1 large sweet red pepper, cut into 1-inch pieces

### Direction

- Mix the first nine ingredients in a small bowl. Transfer a cup of the mixture into a large zip-top bag with the lamb. Seal the bag and turn several times to coat; keep refrigerated for 6-8 hours. Cover the bowl of remaining marinade and store in the refrigerator until ready for basting. Drain the lamb and dispose of the marinade. Alternately thread lamb and vegetables on eight metal or water-soaked wooden skewers. Cook on an uncovered grill at medium heat, basting frequently with reserved marinade, for 8-10 minutes per side or until meat is cooked to liking. A meat thermometer reading of 145 degrees is medium-rare, 160 degrees is medium, and 170 degrees is well-done.

### Nutrition Information

- Calories: 366 calories
- Sodium: 591mg sodium
- Fiber: 2g fiber)
- Total Carbohydrate: 6g carbohydrate (3g sugars
- Cholesterol: 69mg cholesterol
- Protein: 22g protein.
- Total Fat: 28g fat (5g saturated fat)

### 401. Herbed Portobello Pasta

*Serving: 4 servings. | Prep: 20mins | Cook: 15mins | Ready in:*

### Ingredients

- 1/2 pound uncooked multigrain angel hair pasta
- 4 large portobello mushrooms (3/4 pound), stems removed
- 1 tablespoon olive oil
- 2 garlic cloves, minced
- 4 plum tomatoes, chopped
- 1/4 cup pitted Greek olives
- 1/4 cup minced fresh basil

- 1 teaspoon minced fresh rosemary or 1/4 teaspoon dried rosemary, crushed
- 1 teaspoon minced fresh thyme or 1/4 teaspoon dried thyme
- 1/4 teaspoon salt
- 1/8 teaspoon pepper
- 2/3 cup crumbled feta cheese
- 1/4 cup shredded Parmesan cheese

## Direction

- Follow al dente directions on package to cook pasta. In the meantime, cut mushrooms first in half, then thinly slice. Heat oil in a big frying pan on medium heat. Add the mushrooms and sauté 8-10 minutes or until tender. Mix in garlic and cook for 1 more minute. Mix in olives and tomatoes. Put heat on low. Do not cover; cook until thick, 5 minutes. Mix in pepper, herbs, and salt. Drain water from pasta, keep 1/4 cup of cooking water. Mix the pasta into the mushroom mixture, use the cooking water to adjust consistency. Sprinkle on cheeses.

## Nutrition Information

- Calories: 375 calories
- Total Carbohydrate: 48g carbohydrate (5g sugars
- Cholesterol: 14mg cholesterol
- Protein: 18g protein. Diabetic Exchanges: 3 starch
- Total Fat: 12g fat (4g saturated fat)
- Sodium: 585mg sodium
- Fiber: 7g fiber)

## 402. Herbed Seafood Skewers

*Serving: 4 servings. | Prep: 30mins | Cook: 10mins | Ready in:*

## Ingredients

- 1/4 cup canola oil
- 1/4 cup lemon juice
- 1 garlic clove, minced
- 1 teaspoon dried oregano
- 1 teaspoon chicken bouillon granules
- 1/2 teaspoon salt
- 1/2 teaspoon dried basil
- 3/4 pound uncooked large shrimp, peeled and deveined
- 1/2 pound sea scallops
- 1 large sweet yellow pepper, cut into 1-inch pieces
- 1 large green pepper, cut into 1-inch pieces
- 1 small zucchini, cut into 1/4-inch slices
- 1 small yellow summer squash, cut into 1/4-inch slices
- Hot cooked rice, optional

## Direction

- Mix the first seven ingredients in a large bowl. Portion the marinade between two large re-sealable bags. In one bag goes the scallops and the shrimps; in the other goes the vegetables. Seal both bags, turn several times to coat, and refrigerate for 1-2 hours. Drain the seafood and discard its marinade. Drain the vegetables but reserve its marinade for basting later. Alternately thread scallops, shrimps, and vegetables onto eight metal or pre-soaked wooden skewers. Dab the grill rack with an oil-moistened paper towel gripped with a long-handled pair of tongs. Cook skewers on a covered grill over medium heat, or broil 4 in. from the heat, turning and brushing occasionally with reserved marinade, until scallop flesh is firm and opaque, and the shrimp turns pink, about 6-8 minutes. May be served with rice.

## Nutrition Information

- Calories: 217 calories
- Sodium: 684mg sodium
- Fiber: 3g fiber)
- Total Carbohydrate: 10g carbohydrate (0 sugars
- Cholesterol: 120mg cholesterol

- Protein: 22g protein. Diabetic Exchanges: 3 lean meat
- Total Fat: 10g fat (1g saturated fat)

## 403. Herbed Spareribs

*Serving: 4-5 servings. | Prep: 50mins | Cook: 15mins | Ready in:*

### Ingredients

- 4 pounds pork spareribs, cut into serving-size pieces
- 1/4 cup olive oil
- 2 tablespoons lemon juice
- 3 garlic cloves, minced
- 1 teaspoon salt
- 1 teaspoon dried rosemary, crushed
- 1 teaspoon paprika
- 1/2 teaspoon dried oregano
- 1/2 teaspoon dried marjoram

### Direction

- In 2 ungreased, 13x9-inch baking dish, arrange ribs on top; cover. Bake for 45-55 minutes, covered, in a 350 degrees F oven until tender.
- Mix remaining ingredients together in a bowl; spread mixture over ribs. On medium heat, grill ribs without cover for 6-8 minutes until light brown. Occasionally spread the herb mixture over ribs.

### Nutrition Information

- Calories: 717 calories
- Total Fat: 60g fat (20g saturated fat)
- Sodium: 640mg sodium
- Fiber: 0 fiber)
- Total Carbohydrate: 2g carbohydrate (0 sugars
- Cholesterol: 196mg cholesterol
- Protein: 41g protein.

## 404. Honey Barbecued Spareribs

*Serving: 4 servings. | Prep: 5mins | Cook: 01hours30mins | Ready in:*

### Ingredients

- 3 pounds pork spareribs or pork baby back ribs
- 3 tablespoons lemon juice
- 2 tablespoons honey
- 2 tablespoons canola oil
- 1 tablespoon soy sauce
- 1 tablespoon dried minced onion
- 1 teaspoon paprika
- 1 teaspoon salt
- 1/2 teaspoon dried oregano
- 1/8 teaspoon garlic powder

### Direction

- Slice spareribs into serving-size pieces. On a rack set in a shallow roasting pan, put the ribs with the bone side turning down. Put a cover on and bake for 60 minutes at 350°. Drain.
- Mix the rest of the ingredients together, brush on the ribs with some of the glaze. Bake without a cover until the meat is soft, about another 30-45 minutes, brushing sometimes with the leftover glaze.

### Nutrition Information

- Calories: 731 calories
- Protein: 47g protein.
- Total Fat: 55g fat (18g saturated fat)
- Sodium: 968mg sodium
- Fiber: 0 fiber)
- Total Carbohydrate: 11g carbohydrate (9g sugars
- Cholesterol: 191mg cholesterol

## 405. Howard's Sauerbraten

*Serving: 8 servings. | Prep: 20mins | Cook: 03hours00mins | Ready in:*

### Ingredients

- 2-1/2 cups water
- 1-1/2 cups red wine vinegar
- 2 medium onions, sliced
- 1 carrot, finely chopped
- 1 celery rib, finely chopped
- 8 whole cloves
- 4 bay leaves
- 1/2 teaspoon whole peppercorns
- 1 beef rump roast or eye of round (about 3 pounds)
- 1/4 cup butter, cubed
- GINGERSNAP GRAVY:
- 1/2 cup water
- 2 tablespoons sugar
- 1/2 cup gingersnap crumbs (about 12 cookies)

### Direction

- Mix vinegar and water in 4-cup glass measure; put 1/2 in saucepan. Divide each of seasonings and veggies to both mixtures. Boil mixture in saucepan; cool down to room temperature. Cover; in glass measure, refrigerate mixture.
- In big resealable plastic bag, put beef. Add cooled vinegar mixture; flip to coat. Put into baking dish; refrigerate, occasionally turning, for 2 days.
- Drain beef; discard veggies and marinade in bag. Pat dry roast. Brown roast on all sides in butter in a Dutch oven. Add reserved vinegar mixture; boil. Lower heat. Simmer with a cover for 3 hours till meat is tender.
- Gravy: remove roast; keep warm. Strain the cooking liquid; discard seasonings and veggies. Get 1 1/2 cups cooking liquid; put into saucepan. Add sugar and water; boil, mixing to dissolve sugar. Lower heat then add gingersnap crumbs; simmer till gravy thickens and serve with roast.

### Nutrition Information

- Calories:
- Cholesterol:
- Protein:
- Total Fat:
- Sodium:
- Fiber:
- Total Carbohydrate:

## 406. Individual Greek Pizzas

*Serving: 4 servings. | Prep: 5mins | Cook: 25mins | Ready in:*

### Ingredients

- 1 package (6 ounces) fresh baby spinach
- 1 tablespoon olive oil
- 1/2 pound lean ground beef (90% lean)
- 1 can (15 ounces) pizza sauce
- 4 prebaked mini pizza crusts
- 4 plum tomatoes, sliced
- 1 cup crumbled tomato and basil feta cheese
- 1/4 cup pine nuts, toasted

### Direction

- Put oil in a big frying pan and sauté spinach until wilted, 2-3 minutes. Remove spinach and set it aside. Cook beef in same pan on medium heat until not pink. Drain excess grease. Mix in the pizza sauce and cook through, about 5 minutes. Put the crusts in a 15x10x1-in. ungreased pan and spread meat sauce close to edges, within a 1/2 in. Layer spinach, tomatoes, the cheese, and pine nuts on top. Bake in a 450-degree oven until cooked through, 8-10 minutes.

### Nutrition Information

- Calories: 687 calories
- Total Carbohydrate: 77g carbohydrate (8g sugars

- Cholesterol: 43mg cholesterol
- Protein: 35g protein.
- Total Fat: 27g fat (8g saturated fat)
- Sodium: 1436mg sodium
- Fiber: 7g fiber)

## 407. Individual Tuna Casseroles

*Serving: 6 servings. | Prep: 30mins | Cook: 25mins | Ready in:*

### Ingredients

- 1-1/2 cups uncooked whole wheat penne pasta
- 1 can (12 ounces) albacore white tuna in water
- 1 can (10-3/4 ounces) reduced-fat reduced-sodium condensed cream of mushroom soup, undiluted
- 1-1/4 cups water-packed artichoke hearts, rinsed, drained and chopped
- 1/2 cup reduced-fat sour cream
- 1/4 cup roasted sweet red peppers, drained and chopped
- 3 tablespoons chopped onion
- 3 tablespoons sun-dried tomatoes (not packed in oil), chopped
- 2 tablespoons Greek olives, chopped
- 1 tablespoon snipped fresh dill or 1 teaspoon dill weed
- 1 tablespoon capers, drained
- 2 garlic cloves, minced
- 1 teaspoon grated lemon peel
- 1/2 teaspoon crushed red pepper flakes
- 1/2 cup dry bread crumbs
- 1/4 cup grated Parmesan cheese
- 1/2 teaspoon Italian seasoning

### Direction

- Follow package instructions to cook pasta
- At the same time, in a big bowl, mix together pepper flakes, lemon peel, garlic, capers, dill, olives, sun-dried tomatoes, onion, peppers, sour cream, artichokes, soup, and tuna. Drain pasta then mix into tuna mixture. Distribute into six 10-ounce custard cups or ramekins.
- Combine Italian seasoning, cheese, and bread crumbs in a small bowl. Spread over the top of the tuna mixture. Put ramekins (or custard cups) on a baking sheet. Bake at 350 degrees without cover for 25-30 minutes or until golden brown.

### Nutrition Information

- Calories: 321 calories
- Sodium: 801mg sodium
- Fiber: 4g fiber)
- Total Carbohydrate: 38g carbohydrate (4g sugars
- Cholesterol: 35mg cholesterol
- Protein: 24g protein.
- Total Fat: 7g fat (3g saturated fat)

## 408. Irish Stew

*Serving: 6 | Prep: 15mins | Cook: 1hours45mins | Ready in:*

### Ingredients

- 1 tablespoon olive oil
- 2 pounds boneless lamb shoulder, cut into 1 1/2 inch pieces
- 1/2 teaspoon salt
- freshly ground black pepper to taste
- 1 large onion, sliced
- 2 carrots, peeled and cut into large chunks
- 1 parsnip, peeled and cut into large chunks (optional)
- 4 cups water, or as needed
- 3 large potatoes, peeled and quartered
- 1 tablespoon chopped fresh rosemary (optional)
- 1 cup coarsely chopped leeks
- chopped fresh parsley for garnish (optional)

## Direction

- In a Dutch oven or big stockpot, heat the oil over medium heat. Put in pieces of lamb and cook, mixing softly, till evenly browned. Add pepper and salt to season.
- Put in parsnips, carrots and onion, and cook softly alongside of meat for several minutes. Mix in water. Place on the cover and let it come to boil prior to reducing the heat to low. Let it simmer for an hour or more, this will vary on the meat cut you used and the tenderness.
- Mix in potatoes, and let it simmer for 15 to 20 minutes, prior to putting in rosemary and leeks. Keep simmering without a cover, till potatoes are soft but remain whole. Jazz up with fresh parsley and serve piping hot in bowls.

## Nutrition Information

- Calories: 609 calories;
- Total Carbohydrate: 43.4
- Cholesterol: 109
- Protein: 29.8
- Total Fat: 35.1
- Sodium: 325

## 409. Italian Leg Of Lamb With Lemon Sauce

*Serving: 12 servings (2 cups gravy). | Prep: 25mins | Cook: 02hours15mins | Ready in:*

## Ingredients

- 2/3 cup lemon juice
- 1/2 cup canola oil
- 2 tablespoons dried oregano
- 4 teaspoons chopped anchovy fillets
- 3 garlic cloves, minced
- 2 teaspoons ground mustard
- 1 teaspoon salt
- One 2-gallon resealable plastic bag
- 1 boneless leg of lamb (5 to 6 pounds), trimmed
- 1/4 cup all-purpose flour
- 1/4 cup cold water

## Direction

- Mix the first 7 ingredients in a small bowl. In a 2-gal resealable plastic bag, put 2/3 cup marinade. Add lamb; seal bag. Turn to coat; refrigerate for 8 hours – overnight. Cover; refrigerate leftover marinade.
- Preheat an oven to 325°. Drain; remove marinade. Put leg of lamb onto a rack in a roasting pan; bake without cover for 2 1/4-2 3/4 hours, till meat gets desired doneness (meat thermometer should read 170° for well done, 160° for medium and 145° for medium-rare)
- Transfer meat to a serving platter and let it stand for 15 minutes prior slicing.
- Meanwhile, put loosened brown bits and drippings into a 2-cup measuring cup then skim fat. Add reserved marinade and enough water to get 1 3/4 cups.
- Mix cold water and flour till smooth in a small saucepan; mix in drippings slowly. Boil; mix and cook till thickened for 2 minutes; serve with lamb.

## Nutrition Information

- Calories: 319 calories
- Sodium: 262mg sodium
- Fiber: 0 fiber)
- Total Carbohydrate: 3g carbohydrate (0 sugars
- Cholesterol: 115mg cholesterol
- Protein: 36g protein.
- Total Fat: 17g fat (5g saturated fat)

### 410. Juicy & Delicious Mixed Spice Burgers

*Serving: 6 servings. | Prep: 20mins | Cook: 10mins | Ready in:*

Ingredients

- 1 medium onion, finely chopped
- 3 tablespoons minced fresh parsley
- 2 tablespoons minced fresh mint
- 1 garlic clove, minced
- 3/4 teaspoon ground allspice
- 3/4 teaspoon pepper
- 1/2 teaspoon ground cinnamon
- 1/2 teaspoon salt
- 1/4 teaspoon ground nutmeg
- 1-1/2 pounds lean ground beef (90% lean)
- Refrigerated tzatziki sauce, optional

Direction

- Mix the initial 9 ingredients in a big bowl. Put the beef; stir gently yet well. Form into 6 oval patties, 4x2-inch in size.
- Let patties grill with cover, over moderate heat or broil for 4 to 6 minutes per side 4-inch away from the heat or till a thermometer register 160°. If wished, serve along with the sauce.

Nutrition Information

- Calories: 192 calories
- Protein: 22g protein. Diabetic Exchanges: 3 lean meat.
- Total Fat: 9g fat (4g saturated fat)
- Sodium: 259mg sodium
- Fiber: 1g fiber)
- Total Carbohydrate: 3g carbohydrate (2g sugars
- Cholesterol: 71mg cholesterol

### 411. Kathy's Smoked Salmon Pizza

*Serving: 6-8 slices. | Prep: 10mins | Cook: 15mins | Ready in:*

Ingredients

- 1 prebaked 12-inch thin pizza crust
- 1/2 cup ranch salad dressing
- 6 slices tomato
- 1/2 cup crumbled feta cheese
- 1 package (3 ounces) smoked salmon or lox
- 4 slices provolone cheese, cut in half

Direction

- On an ungreased 14-inch Pizza Pan, put the crust. Use ranch dressing to spread on it and put salmon, feta cheese and tomato on top. Arrange provolone cheese on top.
- Bake until the cheese is melted or for 15 to 20 minutes at 425 degrees.

Nutrition Information

- Calories:
- Cholesterol:
- Protein:
- Total Fat:
- Sodium:
- Fiber:
- Total Carbohydrate:

### 412. Lamb Chops With Mint Stuffing

*Serving: 8 servings. | Prep: 20mins | Cook: 60mins | Ready in:*

Ingredients

- 1/4 cup chopped onion
- 1/4 cup chopped celery
- 1/2 cup butter, cubed

- 2/3 cup fresh mint leaves, chopped and packed
- 4 cups white or brown bread, torn in 3/4-in. pieces
- Salt to taste
- Black pepper to taste
- 1 large egg, beaten
- 8 shoulder lamb chops
- 4 teaspoons creme de menthe, optional

## Direction

- Sauté celery and onion in butter; mix with bread and mint. Season with pepper and salt. Add egg; lightly mix.
- Put lamb into shallow baking dish; if desired, brush using crème de menthe. Pile stuffing over chops; bake for 1 hour at 350°.

## Nutrition Information

- Calories:
- Total Carbohydrate:
- Cholesterol:
- Protein:
- Total Fat:
- Sodium:
- Fiber:

### 413. Lamb Fajitas

*Serving: 8 servings. | Prep: 15mins | Cook: 15mins | Ready in:*

## Ingredients

- 1 boneless leg of lamb or lamb shoulder (3 to 4 pounds)
- 1/2 cup canola oil
- 1/2 cup lemon juice
- 1/3 cup soy sauce
- 1/3 cup packed brown sugar
- 1/4 cup vinegar
- 3 tablespoons Worcestershire sauce
- 1 tablespoon ground mustard
- 1/2 teaspoon pepper
- 1 large green pepper, sliced
- 1 large sweet red pepper, sliced
- 1 large onion, sliced
- 16 flour tortillas (7 inches), warmed
- Chopped tomato and cucumber, optional

## Direction

- Cut lamb to thin bite-sized strips. Mix pepper, mustard, Worcestershire, vinegar, sugar, soy sauce, lemon juice and oil in a big resealable plastic bag. Add lamb; seal bag. Turn to coat, refrigerate, occasionally turning, for 3 hours.
- Put marinade and lamb into big saucepan/Dutch oven; boil. Lower heat; cover. Simmer till meat is tender for 8-10 minutes. Add onion and peppers; cook till veggies are crisp tender for 4 minutes.
- Put veggies and meat on tortillas using slotted spoon; if desired, top with cucumber and tomato. Fold in tortilla's sides.

## Nutrition Information

- Calories: 697 calories
- Sodium: 1251mg sodium
- Fiber: 1g fiber)
- Total Carbohydrate: 67g carbohydrate (12g sugars
- Cholesterol: 95mg cholesterol
- Protein: 40g protein.
- Total Fat: 30g fat (6g saturated fat)

### 414. Lamb Kabobs With Bulgur Pilaf

*Serving: 6 servings. | Prep: 15mins | Cook: 35mins | Ready in:*

## Ingredients

- 30 garlic cloves, crushed (1-1/2 to 2 bulbs)

- 1/2 cup balsamic vinegar
- 3/4 cup chopped fresh mint or 1/4 cup dried mint
- 1/4 cup olive oil
- 2 pounds lean boneless lamb, cut into 1-1/2-inch cubes
- PILAF:
- 1/2 cup butter, cubed
- 1 large onion, chopped
- 1 cup uncooked mini spiral pasta
- 2 cups bulgur
- 3 cups beef broth

### Direction

- Combine garlic, oil, vinegar, mint, and lamb in a large re-sealable plastic bag. Seal the bag, turn several times to coat, and refrigerate for several hours up to overnight. Prepare the pilaf: melt butter in a large skillet, add the onions and the pasta. Sauté until pasta is lightly browned. Add in the bulgur and stir to coat. Pour in broth and bring to a boil. Reduce heat to simmer while covered for 25-30 minutes or until bulgur is tender. Remove from heat and let cool for 5 minutes. Fluff with a fork. Drain the lamb and dispose of its marinade. Skewer lamb onto six metal or water-soaked wooden skewers. Cook the kabob on a grill over medium heat, covered, for 8-10 minutes or until meat is at desired doneness, turning frequently. Serve with bulgur pilaf.

### Nutrition Information

- Calories: 626 calories
- Sodium: 644mg sodium
- Fiber: 10g fiber)
- Total Carbohydrate: 52g carbohydrate (4g sugars
- Cholesterol: 132mg cholesterol
- Protein: 38g protein.
- Total Fat: 31g fat (14g saturated fat)

## 415. Lamb Kabobs With Yogurt Sauce

*Serving: 2 servings. | Prep: 20mins | Cook: 10mins | Ready in:*

### Ingredients

- 1/2 cup white wine or chicken broth
- 2 tablespoons olive oil
- 2 teaspoons ground coriander
- 1 teaspoon ground ginger
- 1/2 teaspoon salt
- 1/4 teaspoon ground cinnamon
- 1/2 pound sirloin lamb roast, cut into 1-inch cubes
- 1/2 cup plain yogurt
- 6 medium fresh mushrooms
- 1 medium zucchini, cut into 1/2-inch slices
- 1-1/2 cups hot cooked couscous

### Direction

- Take the first six ingredients and mix together in a small bowl. Pour a third of a cup of the mixture into a large re-sealable plastic bag with the lamb. Close the bag and turn to coat the lamb with the marinade; let it soak in the refrigerator for 15 minutes. Put the yogurt in a small bowl and stir in a tablespoon of marinade. Cover the bowl and refrigerate. Keep the remaining marinade in the refrigerator for basting later. Drain the lamb and discard its marinade. Thread the lamb, zucchini, and mushrooms alternately on two metal or water-soaked wooden skewers. Cook on a covered grill over medium heat for 5-6 minutes per side, or until lamb is cooked to liking, basting often with the reserved marinade. A meat thermometer reading of 145 degrees means medium-rare; 160 degrees is medium, and 170 degrees is well-done. Serve skewers with couscous and yogurt mixture on the side.

### Nutrition Information

- Calories: 500 calories
- Sodium: 572mg sodium
- Fiber: 6g fiber)
- Total Carbohydrate: 40g carbohydrate (6g sugars
- Cholesterol: 72mg cholesterol
- Protein: 31g protein.
- Total Fat: 20g fat (5g saturated fat)

## 416. Lamb Ratatouille

*Serving: 6 servings. | Prep: 30mins | Cook: 20mins | Ready in:*

### Ingredients

- 1 package (6.8 ounces) beef-flavored rice and vermicelli mix
- 2 tablespoons butter
- 2-1/2 cups water
- 3 medium tomatoes, peeled, seeded and chopped
- 1 medium zucchini, sliced
- 1-1/2 cups sliced fresh mushrooms
- 1 small onion, chopped
- 6 green onions, sliced
- 3 garlic cloves, minced
- 2 tablespoons olive oil
- 1 pound cooked lamb or beef, cut into thin strips

### Direction

- Reserve the rice seasoning packet. Sauté rice mix in a big pan with butter until brown. Mix in the seasoning packet contents and water; boil. Lower heat; let it simmer for 15 minutes with cover.
- In the meantime, sauté vegetables in another pan with oil until tender-crisp. Put the vegetables and lamb in the rice; cover. Let it simmer for 5-10 minutes until the rice is tender and the meat is not pink.

## Nutrition Information

- Calories: 369 calories
- Cholesterol: 76mg cholesterol
- Protein: 25g protein.
- Total Fat: 16g fat (6g saturated fat)
- Sodium: 580mg sodium
- Fiber: 3g fiber)
- Total Carbohydrate: 31g carbohydrate (6g sugars

## 417. Lamb And Beef Kabobs

*Serving: 8 servings. | Prep: 25mins | Cook: 10mins | Ready in:*

### Ingredients

- 1/4 cup minced fresh parsley
- 2 tablespoons olive oil
- 4 teaspoons salt
- 2 teaspoons pepper
- 2 teaspoons lemon juice
- 2 pounds boneless lamb, cut into 1-1/2-inch cubes
- 1 pound beef top sirloin steak, cut into 1-1/2-inch cubes
- 6 small onions, cut into wedges
- 2 medium sweet red peppers, cut into 1-inch pieces
- 16 large fresh mushrooms
- 6 pita breads (6 inches), cut into wedges

### Direction

- Mix the first five ingredients in a small bowl. In a big plastic resealable bag, add the beef and lamb. Pour in half of marinade. In a separate plastic resealable bag, add the other half of marinade and vegetables. Seal the bags and coat by turning. Keep in the refrigerator for 1 hour.
- On eight soaked wooden or metal skewers, thread the beef, red peppers, lamb, onions, and mushrooms, alternately. Grill meat with

cover on medium heat, about 5 to 6 minutes per side until cooked to desired degree of doneness and vegetables turn tender. Serve along with the pita bread.

## Nutrition Information

- Calories: 419 calories
- Protein: 40g protein.
- Total Fat: 13g fat (4g saturated fat)
- Sodium: 1524mg sodium
- Fiber: 3g fiber)
- Total Carbohydrate: 34g carbohydrate (5g sugars
- Cholesterol: 105mg cholesterol

## 418. Lamb And Potato Stew

*Serving: 8 servings (2 quarts). | Prep: 5mins | Cook: 01hours30mins | Ready in:*

### Ingredients

- 2 pounds lean lamb stew meat, cut into 1-inch pieces
- 1/2 cup chopped onion
- 4 to 6 medium potatoes, peeled and diced
- 4 carrots, diced
- 1-1/4 cups water
- 1 can (14-1/2 ounces) diced tomatoes, undrained
- 1/2 cup diced celery
- 1-1/2 teaspoon salt
- 1/2 teaspoon pepper
- 1/2 teaspoon garlic powder
- 1/2 teaspoon dried thyme
- 1/2 teaspoon dried basil
- 1 to 2 bay leaves

### Direction

- Combine all ingredients in a Dutch oven or large kettle. Bake, covered for 1.5 to 2.5 hours at 325° or until softened. Remove bay leaves before serving.

## Nutrition Information

- Calories: 266 calories
- Protein: 26g protein.
- Total Fat: 6g fat (2g saturated fat)
- Sodium: 606mg sodium
- Fiber: 4g fiber)
- Total Carbohydrate: 26g carbohydrate (6g sugars
- Cholesterol: 74mg cholesterol

## 419. Lamb With Apricots

*Serving: 8 servings. | Prep: 15mins | Cook: 01hours30mins | Ready in:*

### Ingredients

- 1 large onion, chopped
- 2 tablespoons olive oil
- 1 boneless lamb shoulder roast (2-1/2 to 3 pounds), cubed
- 1 teaspoon each ground cumin, cinnamon and coriander
- Salt and pepper to taste
- 1/2 cup dried apricots, halved
- 1/4 cup orange juice
- 1 tablespoon ground almonds
- 1/2 teaspoon grated orange zest
- 1-1/4 cups chicken broth
- 1 tablespoon sesame seeds, toasted

### Direction

- Place the onion in a big skillet and sauté in oil until softened. Cook the lamb and put in the seasonings. Stir while it cooks for 5 minutes or until the meat becomes brown. Stir in the orange juice, apricots, orange zest and almonds.

- Place on a 2-1/2 quarts. baking dish. Mix in the broth. Let it bake at 350° while covered for 1-1/2 hours or until the lamb is tender. Top it off with sesame seeds.

## Nutrition Information

- Calories: 280 calories
- Sodium: 198mg sodium
- Fiber: 2g fiber)
- Total Carbohydrate: 9g carbohydrate (6g sugars
- Cholesterol: 70mg cholesterol
- Protein: 19g protein.
- Total Fat: 19g fat (7g saturated fat)

## 420. Lamb With Raspberry Sauce

*Serving: 8 servings. | Prep: 10mins | Cook: 20mins | Ready in:*

## Ingredients

- 2 cups fresh or frozen unsweetened raspberries
- 3/4 cup finely chopped seeded peeled cucumber
- 1/2 cup finely chopped peeled tart apple
- 2 tablespoons white grape juice
- 1 to 2 tablespoons sugar
- 4 garlic cloves, minced
- 3 tablespoons olive oil
- 8 lamb loin chops (1 to 1-1/2 inches thick and 6 ounces each)

## Direction

- Put raspberries in a blender; cover and pulse into puree. Sieve pureed raspberries, discarding seeds; pour pureed raspberries into a small saucepan. Whisk in sugar, grape juice, apple, and cucumber. Bring to a boil. Lower heat; simmer without covering until apple and cucumber are tender for 5 to 7 minutes.
- In the meantime, sauté garlic in oil in a large skillet until tender. Put in lamb chops. Cook without covering for 7 to 10 minutes per side until desired doneness of lamb is reached (145° for medium-rare, 160° for medium, and 170° for well done). Spoon raspberry sauce over lamb to serve.

## Nutrition Information

- Calories: 230 calories
- Protein: 22g protein. Diabetic Exchanges: 3 lean meat
- Total Fat: 12g fat (3g saturated fat)
- Sodium: 61mg sodium
- Fiber: 2g fiber)
- Total Carbohydrate: 7g carbohydrate (4g sugars
- Cholesterol: 68mg cholesterol

## 421. Lamb With Spinach And Onions

*Serving: 6 servings. | Prep: 25mins | Cook: 10mins | Ready in:*

## Ingredients

- 1/2 cup lime juice
- 1/4 cup dry red wine or 1 tablespoon red wine vinegar
- 1 small onion, chopped
- 2 tablespoons minced fresh rosemary or 2 teaspoons dried rosemary, crushed
- 2 tablespoons olive oil
- 2 tablespoons Worcestershire sauce
- 3 garlic cloves, minced
- 1 tablespoon minced fresh thyme or 1 teaspoon dried thyme
- 1/4 teaspoon pepper
- Dash Liquid Smoke, optional
- 12 rib lamb chops (1 inch thick)

- ONION SAUCE:
- 2 tablespoons finely chopped green onions
- 1 teaspoon butter
- 1 cup balsamic vinegar
- 1 cup dry red wine or 1/2 cup beef broth and grape juice
- 1/2 cup loosely packed fresh mint leaves, chopped
- 1 tablespoon sugar
- 1 large sweet onion, cut into quarters
- Olive oil
- Salt and pepper to taste
- SPINACH:
- 1/4 cup finely chopped green onions
- 3 garlic cloves, minced
- 3 tablespoons olive oil
- 3 tablespoons butter
- 12 cups fresh baby spinach
- Salt and pepper to taste

## Direction

- Mix the first ten ingredients in a big plastic resealable bag; put in lamb chops. Seal and turn to coat; chill for 8 hrs. or overnight.
- Sauté green onions in a saucepan with butter until tender. Pour in wine and vinegar or grape juice and broth; boil. Put in sugar and mint. Lower the heat; let it simmer for half an hour without a cover until the sauce reduces to 3/4 cup. Strain then get rid of the mint; set aside.
- Onto soaked wood or metal skewers, thread the onion wedges then rub with pepper and salt. Take the lamb out of the marinade. On medium-hot heat, grill chops for 5-6 minutes per side while covering or until it reaches the preferred doneness. A thermometer should register 170 degrees F for well-done or 160 degrees F for medium. Grill the onion skewers for 2-3 mins or until the onions are tender.
- Sauté garlic and green onions in a big skillet with butter and oil until tender. Put in pepper, salt, and spinach; sauté for 2-3 mins until the spinach is thoroughly heated and just starts to wilt. Move onto a serving platter. Take the onion out of the skewers; lay the lamb chops and onion on the spinach.

## Nutrition Information

- Calories:
- Cholesterol:
- Protein:
- Total Fat:
- Sodium:
- Fiber:
- Total Carbohydrate:

## 422. Leg Of Lamb Dinner

*Serving: 10-12 servings. | Prep: 35mins | Cook: 02hours00mins | Ready in:*

## Ingredients

- 1 leg of lamb (5 to 7 pounds)
- 8 garlic cloves, cut into slivers
- 4 teaspoons minced fresh rosemary, divided
- 2 teaspoons ground mustard
- 1-1/2 teaspoons salt, divided
- 1 teaspoon chopped fresh mint or 1/4 teaspoon dried mint flakes
- 1/4 teaspoon pepper
- 1 tablespoon water
- 3 pounds red potatoes, cut into 1-inch slices
- 1 package (16 ounces) baby carrots
- 2 tablespoons olive oil
- 3 cups fresh or frozen peas
- 3 tablespoons cornstarch
- 1 cup beef broth
- 1/2 cup cold water
- 1/3 to 1/2 cup currant jelly

## Direction

- From roast, remove thin fat layer. Create deep cuts in meat; in each, insert garlic sliver. Mix pepper, mint, 1 tsp. salt, mustard and 3 tsp. rosemary; mix in water. Rub on meat. Put onto

- rack in big roasting pan; bake at 350°, uncovered, for 1 1/2 hours.
- Meanwhile, toss salt, leftover rosemary, oil, carrots and potatoes in a big bowl; put into separate greased roasting pan. Bake at 350°, uncovered, for 1-1 3/4 hours.
- Use pan drippings to base roast; bake till meat gets desired doneness, 170° for well done, 160° for medium well, for 30 minutes – 2 hours.
- Put peas in veggie mixture; bake till veggies are tender and browned for 10 minutes. Transfer veggies and roast onto warm serving platter; keep warm.
- Into saucepan, strain pan drippings; skim fat. Mix cold water, broth and cornstarch till smooth in small bowl; add to drippings slowly. Mix in jelly. Boil; mix and cook till thick for 2 minutes. Serve with veggies and roast.

## Nutrition Information

- Calories: 372 calories
- Cholesterol: 93mg cholesterol
- Protein: 31g protein.
- Total Fat: 10g fat (3g saturated fat)
- Sodium: 470mg sodium
- Fiber: 5g fiber)
- Total Carbohydrate: 39g carbohydrate (12g sugars

## 423. Lemon Chicken Skewers

*Serving: 6 servings. | Prep: 10mins | Cook: 15mins | Ready in:*

## Ingredients

- 1/4 cup olive oil
- 3 tablespoons lemon juice
- 1 tablespoon white wine vinegar
- 2 garlic cloves, minced
- 2 teaspoons grated lemon zest
- 1 teaspoon salt
- 1/2 teaspoon sugar
- 1/4 teaspoon dried oregano
- 1/4 teaspoon pepper
- 1-1/2 pounds boneless skinless chicken breasts, cut into 1-1/2-in. pieces
- 3 medium zucchini, halved lengthwise and cut into 1-1/2-inch slices
- 3 medium onions, cut into wedges
- 12 cherry tomatoes

## Direction

- Mix the first nine ingredients in a big bowl and set aside 1/4 cup for basting later. Place chicken and half of the mixture in a separate large bowl; turn to coat chicken pieces evenly. Take the remaining marinade and pour into another big bowl; add the onions, tomatoes, and zucchinis and turn several times to coat. Cover the bowls of chicken and vegetables and refrigerate overnight or for at least 4 hours. Drain, discarding the marinade. Skewer the chicken and vegetables alternately onto metal or wooden skewers that have been soaked. Cook on covered grill, set on medium heat, while brushing the kabobs occasionally with reserved marinade, for 6 minutes per side or until chicken juices are clear.

## Nutrition Information

- Calories: 219 calories
- Total Fat: 6g fat (1g saturated fat)
- Sodium: 278mg sodium
- Fiber: 3g fiber)
- Total Carbohydrate: 12g carbohydrate (0 sugars
- Cholesterol: 66mg cholesterol
- Protein: 29g protein. Diabetic Exchanges: 3 lean meat

### 424. Lemon Chicken With Oregano

*Serving: 4 servings. | Prep: 5mins | Cook: 45mins | Ready in:*

Ingredients

- 4 chicken leg quarters (3-1/2 pounds)
- 3 tablespoons lemon juice
- 2 tablespoons honey
- 1 tablespoon olive oil
- 3 garlic cloves, minced
- 2 to 4 teaspoons dried oregano

Direction

- Cut leg into quarters at the joints, if wanted, using a sharp knife. Put chicken in a 13"x9" baking dish coated with grease. Mix together oregano, garlic, oil, honey and lemon juice, then scoop over chicken.
- Bake at 375 degrees without a cover until a thermometer reaches 180 degrees, while basting with pan juices sometimes, about 45 minutes.

Nutrition Information

- Calories:
- Sodium:
- Fiber:
- Total Carbohydrate:
- Cholesterol:
- Protein:
- Total Fat:

### 425. Lemon Feta Chicken

*Serving: 4 servings. | Prep: 5mins | Cook: 20mins | Ready in:*

Ingredients

- 4 boneless skinless chicken breast halves (4 ounces each)
- 2 to 3 tablespoons lemon juice
- 1/4 cup crumbled feta cheese
- 1 teaspoon dried oregano
- 1/4 to 1/2 teaspoon pepper

Direction

- In a 13x9-in. baking dish coated in cooking spray, put chicken. Put lemon juice on chicken. Sprinkle pepper, oregano and feta cheese on top.
- Bake for 20-25 minutes at 400°, uncovered, till a thermometer registers 170°.

Nutrition Information

- Calories: 143 calories
- Sodium: 122mg sodium
- Fiber: 0 fiber)
- Total Carbohydrate: 1g carbohydrate (0 sugars
- Cholesterol: 66mg cholesterol
- Protein: 24g protein. Diabetic Exchanges: 3 lean meat
- Total Fat: 4g fat (1g saturated fat)

### 426. Lemon Garlic Chicken

*Serving: 3 | Prep: 10mins | Cook: 15mins | Ready in:*

Ingredients

- 2 tablespoons butter
- 3 skinless, boneless chicken breast halves
- 1 1/2 teaspoons salt
- 1 1/2 teaspoons ground black pepper
- 2 tablespoons garlic powder
- 1 lemon, juiced

Direction

- Melt butter over medium-high heat in a skillet.
- Season chicken with pepper and salt. Cook chicken in melted butter in the skillet for about

5 minutes, turning constantly, until browned. Scatter 1 tablespoon of garlic powder over chicken; turn over; scatter another tablespoon of garlic powder on the other side. Cook each side for 2 minutes. Stream lemon juice over each side of chicken; cook for 5 to 10 minutes longer until not pink anymore on the inside and an instant-read thermometer registers at least 165°F (74°C) when inserted into the middle.

## Nutrition Information

- Calories: 214 calories;
- Sodium: 1275
- Total Carbohydrate: 4.7
- Cholesterol: 85
- Protein: 24.7
- Total Fat: 10.5

### 427. Lemon Herb Lamb Chops

*Serving: 2 servings. | Prep: 5mins | Cook: 10mins | Ready in:*

## Ingredients

- 1/4 cup olive oil
- 1 tablespoon lemon juice
- 1 garlic clove, minced
- 1 teaspoon grated lemon peel
- 1/4 teaspoon salt
- 1/4 teaspoon dried basil
- 1/4 teaspoon dried rosemary, crushed
- 1/4 teaspoon pepper
- 2 lamb loin chops (1 inch thick and 6 ounces each)

## Direction

- Mix the first 8 ingredients in a big ziplock bag; put in chops. Seal then turn the bag to coat the chops; chill for at least 2 hours to overnight.

- Drain and get rid of the marinade. Broil the chops for 4-9 minutes per side, three to four inches from heat until it reaches the preferred doneness. The thermometer should register 145 degrees F for medium-rare, 160 degrees F for medium, and 170°C for well-done.

## Nutrition Information

- Calories: 303 calories
- Sodium: 238mg sodium
- Fiber: 0 fiber)
- Total Carbohydrate: 1g carbohydrate (0 sugars
- Cholesterol: 68mg cholesterol
- Protein: 22g protein.
- Total Fat: 23g fat (5g saturated fat)

### 428. Lemon Turkey With Couscous Stuffing

*Serving: 8 servings. | Prep: 15mins | Cook: 01hours25mins | Ready in:*

## Ingredients

- 1 bone-in turkey breast (4 to 4-1/2 pounds)
- 2 teaspoons olive oil
- 1 teaspoon lemon juice
- 1 garlic clove, minced
- 1/2 teaspoon grated lemon peel
- 1/4 teaspoon salt
- 1/8 teaspoon pepper
- STUFFING:
- 1-1/2 cups boiling water
- 1 cup uncooked couscous
- 1 medium carrot, shredded
- 1/2 cup raisins
- 1/3 cup chicken broth
- 1/4 cup slivered almonds, toasted
- 2 tablespoons minced fresh parsley

## Direction

- Loosen the turkey skin carefully but keep it attached to the back. Mix pepper, salt, lemon peel, garlic, lemon juice, and oil; distribute under the turkey skin. Arrange the turkey into one side of a greased shallow roasting pan.
- Pour the boiling water over the couscous in a bowl for the stuffing. Put on a cover and allow to stand until the water is absorbed, 5 minutes. Put in the remaining ingredients and toss them to mix. Add the stuffing to the other side of the pan and form into an 8x5x2-inch mound. Put a cover on the pan and bake for 45 minutes at 325 degrees.
- Remove the cover from the turkey but cover the stuffing. Bake until a thermometer registers 170 degrees, for 40-50 more minutes. Before cutting, use foil to cover the turkey and allow to stand for 15 minutes. Serve alongside the stuffing.

## Nutrition Information

- Calories: 303 calories
- Total Carbohydrate: 26g carbohydrate (0 sugars
- Cholesterol: 94mg cholesterol
- Protein: 38g protein. Diabetic Exchanges: 4 lean meat
- Total Fat: 4g fat (1g saturated fat)
- Sodium: 181mg sodium
- Fiber: 2g fiber)

## 429. Lemon Caper Baked Cod

*Serving: 4 servings. | Prep: 10mins | Cook: 10mins | Ready in:*

## Ingredients

- 1/4 cup butter, cubed
- 2 tablespoons lemon juice
- 1/4 teaspoon garlic pepper blend
- 1/4 teaspoon grated lemon peel
- 2 tablespoons capers, drained
- 4 cod or haddock fillets (6 ounces each)
- 1/2 teaspoon seafood seasoning
- 1 tablespoon crumbled feta cheese

## Direction

- Mix together lemon peel, garlic pepper, lemon juice and butter in a small microwavable bowl. Cook in the microwave on high setting without a cover until butter has melted, or about 45 to 60 seconds, then add capers and stir.
- In an ungreased 13"x9" baking dish, position cod, then use seafood seasoning to sprinkle over. Scoop over fillets with butter mixture, then sprinkle on top with cheese. Bake at 425 degrees without a cover until it is easy to make fish flake using a fork, or about 10 to 15 minutes.

## Nutrition Information

- Calories: 256 calories
- Fiber: 0 fiber)
- Total Carbohydrate: 1g carbohydrate (0 sugars
- Cholesterol: 129mg cholesterol
- Protein: 33g protein.
- Total Fat: 13g fat (8g saturated fat)
- Sodium: 441mg sodium

## 430. Lemon Garlic Pork Tenderloin

*Serving: 2 servings. | Prep: 15mins | Cook: 30mins | Ready in:*

## Ingredients

- 2 tablespoons canola oil
- 1-1/2 teaspoons lemon juice
- 1-1/2 teaspoons grated lemon peel
- 3 garlic cloves, minced
- 1-1/2 teaspoons dried oregano
- 1/4 teaspoon salt

- 1/4 teaspoon pepper
- 1 pork tenderloin (3/4 pound)

### Direction

- Mix the oil, pepper, lemon juice, salt, peel, garlic and oregano in a resealable plastic bag; add pork. Seal and turn to coat; keep cool in refrigerator for 8 hours or overnight.
- Drain and dispose of marinade. Cover and grill over medium heat until juices run clear and a thermometer reads 160deg, about 13-14 minutes on each side. Before slicing, let meat stand for 5 minutes.

### Nutrition Information

- Calories: 239 calories
- Fiber: 0 fiber)
- Total Carbohydrate: 1g carbohydrate (0 sugars
- Cholesterol: 111mg cholesterol
- Protein: 36g protein. Diabetic Exchanges: 4-1/2 lean meat.
- Total Fat: 9g fat (2g saturated fat)
- Sodium: 159mg sodium

### 431. Lemon Herb Leg Of Lamb

*Serving: 12 servings. | Prep: 10mins | Cook: 01hours45mins | Ready in:*

### Ingredients

- 2 teaspoons lemon juice
- 1-1/2 teaspoons grated lemon peel
- 1 teaspoon garlic salt
- 1 teaspoon dried oregano
- 1 teaspoon dried thyme
- 1 teaspoon dried rosemary, crushed
- 1 teaspoon ground mustard
- 1 boneless leg of lamb (4 pounds), rolled and tied

### Direction

- Mix initial 7 ingredients in a small bowl; rub on lamb leg. Cover; refrigerate overnight.
- Preheat an oven to 325°. Put lamb onto rack in shallow roasting pan; bake for 1 3/4-2 1/4 hours, uncovered, till meat gets desired doneness; 170° well-done, 160° medium and 145° for medium-rare on a thermometer.
- Before slicing, stand for 15 minutes.

### Nutrition Information

- Calories: 198 calories
- Total Fat: 8g fat (3g saturated fat)
- Sodium: 225mg sodium
- Fiber: 0 fiber)
- Total Carbohydrate: 0 carbohydrate (0 sugars
- Cholesterol: 92mg cholesterol
- Protein: 28g protein. Diabetic Exchanges: 4 lean meat.

### 432. Lemony Spinach Stuffed Chicken Breasts For Two

*Serving: 2 servings. | Prep: 30mins | Cook: 20mins | Ready in:*

### Ingredients

- 1/4 cup chopped sweet onion
- 1-1/2 teaspoons olive oil, divided
- 3 cups fresh baby spinach, chopped
- 1/2 teaspoon minced garlic
- 1-1/2 teaspoons balsamic vinegar
- 2 tablespoons crumbled feta cheese
- 1/4 teaspoon grated lemon peel
- 1/8 teaspoon salt
- 1/8 teaspoon pepper
- 2 boneless skinless chicken breast halves (6 ounces each)

### Direction

- On medium heat, cook onion for 10-15 minutes while frequently stirring in a small pan with a teaspoon of oil until the onion is golden brown. Put in vinegar, garlic, and spinach; cook for another minute. Take off heat then cool for 5 minutes. Mix in pepper, cheese, salt, and lemon peel.
- Flatten the chicken until a quarter-inch thick; spread the spinach mixture on chicken. Roll up then secure using toothpicks.
- On medium heat, cook chicken for 8-10 minutes per side in a small pan with the remaining oil until the juices are clear. Remove toothpicks.

## Nutrition Information

- Calories: 252 calories
- Sodium: 334mg sodium
- Fiber: 2g fiber)
- Total Carbohydrate: 5g carbohydrate (2g sugars
- Cholesterol: 98mg cholesterol
- Protein: 37g protein. Diabetic Exchanges: 5 lean meat
- Total Fat: 9g fat (2g saturated fat)

## 433. Lentil Vegetable Stew

*Serving: 5 quarts. | Prep: 10mins | Cook: 01hours40mins | Ready in:*

## Ingredients

- 2 cups dried lentils, rinsed
- 3/4 cup uncooked brown rice
- 1 can (28 ounces) diced tomatoes, undrained
- 1 can (48 ounces) tomato or vegetable juice
- 4 cups water
- 3 garlic cloves, minced
- 1 large onion, chopped
- 2 celery ribs, sliced
- 3 medium carrots, sliced
- 1 bay leaf
- 1 teaspoon dried basil
- 1 teaspoon dried oregano
- 1 teaspoon dried thyme
- 1/2 teaspoon pepper
- 3 tablespoons minced fresh parsley
- 1 medium zucchini, sliced
- 2 medium potatoes, peeled and diced
- 2 tablespoons lemon juice
- 1 teaspoon ground mustard
- Salt to taste

## Direction

- Mix first 15 ingredients in a stockpot or 6-qt. Dutch oven. Heat to a boil. Cover, decrease heat, and simmer until lentils and rice are tender, 45-60 minutes. Add more tomato juice or water if needed. Mix in the rest of the ingredients. Place cover and cook for 45 minutes or until veggies are tender.

## Nutrition Information

- Calories:
- Sodium:
- Fiber:
- Total Carbohydrate:
- Cholesterol:
- Protein:
- Total Fat:

## 434. Linguine With Seafood Sauce

*Serving: 6 servings. | Prep: 10mins | Cook: 20mins | Ready in:*

## Ingredients

- 4 green onions, sliced
- 1 garlic clove, minced
- 2 tablespoons butter
- 1 pound cooked medium shrimp, peeled and deveined

- 1 can (6-1/2 ounces) chopped clams, undrained
- 1 cup chicken broth
- 1/2 cup white wine or additional chicken broth
- 2 tablespoons lemon juice
- 1/2 cup minced fresh parsley
- 1 teaspoon dried basil
- 1 teaspoon dried oregano
- 1/2 teaspoon salt
- 1/4 teaspoon pepper
- 12 ounces uncooked linguine
- 2 tablespoons cornstarch
- 2 tablespoons cold water
- 1/4 cup reduced-fat sour cream

## Direction

- Sauté garlic and onions with butter in a big nonstick skillet until softened, about 4 to 5 minutes. Stir in the following ten ingredients, then bring to a boil. Lower heat and simmer without a cover about 5 minutes. At the same time, following package directions to cook linguine.
- Mix water and cornstarch together until smooth, then put into the seafood mixture slowly. Bring the mixture to a boil, then cook and stir until thickened, about 2 minutes. Drain linguine and toss together with sour cream. Put into a serving bowl, then put in seafood sauce and toss to coat well.

## Nutrition Information

- Calories: 337 calories
- Fiber: 2g fiber)
- Total Carbohydrate: 38g carbohydrate (0 sugars
- Cholesterol: 139mg cholesterol
- Protein: 26g protein. Diabetic Exchanges: 2-1/2 starch
- Total Fat: 8g fat (3g saturated fat)
- Sodium: 632mg sodium

## 435. Makeover Greek Chicken Penne

*Serving: 6 servings. | Prep: 20mins | Cook: 20mins | Ready in:*

## Ingredients

- 2 cups uncooked penne pasta
- 1/2 cup sun-dried tomatoes (not packed in oil)
- 1-1/2 cups boiling water
- 1 large onion, chopped
- 3 tablespoons reduced-fat butter
- 1/4 cup all-purpose flour
- 1 can (14-1/2 ounces) reduced-sodium chicken broth
- 3 cups cubed cooked chicken breast
- 1 cup (4 ounces) crumbled feta cheese
- 1 cup water-packed artichoke hearts, rinsed, drained and chopped
- 1/3 cup Greek olives, sliced
- 2 tablespoons minced fresh parsley
- 1/4 teaspoon Greek seasoning

## Direction

- Cook the pasta following the package instructions. In the meantime, in a small bowl, put the tomatoes, then add boiling water. Put cover and allow it to stand for 5 minutes.
- Sauté the onion in butter in a Dutch oven until it becomes tender. Mix in flour until combined and slowly add the broth, then boil. Let it cook and stir for 2 minutes or until it becomes thick. Drain and chop the tomatoes, then add it into the pan. Mix in the leftover ingredients. Drain the pasta, then add it into the pan and heat it through.

## Nutrition Information

- Calories: 343 calories
- Fiber: 3g fiber)
- Total Carbohydrate: 31g carbohydrate (4g sugars

- Cholesterol: 71mg cholesterol
- Protein: 30g protein.
- Total Fat: 11g fat (5g saturated fat)
- Sodium: 813mg sodium

### 436. Makeover Greek Spaghetti

*Serving: 10 servings. | Prep: 30mins | Cook: 25mins | Ready in:*

## Ingredients

- 1 package (16 ounces) spaghetti, broken into 2-inch pieces
- 4 cups cubed cooked chicken breast
- 2 packages (10 ounces each) frozen chopped spinach, thawed and squeezed dry
- 1 can (10-3/4 ounces) reduced-fat reduced-sodium condensed cream of chicken soup, undiluted
- 3/4 cup reduced-fat mayonnaise
- 3/4 cup reduced-fat sour cream
- 3 celery ribs, chopped
- 1 small onion, chopped
- 1/2 cup chopped green pepper
- 1 jar (2 ounces) diced pimientos, drained
- 1/2 teaspoon salt-free lemon-pepper seasoning
- 3 tablespoons all-purpose flour
- 1-1/3 cups fat-free milk
- 1 teaspoon chicken bouillon granules
- 1 cup shredded part-skim mozzarella cheese
- 1/2 cup soft bread crumbs
- 1/4 cup shredded Parmesan cheese

## Direction

- Cook the spaghetti following the package instructions, then drain. Put the spaghetti back into the saucepan. Stir in the lemon-pepper, pimientos, green pepper, onion, celery, sour cream, mayonnaise, soup, spinach and chicken.
- Whisk the milk and flour in a small saucepan until it becomes smooth, then boil on medium heat. Let it cook and stir for 2 minutes or until it becomes thick. Mix in bullion. Pour it on top of the spaghetti mixture and stir well.
- Move to a cooking spray coated 13 by 9-inch baking dish (the dish must be full). Put the Parmesan cheese, breadcrumbs and mozzarella cheese on top. Let it bake for 25 to 30 minutes at 350 degrees without cover or until heated through.

## Nutrition Information

- Calories: 442 calories
- Protein: 31g protein.
- Total Fat: 13g fat (5g saturated fat)
- Sodium: 565mg sodium
- Fiber: 3g fiber)
- Total Carbohydrate: 49g carbohydrate (7g sugars
- Cholesterol: 67mg cholesterol

### 437. Makeover Mediterranean Chicken & Beans

*Serving: 6 servings. | Prep: 25mins | Cook: 20mins | Ready in:*

## Ingredients

- 2 tablespoons all-purpose flour
- 1 teaspoon garlic salt
- 1 teaspoon dried rosemary, crushed
- 1/2 teaspoon pepper
- 6 bone-in chicken thighs (about 2-1/4 pounds), skin removed
- 2 tablespoons olive oil
- 1 can (15 ounces) white kidney or cannellini beans, rinsed and drained
- 1 can (14-1/2 ounces) diced tomatoes, undrained
- 6 slices provolone cheese

### Direction

- Mix together the pepper, rosemary, garlic salt and flour in a big resealable plastic bag; add chicken, a few pieces at a time, then shake until coated.
- Cook the chicken in oil in a big frying pan until browned. Mix in tomatoes and beans, then boil. Lower the heat, put cover on and simmer for 20 to 25 minutes or until the chicken juices run clear. Take away from heat and put cheese on top. Put cover on and allow it to stand for 5 minutes or until the cheese melts.

### Nutrition Information

- Calories: 378 calories
- Total Carbohydrate: 15g carbohydrate (2g sugars
- Cholesterol: 102mg cholesterol
- Protein: 33g protein.
- Total Fat: 20g fat (7g saturated fat)
- Sodium: 690mg sodium
- Fiber: 4g fiber)

## 438. Maple Salmon With Mushroom Couscous

*Serving: 2 servings. | Prep: 5mins | Cook: 15mins | Ready in:*

### Ingredients

- 2 tablespoons maple syrup
- 2 tablespoons reduced-sodium soy sauce
- 1 garlic clove, minced
- 2 salmon fillets (4 ounces each)
- 1 cup reduced-sodium chicken broth
- 1/2 cup sliced fresh mushrooms
- 1/8 teaspoon pepper
- 1/2 cup uncooked couscous

### Direction

- Use foil to line a small baking pan, then spray cooking spray to the foil. Mix together garlic, soy sauce and syrup together in a small bowl. Put on the prepared pan with fillets, skin side down. Brush over salmon with a half of the syrup mixture, then broil about 6 inches from the source of heat about 7 minutes. Brush with the leftover syrup mixture and broil for 6 to 8 more minutes, until it's easy to flake fish with a fork.
- At the same time, bring pepper, mushrooms and broth in a small saucepan to a boil. Lower heat, then cover and simmer until mushrooms are softened, about 5 to 6 minutes. Bring back to a boil and stir in couscous. Cover and take away from the heat, allowing to stand about 5 minutes. Use a fork to fluff and serve together with salmon.

### Nutrition Information

- Calories: 421 calories
- Total Carbohydrate: 44g carbohydrate (8g sugars
- Cholesterol: 67mg cholesterol
- Protein: 32g protein.
- Total Fat: 13g fat (3g saturated fat)
- Sodium: 1017mg sodium
- Fiber: 2g fiber)

## 439. Marinated Chicken Breasts

*Serving: 6 servings. | Prep: 15mins | Cook: 35mins | Ready in:*

### Ingredients

- 1 teaspoon chicken bouillon granules
- 1/2 cup warm apple juice
- 1 cup white wine or chicken broth
- 2 to 4 tablespoons olive oil
- 1 to 2 tablespoons curry powder
- 2 teaspoons celery salt

- 2 teaspoons soy sauce
- 1 garlic clove, peeled and sliced
- 6 bone-in chicken breast halves (6 ounces each)

### Direction

- Dissolve bouillon in apple juice in a small bowl. Put in garlic, soy sauce, celery salt, curry powder, oil and wine. Put into a big resealable plastic bag with 1 cup of marinade, then add chicken into bag. Seal and turn to coat well, then chill overnight. Cover and chill the leftover marinade.
- Drain and get rid of marinade from chicken. Grill with a cover on medium heat until a thermometer reaches 170 degrees while turning basting sometimes with reserved marinade, about 35 to 40 minutes.

### Nutrition Information

- Calories: 214 calories
- Total Carbohydrate: 4g carbohydrate (0 sugars
- Cholesterol: 68mg cholesterol
- Protein: 25g protein. Diabetic Exchanges: 3 lean meat
- Total Fat: 8g fat (1g saturated fat)
- Sodium: 364mg sodium
- Fiber: 1g fiber)

## 440. Marinated Grilled Lamb

*Serving: 10 servings. | Prep: 10mins | Cook: 01hours30mins | Ready in:*

### Ingredients

- 1/4 cup lemon juice
- 1/4 cup dry white wine or chicken broth
- 3 tablespoons olive oil
- 8 garlic cloves, minced
- 3 tablespoons minced fresh rosemary
- 1 tablespoon minced fresh thyme
- 1 tablespoon minced fresh oregano
- 1 teaspoon salt
- 1/2 teaspoon coarsely ground pepper
- 1 boneless leg of lamb (3 to 4 pounds), trimmed and untied
- 1 sprig fresh rosemary
- Additional salt and pepper

### Direction

- Mix together the first nine ingredients in a large resealable plastic bag; add in lamb. Secure the bag and flip the coat; place inside the refrigerator for 4 hours.
- Prepare the grill for indirect medium heat. Strain lamb, getting rid of marinade. Put rosemary sprig on lamb; roll it up and use kitchen string to tie, keep a piece of the sprig exposed. Season with additional pepper and salt if desired.
- Grill the lamb on the indirect medium heat with cover on for 1-1/2 to 2 hours or until meat is doneness desired (a thermometer should read 145°F for medium rare; 160°F for medium; 170°F for well done). Take from grill; use foil to tent and before slicing, let it stand for 15 minutes. Get rid of rosemary sprig before serving.

### Nutrition Information

- Calories: 225 calories
- Total Fat: 12g fat (4g saturated fat)
- Sodium: 304mg sodium
- Fiber: 0 fiber)
- Total Carbohydrate: 2g carbohydrate (0 sugars
- Cholesterol: 82mg cholesterol
- Protein: 26g protein. Diabetic Exchanges: 4 lean meat

## 441. Marinated Lamb Chops

*Serving: Serves 4 | Prep: | Cook: | Ready in:*

### Ingredients

- 1/4 cup olive oil
- 1 tablespoon balsamic vinegar
- 4 garlic cloves, minced
- 8 frenched 1-inch-thick rib lamb chops (about 1 pound total)

## Direction

- Beat together in a small bowl the pepper, salt, garlic, vinegar and oil to taste. Coat lamb chops on both sides with marinade for 30 minutes, and let it sit at room temperature, flipping once, on a plate or in a shallow dish.
- Prepare the broiler by preheating.
- Place chops on rack of broiler pan 2 inches from heat and roast for 7 minutes, flipping after 5 minutes to achieve a medium-rare meat.

## Nutrition Information

- Calories: 11920
- Saturated Fat: 482 g(2412%)
- Sodium: 1777 mg(74%)
- Fiber: 0 g(0%)
- Total Carbohydrate: 2 g(1%)
- Cholesterol: 2409 mg(803%)
- Protein: 460 g(921%)
- Total Fat: 1104 g(1698%)

## 442. Marinated Pork Loin Roast

*Serving: 10 servings. | Prep: 10mins | Cook: 01hours30mins | Ready in:*

## Ingredients

- 3/4 cup ketchup
- 1/4 cup seedless raspberry jam
- 1/4 cup white wine vinegar
- 1/4 cup packed brown sugar
- 1/4 cup maple-flavored syrup
- 2 tablespoons Worcestershire sauce
- 2 tablespoons lemon juice
- 1 teaspoon each dried thyme, oregano and marjoram
- 1 teaspoon salt
- 1 teaspoon pepper
- 1 teaspoon Dijon mustard
- 1 bay leaf
- 1/4 teaspoon ground ginger
- 1 boneless pork loin roast (3 pounds)

## Direction

- Mix all ingredients but pork in a saucepan, boil over medium heat; take off heat. Fully cool. Pour 1 cup sauce into a big resealable plastic bag and add pork; seal bag. Turn to coat. Refrigerate for 8 hours/overnight; refrigerate leftover sauce.
- Drain pork; throw away marinade in bag. Put pork onto greased rack in the shallow roasting pan; bake for 15 minutes at 425°, uncovered. Lower oven to 350°; bake till thermometer reads 145° for 1-1 1/4 hours. Stand before slicing for 10 minutes; serve with reserved sauce.

## Nutrition Information

- Calories: 255 calories
- Sodium: 543mg sodium
- Fiber: 0 fiber)
- Total Carbohydrate: 22g carbohydrate (15g sugars
- Cholesterol: 68mg cholesterol
- Protein: 27g protein.
- Total Fat: 6g fat (2g saturated fat)

## 443. Marinated Pork With Caramelized Fennel

*Serving: 6 servings. | Prep: 20mins | Cook: 30mins | Ready in:*

## Ingredients

- 1/4 cup olive oil
- 1 tablespoon reduced-sodium soy sauce
- 2 garlic cloves, minced
- 2 teaspoons grated lemon peel
- 1 teaspoon ground cumin
- 1 teaspoon fennel seed, crushed
- 1/2 teaspoon salt
- 1/2 teaspoon pepper
- 1/2 teaspoon ground allspice
- 2 pork tenderloins (3/4 pound each)
- FENNEL:
- 2 medium fennel bulbs, halved and cut into 1/2-inch slices
- 4-1/2 teaspoons plus 1 tablespoon olive oil, divided
- 1/4 teaspoon salt
- 1/4 teaspoon pepper
- Fennel fronds, optional

### Direction

- Blend the first 9 ingredients in a big resealable plastic bag; add pork. Seal the bag and flip to coat. Refrigerate for 8 hours to overnight.
- Put the fennel in a big bowl; drizzle with 4 1/2 teaspoons of oil. Dust with pepper and salt; stir to coat. Shift to a 15x10x1-inch ungreased baking pan. Bake for 30 to 35 minutes at 450°, until softened, mixing once.
- In the meantime, drain and remove marinade. Brown pork in the leftover oil on all sides in a big ovenproof skillet. Put skillet in the oven; bake pork until the thermometer shows 145°, about 18 to 22 minutes.
- Allow to stand for 5 minutes prior to cutting. Enjoy with roasted fennel. If required, decorate with fennel fronds.

### Nutrition Information

- Calories: 292 calories
- Sodium: 535mg sodium
- Fiber: 3g fiber)
- Total Carbohydrate: 7g carbohydrate (0 sugars
- Cholesterol: 63mg cholesterol
- Protein: 24g protein.
- Total Fat: 19g fat (3g saturated fat)

### 444. Marrakesh Chicken & Couscous

*Serving: 6 servings. | Prep: 10mins | Cook: 20mins | Ready in:*

### Ingredients

- 1 tablespoon olive oil
- 1 pound boneless skinless chicken thighs, cut into 1-1/4-inch pieces
- 1 can (14-1/2 ounces) diced tomatoes, undrained
- 1 jar (7-1/2 ounces) marinated quartered artichoke hearts, drained
- 1/4 cup lemon juice
- 2 tablespoons apricot preserves
- 1/2 teaspoon salt
- 1/2 teaspoon ground cumin
- 1/4 teaspoon crushed red pepper flakes
- 1/8 teaspoon ground cinnamon
- 1 package (5.8 ounces) roasted garlic and olive oil couscous
- Chopped smoked almonds, optional

### Direction

- Heat oil in a 6-quart stockpot on medium-high heat. Brown both sides of chicken. Mix in seasoning packet from couscous, spices, salt, preserves, lemon juice, artichoke hearts, and tomatoes; boil. Reduce the heat; simmer without a cover for 10 minutes to develop flavors and to cook the chicken through.
- Mix in couscous; take it away from heat. Allow to sit with a cover for 5 minutes. Scatter almonds on top if you wish.

### Nutrition Information

- Calories: 326 calories

- Protein: 19g protein. Diabetic Exchanges: 3 lean meat
- Total Fat: 14g fat (3g saturated fat)
- Sodium: 751mg sodium
- Fiber: 2g fiber)
- Total Carbohydrate: 30g carbohydrate (8g sugars
- Cholesterol: 50mg cholesterol

## 445. Mediterranean Beef Toss

*Serving: 4 servings. | Prep: 5mins | Cook: 20mins | Ready in:*

### Ingredients

- 1/2 pound lean ground beef
- 4 garlic cloves, minced
- 3/4 teaspoon salt, divided
- 1/4 teaspoon pepper
- 3 teaspoons olive oil, divided
- 1 medium red onion, sliced
- 2 medium zucchini, sliced
- 1 medium green pepper, cut into 1-inch pieces
- 1 can (28 ounces) diced tomatoes, undrained
- 1 teaspoon red wine vinegar
- 1 teaspoon dried basil
- 1 teaspoon dried thyme
- Hot cooked spaghetti, optional

### Direction

- On medium heat, cook a quarter teaspoon salt and pepper, garlic, and beef in a non-stick pan with a teaspoon oil until the meat is not pink. Remove the contents and keep warm. Sauté onion for 2 minutes in the same pan with the remaining oil. Add green pepper and zucchini; cook and stir for 4-6 minutes until the veggies are tender-crisp.
- Mix in the remaining salt, tomatoes, thyme, basil, and vinegar; put in beef mixture then heat completely. If desired, served on top of spaghetti.

### Nutrition Information

- Calories: 204 calories
- Sodium: 739mg sodium
- Fiber: 6g fiber)
- Total Carbohydrate: 18g carbohydrate (0 sugars
- Cholesterol: 21mg cholesterol
- Protein: 15g protein. Diabetic Exchanges: 2 lean meat
- Total Fat: 9g fat (3g saturated fat)

## 446. Mediterranean Chicken Bake

*Serving: 4 servings. | Prep: 10mins | Cook: 20mins | Ready in:*

### Ingredients

- 4 boneless skinless chicken breast halves (5 ounces each)
- 2 teaspoons herbes de Provence
- 1/2 teaspoon salt
- 1/4 teaspoon pepper
- 1 tablespoon olive oil
- 1 cup marinated quartered artichoke hearts
- 1/4 cup oil-packed sun-dried tomatoes, coarsely chopped
- 1 cup (4 ounces) crumbled feta cheese

### Direction

- Flatten the chicken until half-inch thick. Mix pepper, salt, and herbes de Provence; scatter over the chicken. Brown both sides of the chicken in a big pan with oil.
- Move to a greased 11-in by 7-in baking dish; add tomatoes, artichokes, and cheese on top. Bake for 15-20 minutes in 425 degrees oven without cover until an inserted thermometer registers 170 degrees.

### Nutrition Information

- Calories: 353 calories
- Protein: 34g protein.
- Total Fat: 20g fat (6g saturated fat)
- Sodium: 835mg sodium
- Fiber: 2g fiber)
- Total Carbohydrate: 6g carbohydrate (0 sugars
- Cholesterol: 93mg cholesterol

## 447. Mediterranean Chicken Orzo

*Serving: 6 servings. | Prep: 15mins | Cook: 04hours00mins | Ready in:*

### Ingredients

- 1-1/2 pounds boneless skinless chicken thighs, cut into 1-inch pieces
- 2 cups reduced-sodium chicken broth
- 2 medium tomatoes, finely chopped
- 1 cup sliced pitted green olives
- 1 cup sliced pitted ripe olives
- 1 large carrot, finely chopped
- 1 small red onion, finely chopped
- 1 tablespoon grated lemon peel
- 3 tablespoons lemon juice
- 2 tablespoons butter
- 1 tablespoon herbes de Provence
- 1 cup uncooked orzo pasta

### Direction

- Mix initial 11 ingredients in a 3-4-qt. slow cooker. Cook for 4-5 hours on low, covered, till veggies, pasta and chicken are tender. At final 30 minutes of cooking time, add orzo.

### Nutrition Information

- Calories: 415 calories
- Total Fat: 19g fat (5g saturated fat)
- Sodium: 941mg sodium
- Fiber: 3g fiber)

- Total Carbohydrate: 33g carbohydrate (4g sugars
- Cholesterol: 86mg cholesterol
- Protein: 27g protein.

## 448. Mediterranean Chicken Pasta

*Serving: 4 servings, 1-3/4 cup each | Prep: 30mins | Cook: | Ready in:*

### Ingredients

- 1 Tbsp. oil
- 4 small boneless skinless chicken breasts (1 lb.)
- 1 pkg. (6.4 oz.) KRAFT Italian Pasta Salad
- 2 cups water
- 1/3 cup KRAFT Zesty Italian Dressing
- 1 tomato, chopped
- 1 small red onion, sliced
- 1 pkg. (4 oz.) ATHENOS Traditional Crumbled Feta Cheese
- 1/2 tsp. dried oregano leaves

### Direction

- On medium heat, heat oil in a big non-stick skillet; cook chicken for 3-4 mins per side or until each side is brown.
- Stir in water and the Pasta and Seasoning pouches contents. Turn to medium heat; cook for 7-9 mins while covering or until the pasta is tender.
- Take the chicken out of the skillet. Mix onions, tomatoes, and dressing into the skillet; transfer the chicken onto the top then cover. Cook for 5 mins or until thoroughly heated. Scatter with oregano, feta, and Parmesan.

### Nutrition Information

- Calories: 460
- Saturated Fat: 6 g

- Sugar: 7 g
- Total Carbohydrate: 38 g
- Total Fat: 18 g
- Sodium: 920 mg
- Fiber: 3 g
- Cholesterol: 90 mg
- Protein: 37 g

### 449. Mediterranean Chicken Stew

*Serving: 6 servings. | Prep: 10mins | Cook: 30mins | Ready in:*

## Ingredients

- 1 medium onion, chopped
- 2 garlic cloves, minced
- 2 tablespoons canola oil
- 1-1/2 pounds boneless skinless chicken breasts, cut into 1-inch pieces
- 2 cans (14-1/2 ounces each) stewed tomatoes
- 1 medium green pepper, julienned
- 1 medium sweet red pepper, julienned
- 1 cup pitted ripe olives
- 1 teaspoon salt
- 1 teaspoon dried oregano
- 2 tablespoons cornstarch
- 3 tablespoons cold water
- Hot cooked rice

## Direction

- Combine garlic and onion in a large skillet, sauté in oil for 3 to 4 minutes until softened. Add chicken and cook for 6 to 8 minutes until juice from chicken runs clear. Stir in oregano, salt, olives, peppers and tomatoes; bring to a boil; lower the heat and simmer, covered, for 10-12 minutes, remember to stir occasionally while simmering.
- Combine water and cornstarch until smooth; slowly stir into chicken. Bring to a boil; cook, stirring, for 1 minute or until thickened. Serve with rice.

## Nutrition Information

- Calories: 236 calories
- Protein: 24g protein.
- Total Fat: 9g fat (2g saturated fat)
- Sodium: 738mg sodium
- Fiber: 3g fiber)
- Total Carbohydrate: 14g carbohydrate (6g sugars
- Cholesterol: 63mg cholesterol

### 450. Mediterranean Chicken Stir Fry

*Serving: 4 servings. | Prep: 15mins | Cook: 15mins | Ready in:*

## Ingredients

- 2 cups water
- 1 cup quick-cooking barley
- 1 pound boneless skinless chicken breasts, cubed
- 3 teaspoons olive oil, divided
- 1 medium onion, chopped
- 2 medium zucchini, chopped
- 2 garlic cloves, minced
- 1 teaspoon dried oregano
- 1/2 teaspoon dried basil
- 1/4 teaspoon salt
- 1/4 teaspoon pepper
- Dash crushed red pepper flakes
- 2 plum tomatoes, chopped
- 1/2 cup pitted Greek olives, chopped
- 1 tablespoon minced fresh parsley

## Direction

- Boil water in a small saucepan. Mix in barley. Lower the heat and cover the pan. Let it simmer for 10-12 minutes until the barley is tender. Remove it from the heat and allow it to stand for 5 minutes.

- In the meantime, stir-fry the chicken in a wok or large skillet with 2 tsp. of oil until the chicken is not anymore pinkish. Remove from the heat and keep it warm.
- In the remaining oil, stir-fry the onion for 3 minutes. Add the garlic, salt, pepper flakes, pepper, oregano, zucchini, and basil. Stir-fry the vegetables for 2-4 minutes until crisp-tender. Add the chicken, parsley, olives, and tomatoes. Serve the mixture with barley.

## Nutrition Information

- Calories: 403 calories
- Fiber: 11g fiber)
- Total Carbohydrate: 44g carbohydrate (5g sugars
- Cholesterol: 63mg cholesterol
- Protein: 31g protein. Diabetic Exchanges: 3 lean meat
- Total Fat: 12g fat (2g saturated fat)
- Sodium: 498mg sodium

## 451. Mediterranean Chicken In Creamy Herb Sauce

*Serving: 6 servings. | Prep: 25mins | Cook: 20mins | Ready in:*

## Ingredients

- 1-1/2 pounds boneless skinless chicken thighs, cut into strips
- 1 teaspoon paprika
- 1/2 teaspoon salt
- 1/2 teaspoon cayenne pepper
- 2 tablespoons all-purpose flour
- 2 tablespoons olive oil
- 3 shallots, thinly sliced
- 4 garlic cloves, minced
- 1-1/2 cups white wine
- 1 can (14 ounces) water-packed artichoke hearts, rinsed, drained and quartered
- 2 sun-dried tomatoes (not packed in oil), chopped
- 1 tablespoon capers, drained
- 1 tablespoon cornstarch
- 1 cup heavy whipping cream
- 3/4 cup pitted Greek olives, halved
- 1/2 cup shredded Asiago cheese, divided
- 3 tablespoons minced fresh basil
- 1 tablespoon minced fresh thyme
- Hot cooked linguine
- Additional minced fresh basil

## Direction

- Sprinkle cayenne, salt and paprika over chicken. In a big resealable plastic bag, place flour. A few pieces at 1 time, add chicken; shake to coat.
- Cook chicken in oil till no pink anymore in a big skillet over medium heat. Add garlic and shallots; cook for 2 minutes more. Mix in capers, tomatoes, artichokes and wine; boil. Lower heat; simmer for 10 minutes, uncovered.
- Mix cream and cornstarch till smooth; mix into skillet. Boil. Lower heat; cook while stirring till thickened for 1-2 minutes. Add thyme, basil, 1/4 cup cheese and olives.
- Serve with linguine; sprinkle with extra minced basil and leftover cheese.

## Nutrition Information

- Calories: 533 calories
- Total Fat: 35g fat (14g saturated fat)
- Sodium: 814mg sodium
- Fiber: 1g fiber)
- Total Carbohydrate: 17g carbohydrate (2g sugars
- Cholesterol: 138mg cholesterol
- Protein: 28g protein.

### 452. Mediterranean Chicken In Eggplant Sauce

*Serving: 8 servings. | Prep: 45mins | Cook: 05hours00mins | Ready in:*

#### Ingredients

- 1/3 cup all-purpose flour
- 2 teaspoons paprika
- 2 teaspoons ground cumin
- 1 teaspoon salt
- 1 teaspoon freshly ground pepper
- 3 pounds boneless skinless chicken thighs, cut into 2-inch pieces
- 2 tablespoons olive oil
- 1-1/4 cups white wine or chicken broth
- 1 small eggplant (1 pound), peeled and cubed
- 1 jar (12 ounces) roasted sweet red peppers, drained
- 1 medium onion, chopped
- 1 jalapeno pepper, seeded and chopped
- 2 tablespoons tomato paste
- 1 tablespoon brown sugar
- 3 garlic cloves, minced
- 1 cup pitted ripe olives, halved
- 1/4 cup minced fresh Italian parsley
- 1 cup (4 ounces) crumbled feta cheese
- 8 naan flatbreads, quartered

#### Direction

- Mix the first 5 ingredients in a big bow; toss in chicken to coat. Cook chicken in batches in a big pan with oil until brown; move to a four-quart slow cooker.
- Stir in wine in the pan to loosen the brown bits. Mix in garlic, eggplant, brown sugar, red peppers, tomato paste, jalapeno, and onion; boil. Lower heat; let it simmer for 5 minutes without cover. Slightly cool then move to a blender. Process with cover until the mixture is pureed; pour all over the chicken.
- Cook for 5-6 hours on low with cover until the chicken is tender. Put in parsley and olives on the final half hour of cooking. Scatter top with feta cheese barely before serving it with naan.

#### Nutrition Information

- Calories: 588 calories
- Protein: 40g protein.
- Total Fat: 23g fat (7g saturated fat)
- Sodium: 1293mg sodium
- Fiber: 4g fiber)
- Total Carbohydrate: 44g carbohydrate (10g sugars
- Cholesterol: 126mg cholesterol

### 453. Mediterranean Chicken With Spaghetti Squash

*Serving: 6 servings. | Prep: 35mins | Cook: 35mins | Ready in:*

#### Ingredients

- 1 medium spaghetti squash
- 1-1/2 pounds boneless skinless chicken breasts, cut into 1/2-inch cubes
- 5 center-cut bacon strips, chopped
- 1 medium leek (white portion only), coarsely chopped
- 4 garlic cloves, minced
- 3 tablespoons all-purpose flour
- 1 cup reduced-sodium chicken broth
- 1/2 cup white wine or additional reduced-sodium chicken broth
- 1/3 cup half-and-half cream
- 2 plum tomatoes, chopped
- 1 can (2-1/4 ounces) sliced ripe olives, drained
- 1/3 cup grated Parmesan cheese
- 1-1/2 teaspoons minced fresh sage or 1/2 teaspoon rubbed sage
- 1 teaspoon minced fresh thyme or 1/4 teaspoon dried thyme
- 1/2 teaspoon salt
- 1/8 teaspoon pepper

#### Direction

- Lengthwise, slice squash in half, remove seeds. Put squash onto a microwave-safe plate, cut side down. Microwave on high, uncovered, till tender for 15-18 minutes.
- Meanwhile, cook chicken on medium heat in a big nonstick skillet coated in cooking spray till it's not pink. Drain. Take out of skillet.
- Cook leek and bacon in the same skillet on medium heat till bacon is crisp. Put bacon mixture onto paper towels with a slotted spoon. Put garlic; cook for a minute. Mix flour in till blended. Add cream, wine and broth gradually; boil. Stir and cook till thick for 1-2 minutes. Mix leftover ingredients in. Add bacon mixture and chicken in; heat through.
- Once squash is cool to the touch, separate strands with a fork. Serve it with chicken mixture.

## Nutrition Information

- Calories: 340 calories
- Cholesterol: 82mg cholesterol
- Protein: 30g protein. Diabetic Exchanges: 4 lean meat
- Total Fat: 12g fat (4g saturated fat)
- Sodium: 656mg sodium
- Fiber: 5g fiber)
- Total Carbohydrate: 27g carbohydrate (2g sugars

### 454. Mediterranean Chickpeas

*Serving: 4 servings. | Prep: 10mins | Cook: 15mins | Ready in:*

## Ingredients

- 1 cup water
- 3/4 cup uncooked whole wheat couscous
- 1 tablespoon olive oil
- 1 medium onion, chopped
- 2 garlic cloves, minced
- 1 can (15 ounces) chickpeas or garbanzo beans, rinsed and drained
- 1 can (14-1/2 ounces) no-salt-added stewed tomatoes, cut up
- 1 can (14 ounces) water-packed artichoke hearts, rinsed, drained and chopped
- 1/2 cup pitted Greek olives, coarsely chopped
- 1 tablespoon lemon juice
- 1/2 teaspoon dried oregano
- Dash pepper
- Dash cayenne pepper

## Direction

- Bring water in a small saucepan to a boil, then stir in couscous. Take away from the heat and allow to stand with a cover until water is absorbed, about 5 to 10 minutes. Use a fork to fluff.
- At the same time, heat oil in a big nonstick skillet on moderately high heat. Put in onion, then cook and stir until softened. Put in garlic and cook for 1 minute more. Stir in remaining ingredients and heat through while stirring sometimes. Serve together with couscous.

## Nutrition Information

- Calories: 340 calories
- Fiber: 9g fiber)
- Total Carbohydrate: 51g carbohydrate (9g sugars
- Cholesterol: 0 cholesterol
- Protein: 11g protein.
- Total Fat: 10g fat (1g saturated fat)
- Sodium: 677mg sodium

### 455. Mediterranean Cod

*Serving: 4 servings. | Prep: 25mins | Cook: 15mins | Ready in:*

## Ingredients

- 4 cups shredded cabbage
- 1 large sweet onion, thinly sliced
- 4 garlic cloves, minced
- 4 cod fillets (6 ounces each)
- 1/4 cup pitted Greek olives, chopped
- 1/2 cup crumbled feta cheese
- 1/4 teaspoon salt
- 1/4 teaspoon pepper
- 4 teaspoons olive oil

## Direction

- Cut a heavy-duty foil or parchment paper into 4, 18-in by 12-in portions; put a cup of cabbage in each piece. Add pepper, onion, salt, garlic, cheese, olives, and cod on top; dribble with oil.
- Fold the parchment or foil over the dish; join the edges together on all sides then flute to enclose, making a packet. Repeat with the rest of the packets then arrange on baking sheets.
- Bake for 12-15 minutes in 450 degrees oven until the cod easily flakes with a fork. Carefully open the packets then let the steam escape.

## Nutrition Information

- Calories: 270 calories
- Sodium: 532mg sodium
- Fiber: 3g fiber)
- Total Carbohydrate: 12g carbohydrate (4g sugars
- Cholesterol: 72mg cholesterol
- Protein: 31g protein. Diabetic Exchanges: 5 lean meat
- Total Fat: 10g fat (3g saturated fat)

## 456. Mediterranean Fettuccine

*Serving: 4 servings. | Prep: 10mins | Cook: 20mins | Ready in:*

## Ingredients

- 1/2 cup vegetable broth
- 8 sun-dried tomatoes (not packed in oil), halved
- 6 ounces uncooked fettuccine
- 1 medium sweet yellow pepper, thinly sliced
- 1 medium sweet red pepper, thinly sliced
- 1 cup chopped green onions
- 1 tablespoon olive oil
- 2 garlic cloves, minced
- 10 Greek olives, pitted and coarsely chopped
- 1/4 cup minced fresh basil
- 1 tablespoon capers, drained
- 1 teaspoon dried oregano
- 1 package (4 ounces) crumbled feta cheese

## Direction

- Bring broth in a small saucepan to a boil, then take away from the heat. Put in tomatoes and allow to stand for 5 to 7 minutes. Cut tomatoes into thin slices and turn back to broth, then set aside.
- Following the package directions to cook fettuccine. At the same time, sauté onions and peppers with oil in a big nonstick skillet coated with cooking spray until softened, about 3 to 4 minutes. Put in garlic and cook for 1 minute more. Lower heat, then stir in reserved tomato mixture, oregano, capers, basil and olives.
- Drain fettuccine and put in a big serving bowl. Put in pepper mixture and cheese, then toss to coat well.

## Nutrition Information

- Calories: 331 calories
- Cholesterol: 15mg cholesterol
- Protein: 14g protein.
- Total Fat: 12g fat (4g saturated fat)
- Sodium: 854mg sodium
- Fiber: 6g fiber)
- Total Carbohydrate: 44g carbohydrate (6g sugars

## 457. Mediterranean Fish Skillet

*Serving: 2 servings. | Prep: 20mins | Cook: 10mins | Ready in:*

### Ingredients

- 1 large tomato, seeded and finely chopped
- 1 small green pepper, finely chopped
- 1 jalapeno pepper, seeded and minced
- 3 tablespoons minced fresh basil
- 3 tablespoons white wine or chicken broth
- 1 shallot, sliced
- 1 garlic clove, minced
- 1/2 teaspoon chili powder, divided
- 2 whitefish fillets (5 ounces each)
- 1 tablespoon olive oil

### Direction

- Mix together 1/4 tsp. of chili powder, garlic, shallot, wine, basil, peppers and tomato in a small bowl, then set aside.
- Sprinkle the remaining chili powder over fillets. Cook fillets in oil in a big skillet on medium high heat until it is easy to use a fork to flake fish, about 4 to 5 minutes per side, while putting in tomato mixture during the final 3 minutes of cooking.

### Nutrition Information

- Calories: 319 calories
- Sodium: 90mg sodium
- Fiber: 2g fiber)
- Total Carbohydrate: 11g carbohydrate (4g sugars
- Cholesterol: 87mg cholesterol
- Protein: 30g protein.
- Total Fat: 16g fat (2g saturated fat)

## 458. Mediterranean One Dish Meal

*Serving: 4 servings. | Prep: 15mins | Cook: 25mins | Ready in:*

### Ingredients

- 3/4 pound Italian turkey sausage links, cut into 1-inch pieces
- 1 medium onion, chopped
- 2 garlic cloves, minced
- 1 can (14-1/2 ounces) no-salt-added diced tomatoes, undrained
- 1/4 cup Greek olives
- 1 teaspoon dried oregano
- 1/2 cup quinoa, rinsed
- 3 cups fresh baby spinach
- 1/2 cup crumbled feta cheese

### Direction

- Use cooking spray to coat a big non-stick pan. On medium heat, cook onion and sausage in the greased pan until the onion is tender and the sausage is brown; put in garlic. Cook for another minute. Mix in oregano, olives, and tomatoes; boil.
- Mix in quinoa then add spinach on top. Lower heat; let it simmer for 12-15 minutes with cover until the liquid is absorbed. Take off heat then use a fork to fluff. Scatter with cheese.

### Nutrition Information

- Calories: 307 calories
- Total Carbohydrate: 26g carbohydrate (6g sugars
- Cholesterol: 58mg cholesterol
- Protein: 21g protein.
- Total Fat: 14g fat (3g saturated fat)
- Sodium: 845mg sodium
- Fiber: 5g fiber)

## 459. Mediterranean Pizza

*Serving: 16 servings | Prep: 10mins | Cook: | Ready in:*

### Ingredients

- 3/4 cup MIRACLE WHIP Dressing
- 1/2 cup KRAFT Shredded Parmesan Cheese
- 1/2 cup KRAFT Shredded Mozzarella Cheese
- 2 cloves garlic, minced
- 1 ready-to-use baked pizza crust (12 inch)
- 10 Kalamata olives, cut in half
- 2 plum tomatoes, seeded, sliced
- 2 Tbsp. thinly sliced fresh basil

### Direction

- 1. Mix the first four ingredients; spread over the pizza crust.
- 2. Put tomatoes and olives on top.
- 3. Bake until the cheese is melted and the edge of crust turns golden brown, about 20 minutes.
- 4. Top with basil.

### Nutrition Information

- Calories: 110
- Total Fat: 6 g
- Sodium: 290 mg
- Fiber: 0 g
- Protein: 4 g
- Saturated Fat: 1.5 g
- Sugar: 1 g
- Total Carbohydrate: 12 g
- Cholesterol: 5 mg

## 460. Mediterranean Pizzas

*Serving: 2 servings. | Prep: 10mins | Cook: 5mins | Ready in:*

### Ingredients

- 2 English muffins, split and toasted
- 2 tablespoons prepared pesto
- 4 slices deli ham (3/4 ounce each)
- 1/4 cup julienned roasted sweet red peppers
- 1/4 cup crumbled feta cheese
- 2 teaspoons minced fresh basil or 1/2 teaspoon dried basil

### Direction

- Spread pesto and cut sides of a muffin; layer with peppers and ham in reverse order. Dust with cheese. Transfer to an ungreased baking sheet. Broil for 2-4 minutes, 4 to 6-inches away from the heat source or until heated through. Dust with basil.

### Nutrition Information

- Calories: 294 calories
- Sodium: 1003mg sodium
- Fiber: 3g fiber)
- Total Carbohydrate: 29g carbohydrate (4g sugars
- Cholesterol: 31mg cholesterol
- Protein: 18g protein.
- Total Fat: 11g fat (4g saturated fat)

## 461. Mediterranean Pork And Orzo

*Serving: 6 servings. | Prep: 15mins | Cook: 15mins | Ready in:*

### Ingredients

- 1-1/2 pounds pork tenderloin
- 1 teaspoon coarsely ground pepper
- 2 tablespoons olive oil
- 3 quarts water
- 1-1/4 cups uncooked orzo pasta
- 1/4 teaspoon salt
- 1 package (6 ounces) fresh baby spinach
- 1 cup grape tomatoes, halved
- 3/4 cup crumbled feta cheese

### Direction

- Massage pepper on pork then slice into one-inch cubes. On medium heat, heat oil in a big non-stick pan; put the pork, cook and stir for 8-10 minutes until the meat is not pink.
- In the meantime, boil water in a Dutch oven; mix in salt and orzo. Cook for 8 minutes without cover; mix in spinach. Cook for another 45-60 seconds until the spinach wilts and the orzo is tender; drain.
- Put tomatoes in the pork; heat completely. Mix in cheese and orzo mixture.

### Nutrition Information

- Calories: 372 calories
- Protein: 31g protein. Diabetic Exchanges: 3 lean meat
- Total Fat: 11g fat (4g saturated fat)
- Sodium: 306mg sodium
- Fiber: 3g fiber)
- Total Carbohydrate: 34g carbohydrate (2g sugars
- Cholesterol: 71mg cholesterol

## 462. Mediterranean Rack Of Lamb

*Serving: 4 servings. | Prep: 15mins | Cook: 30mins | Ready in:*

### Ingredients

- 2 racks of lamb (1-1/2 pounds each)
- 1/4 cup grated lemon zest
- 1/4 cup minced fresh oregano or 4 teaspoons dried oregano
- 6 garlic cloves, minced
- 1 tablespoon olive oil
- 1/4 teaspoon salt
- 1/4 teaspoon pepper
- Fresh oregano and lemon slices, optional

### Direction

- Preheat an oven to 375°. In a shallow roasting pan, put lamb. Mix pepper, salt, oil, garlic, oregano and lemon zest in small bowl; rub over lamb.
- Bake for 30-40 minutes till meat gets desired doneness (thermometer should read 145° for medium well; 140° for medium and 135° for medium rare). Before cutting, stand for 5 minutes; serve with lemon slices and fresh oregano if desired.

### Nutrition Information

- Calories: 307 calories
- Protein: 30g protein.
- Total Fat: 19g fat (6g saturated fat)
- Sodium: 241mg sodium
- Fiber: 1g fiber)
- Total Carbohydrate: 3g carbohydrate (0 sugars
- Cholesterol: 100mg cholesterol

## 463. Mediterranean Roasted Salmon

*Serving: 4 servings. | Prep: 15mins | Cook: 15mins | Ready in:*

### Ingredients

- 4 salmon fillets (6 ounces each)
- 1/2 teaspoon salt, divided
- 1/2 cup olive oil
- 2 tablespoons balsamic vinegar
- 2 teaspoons honey
- 1 teaspoon Dijon mustard
- 3 plum tomatoes, chopped
- 1/4 cup chopped red onion
- 1/4 cup chopped green pepper
- 2 tablespoons chopped pitted green olives
- 2 tablespoons chopped ripe olives

### Direction

- In a greased 15-in by 10-in by 1-in baking pan, lay the salmon then scatter with a quarter teaspoon of salt. Combine the remaining salt, oil, mustard, honey, and vinegar in a small bowl; scoop a tablespoon of mixture on each salmon fillet.
- Mix the remaining oil mixture, tomatoes, olives, green pepper, and onion in a big bowl; scoop on top of the fillets.
- Bake for 12-15 mins in a 425 degrees F oven or until the fillets easily flake using a fork.

## Nutrition Information

- Calories: 550 calories
- Protein: 29g protein.
- Total Fat: 45g fat (7g saturated fat)
- Sodium: 579mg sodium
- Fiber: 1g fiber)
- Total Carbohydrate: 8g carbohydrate (6g sugars
- Cholesterol: 85mg cholesterol

### 464. Mediterranean Seafood Stew

*Serving: 6 servings. | Prep: 5mins | Cook: 25mins | Ready in:*

## Ingredients

- 1 medium onion, finely chopped
- 1 tablespoon olive oil
- 1-1/2 teaspoons minced garlic, divided
- 1/2 pound plum tomatoes, seeded and diced
- 1 teaspoon grated lemon peel
- 1/4 teaspoon crushed red pepper flakes
- 1 cup clam juice
- 1/3 cup white wine or additional clam juice
- 1 tablespoon tomato paste
- 1/2 teaspoon salt
- 1 pound orange roughy or red snapper fillets, cut into 1-inch cubes
- 1 pound uncooked large shrimp, peeled and deveined
- 1/2 pound sea scallops
- 1/3 cup minced fresh parsley
- 1/3 cup reduced-fat mayonnaise

## Direction

- Sauté onion in a Dutch oven with oil until softened. Put in 1/2 tsp. of garlic and cook for 1 more minute. Put in pepper flakes, lemon peel and tomatoes, then cook and stir about 2 minutes. Put in salt, tomato paste, clam juice and wine or more clam juice. Bring the whole mixture to a boil, then lower the heat and simmer until heated through, while covering, or about 10 minutes.
- Put in parsley, scallops, shrimp and fish, then cook, covered, until it is easy to make fish flake using a fork, scallops are opaque and shrimp turn pink, or about 8 to 10 minutes. Mix the leftover garlic with mayonnaise, then dollop on top of each serving.

## Nutrition Information

- Calories: 221 calories
- Protein: 28g protein. Diabetic Exchanges: 4 lean meat
- Total Fat: 8g fat (1g saturated fat)
- Sodium: 607mg sodium
- Fiber: 1g fiber)
- Total Carbohydrate: 7g carbohydrate (0 sugars
- Cholesterol: 123mg cholesterol

### 465. Mediterranean Shrimp 'n' Pasta

*Serving: 4 servings. | Prep: 15mins | Cook: 20mins | Ready in:*

## Ingredients

- 1 cup boiling water

- 1/2 cup dry-pack sun-dried tomatoes, chopped
- 6 ounces uncooked fettuccine
- 1 can (8 ounces) tomato sauce
- 2 tablespoons clam juice
- 2 tablespoons unsweetened apple juice
- 1 teaspoon curry powder
- 1/4 teaspoon pepper
- 1 pound fresh asparagus, trimmed and cut into 1-inch pieces
- 1 tablespoon olive oil
- 1/2 cup thinly sliced green onions
- 2 garlic cloves, minced
- 1 pound uncooked medium shrimp, peeled and deveined

### Direction

- Pour boiling water over sun-dried tomatoes to cover in a small bowl; let steep for 2 minutes. Strain and put to one side. Cook fettuccine as directed on package.
- In the meantime, combine pepper, curry powder, apple juice, clam juice, and tomato sauce in a small bowl; put to one side. Sauté asparagus in oil in a large nonstick skillet greased with cooking spray, about 2 minutes. Add garlic and green onions, cook while stirring for another minute.
- Mix in shrimp. Cook while stirring until shrimp becomes pink, about 3 more minutes. Mix in sun-dried tomatoes and tomato sauce mixture; cook through. Strain fettuccine and add to skillet; coat by tossing.

### Nutrition Information

- Calories: 368 calories
- Protein: 32g protein. Diabetic Exchanges: 3 starch
- Total Fat: 6g fat (1g saturated fat)
- Sodium: 702mg sodium
- Fiber: 5g fiber)
- Total Carbohydrate: 46g carbohydrate (8g sugars
- Cholesterol: 173mg cholesterol

## 466. Mediterranean Shrimp Linguine

*Serving: 8 servings. | Prep: 20mins | Cook: 20mins | Ready in:*

### Ingredients

- 1 package (16 ounces) linguine
- 2 pounds uncooked medium shrimp, peeled and deveined
- 1 medium onion, chopped
- 6 tablespoons olive oil
- 4 garlic cloves, minced
- 1 cup chopped roasted sweet red peppers
- 2 cans (2-1/4 ounces each) sliced ripe olives, drained
- 1/2 cup minced fresh parsley
- 1/2 cup white wine or chicken broth
- 1/2 teaspoon crushed red pepper flakes
- 1/2 teaspoon kosher salt
- 1/2 teaspoon dried oregano
- 1/2 teaspoon pepper
- 3/4 cup crumbled feta cheese
- 2 tablespoons lemon juice

### Direction

- Cook linguine as directed on the package.
- In the meantime, sauté onion and shrimp in oil until shrimp turns pink in a large skillet. Add garlic; cook for 1 more minute. Stir in pepper, oregano, salt, pepper flakes, wine, parsley, olives and red peppers. Lower the heat.
- Drain linguine; set half cup of cooking water aside. Add reserved water and linguine to the skillet. Stir in lemon juice and cheese; cook while stirring until cheese melts.

### Nutrition Information

- Calories: 462 calories
- Fiber: 3g fiber)

- Total Carbohydrate: 48g carbohydrate (4g sugars
- Cholesterol: 144mg cholesterol
- Protein: 28g protein.
- Total Fat: 16g fat (3g saturated fat)
- Sodium: 610mg sodium

### 467. Mediterranean Shrimp And Linguine

*Serving: 6 servings. | Prep: 15mins | Cook: 15mins | Ready in:*

## Ingredients

- 9 ounces uncooked linguine
- 2 tablespoons olive oil
- 1 cup sliced fresh mushrooms
- 1 pound uncooked medium shrimp, peeled and deveined
- 3 medium tomatoes, chopped
- 1 can (14 ounces) water-packed artichoke hearts, rinsed, drained and halved
- 1 can (6 ounces) pitted ripe olives, drained and halved
- 2 garlic cloves, minced
- 1 teaspoon dried oregano
- 1/2 teaspoon salt
- 1/2 teaspoon dried basil
- 1/8 teaspoon pepper

## Direction

- Cook linguine as directed on package. In the meantime, heat oil over medium-high heat in a large skillet. Put in mushrooms, cook while stirring for 4 minutes. Stir in the remaining ingredients; cook until shrimp is pink, about 5 minutes.
- Strain linguine; serve with shrimp mixture.

## Nutrition Information

- Calories: 328 calories
- Sodium: 748mg sodium
- Fiber: 3g fiber)
- Total Carbohydrate: 41g carbohydrate (4g sugars
- Cholesterol: 112mg cholesterol
- Protein: 21g protein. Diabetic Exchanges: 2 starch
- Total Fat: 9g fat (1g saturated fat)

### 468. Mediterranean Shrimp And Pasta

*Serving: 4 | Prep: 25mins | Cook: | Ready in:*

## Ingredients

- 8 ounces fresh or frozen medium shrimp
- Nonstick cooking spray
- 1 (14.5 ounce) can no-salt-added diced tomatoes, drained
- 1 cup sliced zucchini
- 1 large red sweet pepper, chopped (1 cup)
- ½ cup dry white wine or reduced-sodium chicken broth
- 2 cloves garlic, minced
- 8 pitted Kalamata olives, coarsely chopped
- ¼ cup chopped fresh basil
- 1 tablespoon olive oil
- 1½ teaspoons chopped fresh rosemary or ½ teaspoon dried rosemary, crushed
- ¼ teaspoon salt
- 4 ounces dried acini di pepe or whole-wheat acini di pepe, cooked according to package directions
- 2 ounces reduced-fat feta cheese, crumbled

## Direction

- Defrost the shrimp if it is frozen. Peel and devein; cover and chill until ready to use. Lightly grease an unheated 1 1/2-quart slow cooker with cooking spray. Mix garlic, wine, sweet pepper, zucchini and tomatoes in the slow cooker.

- Cook with a cover on low heat setting for 4 hours or on high heat setting for 2 hours (If there is no heat setting, cook for 3 hours). Stir in shrimp. If you use the low-heat setting, switch to the high-heat setting. Cook with a cover for another 30 minutes.
- Stir in salt, rosemary, olive oil, basil and olives. Transfer cooked pasta to a serving bowl and put shrimp mixture on top. Evenly sprinkle all over the pasta with feta cheese.

## Nutrition Information

- Calories: 302 calories;
- Sodium: 571
- Fiber: 4
- Total Carbohydrate: 32
- Protein: 20
- Total Fat: 8
- Cholesterol: 90
- Sugar: 6
- Saturated Fat: 2

## 469. Mediterranean Tilapia

*Serving: 2 | Prep: 10mins | Cook: 15mins | Ready in:*

### Ingredients

- 3 tablespoons sun-dried tomatoes packed in oil, drained and chopped
- 1 tablespoon capers, drained
- 2 tilapia fillets
- 1 tablespoon oil from the jar of sun-dried tomatoes
- 1 tablespoon lemon juice
- 2 tablespoons kalamata olives, pitted and chopped

### Direction

- Set the oven at 190°C (375°F) and start preheating. Add capers, olives and sun-dried tomatoes in a small bowl, mix together and set aside.
- Put the tilapia fillets side by side on a baking tray. Drizzle oil and lemon juice on top.
- Put the tray in the oven and start baking for 10 to 15 minutes, until the fish can be shredded with a fork. Check after 10 minutes to make sure fish are not overcooked, otherwise they will be dry. After baking, serve with tomato mixture on top.

## Nutrition Information

- Calories: 183 calories;
- Total Fat: 7.2
- Sodium: 464
- Total Carbohydrate: 5.4
- Cholesterol: 41
- Protein: 24

## 470. Mediterranean Turkey Potpies

*Serving: 6 servings. | Prep: 30mins | Cook: 20mins | Ready in:*

### Ingredients

- 2 medium onions, thinly sliced
- 2 teaspoons olive oil
- 3 garlic cloves, minced
- 3 tablespoons all-purpose flour
- 1-1/4 cups reduced-sodium chicken broth
- 1 can (14-1/2 ounces) no-salt-added diced tomatoes, undrained
- 2-1/2 cups cubed cooked turkey breast
- 1 can (14 ounces) water-packed artichoke hearts, rinsed, drained and sliced
- 1/2 cup pitted ripe olives, halved
- 1/4 cup sliced pepperoncini
- 1 tablespoon minced fresh oregano or 1 teaspoon dried oregano
- 1/4 teaspoon pepper
- CRUST:

- 1 loaf (1 pound) frozen pizza dough, thawed
- 1 egg white
- 1 teaspoon minced fresh oregano or 1/4 teaspoon dried oregano

## Direction

- Sauté onions in a Dutch oven with oil until tender; put in garlic. Cook for 2 minutes more. Whisk broth and flour in a small bowl until smooth; mix into the onion mixture gradually. Mix in tomatoes then boil. Cook and stir until thick for 2 minutes.
- Take off heat; mix in pepper, turkey, oregano, artichokes, pepperoncini, and olives gently. Split the turkey mixture between 6 ten-ounce ramekins.
- Unroll and fit 2-ounce dough on each ramekin. Set the remaining dough aside for another use. Make slits on the dough then put on top of the filling; pinch edges to seal. Mix oregano and egg white; slather on top of the dough.
- Arrange the ramekins on a baking sheet. Bake for 18-22 minutes in 425 degrees oven until the crusts are golden brown.

## Nutrition Information

- Calories: 326 calories
- Fiber: 3g fiber)
- Total Carbohydrate: 43g carbohydrate (7g sugars
- Cholesterol: 50mg cholesterol
- Protein: 26g protein. Diabetic Exchanges: 2 starch
- Total Fat: 4g fat (1g saturated fat)
- Sodium: 699mg sodium

### 471. Mediterranean Vegetable Casserole

*Serving: 3 servings. | Prep: 25mins | Cook: 30mins | Ready in:*

## Ingredients

- 1 cup uncooked penne pasta
- 1 can (8 ounces) tomato sauce
- 3/4 cup crumbled feta cheese
- 1/2 cup sour cream
- 1/4 cup fresh basil leaves, thinly sliced
- 1/4 cup marinated quartered artichoke hearts, drained
- 1/4 cup oil-packed sun-dried tomatoes, drained and thinly sliced
- 1/4 cup Greek olives, pitted and halved
- 2 tablespoons chopped red onion
- 1-1/2 teaspoons dried oregano
- 1/2 teaspoon dried thyme
- 1/4 teaspoon pepper

## Direction

- Cook pasta following the package instructions. In the meantime, in a large bowl, mix the remaining ingredients.
- Drain the pasta; toss with the sauce mixture. Place in a baking dish (about 1-1/2-qt.) coated with cooking spray. Bake, uncovered, for 30 to 35 minutes at 375°, or until heated through.

## Nutrition Information

- Calories: 341 calories
- Total Fat: 19g fat (9g saturated fat)
- Sodium: 903mg sodium
- Fiber: 4g fiber)
- Total Carbohydrate: 29g carbohydrate (4g sugars
- Cholesterol: 42mg cholesterol
- Protein: 12g protein.

### 472. Mediterranean Style Chicken

*Serving: 2 servings. | Prep: 5mins | Cook: 25mins | Ready in:*

### Ingredients

- 2 bone-in chicken thighs (about 3/4 pounds), skin removed
- 1 teaspoon olive oil
- 2 garlic cloves, minced
- 1 can (14-1/2 ounces) stewed tomatoes, cut up
- 1 bay leaf
- 3/4 teaspoon sugar
- 3/4 teaspoon dried basil
- 1/4 teaspoon salt
- Dash pepper
- Hot cooked spaghetti
- 2 tablespoons sliced pimiento-stuffed olives, optional

### Direction

- Cook chicken with oil in a skillet over medium-high until brown on both sides, about 3 minutes for each side. Put in garlic; cook and stir for about 45 seconds. Mix in pepper, salt, basil, sugar, bay leaf and tomatoes.
- Bring to a boil. Lower heat; cover and let it simmer for 20-25 minutes, or until tender and chicken juices run clear.
- Simmer with no cover, until the sauce has the desired thickness. Remove bay leaf. Serve on top of spaghetti. Add olives to garnish if desired.

### Nutrition Information

- Calories:
- Protein:
- Total Fat:
- Sodium:
- Fiber:
- Total Carbohydrate:
- Cholesterol:

---

### 473. Mediterranean Style Red Snapper

*Serving: 4 servings. | Prep: 10mins | Cook: 20mins | Ready in:*

### Ingredients

- 1 teaspoon lemon-pepper seasoning
- 1/2 teaspoon garlic powder
- 1/2 teaspoon dried thyme
- 1/8 teaspoon cayenne pepper
- 4 red snapper fillets (6 ounces each)
- 2 teaspoons olive oil, divided
- 1/2 medium sweet red pepper, julienned
- 3 green onions, chopped
- 1 garlic clove, minced
- 1 can (14-1/2 ounces) diced tomatoes, undrained
- 1/2 cup chopped pimiento-stuffed olives
- 1/4 cup chopped ripe olives
- 1/4 cup minced chives

### Direction

- Combine cayenne, lemon pepper, thyme, and garlic powder; massage on the fillets. Use cooking spray to coat a big non-stick pan. On medium heat, cook fillets for 4-5 minutes per side in the pan with a teaspoon of oil until the fish easily flakes using a fork. Take it out then retain warmth.
- Sauté onions and red pepper with the remaining oil in the same pan until tender-crisp; Put the garlic, cook for an additional of 1 minute. Mix in tomatoes boil. Lower heat; simmer for minutes with no cover until the liquid evaporates. Serve it with snapper then scatter top with chives and olives.

### Nutrition Information

- Calories: 258 calories
- Protein: 35g protein. Diabetic Exchanges: 5 lean meat
- Total Fat: 9g fat (1g saturated fat)
- Sodium: 754mg sodium

- Fiber: 3g fiber)
- Total Carbohydrate: 10g carbohydrate (4g sugars
- Cholesterol: 60mg cholesterol

## 474. Minted Lamb 'n' Veggie Kabobs

*Serving: 4 servings. | Prep: 30mins | Cook: 10mins | Ready in:*

### Ingredients

- 3 tablespoons olive oil
- 2 tablespoons lemon juice
- 4 garlic cloves, minced
- 2 teaspoons dried basil
- 1 teaspoon dried oregano
- 1 teaspoon pepper
- 1/2 teaspoon salt
- 1/2 teaspoon dried thyme
- 1 pound boneless leg of lamb, cut into 1-inch cubes
- 1 medium sweet red pepper, cut into 1-inch pieces
- 1 medium sweet yellow pepper, cut into 1-inch pieces
- 1 medium zucchini, cut into 1/4-inch slices
- 1 small red onion, cut into chunks
- 16 medium fresh mushrooms
- 1 cup fresh mint leaves
- Hot cooked brown rice

### Direction

- Mix the salt, pepper, basil, garlic, oregano, thyme, oil, and lemon juice in a large re-sealable bag. Add in the lamb, seal the bag and turn to coat the meat. Let stand in refrigerator for 30 minutes. Alternately skewer lamb and vegetables with mint leaves on eight metal or pre-soaked wooden skewers. Grill with cover over medium heat, or broil 4 in. from the heat, for 4-5 minutes per side or until vegetables are tender and meat is done to liking. Serve with warm rice.

### Nutrition Information

- Calories: 305 calories
- Total Carbohydrate: 14g carbohydrate (5g sugars
- Cholesterol: 69mg cholesterol
- Protein: 26g protein.
- Total Fat: 17g fat (4g saturated fat)
- Sodium: 365mg sodium
- Fiber: 5g fiber)

## 475. Minted Meatballs

*Serving: 40 meatballs. | Prep: 15mins | Cook: 20mins | Ready in:*

### Ingredients

- 4 slices bread
- 1/2 cup water
- 1 egg, beaten
- 1 medium onion, finely chopped
- 1/2 cup minced fresh parsley
- 1 garlic clove, minced
- 2 teaspoons dried mint flakes
- 1 teaspoon salt
- 1/8 teaspoon pepper
- 1 pound ground beef
- 1 cup all-purpose flour
- 1/2 cup vegetable oil

### Direction

- Plunge the bread into water, squeeze to remove excess water. Break the bread into crumbs in a big bowl. Mix in the pepper, salt, mint, garlic, parsley, onion and egg. Break the beef into crumbs then mix well into the mixture. Form into 1-inch balls. Roll into flour. Add meatballs to oil in a big frying pan, cook over medium heat until it is not pink any longer, about 15 minutes.

## Nutrition Information

- Calories:
- Cholesterol:
- Protein:
- Total Fat:
- Sodium:
- Fiber:
- Total Carbohydrate:

## 476. Moroccan Apple Beef Stew

*Serving: 8 servings (2 quarts). | Prep: 20mins | Cook: 02hours00mins | Ready in:*

### Ingredients

- 1-1/4 teaspoons salt
- 1/2 teaspoon ground cinnamon
- 1/2 teaspoon pepper
- 1/4 teaspoon ground allspice
- 2-1/2 pounds beef stew meat, cut into 1-inch pieces
- 2 to 3 tablespoons olive oil
- 1 large onion, chopped (about 2 cups)
- 3 garlic cloves, minced
- 1 can (15 ounces) tomato sauce
- 1 can (14-1/2 ounces) beef broth
- 1 cup pitted dried plums, coarsely chopped
- 1 tablespoon honey
- 2 medium Fuji or Gala apples, peeled and cut into 1-1/2-inch pieces
- Hot cooked rice or couscous, optional

### Direction

- Stir allspice, pepper, cinnamon and salt; dust over beef and mix to coat. Heat 2 tablespoons oil over medium heat in a Dutch oven.
- Brown beef in batches, put in extra oil as needed. Take the beef using a slotted spoon.
- In the same pan, put onion; cook and mix for 6-8 minutes or until soft. Put in garlic; cook for another minute. Mix in honey, dried plums, broth and tomato sauce. Bring beef back to the pan; take to a boil. Lower heat; simmer with cover for 1 1/2 hours.
- Put in apples; cook with cover, until apples and beef are soft, about another 30 to 45 minutes. Skim fat. Serve stew with rice if desired. Freezing option: freeze cooled stew in freezer containers. Defrost slightly in refrigerator overnight to use. Heat through in a saucepan, mixing occasionally and, if necessary, add a little broth.

## Nutrition Information

- Calories: 339 calories
- Cholesterol: 88mg cholesterol
- Protein: 29g protein.
- Total Fat: 13g fat (4g saturated fat)
- Sodium: 905mg sodium
- Fiber: 2g fiber)
- Total Carbohydrate: 24g carbohydrate (14g sugars

## 477. Moroccan Beef Kabobs

*Serving: 8 servings. | Prep: 25mins | Cook: 10mins | Ready in:*

### Ingredients

- 1 cup chopped fresh parsley
- 1 cup chopped fresh cilantro
- 1/4 cup grated onion
- 3 tablespoons lemon juice
- 2 tablespoons olive oil
- 1 tablespoon ground cumin
- 1 tablespoon ground coriander
- 1 tablespoon paprika
- 1 tablespoon cider vinegar

- 1 tablespoon ketchup
- 2 garlic cloves, minced
- 1 teaspoon minced fresh gingerroot
- 1 teaspoon Thai red chili paste
- Dash salt and pepper
- 2 pounds beef top sirloin steak, cut into 1-inch pieces

## Direction

- Combine salt, pepper, paprika, cumin, coriander, garlic, onion, ginger, parsley, cilantro, oil, vinegar, lemon juice, ketchup, and chili paste in a large re-sealable bag. Add beef, seal the bag, and turn several times to coat. Keep in refrigerator overnight or for at least 8 hours. Drain marinade, discarding it. Thread beef cubes on eight metal or wooden skewers that have been soaked. Use a long-handled tongs to grip a paper towel, moisten it with oil, and dab on the grates to grease them lightly. Place beef skewers on the grill, cover it, and cook on medium-high heat, turning occasionally, or broil 4 in. away from the heat, for 8-12 minutes or until beef is at preferred doneness.

## Nutrition Information

- Calories: 185 calories
- Cholesterol: 63mg cholesterol
- Protein: 22g protein. Diabetic Exchanges: 3 lean meat
- Total Fat: 9g fat (3g saturated fat)
- Sodium: 91mg sodium
- Fiber: 1g fiber)
- Total Carbohydrate: 3g carbohydrate (1g sugars

## 478. Moroccan Chicken

*Serving: 4 | Prep: 10mins | Cook: 30mins | Ready in:*

## Ingredients

- 1 pound skinless, boneless chicken breast meat - cubed
- 2 teaspoons salt
- 1 onion, chopped
- 2 cloves garlic, chopped
- 2 carrots, sliced
- 2 stalks celery, sliced
- 1 tablespoon minced fresh ginger root
- 1/2 teaspoon paprika
- 3/4 teaspoon ground cumin
- 1/2 teaspoon dried oregano
- 1/4 teaspoon ground cayenne pepper
- 1/4 teaspoon ground turmeric
- 1 1/2 cups chicken broth
- 1 cup crushed tomatoes
- 1 cup canned chickpeas, drained
- 1 zucchini, sliced
- 1 tablespoon lemon juice

## Direction

- In a big saucepan, season the chicken with brown and salt on medium heat, until it is nearly cooked through. Take out the chicken from the pan and put it aside.
- In the same pan, sauté celery, carrots, garlic and onion till tender. Then mix in turmeric, cayenne pepper, oregano, cumin, paprika and ginger. Stir fry it for about a minute, then stir in the tomatoes and broth. Put the chicken back into the pan, minimize the heat to low and let it simmer for about 10 minutes.
- Put zucchini and chickpeas into the pan and let it simmer again. Cook until the zucchini is soft and cooked through, or for about 15 minutes with cover on. Mix in lemon juice then serve.

## Nutrition Information

- Calories: 286 calories;
- Cholesterol: 67
- Protein: 36
- Total Fat: 3.7
- Sodium: 2128
- Total Carbohydrate: 27.9

## 479. Mustard Herb Grilled Tenderloin

*Serving: 6 servings. | Prep: 10mins | Cook: 20mins | Ready in:*

### Ingredients

- 2/3 cup olive oil
- 1/2 cup beef broth
- 3 tablespoons Dijon mustard
- 2 tablespoons red wine vinegar
- 2 tablespoons lemon juice
- 1/2 teaspoon sugar
- 2 garlic cloves, minced
- 1/2 teaspoon salt
- 1/4 teaspoon each dried oregano, summer savory, tarragon and thyme
- 1/8 teaspoon pepper
- 1 beef tenderloin roast (1-1/2 pounds)

### Direction

- Mix seasonings, oil, garlic, broth, sugar, mustard, lemon juice, and vinegar in a small bowl. Transfer 3/4 cup of the mixture into a big plastic resealable bag then put in beef; seal and turn to coat. Chill overnight, flip the bag 1 or 2 times. Cover and chill the rest of the marinade for basting.
- Drain and get rid of the beef marinade. On medium heat, grill beat for 20-25 mins while covering or until it reaches the preferred doneness. An inserted thermometer should register 170 degrees F for well-done, 160 degrees F for medium, and 145 degrees F for medium-rare. Flip one time then use a quarter cup of the reserved marinade to baste on the final 5 mins.
- Let the beef sit for 10 mins then slice. Serve tenderloin slices with the rest of the reserved marinade.

### Nutrition Information

- Calories: 257 calories
- Sodium: 181mg sodium
- Fiber: 0 fiber)
- Total Carbohydrate: 1g carbohydrate (0 sugars
- Cholesterol: 50mg cholesterol
- Protein: 24g protein.
- Total Fat: 16g fat (4g saturated fat)

## 480. Nikki's Perfect Pastitsio

*Serving: 12 servings. | Prep: 45mins | Cook: 50mins | Ready in:*

### Ingredients

- 2-1/2 cups uncooked penne pasta
- 2 tablespoons butter, melted
- 1 cup grated Parmesan cheese
- 1-1/2 pounds ground sirloin
- 1 medium onion, chopped
- 2 garlic cloves, minced
- 1 can (15 ounces) tomato sauce
- 1/2 teaspoon salt
- 1/2 teaspoon ground cinnamon
- 1 cup shredded Parmesan cheese, divided
- BECHAMEL SAUCE:
- 1/2 cup butter, cubed
- 2/3 cup all-purpose flour
- 1/2 teaspoon salt
- 1/4 teaspoon pepper
- 4 cups 2% milk
- 2 large eggs

### Direction

- As package instructions, cook the pasta; drain the pasta. Toss together with butter; put in the grated Parmesan cheese. Place into a 13x9-inch baking dish that's greased.
- Set an oven to 350 degrees and start preheating. Cook the onion and beef on medium heat in a large skillet and crumble the beef until the beef is not pink anymore or 8-10

- minutes; drain. Put in garlic and cook for 2 more minutes. Stir in cinnamon, salt, and tomato sauce; heat thoroughly. Scoop over the pasta. Sprinkle with 1/2 cup of shredded Parmesan cheese.
- Let the butter melt in a large saucepan. Stir in pepper, salt, and flour until they become smooth and slowly pour the milk. Boil; stir and cook until thick or for 1-2 minutes.
- Whisk a small amount of the hot mixture into the eggs in a small bowl; place all back into the pan and whisk constantly. Boil gently; stir and cook for 2 minutes. Place over the beef mixture. Sprinkle with the remaining cheese.
- Put a cover on and bake for 20 minutes. Uncover and bake until golden brown or 30-40 more minutes.

## Nutrition Information

- Calories: 332 calories
- Sodium: 718mg sodium
- Fiber: 1g fiber)
- Total Carbohydrate: 24g carbohydrate (6g sugars
- Cholesterol: 98mg cholesterol
- Protein: 20g protein.
- Total Fat: 18g fat (10g saturated fat)

## 481. North African Chicken And Rice

*Serving: 8 servings. | Prep: 10mins | Cook: 04hours00mins | Ready in:*

## Ingredients

- 1 medium onion, diced
- 1 tablespoon olive oil
- 8 boneless skinless chicken thighs (about 2 pounds)
- 1 tablespoon minced fresh cilantro
- 1 teaspoon ground turmeric
- 1 teaspoon paprika
- 1 teaspoon sea salt
- 1/2 teaspoon pepper
- 1/2 teaspoon ground cinnamon
- 1/2 teaspoon chili powder
- 1 cup golden raisins
- 1/2 to 1 cup chopped pitted green olives
- 1 medium lemon, sliced
- 2 garlic cloves, minced
- 1/2 cup chicken broth or water
- 4 cups hot cooked brown rice

## Direction

- Mix oil and onion in a 3-4-qt. slow cooker. Put chicken thighs over onion. Sprinkle following 7 ingredients on top. Put garlic, lemon, olives and raisins over. Put broth. Cook on low, covered, for 4-5 hours till chicken is tender. Serve this with hot cooked rice.

## Nutrition Information

- Calories: 386 calories
- Fiber: 3g fiber)
- Total Carbohydrate: 44g carbohydrate (12g sugars
- Cholesterol: 76mg cholesterol
- Protein: 25g protein.
- Total Fat: 13g fat (3g saturated fat)
- Sodium: 556mg sodium

## 482. Orange Blossom Lamb

*Serving: 4 servings. | Prep: 5mins | Cook: 25mins | Ready in:*

## Ingredients

- 8 lamb rib chops (6 to 7 ounces each and 1- thick)
- 2 tablespoons butter
- 1 can (6 ounces) orange juice concentrate, thawed
- 1 medium onion, sliced

- 1 to 2 teaspoons soy sauce
- 1 teaspoon salt
- Dash pepper

## Direction

- Brown the lamb chops in butter on medium heat in a big skillet. Add leftover ingredients; stir well. Lower heat; cover. Simmer till meat is tender, flipping once, for 20-25 minutes. Serve: Put sauce on lamb.

## Nutrition Information

- Calories: 442 calories
- Fiber: 1g fiber)
- Total Carbohydrate: 20g carbohydrate (18g sugars
- Cholesterol: 151mg cholesterol
- Protein: 45g protein.
- Total Fat: 20g fat (9g saturated fat)
- Sodium: 847mg sodium

## 483. Oregano Olive Chicken

*Serving: 8 servings. | Prep: 15mins | Cook: 30mins | Ready in:*

## Ingredients

- 1 broiler/fryer chicken (4 pounds), cut up and skin removed
- 1/4 teaspoon pepper
- 2 tablespoons olive oil
- 1/2 cup white wine or reduced-sodium chicken broth
- 1/2 cup chopped pimiento-stuffed olives
- 1/4 cup capers, drained
- 2 tablespoons minced fresh oregano
- 1 tablespoon minced fresh mint
- 1 tablespoon cider vinegar
- 2 garlic cloves, minced
- 1 teaspoon minced fresh thyme

## Direction

- Scatter the chicken with pepper. Brown all sides of the chicken in a cooking-spray-coated big non-stick skillet. Take the chicken out of the skillet then keep warm. Drain the drippings in the skillet.
- Mix the remaining ingredients then add into the skillet; mix to loosen the browned bits then boil. Put the chicken back in the skillet carefully. Lower the heat; let it simmer for 20-25 mins while covering or until the chicken juices are clear.

## Nutrition Information

- Calories: 217 calories
- Cholesterol: 73mg cholesterol
- Protein: 24g protein. Diabetic Exchanges: 3 lean meat
- Total Fat: 11g fat (2g saturated fat)
- Sodium: 370mg sodium
- Fiber: 0 fiber)
- Total Carbohydrate: 2g carbohydrate (0 sugars

## 484. Oregano Lemon Chicken

*Serving: 6 | Prep: 15mins | Cook: 45mins | Ready in:*

## Ingredients

- 3 pounds skinless, boneless chicken breast halves
- 3 tablespoons lemon juice
- 2 tablespoons honey
- 1 tablespoon olive oil
- 3 cloves garlic, minced
- 2 teaspoons dried oregano

## Direction

- Turn the oven to 375°F (190°C) to preheat. Coat a 9x13-in. baking dish with oil.
- In the prepared baking dish, put chicken breast halves. In a bowl, mix together oregano,

garlic, olive oil, honey, and lemon juice and add the mixture to the chicken breasts.
- Put in the preheated oven and bake for 45 minutes until an instant-read meat thermometer displays 180°F (80°C) when you insert it into the thickest section of a breast, the juices run clear and the inside of the chicken is not pink anymore. During baking, baste the pan juices over the chicken every 15 minutes.

## Nutrition Information

- Calories: 277 calories;
- Sodium: 97
- Total Carbohydrate: 7.2
- Cholesterol: 117
- Protein: 44.3
- Total Fat: 6.9

## 485. Pan Fried Chicken Athena

Serving: 4 servings. | Prep: 15mins | Cook: 15mins | Ready in:

## Ingredients

- 4 boneless skinless chicken breast halves (6 ounces each)
- 2 tablespoons butter
- 4-1/2 teaspoons lemon juice
- 4-1/2 teaspoons Worcestershire sauce
- 1/2 teaspoon Dijon mustard
- 1/4 teaspoon salt
- 1 tablespoon minced chives
- 1 tablespoon minced fresh parsley or 1 teaspoon dried parsley flakes
- Lemon wedges

## Direction

- Flatten the chicken breasts to 1/2-in. thick. Cook chicken in butter in big skillet on medium heat till thermometer reads 170° for 5-6 minutes per side. Remove; keep warm.
- Boil salt, mustard, Worcestershire sauce and lemon juice in same skillet. Take off heat; mix parsley and chives in. Put on chicken; serve with lemon wedges.

## Nutrition Information

- Calories: 240 calories
- Fiber: 0 fiber)
- Total Carbohydrate: 2g carbohydrate (1g sugars
- Cholesterol: 109mg cholesterol
- Protein: 34g protein. Diabetic Exchanges: 5 lean meat
- Total Fat: 10g fat (5g saturated fat)
- Sodium: 348mg sodium

## 486. Parmesan Chicken Couscous

Serving: 4 servings. | Prep: 15mins | Cook: 5mins | Ready in:

## Ingredients

- 1/2 cup chopped walnuts
- 2 teaspoons olive oil, divided
- 3 garlic cloves, minced
- 2 cups chopped fresh spinach
- 1-1/2 cups cubed cooked chicken
- 1-1/4 cups water
- 2 teaspoons dried basil
- 1/4 teaspoon pepper
- 1 package (5.9 ounces) Parmesan couscous
- 1/4 cup grated Parmesan cheese

## Direction

- Cook walnuts in a large saucepan over medium heat in 1 teaspoon of oil until toasted or for 2-3 minutes. Take off the heat; set aside.

- Sauté garlic in the same pan for 1 minute with the remaining oil. Stir in pepper, basil, water, chicken and spinach. Bring to a boil. Mix in couscous. Take off the heat; let it stand with a cover until the water is absorbed or for 5-10 minutes. Use a fork to fluff. Add walnuts and stir well; use cheese to sprinkle.

## Nutrition Information

- Calories: 391 calories
- Total Carbohydrate: 34g carbohydrate (1g sugars
- Cholesterol: 51mg cholesterol
- Protein: 25g protein. Diabetic Exchanges: 3 lean meat
- Total Fat: 18g fat (3g saturated fat)
- Sodium: 490mg sodium
- Fiber: 3g fiber)

## 487. Parmesan Chicken With Artichoke Hearts

*Serving: 4 servings. | Prep: 20mins | Cook: 20mins | Ready in:*

## Ingredients

- 4 boneless skinless chicken breast halves (6 ounces each)
- 3 teaspoons olive oil, divided
- 1 teaspoon dried rosemary, crushed
- 1/2 teaspoon dried thyme
- 1/2 teaspoon pepper
- 2 cans (14 ounces each) water-packed artichoke hearts, drained and quartered
- 1 medium onion, coarsely chopped
- 1/2 cup white wine or reduced-sodium chicken broth
- 2 garlic cloves, chopped
- 1/4 cup shredded Parmesan cheese
- 1 lemon, cut into 8 slices
- 2 green onions, thinly sliced

## Direction

- Turn on the oven to 375 degrees to preheat. In a cooking sprayed 15x10x1-in. baking pan, arrange the chicken; use 1-1/2 teaspoons of oil to drizzle. Combine pepper, thyme and rosemary in a small bowl; scatter half of it onto the chicken.
- Mix together the remaining herb mixture, the remaining oil, garlic, wine, onion and artichoke hearts in a large bowl; toss until well-coated. Place around the chicken. Use cheese to sprinkle over chicken and lemon slices to top.
- Put on roast until a thermometer reaches 165 degrees when inserted into the chicken or for 20-25 minutes. Use green onions to sprinkle.

## Nutrition Information

- Calories: 339 calories
- Protein: 42g protein. Diabetic Exchanges: 5 lean meat
- Total Fat: 9g fat (3g saturated fat)
- Sodium: 667mg sodium
- Fiber: 1g fiber)
- Total Carbohydrate: 18g carbohydrate (2g sugars
- Cholesterol: 98mg cholesterol

## 488. Pasta Lamb Skillet

*Serving: 8 servings. | Prep: 15mins | Cook: 0mins | Ready in:*

## Ingredients

- 1 package (8 ounces) small pasta
- 12 ounces ground lamb
- 1 cup chopped onion
- 2 garlic cloves, minced
- 1 tablespoon olive oil
- 1 medium zucchini, quartered and thinly sliced (1-1/4 cups)

- 1 can (14-1/2 ounces) diced tomatoes, undrained
- 1 cup sliced fresh mushrooms
- 3 tablespoons minced fresh basil or 1 tablespoon dried basil
- 1/2 teaspoon pepper
- 1/4 to 1/2 teaspoon seasoned salt
- 1/4 cup sliced ripe olives

## Direction

- Follow package directions to cook pasta. Cook garlic, onion and lamb in oil in a big skillet on medium heat till veggies are tender and meat isn't pink anymore; drain. Put aside; keep warm.
- Mix seasoned salt, pepper, basil, mushrooms, tomatoes and zucchini in same skillet; cover. Cook for 5 minutes on medium heat till veggies are tender. Drain the pasta. Add olives, lamb mixture and pasta to skillet and heat through.

## Nutrition Information

- Calories: 228 calories
- Protein: 12g protein.
- Total Fat: 9g fat (3g saturated fat)
- Sodium: 176mg sodium
- Fiber: 3g fiber)
- Total Carbohydrate: 27g carbohydrate (4g sugars
- Cholesterol: 28mg cholesterol

## 489. Pastry Topped Salmon Casserole

*Serving: 6 servings. | Prep: 20mins | Cook: 30mins | Ready in:*

## Ingredients

- 1 large onion, chopped
- 5 tablespoons butter, divided
- 1 garlic clove, minced
- 1-1/4 cups 2% milk
- 1 package (8 ounces) cream cheese, softened, cubed
- 2 cups frozen peas and carrots, thawed
- 1 can (14-1/2 ounces) diced potatoes, drained
- 2 pouches (6 ounces each) boneless skinless pink salmon, flaked
- 1/2 teaspoon salt
- 1/4 teaspoon pepper
- 10 sheets phyllo dough (14x9-inch size)

## Direction

- Set the oven at 375° to preheat. Sauté onion in 2 tablespoons of butter in a large skillet until crisp-tender, or for 5 minutes. Add garlic, continue to cook for 1 minute more. Stir in milk; over medium heat, heat until bubbles form around the side of the pan. Put in cheese and stir until the cheese is melted. Next, remove from the heat; stir in pepper, salt, salmon, potatoes, carrots, and peas.
- Melt the leftover butter; over the bottom and sides of a 2-1/2-qt. round the baking dish, brush some of the butter. Line with 5 sheets of phyllo dough. Next, pour in the salmon mixture. Put over the filling with the leftover sheets of phyllo dough to cover the top. Fold the edges and sweep the dough with the leftover butter.
- Bake until the crust is lightly browned, or for 30-35 minutes.

## Nutrition Information

- Calories: 417 calories
- Sodium: 943mg sodium
- Fiber: 3g fiber)
- Total Carbohydrate: 28g carbohydrate (7g sugars
- Cholesterol: 90mg cholesterol
- Protein: 19g protein.
- Total Fat: 26g fat (16g saturated fat)

## 490. Pesto Veggie Pizza

*Serving: 6 slices. | Prep: 25mins | Cook: 10mins | Ready in:*

### Ingredients

- 2 cups sliced fresh mushrooms
- 1 cup fresh broccoli florets, chopped
- 3/4 cup thinly sliced zucchini
- 1/2 cup julienned sweet yellow pepper
- 1/2 cup julienned sweet red pepper
- 1 small red onion, thinly sliced and separated into rings
- 1 tablespoon prepared pesto
- 1 prebaked 12-inch thin whole wheat pizza crust
- 1/3 cup pizza sauce
- 2 tablespoons grated Romano or Parmesan cheese
- 1/4 cup sliced ripe olives
- 1/2 cup crumbled reduced-fat feta cheese
- 1/2 cup shredded part-skim mozzarella cheese

### Direction

- Sauté onion, mushrooms, peppers, zucchini, and broccoli in a cooking-spray-coated big non-stick skillet. Take off the heat then mix in pesto.
- On a 12-inch pizza pan, put the crust then spread with pizza sauce. Scatter Romano cheese then add the veggie mixture and olives on top. Scatter mozzarella and feta.
- Bake for 8-12mins in a 450 degrees F oven until the mozzarella melts and the crust is slightly brown.

### Nutrition Information

- Calories: 220 calories
- Sodium: 570mg sodium
- Fiber: 5g fiber)
- Total Carbohydrate: 29g carbohydrate (4g sugars
- Cholesterol: 12mg cholesterol
- Protein: 13g protein. Diabetic Exchanges: 1-1/2 starch
- Total Fat: 8g fat (4g saturated fat)

## 491. Phyllo Chicken

*Serving: 12 servings. | Prep: 15mins | Cook: 35mins | Ready in:*

### Ingredients

- 1/2 cup butter, melted, divided
- 12 sheets phyllo dough (14x9 inches)
- 3 cups diced cooked chicken
- 1/2 pound sliced bacon, cooked and crumbled
- 3 cups frozen chopped broccoli, thawed and drained
- 2 cups shredded cheddar or Swiss cheese
- 6 large eggs
- 1 cup half-and-half cream or evaporated milk
- 1/2 cup whole milk
- 1 teaspoon salt
- 1/2 teaspoon pepper

### Direction

- Brush some of melted butter on the bottom and sides of a 13-in by 9-in baking dish; put a sheet of phyllo on base of dish then spread butter lightly. Repeat with 5 more phyllo sheets. Use plastic wrap and a moist towel to keep the rest of the phyllo covered to avoid drying out.
- Mix cheese, chicken, broccoli, and bacon in a big bowl; evenly slather on top of the phyllo in a baking dish. Beat pepper, eggs, salt, milk, and cream in a small bowl; add on top of the chicken mixture. Use a sheet of phyllo to cover the filling then slather with butter. Repeat with the rest of the phyllo dough then brush the remaining butter on top.
- Bake for 35-40 minutes without cover in 375 degrees oven until a thermometer registers 160 degrees. Let it sit for 5-10 minutes then cut.

### Nutrition Information

- Calories: 373 calories
- Fiber: 1g fiber)
- Total Carbohydrate: 16g carbohydrate (3g sugars
- Cholesterol: 195mg cholesterol
- Protein: 23g protein.
- Total Fat: 24g fat (13g saturated fat)
- Sodium: 659mg sodium

## 492. Phyllo Chicken Potpie

*Serving: 6 servings. | Prep: 35mins | Cook: 10mins | Ready in:*

### Ingredients

- 6 cups water
- 2 cups fresh pearl onions
- 1-1/2 pounds boneless skinless chicken breasts, cubed
- 2 tablespoons canola oil, divided
- 2 medium red potatoes, peeled and chopped
- 1 cup sliced fresh mushrooms
- 1 can (14-1/2 ounces) reduced-sodium chicken broth
- 1/2 pound fresh asparagus, trimmed and cut into 1-inch pieces
- 3 tablespoons sherry or additional reduced-sodium chicken broth
- 3 tablespoons cornstarch
- 1/2 cup fat-free milk
- 1-1/2 teaspoons minced fresh thyme
- 1/2 teaspoon salt
- 1/4 teaspoon pepper
- 10 sheets phyllo dough (14 inches x 9 inches)
- Refrigerated butter-flavored spray

### Direction

- In a Dutch oven, boil water. Put in pearl onions; boil for approximately 3 minutes. Let drain and rinse in cold water; peel and leave aside.
- In a large skillet, cook chicken in 1 tablespoon oil over medium till no longer pink; take out and keep warm. In the same pan, sauté potatoes in remaining oil for around 5 minutes. Put in mushrooms and onions; sauté for an addition of 3 minutes. Put in the asparagus, broth and sherry or additional broth. Let boil. Lower heat; simmering with cover for around 5 minutes till potatoes are soften.
- Combine milk and cornstarch until smooth; stir into skillet. Let boil; cook and stir for nearly 2 minutes till thicken. Let chicken drain; add to onion mixture. Mix in pepper, salt and thyme. Place to a baking dish of 8-inch square covered with cooking spray.
- Stack all 10 phyllo sheets. Roll up, starting at a long side; cut into strips of a half inch. In a large bowl, place strips and toss to separate. Use butter-flavored spray to spritz over. Place over chicken mixture; spritz again.
- Bake with no cover at 425° for around 10 to 15 minutes until it has golden brown color.

### Nutrition Information

- Calories: 325 calories
- Total Fat: 8g fat (1g saturated fat)
- Sodium: 542mg sodium
- Fiber: 2g fiber)
- Total Carbohydrate: 33g carbohydrate (5g sugars
- Cholesterol: 63mg cholesterol
- Protein: 29g protein. Diabetic Exchanges: 3 lean meat

## 493. Phyllo Wrapped Halibut

*Serving: 2 servings. | Prep: 20mins | Cook: 20mins | Ready in:*

### Ingredients

- 4 cups fresh baby spinach

- 3/4 cup chopped sweet red pepper
- 3/4 teaspoon salt-free lemon-pepper seasoning, divided
- 1/2 teaspoon lemon juice
- 6 sheets phyllo dough (14 inches x 9 inches)
- 2 tablespoons reduced-fat butter, melted
- 2 halibut fillets (4 ounces each)
- 1/4 teaspoon salt
- 1/8 teaspoon pepper
- 1/4 cup shredded part-skim mozzarella cheese

### Direction

- Sauté red pepper and spinach in a cooking-spray-coated big non-stick skillet until tender. Add lemon juice and half a teaspoon of lemon pepper. Take off the heat then cool.
- Put foil on a baking sheet then coat with cooking spray; set it aside. On a work surface, put a phyllo sheet then brush with butter. Use plastic wrap and a moist towel to cover the phyllo to avoid drying out prior to using. Put the remaining phyllo on top of the first sheet in a layer, brush butter on each sheet. Halve the stack widthwise.
- In the middle of each square, put a halibut fillet then season with pepper and salt. Add cheese and the spinach mixture on top. Fold the bottom edge and sides over the fillet then roll the square up to enclose. If needed, cut the ends of the phyllo. Brush with the remaining butter then top with sprinkled remaining lemon pepper.
- Arrange on the prepared baking sheet with the seam-side down. Bake for 20-25 mins in a 375 degrees F oven or until golden brown.

### Nutrition Information

- Calories: 330 calories
- Protein: 33g protein. Diabetic Exchanges: 4 lean meat
- Total Fat: 12g fat (6g saturated fat)
- Sodium: 676mg sodium
- Fiber: 4g fiber)
- Total Carbohydrate: 26g carbohydrate (4g sugars
- Cholesterol: 64mg cholesterol

### 494. Pineapple Beef Kabobs

*Serving: 6 servings. | Prep: 20mins | Cook: 10mins | Ready in:*

### Ingredients

- 1 can (6 ounces) unsweetened pineapple juice
- 1/3 cup honey
- 1/3 cup soy sauce
- 3 tablespoons cider vinegar
- 1-1/2 teaspoons minced garlic
- 1-1/2 teaspoons ground ginger
- 1-1/2 pounds beef top sirloin steak, cut into 1-inch pieces
- 1 fresh pineapple, peeled and cut into 1-inch chunks
- 12 large fresh mushrooms
- 1 medium sweet red pepper, cut into 1-inch pieces
- 1 medium sweet yellow pepper, cut into 1-inch pieces
- 1 medium red onion, cut into 1-inch pieces
- 2-1/2 cups uncooked instant rice

### Direction

- Combine first six ingredients in a small bowl. Transfer a quarter cup into a large re-sealable plastic bag and add the beef. Close the bag and turn several times to coat. Keep refrigerated for 1-4 hours. Store covered bowl with remaining marinade in the refrigerator until ready for basting. Drain beef, discarding its marinade. Alternately thread beef, mushrooms, pineapples, onions, and peppers. Dab the grates with oil-moistened paper towel at the end of long-handled tongs. Arrange skewers on the grill, cover it, and cook over medium heat, turning from time to time but basting often using reserved marinade, for 8-10 minutes or until done to liking. Cook rice as directed and serve with the kabobs.

## Nutrition Information

- Calories: 412 calories
- Total Fat: 5g fat (2g saturated fat)
- Sodium: 534mg sodium
- Fiber: 3g fiber)
- Total Carbohydrate: 60g carbohydrate (21g sugars
- Cholesterol: 46mg cholesterol
- Protein: 31g protein.

### 495. Pineapple Pork Kabobs

*Serving: 2 servings. | Prep: 5mins | Cook: 10mins | Ready in:*

## Ingredients

- 1 can (8 ounces) unsweetened pineapple chunks
- 2 tablespoons plus 1-1/2 teaspoons cider vinegar
- 2 tablespoons brown sugar
- Dash pepper
- 1/2 pound pork tenderloin, cut into 1-inch pieces
- 1/2 small sweet red pepper, cut into 1-inch chunks
- 1/2 small green pepper, cut into 1-inch chunks
- Hot cooked rice, optional

## Direction

- Reserve the juice of the canned pineapple and keep the fruit in the refrigerator. Combine the reserved pineapple juice, vinegar, pepper, and brown sugar in a bowl. Place the pork in a large re-sealable plastic bag and pour half of the marinade over the meat. Seal the bag, turn several times to coat, and keep in the refrigerator for 4 hours to marinate. Keep remaining marinade in a covered container in the refrigerator, for basting later. Drain the pork, disposing of marinade. Alternately thread pork, peppers, and pineapples on metal or pre-soaked wooden skewers. Cook in a covered grill over medium heat until vegetables are soft and the pork is not pink anymore, about 10-15 minutes. Turn and baste from time to time while grilling. Serve with rice, if preferred.

## Nutrition Information

- Calories:
- Protein:
- Total Fat:
- Sodium:
- Fiber:
- Total Carbohydrate:
- Cholesterol:

### 496. Plum Glazed Lamb

*Serving: 6 servings. | Prep: 5mins | Cook: 01hours45mins | Ready in:*

## Ingredients

- 1 bone-in leg of lamb (4 to 5 pounds)
- Salt and pepper to taste
- 2 cans (15 ounces each) plums, pitted
- 2 garlic cloves
- 1/4 cup lemon juice
- 2 tablespoons reduced-sodium soy sauce
- 2 teaspoons Worcestershire sauce
- 1 teaspoon dried basil

## Direction

- Preheat an oven to 325°. Put lamb onto rack, fat side up, in shallow baking pan; season with pepper and salt. Bake for 1 3/4-2 1/4 hours, uncovered, till meat gets desired doneness; 170° for well-done, 160° for medium and 145° for medium-rare on a thermometer.
- Meanwhile, drain the plums; save 1/2 cup syrup. Cover and process basil, Worcestershire sauce, soy sauce, lemon juice, garlic, reserved

syrup and plums till smooth in a food processor; put 1/2 plum sauce aside.
- Baste the lamb every 15 minutes through the final hour of roasting. Simmer reserved sauce for 5 minutes in a small saucepan; serve with meat.

## Nutrition Information

- Calories: 338 calories
- Fiber: 2g fiber)
- Total Carbohydrate: 23g carbohydrate (18g sugars
- Cholesterol: 137mg cholesterol
- Protein: 39g protein.
- Total Fat: 10g fat (4g saturated fat)
- Sodium: 283mg sodium

## 497. Pork Kabobs

*Serving: 6-8 servings. | Prep: 10mins | Cook: 10mins | Ready in:*

### Ingredients

- 1/2 cup vegetable oil
- 1/4 cup chopped onion
- 3 tablespoons lemon juice
- 1 tablespoon minced fresh parsley
- 1 garlic clove, minced
- 1/2 teaspoon salt
- 1/2 teaspoon dried marjoram
- 1/8 teaspoon pepper
- 2 pounds boneless pork, cut into 1-inch cubes
- CUCUMBER YOGURT SAUCE:
- 1 cup (8 ounces) plain yogurt
- 1/2 cup chopped cucumber
- 1 tablespoon chopped onion
- 1 tablespoon minced fresh parsley
- 1 teaspoon lemon juice
- 1/8 teaspoon garlic salt
- Pita bread

### Direction

- Take a re-sealable plastic bag or a shallow glass dish and mix together the first eight ingredients and the pork. Seal or cover and refrigerate overnight to marinate. Meantime, combine sauce ingredients and keep in a covered container in the fridge for several hours. Drain the pork, discarding its marinade. Thread the pork on skewers, keeping a small space between pieces. Cook on an open grill over medium heat for 8-10 minutes or until the meat is cooked through, turning often. Serve in pita bread drizzled with sauce.

## Nutrition Information

- Calories:
- Total Fat:
- Sodium:
- Fiber:
- Total Carbohydrate:
- Cholesterol:
- Protein:

## 498. Portobello Lamb Chops

*Serving: 4 servings. | Prep: 10mins | Cook: 20mins | Ready in:*

### Ingredients

- 3/4 cup peach preserves
- 1 tablespoon balsamic vinegar
- 1/4 teaspoon pepper
- 1/8 teaspoon salt
- 4 lamb loin chops (2 inches thick and 5 ounces each
- 1/4 cup olive oil
- 1 teaspoon dried rosemary, crushed
- 4 large portobello mushrooms

### Direction

- Mix all of the first 4 ingredients together in a small bowl. In a big ziplock plastic bag, put in

1/3 cup of the marinade mixture followed by the lamb chops. Seal the ziplock bag and turn it to coat the lamb chops with the marinade mixture; keep it in the fridge for 1-4 hours. Cover the remaining marinade mixture and keep it in the fridge as well.
- Mix the rosemary and oil together in a small bowl then use a brush to coat the mushrooms with the rosemary-oil mixture. Use long-handled tongs to lightly rub a grill rack with a paper towel dampened with cooking oil.
- Put the marinated lamb chops and coated mushrooms onto the prepared grill over medium heat and let it grill without cover, or put the lamb chops and mushrooms in a broiler and let it broil 4 inches away from the heat for 8 to 10 minutes on every side until the preferred meat doneness is achieved (a thermometer inserted on the meat should indicate 170° for well-done, 160° for medium and 145° for medium-rare), use the reserved marinade to baste the lamb chops and mushrooms from time to time.
- Cut the grilled mushrooms into slices and serve it alongside the grilled lamb chops.

## Nutrition Information

- Calories: 429 calories
- Protein: 20g protein.
- Total Fat: 19g fat (4g saturated fat)
- Sodium: 131mg sodium
- Fiber: 1g fiber)
- Total Carbohydrate: 44g carbohydrate (38g sugars
- Cholesterol: 57mg cholesterol

## 499. Pressure Cooker Mediterranean Chicken Orzo

Serving: 6 servings. | Prep: 15mins | Cook: 10mins | Ready in:

## Ingredients

- 6 boneless skinless chicken thighs (about 1-1/2 pounds), cut into 1-inch pieces
- 2 cups reduced-sodium chicken broth
- 2 medium tomatoes, chopped
- 1 cup sliced pitted green olives, drained
- 1 cup sliced pitted ripe olives, drained
- 1 large carrot, halved lengthwise and chopped
- 1 small red onion, finely chopped
- 1 tablespoon grated lemon zest
- 3 tablespoons lemon juice
- 2 tablespoons butter
- 1 tablespoon herbes de Provence
- 1 cup uncooked orzo pasta

## Direction

- Mix initial 11 ingredients in a 6-qt. electric pressure cooker; mix to combine then lock lid. Close vent. Choose manual setting; put pressure on high. Set timer to 8 minutes. When times up, follow manufacturer's direction to quick-release pressure.
- Put orzo then lock lid. Close vent. Choose manual setting. Put pressure on low. Set timer to 3 minutes. When timers up, let pressure release naturally for 4 minutes. Follow manufacturer's directions to quick-release leftover pressure. Before serving, let sit for 8-10 minutes.

## Nutrition Information

- Calories: 415 calories
- Cholesterol: 86mg cholesterol
- Protein: 27g protein.
- Total Fat: 19g fat (5g saturated fat)
- Sodium: 941mg sodium
- Fiber: 3g fiber)
- Total Carbohydrate: 33g carbohydrate (4g sugars

## 500. Pronto Pita Pizzas

*Serving: 4 servings. | Prep: 10mins | Cook: 15mins | Ready in:*

### Ingredients

- 1 pound ground turkey breast
- 1 cup sliced fresh mushrooms
- 1/2 cup chopped onion
- 2 garlic cloves, minced
- 1 can (8 ounces) no-salt-added tomato sauce
- 1/2 teaspoon fennel seed
- 1/4 teaspoon dried oregano
- 4 pita breads, warmed
- 1/2 cup shredded part-skim mozzarella cheese

### Direction

- Brown the turkey in a skillet; drain. Add garlic, onion, and mushrooms; cook until softened. Mix in oregano, fennel seed, and tomato sauce. Simmer for 10 to 15 minutes, covered, or until heated through.
- Put 1 cup meat mixture on each pita and spread; dust with cheese. Serve right away.

### Nutrition Information

- Calories: 358 calories
- Fiber: 0 fiber)
- Total Carbohydrate: 41g carbohydrate (0 sugars
- Cholesterol: 63mg cholesterol
- Protein: 38g protein. Diabetic Exchanges: 4 lean meat
- Total Fat: 5g fat (0 saturated fat)
- Sodium: 187mg sodium

## 501. Quick Marinated Flank Steak

*Serving: 6 servings. | Prep: 5mins | Cook: 15mins | Ready in:*

### Ingredients

- 2/3 cup olive oil
- 1/4 cup lemon juice
- 2 tablespoons red wine vinegar
- 1 tablespoon Worcestershire sauce
- 1 tablespoon soy sauce
- 1 tablespoon Dijon mustard
- 1 teaspoon dried basil
- 1/2 teaspoon dried oregano
- 1/4 teaspoon dried thyme
- 1 beef flank steak (about 1-1/2 pounds)

### Direction

- Mix the initial nine ingredients together in a big resealable plastic bag before adding the steak. Turn to coat the meat and seal the bag up. Keep refrigerated for 8 hours or through the night, turning it from time to time. Drain the meat and throw the marinade away. Over medium-hot heat, grill the steak with a cover on until the meat is at desired doneness, about 6 to 10 minutes on each side. For medium-rare meat, a thermometer should register at 145°F and for medium, it should be 160°F. For well-done meat, it should read 170°F. Cut across the grain in thin slices and serve.

### Nutrition Information

- Calories: 392 calories
- Protein: 23g protein.
- Total Fat: 32g fat (7g saturated fat)
- Sodium: 312mg sodium
- Fiber: 0 fiber)
- Total Carbohydrate: 2g carbohydrate (0 sugars
- Cholesterol: 54mg cholesterol

## 502. Rack Of Lamb

*Serving: 4 servings | Prep: 15mins | Cook: | Ready in:*

### Ingredients

- 1 rack of lamb (2 lb.)
- 1 cup A.1. Garlic & Herb Marinade

### Direction

- Arrange lamb rack in a shallow dish, meat side down. Stream marinade over lamb. Allow lamb to marinate in the fridge, flipping every 1 1/2 hours.
- Turn oven to 375°F to preheat. Take lamb out of the marinade; dispose used marinade. Arrange meat in a shallow roasting pan.
- Bake lamb in the preheated oven until its internal temperature reaches 160°F for 30 to 45 minutes. Take out of the oven; allow to stand, covered, for 15 minutes before serving.

### Nutrition Information

- Calories: 220
- Total Carbohydrate: 8 g
- Protein: 21 g
- Total Fat: 11 g
- Sodium: 620 mg
- Sugar: 4 g
- Cholesterol: 70 mg
- Saturated Fat: 4 g
- Fiber: 1 g

## 503. Rack Of Lamb With Figs

*Serving: 6-8 servings. | Prep: 30mins | Cook: 45mins | Ready in:*

### Ingredients

- 2 racks of lamb (2 pounds each)
- 1 teaspoon salt, divided
- 1 cup water
- 1 small onion, finely chopped
- 1 tablespoon canola oil
- 1 garlic clove, minced
- 2 tablespoons cornstarch
- 1 cup port wine or 1/2 cup grape juice plus 1/2 cup reduced-sodium beef broth
- 10 dried figs, halved
- 1/4 teaspoon pepper
- 1/2 cup coarsely chopped walnuts, toasted

### Direction

- Use 1/2 tsp. of salt to rub lamb. On a rack set in a roasting pan coated with grease, arrange lamb with meat side facing up. Bake at 375 degrees without a cover until reaching desired doneness (for medium-rare, a thermometer should register 145 degrees; medium, 160 degrees and well-done, 170 degrees), about 45 to 60 minutes.
- Transfer to a serving platter and use foil to cover loosely. Put 1 cup of water into the roasting pan, then stir to loosen any browned bits from pan. Strain the mixture with a fine sieve, then put drippings aside.
- Sauté onion in a small saucepan with oil until soft. Put in garlic and cook for 1 minute more. Stir in cornstarch until combined, then put in leftover salt, pepper, figs, drippings and wine gradually. Bring the mixture to a boil. Lower heat to moderately low and cook without a cover for 10 minutes, until sauce is thickened and figs are soft, while stirring sometimes.
- Sprinkle walnuts over lamand serve together with fig sauce.

### Nutrition Information

- Calories: 363 calories
- Sodium: 362mg sodium
- Fiber: 3g fiber)
- Total Carbohydrate: 23g carbohydrate (14g sugars
- Cholesterol: 66mg cholesterol
- Protein: 23g protein.
- Total Fat: 16g fat (4g saturated fat)

## 504. Roast Lamb With Plum Sauce

*Serving: 11 servings. | Prep: 30mins | Cook: 02hours30mins | Ready in:*

### Ingredients

- 1 leg of lamb (5 to 6 pounds)
- 3 garlic cloves, slivered
- 1/2 cup thinly sliced green onions
- 1/4 cup butter
- 1 jar (12 ounces) plum jam
- 1/2 cup chili sauce
- 1/4 cup white grape juice
- 1 tablespoon lemon juice
- 1/2 teaspoon ground allspice
- 1 tablespoon dried parsley flakes

### Direction

- Remove thin fat covering from roast. In meat, make slits; insert a garlic sliver into each. Put onto a rack in big roasting pan; bake for 1 1/2 hours at 325°, uncovered.
- Meanwhile, to make plum sauce, sauté onions in butter till tender in a medium saucepan. Add allspice, lemon juice, grape juice, chili sauce and jam; boil, occasionally mixing. Simmer for 10 minutes, uncovered.
- Use sauce to baste roast; bake for 1 hour, occasionally basting with plum sauce, till meat gets desired doneness (170° for well-done, 160° for medium on a thermometer). Boil leftover sauce; mix in parsley. Stand roast for 10-15 minutes then carve; serve roast with leftover sauce.

### Nutrition Information

- Calories: 300 calories
- Total Carbohydrate: 25g carbohydrate (22g sugars
- Cholesterol: 104mg cholesterol
- Protein: 26g protein.
- Total Fat: 11g fat (5g saturated fat)
- Sodium: 253mg sodium
- Fiber: 0 fiber)

## 505. Roast Leg Of Lamb

*Serving: 12 | Prep: 15mins | Cook: 1hours45mins | Ready in:*

### Ingredients

- 4 cloves garlic, sliced
- 2 tablespoons fresh rosemary
- salt to taste
- ground black pepper to taste
- 5 pounds leg of lamb

### Direction

- Set oven to 350°F (175°C) to preheat.
- Make slits every 3 to 4 inches over top of the lamb's leg, deep enough to push slices of garlic down into the meat. Liberally sprinkle pepper and salt over top of lamb to season; arrange several fresh rosemary sprigs over top and bottom of the lamb. Position lamb on a roasting pan.
- Roast lamb for about 1-3/4 to 2 hours in preheated oven until desired doneness is reached. Do not overcook the lamb. Keep the lamb meat slightly pink for the best flavor. Allow meat to stand for at least 10 minutes before cutting to serve.

### Nutrition Information

- Calories: 382 calories;
- Cholesterol: 136
- Protein: 35.8
- Total Fat: 25.3
- Sodium: 136
- Total Carbohydrate: 0.4

### 506. Roast Leg Of Lamb With Rosemary

*Serving: 6 | Prep: 15mins | Cook: 1hours20mins | Ready in:*

#### Ingredients

- 1/4 cup honey
- 2 tablespoons prepared Dijon-style mustard
- 2 tablespoons chopped fresh rosemary
- 1 teaspoon freshly ground black pepper
- 1 teaspoon lemon zest
- 3 cloves garlic, minced
- 5 pounds whole leg of lamb
- 1 teaspoon coarse sea salt

#### Direction

- Mix garlic, lemon zest, ground black pepper, rosemary, mustard and honey well in a small bowl; apply to lamb. Cover; marinate overnight in the fridge.
- Preheat an oven to 230°C/450°F.
- Put lamb onto a rack in a roasting pan; sprinkle salt to taste.
- Bake for 20 minutes at 230°C/450°F; lower heat to 200°C/400°F. Roast to get medium-rare for 55-60 minutes; internal temperature should be at least 63°C/145°F using a meat thermometer. Rest roast for 10 minutes; carve.

#### Nutrition Information

- Calories: 922 calories;
- Total Fat: 64.6
- Sodium: 631
- Total Carbohydrate: 13.6
- Cholesterol: 261
- Protein: 67.9

### 507. Roast Pork With Currant Sauce

*Serving: 6 servings. | Prep: 10mins | Cook: 60mins | Ready in:*

#### Ingredients

- 1-1/2 cups orange juice
- 1/4 cup lemon juice
- 2 teaspoons minced fresh gingerroot
- 2 teaspoons minced garlic, divided
- 1 teaspoon dried oregano
- 1 teaspoon ground cinnamon
- 1/2 teaspoon ground coriander
- 1 boneless pork loin roast (2 pounds)
- 1 small onion, sliced
- 1 shallot, chopped
- 1 tablespoon butter
- 1 tablespoon all-purpose flour
- 1/2 cup reduced-sodium chicken broth
- 1/2 cup red currant jelly

#### Direction

- Combine oregano, coriander, cinnamon, 1 teaspoon garlic, ginger, lemon juice, and orange juice in a bowl. Cover and chill 1 cup for the sauce. Next, pour the leftover marinade into a large resealable plastic bag; add onion and pork. Seal it and flip to coat; chill for 4 hours, occasionally turning.
- Let drain and discard the marinade; arrange the roast on a rack in a shallow roasting pan coated with cooking spray. Bake at 350° until a thermometer states 160°, for 60 minutes. Allow to stand for 10 minutes before slicing.
- Sauté the remaining garlic and shallot in butter in a small nonstick saucepan for a minute. Dust with flour; then cook and stir until combined. Stir in the reserved juice mixture, jelly, and broth gradually. Boil; cook and stir until thickened, for around 2 minutes. Enjoy with pork.

#### Nutrition Information

- Calories: 307 calories
- Fiber: 0 fiber)
- Total Carbohydrate: 26g carbohydrate (21g sugars
- Cholesterol: 80mg cholesterol
- Protein: 30g protein. Diabetic Exchanges: 4 lean meat
- Total Fat: 9g fat (4g saturated fat)
- Sodium: 115mg sodium

## 508. Roast Rack Of Lamb With Herb Sauce

*Serving: 4 servings (1-3/4 cups sauce). | Prep: 35mins | Cook: 35mins | Ready in:*

### Ingredients

- 1/4 cup minced fresh rosemary
- 1-1/2 teaspoons coarsely ground pepper
- 1-1/2 teaspoons salt
- 2 racks of lamb (1-1/2 pounds each)
- 1 tablespoon olive oil
- SAUCE:
- 3/4 cup fresh parsley leaves
- 2/3 cup fresh basil leaves
- 1/3 cup each fresh cilantro leaves, mint leaves, oregano leaves and thyme leaves
- 1/3 cup coarsely chopped fresh chives
- 1/3 cup chopped shallots
- 2 garlic cloves, crushed
- 3 tablespoons grated lemon peel
- 1/2 cup lemon juice
- 2 tablespoons Dijon mustard
- 3/4 teaspoon salt
- 1/2 teaspoon pepper
- 1/3 cup olive oil

### Direction

- Mix salt, pepper and rosemary; rub on lamb. Refrigerate for 8 hours or overnight, covered.
- Preheat an oven to 375°. Put lamb, fat side up, into a shallow roasting pan; drizzle with oil.
- Roast for 35-45 minutes till meat gets desired doneness (170°: well-done, 160°: medium, 145°: medium-rare on a thermometer). Take off lamb from oven; use foil to tent. Let sit for 10 minutes then serve.
- Meanwhile, pulse garlic, shallots and herbs till herbs are chopped in a food processor. Add pepper, salt, mustard, lemon juice and lemon peel; process till blended. In a steady stream, gradually add oil while processing; serve lamb with sauce.

### Nutrition Information

- Calories:
- Protein:
- Total Fat:
- Sodium:
- Fiber:
- Total Carbohydrate:
- Cholesterol:

## 509. Rocky Mountain Grill

*Serving: 4 servings. | Prep: 5mins | Cook: 10mins | Ready in:*

### Ingredients

- 2 tablespoons water
- 2 tablespoons red wine vinegar
- 2 tablespoons canola oil
- 1-1/2 teaspoons rubbed sage
- 1 teaspoon grated onion
- 1/2 teaspoon lemon-pepper seasoning
- 1/2 teaspoon Dijon mustard
- 1/8 to 1/4 teaspoon cayenne pepper
- 4 lamb loin chops (1 pound)

### Direction

- Mix the first 8 ingredients in a big plastic resealable bag; take out 3 tbsp. for basting then chill. Put the lamb chop into the rest of the

marinade then turn to coat; seal then chill overnight.
- Drain then get rid of the marinade. On medium-hot heat, grill chops for 4 mins while covering. Flip then use the reserved marinade to baste; grill for 4 mins. Flip then grill for another minute or until it reaches the preferred doneness. A thermometer should register 170 degrees F for well-done, 160 degrees F for medium, and 145 degrees for medium-rare.

## Nutrition Information

- Calories: 233 calories
- Sodium: 86mg sodium
- Fiber: 0 fiber)
- Total Carbohydrate: 0 carbohydrate (0 sugars
- Cholesterol: 78mg cholesterol
- Protein: 24g protein. Diabetic Exchanges: 1 fat
- Total Fat: 15g fat (0 saturated fat)

### 510. Rosemary Leg Of Lamb

*Serving: 10-12 servings. | Prep: 10mins | Cook: 01hours30mins | Ready in:*

## Ingredients

- 4 garlic cloves, minced
- 1 to 2 tablespoons minced fresh rosemary or 1 teaspoon dried rosemary, crushed
- 1 teaspoon salt
- 1/2 teaspoon pepper
- 1 bone-in leg of lamb (7 to 9 pounds), trimmed
- 1 teaspoon cornstarch
- 1/4 cup beef broth

## Direction

- Preheat an oven to 350°. Mix pepper, salt, rosemary and garlic in a small bowl; rub on meat. Put onto rack in the big roasting pan.
- Bake for 1 1/2-2 1/2 hours, uncovered, till meat gets desired doneness; 170° well done, 160° medium and 145° for medium rare on a thermometer. Before slicing, stand for 10 minutes.
- Meanwhile, put loosened brown bits and pan drippings in a small saucepan and skim fat. Mix broth and cornstarch till smooth; whisk into drippings. Boil; mix and cook till thick for 1-2 minutes; serve with lamb.

## Nutrition Information

- Calories: 220 calories
- Total Fat: 8g fat (4g saturated fat)
- Sodium: 268mg sodium
- Fiber: 0 fiber)
- Total Carbohydrate: 1g carbohydrate (0 sugars
- Cholesterol: 119mg cholesterol
- Protein: 33g protein.

### 511. Rosemary Seasoned Lamb

*Serving: 12 servings. | Prep: 10mins | Cook: 01hours45mins | Ready in:*

## Ingredients

- 2 tablespoons chopped fresh rosemary
- 1 teaspoon coarsely ground pepper
- 3/4 teaspoon salt
- 1/2 teaspoon ground mustard
- 1/2 teaspoon dried oregano
- 1/2 teaspoon garlic powder
- 1/4 teaspoon white pepper
- 1/8 teaspoon cayenne pepper
- 1 boneless leg of lamb (about 4 pounds)

## Direction

- Mix seasonings in a spice mill/blender with cover till coarsely ground. Untie leg of lamb; unroll. On both sides of the meat, rub spice blend. Reroll; tie using kitchen string.

- In shallow a roasting pan, put onto a rack; bake without cover for 1 3/4-2 1/4 hours at 350° till meat gets desired doneness (170° for well-done, 160° for medium and 145° for medium-rare on a thermometer). Stand for 10-15 minutes; slice.

## Nutrition Information

- Calories: 181 calories
- Total Carbohydrate: 0 carbohydrate (0 sugars
- Cholesterol: 81mg cholesterol
- Protein: 25g protein. Diabetic Exchanges: 3 lean meat.
- Total Fat: 8g fat (3g saturated fat)
- Sodium: 209mg sodium
- Fiber: 0 fiber)

## 512. Rosemary Rubbed Lamb Chops

*Serving: 4-6 servings. | Prep: 30mins | Cook: 15mins | Ready in:*

## Ingredients

- 2 frenched racks of lamb (1-1/2 pounds each)
- 2 tablespoons olive oil
- 2 tablespoons Dijon mustard
- 4 garlic cloves, minced
- 1 tablespoon minced fresh rosemary
- 1 tablespoon minced fresh marjoram
- 1 teaspoon soy sauce
- 1/2 teaspoon salt
- 1/4 teaspoon pepper

## Direction

- Slice each rack of lamb into individual chops using a sharp knife. Mix the remaining ingredients in a small bowl and then massage onto each side of the chops; transfer onto a rack in a shallow roasting pan. Cover the pan and chill for two hours.

- Bake while uncovered for 14 to 16 minutes at 400° or until the meat reaches the doneness desired (for medium-rare, a thermometer should indicate 145°; well-done, 170°; medium, 160°).

## Nutrition Information

- Calories: 139 calories
- Total Carbohydrate: 2g carbohydrate (0 sugars
- Cholesterol: 33mg cholesterol
- Protein: 10g protein.
- Total Fat: 10g fat (2g saturated fat)
- Sodium: 405mg sodium
- Fiber: 0 fiber)

## 513. Rosemary Skewered Artichoke Chicken

*Serving: 6 servings. | Prep: 20mins | Cook: 20mins | Ready in:*

## Ingredients

- 1/3 cup olive oil
- 2 tablespoons snipped fresh dill
- 1 tablespoon minced fresh oregano
- 2 teaspoons grated lemon peel
- 2 garlic cloves, minced
- 1/2 teaspoon salt
- 1/4 teaspoon pepper
- 1-1/2 pounds boneless skinless chicken breasts, cut into 1-inch cubes
- 6 fresh rosemary stems (18 inches)
- 1 can (14 ounces) water-packed artichoke hearts, rinsed, drained and halved
- 2 medium yellow summer squash, cut into 1-inch slices
- 6 cherry tomatoes

## Direction

- Mix garlic, pepper, salt, lemon peel, oil, oregano, and dill in a large resealable plastic

bag. Add the chicken. Seal the bag and flip it to coat. Store it inside the refrigerator for at least 2 hours.
- Peel the bark from the bottom half of each of the rosemary stem using a vegetable peeler. Make a point on each end and soak it in water until ready to use.
- Drain the chicken, discarding the marinade. Thread the chicken, artichokes, squash, and tomatoes alternately on the soaked rosemary steams. Make sure that the position of the leaf parts of the rosemary stems is placed outside the grill cover.
- Moisten a paper towel with cooking oil. Use the long-handled tongs to wipe the towel into the grill rack. Grill the chicken while covered over medium heat. You can also cook them on a broiler for 10-15 minutes per side, positioning them 4-inches away from the heat source until the vegetables are tender and the chicken is no longer pink.

## Nutrition Information

- Calories: 215 calories
- Cholesterol: 63mg cholesterol
- Protein: 25g protein. Diabetic Exchanges: 3 lean meat
- Total Fat: 9g fat (2g saturated fat)
- Sodium: 321mg sodium
- Fiber: 1g fiber)
- Total Carbohydrate: 8g carbohydrate (2g sugars

### 514. Rosemary Thyme Lamb Chops

*Serving: 4 servings. | Prep: 15mins | Cook: 15mins | Ready in:*

## Ingredients

- 8 lamb loin chops (3 ounces each)
- 1/2 teaspoon pepper
- 1/4 teaspoon salt
- 3 tablespoons Dijon mustard
- 1 tablespoon minced fresh rosemary
- 1 tablespoon minced fresh thyme
- 3 garlic cloves, minced

## Direction

- Season lamb chops with salt and pepper. Combine in a small bowl the garlic, thyme, rosemary and mustard.
- Place chops on the grill and cook on a greased rack over medium heat for six minutes, covered. Flip; spread the herb mixture over lamb. Cook for 6-8 minutes or until meat achieves doneness desired (a thermometer should read 135°F for medium rare; 140°F for medium; and 145°F for medium well).

## Nutrition Information

- Calories: 231 calories
- Sodium: 493mg sodium
- Fiber: 0 fiber)
- Total Carbohydrate: 3g carbohydrate (0 sugars
- Cholesterol: 97mg cholesterol
- Protein: 32g protein. Diabetic Exchanges: 4 lean meat.
- Total Fat: 9g fat (4g saturated fat)

### 515. Rubbed Sage Lamb Chops

*Serving: 2 servings. | Prep: 10mins | Cook: 10mins | Ready in:*

## Ingredients

- 2 tablespoons water
- 2 tablespoons red wine vinegar
- 2 tablespoons canola oil
- 1-1/2 teaspoons rubbed sage
- 1 teaspoon grated onion
- 1/2 teaspoon lemon-pepper seasoning

- 1/2 teaspoon Dijon mustard
- 1/8 to 1/4 teaspoon cayenne pepper
- 4 bone-in lamb loin chops (1 inch thick and 4 ounces each)

## Direction

- Mix seasonings, oil, vinegar and water together in a small bowl. Pour a quarter cup into a big resealable plastic bag; put in the lamb. Enclose bag and coat by flipping; chill in the fridge overnight. Put on a cover and chill the rest of the marinade in the fridge for basting.
- Let drain and put away the marinade. With cooking oil, dampen one paper towel and coat grill rack lightly using tongs with long handle. Grill chops with a cover over moderate heat or broil for 4 minutes per side 4-inch away from the heat, basting from time to time with reserved marinade.
- Grill for an additional of 1 to 2 minutes or until meat achieves preferred doneness (a thermometer must register 145° for medium-rare, 160° for medium and 170° for well-done).

## Nutrition Information

- Calories: 305 calories
- Total Carbohydrate: 1g carbohydrate (0 sugars
- Cholesterol: 90mg cholesterol
- Protein: 29g protein.
- Total Fat: 20g fat (4g saturated fat)
- Sodium: 189mg sodium
- Fiber: 0 fiber)

## 516. Rustic Phyllo Vegetable Pie

*Serving: 6 servings. | Prep: 30mins | Cook: 50mins | Ready in:*

## Ingredients

- 1 large egg, lightly beaten
- 2 cups cooked long grain rice
- 1 cup 1% cottage cheese
- 1 cup shredded part-skim mozzarella cheese, divided
- 1 tablespoon lemon juice
- 1 teaspoon grated lemon peel
- 1 medium onion, chopped
- 4 garlic cloves, minced
- 1 tablespoon olive oil
- 2 packages (10 ounces each) fresh spinach, torn
- 1/2 cup golden raisins
- 1/4 teaspoon ground cinnamon
- 1/8 teaspoon salt
- 12 sheets phyllo dough (14 inches x 9 inches)
- Butter-flavored cooking spray
- 1-1/2 cups meatless spaghetti sauce

## Direction

- Mix lemon juice and peel, 1/2 cup mozzarella, cottage cheese, rice and the egg in a large bowl; put aside. Sauté garlic and onion in oil in a Dutch oven until tender. Add salt, cinnamon, raisins and spinach. Cook while stirring for about 3 minutes or until spinach is wilted. Take away from the heat; stir in remaining mozzarella.
- With butter-flavored spray, spritz one sheet of phyllo dough. Use cooking spray to spray a 9-in. deep-dish pie plate and put the dough in the pie plate, with short sides of dough hanging over edges. (Keep covering the remaining phyllo with plastic wrap and a damp towel so that it will not dry out.). Transfer the remaining phyllo sheets to the pie plate in a crisscross fashion like the spokes of a wheel, and spritz between layers with butter-flavored spray. Fill 1/2 of the rice mixture into crust; top with 1/2 spinach mixture and 1/2 of spaghetti sauce. Repeat layers.
- Fold the dough edges gently over filling without covering the pie's center. Spritz with butter-flavored spray. Use foil to loosely cover, bake for 45 minutes at 350°. Bake without a cover until filling reaches 160°, about 5-10

more minute. Allow to sit for 10 minutes before cutting.

## Nutrition Information

- Calories: 341 calories
- Fiber: 5g fiber)
- Total Carbohydrate: 51g carbohydrate (17g sugars
- Cholesterol: 48mg cholesterol
- Protein: 18g protein.
- Total Fat: 8g fat (3g saturated fat)
- Sodium: 745mg sodium

### 517. Salmon Couscous Supper

*Serving: 2 servings. | Prep: 10mins | Cook: 15mins | Ready in:*

## Ingredients

- 1/2 cup fresh broccoli florets
- 1/2 cup sliced fresh carrot
- 1/2 cup sliced fresh mushrooms
- 2 garlic cloves, minced
- 10 ounces fully cooked salmon, cut into chunks
- 1/2 cup cooked couscous
- 3 tablespoons reduced-sodium soy sauce

## Direction

- In a steamer basket, add broccoli, then set a small saucepan over 1 inch of water. Bring water to a boil, then cover and steam until broccoli is tender yet still crisp, 6 to 8 minutes.
- Sauté garlic and mushrooms in a big skillet sprayed with cooking spray for 2 minutes. Put in carrot and broccoli, then sauté for 2 more minutes. Stir in soy sauce, couscous and salmon, then heat through.

## Nutrition Information

- Calories: 345 calories
- Total Carbohydrate: 16g carbohydrate (3g sugars
- Cholesterol: 84mg cholesterol
- Protein: 33g protein.
- Total Fat: 16g fat (3g saturated fat)
- Sodium: 1010mg sodium
- Fiber: 2g fiber)

### 518. Salmon Spirals With Cucumber Sauce

*Serving: 4 skewers (1-1/3 cups sauce). | Prep: 20mins | Cook: 10mins | Ready in:*

## Ingredients

- 1 salmon fillet (1 pound)
- 8 fresh dill sprigs
- 1/4 cup lime juice
- 1 tablespoon olive oil
- 2 teaspoons Dijon mustard
- SAUCE:
- 1 cup (8 ounces) fat-free plain yogurt
- 1/4 cup fat-free mayonnaise
- 2 tablespoons finely chopped seeded peeled cucumber
- 2 tablespoons snipped fresh dill
- 1 tablespoon lemon juice

## Direction

- Remove fillet skin and get rid of the skin. Chop the fillet lengthwise into 4 strips. Put 2 dill sprigs onto each strip and then roll up. Thread the salmon over 4 metal or soaked wooden skewers.
- Mix the mustard, oil, and lime juice in a large plastic bag that is sealable. Place in salmon, seal the bag and flip to coat. Chill for 30 minutes while turning often.
- Drain the fish and get rid of the marinade. Use cooking oil to moisten a paper towel with long-handled tongs and then coat the grill rack lightly. Grill the salmon while covered on top

- of high heat or broil the fish for 4 to 5 minutes per side at 3-4 in. away from the heat source or until the fish easily flakes with a fork.
- In the meantime, mix the sauce ingredients in a small bowl. Then serve together with salmon.

## Nutrition Information

- Calories: 253 calories
- Protein: 25g protein.
- Total Fat: 13g fat (3g saturated fat)
- Sodium: 233mg sodium
- Fiber: 0 fiber)
- Total Carbohydrate: 8g carbohydrate (5g sugars
- Cholesterol: 70mg cholesterol

### 519. Salmon And Asparagus In Phyllo

*Serving: 4 servings. | Prep: 30mins | Cook: 15mins | Ready in:*

## Ingredients

- 4 cups water
- 12 asparagus spears, trimmed and halved widthwise
- 4 ounces reduced-fat cream cheese
- 2 tablespoons egg substitute
- 1 tablespoon finely chopped onion
- 1 teaspoon dried tarragon
- 1/4 teaspoon salt
- 1/4 teaspoon pepper
- 8 sheets phyllo dough (14 inches x 9 inches)
- 4 salmon fillets (4 ounces each)

## Direction

- Boil water in a big saucepan. Put in boiling water and cook asparagus for 3 minutes until tender-crisp; drain then rinse asparagus in cold water. Pat it dry then set aside.
- Mix pepper, cream cheese, salt, egg substitute, tarragon, and onion; set aside. On a work surface, put one phyllo sheet with the short side facing the bottom; coat with cooking spray. Repeat with another phyllo sheet. Use plastic wrap and a moist towel to cover the remaining phyllo to avoid drying.
- Slather cream cheese mixture in two rounded tablespoons on the lower third of the rectangle approximately the size of the fillet. Add a salmon fillet and 6 asparagus halves on top; fold the sides and lower edge over the fillet. Roll to surround the salmon. If needed, trim the phyllo ends. Coat with cooking spray.
- Arrange on an ungreased baking sheet with the seam-side down; repeat with the rest of the ingredients. Bake for 15-20 minutes in 400 degrees oven until golden brown.

## Nutrition Information

- Calories: 355 calories
- Total Fat: 19g fat (7g saturated fat)
- Sodium: 445mg sodium
- Fiber: 1g fiber)
- Total Carbohydrate: 16g carbohydrate (3g sugars
- Cholesterol: 87mg cholesterol
- Protein: 30g protein. Diabetic Exchanges: 3 lean meat

### 520. Salmon With Cucumber Dill Sauce

*Serving: 4 servings. | Prep: 20mins | Cook: 15mins | Ready in:*

## Ingredients

- 1/4 cup lemon juice
- 2 tablespoons canola oil
- 1 teaspoon dill weed
- 1 teaspoon grated lemon peel
- 1 garlic clove, minced

- 4 salmon fillets (4 ounces each)
- CUCUMBER SAUCE:
- 2/3 cup finely chopped seeded peeled cucumber
- 1/3 cup reduced-fat sour cream
- 1 tablespoon chopped green onion
- 1-1/2 teaspoons reduced-fat mayonnaise
- 1/2 teaspoon lemon juice
- 1/8 teaspoon salt
- 1/8 teaspoon white pepper
- 1/8 teaspoon Worcestershire sauce

## Direction

- Combine first five ingredients in a big plastic resealable bag. Add the salmon, seal the bag and flip to completely coat. Store in the refrigerator for 30 minutes, occasionally turning. Meanwhile, combine the ingredients for the cucumber sauce in a small bowl. Cover the bowl and keep refrigerated until it's time to serve.
- Take salmon from the fridge and drain marinade. Grease grill rack with tongs and a paper towel saturated with cooking oil. Lay salmon on the rack skin down.
- Cover and grill on medium heat or broil fish 4 inches from heat until with fork the fish easily flakes, 12 to 15 minutes. Serve fish with the cucumber sauce.

## Nutrition Information

- Calories: 261 calories
- Total Carbohydrate: 3g carbohydrate (2g sugars
- Cholesterol: 74mg cholesterol
- Protein: 24g protein. Diabetic Exchanges: 3 meat
- Total Fat: 16g fat (4g saturated fat)
- Sodium: 172mg sodium
- Fiber: 0 fiber)

## 521. Sausage & Feta Stuffed Tomatoes

*Serving: 4 servings. | Prep: 15mins | Cook: 10mins | Ready in:*

### Ingredients

- 3 Italian turkey sausage links (4 ounces each), casings removed
- 1 cup (4 ounces) crumbled feta cheese, divided
- 8 plum tomatoes
- 1/4 teaspoon salt
- 1/4 teaspoon pepper
- 3 tablespoons balsamic vinegar
- Minced fresh parsley

### Direction

- Set the oven at 350° and start preheating. In a large skillet over medium heat, cook sausage, breaking into crumbles, until not pink anymore, 4-6 minutes. Move to a small bowl; mix in 1/2 cup of cheese.
- Cut tomatoes lengthwise in half. Scoop out pulp but leave a 1/2-in. shell; remove and discard pulp. Sprinkle pepper and salt over the tomatoes; arrange on an ungreased 13x9-in. baking dish. Transfer the sausage mixture to the tomato shells with a spoon; drizzle with vinegar. Sprinkle the remaining cheese over top.
- Bake without a cover till heated through, 10-12 minutes. Sprinkle parsley over top.

### Nutrition Information

- Calories: 200 calories
- Sodium: 777mg sodium
- Fiber: 3g fiber)
- Total Carbohydrate: 12g carbohydrate (8g sugars
- Cholesterol: 46mg cholesterol
- Protein: 16g protein. Diabetic Exchanges: 2 medium-fat meat
- Total Fat: 10g fat (4g saturated fat)

## 522. Sausage Florentine Potpie

*Serving: 6 servings. | Prep: 30mins | Cook: 25mins | Ready in:*

### Ingredients

- 1 pound Johnsonville® Ground Mild Italian sausage
- 2-1/2 cups sliced fresh mushrooms
- 1 medium red onion, chopped
- 3 garlic cloves, minced
- 1 can (10-3/4 ounces) reduced-fat reduced-sodium condensed cream of mushroom soup, undiluted
- 1 package (10 ounces) frozen chopped spinach, thawed and squeezed dry
- 1 cup half-and-half cream
- 1 cup shredded part-skim mozzarella cheese
- 1/2 cup shredded Parmesan cheese
- TOPPING:
- 5 sheets phyllo dough (14 inches x 9 inches)
- 2 tablespoons butter, melted
- 1 egg
- 1 tablespoon water

### Direction

- Cook garlic, onion, mushrooms and sausage in a big skillet on medium heat till it is not pink anymore; drain. Add cheeses, cream, spinach and soup; mix and cook till cheese melts.
- Put into an oiled 11x7-in. baking dish. Put a phyllo sheet over; brush with some butter. Repeat using reserved butter and phyllo dough; crimp dough edges.
- Whisk water and egg; brush over top. Bake without cover till golden brown for 25-30 minutes at 350°. Let it stand for 10 minutes; serve.

### Nutrition Information

- Calories: 610 calories
- Total Fat: 39g fat (17g saturated fat)
- Sodium: 1201mg sodium
- Fiber: 4g fiber)
- Total Carbohydrate: 38g carbohydrate (6g sugars
- Cholesterol: 114mg cholesterol
- Protein: 27g protein.

## 523. Sausage Marinara Over Pasta

*Serving: 6 servings. | Prep: 15mins | Cook: 25mins | Ready in:*

### Ingredients

- 1 pound turkey Italian sausage links
- 4 cups uncooked spiral pasta
- 1/2 pound fresh mushrooms, sliced
- 1 large onion, chopped
- 1 medium sweet red pepper, chopped
- 1 medium green pepper, chopped
- 3 large garlic cloves, minced
- 1 tablespoon olive oil
- 1 jar (26 ounces) meatless spaghetti sauce
- 1 tablespoon dried basil
- 1 tablespoon dried oregano
- 1 teaspoon pepper
- 1/3 cup crumbled feta cheese

### Direction

- Brown sausage for 12 to 14 minutes over medium heat in a large nonstick skillet greased with cooking spray, turning 2 times while cooking. Allow to cool; cut sausage into slices and put to one side. Cook pasta as directed on the package.
- Sauté garlic, peppers, onion, and mushrooms in oil the same skillet until tender. Mix in reserved sausage, pepper, oregano, basil, and spaghetti sauce. Bring to a boil. Lower the heat; simmer without covering, stirring occasionally, for 5 minutes. Strain the pasta. Ladle sauce over pasta to serve. Sprinkle top with feta cheese.

### Nutrition Information

- Calories: 372 calories
- Protein: 22g protein. Diabetic Exchanges: 2-1/2 starch
- Total Fat: 12g fat (4g saturated fat)
- Sodium: 1mg sodium
- Fiber: 6g fiber)
- Total Carbohydrate: 45g carbohydrate (0 sugars
- Cholesterol: 48mg cholesterol

## 524. Savory Marinated Flank Steak

*Serving: 6 servings. | Prep: 10mins | Cook: 15mins | Ready in:*

### Ingredients

- 3 tablespoons canola oil
- 2 tablespoons lemon juice
- 2 tablespoons Worcestershire sauce
- 1 tablespoon dried minced garlic
- 1 tablespoon Greek seasoning
- 1 tablespoon brown sugar
- 1 teaspoon onion powder
- 1 beef flank steak (1-1/2 pounds)

### Direction

- Mix all the initial 7 ingredients together in a big Ziplock plastic bag then put in the steak. Seal the Ziplock bag and turn to coat the steak with the marinade then keep it in the fridge for 6 hours or throughout the night.
- Drain the marinated steak and throw away the marinade mixture. Use tongs to lightly rub an oiled paper towel on the grill rack. Put the marinated steak on a grill over medium heat then cover and grill or put the steak in a broiler and let it broil 4 inches away from the heat for 6 to 8 minutes on every side until the preferred meat doneness is achieved (a thermometer inserted on the meat should indicate 170°F for well-done, 160°F for medium and 145°F for medium-rare).
- Cut the steak into thin slices perpendicular to the grain then serve.

### Nutrition Information

- Calories: 196 calories
- Protein: 22g protein. Diabetic Exchanges: 3 lean meat
- Total Fat: 11g fat (4g saturated fat)
- Sodium: 269mg sodium
- Fiber: 0 fiber)
- Total Carbohydrate: 2g carbohydrate (1g sugars
- Cholesterol: 54mg cholesterol

## 525. Sea Bass With Shrimp And Tomatoes

*Serving: 2 servings. | Prep: 5mins | Cook: 45mins | Ready in:*

### Ingredients

- 2 sea bass or halibut steaks (8 to 10 ounces each)
- 6 to 8 large uncooked shrimp, peeled and deveined
- 1/2 small red or sweet onion, thinly sliced
- 1 can (14-1/2 ounces) Italian-style stewed tomatoes
- 1 package (4 ounces) crumbled feta cheese

### Direction

- Arrange fish in an oiled 8x8-inch baking dish. Top with feta cheese, tomatoes, onion, and shrimp. Bake without covering for 45 to 50 minutes at 325° until fish is easily flaked using a fork.

## Nutrition Information

- Calories: 348 calories
- Sodium: 1402mg sodium
- Fiber: 6g fiber)
- Total Carbohydrate: 17g carbohydrate (11g sugars
- Cholesterol: 158mg cholesterol
- Protein: 42g protein.
- Total Fat: 12g fat (7g saturated fat)

## 526. Shrimp Orzo With Feta

*Serving: 4 servings. | Prep: 10mins | Cook: 15mins | Ready in:*

### Ingredients

- 1-1/4 cups uncooked whole wheat orzo pasta
- 2 tablespoons olive oil
- 2 garlic cloves, minced
- 2 medium tomatoes, chopped
- 2 tablespoons lemon juice
- 1-1/4 pounds uncooked shrimp (26-30 per pound), peeled and deveined
- 2 tablespoons minced fresh cilantro
- 1/4 teaspoon pepper
- 1/2 cup crumbled feta cheese

### Direction

- Cook orzo as directed on the package. In the meantime, in a large skillet over medium heat, heat oil. Add garlic; cook while stirring for a minute. Add lemon juice and tomatoes. Bring to a boil. Stir in shrimp. Lower the heat; simmer without a cover for 4-5 minutes or until shrimp turns pink.
- Drain orzo. Add pepper, cilantro and orzo to shrimp mixture; heat through. Top with feta cheese.

## Nutrition Information

- Calories: 406 calories
- Sodium: 307mg sodium
- Fiber: 9g fiber)
- Total Carbohydrate: 40g carbohydrate (2g sugars
- Cholesterol: 180mg cholesterol
- Protein: 33g protein. Diabetic Exchanges: 4 lean meat
- Total Fat: 12g fat (3g saturated fat)

## 527. Shrimp Scampi With Lemon Couscous

*Serving: 6 servings. | Prep: 10mins | Cook: 10mins | Ready in:*

### Ingredients

- 1 cup chicken broth
- 3 tablespoons lemon juice, divided
- 1 cup uncooked couscous
- 5 tablespoons butter, divided
- 3 tablespoons minced fresh parsley, divided
- 1 teaspoon grated lemon peel
- 2 tablespoons olive oil
- 1-1/2 teaspoons minced garlic
- 2 pounds cooked jumbo shrimp, peeled and deveined
- 1/3 cup white wine or additional chicken broth
- 1/4 teaspoon salt
- 1/8 teaspoon pepper
- 1/4 cup shredded Asiago cheese

### Direction

- Bring 1 tbsp. of lemon juice and broth in a small saucepan to a boil. Stir in lemon peel, 1 tbsp. of parsley, 1 tbsp. of butter and couscous. Cover and take away from the heat, then allow to stand until liquid is absorbed, about 5 minutes.
- At the same time, stir leftover butter and oil in a big skillet on moderately high heat until butter is melted. Put in garlic, then cook and stir until softened. Put in shrimp and cook

until shrimp turn pink, about 1 minute per side.
- Put in leftover lemon juice, pepper, salt and wine, then cook until heated through, about 2 to 3 more minutes. Serve together with couscous. Sprinkle leftover parsley and cheese on top.

## Nutrition Information

- Calories: 379 calories
- Total Carbohydrate: 25g carbohydrate (1g sugars
- Cholesterol: 254mg cholesterol
- Protein: 30g protein.
- Total Fat: 17g fat (8g saturated fat)
- Sodium: 624mg sodium
- Fiber: 1g fiber)

## 528. Shrimp Stew

*Serving: 2 servings. | Prep: 5mins | Cook: 25mins | Ready in:*

## Ingredients

- 1 small onion, chopped
- 2 garlic cloves, minced
- 1-1/2 teaspoons olive oil
- 1-1/2 cups diced fresh tomatoes
- 1/2 cup tomato sauce
- 4-1/2 teaspoons minced fresh dill or 1 teaspoon dill weed
- 1 teaspoon Dijon mustard
- 1/2 teaspoon honey
- 1/4 teaspoon salt
- 1/2 pound cooked medium shrimp, peeled and deveined
- 1/2 cup crumbled feta cheese
- 1/2 cup minced fresh parsley

## Direction

- Sauté garlic and onion with oil in a big saucepan for 5 minutes. Stir in salt, honey, mustard, dill, tomato sauce, and tomatoes, then set to boil. Lower the heat and simmer while uncovered for 10 minutes. Add in the parsley, cheese, and shrimp, then simmer for another 5 minutes.

## Nutrition Information

- Calories: 296 calories
- Sodium: 1098mg sodium
- Fiber: 4g fiber)
- Total Carbohydrate: 18g carbohydrate (9g sugars
- Cholesterol: 187mg cholesterol
- Protein: 31g protein.
- Total Fat: 11g fat (4g saturated fat)

## 529. Shrimp And Feta Linguine

*Serving: 4 servings. | Prep: 15mins | Cook: 15mins | Ready in:*

## Ingredients

- 6 ounces uncooked linguine
- 1 pound uncooked medium shrimp, peeled and deveined
- 1/2 cup chopped onion
- 1 garlic clove, minced
- 1 tablespoon olive oil
- 3 cups sliced plum tomatoes
- 1/2 cup white wine or reduced-sodium chicken broth
- 1 tablespoon tomato paste
- 1 teaspoon dried oregano
- 1/2 teaspoon salt
- 1/4 teaspoon crushed red pepper flakes
- 1/4 cup crumbled feta cheese
- 2 tablespoons minced fresh parsley

## Direction

- Following package directions to cook linguine. At the same time, sauté garlic, onion and shrimp with oil in a big nonstick skillet until shrimp are pink, about 3 to 5 minutes.
- Put in pepper flakes, salt, oregano, tomato paste, broth or wine and tomatoes, then bring the mixture to a boil. Lower heat and simmer without a cover about 10 minutes. Drain linguine and put shrimp mixture on top. Sprinkle over with parsley and feta cheese.

## Nutrition Information

- Calories: 348 calories
- Total Fat: 7g fat (2g saturated fat)
- Sodium: 576mg sodium
- Fiber: 4g fiber)
- Total Carbohydrate: 41g carbohydrate (7g sugars
- Cholesterol: 172mg cholesterol
- Protein: 27g protein. Diabetic Exchanges: 3 lean meat

## 530. Simple Mediterranean Chicken

*Serving: 4-6 servings. | Prep: 5mins | Cook: 50mins | Ready in:*

## Ingredients

- 1 broiler/fryer chicken (3-1/2 to 4 pounds), cut up
- 3 tablespoons vegetable oil, divided
- 3 medium onions, thinly sliced
- 3 garlic cloves, minced
- 1/4 cup minced fresh parsley
- 1 tablespoon minced fresh tarragon or 1 teaspoon dried tarragon
- 1 teaspoon salt
- 1/2 teaspoon pepper
- 1 cup chopped pimiento-stuffed olives
- Hot cooked rice or noodles

## Direction

- On medium heat, brown chicken in a big pan with 2 tbsp. oil. Take out the chicken then set aside. Pour the rest of the oil in the skillet; sauté garlic and onions until tender. Mix in pepper, parsley, salt, and tarragon, toss well.
- Place the chicken back in the skillet then coat in onion mixture. Use olives to sprinkle. Lower the heat; let it simmer for 40-45mins while covering or until the juices are clear and the chicken is tender. Serve chicken on top of noodles or rice.

## Nutrition Information

- Calories: 425 calories
- Cholesterol: 102mg cholesterol
- Protein: 34g protein.
- Total Fat: 28g fat (5g saturated fat)
- Sodium: 965mg sodium
- Fiber: 2g fiber)
- Total Carbohydrate: 10g carbohydrate (5g sugars

## 531. Sirloin Squash Shish Kabobs

*Serving: 4 servings. | Prep: 10mins | Cook: 10mins | Ready in:*

## Ingredients

- 1 cup packed brown sugar
- 1 cup soy sauce
- 1 teaspoon each garlic powder, ground mustard and ground ginger
- 1 pound beef top sirloin steak, cut into 1-inch pieces
- 1 medium zucchini, cut into 1/4-inch slices
- 1 medium yellow summer squash, cut into 1/4-inch slices
- 1 medium sweet red pepper, cut into 1-inch pieces

- 1 medium red onion, cut into eight wedges, optional

## Direction

- Mix together the soy sauce, brown sugar, mustard, garlic powder, and ginger in a small bowl. Put the beef in a large re-sealable plastic bag and pour in a cup of the marinade. Close the bag and turn several times to coat. Pour in the remaining marinade in another re-sealable plastic bag with the yellow squash, zucchini, onion (if desired), and red pepper. Seal the bag and toss to coat. Keep both bags in the fridge for at least 4 hours, turning occasionally to let marinade cover the solids from all sides. Drain both bags, disposing of the marinade. Alternately thread beef and vegetables on eight metal or water-soaked wooden skewers. Cook in a covered grill over medium heat, or broil 4-6 in. from the heat, for 10 minutes or until meat is done to liking. Turn the skewers from time to time while cooking.

## Nutrition Information

- Calories:
- Protein:
- Total Fat:
- Sodium:
- Fiber:
- Total Carbohydrate:
- Cholesterol:

### 532. Skewered Lamb With Blackberry Balsamic Glaze

*Serving: 6 servings. | Prep: 10mins | Cook: 10mins | Ready in:*

## Ingredients

- 1/2 cup seedless blackberry spreadable fruit
- 1/3 cup balsamic vinegar
- 1 tablespoon minced fresh rosemary or 1 teaspoon dried rosemary, crushed
- 1 tablespoon Dijon mustard
- 1-1/2 pounds lean boneless lamb, cut into 1-inch cubes
- 1/4 teaspoon salt

## Direction

- Mix together vinegar, the spreadable fruit, mustard, and rosemary. Take 2/3 cup of this marinade and pour into a large re-sealable plastic bag with the lamb. Zip the bag and turn several times to coat; let marinate in the fridge for at least an hour. Store leftover marinade in a covered container in the refrigerator. Drain the lamb and discard its marinade. Take six metal or pre-soaked wooden skewers and cue the lamb pieces. Arrange the kabobs on greased grill rack, and cook, covered, over medium heat or broil 4 in. from the heat for 10-12 minutes or until lamb is done to liking - for medium-rare, a meat thermometer should read 145 degrees; medium at 160 degrees; well-done at 170 degrees. Turn once but baste often with the reserved marinade. Salt the kabobs before serving.

## Nutrition Information

- Calories: 255 calories
- Total Fat: 9g fat (4g saturated fat)
- Sodium: 264mg sodium
- Fiber: 0 fiber)
- Total Carbohydrate: 9g carbohydrate (7g sugars
- Cholesterol: 103mg cholesterol
- Protein: 32g protein. Diabetic Exchanges: 5 lean meat

### 533. Skillet Lamb Chops

*Serving: 2 servings. | Prep: 5mins | Cook: 40mins | Ready in:*

### Ingredients

- 2 lamb shoulder blade chops (8 ounces each)
- 2 tablespoons canola oil
- 1/2 cup warm water
- 1 teaspoon lemon juice
- 1 teaspoon dried minced onion
- 1/2 teaspoon dried oregano
- 1/4 teaspoon salt
- 1/8 teaspoon pepper

### Direction

- Brown the lamb chops in oil in a big skillet. Add leftover ingredients; boil. Lower heat; cover. Simmer till meat attains the desired doneness (for well-done 170° on a thermometer, 160° for medium and 145° for medium rare) for 30-35 minutes.

### Nutrition Information

- Calories: 288 calories
- Total Carbohydrate: 1g carbohydrate (0 sugars
- Cholesterol: 56mg cholesterol
- Protein: 14g protein.
- Total Fat: 25g fat (7g saturated fat)
- Sodium: 332mg sodium
- Fiber: 0 fiber)

## 534. Slow Cook Lamb Chops

*Serving: 4 servings. | Prep: 10mins | Cook: 05hours30mins | Ready in:*

### Ingredients

- 4 bacon strips
- 4 lamb shoulder blade chops, trimmed
- 2-1/4 cups thinly sliced peeled potatoes
- 1 cup thinly sliced carrots
- 1/2 teaspoon dried rosemary, crushed
- 1/4 teaspoon garlic powder
- 1/4 teaspoon salt
- 1/4 teaspoon pepper
- 1/4 cup chopped onion
- 2 garlic cloves, minced
- 1 can (10-3/4 ounces) condensed cream of mushroom soup, undiluted
- 1/3 cup 2% milk
- 1 jar (4-1/2 ounces) sliced mushrooms, drained

### Direction

- Bind the lamb chops in bacon then secure using toothpicks; put in a 3-quart slow cooker. Cook for 1 1/2 hours on High with cover.
- Take the chops out then remove the bacon and toothpicks; drain the liquid in the cooker. Put carrot and potatoes then place the lamb chops on top. Sprinkle garlic, rosemary, onion, garlic powder, pepper, and salt.
- Mix milk and soup in a small bowl; put in mushrooms. Pour the mixture on top of the chops; cover. Cook for 4-6 hours on Low until the veggies and meat are tender.

### Nutrition Information

- Calories:
- Sodium:
- Fiber:
- Total Carbohydrate:
- Cholesterol:
- Protein:
- Total Fat:

## 535. Slow Cooked Chicken Marbella

*Serving: 6 servings. | Prep: 30mins | Cook: 04hours00mins | Ready in:*

### Ingredients

- 1 cup pitted green olives, divided
- 1 cup pitted dried plums, divided
- 2 tablespoons dried oregano

- 2 tablespoons brown sugar
- 2 tablespoons capers, drained
- 2 tablespoons olive oil
- 4 garlic cloves, minced
- 1/2 teaspoon salt
- 1/2 teaspoon pepper
- 6 bone-in chicken thighs (about 2 pounds), skin removed
- 1/4 cup reduced-sodium chicken broth
- 1 tablespoon minced fresh parsley
- 1 tablespoon white wine
- 1 tablespoon lemon juice
- Hot cooked couscous

## Direction

- Put the pepper, salt, garlic, oil, capers, brown sugar, oregano, half a cup of dried plums and half a cup of olives into a food processor; blend until smooth. Move mixture to a 4-quart slow cooker. Put the chicken into the slow cooker. Cover and cook for 4 to 5 hours on low until chicken is tender.
- Chop dried plums and the rest of olives. Take chicken out of the slow cooker and keep warm. Mix the rest of plums and olives, the lemon juice, wine, parsley and chicken broth into the olive mixture. Serve along with couscous and chicken.

## Nutrition Information

- Calories: 372 calories
- Total Carbohydrate: 26g carbohydrate (13g sugars
- Cholesterol: 87mg cholesterol
- Protein: 25g protein.
- Total Fat: 18g fat (3g saturated fat)
- Sodium: 845mg sodium
- Fiber: 2g fiber)

### 536. Slow Cooked Lamb Chops

*Serving: 4 servings. | Prep: 10mins | Cook: 04hours00mins | Ready in:*

## Ingredients

- 1 medium onion, sliced
- 1 teaspoon dried oregano
- 1/2 teaspoon dried thyme
- 1/2 teaspoon garlic powder
- 1/4 teaspoon salt
- 1/8 teaspoon pepper
- 8 lamb loin chops (about 1-3/4 pounds)
- 2 garlic cloves, minced

## Direction

- Put onion into a 3-quart slow cooker. Mix pepper, salt, garlic powder, thyme, and oregano together; rub lamb chops with the spice mixture. Arrange lamb chops over onion. Place garlic atop chops. Cook, covered, for 4 to 6 hours on low setting until meat is tender.

## Nutrition Information

- Calories: 201 calories
- Total Carbohydrate: 5g carbohydrate (2g sugars
- Cholesterol: 79mg cholesterol
- Protein: 26g protein.
- Total Fat: 8g fat (3g saturated fat)
- Sodium: 219mg sodium
- Fiber: 1g fiber)

### 537. Slow Cooked Lemon Chicken

*Serving: 6 servings. | Prep: 20mins | Cook: 05hours15mins | Ready in:*

## Ingredients

- 6 bone-in chicken breast halves (12 ounces each), skin removed
- 1 teaspoon dried oregano
- 1/2 teaspoon seasoned salt
- 1/4 teaspoon pepper
- 2 tablespoons butter
- 1/4 cup water
- 3 tablespoons lemon juice
- 2 garlic cloves, minced
- 1 teaspoon chicken bouillon granules
- 2 teaspoons minced fresh parsley
- Hot cooked rice

### Direction

- Remove any excess water from chicken by patting with paper towels. After combining, rub oregano, pepper, and seasoned salt on chicken. Brown chicken in butter in a frying pan on medium heat. Place in a 5-qt. slow cooker. In the frying pan, add bouillon, water, garlic, and lemon juice. Bring mixture to a boil mixing to remove browned bits. Pour water mixture over chicken, cover, and cook for 5-6 hours on low. Once cooked, use cooking juices to baste chicken. Throw in parsley, replace cover and cook until the meat juices are clear about 15-30 minutes. Tastes best with rice. (Cooking juices can also be thickened).

### Nutrition Information

- Calories: 336 calories
- Sodium: 431mg sodium
- Fiber: 0 fiber)
- Total Carbohydrate: 1g carbohydrate (0 sugars
- Cholesterol: 164mg cholesterol
- Protein: 56g protein.
- Total Fat: 10g fat (4g saturated fat)

## 538. Slow Cooked Moroccan Chicken

*Serving: 4 servings. | Prep: 20mins | Cook: 06hours00mins | Ready in:*

### Ingredients

- 4 medium carrots, sliced
- 2 large onions, halved and sliced
- 1 broiler/fryer chicken (3 to 4 pounds), cut up, skin removed
- 1/2 teaspoon salt
- 1/2 cup chopped dried apricots
- 1/2 cup raisins
- 1 can (14-1/2 ounces) reduced-sodium chicken broth
- 1/4 cup tomato paste
- 2 tablespoons all-purpose flour
- 2 tablespoons lemon juice
- 2 garlic cloves, minced
- 1-1/2 teaspoons ground ginger
- 1-1/2 teaspoons ground cumin
- 1 teaspoon ground cinnamon
- 3/4 teaspoon pepper
- Hot cooked couscous

### Direction

- Add onions and carrots to a greased 5-quart slow cooker. Sprinkle salt over the chicken and put into the slow cooker. Sprinkle raisins and apricots on top. Stir together the seasonings, garlic, lemon juice, flour, tomato paste and broth until combined, then pour into the slow cooker.
- Cook while covering for 6-7 hours on low until the chicken becomes soft. Serve with couscous.

### Nutrition Information

- Calories: 435 calories
- Cholesterol: 110mg cholesterol
- Protein: 42g protein.
- Total Fat: 9g fat (3g saturated fat)
- Sodium: 755mg sodium
- Fiber: 6g fiber)

- Total Carbohydrate: 47g carbohydrate (27g sugars

### 539. Southwestern Lamb Chops

*Serving: 4 servings. | Prep: 15mins | Cook: 15mins | Ready in:*

## Ingredients

- 1 cup orange juice
- 2 jalapeno peppers, seeded and finely chopped
- 1 teaspoon ground cumin
- 1/2 teaspoon salt, optional
- Dash pepper
- 3/4 cup halved sliced sweet onion
- 4 teaspoons cornstarch
- 1/4 cup cold water
- 1 cup fresh orange sections
- 2 tablespoons minced fresh cilantro
- 8 lamb loin chops (1 inch thick and 4 ounces each)

## Direction

- Mix the cumin, orange juice, pepper, salt (optional) and jalapeño together in a small saucepan. Let the mixture cook over medium-high heat setting until it is starting to simmer. Add in the onion and give it a mix.
- Mix the water and cornstarch together until it is smooth in consistency then put it slowly into the orange juice mixture. Let the mixture boil and cook it for 2 minutes while stirring it over medium heat until the sauce mixture is bubbling and is thick in consistency. Remove the pan away from the heat. Mix in the cilantro and oranges and keep the temperature of the sauce mixture warm.
- Put the lamb chops onto the grill over medium heat then cover and let it grill, or put the lamb chops in a broiler and let it broil 4-6 inches away from the heat for 4 to 9 minutes on every side until the preferred meat doneness is achieved (a thermometer inserted on the meat should indicate 170° for well-done, 160° for medium and 145° for medium-rare).
- Serve the grilled lamb chops along with the prepared orange sauce.

## Nutrition Information

- Calories: 281 calories
- Protein: 30g protein. Diabetic Exchanges: 4 lean meat
- Total Fat: 10g fat (3g saturated fat)
- Sodium: 83mg sodium
- Fiber: 2g fiber)
- Total Carbohydrate: 18g carbohydrate (11g sugars
- Cholesterol: 90mg cholesterol

### 540. Spaghetti Squash With Balsamic Vegetables And Toasted Pine Nuts

*Serving: 6 servings. | Prep: 20mins | Cook: 15mins | Ready in:*

## Ingredients

- 1 medium spaghetti squash (about 4 pounds)
- 1 cup chopped carrots
- 1 small red onion, halved and sliced
- 1 tablespoon olive oil
- 4 garlic cloves, minced
- 1 can (15-1/2 ounces) great northern beans, rinsed and drained
- 1 can (14-1/2 ounces) diced tomatoes, drained
- 1 can (14 ounces) water-packed artichoke hearts, rinsed, drained and halved
- 1 medium zucchini, chopped
- 3 tablespoons balsamic vinegar
- 2 teaspoons minced fresh thyme or 1/2 teaspoon dried thyme
- 1/4 teaspoon salt
- 1/4 teaspoon pepper

- 1/2 cup pine nuts, toasted

## Direction

- Lengthwise, cut squash in half; throw seeds. Put squash on microwave-safe plate, cut side down. Microwave on high, uncovered, till tender for 15-18 minutes.
- Meanwhile, sauté onion and carrots in oil in big nonstick skillet till tender. Add garlic; cook for a minute. Mix pepper, salt, thyme, vinegar, zucchini, artichokes, tomatoes and beans in; mix and cook on medium heat till heated through for 8-10 minutes.
- Use fork to separate strands when squash is cool enough to touch. Serve with bean mixture then sprinkle nuts.

## Nutrition Information

- Calories: 275 calories
- Total Carbohydrate: 41g carbohydrate (6g sugars
- Cholesterol: 0 cholesterol
- Protein: 11g protein. Diabetic Exchanges: 2-1/2 starch
- Total Fat: 10g fat (1g saturated fat)
- Sodium: 510mg sodium
- Fiber: 10g fiber)

## 541. Spanako Pasta

*Serving: 4 servings. | Prep: 20mins | Cook: 15mins | Ready in:*

## Ingredients

- 4-1/2 cups uncooked whole wheat spiral pasta
- 1 medium onion, chopped
- 2 teaspoons olive oil
- 2 garlic cloves, minced
- 2 tablespoons all-purpose flour
- 3/4 cup reduced-sodium chicken broth or vegetable broth
- 3/4 cup fat-free milk
- 1 package (10 ounces) frozen chopped spinach, thawed and squeezed dry
- 1/4 cup grated Parmesan cheese
- 2 ounces reduced-fat cream cheese
- 2 tablespoons lemon juice
- 2 tablespoons snipped fresh dill
- 1/4 teaspoon ground nutmeg
- 1/4 teaspoon salt
- Dash cayenne pepper
- 3/4 cup crumbled feta cheese

## Direction

- Prepare the pasta following the package instructions. In the meantime, sauté onion in a big pan with oil until tender; put in garlic. Cook for another minute; mix in flour until combined. Pour in milk and broth gradually; boil. Cook and stir for 2 minutes until thick.
- Add cayenne, spinach, salt, Parmesan cheese, nutmeg, cream cheese, dill, and lemon juice; completely heat. Drain the pasta then save a cup of liquid. Mix the spinach mixture and pasta. If needed, mix in some of the reserved liquid. Scatter with feta cheese.

## Nutrition Information

- Calories: 435 calories
- Sodium: 667mg sodium
- Fiber: 11g fiber)
- Total Carbohydrate: 61g carbohydrate (7g sugars
- Cholesterol: 27mg cholesterol
- Protein: 23g protein.
- Total Fat: 12g fat (6g saturated fat)

## 542. Speedy Hummus Pizza

*Serving: 6 slices. | Prep: 10mins | Cook: 10mins | Ready in:*

## Ingredients

- 1 prebaked 12-inch pizza crust
- 1 cup hummus
- 3/4 teaspoon dried oregano
- 1/4 teaspoon crushed red pepper flakes
- 1/2 cup crumbled feta cheese
- 1/2 cup oil-packed sun-dried tomatoes, chopped
- 1/2 cup pitted Greek olives, chopped
- 1 tablespoon olive oil

### Direction

- Start oven to 450 degrees and start preheating. On a 12-in. pizza pan or ungreased cookie sheet put the crust. In a bowl, stir together oregano, pepper flakes, and hummus. Spread like sauce on crust. Sprinkle with cheese and place olives and tomatoes on top. Bake until heated; 8-10 minutes. Drizzle oil on top.

### Nutrition Information

- Calories:
- Total Fat:
- Sodium:
- Fiber:
- Total Carbohydrate:
- Cholesterol:
- Protein:

## 543. Spiced Lamb Stew With Apricots

*Serving: 5 servings. | Prep: 30mins | Cook: 05hours00mins | Ready in:*

### Ingredients

- 2 pounds lamb stew meat, cut into 3/4-inch cubes
- 3 tablespoons butter
- 1-1/2 cups chopped sweet onion
- 3/4 cup dried apricots
- 1/2 cup orange juice
- 1/2 cup chicken broth
- 2 teaspoons paprika
- 2 teaspoons ground allspice
- 2 teaspoons ground cinnamon
- 1-1/2 teaspoons salt
- 1 teaspoon ground cardamom
- Hot cooked couscous
- Chopped dried apricots, optional

### Direction

- Set a large frying pan, put lamb and brown it in butter in batches. Use a slotted spoon to move it to a 3-qt. slow cooker. In exactly the same frying pan, sauté onion in drippings till tender. Mix in seasonings, broth, orange juice and apricots; drizzle over lamb.
- Cook on high heat with a cover for 5-6 hours or till meat is tender. Serve with couscous. Drizzle chopped apricots on top if desired.

### Nutrition Information

- Calories: 404 calories
- Protein: 38g protein.
- Total Fat: 17g fat (8g saturated fat)
- Sodium: 975mg sodium
- Fiber: 5g fiber)
- Total Carbohydrate: 24g carbohydrate (15g sugars
- Cholesterol: 136mg cholesterol

## 544. Spicy Chicken Breasts

*Serving: 4 | Prep: 15mins | Cook: 15mins | Ready in:*

### Ingredients

- 2 1/2 tablespoons paprika
- 2 tablespoons garlic powder
- 1 tablespoon salt
- 1 tablespoon onion powder
- 1 tablespoon dried thyme
- 1 tablespoon ground cayenne pepper

- 1 tablespoon ground black pepper
- 4 skinless, boneless chicken breast halves

## Direction

- Combine the ground black pepper, cayenne pepper, thyme, onion powder, salt, garlic powder and paprika in a medium bowl. Reserve around 3 tbsp. of this seasoning mixture to use for the chicken. Store the leftover in an airtight container to use later (for seasoning the vegetables, meats or fish).
- Set the grill to preheat to medium-high heat. Rub some of the reserved 3 tbsp. of seasoning on both sides of the chicken breasts.
- Oil the grill grate lightly. Put the chicken on the grill and let it cook for 6-8 minutes per side, until the juices run clear.

## Nutrition Information

- Calories: 173 calories;
- Protein: 29.2
- Total Fat: 2.4
- Sodium: 1826
- Total Carbohydrate: 9.2
- Cholesterol: 68

## 545. Spicy Lamb Kabobs

*Serving: 8 servings. | Prep: 40mins | Cook: 10mins | Ready in:*

## Ingredients

- 1 large cucumber
- 2 cups (8 ounces) sour cream or plain yogurt
- 2 teaspoons lemon juice
- 1/2 teaspoon salt
- 1/8 teaspoon garlic powder
- 1/8 teaspoon dill weed
- 1/8 teaspoon pepper
- KABOBS:
- 2 cups buttermilk
- 2 teaspoons ground turmeric
- 2 teaspoons curry powder
- 1 teaspoon coarsely ground pepper
- 1 teaspoon chili powder
- 1 teaspoon minced fresh sage
- 1/2 teaspoon salt
- 2-1/2 pounds lean boneless lamb, cut into 1-inch cubes
- 16 cubes fresh pineapple (1-inch)
- 16 cherry tomatoes
- SALAD:
- 8 cups torn leaf lettuce
- 2 cups torn romaine
- 2 cups torn Bibb or Boston lettuce
- 1/2 large sweet onion, sliced
- 1/2 medium red onion, finely chopped
- 1 medium tomato, chopped
- 1/2 cup bean sprouts
- 1/2 cup green grapes, quartered
- 1/2 cup chopped walnuts
- 1/2 cup crumbled feta cheese
- 1/4 cup butter, softened
- 2 tablespoons honey
- 4 pita breads (6 inches), halved and warmed

## Direction

- Peel the cucumber, removing its seeds. Process the peeled and de-seeded cucumbers in a food processor until finely chopped. Set aside half then puree the rest. Stir together the pureed cucumber and the chopped cucumber, then the sour cream, seasonings, and lemon juice. Keep in the refrigerator for at least 60 minutes. Combine the first seven kabob ingredients in a small bowl. Place the lambs in a large zip-top bag and pour 1 1/2 cups of the marinade over the meat. Zip the bag, turn to coat, and refrigerate for at least an hour. Keep the remaining marinade in a covered container in the refrigerator, for use in basting later. Drain and discard marinade from the lamb. Take eight metal or pre-soaked wooden skewers and alternately thread lamb, tomatoes, and pineapples. Put out a large bowl and mix together the lettuces, tomatoes, onions, grapes, sprouts, and walnuts, then scatter cheese over it. Set aside. Cook kabobs in a covered gill over medium heat for 5-6 minutes per side or until lamb is cooked to liking. A meat thermometer should read 145 deg for medium-rare, 160 deg for medium, and 170 deg for well-done. Brush often with reserved marinade. Beat honey and butter until well-blended and brush this over the pitas. Serve kabobs with honey-glazed pita, salad greens, and sauce.

## Nutrition Information

- Calories: 610 calories
- Total Fat: 30g fat (15g saturated fat)
- Sodium: 729mg sodium
- Fiber: 5g fiber)
- Total Carbohydrate: 43g carbohydrate (19g sugars
- Cholesterol: 147mg cholesterol
- Protein: 39g protein.

## 546. Spicy Shrimp Fettuccine

*Serving: 4 servings. | Prep: 10mins | Cook: 20mins | Ready in:*

## Ingredients

- 8 ounces uncooked fettuccine
- 1 medium onion, chopped
- 1 garlic clove, minced
- 1 tablespoon olive oil
- 4 plum tomatoes, chopped
- 1 cup chicken broth
- 2 cups coarsely chopped fresh spinach
- 3/4 pound cooked medium shrimp, peeled and deveined
- 2 tablespoons minced fresh parsley
- 1 tablespoon balsamic vinegar
- 1 tablespoon butter
- 1/2 teaspoon salt
- 1/4 teaspoon pepper
- 1/8 teaspoon cayenne pepper
- 2 ounces feta cheese, crumbled

## Direction

- Following package directions to cook fettuccine. In the meantime, saute garlic and onion in a big nonstick skillet with oil until softened. Put in broth and tomatoes, then bring to a boil. Lower heat and simmer without a cover about 3 minutes.
- Put in vinegar, parsley, shrimp and spinach. Simmer without a cover until shrimp is heated through, about 2 minutes. Add cayenne, pepper, salt and butter, stir. Drain the fettuccine and serve together with feta cheese as well as shrimp mixture.

## Nutrition Information

- Calories: 419 calories
- Protein: 28g protein. Diabetic Exchanges: 3 lean meat
- Total Fat: 12g fat (5g saturated fat)
- Sodium: 861mg sodium
- Fiber: 4g fiber)
- Total Carbohydrate: 49g carbohydrate (0 sugars
- Cholesterol: 150mg cholesterol

## 547. Spiedis

*Serving: 8 servings. | Prep: 10mins | Cook: 10mins | Ready in:*

## Ingredients

- 1 cup vegetable oil
- 2/3 cup cider vinegar
- 2 tablespoons Worcestershire sauce
- 1/2 medium onion, finely chopped
- 1/2 teaspoon salt
- 1/2 teaspoon sugar
- 1/2 teaspoon dried basil
- 1/2 teaspoon dried marjoram
- 1/2 teaspoon dried rosemary, crushed

- 2-1/2 pounds boneless lean pork, beef, lamb, venison, chicken or turkey, cut into 1-1/2- to 2-inch cubes
- Italian rolls or hot dog buns

## Direction

- Mix the initial nine ingredients in a plastic or glass bowl. Combine with meat and toss together to coat evenly. Keep covered to marinate for 24 hours, with periodic stirs.
- Once ready to grill, skewer meat on metal skewers and cook by grilling at high heat for 10-15 minutes until the meat is cooked to preference. Remove skewers from meat and consume while placed on hot dog buns or long Italian rolls.

## Nutrition Information

- Calories: 205 calories
- Sodium: 104mg sodium
- Fiber: 0 fiber)
- Total Carbohydrate: 1g carbohydrate (0 sugars
- Cholesterol: 42mg cholesterol
- Protein: 22g protein. Diabetic Exchanges: 2 lean meat
- Total Fat: 12g fat (0 saturated fat)

## 548. Spinach & Chicken Phyllo Pie

*Serving: 8 servings. | Prep: 35mins | Cook: 35mins | Ready in:*

## Ingredients

- 2 pounds ground chicken
- 1 large onion, chopped
- 1 teaspoon pepper
- 1 teaspoon dried oregano
- 3/4 teaspoon salt
- 1/2 teaspoon ground nutmeg
- 1/4 teaspoon crushed red pepper flakes
- 3 packages (10 ounces each) frozen chopped spinach, thawed and squeezed dry
- 4 large eggs, lightly beaten
- 3 cups crumbled feta cheese
- 20 sheets phyllo dough (14x9-inch size)
- Cooking spray

## Direction

- Preheat an oven to 375°. Cook chicken and onion in a big skillet over medium-high heat till chicken isn't pink anymore for 7-9 minutes, breaking up chicken into crumbles; drain. Mix in seasonings. Add the spinach; cook while stirring till liquid evaporates. Put into a big bowl; slightly cool. Mix in cheese and beaten eggs.
- Layer 10 phyllo dough sheets into a 13x9-in. greased baking dish, spritzing cooking spray on each; keep leftover phyllo covered in plastic wrap and a damp towel to avoid drying out. Spread the spinach mixture on phyllo. Put leftover phyllo sheets on top; spritz cooking spray on each. Cut into 8 rectangles.
- Bake till golden brown for 35-40 minutes, uncovered; recut rectangles before serving, if needed.

## Nutrition Information

- Calories: 442 calories
- Protein: 35g protein.
- Total Fat: 23g fat (8g saturated fat)
- Sodium: 921mg sodium
- Fiber: 6g fiber)
- Total Carbohydrate: 25g carbohydrate (3g sugars
- Cholesterol: 191mg cholesterol

## 549. Spinach Beef Biscuit Bake

*Serving: 6 servings. | Prep: 15mins | Cook: 25mins | Ready in:*

### Ingredients

- 2 tubes (6 ounces each) refrigerated buttermilk biscuits
- 1-1/2 pounds ground beef
- 1/2 cup finely chopped onion
- 2 eggs
- 1 package (10 ounces) frozen chopped spinach, thawed and squeezed dry
- 1 can (4 ounces) mushroom stems and pieces, drained
- 4 ounces crumbled feta cheese
- 1/4 cup grated Parmesan cheese
- 1-1/2 teaspoons garlic powder
- Salt and pepper to taste
- 1 to 2 tablespoons butter, melted

### Direction

- Flatten and pack the biscuits on the sides and bottom of an oil 11-in by 7-in baking dish; set it aside.
- On medium heat, cook onion and beef in a pan until the meat is not pink; drain.
- Whisk eggs in a bowl; stir in mushrooms and spinach thoroughly. Mix in beef mixture, cheeses, pepper, salt, and garlic powder to combine well; scoop to the prepared crust then sprinkle with butter.
- Bake for 25-30 minutes in 375 degrees oven without cover until the crust is pale brown.

### Nutrition Information

- Calories: 418 calories
- Sodium: 686mg sodium
- Fiber: 3g fiber)
- Total Carbohydrate: 19g carbohydrate (1g sugars
- Cholesterol: 164mg cholesterol
- Protein: 34g protein.
- Total Fat: 22g fat (10g saturated fat)

## 550. Spinach Cheese Phyllo Squares

*Serving: 12 servings. | Prep: 20mins | Cook: 40mins | Ready in:*

### Ingredients

- 6 sheets phyllo dough (14x9 inches)
- 1 package (10 ounces) frozen chopped spinach, thawed and squeezed dry
- 2-1/2 cups shredded part-skim mozzarella cheese
- 1-1/2 cups shredded reduced-fat cheddar cheese
- 1-1/2 cups (12 ounces) fat-free cottage cheese
- 4 large eggs
- 1-1/2 teaspoons dried parsley flakes
- 3/4 teaspoon salt
- 6 large egg whites
- 1-1/2 cups fat-free milk

### Direction

- In a greased 13x9-in. pan layer three phyllo sheets. Spray a little grease on the top of each phyllo sheet. Mix cheese, salt, spinach, 2 eggs, and parsley flakes in a big bowl. Spread mixture over phyllo dough. Put the rest of the phyllo sheets on top, make sure to lightly spray the top of each one. Cut into 12 squares with a knife. Cover; put in refrigerator and chill for 1 hour. Beat milk, the rest of the eggs, and egg whites in a big bowl until combined. Pour on top of the phyllo. Cover and put back in refrigerator overnight. Take it out about 1 hour before baking. Do not cover; bake in a 375-degree oven until a knife poked into the middle comes out clean, 40-50 minutes. Before cutting, let it cool for 10 minutes.

### Nutrition Information

- Calories: 187 calories
- Total Fat: 9g fat (5g saturated fat)
- Sodium: 593mg sodium
- Fiber: 1g fiber)

- Total Carbohydrate: 9g carbohydrate (0 sugars
- Cholesterol: 97mg cholesterol
- Protein: 19g protein. Diabetic Exchanges: 2 lean meat

- Sodium: 936mg sodium
- Fiber: 4g fiber)
- Total Carbohydrate: 51g carbohydrate (7g sugars

## 551. Spinach Feta Turnovers

*Serving: 4 servings. | Prep: 20mins | Cook: 10mins | Ready in:*

### Ingredients

- 2 large eggs
- 1 package (10 ounces) frozen leaf spinach, thawed, squeezed dry and chopped
- 3/4 cup crumbled feta cheese
- 2 garlic cloves, minced
- 1/4 teaspoon pepper
- 1 tube (13.8 ounces) refrigerated pizza crust
- Refrigerated tzatziki sauce, optional

### Direction

- Beat eggs in a bowl; reserve a tablespoon. Mix pepper, spinach, garlic, and feta cheese in the remaining beaten eggs.
- Roll the pizza dough out and form into a twelve-inch square; slice into 4 three-inch squares. Put 1/3 cup of the spinach mixture on top of each square. Fold the square into a triangle then press edges to enclose; make slashes on top. Slather with the reserved beaten egg.
- Arrange on a greased baking sheet; bake for 10-12 minutes in a 425 degrees F oven until golden brown. Serve along with tzatziki sauce if desired.

### Nutrition Information

- Calories: 361 calories
- Cholesterol: 104mg cholesterol
- Protein: 17g protein.
- Total Fat: 9g fat (4g saturated fat)

## 552. Spinach Ricotta Tart

*Serving: 6 servings. | Prep: 25mins | Cook: 25mins | Ready in:*

### Ingredients

- 2 pounds fresh spinach, torn
- 3 eggs, lightly beaten
- 1 carton (15 ounces) part-skim ricotta cheese
- 1 medium onion, chopped
- 2 tablespoons minced fresh basil
- 1 teaspoon salt
- 1/8 teaspoon pepper
- Dash ground nutmeg
- 4 sheets phyllo dough (14 inches x 9 inches)
- 3 medium tomatoes, halved, seeded and sliced
- 2 tablespoons crumbled blue cheese

### Direction

- In a steamer basket, put spinach. Move into a saucepan over 1-in. of water; allow to boil. Steam with a cover till wilted, 2-3 minutes; strain well. Chop the spinach; squeeze dry; set aside. Mix together nutmeg, pepper, salt, basil, onion, ricotta cheese and eggs in a large bowl; combine properly. Chop spinach. Squeeze dry and set aside. In large bowl, combine the eggs, ricotta cheese, onion, basil, salt, pepper and nutmeg; mix well. Add the spinach.
- Coat a 9-in. pie plate with cooking spray; arrange one sheet of phyllo dough on it; using cooking spray, spray the phyllo dough. Arrange another sheet across the first sheet of phyllo; use cooking spray to spray. Repeat with the remaining phyllo. Transfer the spinach mixture into the phyllo crust. To form a rim, fold the excess dough under the crust; use cooking spray to spray the rim. Place

tomato slices over the tart. Bake at 400° till set, 35-40 minutes. Sprinkle blue cheese over. Allow to stand for 10 minutes before cutting.

## Nutrition Information

- Calories: 221 calories
- Protein: 18g protein. Diabetic Exchanges: 2 lean meat
- Total Fat: 10g fat (5g saturated fat)
- Sodium: 706mg sodium
- Fiber: 5g fiber)
- Total Carbohydrate: 19g carbohydrate (0 sugars
- Cholesterol: 130mg cholesterol

## 553. Spinach Tomato Linguine

*Serving: 4 servings. | Prep: 10mins | Cook: 15mins | Ready in:*

### Ingredients

- 8 ounces uncooked linguine
- 3 cups chopped seeded plum tomatoes
- 1 package (10 ounces) frozen chopped spinach, thawed and squeezed dry
- 1/2 cup chopped green onions
- 1 teaspoon olive oil
- 1/4 teaspoon salt
- 1/4 teaspoon garlic salt
- 4 ounces crumbled feta cheese

### Direction

- Following the package directions to cook linguine. In the meantime, sauté onions, spinach and tomatoes with oil in a large nonstick skillet until the tomatoes have softened. Sprinkle garlic salt and salt over. Lower the heat. Mix in cheese till heated through.
- Strain the linguine; move to serving bowl. Put in tomato mixture; coat by tossing.

## Nutrition Information

- Calories: 357 calories
- Fiber: 6g fiber)
- Total Carbohydrate: 52g carbohydrate (0 sugars
- Cholesterol: 25mg cholesterol
- Protein: 15g protein. Diabetic Exchanges: 2-1/2 starch
- Total Fat: 11g fat (5g saturated fat)
- Sodium: 646mg sodium

## 554. Spinach And Feta Flank Steak

*Serving: 6 servings. | Prep: 15mins | Cook: 50mins | Ready in:*

### Ingredients

- 1 beef flank steak (1-1/2 to 2 pounds)
- 1 package (10 ounces) frozen chopped spinach, thawed and squeezed dry
- 1 package (4 ounces) crumbled feta cheese
- 1/3 cup minced fresh parsley
- 3 tablespoons snipped fresh dill
- 3 tablespoons chopped green onions
- 1 teaspoon salt
- 1/2 teaspoon pepper
- 1 tablespoon olive oil

### Direction

- From a long side, horizontally cut steak within 1/2-in. from opposing side; open steak and let it lie flat. Cover using plastic wrap then flatten to 1/4-in. thick; remove the plastic.
- Mix onions, dill, parsley, cheese and spinach; within 1-in. from edges, spread on steak. Roll up, starting at short side, jellyroll style; tie using kitchen string. Sprinkle pepper and salt.

- Brown meat on all sides in oil in a big skillet; put onto greased rack of the shallow roasting pan. Bake for 40-45 minutes at 400° till meat gets desired doneness; 145° medium-well, 140° medium and 135° for medium-rare on a thermometer. Remove from oven; stand for 15 minutes. Serve; remove string to cut to 1-inch thick slices.

## Nutrition Information

- Calories: 242 calories
- Protein: 24g protein.
- Total Fat: 14g fat (6g saturated fat)
- Sodium: 662mg sodium
- Fiber: 2g fiber)
- Total Carbohydrate: 3g carbohydrate (0 sugars
- Cholesterol: 58mg cholesterol

### 555. Spinach Stuffed Lamb

*Serving: 8-10 servings. | Prep: 30mins | Cook: 01hours15mins | Ready in:*

## Ingredients

- 3 tablespoons minced garlic
- 1 tablespoon olive oil
- 2 packages (10 ounces each) frozen chopped spinach, thawed and squeezed dry
- 2 logs (4 ounces each) fresh goat cheese, crumbled
- 3/4 teaspoon salt, divided
- 1/4 teaspoon pepper, divided
- 1 boneless butterflied leg of lamb (4 to 5 pounds), trimmed
- 3 garlic cloves, slivered
- 3 tablespoons minced fresh rosemary

## Direction

- Sauté minced garlic for 2-3 minutes in oil in a small skillet. Take off heat; mix in 1/8 tsp. pepper, 1/2 tsp. salt, cheese and spinach.
- Untie lamb. So it lies flat, open; flatten to 3/4-in. thick. Spread meat within 1-in. of edges with spinach mixture. Roll up lamb beginning at 1 short side. Tuck ends in; at 2-in. intervals, tie with kitchen string. Create slits on outside of meat with a sharp knife; insert garlic slivers. Sprinkle leftover pepper and salt and rosemary.
- Put onto rack in shallow roasting pan, seam side down; cover. Bake for 1 hour at 425°. Uncover; bake, basting with pan juices occasionally, till thermometer reads 160° and browned for 15-30 minutes. Stand before slicing for 10-15 minutes.

## Nutrition Information

- Calories: 343 calories
- Total Fat: 18g fat (9g saturated fat)
- Sodium: 404mg sodium
- Fiber: 1g fiber)
- Total Carbohydrate: 3g carbohydrate (1g sugars
- Cholesterol: 128mg cholesterol
- Protein: 40g protein.

### 556. Spinach Tomato Phyllo Bake

*Serving: 6 servings. | Prep: 25mins | Cook: 55mins | Ready in:*

## Ingredients

- 4 large eggs, lightly beaten
- 2 packages (10 ounces each) frozen chopped spinach, thawed and squeezed dry
- 1 cup (4 ounces) crumbled feta cheese
- 1/2 cup 1% cottage cheese
- 3 green onions, sliced
- 1 teaspoon dill weed
- 1/2 teaspoon salt
- 1/4 teaspoon pepper
- 1/4 teaspoon ground nutmeg

- 10 sheets phyllo dough (14x9-inch size)
- Butter-flavored cooking spray
- 3 large tomatoes, sliced

## Direction

- Set the oven at 350° and start preheating. Mix together the first nine ingredients in a large bowl; set aside.
- Using butter-flavored cooking spray, spritz one sheet of phyllo dough. Arrange on a greased 8-in. square baking dish; keep one end of the dough hang over the edge of the dish. Repeat with 4 additional phyllo sheets; stagger the overhanging phyllo around the edges of the dish. (Cover the remaining phyllo with a plastic wrap and prevent it from drying out with a damp towel.) Spoon 1/3 of the spinach mixture into the crust. Add layers of half of the tomatoes, another 1/3 of the spinach mixture, the remaining tomatoes and the remaining spinach mixture. Spritz and layer the remaining phyllo dough as previously.
- Carefully fold the ends of the dough over the filling and toward the center of the baking dish; use butter-flavored spray to spritz. Use foil to cover the edges. Bake till a thermometer reads 160°, 55-60 minutes. Allow to sit for 15 minutes before cutting.

## Nutrition Information

- Calories: 216 calories
- Total Fat: 9g fat (3g saturated fat)
- Sodium: 652mg sodium
- Fiber: 5g fiber)
- Total Carbohydrate: 21g carbohydrate (5g sugars
- Cholesterol: 153mg cholesterol
- Protein: 15g protein. Diabetic Exchanges: 2 medium-fat meat

## 557. Spit Roasted Lemon Rosemary Chicken

*Serving: 6 servings. | Prep: 20mins | Cook: 01hours15mins | Ready in:*

## Ingredients

- 8 cups warm water (110° to 115°)
- 1/2 cup kosher salt
- 1/4 cup packed brown sugar
- 3 tablespoons molasses
- 1 tablespoon whole peppercorns, crushed
- 1 tablespoon whole allspice, crushed
- 2 teaspoons ground ginger
- 1 broiler/fryer chicken (3-1/2 to 4 pounds)
- 2 medium lemons
- 3 teaspoons minced fresh rosemary, divided
- 1/2 teaspoon salt, divided
- 1/2 teaspoon pepper, divided
- 1/4 cup olive oil

## Direction

- To make brine, in a big kettle, mix the first 7 ingredients together. Bring the mixture to a boil, then cook and stir until salt is dissolved. Take away from the heat and allow to cool to room temperature. At the same time, grate peel from lemons. Juice lemons and save juiced lemon halves, then set aside.
- Get rid of giblets from chicken. Put into a 2-gal. resealable plastic bag with cold water, then add in chicken. Put in a roasting pan. Pour cooled brine into bag carefully and squeeze out as much air as you can, then seal and turn to coat well. Chill about 3 to 4 hours while turning a few times.
- Get rid of brine. Rinse the chicken with water and pat it dry. Use 1/8 tsp. of each pepper and salt and 1 tsp. of rosemary to rub the inside of chicken, then put the juiced lemon halves in cavity. Skewer chicken openings and tie together.
- Following the manufacturer's directions to put chicken on rotisserie rod on grill using a drip pan. Mix together pepper, salt, leftover

rosemary, lemon peel and juice, and olive oil, then brush the mixture over chicken. Grill until chicken juices run clear, about 1-1 1/2 hours.

## Nutrition Information

- Calories:
- Total Carbohydrate:
- Cholesterol:
- Protein:
- Total Fat:
- Sodium:
- Fiber:

### 558. Spring Lamb Supper

*Serving: 4 servings. | Prep: 20mins | Cook: 0mins | Ready in:*

## Ingredients

- 1 pound boneless lamb, cut into cubes
- 2 teaspoons olive oil
- 2 cups thinly sliced yellow summer squash
- 1/2 pound fresh mushrooms, sliced
- 2 medium tomatoes, seeded and chopped
- 1/2 cup sliced green onions
- 3 cups cooked brown rice
- 1 teaspoon salt
- 1/2 teaspoon garlic powder
- 1/2 teaspoon pepper
- 1/2 teaspoon dried rosemary, crushed

## Direction

- Sauté lamb in a large skillet with oil till not pink anymore; using a slotted spoon, take lamb out of the skillet. In the same skillet, stir-fry onions, tomatoes, mushrooms and squash till tender, or for 2-3 minutes. Turn the lamb back to the skillet. Mix in seasonings and rice; cook while stirring till heated through.

## Nutrition Information

- Calories: 376 calories
- Sodium: 659mg sodium
- Fiber: 6g fiber)
- Total Carbohydrate: 44g carbohydrate (5g sugars
- Cholesterol: 63mg cholesterol
- Protein: 27g protein.
- Total Fat: 11g fat (3g saturated fat)

### 559. Stuffed Sweet Peppers

*Serving: 5 servings. | Prep: 15mins | Cook: 04hours00mins | Ready in:*

## Ingredients

- 3 medium sweet red peppers
- 2 medium sweet yellow peppers
- 1 jar (14 ounces) spaghetti sauce, divided
- 3/4 pound Italian turkey sausage links, casings removed
- 3/4 cup uncooked instant rice
- 1/2 cup crumbled feta cheese
- 1/2 cup chopped onion
- 1/4 cup chopped tomato
- 1/4 cup minced fresh parsley
- 2 tablespoons sliced ripe olives
- 1/4 to 1/2 teaspoon garlic powder
- 1/2 teaspoon salt
- 1/2 teaspoon Italian seasoning
- 1/2 teaspoon crushed red pepper flakes

## Direction

- Slice off the pepper tops; chop the tops then reserve. Remove the seeds and stems; set aside the pepper cups. Reserve 3/4 cup spaghetti sauce then add the rest in a five-quart slow cooker.
- Combine the reserved spaghetti sauce, sausage, reserved chopped peppers, rice, pepper flakes, cheese, Italian seasoning, onion,

salt, tomato, garlic powder, olives, and parsley; scoop into peppers.
- Move the peppers in the slow cooker; cover. Cook for 4-5 hours on low until the peppers are tender and the sausage is not pink.

## Nutrition Information

- Calories: 292 calories
- Cholesterol: 48mg cholesterol
- Protein: 17g protein.
- Total Fat: 12g fat (3g saturated fat)
- Sodium: 1182mg sodium
- Fiber: 4g fiber)
- Total Carbohydrate: 30g carbohydrate (10g sugars

## 560. Stuffed Olive Cod

*Serving: 4 servings. | Prep: 15mins | Cook: 10mins | Ready in:*

### Ingredients

- 4 cod fillets (6 ounces each)
- 1 teaspoon dried oregano
- 1/4 teaspoon salt
- 1 medium lemon, thinly sliced
- 1 shallot, thinly sliced
- 1/3 cup garlic-stuffed olives, halved
- 2 tablespoons water
- 2 tablespoons olive juice

### Direction

- In a big nonstick skillet sprayed with cooking spray, position fillets. Top with salt and oregano, then put shallot and lemon on top.
- Scatter around fish with olives, then put in olive juice and water. Bring to a boil, then lower heat to low and cook gently with a cover until fish starts to flake easily with a fork, about 8 to 10 minutes.

## Nutrition Information

- Calories: 163 calories
- Protein: 27g protein. Diabetic Exchanges: 4 lean meat.
- Total Fat: 3g fat (0 saturated fat)
- Sodium: 598mg sodium
- Fiber: 0 fiber)
- Total Carbohydrate: 4g carbohydrate (1g sugars
- Cholesterol: 65mg cholesterol

## 561. Sun Dried Tomato Chicken

*Serving: 6 | Prep: 20mins | Cook: 40mins | Ready in:*

### Ingredients

- 2 tablespoons olive oil
- 4 skinless, boneless chicken breast halves - cut into 1 1/2 inch pieces
- 4 cloves garlic, minced
- 1 cup heavy cream
- 1 (9 ounce) jar sun-dried tomato pesto
- 1 (12 ounce) jar roasted red peppers, drained and chopped
- 1 cup chopped fresh basil
- 1 teaspoon cayenne pepper
- 1 pound dry penne pasta

### Direction

- In a skillet, heat the olive oil over medium heat, cook and stir the chicken breast until browned, around 10 minutes. Put in garlic, cook, stirring with the chicken for 1 minute, then pour in the cream. Next, mix in cayenne pepper, basil, roasted peppers, and sun-dried tomato pesto; over low heat, simmer until the sauce has thickened, 30 minutes.
- While simmering the sauce, pour lightly salted water to fill a large pot, over high heat, bring to a rolling boil. Mix in the penne, and bring back to a boil. Uncover and cook the pasta,

occasionally stirring for about 11 minutes, until the pasta has cooked through yet still firm to the bite. Drain well.
- Serve the cooked penne with the sauce.

## Nutrition Information

- Calories: 599 calories;
- Cholesterol: 97
- Protein: 29
- Total Fat: 25.7
- Sodium: 650
- Total Carbohydrate: 63.9

### 562. Sunday Paella

*Serving: 8 servings. | Prep: 25mins | Cook: 40mins | Ready in:*

## Ingredients

- 1-1/2 pounds boneless skinless chicken breasts, cubed
- 3 tablespoons canola oil
- 1 pound Johnsonville® Fully Cooked Smoked Sausage Rope, cut into 1/4-inch slices
- 1 small onion, chopped
- 1-1/2 cups uncooked long grain rice
- 2 teaspoons Italian seasoning
- 1/4 teaspoon ground turmeric
- 1/4 teaspoon pepper
- 3 cups chicken broth
- 1-1/2 pounds uncooked medium shrimp, peeled and deveined
- 1 can (28 ounces) diced tomatoes, undrained
- 1-1/2 cups frozen peas, thawed
- 1 tablespoon sugar

## Direction

- Cook while mixing chicken in oil over medium heat in a Dutch oven until not pink anymore. Add onion and sausage; cook for 3 to 4 more minutes. Add pepper, turmeric, Italian seasoning, and rice; cook and mix until rice turn brown lightly, or for 3 to 4 minutes longer.
- Pour in broth. Bring to a boil. Lower the heat; simmer, covered until rice is nearly tender, or for 14 to 18 minutes. Mix in sugar, peas, tomatoes, and shrimp; cook, covered, turning occasionally, for 10 to 15 minutes or until shrimp has a pink color.

## Nutrition Information

- Calories: 570 calories
- Cholesterol: 190mg cholesterol
- Protein: 44g protein.
- Total Fat: 24g fat (8g saturated fat)
- Sodium: 1309mg sodium
- Fiber: 4g fiber)
- Total Carbohydrate: 41g carbohydrate (8g sugars

### 563. Supreme Kabobs

*Serving: 8 servings. | Prep: 5mins | Cook: 20mins | Ready in:*

## Ingredients

- 3/4 cup canola oil
- 1/3 cup soy sauce
- 1/4 cup red wine vinegar
- 1/4 cup lemon juice
- 2 tablespoons Worcestershire sauce
- 2 teaspoons ground mustard
- 1 teaspoon pepper
- 1 teaspoon dried parsley flakes
- 2 pounds boneless skinless chicken breasts, cut into 1-inch cubes
- 12 ounces small fresh mushrooms
- 1 medium green or sweet red pepper, cut into 1-inch pieces
- 2 small onions, cut into 1-inch pieces
- 1 can (8 ounces) pineapple chunks, drained

## Direction

- Combine the first eight ingredients in a small bowl. Divide the mixture into two large resealable plastic bags; chicken goes into one bag and mushrooms, onions, and peppers go in the other. Seal both bags and turn several times to coat; store in the fridge to marinate for 6 hours, minimum. Drain both bags, discarding the marinade. Alternately thread chicken, pineapple, and vegetables on skewers. Cook in a covered grill over medium-low heat, turning often for 16-20 minutes or until chicken is cooked through.

## Nutrition Information

- Calories: 274 calories
- Cholesterol: 97mg cholesterol
- Protein: 38g protein. Diabetic Exchanges: 4 lean meat
- Total Fat: 9g fat (0 saturated fat)
- Sodium: 235mg sodium
- Fiber: 0 fiber)
- Total Carbohydrate: 8g carbohydrate (0 sugars

## 564. Sweet 'n' Zesty Chicken Breasts

*Serving: 2 servings. | Prep: 5mins | Cook: 15mins | Ready in:*

## Ingredients

- 2 boneless skinless chicken breast halves (6 ounces each)
- 1 medium onion, sliced
- 1 tablespoon canola oil
- 1 cup water
- 1 package (2.4 ounces) tomato-basil soup mix
- 2 tablespoons brown sugar
- 1/4 to 1/2 teaspoon hot pepper sauce
- Hot cooked couscous, optional

## Direction

- Cook chicken and onion in a non-stick pan with oil until both sides are brown; take it out of the pan then set aside. Boil hot pepper sauce, water, brown sugar, and soup mix in the same pan while constantly mixing. Place the chicken back in the pan. Lower heat; let it simmer for 5-7 minutes with cover until the chicken juices are clear. If desired, serve on top of couscous.

## Nutrition Information

- Calories: 452 calories
- Fiber: 3g fiber)
- Total Carbohydrate: 42g carbohydrate (18g sugars
- Cholesterol: 98mg cholesterol
- Protein: 40g protein. Diabetic Exchanges: 4 lean meat
- Total Fat: 13g fat (2g saturated fat)
- Sodium: 825mg sodium

## 565. Swordfish Shrimp Kabobs

*Serving: 2 servings. | Prep: 20mins | Cook: 10mins | Ready in:*

## Ingredients

- 1/4 cup olive oil
- 2 tablespoons balsamic vinegar
- 1/2 teaspoon crushed red pepper flakes
- 1/2 teaspoon dried oregano
- 1/4 teaspoon salt
- 1/8 teaspoon pepper
- 1/2 pound swordfish steak, skin removed and cut into 1-inch chunks
- 8 uncooked large shrimp, peeled and deveined
- 8 cherry tomatoes
- 1/2 medium red onion, cut into 4 wedges
- 1/2 medium sweet yellow pepper, cut into 8 chunks

### Direction

- Combine vinegar, oil, and seasonings in a small bowl. Take 3 tablespoons of the mixture and put in a large re-sealable bag with the swordfish and shrimp. Seal, turn several times to coat, and refrigerate up to 1 hour. Keep remaining marinade for basting. Thread swordfish, onions, tomatoes, shrimps, and yellow peppers onto four metal or wooden skewers that have been soaked. Use long-handled tongs to grip an oil-moistened paper towel and wipe the rack to lightly oil it. Cooks the kabobs on an uncovered grill at medium heat, or broil 4 in from the heat, for 3 minutes. Baste frequently with the reserved marinade. Grill for another 3-4 minutes, turning and basting, until fish meat just turns milky in color and the shrimps turn pink.

### Nutrition Information

- Calories: 426 calories
- Fiber: 2g fiber)
- Total Carbohydrate: 8g carbohydrate (6g sugars
- Cholesterol: 84mg cholesterol
- Protein: 27g protein.
- Total Fat: 32g fat (5g saturated fat)
- Sodium: 451mg sodium

## 566. Swordfish With Fennel And Tomatoes

*Serving: 4 servings. | Prep: 15mins | Cook: 10mins | Ready in:*

### Ingredients

- 1 medium onion, halved and thinly sliced
- 1 fennel bulb, halved and thinly sliced
- 3 tablespoons olive oil
- 1 garlic clove, minced
- 1 can (28 ounces) whole tomatoes, drained
- 2 tablespoons chicken broth
- 2 tablespoons white wine
- 3/4 teaspoon pepper
- 1/2 teaspoon kosher salt
- 1/2 cup loosely packed basil leaves, thinly sliced
- 1 tablespoon butter
- FISH:
- 4 swordfish steaks (8 ounces each)
- 2 tablespoons olive oil
- 1/2 teaspoon kosher salt
- 1/4 teaspoon pepper

### Direction

- Sauté fennel and onion with oil in a large skillet till softened. Add garlic in; allow to cook for another 1 minute. Mix salt, pepper, wine, broth, and tomatoes in. Bring to a boil. Lower heat; let simmer for 5 minutes, uncovered. Mix butter and basil in. Remove from the heat and put aside.
- Use oil to brush steaks; use pepper and salt to drizzle on. Moisten a paper towel with cooking oil and cover the grill rack lightly using long-handled tongs. Cover and broil swordfish 4 inches from the heat or grill over medium-hot heat for 5-7 minutes on every side or till fish just turns opaque. Serve along with tomato mixture.

### Nutrition Information

- Calories: 512 calories
- Total Fat: 28g fat (6g saturated fat)
- Sodium: 1225mg sodium
- Fiber: 5g fiber)
- Total Carbohydrate: 17g carbohydrate (7g sugars
- Cholesterol: 90mg cholesterol
- Protein: 45g protein.

## 567. Swordfish With Sauteed Vegetables

*Serving: 4 servings. | Prep: 20mins | Cook: 10mins | Ready in:*

### Ingredients

- 1/2 cup olive oil
- 2 green onions, sliced
- 2 tablespoons minced fresh rosemary or 2 teaspoons dried rosemary, crushed
- 2 tablespoons lime juice
- 2 tablespoons Dijon mustard
- 6 swordfish or halibut steaks (6 ounces each)
- VEGETABLES:
- 2 small zucchini
- 2 small yellow summer squash
- 1/4 cup sliced green onions
- 1 to 2 tablespoons minced fresh rosemary or 2 teaspoons dried rosemary, crushed
- 3 tablespoons olive oil
- 1 pound small red potatoes, cooked and cut into 1/2-inch slices
- 2 cups halved cherry tomatoes
- 1/2 to 3/4 teaspoon salt
- 1/4 teaspoon pepper

### Direction

- Mix the first 5 ingredients together in a large resealable plastic bag; place swordfish in. Seal bag and turn to cover; let sit for 30-45 minutes in the refrigerator.
- Strain and discard marinade. Moisten a paper towel with cooking oil and cover the grill rack lightly using long-handled tongs. Cover and broil swordfish 4 inches from the heat or grill over medium-hot heat till fish just turns opaque, or for 5-7 minutes each side.
- Slice yellow squash and zucchini lengthwise into 1/4-inch slices, then slice widthwise into 3-inch pieces. Sauté rosemary and onions with oil in a large skillet till onions get tender or for 1-2 minutes. Add squash in; sauté till crisp-tender or for 5-6 minutes. Add tomatoes and potatoes; allow to cook just till thoroughly heated. Use pepper and salt to drizzle on; toss to cover. Pair with swordfish when serving.

### Nutrition Information

- Calories:
- Sodium:
- Fiber:
- Total Carbohydrate:
- Cholesterol:
- Protein:
- Total Fat:

## 568. Tangy Lamb Tagine

*Serving: 8 servings. | Prep: 40mins | Cook: 08hours00mins | Ready in:*

### Ingredients

- 3 pounds lamb stew meat, cut into 1-1/2-inch cubes
- 1 teaspoon salt
- 1 teaspoon pepper
- 4 tablespoons olive oil, divided
- 6 medium carrots, sliced
- 2 medium onions, chopped
- 6 garlic cloves, minced
- 2 teaspoons grated lemon zest
- 1/4 cup lemon juice
- 1 tablespoon minced fresh gingerroot
- 1-1/2 teaspoons ground cinnamon
- 1-1/2 teaspoons ground cumin
- 1-1/2 teaspoons paprika
- 2-1/2 cups reduced-sodium chicken broth
- 1/4 cup sweet vermouth
- 1/4 cup honey
- 1/2 cup pitted dates, chopped
- 1/2 cup sliced almonds, toasted

### Direction

- Sprinkle pepper and salt over the lamb. Brown meat in batches in a Dutch oven with 2

tablespoons of oil. Move the meat to a 4 or 5-quart slow cooker using a slotted spoon.
- Sauté lemon zest, carrots, garlic, and onion in a Dutch oven with the remaining oil until tender-crisp. Put in paprika, lemon juice, cumin, cinnamon, and ginger; cook and stir for another 2 minutes. Move to the slow cooker.
- Mix in date, broth, honey, and vermouth; cover. Cook for 8-10 hours on low until the meat is tender. Scatter top with almonds.

## Nutrition Information

- Calories: 440 calories
- Protein: 38g protein.
- Total Fat: 19g fat (4g saturated fat)
- Sodium: 620mg sodium
- Fiber: 4g fiber)
- Total Carbohydrate: 28g carbohydrate (21g sugars
- Cholesterol: 111mg cholesterol

## 569. Tangy Lemon Catfish

*Serving: 2 servings. | Prep: 10mins | Cook: 10mins | Ready in:*

## Ingredients

- 2 tablespoons lemon juice
- 1 garlic clove, minced
- 1/4 teaspoon salt
- Dash dried oregano
- 1/2 pound catfish or whitefish fillets
- 1/4 cup cornmeal
- 2 tablespoons all-purpose flour
- 1-1/2 teaspoons canola oil
- 1-1/2 teaspoons butter
- TARTAR SAUCE:
- 1/4 cup mayonnaise
- 1 tablespoon finely chopped dill pickle
- 2 teaspoons finely chopped onion
- 2 teaspoons minced fresh dill or 3/4 teaspoon dill weed

## Direction

- Mix the garlic, oregano, salt and lemon juice in a resealable plastic bag. Add in the fillets then seal the plastic bag. Place inside a refrigerator for 30 minutes to an hour and turn it a few times.
- Drain the fillets and throw the marinade. Use a shallow bowl to mix flour and cornmeal. Coat the fillets with the cornmeal mixture. Use oil and butter to cook the fillets in a frying pan. Cook each side for about five minutes or until it turns golden brown.
- Prepare the tartar sauce by combining the pickle, onion, mayonnaise and dill. Serve the fish with the sauce.

## Nutrition Information

- Calories: 287 calories
- Cholesterol: 63mg cholesterol
- Protein: 22g protein. Diabetic Exchanges: 3 lean meat
- Total Fat: 10g fat (3g saturated fat)
- Sodium: 717mg sodium
- Fiber: 2g fiber)
- Total Carbohydrate: 26g carbohydrate (0 sugars

## 570. Tapenade Stuffed Chicken Breasts

*Serving: 4 servings. | Prep: 10mins | Cook: 20mins | Ready in:*

## Ingredients

- 4 oil-packed sun-dried tomatoes
- 4 pitted Greek olives
- 4 pitted Spanish olives
- 4 pitted ripe olives
- 1/4 cup roasted sweet red peppers, drained
- 4 garlic cloves, minced
- 1 tablespoon olive oil

- 2 teaspoons balsamic vinegar
- 4 boneless skinless chicken breast halves (6 ounces each)
- Grated Parmesan cheese

## Direction

- In a food processor, pulse the first 8 ingredients until the olives and tomatoes are chopped coarsely. Horizontally slice a pocket on the thickest area of each chicken breast then fill the olive mixture in the pockets. Use toothpicks to secure.
- Use cooking oil to grease a grill rack lightly. On medium heat, grill chicken while covering or broil four inches from heat for 8-10 mins per side or until an inserted thermometer in the stuffing registers 165 degrees F. Top with sprinkled cheese. Remove the toothpicks then serve.

## Nutrition Information

- Calories: 264 calories
- Sodium: 367mg sodium
- Fiber: 1g fiber)
- Total Carbohydrate: 5g carbohydrate (1g sugars
- Cholesterol: 94mg cholesterol
- Protein: 35g protein. Diabetic Exchanges: 5 lean meat
- Total Fat: 11g fat (2g saturated fat)

## 571. Tarragon Chicken Kiev

*Serving: 4 servings. | Prep: 01hours30mins | Cook: 20mins |Ready in:*

## Ingredients

- 6 tablespoons butter, softened, divided
- 1-1/2 teaspoons minced fresh tarragon or 1/2 teaspoon dried tarragon
- 4 boneless skinless chicken breast halves
- Salt, pepper and ground nutmeg to taste
- 1 egg
- 2 tablespoons water
- 1/2 cup all-purpose flour
- 1/2 cup dry bread crumbs
- LEMON TARRAGON SAUCE:
- 3 tablespoons butter
- 4-1/2 teaspoons all-purpose flour
- 1/2 teaspoon ground mustard
- 1-1/4 cups chicken broth
- 1-1/2 teaspoons minced fresh tarragon or 1/2 teaspoon dried tarragon
- 2 egg yolks
- 1 tablespoon lemon juice

## Direction

- Mix tarragon and 3 tablespoons butter in a small bowl; refrigerate. Form 4 two-inch logs from the tarragon butter; place in the freezer until firm. Pound the chicken until 1/8-inch thick; sprinkle nutmeg, pepper, and salt. Place each butter log in the middle of each chicken breast. Roll up and tuck at the end then use a toothpick to secure. Whisk water and egg in a shallow bowl. Dredge the chicken in flour then submerge in egg mixture; dredge in bread crumbs. Cook chicken in a pan with the remaining butter until golden brown; move to a greased eight-inch square baking pan. Bake for 20 minutes in 350 degrees oven without cover until the juices run clear.
- In the meantime, on low heat, melt butter in a pot to make the sauce. Mix in mustard and flour until smooth. Mix in tarragon and broth gradually; boil. Cook and stir for 2 minutes until thick; lower heat. Mix lemon juice and egg yolks in a bowl; beat in a small amount of hot mixture gradually. Pour the mixture in the pan while constantly mixing. Cook and stir for a minute until it reaches 160 degrees. Remove the toothpicks from the chicken then serve with sauce.

## Nutrition Information

- Calories: 434 calories

- Total Carbohydrate: 25g carbohydrate (1g sugars
- Cholesterol: 244mg cholesterol
- Protein: 13g protein.
- Total Fat: 31g fat (17g saturated fat)
- Sodium: 701mg sodium
- Fiber: 1g fiber)

### 572. Tasty Shrimp Penne

*Serving: 6 servings. | Prep: 10mins | Cook: 20mins | Ready in:*

## Ingredients

- 1-1/2 cups uncooked penne pasta
- 1/2 cup each chopped broccoli, zucchini and carrot
- 1/2 pound cooked medium shrimp, peeled and deveined
- 1-1/2 teaspoons minced garlic
- 1/2 teaspoon dried basil
- 1-1/2 teaspoons olive oil
- 1 cup spaghetti sauce
- 1/2 cup crumbled feta cheese
- Salt and pepper to taste

## Direction

- Following package directions to cook pasta, putting in vegetables during the final 5 minutes of cooking process. In the meantime, cook together basil, garlic and shrimp in a big skillet with oil until heated through, or about 1 to 2 minutes. Put in spaghetti sauce and bring to a boil. Lower the heat to low. Drain pasta and vegetables, then stir into the shrimp mixture. Put in pepper, salt and feta cheese.

## Nutrition Information

- Calories: 178 calories
- Sodium: 388mg sodium
- Fiber: 2g fiber)

- Total Carbohydrate: 19g carbohydrate (4g sugars
- Cholesterol: 80mg cholesterol
- Protein: 13g protein.
- Total Fat: 5g fat (2g saturated fat)

### 573. Tender Lamb With Mint Salsa

*Serving: 4 servings. | Prep: 15mins | Cook: 20mins | Ready in:*

## Ingredients

- 1 tablespoon plus 2 teaspoons olive oil
- 2 garlic cloves, minced
- 1 teaspoon each dried basil, thyme and rosemary, crushed
- 1/2 teaspoon salt
- 1/4 teaspoon pepper
- 2 racks of lamb (1 to 1-1/2 pounds each)
- SALSA:
- 1 cup minced fresh mint
- 1 small cucumber, peeled, seeded and chopped
- 1/2 cup seeded chopped tomato
- 1/3 cup finely chopped onion
- 1/3 cup chopped sweet yellow pepper
- 1 jalapeno pepper, seeded and chopped
- 3 tablespoons lemon juice
- 2 tablespoons sugar
- 2 garlic cloves, minced
- 3/4 teaspoon ground ginger
- 1/4 teaspoon salt

## Direction

- Mix seasonings, garlic and oil in a small bowl. Massage atop lamb. Put in a roasting pan, then cover and chill for one hour. Mix the salsa ingredients in a bowl, cover and then chill until serving.
- Bake the lamb while uncovered for 30 to 35 minutes at 375° or until the meat reaches the doneness desired (for medium-rare, the

internal temperature from the thermometer should be 145°; well-done, 170°; medium, 160°). Take out from oven and loosely cover with foil. Leave to stand for 5 to 10 minutes prior to cutting. Serve together with salsa.

## Nutrition Information

- Calories: 283 calories
- Protein: 21g protein.
- Total Fat: 16g fat (4g saturated fat)
- Sodium: 510mg sodium
- Fiber: 2g fiber)
- Total Carbohydrate: 14g carbohydrate (8g sugars
- Cholesterol: 66mg cholesterol

## 574. Tex Mex Chicken Starter

*Serving: 6 cups. | Prep: 10mins | Cook: 15mins | Ready in:*

### Ingredients

- 1/2 cup lemon juice
- 1/2 cup canola oil
- 3 tablespoons chili powder
- 1-1/2 teaspoons each garlic powder, ground cumin, dried coriander and dried oregano
- 3/4 teaspoon salt
- 3/4 teaspoon pepper
- 1/4 to 1/2 teaspoon cayenne pepper, optional
- 3 pounds boneless skinless chicken breasts, cut into 1-inch strips
- 3 medium onions, halved and sliced into rings
- 4 garlic cloves, minced

### Direction

- Mix seasonings, oil, and lemon juice in a big ziplock bag; put in chicken. Seal then turn the bag to coat the chicken; chill for an hour.
- On medium-high heat, boil marinade and chicken in batches in a big pan. Lower heat; cook and stir until the juices run clear for 6 minutes. Use tongs to move the chicken to a big bowl.
- Sauté garlic and onions in the drippings until the onions are tender-crisp; Put on chicken and mix thoroughly. Cool for half an hour.
- Split the mixture between 3 freezer containers; cover. Place in the freezer for up to three months. Thaw the mixture before using.

## Nutrition Information

- Calories: 231 calories
- Total Fat: 12g fat (2g saturated fat)
- Fiber: 2g fiber)
- Protein: 24g protein.
- Sodium: 224mg sodium
- Total Carbohydrate: 6g carbohydrate (3g sugars
- Cholesterol: 63mg cholesterol

## 575. Thick Beef Stew

*Serving: 3 servings. | Prep: 5mins | Cook: 20mins | Ready in:*

### Ingredients

- 1 portion Triple-Batch Beef, thawed
- 3 medium red potatoes, quartered and cut into 1/4-inch slices
- 1-1/4 cups water
- 1 to 1-1/2 teaspoons dried oregano
- 1 teaspoon salt
- 1 cup frozen peas
- 1 tablespoon cornstarch
- 2 tablespoons lemon juice

### Direction

- Mix salt, oregano, water, potatoes, and beef together in a big saucepan. Boil it. Lower the heat, simmer with a cover until the potatoes

are soft, about 10-15 minutes. Put in peas and heat through.
- Mix lemon juice and cornstarch until the mixture is smooth; slowly pour in the beef mixture. Boil it, cook while stirring until bubbly and thickened, about 2 minutes.

## Nutrition Information

- Calories:
- Total Fat:
- Sodium:
- Fiber:
- Total Carbohydrate:
- Cholesterol:
- Protein:

### 576. Tomato Dill Shrimp Stew

*Serving: 4 servings. | Prep: 5mins | Cook: 25mins | Ready in:*

## Ingredients

- 1 large onion, chopped
- 4 garlic cloves, minced
- 1 tablespoon olive oil
- 3 cups diced fresh tomatoes
- 1 can (8 ounces) tomato sauce
- 3 tablespoons minced fresh dill or 2 teaspoons dill weed
- 2 teaspoons Dijon mustard
- 1 teaspoon honey
- 1/2 teaspoon salt
- 1 pound cooked medium shrimp, peeled and devined
- 4 ounces crumbled feta cheese
- 1 cup minced fresh parsley

## Direction

- Sauté garlic and onion in a large saucepan with oil for 5 mins. Mix in salt, honey, mustard, dill, tomato sauce and tomatoes. Boil.

Lower the heat and simmer, uncovered, about 20 mins. Put in parsley, cheese and shrimp; simmer for 5 more mins.

## Nutrition Information

- Calories: 306 calories
- Sodium: 1282mg sodium
- Fiber: 4g fiber)
- Total Carbohydrate: 21g carbohydrate (0 sugars
- Cholesterol: 246mg cholesterol
- Protein: 31g protein.
- Total Fat: 11g fat (5g saturated fat)

### 577. Tomato Poached Halibut

*Serving: 4 servings. | Prep: 15mins | Cook: 15mins | Ready in:*

## Ingredients

- 1 tablespoon olive oil
- 2 poblano peppers, finely chopped
- 1 small onion, finely chopped
- 1 can (14-1/2 ounces) fire-roasted diced tomatoes, undrained
- 1 can (14-1/2 ounces) no-salt-added diced tomatoes, undrained
- 1/4 cup chopped pitted green olives
- 3 garlic cloves, minced
- 1/4 teaspoon pepper
- 1/8 teaspoon salt
- 4 halibut fillets (4 ounces each)
- 1/3 cup chopped fresh cilantro
- 4 lemon wedges
- Crusty whole grain bread, optional

## Direction

- Heat oil in a big nonstick skillet on moderately high heat. Put in onion and poblano peppers, then cook and stir until softened, about 4 to 6 minutes.

- Stir in salt, pepper, garlic, olives and tomatoes, then bring all to a boil. Lower heat to maintain a gentle simmer. Put in fillets and cook with a cover until it is easy for fish to flake using a fork, about 8 to 10 minutes. Sprinkle with cilantro and serve together with lemon wedges and bread, if wanted.

## Nutrition Information

- Calories: 224 calories
- Cholesterol: 56mg cholesterol
- Protein: 24g protein. Diabetic Exchanges: 3 lean meat
- Total Fat: 7g fat (1g saturated fat)
- Sodium: 651mg sodium
- Fiber: 4g fiber)
- Total Carbohydrate: 17g carbohydrate (8g sugars

## 578. Traditional Lamb Stew

*Serving: 4 servings. | Prep: 10mins | Cook: 60mins | Ready in:*

## Ingredients

- 1-1/2 pounds lamb stew meat
- 2 tablespoons olive oil, divided
- 3 large onions, quartered
- 3 medium carrots, cut into 1-inch pieces
- 4 small potatoes, peeled and cubed
- 1 can (14-1/2 ounces) beef broth
- 1 teaspoon salt
- 1/4 teaspoon pepper
- 1 tablespoon butter
- 1 tablespoon all-purpose flour
- 1-1/2 teaspoons minced fresh parsley
- 1-1/2 teaspoons minced chives
- 1/2 teaspoon minced fresh thyme

## Direction

- Brown meat in 1 tbsp. oil till meat isn't pink in a Dutch oven on medium heat. Use a slotted spoon to remove; put aside. Add leftover oil, carrots and onions to pan; cook, occasionally mixing, till onions are tender for 5 minutes. Add lamb, pepper, broth, salt and potatoes; boil.
- Take off heat; cover. Bake at 350° till veggies and meat are tender for 50-60 minutes.
- Remove veggies and meat into a big bowl with a slotted spoon; put aside. Keep warm. Put pan juices into separate bowl; put aside.
- Melt butter on medium heat in a Dutch oven; mix in flour till smooth. Whisk in pan juices slowly; boil. Mix and cook till thick for 2 minutes. Mix in veggies, meat, thyme, chives and parsley; heat through.

## Nutrition Information

- Calories:
- Fiber:
- Total Carbohydrate:
- Cholesterol:
- Protein:
- Total Fat:
- Sodium:

## 579. Tropical Lime Chicken

*Serving: 4 servings (1 cup salsa). | Prep: 20mins | Cook: 10mins | Ready in:*

## Ingredients

- SALSA:
- 1/2 cup pineapple tidbits
- 1 medium kiwifruit, peeled and chopped
- 1/4 cup chopped sweet red pepper
- 1 tablespoon lime juice
- 1 tablespoon white wine vinegar
- 1 tablespoon honey
- 1 teaspoon crushed red pepper flakes
- CHICKEN:

- 3 tablespoons plus 1-1/2 teaspoons lime juice
- 1 tablespoon canola oil
- 1 teaspoon grated lime zest
- 1/8 teaspoon salt
- 1/8 teaspoon pepper
- 4 boneless skinless chicken breast halves (4 ounces each)
- 1 cup uncooked couscous

## Direction

- Mix the salsa ingredients in a small bowl; cover then chill until serving.
- Mix pepper, lime juice, salt, lime zest, and oil in a big bowl; put in chicken and flip to coat. Cover and chill for 2-4 hours.
- Drain and get rid of the marinade. Put the chicken on a cooking-spray-coated broiler pan. Broil for 5-6 minutes per side, three inches from heat until the juices are clear. In the meantime, cook couscous following the package instructions. Serve with salsa and chicken.

## Nutrition Information

- Calories: 371 calories
- Cholesterol: 63mg cholesterol
- Protein: 30g protein.
- Total Fat: 7g fat (1g saturated fat)
- Sodium: 135mg sodium
- Fiber: 3g fiber)
- Total Carbohydrate: 49g carbohydrate (13g sugars

## 580. Tuna With Tuscan White Bean Salad

Serving: 4 servings. | Prep: 20mins | Cook: 10mins | Ready in:

## Ingredients

- 1 can (15 ounces) white kidney or cannellini beans, rinsed and drained
- 3 celery ribs, finely chopped
- 1 medium sweet red pepper, finely chopped
- 1 plum tomato, seeded and finely chopped
- 1/2 cup fresh basil leaves, thinly sliced
- 1/4 cup finely chopped red onion
- 3 tablespoons olive oil
- 2 tablespoons red wine vinegar
- 1 tablespoon lemon juice
- 1/4 teaspoon salt
- 1/4 teaspoon pepper
- TUNA:
- 4 tuna steaks (6 ounces each)
- 1 tablespoon olive oil
- 1/4 teaspoon salt
- 1/4 teaspoon pepper

## Direction

- Stir the first six ingredients together in a large bowl. Mix pepper, salt, lemon juice, vinegar, and oil together in a small bowl. Spoon over bean mixture; toss to cover. Let sit in the refrigerator till serving time.
- Use oil to brush tuna. Use pepper and salt to drizzle on; lay onto greased grill rack. Cover and broil 3-4 inches from the heat or grill over high heat till the center gets pink slightly, or for 3-4 minutes on every side for medium-rare. Pair with salad and serve.

## Nutrition Information

- Calories: 409 calories
- Total Fat: 16g fat (2g saturated fat)
- Sodium: 517mg sodium
- Fiber: 6g fiber)
- Total Carbohydrate: 20g carbohydrate (3g sugars
- Cholesterol: 77mg cholesterol
- Protein: 45g protein. Diabetic Exchanges: 5 lean meat

## 581. Turkey Gyro Pizza

*Serving: 6 servings. | Prep: 10mins | Cook: 25mins | Ready in:*

### Ingredients

- 2 cups biscuit/baking mix
- 6 tablespoons cold water
- 1/4 teaspoon dried oregano
- 1/4 cup Greek vinaigrette
- 1/2 cup pitted Greek olives, sliced
- 1/2 cup thinly sliced roasted sweet red pepper
- 1-1/2 cups shredded part-skim mozzarella cheese
- 1/2 cup crumbled feta cheese
- 1/2 cup chopped cucumber
- 1 small tomato, chopped
- Additional Greek vinaigrette, optional

### Direction

- Heat the oven to 425 degrees. Mix oregano, water, and biscuit mix in a small bowl to make a soft dough. Press the dough to fit a 12-inch greased pizza pan; press edge to shape a rim. Bake for 10-12 minutes or until light brown.
- Use 1/4 cup vinaigrette to brush over crust; place cheeses, red pepper, and olives on top. Bake for 8-10 minutes or until the crust turns light brown and cheese melts.
- Scatter with tomato and cucumber before serving. Sprinkle with additional vinaigrette, if wished.

### Nutrition Information

- Calories: 524 calories
- Protein: 18g protein.
- Total Fat: 28g fat (10g saturated fat)
- Sodium: 1716mg sodium
- Fiber: 3g fiber)
- Total Carbohydrate: 48g carbohydrate (4g sugars
- Cholesterol: 35mg cholesterol

## 582. Turkey Spinach Meat Loaf

*Serving: 10 slices. | Prep: 20mins | Cook: 30mins | Ready in:*

### Ingredients

- 1 medium onion, finely chopped
- 1 tablespoon canola oil
- 2 eggs
- 1/2 cup 2% milk
- 2 teaspoons lemon juice
- 1 teaspoon salt
- 1 teaspoon dried basil
- 1/2 teaspoon dried oregano
- 1/2 teaspoon pepper
- 2 cups soft whole wheat bread crumbs (about 5 slices)
- 1 package (10 ounces) frozen chopped spinach, thawed and squeezed dry
- 2-1/2 pounds lean ground turkey
- 1/2 cup salsa
- 1 tablespoon butter, melted

### Direction

- Sauté onion in oil in a small skillet until soft; put aside. Combine pepper, oregano, basil, salt, lemon juice, milk, and eggs in a small bowl. Stir in the reserved onion, spinach, and bread crumbs. Crumble turkey over the mixture and blend well.
- Form into a 12x5-in. loaf; arrange in a 13x9-in. baking dish greased with cooking spray. Next, scoop over top with salsa.
- Uncover and bake for a half-hour at 350°. Spray with butter and continue to bake until no pink remains and a thermometer states 165°, or for 30-35 more minutes.

### Nutrition Information

- Calories: 299 calories
- Sodium: 598mg sodium

- Fiber: 4g fiber)
- Total Carbohydrate: 17g carbohydrate (3g sugars
- Cholesterol: 136mg cholesterol
- Protein: 25g protein. Diabetic Exchanges: 3 lean meat
- Total Fat: 14g fat (4g saturated fat)

### 583. Tuscan Roast Pork Tenderloin

*Serving: 6 servings. | Prep: 10mins | Cook: 30mins | Ready in:*

## Ingredients

- 1-1/3 cups (2.8 ounces) French's® Original French Fried Onions
- 1 teaspoon dried rosemary, crushed
- 1/2 teaspoon garlic powder
- 1/4 teaspoon pepper
- 1-1/2 pounds pork tenderloin
- 2 tablespoons spicy brown or honey mustard

## Direction

- In a resealable plastic bag, put pepper, garlic, rosemary and onions. Seal the bag; crush with a rolling pin or with hands. Brush the pork with mustard. Allow to coat in seasoned onion crumbs; firmly press to adhere.
- Arrange the pork on a foil-lined baking sheet. Bake without a cover for 30 minutes at 400°, or till a meat thermometer reads 160°. Allow to stand for 10 minutes before slicing. Serve with more mustard to your preference.

## Nutrition Information

- Calories:
- Total Carbohydrate:
- Cholesterol:
- Protein:
- Total Fat:

- Sodium:
- Fiber:

### 584. Vegetable Stew

*Serving: about 8-10 servings (3-1/2 quarts). | Prep: 5mins | Cook: 01hours45mins | Ready in:*

## Ingredients

- 1-1/2 pounds lean boneless lamb or pork, cut into 1-inch cubes
- 2 tablespoons vegetable oil
- 1 medium onion, chopped
- 2 medium potatoes, peeled and cubed
- 1 medium leek, sliced
- 6 cups beef broth
- 2 tablespoons tomato paste
- 1 teaspoon salt
- 1/2 teaspoon dried thyme
- 1/4 teaspoon pepper
- 4 cups chopped cabbage
- 2 to 3 cups cauliflower florets
- 3 carrots, sliced
- 1 celery rib, sliced
- 1 package (9 ounces) frozen cut green beans, thawed
- Minced fresh parsley
- Cornstarch and water, optional

## Direction

- Brown meat in oil on medium high heat in a Dutch oven. Add onion. Cook till tender; drain. Add next 7 ingredients; cover. Simmer for 1 hour till meat is tender. Add parsley, beans, celery, carrots, cauliflower and cabbage; cover. Simmer for 30 minutes till veggies are tender. Thicken with cornstarch dissolved in water if desired.

## Nutrition Information

- Calories: 141 calories

- Sodium: 595mg sodium
- Fiber: 3g fiber)
- Total Carbohydrate: 12g carbohydrate (4g sugars
- Cholesterol: 32mg cholesterol
- Protein: 12g protein.
- Total Fat: 5g fat (1g saturated fat)

### 585. Wyoming Lamb Stew

*Serving: 6 servings. | Prep: 30mins | Cook: 02hours00mins | Ready in:*

## Ingredients

- 5 bacon strips, diced
- 1/4 cup all-purpose flour
- 1 teaspoon salt
- 1/2 teaspoon pepper
- 6 lamb shanks (about 6 pounds)
- 1 can (28 ounces) diced tomatoes, undrained
- 1 can (14-1/2 ounces) beef broth
- 1 can (8 ounces) tomato sauce
- 2 cans (4 ounces each) mushroom stems and pieces, drained
- 2 medium onions, chopped
- 1 cup chopped celery
- 1/2 cup minced fresh parsley
- 2 tablespoons prepared horseradish
- 1 tablespoon cider vinegar
- 2 teaspoon Worcestershire sauce
- 1 garlic clove, minced

## Direction

- Cook bacon over medium heat in a Dutch oven until crispy. Transfer bacon to paper towels to drain with a slotted spoon, saving drippings. Set bacon aside for garnish; chill in the fridge.
- Combine pepper, salt, and flour in a big resealable plastic bag; put in lamb shanks, one by one, and shake until well coated. Cook shanks in the reserve bacon drippings until all sides are browned; drain. Put in the rest of ingredients. Bring to a boil.
- Bake, covered, for 2 to 2.5 hours at 325° until meat is very tender; skim fat. Sprinkle top with the reserved bacon to garnish.

## Nutrition Information

- Calories: 569 calories
- Protein: 49g protein.
- Total Fat: 31g fat (13g saturated fat)
- Sodium: 1423mg sodium
- Fiber: 5g fiber)
- Total Carbohydrate: 21g carbohydrate (9g sugars
- Cholesterol: 171mg cholesterol

# Chapter 7: Greek Vegetarian Recipes

\*\*\*

### 586. A Touch Of Greek Dip

*Serving: 1-1/4 cups. | Prep: 10mins | Cook: 0mins | Ready in:*

## Ingredients

- 1/2 cup 1% cottage cheese
- 1/2 cup crumbled feta cheese
- 1/4 cup fat-free milk
- 1 teaspoon dried oregano
- 1/4 teaspoon grated lemon peel
- Pepper to taste
- Assorted fresh vegetables

## Direction

- Combine pepper, lemon peel, oregano, feta cheese, cottage cheese and milk in a blender. Process, covered, till smooth. In a small bowl, place the mixture. Serve with vegetables.

## Nutrition Information

- Calories: 54 calories
- Sodium: 213mg sodium
- Fiber: 1g fiber)
- Total Carbohydrate: 2g carbohydrate (2g sugars
- Cholesterol: 7mg cholesterol
- Protein: 6g protein. Diabetic Exchanges: 1/2 milk.
- Total Fat: 2g fat (1g saturated fat)

## 587. Almond "Feta" With Herb Oil

*Serving: 1-1/2 cups. | Prep: 25mins | Cook: 35mins | Ready in:*

## Ingredients

- 1 cup blanched almonds
- 1/2 cup water
- 1/4 cup lemon juice
- 5 tablespoons olive oil, divided
- 1 garlic clove
- 1-1/4 teaspoons salt
- 1-1/2 teaspoons minced fresh thyme or 1/2 teaspoon dried thyme
- 1/2 teaspoon minced fresh rosemary or 1/8 teaspoon dried rosemary, crushed
- Assorted crackers

## Direction

- In cold water, rinse almonds then put in a big bowl; pour in water to submerge by three inches. Cover then let it sit overnight.
- Drain the almonds then rinse; get rid of the liquid. Puree the almonds, salt, half cup water, garlic, 3 tablespoons oil and lemon juice in a food processor with cover for 5-6 minutes.
- Line four cheesecloth layers in a big strainer then set over a big bowl; add the almond mixture. Lift the sides of the cloth then bind with a string to make a bag. Chill overnight.
- Squeeze any liquid out then remove the cloth bag; remove the liquid in the bowl. Place ball in a baking sheet lined with parchment paper. Slightly flatten to a six-inch round.
- Bake for 35-40 minutes in a 200 degrees F oven until firm; cool. Refrigerate to chill.
- On medium heat, heat the remaining oil, rosemary, and thyme for 2 minutes in a small pan. Cool the mixture to room temperature then sprinkle on top of the almond mixture. Serve it with crackers.

## Nutrition Information

- Calories: 122 calories
- Cholesterol: 0 cholesterol
- Protein: 3g protein.
- Total Fat: 12g fat (1g saturated fat)
- Sodium: 249mg sodium
- Fiber: 1g fiber)
- Total Carbohydrate: 3g carbohydrate (1g sugars

## 588. Anytime Frittata

*Serving: 4 servings. | Prep: 25mins | Cook: 5mins | Ready in:*

## Ingredients

- 1-1/4 cups egg substitute
- 2 large eggs
- 1/2 teaspoon dried oregano
- 1/8 teaspoon pepper
- 1 small onion, chopped
- 1 garlic clove, minced
- 1 teaspoon butter
- 3 plum tomatoes, chopped

- 1/2 cup crumbled feta cheese
- 2 tablespoons capers, drained

### Direction

- Mix pepper, oregano, eggs and egg substitute together in a small-sized bowl; put aside. In one 10-in. oven-proof skillet, sauté garlic and onion in butter for 2 minutes. Mix in tomatoes; heat through.
- Add reserved egg mixture to the skillet. Lower the heat; keep it covered and let cook till almost set, about 4 to 6 minutes.
- Drizzle with capers and cheese. Broil 3-4 inches away from the heat till eggs become set totally, about 2 to 3 minutes. Allow it to rest for 5 minutes. Chop into wedges.

### Nutrition Information

- Calories: 138 calories
- Protein: 14g protein. Diabetic Exchanges: 2 lean meat
- Total Fat: 6g fat (3g saturated fat)
- Sodium: 465mg sodium
- Fiber: 2g fiber)
- Total Carbohydrate: 6g carbohydrate (4g sugars
- Cholesterol: 116mg cholesterol

## 589. Apple Goat Cheese Bruschetta

*Serving: 16 appetizers. | Prep: 15mins | Cook: 5mins | Ready in:*

### Ingredients

- 16 slices French bread (1/2 inch thick)
- 1 medium Fuji apple, chopped
- 1/4 cup crumbled goat cheese
- 3/4 teaspoon minced fresh thyme
- 1/2 teaspoon minced fresh oregano
- 1/4 teaspoon coarsely ground pepper

### Direction

- Arrange the bread onto a baking sheet with no grease. Broil until golden brown for 1 to 2 minutes, 3 to 4 inches away from the heat source. Combine pepper, oregano, thyme, goat cheese, and apples; then sprinkle the mixture over the bread. Broil until cheese has softened, about 1 more minute.

### Nutrition Information

- Calories: 157 calories
- Sodium: 206mg sodium
- Fiber: 2g fiber)
- Total Carbohydrate: 24g carbohydrate (2g sugars
- Cholesterol: 6mg cholesterol
- Protein: 4g protein.
- Total Fat: 5g fat (2g saturated fat)

## 590. Around The World Tapenade

*Serving: 16 appetizers. | Prep: 10mins | Cook: 0mins | Ready in:*

### Ingredients

- 1/2 cup chopped roasted sweet red pepper
- 1/2 cup pitted Greek olives
- 1/4 cup chopped poblano pepper
- 2 tablespoons lemon juice
- 2 tablespoons olive oil
- 1 tablespoon minced fresh parsley
- 1 tablespoon capers, drained
- 2 garlic cloves, minced
- 1/4 teaspoon dried thyme
- 16 slices French bread baguette (1/2 inch thick), toasted

### Direction

- Process the first 9 ingredients in a food processor with cover to combine. Put a tablespoon of tapenade over each slice of baguette.

## Nutrition Information

- Calories: 63 calories
- Cholesterol: 0 cholesterol
- Protein: 1g protein. Diabetic Exchanges: 1/2 starch
- Total Fat: 3g fat (0 saturated fat)
- Sodium: 183mg sodium
- Fiber: 0 fiber)
- Total Carbohydrate: 7g carbohydrate (0 sugars

## 591. Artichoke Tomato Salad

*Serving: 8 servings. | Prep: 20mins | Cook: 0mins | Ready in:*

## Ingredients

- 5 large tomatoes (about 2 pounds), cut into wedges
- 1/4 teaspoon salt
- 1/4 teaspoon pepper
- 1 jar (7-1/2 ounces) marinated quartered artichoke hearts, drained
- 1 can (2-1/4 ounces) sliced ripe olives, drained
- 2 tablespoons minced fresh parsley
- 2 tablespoons white wine vinegar
- 2 garlic cloves, minced

## Direction

- Lay tomato wedges on a large platter; use salt and pepper to sprinkle. Toss remaining ingredients in a small bowl; transfer the mixture over tomatoes.

## Nutrition Information

- Calories: 74 calories
- Protein: 1g protein. Diabetic Exchanges: 1 vegetable
- Total Fat: 5g fat (1g saturated fat)
- Sodium: 241mg sodium
- Fiber: 2g fiber)
- Total Carbohydrate: 7g carbohydrate (3g sugars
- Cholesterol: 0 cholesterol

## 592. Artichokes With Lemon Mint Dressing

*Serving: 4 servings (1 cup dressing). | Prep: 10mins | Cook: 20mins | Ready in:*

## Ingredients

- 4 medium artichokes
- 1 package (12.3 ounces) silken firm tofu
- 4 teaspoons minced fresh mint or 1-1/4 teaspoons dried mint
- 4 teaspoons lemon juice
- 1 tablespoon olive oil
- 2-1/2 teaspoons honey mustard
- 1 teaspoon grated lemon peel
- 3/4 teaspoon salt
- 1/4 teaspoon curry powder
- 1/4 teaspoon pepper

## Direction

- In a steamer basket, arrange the artichokes upside down; set the steamer basket over a pot with an inch of boiling water. Cover; steam the artichokes for 20-25 minutes until tender.
- In the meantime, process the remaining ingredients in a food processor or blender with cover until smooth to make the dressing. Serve it with artichokes.

## Nutrition Information

- Calories: 154 calories
- Sodium: 615mg sodium
- Fiber: 7g fiber)

- Total Carbohydrate: 18g carbohydrate (4g sugars
- Cholesterol: 0 cholesterol
- Protein: 10g protein. Diabetic Exchanges: 1 vegetable
- Total Fat: 6g fat (1g saturated fat)

### 593. Asparagus Cheese Bundles

*Serving: 8 servings. | Prep: 20mins | Cook: 10mins | Ready in:*

## Ingredients

- 1 cup water
- 1/2 pound fresh asparagus, trimmed and cut into 2-inch pieces
- 2 medium carrots, julienned
- 1 package (8 ounces) cream cheese, softened
- 1 egg
- 2 tablespoons minced fresh basil or 2 teaspoons dried basil
- 1/2 cup crumbled feta cheese
- 8 flour tortillas (8 inches), warrmed
- 2 tablespoons milk
- 2 teaspoons sesame seeds

## Direction

- Bring water in a big saucepan to a boil. Put in carrots and asparagus, and then cook without a cover for about 5 minutes. Drain.
- Beat together bail, egg and cream cheese in a small bowl, and then stir in feta cheese.
- Put in the center of each tortilla with a mound of vegetables, and then place 2 rounded tablespoonfuls of cheese mixture on top. Fold the ends as well as sides over filling then roll it up.
- Arrange on an ungreased baking sheet with seam-side facing down. Use milk to brush over and sprinkle with sesame seeds. Bake at 425 degrees until they turn golden brown and heated through, about 10 to 14 minutes.

## Nutrition Information

- Calories: 288 calories
- Fiber: 1g fiber)
- Total Carbohydrate: 29g carbohydrate (2g sugars
- Cholesterol: 62mg cholesterol
- Protein: 9g protein.
- Total Fat: 15g fat (8g saturated fat)
- Sodium: 417mg sodium

### 594. Asparagus Phyllo Bake

*Serving: 12 servings. | Prep: 25mins | Cook: 50mins | Ready in:*

## Ingredients

- 2 pounds fresh asparagus, trimmed and cut into 1-inch pieces
- 5 large eggs, lightly beaten
- 1 carton (15 ounces) ricotta cheese
- 1 cup shredded Swiss cheese
- 2 tablespoons grated Parmesan cheese
- 2 garlic cloves, minced
- 1/2 teaspoon salt
- 1/2 teaspoon grated lemon peel
- 1/2 teaspoon pepper
- 1/2 cup slivered almonds, toasted
- 3/4 cup butter, melted
- 16 sheets phyllo dough (14x9 inches)

## Direction

- Boil 8 cups water in a big saucepan. Put in asparagus, cook without a cover just until the asparagus are bright green, about 30 seconds. Take the asparagus out and immediately put into ice water. Strain and tap dry. Combine seasonings, cheeses, and eggs in a big bowl, mix in asparagus and almonds.
- Start preheating the oven to 375°. Brush some of the butter over a 13x9-inch baking dish. Roll

out the phyllo dough. In the prepared dish, put 8 sheets of phyllo, brush butter over each phyllo sheets. Cover the rest of the phyllo in plastic wrap and a moist towel so they don't dry out.
- Spread the phyllo layers with the ricotta mixture. Put the leftover phyllo sheets on top, brush butter over each phyllo sheets. Slice into 12 rectangles. Bake until turning golden brown, about 50-55 minutes.

## Nutrition Information

- Calories: 295 calories
- Cholesterol: 142mg cholesterol
- Protein: 13g protein.
- Total Fat: 22g fat (12g saturated fat)
- Sodium: 351mg sodium
- Fiber: 2g fiber)
- Total Carbohydrate: 13g carbohydrate (4g sugars

## 595. Asparagus Spanakopita

*Serving: 12 servings. | Prep: 30mins | Cook: 30mins | Ready in:*

## Ingredients

- 2 cups cut fresh asparagus (1-inch pieces)
- 20 sheets phyllo dough, (14 inches x 9 inches)
- Nonstick cooking spray
- Refrigerated butter-flavored spray
- 2 cups torn fresh spinach
- 3 ounces crumbled feta cheese
- 2 tablespoons butter
- 1/4 cup all-purpose flour
- 1-1/2 cups fat-free milk
- 3 tablespoons lemon juice
- 1 teaspoon dill weed
- 1 teaspoon dried thyme
- 1/4 teaspoon salt

## Direction

- In a steamer basket, put the asparagus and place it on top of a saucepan with 1-inch of water, then boil. Put cover and let it steam for 5 minutes or until it becomes crisp-tender.
- Put 1 sheet of phyllo dough in a cooking spray coated 13x9-inch baking dish, then cut if needed. Use butter-flavored spray to spritz the dough. Redo the layers 9 times. Lay out the asparagus, feta cheese and spinach on top. Cover it using a sheet of phyllo dough, then spritz it using butter-flavored spray. Redo the process using the leftover phyllo. Slice it into 12 pieces. Let it bake for 30-35 minutes at 350 degrees without cover, or until it turns golden brown.
- To make the sauce, in a small saucepan, melt the butter. Mix in the flour until it becomes smooth, then slowly add the milk. Stir in salt, thyme, dill and lemon juice, then boil. Let it cook and stir for 1 to 2 minutes until it becomes thick. Serve the spanakopita with the sauce.

## Nutrition Information

- Calories: 112 calories
- Fiber: 1g fiber)
- Total Carbohydrate: 15g carbohydrate (0 sugars
- Cholesterol: 12mg cholesterol
- Protein: 5g protein. Diabetic Exchanges: 1 starch
- Total Fat: 4g fat (2g saturated fat)
- Sodium: 242mg sodium

## 596. Asparagus Fennel Pasta Salad

*Serving: 14 servings. | Prep: 25mins | Cook: 20mins | Ready in:*

## Ingredients

- 1 pound fresh asparagus, trimmed and cut into 3/4-inch pieces
- 2 medium onions, halved and thinly sliced
- 1 small fennel bulb, sliced
- 2 tablespoons olive oil
- 8 ounces uncooked penne pasta
- 4 medium tomatoes, seeded and diced
- 12 pitted Greek olives, sliced
- 1 cup minced fresh parsley
- VINAIGRETTE:
- 1/4 cup olive oil
- 1/4 cup lemon juice
- 2 garlic cloves, minced
- 1/2 teaspoon Dijon mustard
- 1/2 teaspoon salt
- 1/4 teaspoon pepper
- 1 cup (4 ounces) crumbled feta cheese

### Direction

- Place fennel, onions, and asparagus in a 15x10x1-inch baking pan. Drizzle oil over the vegetables and stir until evenly coated. Bake for 20 to 25 minutes at 400 degrees or until crisp-tender and lightly brown, stirring sometimes.
- In the meantime, cook pasta as directed on the package. Drain off water and transfer pasta into a large serving bowl. Add roasted vegetables, parsley, olives, and tomatoes.
- Combine pepper, salt, mustard, garlic, lemon juice, and oil in a small bowl, stir properly. Pour dressing over salad and toss until evenly coated. Top with feta cheese before serving.

### Nutrition Information

- Calories: 167 calories
- Total Fat: 8g fat (2g saturated fat)
- Sodium: 278mg sodium
- Fiber: 3g fiber)
- Total Carbohydrate: 19g carbohydrate (3g sugars
- Cholesterol: 4mg cholesterol
- Protein: 5g protein. Diabetic Exchanges: 1-1/2 fat

## 597. Balsamic Cucumber Salad

*Serving: 6 servings. | Prep: 15mins | Cook: 0mins | Ready in:*

### Ingredients

- 1 large English cucumber, halved and sliced
- 2 cups grape tomatoes, halved
- 1 medium red onion, halved and thinly sliced
- 1/2 cup balsamic vinaigrette
- 3/4 cup crumbled reduced-fat feta cheese

### Direction

- Mix onion, tomatoes, and cucumber in a big bowl. Add in vinaigrette and mix to coat. Put in the fridge, cover it until serving. Mix in cheese before eating. Use a slotted spoon to eat.

### Nutrition Information

- Calories: 90 calories
- Sodium: 356mg sodium
- Fiber: 1g fiber)
- Total Carbohydrate: 9g carbohydrate (5g sugars
- Cholesterol: 5mg cholesterol
- Protein: 4g protein. Diabetic Exchanges: 1 vegetable
- Total Fat: 5g fat (1g saturated fat)

## 598. Bean Spread On Pita Crackers

*Serving: 3 cups. | Prep: 20mins | Cook: 30mins | Ready in:*

### Ingredients

- 1 cup chopped onion
- 1 garlic clove, minced
- 3 tablespoons olive oil
- 2 cans (15-1/2 ounces each) great northern beans, rinsed and drained
- 3/4 cup chicken or vegetable broth
- 1 teaspoon minced fresh rosemary
- 1/2 teaspoon salt
- 1/4 teaspoon pepper
- PITA CRACKERS:
- 4 pita breads (6 inches)
- 1/4 cup olive oil
- 1 tablespoon sesame seeds, toasted
- 2 teaspoons onion powder
- 1-1/2 teaspoons poppy seeds
- 1 teaspoon dried thyme
- 1/2 teaspoon kosher salt

## Direction

- Sauté garlic and onion with oil in a big skillet until softened, about 3 minutes. Put in pepper, salt, rosemary, broth and beans, then bring to a boil. Lower heat and simmer about 20 minutes. Allow to cool somewhat, then put half of the mixture into a food processor or blender. Cover and process until smooth, then turn to a bowl. Repeat. Allow to cool to room temperature.
- For crackers, split each pita bread horizontally in half into 2 rounds, then brush with oil. Mix together salt, thyme, poppy seeds, onion powder and sesame seeds and sprinkle over pitas. Broil 3 to 4 inches far from the source of heat until crisp and browned a little, about 2 minutes. Allow to cool on wire racks, then break into big pieces and serve with spread.

## Nutrition Information

- Calories: 197 calories
- Sodium: 517mg sodium
- Fiber: 4g fiber)
- Total Carbohydrate: 24g carbohydrate (1g sugars
- Cholesterol: 0 cholesterol
- Protein: 6g protein.
- Total Fat: 9g fat (1g saturated fat)

### 599. Berries In A Nest

*Serving: 8 servings. | Prep: 15mins | Cook: 7mins | Ready in:*

## Ingredients

- 4 cups halved fresh strawberries
- 1 cup fresh blackberries
- 1 cup fresh raspberries
- 1/3 cup sugar
- 3 tablespoons balsamic vinegar
- 1/4 to 1/2 teaspoon coarsely ground pepper
- PHYLLO NESTS:
- 8 sheets phyllo dough (14 inches x 9 inches)
- Cooking spray
- 2 teaspoons sugar
- 1/4 teaspoon ground cinnamon

## Direction

- Combine raspberries, blackberries and strawberries in a large bowl. Sprinkle with sugar and toss gently until well coated. Allow to stand for 20 minutes. Add vinegar to berries mixture and sprinkle with pepper. Toss gently until well coated. Cover and chill in refrigerator for 2 hours.
- To make phyllo nests, use cooking spray to coat giant nonstick muffin cups; set aside. Unroll phyllo dough sheets; remove one sheet (keep remaining dough covered with a damp cloth and plastic wrap while assembling). For each nest, cut one sheet in half lengthwise and cut in thirds widthwise. Stack 3 sections then place in a prepared cup; coat with cooking spray. Stack the remaining three sections and put in cup, alternating points. Coat with cooking spray. Mix cinnamon and sugar together; sprinkle about 1/4 teaspoon sugar-cinnamon over dough. Repeat until no dough sheet is left.

- Bake at 375° for 7 to 8 minutes or until dough turns golden brown. Let cool for 5 minutes then carefully transfer to a wire rack and allow to rest until completely cooled.
- Stuff each nest with about 3/4 cup berry mixture with a slotted spoon. Add a small amount of juice on top. Serve right away.

## Nutrition Information

- Calories: 142 calories
- Sodium: 92mg sodium
- Fiber: 4g fiber)
- Total Carbohydrate: 33g carbohydrate (0 sugars
- Cholesterol: 0 cholesterol
- Protein: 3g protein. Diabetic Exchanges: 1 starch
- Total Fat: 1g fat (1g saturated fat)

### 600. Black Bean Pineapple Salad

*Serving: 6 servings. | Prep: 10mins | Cook: 0mins | Ready in:*

## Ingredients

- 6 cups fresh baby spinach
- 1 can (15-1/2 ounces) unsweetened pineapple chunks, drained
- 1 can (15 ounces) black beans, rinsed and drained
- 1/2 cup each chopped sweet red and orange peppers
- 1/2 cup crumbled feta cheese
- 1/4 cup prepared balsamic vinaigrette

## Direction

- Combine cheese, pepper, beans, pineapple and spinach in a large bowl. Pour vinaigrette over salad and toss until well coated. Serve right away.

## Nutrition Information

- Calories: 149 calories
- Fiber: 5g fiber)
- Total Carbohydrate: 23g carbohydrate (10g sugars
- Cholesterol: 5mg cholesterol
- Protein: 6g protein. Diabetic Exchanges: 1 lean meat
- Total Fat: 3g fat (1g saturated fat)
- Sodium: 338mg sodium

### 601. Blarney Stone Appetizer

*Serving: about 6-1/2 dozen. | Prep: 10mins | Cook: 45mins | Ready in:*

## Ingredients

- 1 large onion, chopped
- 3 tablespoons butter
- 2 packages (10 ounces each) frozen chopped spinach, thawed and squeezed dry
- 1 can (10-3/4 ounces) condensed cream of mushroom soup, undiluted
- 4 eggs, lightly beaten
- 1 cup sliced fresh mushrooms
- 1/4 cup dried bread crumbs
- 1/4 cup crumbled feta cheese
- 1/8 teaspoon dried oregano
- 1/8 teaspoon dried basil
- Dash ground nutmeg
- Salt and pepper to taste
- 2 tablespoons grated Parmesan cheese

## Direction

- Sauté onion in a big pan with butter; put in pepper, spinach, salt, soup, nutmeg, eggs, basil, mushrooms, oregano, feta cheese, and crumbs. Scoop to a greased 9-inch square baking pan then scatter with Parmesan cheese.

- Bake for 45-50 minutes in a 325 degrees F oven without cover until an inserted knife in the middle comes out without residue. Slice into one-inch squares.

## Nutrition Information

- Calories: 47 calories
- Protein: 2g protein.
- Total Fat: 3g fat (1g saturated fat)
- Sodium: 140mg sodium
- Fiber: 1g fiber)
- Total Carbohydrate: 3g carbohydrate (1g sugars
- Cholesterol: 38mg cholesterol

## 602. Bow Tie & Spinach Salad

*Serving: 6 servings. | Prep: 15mins | Cook: 15mins | Ready in:*

### Ingredients

- 2 cups uncooked multigrain bow tie pasta
- 1 can (15 ounces) chickpeas or garbanzo beans, rinsed and drained
- 6 cups fresh baby spinach (about 6 ounces)
- 2 cups fresh broccoli florets
- 2 plum tomatoes, chopped
- 1 medium sweet red pepper, chopped
- 1/2 cup cubed part-skim mozzarella cheese
- 1/2 cup pitted Greek olives, halved
- 1/4 cup minced fresh basil
- 1/3 cup reduced-fat sun-dried tomato salad dressing
- 1/4 teaspoon salt
- 1/4 cup chopped walnuts, toasted

### Direction

- Cook pasta as directed on package. Drain off water and transfer pasta into a large bowl Add basil, olives, cheese, vegetables, and beans to the pasta. Pour the dressing over the pasta mixture and season with salt; stir well to coat. Garnish with walnuts, then enjoy.

## Nutrition Information

- Calories: 319 calories
- Cholesterol: 6mg cholesterol
- Protein: 14g protein. Diabetic Exchanges: 2 starch
- Total Fat: 13g fat (2g saturated fat)
- Sodium: 660mg sodium
- Fiber: 7g fiber)
- Total Carbohydrate: 39g carbohydrate (6g sugars

## 603. Brown Rice, Tomato & Basil Salad

*Serving: 10 servings. | Prep: 20mins | Cook: 30mins | Ready in:*

### Ingredients

- 2 cups uncooked brown basmati rice
- 2 tablespoons olive oil
- 1 medium onion, finely chopped
- 3 cups grape tomatoes, halved
- 3 garlic cloves, minced
- 1 tablespoon balsamic vinegar
- 6 ounces feta cheese, cut into 1/2-inch cubes
- 1/2 cup fresh basil leaves, thinly sliced
- 1/4 cup pitted Greek olives, coarsely chopped
- 1 teaspoon salt
- 1/2 teaspoon pepper

### Direction

- Following the instruction on the package, cook rice. At the same time, over medium heat, heat oil in a big skillet. Put in onion; cook and mix till soft. Put in garlic and tomatoes; cook for 1 more minute. Take away from heat; mix in vinegar.

- In a big bowl, add rice. Put in pepper, salt, olives, basil, cheese and tomato mixture; coat by lightly mixing. Serve when still warm or at room temperature.

## Nutrition Information

- Calories: 256 calories
- Protein: 6g protein.
- Total Fat: 11g fat (3g saturated fat)
- Sodium: 516mg sodium
- Fiber: 2g fiber)
- Total Carbohydrate: 34g carbohydrate (3g sugars
- Cholesterol: 15mg cholesterol

## 604. Bulgur Salad In Lemon Baskets

*Serving: 12 servings. | Prep: 15mins | Cook: 0mins | Ready in:*

## Ingredients

- 2/3 cup uncooked bulgur
- 2 cups boiling water
- 1-1/3 cups diced seeded tomatoes
- 2 tablespoons sliced green onions
- 1/2 cup diced peeled cucumber
- 1/3 cup minced fresh parsley
- 3 tablespoons vegetable oil
- 3 tablespoons lemon juice
- 2 teaspoons sugar
- 1/2 teaspoon salt
- 1/2 teaspoon oregano
- 1/4 teaspoon pepper
- 12 medium lemons

## Direction

- In a bowl, put bulgur. Mix in water, put a cover on and let it sit until the bulgur has soaked up most of the water, or for about 30 minutes. Strain and squeeze dry. Mix in parsley, cucumber, onions, and tomatoes. Mix pepper, oregano, salt, sugar, lemon juice, and oil together in a tightly fitting lidded jar; shake well. Put on the bulgur mixture and coat by tossing. Chill.
- Carve a 1/2-in.-wide strip around the top of lemons to resemble basket handles. Carve the skin, start from the bottom of the handle on one side to the other side. Slice along the lines using a sharp knife. Take away the skin. Do the same on the other side. Remove the pulp inside the basket and below the handle with a spoon and sharp knife. Use the salad to stuff in.

## Nutrition Information

- Calories: 66 calories
- Sodium: 103mg sodium
- Fiber: 2g fiber)
- Total Carbohydrate: 8g carbohydrate (1g sugars
- Cholesterol: 0 cholesterol
- Protein: 1g protein.
- Total Fat: 4g fat (0 saturated fat)

## 605. Bulgur Wheat Salad

*Serving: 6 servings. | Prep: 35mins | Cook: 0mins | Ready in:*

## Ingredients

- 1 cup bulgur
- 1 cup boiling water
- 2 tablespoons lemon juice
- 2 tablespoons olive oil
- 1 garlic clove, minced
- 1/2 teaspoon salt
- 1/2 cup minced fresh parsley
- 2 medium tomatoes, chopped
- 4 green onions, chopped

## Direction

- Use a large bowl to contain bulgur; pour water in the bowl and stir well. Cover and set aside until water is absorbed, or for 30 minutes.
- Combine salt, garlic, oil, and lemon juice in a small bowl. Add bulgur and stir well. Sprinkle parsley. Cover and chill in the fridge for at least 1 hour. Stir in onions and tomatoes just before serving.

## Nutrition Information

- Calories: 137 calories
- Sodium: 210mg sodium
- Fiber: 5g fiber)
- Total Carbohydrate: 22g carbohydrate (2g sugars
- Cholesterol: 0 cholesterol
- Protein: 4g protein. Diabetic Exchanges: 1-1/2 starch
- Total Fat: 5g fat (1g saturated fat)

### 606. Buttercup Squash Coffee Cake

*Serving: 10-12 servings. | Prep: 15mins | Cook: 55mins | Ready in:*

## Ingredients

- CRUMB MIXTURE:
- 1/4 cup packed brown sugar
- 1/4 cup sugar
- 1/4 cup all-purpose flour
- 1/4 cup quick-cooking oats
- 1/4 cup chopped nuts
- 1-1/2 teaspoons ground cinnamon
- 3 tablespoons cold butter
- CAKE:
- 1/2 cup butter-flavored shortening
- 1 cup sugar
- 2 large eggs
- 1 cup mashed cooked buttercup squash
- 1 teaspoon vanilla extract
- 2 cups all-purpose flour
- 2 teaspoons baking powder
- 1-1/2 teaspoons ground cinnamon
- 1/2 teaspoon baking soda
- 1/2 teaspoon salt
- 1/4 teaspoon ground ginger
- 1/4 teaspoon ground nutmeg
- Pinch ground cloves
- 1/2 cup unsweetened applesauce
- GLAZE:
- 1/2 cup confectioners' sugar
- 1/4 teaspoon vanilla extract
- 1-1/2 teaspoons hot water

## Direction

- Mix the first 6 ingredients in a small bowl; cut in butter until the mixture is crumbly. Set it aside. Cream sugar and shortening in a big bowl until fluffy and light. Whisk in one egg at a time, whip well before adding another. Whip in vanilla and squash. Mix the dry ingredients then stir into the creamed mixture gradually until well blended. Scoop 1/2 in a greased 9-inch springform pan.
- Scatter applesauce all over the batter then scatter top with 1/2 of the crumb mixture. Evenly scoop the remaining batter on top of the crumb mixture. Add the remaining crumb mixture on top.
- Bake for 50-55 minutes in 350 degrees oven until an inserted toothpick in the middle comes out without residue. Cool in the pan for 10 minutes then remove the sides.
- Mix extract, confectioners' sugar, and just enough water to get the preferred consistency; sprinkle over the coffee cake.

## Nutrition Information

- Calories: 351 calories
- Protein: 5g protein.
- Total Fat: 14g fat (4g saturated fat)
- Sodium: 260mg sodium
- Fiber: 2g fiber)
- Total Carbohydrate: 53g carbohydrate (32g sugars

- Cholesterol: 43mg cholesterol

## 607. Calico Cranberry Couscous Salad

*Serving: 6 servings. | Prep: 20mins | Cook: 0mins | Ready in:*

### Ingredients

- 1 cup water
- 3/4 cup uncooked couscous
- 1/2 cup dried cranberries
- 1/2 cup chopped celery
- 1/2 cup shredded carrot
- 1/4 cup chopped green onions
- 1/4 cup slivered almonds, toasted
- DRESSING:
- 3 tablespoons red wine vinegar
- 1 tablespoon olive oil
- 1 tablespoon Dijon mustard
- 1/4 teaspoon salt
- 1/4 teaspoon pepper

### Direction

- Bring water to a boil in a small saucepan. Stir in couscous; cover and remove from the heat.
- Allow to stand for 5 minutes. Use a fork to fluff couscous; cool.
- Combine almonds, onions, carrot, celery, cranberries and couscous in a serving bowl.
- Whisk together the dressing ingredients in a small bowl. Add to salad mixture and toss until well coated. Serve chilled or at room temperature.

### Nutrition Information

- Calories: 171 calories
- Protein: 5g protein. Diabetic Exchanges: 2 starch
- Total Fat: 5g fat (1g saturated fat)
- Sodium: 176mg sodium
- Fiber: 3g fiber)
- Total Carbohydrate: 29g carbohydrate (8g sugars
- Cholesterol: 0 cholesterol

## 608. Cashew & Olive Feta Cheese Dip

*Serving: 1-1/2 cups. | Prep: 10mins | Cook: 5mins | Ready in:*

### Ingredients

- 1-1/2 cups (6 ounces) crumbled feta cheese
- 1/2 cup lightly salted cashews
- 1/4 cup 2% milk
- 1 tablespoon lemon juice
- 1 teaspoon dried oregano
- 1/4 teaspoon crushed red pepper flakes
- 1/4 teaspoon pepper
- 3 tablespoons chopped pitted green olives, divided
- 3 tablespoons chopped pitted kalamata olives, divided
- Baked pita chips

### Direction

- In a food processor, place the initial 7 ingredients and process till smooth. Place in 2 tbsp. of kalamata olives and 2 tbsp. of green olives, pulse to combine.
- Place into a serving dish and sprinkle the leftover olives over. Serve with pita chips. Store the remainings in the fridge.

### Nutrition Information

- Calories:
- Fiber:
- Total Carbohydrate:
- Cholesterol:
- Protein:
- Total Fat:

- Sodium:

### 609. Cheese Boereg

*Serving: 16-20 servings. | Prep: 20mins | Cook: 25mins | Ready in:*

#### Ingredients

- 1 large egg, lightly beaten
- 1 large egg white, lightly beaten
- 1 cup ricotta cheese
- 1/4 cup minced fresh parsley
- 4 cups shredded part-skim mozzarella or Muenster cheese
- 10 sheets phyllo dough (18x14 inches)
- 1/2 cup butter, melted

#### Direction

- Mix parsley, egg, ricotta and egg white in a big bowl; mix in mozzarella cheese. Set the mixture aside.
- Unroll the phyllo dough; halve the sheet stack widthwise. On a greased 13-in by 9-in baking pan, put a phyllo sheet then brush with butter. Repeat 9 more times. Use plastic wrap to cover the remaining dough to avoid drying out.
- Evenly spread cheese mixture on top. Put the remaining phyllo in a layer, brush butter on every other phyllo sheet.
- Bake for 25-30mins in a 350 degrees F oven or until golden brown. Slice into squares or triangles.

#### Nutrition Information

- Calories: 150 calories
- Total Fat: 10g fat (6g saturated fat)
- Sodium: 218mg sodium
- Fiber: 0 fiber)
- Total Carbohydrate: 8g carbohydrate (2g sugars
- Cholesterol: 41mg cholesterol

- Protein: 8g protein.

### 610. Cheese Spread Pinecone

*Serving: 3-1/2 cups. | Prep: 20mins | Cook: 0mins | Ready in:*

#### Ingredients

- 2 packages (8 ounces each) cream cheese, softened
- 1/4 cup milk
- 1 cup crumbled feta cheese
- 1 cup shredded part-skim mozzarella cheese
- 2 tablespoons dried minced onion
- 1/4 teaspoon cayenne pepper
- 2/3 cup sliced almonds, toasted
- 1 cinnamon stick
- Fresh dill sprigs
- Breadsticks, crackers and/or raw vegetables

#### Direction

- Beat cream cheese and milk in a large bowl until smooth. Add the mozzarella, feta, cayenne, and onion; mix well. Cover and chill in the refrigerator until firm or for 2 hours.
- Form cheese mixture into a pinecone shape on a serving plate. Arrange almonds in overlapping rows, beginning at the narrow end. Add cinnamon stick and dill for the pine needles and stem. Serve with breadsticks, crackers and/or vegetables.

#### Nutrition Information

- Calories: 64 calories
- Total Fat: 5g fat (3g saturated fat)
- Sodium: 83mg sodium
- Fiber: 0 fiber)
- Total Carbohydrate: 1g carbohydrate (1g sugars
- Cholesterol: 14mg cholesterol
- Protein: 3g protein.

## 611. Cheese Tortellini Salad

*Serving: 8 | Prep: 15mins | Cook: 10mins | Ready in:*

### Ingredients

- 3 (250 g) packages cheese tortellini
- 1/2 pound pepperoni, chopped
- 1/2 pound provolone cheese, chopped
- 2 (6.5 ounce) jars marinated artichoke hearts, drained and chopped
- 1 (6 ounce) can sliced black olives
- 1/2 (8 ounce) bottle Italian-style salad dressing, or more to taste
- 1 (.7 ounce) package dry Italian salad dressing mix (such as Good Seasons®)
- ground black pepper to taste

### Direction

- Boil lightly salted water in a large pot. Cook the tortellini at a boil and stir occasionally, for 6 to 8 minutes until the pasta floats to the top and the filling is hot, then drain. Rinse the tortellini With cool water until they are completely cooled. Drain. Transfer the drained pasta to a larger bowl.
- Stir tortellini with black pepper, dry Italian dressing mix, Italian-style salad dressing, black olives, artichoke hearts, provolone cheese and pepperoni. Prior to serving, add more Italian dressing if wished.

### Nutrition Information

- Calories: 641 calories;
- Total Fat: 36.8
- Sodium: 2047
- Total Carbohydrate: 52.4
- Cholesterol: 90
- Protein: 28.3

## 612. Cheese Stuffed Cherry Tomatoes

*Serving: about 1 dozen. | Prep: 15mins | Cook: 0mins | Ready in:*

### Ingredients

- 1 pint cherry tomatoes
- 1 package (4 ounces) crumbled feta cheese
- 1/2 cup finely chopped red onion
- 1/2 cup olive oil
- 1/4 cup red wine vinegar
- 1 tablespoon dried oregano
- Salt and pepper to taste

### Direction

- Trim a thin slice off the top of each tomato. Spoon out flesh and discard. Turn tomatoes upside down onto paper towels to drain. Mix onion and cheese together; fill into hollowed tomatoes.
- Stir pepper, salt, oregano, vinegar, and oil together in a small mixing bowl. Spread over tomatoes. Chill, covered, for half until hour or until serving.

### Nutrition Information

- Calories:
- Total Fat:
- Sodium:
- Fiber:
- Total Carbohydrate:
- Cholesterol:
- Protein:

## 613. Cheese Stuffed Sweet Onions

*Serving: 8 servings. | Prep: 25mins | Cook: 04hours00mins | Ready in:*

### Ingredients

- 4 large Vidalia or other sweet onions
- 3/4 cup crumbled goat cheese
- 3/4 cup crumbled blue cheese
- 1 teaspoon minced fresh thyme
- 2 cups vegetable stock
- 1 tablespoon olive oil
- 1/4 teaspoon salt
- 1/8 teaspoon pepper
- 1/4 cup grated Romano or Parmesan cheese
- Fresh thyme leaves

### Direction

- Rind onions and cut off top of each onion with a 1/2-inch slice, then use a melon baller to take out the centers to leave shells with 1/2 inch size. Chop the removed onion and save 3 cups (reserve leftover onion for another use). Combine 3 cups of reserved onion, minced thyme, blue and goat cheeses together then scoop into onions.
- In a 6-quart slow cooker, add stock and onions, then use oil to drizzle over. Sprinkle onions with Romano cheese, pepper and salt, then cook with a cover on low setting for 4 to 5 hours, until onions are softened. Halve the onions to serve and sprinkle with thyme leaves.

### Nutrition Information

- Calories: 137 calories
- Total Carbohydrate: 8g carbohydrate (3g sugars
- Cholesterol: 23mg cholesterol
- Protein: 7g protein.
- Total Fat: 9g fat (5g saturated fat)
- Sodium: 471mg sodium
- Fiber: 2g fiber)

## 614. Cheesy Chive Potatoes

*Serving: 6 servings. | Prep: 15mins | Cook: 15mins | Ready in:*

### Ingredients

- 6 medium potatoes, peeled and cubed
- 1/2 cup fat-free milk
- 1/2 cup crumbled feta cheese
- 1 tablespoon butter
- 1/2 teaspoon salt
- 1/8 teaspoon pepper
- 2 tablespoons minced chives

### Direction

- In a big saucepan, put tomatoes, pour in water to cover; heat to a boil. Decrease heat and cook with cover until tender, or about 10-15 minutes.
- Drain potatoes. Put in pepper, salt, butter, cheese, and milk then mash. Mix in chives.

### Nutrition Information

- Calories: 171 calories
- Total Carbohydrate: 30g carbohydrate (3g sugars
- Cholesterol: 10mg cholesterol
- Protein: 5g protein. Diabetic Exchanges: 2 starch
- Total Fat: 4g fat (2g saturated fat)
- Sodium: 313mg sodium
- Fiber: 2g fiber)

## 615. Cheesy Herbed Eggs

*Serving: 6-8 servings. | Prep: 10mins | Cook: 15mins | Ready in:*

### Ingredients

- 1-1/3 cups half-and-half cream
- 1 teaspoon grated lemon zest

- 16 large eggs, lightly beaten
- 1 teaspoon salt
- 1/2 teaspoon white pepper
- 1/4 teaspoon dried basil
- 1/4 teaspoon dried oregano
- 1/4 teaspoon dried rosemary, crushed
- 1/2 cup shredded cheddar cheese
- 1/2 cup grated Parmesan cheese
- 1/4 cup butter
- Tomato wedges, optional

## Direction

- Mix together the lemon zest and cream in a big bowl, then add the seasonings and eggs and stir well. Mix in the cheeses.
- Melt the butter in a big skillet, then pour it in the egg mixture. Cook and gently stir for about 15 minutes on medium heat, until the eggs become set. If preferred, put tomato wedges as garnish.

## Nutrition Information

- Calories: 301 calories
- Total Carbohydrate: 3g carbohydrate (3g sugars
- Cholesterol: 472mg cholesterol
- Protein: 17g protein.
- Total Fat: 23g fat (12g saturated fat)
- Sodium: 634mg sodium
- Fiber: 0 fiber)

## 616.    Chickpea & Feta Salad

*Serving: 12 servings (3/4 cup each). | Prep: 20mins | Cook: 0mins | Ready in:*

## Ingredients

- 1/2 cup olive oil
- 1/4 cup minced fresh chives
- 4 garlic cloves, minced
- 2 tablespoons minced fresh oregano or 2 teaspoons dried oregano
- 2 teaspoons grated lemon peel
- 3 tablespoons lemon juice
- 1/2 teaspoon salt
- 1/2 teaspoon pepper
- 2 cans (15 ounces each) chickpeas or garbanzo beans, rinsed and drained
- 2 cups (8 ounces) crumbled feta cheese
- 2 celery ribs, finely chopped
- 1 large red onion, finely chopped
- 1 medium cucumber, peeled and chopped

## Direction

- Whisk the first eight ingredients together in a small bowl. Combine remaining ingredients in a large bowl. Add dressing to salad mixture and toss lightly until well combined.

## Nutrition Information

- Calories: 206 calories
- Total Carbohydrate: 15g carbohydrate (3g sugars
- Cholesterol: 10mg cholesterol
- Protein: 7g protein.
- Total Fat: 13g fat (3g saturated fat)
- Sodium: 381mg sodium
- Fiber: 4g fiber)

## 617.    Chickpea Cucumber Salad

*Serving: 12 servings (3/4 cup each). | Prep: 10mins | Cook: 0mins | Ready in:*

## Ingredients

- 3 cans (15 ounces each) chickpeas or garbanzo beans, rinsed and drained
- 4 large cucumbers, seeded and cut into 1/2-inch pieces

- 2 packages (3-1/2 ounces each) crumbled reduced-fat feta cheese (about 1-1/3 cups)
- 1 cup finely chopped red onion
- 1/2 cup reduced-fat ranch salad dressing
- 2 tablespoons snipped fresh dill
- 3/4 teaspoon salt
- 1/4 teaspoon pepper

## Direction

- Mix onion, cheese, cucumbers, and chickpeas together. In the second bowl, mix pepper, salt, dill, and ranch dressing together. Pour over salad; toss to coat. Before serving, cover and let sit in the refrigerator for an hour.

## Nutrition Information

- Calories:
- Total Carbohydrate:
- Cholesterol:
- Protein:
- Total Fat:
- Sodium:
- Fiber:

### 618. Chickpea Patties With Yogurt Sauce

*Serving: 1 dozen (1 cup sauce). | Prep: 25mins | Cook: 10mins | Ready in:*

## Ingredients

- 1 can (15 ounces) chickpeas or garbanzo beans, rinsed and drained, divided
- 2 green onions, chopped
- 2 tablespoons dry bread crumbs
- 2 tablespoons snipped fresh dill or 2 teaspoons dill weed
- 2 tablespoons lemon juice
- 2 tablespoons tahini
- 1/2 teaspoon salt
- 1/2 teaspoon ground cumin
- 1/4 teaspoon pepper
- 4 teaspoons canola oil
- SAUCE:
- 1 cup (8 ounces) fat-free plain yogurt
- 2 garlic cloves, minced
- 1/4 teaspoon curry powder
- Dash crushed red pepper flakes

## Direction

- In a food processor, put the onions and 1/2 of the chickpeas. Put cover and process until chopped. Move to a small bowl and mix in the lemon juice, dill and breadcrumbs, then put aside.
- In the food processor, put the leftover chickpeas, pepper, cumin, salt and tahini. Put cover and process until combined. Add it to the chopped chickpea mixture and mix to blend. Form it into 12 patties.
- Cook the patties in oil in a big nonstick frying pan coated with cooking spray for 4-5 minutes per side on medium heat in batches or until it turns golden brown in color. In the meantime, mix together the sauce ingredients in a small bowl, then serve it with patties.

## Nutrition Information

- Calories: 159 calories
- Total Fat: 8g fat (1g saturated fat)
- Sodium: 332mg sodium
- Fiber: 4g fiber)
- Total Carbohydrate: 18g carbohydrate (4g sugars
- Cholesterol: 1mg cholesterol
- Protein: 6g protein. Diabetic Exchanges: 1-1/2 fat

### 619. Cilantro Couscous Salad

*Serving: 12 servings (2/3 cup each). | Prep: 20mins | Cook: 5mins | Ready in:*

### Ingredients

- 1 package (10 ounces) couscous
- 1 medium cucumber, finely chopped
- 2 medium tomatoes, seeded and finely chopped
- 2/3 cup minced fresh cilantro
- 1/3 cup olive oil
- 1/4 cup lemon juice
- 3 garlic cloves, minced
- 1 package (8 ounces) feta cheese, crumbled

### Direction

- Prepare couscous following package directions; allow to cool to room temperature.
- Combine couscous, cilantro, tomatoes and cucumber in a large serving bowl. In a small bowl, whisk together garlic, lemon juice and oil. Add dressing to salad mixture and toss until well coated. Add cheese and toss gently until well combined. Refrigerate until serving.

### Nutrition Information

- Calories: 196 calories
- Total Carbohydrate: 21g carbohydrate (3g sugars
- Cholesterol: 17mg cholesterol
- Protein: 6g protein.
- Total Fat: 10g fat (4g saturated fat)
- Sodium: 215mg sodium
- Fiber: 2g fiber)

## 620. Citrus Spiced Olives

*Serving: 4 cups. | Prep: 20mins | Cook: 0mins | Ready in:*

### Ingredients

- 1/2 cup white wine
- 1/4 cup canola oil
- 3 tablespoons salt-free seasoning blend
- 4 garlic cloves, minced
- 1/2 teaspoon crushed red pepper flakes
- 2 teaspoons each grated orange, lemon and lime peels
- 3 tablespoons each orange, lemon and lime juices
- 4 cups mixed pitted olives

### Direction

- Mix the first 5 ingredients in a big bowl. Put in citrus juices and peels, then whisk until combined. Put in olives and toss to coat, then chill with a cover for a minimum of 4 hours before serving.

### Nutrition Information

- Calories: 74 calories
- Protein: 0 protein.
- Total Fat: 7g fat (1g saturated fat)
- Sodium: 248mg sodium
- Fiber: 1g fiber)
- Total Carbohydrate: 3g carbohydrate (1g sugars
- Cholesterol: 0 cholesterol

## 621. Classic Hummus

*Serving: 6 | Prep: | Cook: 10mins | Ready in:*

### Ingredients

- 1 clove garlic, smashed and peeled
- 1 15-ounce can chickpeas, rinsed
- 3 tablespoons fresh lemon juice
- 3 tablespoons extra-virgin olive oil
- 1 tablespoon tahini (see Note)
- ½ teaspoon salt

### Direction

- In a food processor with steel blade attachment, drop the garlic through the feed tube while the machine is running, and process until minced finely. Scrape down the bowl's side then stir in salt, tahini, oil, lemon juice and chickpeas, and blend for 1-2 minutes until it becomes fully smooth. If needed, scrape down the sides of the bowl.

## Nutrition Information

- Calories: 144 calories;
- Cholesterol: 0
- Sugar: 0
- Total Fat: 9
- Saturated Fat: 1
- Sodium: 298
- Protein: 3
- Fiber: 2
- Total Carbohydrate: 13

### 622. Cold Bean Salad

*Serving: 6 servings. | Prep: 20mins | Cook: 0mins | Ready in:*

## Ingredients

- 1 can (15 ounces) garbanzo beans or chickpeas, rinsed and drained
- 1 can (15 ounces) black beans, rinsed and drained
- 2/3 cup shredded Swiss cheese
- 1/2 cup chopped onion
- 1 can (3.8 ounces) sliced ripe olives, drained
- 1/4 cup chopped celery
- 1/4 cup each chopped green, sweet red and orange peppers
- 1/3 cup balsamic vinaigrette

## Direction

- Combine peppers, celery, olives, onion, cheese and beans in a large bowl. Add vinaigrette to salad dressing and toss until well coated. Chill until serving.

## Nutrition Information

- Calories: 225 calories
- Total Carbohydrate: 27g carbohydrate (6g sugars
- Cholesterol: 11mg cholesterol
- Protein: 10g protein.
- Total Fat: 9g fat (3g saturated fat)
- Sodium: 529mg sodium
- Fiber: 7g fiber)

### 623. Colorful Garbanzo Bean Salad

*Serving: 4 servings. | Prep: 20mins | Cook: 10mins | Ready in:*

## Ingredients

- 1 medium sweet red pepper
- 1 can (15 ounces) garbanzo beans or chickpeas, rinsed and drained
- 6 cherry tomatoes, halved
- 2 tablespoons minced fresh basil or 2 teaspoons dried basil
- 2 tablespoons olive oil
- 1 tablespoon lemon juice
- 1 tablespoon red wine vinegar
- 1/2 teaspoon salt
- 1/2 teaspoon grated lemon peel
- 1/4 teaspoon pepper

## Direction

- Broil pepper 4 inches from the heat for about 5 minutes until skin blisters. Rotate pepper 1/4 turn with tongs. Keep rotating and broiling pepper until all sides are darken and blistered. Instantly transfer pepper into a small bowl; cover and set aside for 20 minutes.
- Remove and throw the burned skin away. Remove seeds and stem; chop. Mix basil, tomatoes, garbanzo beans, and pepper together in a large bowl. Whisk pepper, lemon peel, salt, vinegar, lemon juice, and oil together in a small mixing bowl. Drizzle over

bean mixture and stir until evenly coated. Refrigerate until chilled before serving.

## Nutrition Information

- Calories: 174 calories
- Sodium: 436mg sodium
- Fiber: 5g fiber)
- Total Carbohydrate: 20g carbohydrate (4g sugars
- Cholesterol: 0 cholesterol
- Protein: 5g protein. Diabetic Exchanges: 1-1/2 fat
- Total Fat: 9g fat (1g saturated fat)

## 624. Colorful Greek Orzo Salad

*Serving: 8 servings. | Prep: 20mins | Cook: 0mins | Ready in:*

### Ingredients

- 1 cup uncooked orzo pasta
- 2 cups frozen corn, thawed
- 1/2 cup chopped sweet red pepper
- 1/2 cup grape or cherry tomatoes
- 1/2 cup pitted Greek olives, halved
- 1/4 cup chopped sweet onion
- 1/4 cup minced fresh basil or 4 teaspoons dried basil
- 2 tablespoons minced fresh parsley
- 3 tablespoons olive oil
- 2 tablespoons balsamic vinegar
- 1/4 teaspoon salt
- 1/4 teaspoon pepper

### Direction

- Cook pasta following package directions; drain and rinse under cold water. Place in a large serving bowl; add parsley, basil, onion, olives, tomatoes, red pepper and corn. Combine pepper, salt, vinegar and oil in a jar that comes with a tight-fitting lid; cover and shake properly. Add to salad mixture and toss until well coated.

## Nutrition Information

- Calories: 210 calories
- Fiber: 2g fiber)
- Total Carbohydrate: 31g carbohydrate (3g sugars
- Cholesterol: 0 cholesterol
- Protein: 5g protein.
- Total Fat: 8g fat (1g saturated fat)
- Sodium: 219mg sodium

## 625. Confetti Couscous

*Serving: 6 servings. | Prep: 15mins | Cook: 0mins | Ready in:*

### Ingredients

- 1 can (14-1/2 ounces) chicken or vegetable broth
- 2 tablespoons water
- 2 tablespoons lemon juice
- 1 teaspoon grated lemon peel
- 1/2 teaspoon salt
- 1 package (10 ounces) couscous
- 2 cups frozen peas, thawed
- 1/2 cup slivered almonds, toasted
- 1 jar (4 ounces) diced pimientos, drained

### Direction

- Bring lemon juice, water, broth, salt, and peel to a boil in a large saucepan. Mix in peas and couscous. Cover the pan; put off the heat and set aside for 5 minutes. Mix in pimientos and almonds just before serving.

## Nutrition Information

- Calories: 294 calories

- Sodium: 570mg sodium
- Fiber: 6g fiber)
- Total Carbohydrate: 47g carbohydrate (0 sugars
- Cholesterol: 0 cholesterol
- Protein: 12g protein. Diabetic Exchanges: 3 starch
- Total Fat: 6g fat (0 saturated fat)

- Cholesterol: 4mg cholesterol
- Protein: 7g protein.
- Total Fat: 7g fat (1g saturated fat)
- Sodium: 358mg sodium
- Fiber: 4g fiber)
- Total Carbohydrate: 29g carbohydrate (4g sugars

## 626. Cool Couscous Salad

*Serving: 2 servings. | Prep: 10mins | Cook: 5mins | Ready in:*

### Ingredients

- 1/3 cup water
- 1/4 cup uncooked couscous
- 1/3 cup garbanzo beans or chickpeas, rinsed and drained
- 1/4 cup seeded chopped cucumber
- 1 small plum tomato, seeded and chopped
- 1/4 cup prepared balsamic vinaigrette
- 2 lettuce leaves
- 2 tablespoons crumbled feta cheese

### Direction

- Bring water to a boil in a small saucepan. Stir in couscous. Cover and remove from the heat; allow to stand for 5 to 10 minutes until water is fully absorbed. Fluff with a pork; Cover and keep cold in refrigerator for a minimum of 1 hour.
- In a small bowl, combine couscous, tomato, cucumber and garbanzo beans. Add dressing to couscous mixture and toss until well coated. Line lettuce leaves on two individual serving plates. Add couscous mixture on top and sprinkle with cheese.

### Nutrition Information

- Calories: 204 calories

## 627. Cool Tomato Soup

*Serving: 9 servings. | Prep: 30mins | Cook: 0mins | Ready in:*

### Ingredients

- 4 cups tomato juice, divided
- 5 medium tomatoes, peeled, seeded and chopped
- 2 medium cucumbers, peeled, seeded and cut into chunks
- 1 medium green pepper, quartered
- 1 medium sweet red pepper, quartered
- 1 medium onion, peeled and quartered
- 2 garlic cloves, peeled
- 1 tablespoon minced fresh thyme
- 1/4 cup white balsamic vinegar
- 4 cups cubed bread, crusts removed
- 2 tablespoons olive oil
- 1/4 teaspoon pepper
- Fat-free sour cream, fat-free croutons and parsley, optional

### Direction

- Cover and blend together half of the thyme, garlic, onion, peppers, cucumbers, tomatoes and 1 cup of tomato juice in a blender, until all are chopped. Remove to a big bowl, then repeat the process as above.
- In a blender, add leftover tomato juice and vinegar. Put in bread, then place a cover and process until the mixture is smooth. Put into the vegetable mixture and stir in pepper and oil.

- Cover and chill about 1 to 2 hours before serving. Use parsley, croutons and sour cream to decorate, if you want.

## Nutrition Information

- Calories: 124 calories
- Fiber: 3g fiber)
- Total Carbohydrate: 21g carbohydrate (10g sugars
- Cholesterol: 0 cholesterol
- Protein: 4g protein. Diabetic Exchanges: 2 vegetable
- Total Fat: 4g fat (1g saturated fat)
- Sodium: 405mg sodium

### 628. Couscous Salad

*Serving: 8 servings. | Prep: 15mins | Cook: 0mins | Ready in:*

## Ingredients

- 1-2/3 cups water
- 1-1/4 cups uncooked couscous
- 4 medium tomatoes, seeded and chopped
- 1 large red onion, chopped
- 2 tablespoons minced fresh parsley
- 2 tablespoons minced fresh cilantro
- 1 teaspoon minced fresh mint or 1/4 teaspoon dried mint
- 1/3 cup lemon juice
- 3 tablespoons olive oil
- 1/2 teaspoon salt
- 1/4 teaspoon pepper

## Direction

- Add water to a saucepan and boil it. Mix in couscous and put a cover on. Take away from heat and let it sit for 5 minutes.
- Mix herbs, onion, tomatoes, and couscous together in a bowl. Combine pepper, salt, oil,

and lemon juice. Put on the couscous mixture and coat by tossing. Refrigerate overnight.

## Nutrition Information

- Calories: 168 calories
- Sodium: 156mg sodium
- Fiber: 2g fiber)
- Total Carbohydrate: 26g carbohydrate (0 sugars
- Cholesterol: 0 cholesterol
- Protein: 4g protein. Diabetic Exchanges: 1-1/2 starch
- Total Fat: 5g fat (1g saturated fat)

### 629. Couscous Salad With Olives & Raisins

*Serving: 8 servings. | Prep: 15mins | Cook: 5mins | Ready in:*

## Ingredients

- 2 cups vegetable stock
- 1 package (10 ounces) couscous
- 2 tablespoons olive oil
- 1 teaspoon grated lemon peel
- 2 tablespoons lemon juice
- 1/2 teaspoon salt
- 1/4 teaspoon pepper
- 2 plum tomatoes, seeded and chopped
- 3/4 cup sliced Greek olives
- 2/3 cup raisins
- 4 teaspoons finely chopped fresh mint

## Direction

- Bring stock to a boil in a large saucepan. Stir in couscous. Remove from heat; cover and allow to stand for 5 to 10 minutes or until stock is fully absorbed. Fluff with a fork. Cool completely.
- In a small bowl, whisk together pepper, salt, lemon juice, lemon peel and oil until well

blended; stir into couscous. Stir in remaining ingredients.

## Nutrition Information

- Calories:
- Protein:
- Total Fat:
- Sodium:
- Fiber:
- Total Carbohydrate:
- Cholesterol:

### 630. Couscous Tabbouleh With Fresh Mint & Feta

*Serving: 2 servings. | Prep: 10mins | Cook: 10mins | Ready in:*

## Ingredients

- 3/4 cup water
- 1/2 cup uncooked couscous
- 1 can (15 ounces) chickpeas, rinsed and drained
- 1 large tomato, chopped
- 1/2 English cucumber, halved and thinly sliced
- 3 tablespoons lemon juice
- 2 teaspoons grated lemon peel
- 2 teaspoons olive oil
- 2 teaspoons minced fresh mint
- 2 teaspoons minced fresh parsley
- 1/4 teaspoon salt
- 1/8 teaspoon pepper
- 3/4 cup crumbled feta cheese

## Direction

- Bring water to a boil in a small saucepan. Stir in couscous. Remove from the heat; cover and allow couscous to sit for 5 to 8 minutes until water is fully absorbed. Fluff with a fork.
- Combine cucumber, tomato and beans in a large bowl. In a small bowl, whisk together seasoning, oil, lemon peel and lemon juice. Add to bean mixture. Add couscous and toss until well combined. Serve right away or keep in refrigerator until chilled. Add cheese on top before serving.

## Nutrition Information

- Calories: 531 calories
- Sodium: 984mg sodium
- Fiber: 13g fiber)
- Total Carbohydrate: 75g carbohydrate (9g sugars
- Cholesterol: 23mg cholesterol
- Protein: 23g protein.
- Total Fat: 16g fat (5g saturated fat)

### 631. Couscous With Feta 'n' Tomatoes

*Serving: 6 servings. | Prep: 10mins | Cook: 10mins | Ready in:*

## Ingredients

- 1 cup boiling water
- 1/2 cup sun-dried tomatoes (not packed in oil)
- 1 can (14-1/2 ounces) vegetable broth
- 1-1/4 cups uncooked couscous
- 1/2 cup crumbled feta cheese
- 1/4 cup minced fresh parsley
- 1-1/2 teaspoons minced fresh oregano or 1/2 teaspoon dried oregano
- 3 teaspoons lemon juice
- 1 teaspoon water
- 1 teaspoon olive oil

## Direction

- Stream boiling water over tomatoes in a small bowl; allow to sit for 5 minutes. In the meantime, bring broth to a boil in a small

saucepan. Add couscous and stir well. Put off the heat; put on the cover and allow to sit until liquid is absorbed, about 5 minutes.
- Drain tomatoes and chop; add chopped tomatoes to couscous. Gently mix in the remaining ingredients. Enjoy the pasta warm or chilled.

## Nutrition Information

- Calories: 187 calories
- Cholesterol: 5mg cholesterol
- Protein: 8g protein. Diabetic Exchanges: 2 starch
- Total Fat: 3g fat (1g saturated fat)
- Sodium: 481mg sodium
- Fiber: 3g fiber)
- Total Carbohydrate: 33g carbohydrate (3g sugars

## 632. Couscous With Grilled Vegetables

*Serving: 8 servings. | Prep: 15mins | Cook: 15mins | Ready in:*

## Ingredients

- 2 small zucchini, quartered lengthwise
- 1/2 medium eggplant, sliced widthwise 1/2 inch thick
- 1 medium sweet red pepper, quartered
- 1 small onion, sliced 1/2 inch thick
- Cooking spray
- 3/4 teaspoon salt, divided
- 1/2 teaspoon pepper, divided
- 2 cups reduced-sodium chicken or vegetable broth
- 1 package (10 ounces) couscous
- 1/2 cup chopped green onions
- 4-1/2 teaspoons lemon juice
- 2-1/4 teaspoons minced fresh thyme or 1/2 teaspoon dried thyme

## Direction

- Spray vegetables using cooking spray. Sprinkle with 1/4 teaspoon pepper and 1/4 teaspoon salt to taste. Moisten a paper towel with cooking oil using long-handle tongs and coat the grill rack lightly. Use a drip pan to prepare for indirect heat.
- Distribute vegetables over the drip pan; cover and grill for 8 to 10 minutes over indirect medium heat, turning sometimes, or until softened. Allow to cool until handleable.
- Bring broth in a large saucepan to a boil. Mix in couscous. Turn off the heat; allow to stand, covered until liquid has been absorbed, or for 5 minutes.
- Chop grilled vegetables into 1/2-inch pieces. Use a fork to fluff couscous. Add pepper, the remaining salt, thyme, lemon juice, green onions, and vegetables; stir until incorporated.

## Nutrition Information

- Calories: 163 calories
- Fiber: 4g fiber)
- Total Carbohydrate: 34g carbohydrate (4g sugars
- Cholesterol: 0 cholesterol
- Protein: 7g protein. Diabetic Exchanges: 2 starch
- Total Fat: 0 fat (0 saturated fat)
- Sodium: 384mg sodium

## 633. Couscous Stuffed Mushrooms

*Serving: 6 servings. | Prep: 30mins | Cook: 15mins | Ready in:*

## Ingredients

- 18 medium fresh mushrooms
- 3 green onions, chopped
- 2 garlic cloves, minced

- 1 tablespoon olive oil
- 1 cup dry white wine or chicken broth
- 2 tablespoons reduced-sodium soy sauce
- FILLING:
- 1/2 cup reduced-sodium chicken broth
- 1/4 cup uncooked couscous
- 1/3 cup minced fresh parsley
- 2 tablespoons chopped fresh basil or 2 teaspoons dried basil
- 1/4 cup grated Romano cheese
- 1 egg white, lightly beaten
- 2 tablespoons chopped walnuts, toasted
- 1/4 teaspoon salt
- 1/8 teaspoon pepper

## Direction

- Take off the mushroom stems and get rid of it or reserve for later use. Put the cups aside. Sauté the garlic and onions in oil in a big nonstick frying pan for 1 minute. Stir in soy sauce and broth or wine and add the mushroom caps, then boil. Lower the heat, put cover and let it simmer for 5 to 6 minutes or until the mushrooms become tender. Using a slotted spoon, take out the mushrooms and set aside the liquid in the frying pan. Put the mushrooms on the paper towels, stem side down.
- Boil the broth in a big saucepan. Mix in couscous. Take it out of the heat, put cover and allow it to stand for 5 minutes. Fluff it using a fork, then add it to the reserved mushroom liquid. Put cover and let it cook for about 5 minutes on low until the liquid was absorbed. Add the succeeding 5 ingredients and gently toss.
- Sprinkle pepper and salt on the inside of mushroom caps, then stuff it with couscous mixture. Put it in a cooking spray coated 11x7-inch baking pan. Let it bake for 15 to 20 minutes at 350 degrees or until the stuffing turns light brown.

## Nutrition Information

- Calories: 113 calories
- Protein: 5g protein.
- Total Fat: 5g fat (1g saturated fat)
- Sodium: 416mg sodium
- Fiber: 2g fiber)
- Total Carbohydrate: 10g carbohydrate (0 sugars
- Cholesterol: 4mg cholesterol

### 634. Cranberry Couscous Salad

*Serving: 6 servings, about 2/3 cup each | Prep: 20mins | Cook: | Ready in:*

## Ingredients

- 3/4 cup couscous, uncooked
- 2 stalks celery, chopped
- 2 carrot s, shredded
- 2 green onions, sliced
- 1/2 cup dried cranberries
- 1/4 cup PLANTERS Sliced Almonds, toasted
- 1/4 cup KRAFT Light Mayo Reduced Fat Mayonnaise
- 2 Tbsp. KRAFT Lite Zesty Italian Dressing
- 2 tsp. GREY POUPON Dijon Mustard

## Direction

- 1. Follow the directions on the package to cook couscous; transfer into a medium bowl and allow to cool.
- 2. Add nuts, cranberries, and vegetables, stir well.
- 3. Combine mustard, dressing, and mayonnaise until incorporated. Gently mix with couscous mixture.

## Nutrition Information

- Calories: 190
- Saturated Fat: 0.5 g
- Sodium: 190 mg
- Fiber: 3 g

- Total Carbohydrate: 30 g
- Cholesterol: 0 mg
- Protein: 4 g
- Total Fat: 5 g
- Sugar: 11 g

### 635. Cranberry Feta Cheesecake

*Serving: 24-30 servings. | Prep: 25mins | Cook: 30mins | Ready in:*

#### Ingredients

- 7 crisp sesame breadsticks, crushed (about 2/3 cup)
- 3 tablespoons butter, melted
- 1 cup ricotta cheese
- 8 ounces crumbled feta cheese
- 1/2 cup heavy whipping cream
- 1 tablespoon cornstarch
- 1 teaspoon prepared horseradish
- 2 eggs, lightly beaten
- 1 carton (12 ounces) cranberry-orange sauce
- 1/2 cup chopped pecans, toasted
- 1 teaspoon minced fresh thyme
- 1/2 teaspoon minced fresh rosemary
- Assorted crackers

#### Direction

- Mix butter and breadstick crumbs in a small bowl; press on a greased nine-inch springform pan, an inch up the sides and all over the bottom. Put the pan on a baking sheet; bake for 5 minutes in 350 degrees oven. Place on a wire rack to cool.
- Whip cream, feta, and ricotta in a big bowl until smooth. Mix in horseradish and cornstarch well. On low speed, beat in eggs barely until blended. Fold in rosemary, cranberry-orange sauce, thyme, and pecans; scoop into crust. Put the pan on a baking sheet.
- Bake for 30-35 minutes in 350 degrees oven until the middle is nearly set. Cool for 10 minutes on a wire rack. Slide a knife carefully around the sides of the pan to loosen; cool for another hour.
- Cover then chill overnight. Let it sit for half an hour at room temperature before serving. Serve cheesecake with crackers.

#### Nutrition Information

- Calories: 98 calories
- Total Carbohydrate: 7g carbohydrate (6g sugars
- Cholesterol: 30mg cholesterol
- Protein: 3g protein.
- Total Fat: 7g fat (3g saturated fat)
- Sodium: 111mg sodium
- Fiber: 0 fiber)

### 636. Cranberry Brie Phyllo Triangles

*Serving: about 4-1/2 dozen. | Prep: 30mins | Cook: 10mins | Ready in:*

#### Ingredients

- 1 to 1-1/4 cups butter, melted
- 1 package (16 ounces, 18-inches x 14-inches sheet size) frozen phyllo dough, thawed
- 1 to 1-1/2 cups cranberry-orange sauce or whole-berry cranberry sauce
- 8 ounces Brie cheese, rind removed, cubed

#### Direction

- Slice the phyllo sheets into 2-inch strips lengthwise; halve each strip crosswise. Working with 5 strips at a time, slather butter on each strip then pile on top of each other. Use waxed paper to cover the remaining phyllo to keep from drying. Put 1 teaspoon

cranberry sauce on 1-2 cheese cubes at the end of each stack; fold like a flag into a triangle.
- Arrange in an ungreased 15-in by 10-in by 1-in baking pan; slather with butter. Bake for 10 minutes in 400 degrees oven until golden brown. Let it sit for 5 minutes before serving.

## Nutrition Information

- Calories: 232 calories
- Protein: 5g protein.
- Total Fat: 14g fat (8g saturated fat)
- Sodium: 298mg sodium
- Fiber: 1g fiber)
- Total Carbohydrate: 22g carbohydrate (8g sugars
- Cholesterol: 40mg cholesterol

## 637. Creamy Basil Feta Spread

*Serving: 4 cups. | Prep: 15mins | Cook: 0mins | Ready in:*

### Ingredients

- 2 packages (8 ounces each) cream cheese, softened
- 2 cups (8 ounces) crumbled feta cheese
- 1 jar (7 ounces) oil-packed sun-dried tomatoes, drained and chopped
- 1 cup minced fresh basil
- Wheat crackers

### Direction

- Beat cream cheese in a big bowl until smooth. Put in basil, tomatoes and feta cheese, then beat until blended. Turn to a serving dish and refrigerate until ready to serve. Serve together with crackers.

### Nutrition Information

- Calories: 79 calories
- Total Carbohydrate: 2g carbohydrate (0 sugars

- Cholesterol: 19mg cholesterol
- Protein: 3g protein.
- Total Fat: 7g fat (4g saturated fat)
- Sodium: 124mg sodium
- Fiber: 1g fiber)

## 638. Creamy Feta Spinach Dip

*Serving: 2 cups. | Prep: 15mins | Cook: 0mins | Ready in:*

### Ingredients

- 1 cup fat-free plain yogurt
- 3/4 cup crumbled feta cheese
- 2 ounces reduced-fat cream cheese, cubed
- 1/4 cup reduced-fat sour cream
- 1 garlic clove, minced
- 1-1/2 cups finely chopped fresh spinach
- 1 teaspoon dill weed
- 1/8 teaspoon pepper
- Fresh vegetables and/or sliced bread

### Direction

- Line 1 coffee filter or 4 cheesecloth layers on a strainer and set over a bowl. In the prepped strainer, place yogurt and use cheesecloth's edges to cover the yogurt. Store for 2 hours in the fridge to thicken the yogurt to the whipped cream's consistency.
- In a food processor, place the yogurt and remove the liquid from bowl. Add garlic, sour cream, cream cheese and feta cheese then process, covered, till smooth.
- In a small bowl, place the mixture and stir in pepper, dill and spinach. Store in the fridge, covered, to chill. Serve with bread or/and vegetables.

### Nutrition Information

- Calories: 68 calories
- Protein: 5g protein. Diabetic Exchanges: 1/2 starch

- Total Fat: 4g fat (3g saturated fat)
- Sodium: 158mg sodium
- Fiber: 1g fiber)
- Total Carbohydrate: 4g carbohydrate (2g sugars
- Cholesterol: 14mg cholesterol

## 639. Cucumber Couscous Salad

*Serving: 8 servings. | Prep: 25mins | Cook: 0mins | Ready in:*

### Ingredients

- 1-1/4 cups water
- 1 cup uncooked couscous
- 2 medium cucumbers, peeled, quartered lengthwise and sliced
- 1 cup chopped sweet red pepper
- 1/4 cup thinly sliced green onions
- 1/2 cup buttermilk
- 1/4 cup reduced-fat plain yogurt
- 2 tablespoons minced fresh dill
- 2 tablespoons white vinegar
- 1 tablespoon olive oil
- 1/2 teaspoon salt
- 1/4 teaspoon pepper

### Direction

- Boil water in a small saucepan. Mix in couscous. Take away from heat; put a cover on and let it sit for 5 minutes. Use a fork to fluff. Let it cool to room temperature.
- Mix onions, red pepper, cucumbers, and couscous together in a big bowl. Mix together pepper, salt, oil, vinegar, dill, yogurt, and buttermilk. Put on the couscous mixture. Put a cover on and chill for a minimum of 1 hour.

### Nutrition Information

- Calories: 126 calories

- Fiber: 2g fiber)
- Total Carbohydrate: 22g carbohydrate (4g sugars
- Cholesterol: 1mg cholesterol
- Protein: 5g protein. Diabetic Exchanges: 1 starch
- Total Fat: 2g fat (0 saturated fat)
- Sodium: 172mg sodium

## 640. Curried Couscous

*Serving: Serves 2 | Prep: | Cook: | Ready in:*

### Ingredients

- 2 teaspoons olive oil
- 1/2 cup finely chopped onion
- 1 garlic clove, minced and mashed into a paste
- 1/2 teaspoon curry powder
- 3/4 cup chicken broth
- 3 tablespoons raisins
- 1/2 cup couscous
- 1/4 cup finely chopped fresh mint leaves

### Direction

- Heat oil in a nonstick skillet over moderately high heat until hot but not smoking, cook onion and salt to taste, stirring, until turning light brown. Lower the heat to moderate. Add curry powder and garlic paste; cook while stirring until the garlic paste turns golden. Take the frying pan away from heat and keep the mixture warm.
- Boil a small saucepan of broth. Mix in couscous and raisins, put a cover on and let sit without heating, about 5 minutes. Using 1 fork, fluff the couscous and transfer to a bowl. Mix in mint and the onion mixture, pepper and salt to taste.

### Nutrition Information

- Calories: 300

- Saturated Fat: 1 g(5%)
- Sodium: 140 mg(6%)
- Fiber: 4 g(18%)
- Total Carbohydrate: 53 g(18%)
- Cholesterol: 3 mg(1%)
- Protein: 9 g(18%)
- Total Fat: 6 g(9%)

## 641. Dad's Greek Salad

*Serving: 8 servings. | Prep: 20mins | Cook: 0mins | Ready in:*

### Ingredients

- 4 large tomatoes, seeded and coarsely chopped
- 2-1/2 cups (about 6) thinly sliced English cucumbers
- 1 small red onion, halved and thinly sliced
- 1/4 cup olive oil
- 3 tablespoons red wine vinegar
- 1/4 teaspoon salt
- 1/8 teaspoon pepper
- 1/4 teaspoon dried oregano, optional
- 3/4 cup pitted Greek olives
- 3/4 cup crumbled feta cheese

### Direction

- In a large bowl, put in onion, cucumbers and tomatoes. Add in salt, pepper, vinegar, oil and oregano if desired; whisk until combined. Pour the dressing over salad; toss to coat. Put cheese and olives on top.

### Nutrition Information

- Calories: 148 calories
- Fiber: 2g fiber)
- Total Carbohydrate: 7g carbohydrate (3g sugars
- Cholesterol: 6mg cholesterol
- Protein: 3g protein. Diabetic Exchanges: 2 vegetable
- Total Fat: 12g fat (2g saturated fat)
- Sodium: 389mg sodium

## 642. Dilled Potatoes With Feta

*Serving: 4 servings. | Prep: 15mins | Cook: 10mins | Ready in:*

### Ingredients

- 1 pound small red potatoes, halved
- 1 cup (4 ounces) crumbled feta cheese
- 1/4 cup snipped fresh dill
- 2 tablespoons olive oil
- 1 tablespoon lemon juice
- 1/4 teaspoon salt
- 1/4 teaspoon pepper

### Direction

- In a big saucepan, put potatoes and fill with water to cover. Boil it. Decrease the heat, put a cover on and cook until softened, or for 10-15 minutes. Strain.
- Mix pepper, salt, lemon juice, oil, dill, and cheese together in a serving bowl. Add potatoes and mix lightly to coat.

### Nutrition Information

- Calories: 221 calories
- Fiber: 3g fiber)
- Total Carbohydrate: 22g carbohydrate (2g sugars
- Cholesterol: 15mg cholesterol
- Protein: 7g protein.
- Total Fat: 11g fat (4g saturated fat)
- Sodium: 425mg sodium

## 643. Dilled Potatoes With Feta For Two

*Serving: 2 servings. | Prep: 15mins | Cook: 10mins | Ready in:*

### Ingredients

- 1/2 pound small red potatoes, halved
- 1/2 cup crumbled feta cheese
- 2 tablespoons snipped fresh dill
- 1 tablespoon olive oil
- 1-1/2 teaspoons lemon juice
- 1/8 teaspoon salt
- 1/8 teaspoon pepper

### Direction

- In a small saucepan, pour water over potatoes then bring to a boil. Lower the heat; cook covered until tender or for 10 to 15 minutes, drain off the water.
- Combine pepper, salt, lemon juice, oil, dill, and cheese in a serving bowl. Pour potatoes into the bowl and stir to evenly coat.

### Nutrition Information

- Calories: 213 calories
- Total Carbohydrate: 19g carbohydrate (1g sugars
- Cholesterol: 15mg cholesterol
- Protein: 7g protein.
- Total Fat: 11g fat (4g saturated fat)
- Sodium: 425mg sodium
- Fiber: 3g fiber)

## 644. Easy Colorful Bean Salad

*Serving: 6 servings. | Prep: 20mins | Cook: 5mins | Ready in:*

### Ingredients

- 3/4 pound fresh green beans, trimmed
- 2-1/4 cups canned white kidney or cannellini beans, rinsed and drained
- 1/4 cup julienned roasted sweet red peppers
- 3/4 cup pitted Greek olives, halved
- 3 tablespoons olive oil
- 4 teaspoons lemon juice
- 6 fresh basil leaves, thinly sliced
- Salt and pepper to taste

### Direction

- In a steamer basket placed over 1 inch of water in a big saucepan, add green beans then bring to a boil. Cover and steam until crisp-tender, about 5 to 6 minutes, then allow to cool.
- Mix together olives, red peppers, kidney beans and green beans in a big bowl. Mix pepper, salt, basil, lemon juice and oil together in a small bowl, then drizzle over bean mixture and toss to coat well. Serve at room temperature.

### Nutrition Information

- Calories: 202 calories
- Total Carbohydrate: 19g carbohydrate (2g sugars
- Cholesterol: 0 cholesterol
- Protein: 5g protein.
- Total Fat: 12g fat (1g saturated fat)
- Sodium: 439mg sodium
- Fiber: 6g fiber)

## 645. Easy Garden Tomatoes

*Serving: 6 servings. | Prep: 15mins | Cook: 0mins | Ready in:*

### Ingredients

- 3 large tomatoes, thinly sliced
- 1 large red onion, thinly sliced
- 1/3 cup olive oil
- 1/4 cup red wine vinegar

- 2 garlic cloves, minced
- 1 tablespoon minced fresh basil or 1 teaspoon dried basil
- 1-1/2 teaspoons minced fresh oregano or 1/2 teaspoon dried oregano
- 3/4 cup crumbled feta cheese
- 1 can (2-1/4 ounces) sliced ripe olives, drained

### Direction

- Assemble onion and tomatoes onto a serving platter. Mix oregano, basil, garlic, vinegar, and oil in a small bowl. Drizzle on salad. Top with olives and cheese. Chill before serving.

### Nutrition Information

- Calories: 184 calories
- Cholesterol: 8mg cholesterol
- Protein: 4g protein.
- Total Fat: 16g fat (3g saturated fat)
- Sodium: 234mg sodium
- Fiber: 2g fiber)
- Total Carbohydrate: 8g carbohydrate (3g sugars

## 646. Eggplant Dip

*Serving: Makes 4 servings | Prep: | Cook: | Ready in:*

### Ingredients

- 1 1/2 large eggplants, halved
- Olive oil cooking spray
- 1 tablespoon olive oil
- 1 spring onion, coarsely chopped
- 1 clove garlic, minced
- 1 1/2 heirloom tomatoes, coarsely chopped
- 1/2 teaspoon hot paprika
- 1 tablespoon plus 1/2 teaspoon plain lowfat yogurt
- Coarsely ground black pepper
- 1 tablespoon plus 1/2 teaspoon sliced basil

### Direction

- Preheat the oven to 350 degrees F. Use cooking spray to coat eggplants then roast for an hour. Scoop out the pulp then place on a cheesecloth-lined sieve; drain for an hour. Transfer the pulp in a food processor, puree then move to a bowl. On medium heat, heat oil in a sauté pan. Cook onion in the pan until soft for 5 minutes; put in garlic. Cook for 3 minutes until soft; put in paprika and tomatoes. Cook for 3-5 minutes then cool. Mix yogurts in the puree then put in tomatoes and onion; sprinkle pepper and salt. Refrigerate for half an hour. Top with basil then serve with raw veggies.

## 647. Fast Marinated Tomatoes

*Serving: 4-6 servings. | Prep: 10mins | Cook: 0mins | Ready in:*

### Ingredients

- 6 plum tomatoes, sliced
- Red leaf lettuce
- 8 pitted kalmata olives or ripe olives, chopped
- 1 tablespoon balsamic or red wine vinegar
- 1 tablespoon olive oil
- 1 tablespoon grated onion
- 1 tablespoon honey
- 1 garlic clove, minced
- 1/2 teaspoon salt
- 1/4 teaspoon pepper
- 1/8 to 1/4 teaspoon ground cinnamon
- Minced fresh parsley

### Direction

- Place tomatoes on a lettuce-lined serving plate. Add olives on top. Combine cinnamon, pepper, salt, garlic, honey, onion, oil and vinegar in a small bowl. Pour dressing on top of olives and tomatoes. Add parsley on top.

Cover and chill for a minimum of 1 hour before serving.

## Nutrition Information

- Calories: 61 calories
- Protein: 1g protein.
- Total Fat: 4g fat (0 saturated fat)
- Sodium: 285mg sodium
- Fiber: 1g fiber)
- Total Carbohydrate: 7g carbohydrate (5g sugars
- Cholesterol: 0 cholesterol

---

**648.  Favorite Mediterranean Salad**

---

*Serving: 28 servings (3/4 cup each). | Prep: 20mins | Cook: 0mins | Ready in:*

## Ingredients

- 18 cups torn romaine (about 2 large bunches)
- 1 medium cucumber, sliced
- 1 cup crumbled feta cheese
- 1 cup cherry tomatoes, quartered
- 1 small red onion, thinly sliced
- 1/2 cup julienned roasted sweet red peppers
- 1/2 cup pitted Greek olives, halved
- DRESSING:
- 2/3 cup olive oil
- 1/4 cup red wine vinegar
- 1 garlic clove, minced
- 1 teaspoon Italian seasoning
- 1/4 teaspoon salt
- 1/4 teaspoon pepper

## Direction

- Mix the first seven ingredients together in a really big salad bowl. Combine the dressing ingredients in a small bowl. Drizzle over the salad and coat by tossing.

## Nutrition Information

- Calories: 69 calories
- Total Carbohydrate: 2g carbohydrate (1g sugars
- Cholesterol: 2mg cholesterol
- Protein: 1g protein.  Diabetic Exchanges: 1 vegetable
- Total Fat: 6g fat (1g saturated fat)
- Sodium: 117mg sodium
- Fiber: 1g fiber)

---

**649.  Favorite Raspberry Tossed Salad**

---

*Serving: 8 servings. | Prep: 10mins | Cook: 0mins | Ready in:*

## Ingredients

- 4 cups torn red leaf lettuce
- 1 package (5 ounces) spring mix salad greens
- 1 cup fresh raspberries
- 1 cup sliced fresh mushrooms
- 1/2 cup julienned red onion
- 1/4 cup crumbled feta cheese
- 1/4 cup pecan halves, toasted
- 2 tablespoons 100% raspberry fruit spread, melted
- 2 tablespoons raspberry vinegar
- 2 tablespoons canola oil
- 1/8 teaspoon salt
- Dash pepper

## Direction

- Mix the initial 7 ingredients in a big salad bowl. Combine pepper, salt, oil, vinegar and fruit spread in a small bowl. Put on top of the salad and coat by gently tossing.

## Nutrition Information

- Calories: 102 calories

- Total Carbohydrate: 8g carbohydrate (0 sugars
- Cholesterol: 4mg cholesterol
- Protein: 3g protein. Diabetic Exchanges: 1-1/2 fat
- Total Fat: 7g fat (1g saturated fat)
- Sodium: 108mg sodium
- Fiber: 3g fiber)

## 650. Feta 'n' Chive Muffins

*Serving: 1 dozen. | Prep: 15mins | Cook: 20mins | Ready in:*

### Ingredients

- 1-1/2 cups all-purpose flour
- 3 teaspoons baking powder
- 1/4 teaspoon salt
- 2 large eggs
- 1 cup whole milk
- 2 tablespoons butter, melted
- 1/2 cup crumbled feta cheese
- 3 tablespoons minced chives

### Direction

- Mix salt, baking powder, and flour in a big bow. Mix butter, milk, and eggs in a separate bowl; combine with the dry ingredients to just moisten. Fold in chives and feta cheese.
- Pour mixture in paper-lined or greased muffin cups until 2/3 full. Bake for 18-22 minutes at 400 degrees until an inserted toothpick in the middle comes out without residue. Cool in the pan for 5 minutes then move to wire rack. Serve the muffins warm. Chill any leftovers.

### Nutrition Information

- Calories: 105 calories
- Sodium: 235mg sodium
- Fiber: 1g fiber)
- Total Carbohydrate: 13g carbohydrate (1g sugars

- Cholesterol: 43mg cholesterol
- Protein: 4g protein. Diabetic Exchanges: 1 starch
- Total Fat: 4g fat (2g saturated fat)

## 651. Feta Artichoke Bites

*Serving: about 12 servings. | Prep: 20mins | Cook: 5mins | Ready in:*

### Ingredients

- 1 jar (7-1/2 ounces) marinated artichoke hearts
- 1 cup diced seeded tomatoes
- 1 cup (4 ounces) crumbled feta cheese
- 1/3 cup grated Parmesan cheese
- 2 green onions, thinly sliced
- 1 loaf sourdough baguette (about 20 inches long)

### Direction

- Strain artichokes, save 2 tablespoons marinade. Slice the artichokes and put in a big bowl. Combine reserved marinade, onions, cheeses and tomatoes. Cover and cool for an hour in refrigerator.
- Chop baguette into 1/2 inch slices. Pour artichoke mixture over and spread out. Put on an ungreased sheet baking sheet. Broil for 4-5 minutes 4-6 inches from the heat, or until brown at the edges of the bread. Serve right away.

### Nutrition Information

- Calories: 81 calories
- Protein: 3g protein.
- Total Fat: 5g fat (2g saturated fat)
- Sodium: 252mg sodium
- Fiber: 1g fiber)
- Total Carbohydrate: 5g carbohydrate (1g sugars
- Cholesterol: 7mg cholesterol

## 652. Feta Bruschetta

*Serving: Makes 1-1/4 cups or 10 servings, 2 Tbsp. topping and 5 crackers each. | Prep: 10mins | Cook: | Ready in:*

### Ingredients

- 1 large tomato, seeded, chopped
- 1/2 cup ATHENOS Traditional Crumbled Feta Cheese
- 1/4 cup chopped Kalamata olives
- 1/4 cup KRAFT Italian Vinaigrette Dressing made with Extra Virgin Olive Oil
- 1 Tbsp. chopped fresh basil
- RITZ Snowflake Cracker s

### Direction

- Gather all the ingredients and combine them together, excluding the crackers.
- Chill in the refrigerator for 1 hour.
- Spoon the mixture on top of the crackers, then serve.

### Nutrition Information

- Calories: 120
- Saturated Fat: 2 g
- Protein: 3 g
- Total Fat: 7 g
- Sodium: 320 mg
- Fiber: 1 g
- Sugar: 2 g
- Total Carbohydrate: 12 g
- Cholesterol: 5 mg

## 653. Feta Cheese Mashed Potatoes

*Serving: 6 servings. | Prep: 15mins | Cook: 15mins | Ready in:*

### Ingredients

- 2-1/2 pounds Yukon Gold potatoes, cubed
- 4 to 6 garlic cloves, peeled
- 1 package (4 ounces) crumbled feta cheese
- 1/2 cup heavy whipping cream
- 1/4 teaspoon salt
- 1/4 teaspoon pepper

### Direction

- In a big saucepan, add garlic, potatoes and water to cover. Bring to a boil on moderately high heat, then lower heat and cook, covered, until softened, or for about 10 to 15 minutes.
- Drain and turn to a big bowl to mash. Put in pepper, salt, cream and cheese then beat together until fluffy.

### Nutrition Information

- Calories: 181 calories
- Sodium: 374mg sodium
- Fiber: 3g fiber)
- Total Carbohydrate: 32g carbohydrate (3g sugars
- Cholesterol: 8mg cholesterol
- Protein: 8g protein. Diabetic Exchanges: 2 starch
- Total Fat: 3g fat (2g saturated fat)

## 654. Feta Cucumber Salad

*Serving: 4-5 servings. | Prep: 10mins | Cook: 0mins | Ready in:*

### Ingredients

- 2 medium cucumbers
- 1/2 teaspoon salt
- 1/4 cup chopped green onions
- 1 cup (4 ounces) crumbled feta cheese
- 2 tablespoons lemon juice
- 1 tablespoon olive oil
- 1/8 to 1/4 teaspoon coarsely ground pepper

### Direction

- Slice cucumbers into two lengthwise. Take the seeds out with a spoon and throw away. Slice the cucumbers into 1/2-in. cubes and put in a bowl. Use salt to season. Mix in onions. Mix pepper, oil, lemon juice, and cheese together; put on the cucumber mixture and toss lightly.

### Nutrition Information

- Calories: 101 calories
- Fiber: 2g fiber)
- Total Carbohydrate: 5g carbohydrate (3g sugars
- Cholesterol: 12mg cholesterol
- Protein: 5g protein.
- Total Fat: 6g fat (3g saturated fat)
- Sodium: 453mg sodium

## 655. Feta Frittata

*Serving: 2 servings. | Prep: 15mins | Cook: 10mins | Ready in:*

### Ingredients

- 1 green onion, thinly sliced
- 1 small garlic clove, minced
- 2 large eggs
- 1/2 cup egg substitute
- 4 tablespoons crumbled feta cheese, divided
- 1/3 cup chopped plum tomato
- 4 thin slices peeled avocado
- 2 tablespoons reduced-fat sour cream

### Direction

- On medium heat, heat a 6-in. nonstick skillet coated with cooking spray. Sauté garlic and onion until tender. Whisk 3 tablespoons feta cheese, egg substitute and the eggs. In skillet, pour egg mixture (edges should set immediately). Cover and cook until eggs are nearly set, about 4-6 minutes longer. Spread remaining feta cheese and tomato on. Cover and cook until eggs are completely set, about 2-3 minutes. Allow to stand for 5 minutes. Slice in half; eat with sour cream and avocado.

### Nutrition Information

- Calories: 203 calories
- Sodium: 345mg sodium
- Fiber: 3g fiber)
- Total Carbohydrate: 7g carbohydrate (3g sugars
- Cholesterol: 224mg cholesterol
- Protein: 17g protein. Diabetic Exchanges: 2 medium-fat meat
- Total Fat: 12g fat (4g saturated fat)

## 656. Feta Olive Dip

*Serving: about 1-1/2 cups. | Prep: 5mins | Cook: 0mins | Ready in:*

### Ingredients

- 4 ounces reduced-fat cream cheese
- 1/2 cup crumbled feta cheese
- 1/2 cup reduced-fat sour cream
- 1/4 cup sliced ripe olives
- 2 garlic cloves, minced
- 2 teaspoons dried oregano
- 1 teaspoon minced fresh parsley
- 1/4 teaspoon salt
- 1/4 to 1/2 teaspoon hot pepper sauce
- Baked pita chips

### Direction

- Combine the initial 9 ingredients in a food processor and process, covered, till blended. Place into a large bowl and store for at least 1 hour in the fridge before serving, covered. Serve with pita chips.

### Nutrition Information

- Calories: 56 calories
- Protein: 3g protein. Diabetic Exchanges: 1 fat.
- Total Fat: 4g fat (3g saturated fat)
- Sodium: 183mg sodium
- Fiber: 0 fiber)
- Total Carbohydrate: 2g carbohydrate (0 sugars
- Cholesterol: 14mg cholesterol

## 657. Feta Pitas

*Serving: 6 servings. | Prep: 10mins | Cook: 10mins | Ready in:*

### Ingredients

- 6 whole pita breads
- 1-1/2 cups (6 ounces) crumbled feta cheese
- 3 teaspoons Italian seasoning
- 3/4 cup thinly sliced red onion
- 1 small tomato, thinly sliced

### Direction

- On an ungreased baking sheet, put pita breads then scatter with Italian seasoning and cheese. Add tomato and onion on top.
- Bake for 10-12 minutes in 350 degrees oven. If desired, slice into wedges then serve right away.

### Nutrition Information

- Calories:
- Protein:
- Total Fat:
- Sodium:
- Fiber:
- Total Carbohydrate:
- Cholesterol:

## 658. Feta Romaine Salad

*Serving: 6 servings. | Prep: 15mins | Cook: 0mins | Ready in:*

### Ingredients

- 1 bunch romaine, chopped
- 3 plum tomatoes, seeded and chopped
- 1 cup (4 ounces) crumbled feta cheese
- 1 cup chopped seeded cucumber
- 1/2 cup Greek olives, chopped
- 2 tablespoons minced fresh parsley
- 2 tablespoons minced fresh cilantro
- 3 tablespoons lemon juice
- 2 tablespoons olive oil
- 1/4 teaspoon pepper

### Direction

- Combine the first seven ingredients in a large bowl. Whisk the remaining ingredients together in a small bowl. Add dressing to salad mixture and toss until well coated. Serve right away.

### Nutrition Information

- Calories: 139 calories
- Total Carbohydrate: 6g carbohydrate (2g sugars
- Cholesterol: 10mg cholesterol
- Protein: 5g protein. Diabetic Exchanges: 2 fat
- Total Fat: 11g fat (3g saturated fat)
- Sodium: 375mg sodium
- Fiber: 3g fiber)

## 659. Feta Scrambled Egg Wraps

*Serving: 4 servings. | Prep: 10mins | Cook: 5mins | Ready in:*

### Ingredients

- 1-1/2 cups Southwestern-style egg substitute
- 3/4 cup crumbled feta cheese
- 2 tablespoons sliced pepperoncini, chopped
- 4 whole wheat tortillas (8 inches), warmed

## Direction

- Bring a greased large non-stick skillet on medium heat. Add egg substitute; cook, stirring, until thick and no liquid egg remains. Gently whisk in pepperoncini and cheese, then cook until heated through. Place inside tortillas, then serve.

## Nutrition Information

- Calories: 239 calories
- Cholesterol: 11mg cholesterol
- Protein: 17g protein. Diabetic Exchanges: 2 lean meat
- Total Fat: 6g fat (2g saturated fat)
- Sodium: 560mg sodium
- Fiber: 3g fiber)
- Total Carbohydrate: 24g carbohydrate (3g sugars

## 660. Feta Spinach Pizza

Serving: 12 pieces. | Prep: 15mins | Cook: 15mins | Ready in:

## Ingredients

- 1 tube (13.8 ounces) refrigerated pizza crust
- 1 tablespoon olive oil
- 1 teaspoon minced garlic
- 1 can (15 ounces) pizza sauce
- 2 cups chopped fresh spinach
- 3/4 cup sliced red onion, separated into rings
- 1 cup sliced fresh mushrooms
- 1 cup shredded part-skim mozzarella cheese
- 1/2 cup crumbled feta cheese
- 1 teaspoon dried basil
- 1 teaspoon Italian seasoning
- Crushed red pepper flakes, optional

## Direction

- In a greased 15x10x1-inch baking pan, unroll the crust. Flatten the dough and slightly build up its edges. Then brush with oil and sprinkle garlic. Spread the pizza sauce.
- Layer with cheeses, mushrooms, onion and spinach. If desired, sprinkle with pepper flakes, Italian seasoning and basil. Bake until golden brown or for 15 to 18 minutes at 400 degrees.

## Nutrition Information

- Calories: 122 calories
- Protein: 6g protein. Diabetic Exchanges: 1 starch
- Total Fat: 4g fat (1g saturated fat)
- Sodium: 366mg sodium
- Fiber: 1g fiber)
- Total Carbohydrate: 15g carbohydrate (3g sugars
- Cholesterol: 7mg cholesterol

## 661. Feta Olive Romaine Salad

Serving: 4-6 servings. | Prep: 15mins | Cook: 0mins | Ready in:

## Ingredients

- 6 cups torn romaine
- 2/3 cup diced sweet red pepper
- 1/3 cup diced green pepper
- 3 tablespoons chopped ripe olives
- 1/4 cup olive oil
- 1/4 cup balsamic vinegar
- 1/3 cup tomato and basil feta cheese, crumbled

## Direction

- Mix olives, peppers, and romaine together in a salad bowl; toss. Mix vinegar and oil together in a tightly fitting lidded jar and shake well. Drizzle over the salad and coat by tossing. Use feta cheese to sprinkle.

## Nutrition Information

- Calories: 121 calories
- Total Fat: 11g fat (2g saturated fat)
- Sodium: 104mg sodium
- Fiber: 2g fiber)
- Total Carbohydrate: 5g carbohydrate (3g sugars
- Cholesterol: 3mg cholesterol
- Protein: 2g protein.

## 662. Feta Spinach Melts

*Serving: 10 servings. | Prep: 20mins | Cook: 5mins | Ready in:*

## Ingredients

- 3 packages (6 ounces each) fresh baby spinach, chopped
- 1 teaspoon water
- 1/2 cup crumbled feta cheese
- 1 plum tomatoes, seeded and chopped
- 1/4 cup finely chopped red onion
- 3 tablespoons fat-free mayonnaise
- 3 tablespoons fat-free sour cream
- 1 garlic clove, minced
- 1/2 teaspoon salt
- 1/2 teaspoon dill weed
- 20 slices French baguette (1/2 inch thick)

## Direction

- Mix spinach with water in a big microwave-safe bowl. Cover and microwave at high heat until spinach is diminished, for 1 1/2 to 2 minutes, stir twice then drain and squeeze. Mix in the dill weed, salt, garlic, sour cream, mayonnaise, onion, tomato and feta cheese; put aside.
- Lay bread on a baking tray. Put the tray 4 inches away from the heat source and broil until bread is toasted slightly, for 1 to 2 minutes. Add about 1 tablespoon of the spinach mixture over each bread. Broil for 3 to 4 more minutes until cooked through.

## Nutrition Information

- Calories: 100 calories
- Protein: 4g protein. Diabetic Exchanges: 1 starch
- Total Fat: 3g fat (1g saturated fat)
- Sodium: 400mg sodium
- Fiber: 2g fiber)
- Total Carbohydrate: 15g carbohydrate (0 sugars
- Cholesterol: 8mg cholesterol

## 663. Feta Topped Asparagus

*Serving: 4 servings. | Prep: 15mins | Cook: 0mins | Ready in:*

## Ingredients

- 1-1/2 pounds fresh asparagus
- 1 medium red onion, sliced and separated into rings
- 2 tablespoons olive oil
- Salt and pepper to taste
- 1/4 cup crumbled feta cheese

## Direction

- Place asparagus into a large skillet and pour in 1/2 in. of water; allow to boil. Lower the heat; simmer with a cover till crisp-tender, 3-5 minutes; strain. Take out the asparagus, keep warm.
- Sauté onion till crisp-tender in the same pan. Put the asparagus back to the pan. Sprinkle with cheese, pepper and salt.

### Nutrition Information

- Calories: 108 calories
- Cholesterol: 4mg cholesterol
- Protein: 4g protein.
- Total Fat: 8g fat (2g saturated fat)
- Sodium: 78mg sodium
- Fiber: 2g fiber)
- Total Carbohydrate: 6g carbohydrate (3g sugars

## 664. Flavorful Rice Salad

*Serving: 6 servings. | Prep: 15mins | Cook: 0mins | Ready in:*

### Ingredients

- 1 can (15 ounces) black beans, rinsed and drained
- 1-1/2 cups cold cooked long grain rice
- 1-1/2 cups chopped fresh tomatoes (about 4 medium)
- 4 green onions, chopped
- 1 celery rib, chopped
- 1/2 cup chopped fresh spinach
- 2 tablespoons minced fresh cilantro
- 1/2 cup fat-free Italian salad dressing
- 1 cup (4 ounces) crumbled feta cheese

### Direction

- Mix cilantro, spinach, celery, onions, tomatoes, rice and beans in a large bowl. Drizzle dressing over salad and toss to coat. Keep covered for 1 hour in the refrigerator.
- Add a sprinkle of cheese right before serving.

### Nutrition Information

- Calories: 181 calories
- Sodium: 617mg sodium
- Fiber: 5g fiber)
- Total Carbohydrate: 27g carbohydrate (4g sugars
- Cholesterol: 11mg cholesterol
- Protein: 9g protein. Diabetic Exchanges: 2 starch
- Total Fat: 3g fat (2g saturated fat)

## 665. Fresh Greek Garden Salad

*Serving: 2 servings. | Prep: 15mins | Cook: 0mins | Ready in:*

### Ingredients

- 1 medium tomato, chopped
- 1/3 cup chopped cucumber
- 1/4 cup chopped green pepper
- 1/4 cup chopped sweet red pepper
- 1/4 cup crumbled feta cheese
- 2 tablespoons sliced pimiento-stuffed olives
- 2 tablespoons sliced ripe olives
- 1/4 cup Italian salad dressing
- Dash dried oregano

### Direction

- Mix the first 7 ingredients in a bowl. Before serving, add oregano and salad dressing. Toss until coated.

### Nutrition Information

- Calories: 110 calories
- Sodium: 826mg sodium
- Fiber: 3g fiber)
- Total Carbohydrate: 12g carbohydrate (6g sugars
- Cholesterol: 8mg cholesterol
- Protein: 4g protein.
- Total Fat: 5g fat (2g saturated fat)

## 666. Fresh Tomato & Cucumber Salad

*Serving: 6 servings. | Prep: 20mins | Cook: 0mins | Ready in:*

### Ingredients

- 1/4 cup lemon juice
- 1/4 cup olive oil
- 1 tablespoon minced fresh basil or 1 teaspoon dried basil
- 1 tablespoon white wine vinegar
- 1 garlic clove, minced
- 1 teaspoon minced fresh mint or 1/4 teaspoon dried mint
- 1/8 teaspoon kosher salt
- 1/8 teaspoon coarsely ground pepper
- 4 plum tomatoes, seeded and chopped
- 2 medium cucumbers, chopped
- 1/2 cup Greek olives, sliced
- 2 cups torn mixed salad greens
- 3/4 cup crumbled feta cheese
- 1/4 cup pine nuts, toasted

### Direction

- Mix the first 8 ingredients together in a small bowl, put aside.
- In a big bowl, mix olives with tomatoes and cucumbers. Use half of the dressing to sprinkle; mix to combine. Transfer the salad greens onto a big serving dish; put the tomato mixture on top. Use the rest of the dressing, pine nuts and cheese to sprinkle.

### Nutrition Information

- Calories: 209 calories
- Sodium: 366mg sodium
- Fiber: 3g fiber)
- Total Carbohydrate: 9g carbohydrate (4g sugars
- Cholesterol: 8mg cholesterol
- Protein: 6g protein.
- Total Fat: 17g fat (4g saturated fat)

## 667. Fresh As Summer Salad

*Serving: 8 servings. | Prep: 25mins | Cook: 0mins | Ready in:*

### Ingredients

- 2 romaine hearts, torn
- 2 tablespoons olive oil
- 3/4 cup chopped fresh cilantro, mint, sorrel and/or lemon balm
- 3 green onions, thinly sliced
- 1/2 cup plain Greek yogurt
- 1 teaspoon lemon juice
- 3/4 teaspoon salt
- 1/2 teaspoon ground nutmeg
- 1/4 teaspoon pepper
- 1 cup canned garbanzo beans or chickpeas
- 3 tablespoons pistachios
- 3 lemon wedges

### Direction

- In a big bowl, put romaine, use oil to sprinkle and toss to coat.
- Add onions and herbs, toss to blend. Combine pepper, nutmeg, salt, lemon juice, and yogurt; and put on the romaine mixture and toss to coat.
- Move to a serving platter. Put pistachios and garbanzo beans on top. Use lemon wedges to squeeze over the top. Enjoy immediately.

### Nutrition Information

- Calories: 104 calories
- Protein: 3g protein. Diabetic Exchanges: 1 fat
- Total Fat: 7g fat (2g saturated fat)
- Sodium: 289mg sodium
- Fiber: 3g fiber)
- Total Carbohydrate: 9g carbohydrate (2g sugars
- Cholesterol: 4mg cholesterol

## 668. Fruit 'N' Feta Tossed Salad

*Serving: 12 servings. | Prep: 15mins | Cook: 0mins | Ready in:*

### Ingredients

- CREAMY RASPBERRY VINAIGRETTE:
- 1 package (10 ounces) frozen sweetened raspberries, thawed
- 1 cup (8 ounces) reduced-fat plain yogurt
- 2 tablespoons cider vinegar
- 1/2 teaspoon dried tarragon
- SALAD:
- 9 cups torn mixed salad greens
- 1-1/2 cups shredded carrots
- 2 Red Delicious apples, chopped
- 1 Golden Delicious apple, chopped
- 3/4 cup crumbled feta cheese

### Direction

- Drain raspberries, saving juice; pick out pulp and seeds. Combine raspberry juice, tarragon, vinegar, and yogurt in a small bowl until smooth. In a large bowl, mix together apples, carrot, and salad greens. Garnish with feta cheese on top. Serve right away with dressing.

### Nutrition Information

- Calories: 94 calories
- Protein: 3g protein. Diabetic Exchanges: 1 fruit
- Total Fat: 2g fat (2g saturated fat)
- Sodium: 126mg sodium
- Fiber: 3g fiber)
- Total Carbohydrate: 16g carbohydrate (0 sugars
- Cholesterol: 10mg cholesterol

## 669. Fruited Feta Spread

*Serving: 4 cups. | Prep: 20mins | Cook: 0mins | Ready in:*

### Ingredients

- 1 package (8 ounces) cream cheese, softened
- 1 package (4 ounces) crumbled feta cheese
- 1 cup seedless red grapes, diced
- 1 large tart apple, diced
- 3/4 cup chopped pecans, toasted
- 1 jar (4 ounces) diced pimientos, drained
- 1/4 cup mayonnaise
- 3 tablespoons honey
- 2 tablespoons minced fresh parsley
- Assorted crackers

### Direction

- Beat cream cheese and feta in a small bowl until smooth. Stir in the pecans, honey, grapes, pimientos, mayonnaise, apple, and parsley. Chill until you serve. Enjoy with crackers.

### Nutrition Information

- Calories: 159 calories
- Protein: 3g protein.
- Total Fat: 13g fat (5g saturated fat)
- Sodium: 131mg sodium
- Fiber: 1g fiber)
- Total Carbohydrate: 9g carbohydrate (7g sugars
- Cholesterol: 21mg cholesterol

## 670. Fruity Greek Salad

*Serving: 12 servings. | Prep: 10mins | Cook: 0mins | Ready in:*

### Ingredients

- 12 cups torn romaine
- 1 can (11 ounces) mandarin oranges, drained
- 2 celery ribs, sliced

- 1 cup sliced carrots
- 1 small red onion, thinly sliced
- 1/2 cup canned unsweetened peach slices, cut into thirds
- 10 pitted whole ripe olives
- 3 ounces crumbled feta cheese
- 1/4 cup olive oil
- 1/2 teaspoon sugar
- 1/4 teaspoon dried basil
- 1/4 teaspoon dried oregano
- 1/4 teaspoon salt

### Direction

- Mix the first 8 ingredients together in a large salad bowl. In an air-tight jar, combine seasonings, sugar, vinegar, and oil; shake properly. Pour over salad and stir until evenly coated.

### Nutrition Information

- Calories: 94 calories
- Protein: 2g protein. Diabetic Exchanges: 1-1/2 fat
- Total Fat: 7g fat (2g saturated fat)
- Sodium: 178mg sodium
- Fiber: 2g fiber)
- Total Carbohydrate: 8g carbohydrate (0 sugars
- Cholesterol: 6mg cholesterol

## 671. Garbanzo Bean Pitas

Serving: 4 servings. | Prep: 20mins | Cook: 0mins | Ready in:

### Ingredients

- 1 can (15 ounces) garbanzo beans or chickpeas, rinsed and drained
- 1/2 cup fat-free mayonnaise
- 1 tablespoon water
- 2 tablespoons minced fresh parsley
- 2 tablespoons chopped walnuts

- 1 tablespoon chopped onion
- 1 garlic clove, minced
- 1/8 teaspoon pepper
- 4 whole wheat pita pocket halves
- 4 lettuce leaves
- 1/2 small cucumber, thinly sliced
- 1 small tomato, seeded and chopped
- 1/4 cup fat-free ranch salad dressing, optional

### Direction

- Mix together the initial 8 ingredients in a blender. Put on a cover and process until combined. On each pita half, place 1/3 cup of the bean mixture, then put lettuce, cucumber and tomato on top. If preferred, serve with ranch dressing.

### Nutrition Information

- Calories: 241 calories
- Protein: 9g protein. Diabetic Exchanges: 3 starch
- Total Fat: 6g fat (0 saturated fat)
- Sodium: 552mg sodium
- Fiber: 8g fiber)
- Total Carbohydrate: 41g carbohydrate (6g sugars
- Cholesterol: 3mg cholesterol

## 672. Garbanzo Bean Salad With Citrusy Dressing

Serving: 4 servings. | Prep: 10mins | Cook: 0mins | Ready in:

### Ingredients

- 1 can (15 ounces) garbanzo beans or chickpeas, rinsed and drained
- 1/2 cup chopped red onion
- 2 tablespoons minced fresh parsley
- 1 tablespoon minced fresh mint
- 2 tablespoons lemon juice

- 2 tablespoons olive oil
- 1 garlic clove, minced
- 1/2 teaspoon sugar
- 1/2 teaspoon salt
- 1/4 teaspoon pepper
- Leaf lettuce

### Direction

- Combine mint, parsley, onion, and beans in a bowl. Add pepper, salt, sugar, garlic, oil, and lemon juice into an air-tight jar; shake properly. Drizzle dressing over salad and stir until evenly coated. Cover and chill in the fridge for at least 2 hours. Place salad on plates lined with lettuce to serve.

### Nutrition Information

- Calories: 167 calories
- Sodium: 616mg sodium
- Fiber: 5g fiber)
- Total Carbohydrate: 19g carbohydrate (0 sugars
- Cholesterol: 0 cholesterol
- Protein: 6g protein. Diabetic Exchanges: 1-1/2 fat
- Total Fat: 8g fat (1g saturated fat)

## 673. Garbanzo Beans 'N' Rice

*Serving: 6 servings. | Prep: 5mins | Cook: 10mins | Ready in:*

### Ingredients

- 1 medium onion, chopped
- 2 garlic cloves, minced
- 1 tablespoon canola oil
- 2 medium tomatoes, chopped
- 1 medium zucchini, chopped
- 1/2 teaspoon dried oregano
- 1 can (15 ounces) garbanzo beans or chickpeas, rinsed and drained
- 1/2 teaspoon salt
- 1/4 teaspoon pepper
- 3 cups cooked rice
- 1 cup shredded reduced-fat cheddar cheese

### Direction

- Allow to sauté garlic and onion in oil in a non-stick skillet until becoming tender. Stir in the oregano, zucchini, and tomatoes. Cook and stir occasionally, covered, until the zucchini becomes tender-crisp, or for 4-6 minutes.
- Put in the pepper, salt, and beans; stir and cook until heated through. Let serve over the rice. Use cheese to dust.

### Nutrition Information

- Calories: 286 calories
- Cholesterol: 10mg cholesterol
- Protein: 12g protein. Diabetic Exchanges: 2 starch
- Total Fat: 7g fat (2g saturated fat)
- Sodium: 445mg sodium
- Fiber: 5g fiber)
- Total Carbohydrate: 46g carbohydrate (0 sugars

## 674. Garden Barley Salad

*Serving: 3 servings. | Prep: 10mins | Cook: 15mins | Ready in:*

### Ingredients

- 1-1/2 cups water
- 3/4 cup quick-cooking barley
- 1/4 teaspoon salt
- 4 cherry tomatoes, halved
- 2 green onions, chopped
- 4-1/2 teaspoons olive oil
- 1 tablespoon minced fresh parsley
- 1 tablespoon lemon juice
- 1/8 teaspoon pepper

### Direction

- Boil water in a small saucepan. Mix in salt and barley. Reduce heat, cover and simmer until barley is tender, for about 10-12 minutes. Take off heat, let stand for about 5 minutes. Fluff using a fork. Mix in the rest of the ingredients.

### Nutrition Information

- Calories: 232 calories
- Total Fat: 8g fat (1g saturated fat)
- Sodium: 207mg sodium
- Fiber: 9g fiber)
- Total Carbohydrate: 36g carbohydrate (1g sugars
- Cholesterol: 0 cholesterol
- Protein: 6g protein.

## 675. Garden Cucumber Salad

*Serving: 12 servings (3/4 cup each). | Prep: 10mins | Cook: 0mins | Ready in:*

### Ingredients

- 4 medium cucumbers, cut into 1/2-inch pieces (about 7 cups)
- 2 medium sweet red peppers, chopped
- 1 cup cherry tomatoes, halved
- 1 cup crumbled feta cheese
- 1/2 cup finely chopped red onion
- 1/2 cup olive oil
- 1/4 cup lemon juice
- 1 tablespoon Greek seasoning
- 1/2 teaspoon salt

### Direction

- Put all ingredients in a big bowl. Gently toss to combine. Keep in fridge for at least half an hour, covered, before serving.

### Nutrition Information

- Calories: 125 calories
- Protein: 3g protein. Diabetic Exchanges: 2 fat
- Total Fat: 11g fat (2g saturated fat)
- Sodium: 431mg sodium
- Fiber: 2g fiber)
- Total Carbohydrate: 5g carbohydrate (3g sugars
- Cholesterol: 5mg cholesterol

## 676. Garden Herb Rice Salad

*Serving: 4-6 servings. | Prep: 20mins | Cook: 0mins | Ready in:*

### Ingredients

- 3 cups cooked long grain rice, chilled
- 1 large tomato, chopped
- 1 medium sweet yellow pepper, diced
- 1 small cucumber, peeled, seeded and diced
- 1/2 cup diced mozzarella cheese
- 1/2 cup sliced ripe olives, drained
- 1/4 to 1/3 cup snipped fresh basil
- 1/4 cup snipped fresh mint
- 1/3 cup olive oil
- 1/4 cup lemon juice
- Salt and pepper to taste

### Direction

- Combine the first 8 ingredients in a big salad bowl. Whisk pepper, salt, lemon juice, and oil. Pour on salad then toss well. Chill for half an hour.

### Nutrition Information

- Calories: 267 calories
- Total Carbohydrate: 28g carbohydrate (2g sugars
- Cholesterol: 7mg cholesterol
- Protein: 5g protein.
- Total Fat: 16g fat (3g saturated fat)
- Sodium: 138mg sodium

- Fiber: 2g fiber)

## 677. Garden Vegetable Pasta Salad

*Serving: 4 servings | Prep: 20mins | Cook: | Ready in:*

### Ingredients

- 1-3/4 cups farfalle (bow-tie pasta), uncooked
- 2 cups cut-up fresh asparagus spears (1 inch lengths)
- 1/4 cup KRAFT Classic Ranch Dressing
- 1/4 cup KRAFT Real Mayo Mayonnaise
- 1/2 cup finely chopped red onion s
- 2 cups halved cherry tomatoes
- 1/4 cup KRAFT Grated Parmesan Cheese
- 1/4 cup chopped fresh basil

### Direction

- Follow packaging directions to cook pasta, don't add salt and put asparagus into boiling water for the last 3 minutes.
- While waiting, in a big bowl, combine mayo and dressing. Stir in the onions and toss in tomatoes, basil, cheese, and pasta mixture; stir lightly.
- Serve immediately or keep in the refrigerator with cover until time to serve.

### Nutrition Information

- Calories: 430
- Total Carbohydrate: 52 g
- Cholesterol: 15 mg
- Sugar: 8 g
- Protein: 13 g
- Total Fat: 19 g
- Saturated Fat: 4 g
- Sodium: 360 mg
- Fiber: 5 g

## 678. Garlic Artichoke Dip

*Serving: 2-1/2 cups. | Prep: 25mins | Cook: 0mins | Ready in:*

### Ingredients

- 1 large onion, chopped
- 1/2 teaspoon dried oregano
- 1/2 teaspoon dried thyme
- 2 tablespoons olive oil
- 5 garlic cloves, minced
- 1 can (15 ounces) white kidney or cannellini beans, rinsed and drained
- 1 can (14 ounces) water-packed artichoke hearts, rinsed and drained
- 1 tablespoon lemon juice
- 1/2 teaspoon salt
- 1/8 teaspoon cayenne pepper
- Assorted fresh vegetables and/or baked pita chips

### Direction

- Sauté thyme, oregano, onion in oil in a small, nonstick skillet until the onions become tender. Place in garlic and cook for another minute. Take off heat and slightly cool.
- Mix onion mix, cayenne, salt, lemon juice, artichokes, and beans in a food processor. Cover it and process until it's pureed.
- Move to a small bowl. Place on a cover and keep it in the fridge for at least 2 hours and serve. Eat with pita chips or veggies.

### Nutrition Information

- Calories: 81 calories
- Sodium: 271mg sodium
- Fiber: 2g fiber)
- Total Carbohydrate: 11g carbohydrate (1g sugars
- Cholesterol: 0 cholesterol
- Protein: 3g protein. Diabetic Exchanges: 1 vegetable

- Total Fat: 3g fat (0 saturated fat)

### 679. Garlic Cucumber Dip

*Serving: 16 | Prep: 15mins | Cook: | Ready in:*

#### Ingredients

- 4 ounces cream cheese, softened
- 4 ounces sour cream
- 1/2 large cucumber, peeled and diced
- 1 clove garlic, minced
- 1/4 small onion, diced
- salt and pepper to taste

#### Direction

- Combine sour cream and cream cheese in a medium bowl; stir in pepper, cucumber, salt, onion, and garlic. Chill until ready to serve.

#### Nutrition Information

- Calories: 42 calories;
- Total Carbohydrate: 0.9
- Cholesterol: 11
- Protein: 0.8
- Total Fat: 4
- Sodium: 25

### 680. Garlic Feta Spread

*Serving: 1-1/4 cups. | Prep: 10mins | Cook: 0mins | Ready in:*

#### Ingredients

- 4 ounces reduced-fat cream cheese
- 1/3 cup fat-free mayonnaise
- 1 to 2 garlic cloves, minced
- 1/4 teaspoon dried basil, crushed
- 1/4 teaspoon dried oregano, crushed
- 1/8 teaspoon dill weed
- 1/8 teaspoon dried thyme, crushed
- 4 ounces crumbled feta cheese
- Fresh vegetables and/or crackers

#### Direction

- Mix the first 7 ingredients in a food processor, then cover and process until smooth. Turn the mixture to a small bowl then stir in feta cheese. Serve along with vegetables and/or crackers.

#### Nutrition Information

- Calories: 63 calories
- Total Fat: 5g fat (3g saturated fat)
- Sodium: 224mg sodium
- Fiber: 0 fiber)
- Total Carbohydrate: 2g carbohydrate (2g sugars
- Cholesterol: 17mg cholesterol
- Protein: 3g protein. Diabetic Exchanges: 1 fat.

### 681. Garlic Garbanzo Bean Spread

*Serving: 1-1/2 cups. | Prep: 10mins | Cook: 0mins | Ready in:*

#### Ingredients

- 1 can (15 ounces) garbanzo beans or chickpeas, rinsed and drained
- 1/2 cup olive oil
- 2 tablespoons minced fresh parsley
- 1 tablespoon lemon juice
- 1 green onion, cut into three pieces
- 1 to 2 garlic cloves, peeled
- 1/4 teaspoon salt
- Assorted fresh vegetables and baked pita chips

#### Direction

- Process the first 7 ingredients in a food processor with cover until combined; move to a bowl. Chill until ready to serve. Serve with pita chips and veggies.

## Nutrition Information

- Calories: 114 calories
- Total Fat: 10g fat (1g saturated fat)
- Sodium: 96mg sodium
- Fiber: 1g fiber)
- Total Carbohydrate: 6g carbohydrate (1g sugars
- Cholesterol: 0 cholesterol
- Protein: 1g protein.

## 682. Garlic Lemon Dip

Serving: About 1-1/2 cups. | Prep: 30mins | Cook: 0mins | Ready in:

### Ingredients

- 1/4 pound day-old Italian bread, crusts removed and cut into large pieces
- 2 cups water
- 3 to 4 tablespoons lemon juice
- 2 medium red potatoes, peeled, cubed, cooked and cooled
- 5 to 6 garlic cloves, halved
- 1/2 teaspoon salt
- 1/2 cup olive oil
- Chopped walnuts or almonds, optional
- Pita chips or crackers

### Direction

- Soak bread in a big bowl with water about 15 minutes. Squeeze bread and put in a small bowl, then put aside. You should make about 1 cup of bread.
- Mix together salt, garlic, potatoes and lemon juice in a blender, then place a cover and process until smooth. Put in bread and process, covered, until mixed. Put in oil gradually while processing, until combined.

- Remove to a serving bowl and sprinkle nuts over top, if wanted. Serve together with crackers or pita chips. Keep in the fridge.

## Nutrition Information

- Calories: 122 calories
- Protein: 1g protein.
- Total Fat: 9g fat (1g saturated fat)
- Sodium: 155mg sodium
- Fiber: 1g fiber)
- Total Carbohydrate: 8g carbohydrate (0 sugars
- Cholesterol: 0 cholesterol

## 683. Garlic And Artichoke Roasted Potatoes

Serving: 10 servings. | Prep: 15mins | Cook: 35mins | Ready in:

### Ingredients

- 2-1/2 pounds medium red potatoes, cut into 1-1/2-inch cubes
- 2 packages (8 ounces each) frozen artichoke hearts
- 8 garlic cloves, halved
- 3 tablespoons olive oil
- 3/4 teaspoon salt
- 1/4 teaspoon pepper
- 1/4 cup lemon juice
- 2 tablespoons minced fresh parsley
- 1 teaspoon grated lemon peel

### Direction

- Put in a 15"x10"x1" baking pan coated with cooking spray with garlic, artichokes and potatoes. Mix together pepper, salt and oil then pour over the vegetables and toss to coat well.
- Bake at 425° without a cover, until softened while stirring sometimes, about 35 to 40 minutes. Turn to a big bowl then put in lemon

peel, parsley and lemon juice then toss to coat well. Serve while still warm.

## Nutrition Information

- Calories: 143 calories
- Sodium: 209mg sodium
- Fiber: 4g fiber)
- Total Carbohydrate: 24g carbohydrate (2g sugars
- Cholesterol: 0 cholesterol
- Protein: 4g protein. Diabetic Exchanges: 1 starch
- Total Fat: 4g fat (1g saturated fat)

## 684. Garlic Herb Bagel Spread

Serving: 1 cup, 8 servings, 2 tablespoons per serving. | Prep: 10mins | Cook: 0mins | Ready in:

### Ingredients

- 3 ounces cream cheese, softened
- 1/3 cup sour cream
- 1/4 cup crumbled feta cheese
- 2 garlic cloves, minced
- 1/2 teaspoon each garlic powder, dried oregano and basil
- Bagels, split

### Direction

- Beat the cream cheese until smooth in a small bowl. Mix seasonings with garlic, feta cheese, and the sour cream properly. Toast bagels as desired; Place spread on top.

### Nutrition Information

- Calories: 38 calories
- Cholesterol: 8mg cholesterol
- Protein: 3g protein. Diabetic Exchanges: 1 fat.
- Total Fat: 2g fat (1g saturated fat)
- Sodium: 117mg sodium
- Fiber: 0 fiber)
- Total Carbohydrate: 2g carbohydrate (0 sugars

## 685. Garlic Kissed Tomatoes

Serving: 12 servings. | Prep: 15mins | Cook: 0mins | Ready in:

### Ingredients

- 6 medium tomatoes
- 1/4 cup canola oil
- 3 tablespoons lemon juice
- 2 garlic cloves, thinly sliced
- 1/2 teaspoon salt
- 1/2 teaspoon dried oregano
- 1/8 teaspoon pepper

### Direction

- Peel tomatoes and halve them horizontally. Squeeze tomatoes gently to take seeds out. Get rid of both seeds and juices. Put tomato halves in a container with a tight-fitting lid.
- Mix together pepper, oregano, salt, garlic, lemon juice and oil in a small bowl, then drizzle over tomatoes. Close lid and turn to coat. Chill for a minimum of 4 hours and maximum of 2 days, turning sometimes.

### Nutrition Information

- Calories: 58 calories
- Cholesterol: 0 cholesterol
- Protein: 1g protein.
- Total Fat: 5g fat (1g saturated fat)
- Sodium: 105mg sodium
- Fiber: 1g fiber)
- Total Carbohydrate: 4g carbohydrate (2g sugars

## 686. Garlic Sesame Pita Chips

*Serving: about 4 dozen. | Prep: 10mins | Cook: 5mins | Ready in:*

### Ingredients

- 2 whole wheat pita breads (6 inches)
- 3 tablespoons olive oil
- 1 teaspoon sesame oil
- 1 tablespoon sesame seeds
- 1/2 teaspoon garlic salt

### Direction

- Halve pita breads. Separate each half in two; slice into strips. Put on ungreased baking sheets. Mix the oils in a small bowl, spread over strips. Sprinkle garlic salt and sesame seeds over the strips.
- Bake for 3 to 5 minutes at 400deg until golden brown. Place on wire racks.

### Nutrition Information

- Calories: 195 calories
- Protein: 4g protein.
- Total Fat: 13g fat (2g saturated fat)
- Sodium: 398mg sodium
- Fiber: 2g fiber)
- Total Carbohydrate: 18g carbohydrate (0 sugars
- Cholesterol: 0 cholesterol

## 687. Garlicky Kale

*Serving: 6 servings. | Prep: 20mins | Cook: 15mins | Ready in:*

### Ingredients

- 3 cups water
- 2 bunches kale, trimmed and coarsely chopped
- 4 garlic cloves, minced
- 1 teaspoon olive oil
- 1/2 cup golden raisins
- 1/4 cup pitted ripe olives, sliced
- 1/4 teaspoon salt
- 1/4 teaspoon crushed red pepper flakes

### Direction

- Boil water in a big saucepan; mix in kale then cover. Cook for 6-8 minutes until nearly tender; drain then set the kale aside.
- Use cooking spray to coat a big non-stick pan; cook garlic in oil for a minute. Mix in pepper flakes, raisins, salt, and olives; cook for another minute. Mix in kale then cook for 3-4 minutes until tender.

### Nutrition Information

- Calories: 88 calories
- Sodium: 187mg sodium
- Fiber: 2g fiber)
- Total Carbohydrate: 17g carbohydrate (8g sugars
- Cholesterol: 0 cholesterol
- Protein: 3g protein. Diabetic Exchanges: 2 vegetable
- Total Fat: 2g fat (0 saturated fat)

## 688. Goat Cheese 'n' Veggie Quesadillas

*Serving: 2 dozen appetizers. | Prep: 55mins | Cook: 5mins | Ready in:*

### Ingredients

- 1 small eggplant, peeled, quartered and cut into 1/2-inch slices
- 1 medium zucchini, cut into 1/4-inch slices
- 1 medium sweet red pepper, chopped
- 1 medium onion, chopped
- 1/4 cup chopped ripe olives
- 2 garlic cloves, minced

- 2 tablespoons olive oil
- 1 tablespoon lemon juice
- 1/2 teaspoon chili powder
- 1/2 teaspoon cayenne pepper
- 1 tablespoon minced fresh cilantro
- 1/2 cup crumbled goat cheese
- 8 whole wheat tortillas (8 inches)

## Direction

- In an ungreased 15-in by 10-in by 1-in baking pan, put the first 6 ingredients. Mix cayenne, oil, chili powder, and lemon juice; sprinkle on top of vegetable and toss to coat. Bake for 35-40 minutes in 400 degrees oven without cover until tender, mix once. Mix in cilantro.
- Slather 1 tablespoon goat cheese on one side of every tortilla; arrange on an ungreased baking sheet with the plain-side down. Slather 2/3 cup veggie mixture over each then put another tortilla on top. Repeat. Bake for 5-10 minutes in 400 degrees oven until golden brown. Slice each quesadilla to 6 wedges. Serve the wedges warm.

## Nutrition Information

- Calories: 171 calories
- Fiber: 3g fiber)
- Total Carbohydrate: 20g carbohydrate (3g sugars
- Cholesterol: 7mg cholesterol
- Protein: 6g protein.
- Total Fat: 8g fat (2g saturated fat)
- Sodium: 191mg sodium

## 689. Goat Cheese Wontons

*Serving: 16 wontons. | Prep: 20mins | Cook: 10mins | Ready in:*

## Ingredients

- 1 cup crumbled goat cheese

- 1 teaspoon each minced fresh basil, parsley and chives
- 1 garlic clove, minced
- Dash salt and pepper
- 1 egg, beaten
- 1 tablespoon water
- 16 wonton wrappers
- Oil for deep-fat frying

## Direction

- Mix pepper, cheese, salt, garlic, and herbs in a small bowl. Whisk water and egg.
- In the middle a wonton wrapper, put 1 tablespoon of the cheese mixture. Use a damp paper towel to cover the rest of the wrappers until ready to use. Fold the bottom side of the wrapper over the filling then fold the sides to the middle over the filling. Use egg to dampen the remaining side then tightly roll to seal.
- Heat oil in a deep-fat fryer or electric pan to 375 degrees. Fry a few wontons at a time until golden brown for half to a full minute per side; place on paper towels to drain.

## Nutrition Information

- Calories: 99 calories
- Cholesterol: 15mg cholesterol
- Protein: 4g protein.
- Total Fat: 7g fat (3g saturated fat)
- Sodium: 129mg sodium
- Fiber: 0 fiber)
- Total Carbohydrate: 5g carbohydrate (0 sugars

## 690. Goat Cheese, Pear & Onion Pizza

*Serving: 12 slices. | Prep: 30mins | Cook: 10mins | Ready in:*

## Ingredients

- 3 cups thinly sliced red onions

- 3 teaspoons olive oil, divided
- 2 garlic cloves, minced
- 1 prebaked 12-inch thin pizza crust
- 2 medium pears, peeled and sliced
- 3/4 cup shredded part-skim mozzarella cheese
- 1/3 cup goat cheese
- 8 fresh basil leaves, thinly sliced
- 1 teaspoon dried oregano
- 1/4 teaspoon pepper

## Direction

- Sauté onions in 2 teaspoons of oil until tender in a big nonstick skillet coated with cooking spray. Put garlic then sauté for another 2 to 3 minutes. On an ungreased 12-inch pizza pan, put the crust on then spread the onion mixture to within an inch of the edges.
- Sauté pears until tender in the same skillet with the remaining oil. Put it on top of the onion mixture. Use cheeses to sprinkle.
- Bake until edges are lightly browned or for 10 to 12 minutes at 450 degrees. Use pepper, oregano and basil to sprinkle.

## Nutrition Information

- Calories: 154 calories
- Fiber: 2g fiber)
- Total Carbohydrate: 20g carbohydrate (5g sugars
- Cholesterol: 9mg cholesterol
- Protein: 6g protein.
- Total Fat: 6g fat (2g saturated fat)
- Sodium: 204mg sodium

### 691. Golden Greek Lemon Potatoes

*Serving: 4 servings. | Prep: 20mins | Cook: 10mins | Ready in:*

## Ingredients

- 2 tablespoons olive oil
- 1 tablespoon butter
- 1/4 cup chopped onion
- 1-1/4 pounds baby Yukon Gold potatoes
- 1/4 cup water
- 3 tablespoons minced fresh chives or 2 green onions, thinly sliced
- 1-1/2 teaspoons Greek seasoning
- 1 to 1-1/2 teaspoons grated lemon peel
- 1 garlic clove, minced
- 1/2 teaspoon pepper
- 1/4 teaspoon kosher salt
- 1 to 2 tablespoons lemon juice
- 1 tablespoon minced fresh parsley

## Direction

- In the small-sized skillet, heat the butter and oil on medium heat. Put in the onion; cook and stir till becoming tender or for 1 to 2 minutes. Lower the heat to medium low; cook till turning deep golden brown or for 12 to 15 minutes, mixing once in a while.
- At the same time, add the water and potatoes into the big microwave safe dish. Microwave them, while covered, over high heat till becoming soft or for 6 to 8 minutes.
- Put the salt, pepper, garlic, lemon peel, Greek seasoning and chives into the onion mixture; cook and stir for 60 seconds more. Drain off the potatoes; put in the onion mixture. Flatten the potatoes using a fork, coat by tossing along with the onion mixture. Put in the parsley and lemon juice; combine by tossing.

## Nutrition Information

- Calories:
- Protein:
- Total Fat:
- Sodium:
- Fiber:
- Total Carbohydrate:
- Cholesterol:

## 692. Gourmet Garden Tomato Salad

*Serving: 6 servings. | Prep: 15mins | Cook: 0mins | Ready in:*

### Ingredients

- 1-1/2 pounds red, yellow and/or orange tomatoes, cut into 1/4-inch slices
- 1/3 cup olive oil
- 1/3 cup balsamic vinegar
- 1 tablespoon sugar
- 1/4 teaspoon salt
- 1/4 teaspoon pepper
- 1/2 cup crumbled feta cheese
- 1/3 cup fresh basil leaves, thinly sliced

### Direction

- Place tomatoes onto a serving platter. Mix pepper, salt, sugar, vinegar, and oil in a small bowl. Drizzle on tomatoes. Sprinkle basil and cheese.

### Nutrition Information

- Calories: 167 calories
- Protein: 3g protein.
- Total Fat: 14g fat (3g saturated fat)
- Sodium: 198mg sodium
- Fiber: 2g fiber)
- Total Carbohydrate: 9g carbohydrate (7g sugars
- Cholesterol: 5mg cholesterol

## 693. Gourmet Grilled Cheese Sandwich

*Serving: 1 serving. | Prep: 10mins | Cook: 5mins | Ready in:*

### Ingredients

- 2 slices sweet onion
- 1 teaspoon plus 1 tablespoon butter, divided
- 5 Greek olives, sliced
- 2 teaspoons spicy brown mustard
- 2 slices rye or pumpernickel bread
- 3 tablespoons crumbled feta cheese
- 2 slices Swiss cheese

### Direction

- In a small frying pan with 1 tsp butter, sauté the onion until it turns light brown and becomes soft. Add olives and let it cook for 1 minute more. Spread the mustard on top of the slices of bread, then layer one slice with onion mixture and cheeses. Put the leftover bread on top, then spread the leftover butter on the exterior of the sandwich.
- In a small frying pan, toast the sandwich for 2-4 minutes per side on medium heat or until the cheese melts.

### Nutrition Information

- Calories:
- Cholesterol:
- Protein:
- Total Fat:
- Sodium:
- Fiber:
- Total Carbohydrate:

## 694. Grecian Garden Salad

*Serving: 6 servings. | Prep: 10mins | Cook: 10mins | Ready in:*

### Ingredients

- 1-1/2 cups cut fresh asparagus (1-inch pieces)
- 3 medium tomatoes, seeded and chopped
- 2 tablespoons balsamic vinegar

- 4-1/2 teaspoons minced fresh basil or 1-1/2 teaspoons dried basil
- 1 tablespoon olive oil
- 1 teaspoon salt
- 1/2 teaspoon pepper
- 1 cup (4 ounces) crumbled feta cheese

## Direction

- Boil 3 cups of water in a big saucepan. Add asparagus, put a cover on and boil for 3 minutes. Strain and put in ice water immediately. Strain and tap dry. Move to a serving bowl. Mix in tomatoes.
- Combine pepper, salt, oil, basil, and vinegar in a small bowl. Sprinkle over the vegetables, toss to coat. Put a cover on and chill for a minimum of 1 hour. Mix in cheese right before eating.

## Nutrition Information

- Calories: 92 calories
- Fiber: 2g fiber)
- Total Carbohydrate: 6g carbohydrate (3g sugars
- Cholesterol: 10mg cholesterol
- Protein: 5g protein. Diabetic Exchanges: 1 vegetable
- Total Fat: 5g fat (2g saturated fat)
- Sodium: 579mg sodium

## 695. Grecian Potato Cups

*Serving: 8 servings. | Prep: 25mins | Cook: 01hours10mins | Ready in:*

## Ingredients

- 8 medium red potatoes (about 2-1/4 pounds)
- 4 tablespoons olive oil, divided
- 1 teaspoon salt
- 3/4 teaspoon pepper
- 1 medium onion, finely chopped
- 1 teaspoon dried oregano
- 2 garlic cloves, minced
- 1 package (10 ounces) frozen chopped spinach, thawed and squeezed dry
- 1 tablespoon lemon juice
- 1-1/2 cups (6 ounces) crumbled feta cheese

## Direction

- To preheat: set oven to 425°C. Scrub potatoes and use a fork to pierce a few times. Use foil to line a 15x10x1-in. baking pan, put potatoes in the pan and bake potatoes till they become soft, or for 40 to 45 minutes.
- Set the temperature of the oven to 450°. Halve each potatoes crosswise when they are cool enough to handle. Spoon out the pulp, leave 1/4-in.-thick shells. (Don't throw way the removed potatoes, save them for other use). If required, trim the bottom of cups carefully to let potatoes sit upright. Use 3 tablespoons oil to rub over inside and outside of potatoes.
- Arrange potato cups on two 15x10x1-in. baking pans, remember let cut side down; use salt and pepper to sprinkle. Put baking pans into the preheated oven and bake till potatoes skins become crisp, or for 8-10 minutes. Turn potatoes over then bake for 10 to 12 minutes longer or till potatoes skin changes to golden brown color. Take out of the oven. Decrease oven setting to 350°.
- Pour the remaining oil in a large skillet and heat on medium-high heat. Put in oregano and onion, cook and stir till onion becomes soft, or for 2 to 3 minutes. Put in garlic and cook for one minute longer. Put in lemon juice and spinach then stir, heat through. Take the skillet off heat, put in cheese and stir. Spoon the mixture into potato cups. Bake for 8 to 10 minutes or till heated through.

## Nutrition Information

- Calories:
- Cholesterol:
- Protein:
- Total Fat:

- Sodium:
- Fiber:
- Total Carbohydrate:

### 696. Greek Bruschetta

*Serving: Makes 12 servings. | Prep: 5mins | Cook: | Ready in:*

### Ingredients

- 12 Italian-style crostini toast
- 3/4 cup ATHENOS Roasted Red Pepper Hummus
- 1/4 cup finely chopped tomato es
- 2 Tbsp. shredded fresh basil

### Direction

- Scatter hummus on toast.
- Atop with basil and tomatoes.

### Nutrition Information

- Calories: 60
- Protein: 2 g
- Total Fat: 2 g
- Fiber: 1 g
- Sugar: 1 g
- Total Carbohydrate: 8 g
- Saturated Fat: 0 g
- Sodium: 140 mg
- Cholesterol: 0 mg

### 697. Greek Cheese Balls

*Serving: 2 cheese balls (2-1/4 cups each). | Prep: 15mins | Cook: 0mins | Ready in:*

### Ingredients

- 2 packages (8 ounces each) cream cheese, softened
- 2 cups (8 ounces) crumbled feta cheese
- 1 can (4-1/4 ounces) chopped ripe olives
- 1/2 cup finely chopped cucumber
- 1/2 cup chopped roasted sweet red peppers
- 1 teaspoon pepper
- 2 cups finely chopped walnuts, toasted
- Assorted crackers

### Direction

- Beat cream cheese in a big bowl until fluffy. Fold in pepper, red peppers, cucumber, olives and feta cheese, then make into 2 balls. Roll the balls in walnuts and use plastic wrap to wrap them tightly. Refrigerate until serving, and serve along with crackers.

### Nutrition Information

- Calories: 107 calories
- Protein: 4g protein.
- Total Fat: 10g fat (4g saturated fat)
- Sodium: 139mg sodium
- Fiber: 1g fiber)
- Total Carbohydrate: 2g carbohydrate (0 sugars
- Cholesterol: 17mg cholesterol

### 698. Greek Chickpea & Walnut Burgers

*Serving: 5 servings. | Prep: 30mins | Cook: 10mins | Ready in:*

### Ingredients

- 2 eggs
- 1/2 cup dry bread crumbs
- 1/2 cup chopped walnuts
- 1 medium carrot, shredded
- 1/3 cup crumbled reduced-fat feta cheese
- 1/4 cup coarsely chopped onion
- 1/4 cup Greek olives

- 4 sprigs fresh parsley, stems removed
- 1 tablespoon lemon juice
- 2 garlic cloves, minced
- 1/4 teaspoon each salt and pepper
- 1 can (15 ounces) chickpeas or garbanzo beans, rinsed and drained
- TZATZIKI SAUCE:
- 1 cup finely chopped cucumber
- 1/2 cup reduced-fat plain yogurt
- 1/4 cup fat-free sour cream
- 1 tablespoon minced fresh mint or 1 teaspoon dried mint
- 1 tablespoon lemon juice
- 1 garlic clove, minced
- 1/4 teaspoon salt
- BURGERS:
- 5 whole wheat hamburger buns, split
- 5 lettuce leaves
- 5 slices tomato

## Direction

- Mix together the initial 11 ingredients in a food processor, put cover and pulse 4 times. Add the chickpeas and pulse until chopped. Let it chill in the fridge for a minimum of 45 minutes. Mix together the sauce ingredients and let it chill in the fridge until ready to serve.
- Form the chickpea mixture by two-third cupfuls into patties. Use cooking oil to moisten a paper towel using long handled tongs and coat the grill rack lightly.
- Grill the burgers on medium heat with a cover or let it broil for 3 to 5 minutes per side, placed 4 inches from the heat source or until a thermometer registers 160 degrees.
- Served with tomato and lettuce on buns, then top each with 1/4 cup of tzatziki sauce.

## Nutrition Information

- Calories: 425 calories
- Protein: 19g protein.
- Total Fat: 17g fat (3g saturated fat)
- Sodium: 908mg sodium
- Fiber: 9g fiber)
- Total Carbohydrate: 53g carbohydrate (11g sugars
- Cholesterol: 93mg cholesterol

## 699. Greek Country Salad

*Serving: Makes 8 servings | Prep: | Cook: | Ready in:*

## Ingredients

- 1 tablespoon fresh lemon juice
- 1/2 teaspoon salt
- 1 teaspoon honey
- 1/3 cup extra-virgin olive oil
- 1/2 lb escarole (preferably pale inner leaves), chopped (4 cups)
- 1/4 lb tender young mustard greens, trimmed and finely chopped (2 cups)
- 1/2 lb dandelion greens, tough stems discarded and leaves cut crosswise into 1/4-inch slices (2 cups)
- 2 oz baby spinach (2 cups)
- 1 cup watercress sprigs, trimmed
- 1/2 cup chopped fresh dill
- 1/4 cup fresh flat-leaf parsley
- 1/4 cup thinly sliced scallion

## Direction

- To make dressing: In a big salad bowl, whisk honey, salt and lemon juice. Slowly add oil to the mixture, whisking until well blended.
- To make salad: Add salad ingredients to dressing and toss until well coated. Add salt and pepper to season.

## Nutrition Information

- Calories: 111
- Protein: 2 g(4%)
- Total Fat: 9 g(14%)
- Saturated Fat: 1 g(7%)
- Sodium: 180 mg(8%)

- Fiber: 3 g(13%)
- Total Carbohydrate: 7 g(2%)

## 700. Greek Couscous Salad

*Serving: 12 servings. | Prep: 15mins | Cook: 5mins | Ready in:*

### Ingredients

- 1 can (14-1/2 ounces) reduced-sodium chicken broth
- 1-3/4 cups uncooked whole wheat couscous (about 11 ounces)
- DRESSING:
- 1/2 cup olive oil
- 1-1/2 teaspoons grated lemon zest
- 1/4 cup lemon juice
- 1 teaspoon adobo seasoning
- 1/4 teaspoon salt
- SALAD:
- 1 English cucumber, halved lengthwise and sliced
- 2 cups grape tomatoes, halved
- 1 cup coarsely chopped fresh parsley
- 1 can (6-1/2 ounces) sliced ripe olives, drained
- 4 green onions, chopped
- 1/2 cup crumbled feta cheese

### Direction

- Bring broth in a large saucepan to a boil. Add couscous and stir well. Turn the heat off, cover and set aside, wait for about 5 minutes until liquid is absorbed. Remove couscous into a large bowl; allow to cool entirely. Mix dressing ingredients together. Combine couscous with green onions, olives, parsley, tomatoes, and cucumber. Pour dressing over the couscous mixture and stir until incorporated. Add cheese and mix gently. Serve chilled or right away at room temperature.

### Nutrition Information

- Calories: 335 calories
- Fiber: 7g fiber)
- Total Carbohydrate: 39g carbohydrate (3g sugars
- Cholesterol: 4mg cholesterol
- Protein: 9g protein.
- Total Fat: 18g fat (3g saturated fat)
- Sodium: 637mg sodium

## 701. Greek Crostini

*Serving: 2 dozen. | Prep: 15mins | Cook: 10mins | Ready in:*

### Ingredients

- 1 package (8 ounces) cream cheese, softened
- 1/4 cup Greek vinaigrette
- 1/4 teaspoon dried minced garlic
- 1/2 cup Greek pitted olives, chopped
- 1/2 cup roasted sweet red peppers, drained
- 3 tablespoons butter, softened
- 24 slices French bread baguette (1/4 inch thick)
- 3/4 cup crumbled goat or crumbled feta cheese

### Direction

- Put together the garlic, vinaigrette and cream cheese in small bowl. Mix in red peppers and olives just till incorporated.
- Scatter butter on top of baguette slices; put on ungreased baking sheet. Bake at 400° for 3 to 4 minutes till browned lightly. Scatter cream cheese mixture on top of toasts; scatter goat cheese over. Allow to bake for 2 to 3 minutes more till cheese is softened.

### Nutrition Information

- Calories: 100 calories
- Total Carbohydrate: 5g carbohydrate (0 sugars
- Cholesterol: 19mg cholesterol

- Protein: 2g protein.
- Total Fat: 8g fat (4g saturated fat)
- Sodium: 182mg sodium
- Fiber: 1g fiber)

## 702. Greek Deviled Eggs

*Serving: 24 | Prep: 20mins | Cook: 15mins | Ready in:*

### Ingredients

- 12 eggs
- 3/4 cup mayonnaise
- 3/4 cup crumbled feta cheese, or to taste
- 1/2 cup chopped fresh basil, or to taste
- 1 tomato, diced
- 10 black olives, diced
- 2 tablespoons balsamic vinegar
- 1 tablespoon ground black pepper, or to taste

### Direction

- In a saucepan, lay eggs and add water to cover. Bring to a boil, remove from heat, and allow eggs to sit for 15 minutes in hot water. Take out, run cold water over eggs to cool, and remove eggshells.
- Slice every egg in half lengthways; remove egg yolks to a bowl. Use a fork to mash yolks.
- In a bowl, mix balsamic vinegar, black olives, tomato, basil, feta cheese, and mayonnaise together; mix mashed yolks in. In a plastic zip bag, add yolk mixture; on a corner of the bag, cut a small hole.
- On a serving platter, lay egg whites, cut-side up. Fill egg whites with yolk mixture. Use black pepper to season deviled eggs; use extra crumbled feta cheese and chopped basil for garnish.

### Nutrition Information

- Calories: 103 calories;
- Total Carbohydrate: 1.4

- Cholesterol: 100
- Protein: 4
- Total Fat: 9.2
- Sodium: 145

## 703. Greek Feta Salad

*Serving: 7 servings, 1 cup each. | Prep: 15mins | Cook: | Ready in:*

### Ingredients

- 2 cucumber s, cut into bite-size chunks
- 4 plum tomatoes, cut into wedges
- 1/2 cup thinly sliced red onion s
- 1/2 cup pitted Kalamata olives
- 1/3 cup KRAFT Greek Vinaigrette Dressing
- 1 cup KRAFT Natural Feta Cheese Crumbles

### Direction

- In a big bowl, mix together the first 4 ingredients.
- Add the dressing, toss to coat.
- Right before eating, put cheese on top.

### Nutrition Information

- Calories: 140
- Total Carbohydrate: 8 g
- Protein: 5 g
- Total Fat: 10 g
- Fiber: 2 g
- Sodium: 440 mg
- Sugar: 4 g
- Cholesterol: 15 mg
- Saturated Fat: 3 g

## 704. Greek Garden Salad

*Serving: 6 servings. | Prep: 15mins | Cook: 0mins | Ready in:*

### Ingredients

- 2 large tomatoes, chopped
- 3/4 cup chopped cucumber
- 1/2 cup chopped green pepper
- 1/2 cup chopped sweet red pepper
- 1/2 cup crumbled feta cheese
- 1/4 cup thinly sliced green onions
- 1/4 cup sliced ripe olives
- 1/2 cup Italian salad dressing
- 1/8 teaspoon dried oregano
- Leaf lettuce, optional

### Direction

- Mix the first 7 ingredients in a big bowl. Before serving, add oregano and salad dressing. Toss to coat. Put in a bowl lined with lettuce if preferred.

### Nutrition Information

- Calories: 69 calories
- Protein: 3g protein. Diabetic Exchanges: 1 vegetable
- Total Fat: 4g fat (0 saturated fat)
- Sodium: 389mg sodium
- Fiber: 2g fiber)
- Total Carbohydrate: 7g carbohydrate (0 sugars
- Cholesterol: 11mg cholesterol

## 705. Greek Garden Salad With Dressing

*Serving: 4 servings. | Prep: 25mins | Cook: 0mins | Ready in:*

### Ingredients

- 3 cups torn romaine
- 1 plum tomato, sliced
- 1/2 cup julienned sweet red pepper
- 1/2 cup sliced seeded peeled cucumber
- 1/3 cup garbanzo beans or chickpeas, rinsed and drained
- 1/4 cup sliced fennel bulb
- 1/4 cup chopped celery
- 6 pitted ripe or Greek olives
- 1 green onion, thinly sliced
- DRESSING:
- 2 tablespoons lemon juice
- 1 tablespoon olive oil
- 1 garlic clove, minced
- 1 teaspoon minced fresh cilantro
- 1 teaspoon water
- 1/2 teaspoon minced fresh mint or 1/8 teaspoon dried mint
- 1/2 teaspoon minced fresh oregano or 1/8 teaspoon dried oregano
- 1/2 teaspoon grated lemon peel
- Dash each salt and pepper
- 1 tablespoon crumbled reduced-fat feta cheese

### Direction

- Mix the first 9 ingredients in a big serving bowl.
- Mix pepper, salt, lemon peel, oregano, water, mint, cilantro, garlic, oil, and lemon juice in a small bowl for dressing. Pour on salad while tossing to coat. Top with cheese.

### Nutrition Information

- Calories: 90 calories
- Protein: 3g protein. Diabetic Exchanges: 2 vegetable
- Total Fat: 5g fat (1g saturated fat)
- Sodium: 172mg sodium
- Fiber: 4g fiber)
- Total Carbohydrate: 11g carbohydrate (2g sugars
- Cholesterol: 1mg cholesterol

## 706. Greek Green Beans

*Serving: 8 | Prep: 20mins | Cook: 55mins | Ready in:*

## Ingredients

- 3/4 cup olive oil
- 2 cups chopped onions
- 1 clove garlic, minced
- 2 pounds fresh green beans, rinsed and trimmed
- 3 large tomatoes, diced
- 2 teaspoons sugar
- salt to taste

## Direction

- In a big skillet, heat the olive oil over medium heat. Cook and mix in the garlic and onions in the skillet until they become tender.
- IStir the salt, sugar, tomatoes and green beans into the skillet. Turn heat down to low then keep on cooking until beans become soft, another 45 minutes.

## Nutrition Information

- Calories: 243 calories;
- Protein: 3
- Total Fat: 20.6
- Sodium: 12
- Total Carbohydrate: 14.6
- Cholesterol: 0

## 707. Greek Hero

*Serving: 4 servings. | Prep: 15mins | Cook: 0mins | Ready in:*

## Ingredients

- HUMMUS:
- 2 tablespoons lemon juice
- 1 tablespoon olive oil
- 1 can (15 ounces) garbanzo beans or chickpeas, rinsed and drained
- 2 garlic cloves, minced
- 1 teaspoon dried oregano
- 1/4 teaspoon salt
- 1/8 teaspoon pepper
- SANDWICH:
- 1 loaf (8 ounces) unsliced French bread
- 2 medium sweet red peppers, cut into thin strips
- 1/2 medium cucumber, sliced
- 2 small tomatoes, sliced
- 1/4 cup thinly sliced red onion
- 1/4 cup chopped ripe olives
- 1/4 cup chopped pimiento-stuffed olives
- 1/2 cup crumbled feta cheese
- 4 lettuce leaves

## Direction

- To make hummus: Mix the beans, oil and lemon juice in a food processor, put on a cover and process until smooth. Mix in the pepper, salt, oregano and garlic.
- Halve the bread horizontally. Hollow out the bottom half gently and leave a 1/2-inch shell. Fill the shell with hummus. Layer it with red peppers, cucumber, tomatoes, onion, olives, cheese and lettuce, then place back the bread top. Slice it into quarters.

## Nutrition Information

- Calories: 350 calories
- Protein: 12g protein.
- Total Fat: 12g fat (4g saturated fat)
- Sodium: 1219mg sodium
- Fiber: 9g fiber)
- Total Carbohydrate: 50g carbohydrate (0 sugars
- Cholesterol: 17mg cholesterol

## 708. Greek Lettuce Salad

*Serving: 6-8 servings. | Prep: 10mins | Cook: 0mins | Ready in:*

## Ingredients

- 6 cups torn romaine
- 1 cup chopped tomato
- 3/4 cup thinly sliced red onion
- 3/4 cup cubed cucumber
- 3/4 cup cubed feta cheese
- 18 pitted kalmata or ripe olives
- 3 tablespoons olive oil
- 1 tablespoon lemon juice
- 1-1/2 teaspoons dried oregano
- 1-1/2 teaspoons prepared mustard
- 1/4 teaspoon salt

### Direction

- Combine the first six ingredients in a bowl. In a small bowl, whisk the remaining ingredients together. Add to salad and toss until well coated. Serve right away.

### Nutrition Information

- Calories:
- Protein:
- Total Fat:
- Sodium:
- Fiber:
- Total Carbohydrate:
- Cholesterol:

## 709. Greek Loaf

*Serving: 1 loaf. | Prep: 10mins | Cook: 03hours00mins | Ready in:*

### Ingredients

- 1 cup milk (70° to 80°)
- 1 tablespoon olive oil
- 1/2 to 1-1/2 teaspoon salt
- 3/4 cup crumbled feta cheese
- 3 cups bread flour
- 1 tablespoon sugar
- 2-1/4 teaspoons active dry yeast
- 1/4 cup sliced ripe olives

### Direction

- Put the first 7 ingredients into the pan of the bread machine following the order recommended by the manufacturer. Choose the Basic Bread setting on the machine. Select the loaf size and the crust color if the machine used has these options. Follow the instructions on the bread machine to bake the bread (after 5 minutes of the cycle, check on the dough and put 1-2 tablespoons of flour or water if necessary).
- Put in the olives right before the last kneading process (you'll hear the machine's signal for this).

### Nutrition Information

- Calories: 114 calories
- Total Fat: 3g fat (1g saturated fat)
- Sodium: 179mg sodium
- Fiber: 1g fiber)
- Total Carbohydrate: 19g carbohydrate (0 sugars
- Cholesterol: 7mg cholesterol
- Protein: 5g protein. Diabetic Exchanges: 1 starch

## 710. Greek Macaroni Salad

*Serving: 8 servings. | Prep: 15mins | Cook: 0mins | Ready in:*

### Ingredients

- 1 cup uncooked elbow macaroni
- 4 medium plum tomatoes, chopped
- 1 can (15 ounces) garbanzo beans or chickpeas, rinsed and drained
- 1 medium onion, chopped
- 1 can (6 ounces) pitted ripe olives
- 1 package (4 ounces) crumbled feta cheese
- 1 teaspoon salt
- 1/2 teaspoon pepper

- 1 garlic clove, minced
- 1/2 cup olive oil
- 1/4 cup lemon juice

### Direction

- Following the instructions on the package, cook the macaroni; drain off the water and wash under cold water. In a big bowl, mix garlic, pepper, salt, feta cheese, olives, onion, beans, tomatoes and macaroni.
- Mix lemon juice and oil in a small bowl. Put on top of the salad; coat by tossing. Keep it covered and refrigerated until chilled. Mix prior to serving.

### Nutrition Information

- Calories: 278 calories
- Cholesterol: 8mg cholesterol
- Protein: 7g protein.
- Total Fat: 19g fat (4g saturated fat)
- Sodium: 690mg sodium
- Fiber: 4g fiber)
- Total Carbohydrate: 21g carbohydrate (4g sugars

## 711. Greek Olive Bread

*Serving: 1 loaf (16 slices). | Prep: 25mins | Cook: 25mins | Ready in:*

### Ingredients

- 1 package (1/4 ounce) active dry yeast
- 1/4 cup warm water (110° to 115°)
- 1 cup warm 2% milk (110° to 115°)
- 6 tablespoons olive oil, divided
- 1 tablespoon sugar
- 1 teaspoon salt
- 3-1/2 cups all-purpose flour
- 1/2 cup crumbled feta cheese
- 1/3 cup Greek olives

### Direction

- Dissolve yeast in a big bowl with warm water. Put in 1 1/2 cup flour, milk, salt, sugar, and 4 tablespoons oil; beat for 3 minutes on medium speed. Mix in just enough of the remaining dough until a soft dough forms.
- Transfer dough on a floured surface and knead for 6-8 minutes until elastic and smooth. Move to a greased bowl then flip one time to coat the top; cover. Set aside for an hour in a warm area until it doubles.
- Press the dough down; scatter olives and cheese. Fold and lightly knead until blended then form into an 8-inch circle loaf. Put on a greased baking sheet then spread the remaining oil; cover. Allow to rise for 40 minutes in a warm area until it doubles.
- Form 4 shallow slits along top of loaf with a sharp knife. Bake for 25-30 minutes in 375 degrees oven until golden brown. Transfer from pan onto a wire rack then cool.

### Nutrition Information

- Calories: 178 calories
- Protein: 4g protein.
- Total Fat: 7g fat (1g saturated fat)
- Sodium: 266mg sodium
- Fiber: 1g fiber)
- Total Carbohydrate: 23g carbohydrate (2g sugars
- Cholesterol: 3mg cholesterol

## 712. Greek Orzo Salad

*Serving: 6 | Prep: 1hours10mins | Cook: 10mins | Ready in:*

### Ingredients

- 1 1/2 cups uncooked orzo pasta
- 2 (6 ounce) cans marinated artichoke hearts
- 1 tomato, seeded and chopped

- 1 cucumber, seeded and chopped
- 1 red onion, chopped
- 1 cup crumbled feta cheese
- 1 (2 ounce) can black olives, drained
- 1/4 cup chopped fresh parsley
- 1 tablespoon lemon juice
- 1/2 teaspoon dried oregano
- 1/2 teaspoon lemon pepper

## Direction

- Boil a big pot of lightly salted water, then add the pasta and let it cook until al dente or for 8-10 minutes; drain. Drain the artichoke hearts; set the liquid aside.
- Mix lemon pepper, oregano, lemon juice, parsley, olives, feta, onion, cucumber, tomato, artichoke hearts and pasta together in a big bowl. Toss it and place it in the refrigerator for an hour.
- Drizzle the reserved artichoke marinade on top of the salad just prior to serving.

## Nutrition Information

- Calories: 348 calories;
- Sodium: 615
- Total Carbohydrate: 53.2
- Cholesterol: 22
- Protein: 13.9
- Total Fat: 10.2

---

### 713. Greek Orzo And Broccoli

*Serving: 6 servings. | Prep: 30mins | Cook: 0mins | Ready in:*

## Ingredients

- 3/4 cup uncooked orzo pasta
- 2 cups fresh broccoli florets
- 1/3 cup pitted Greek olives
- 1/4 cup crumbled feta cheese
- 1/4 cup grated Parmesan cheese
- 2 tablespoons minced fresh basil
- 4-1/2 teaspoons slivered almonds, toasted
- 1 tablespoon olive oil
- 1/4 teaspoon crushed red pepper flakes
- 1/4 teaspoon pepper

## Direction

- Cook the pasta in the boiling water in a large saucepan for 7 minutes. Add in the broccoli and cook until the pasta becomes tender, or for 2-3 more minutes; let drain. At the same time, blend the basil, Parmesan cheese, feta cheese, and olives in a small bowl.
- Sauté the almonds in oil in a small non-stick skillet for around a minute. Stir in the pepper and red pepper flakes; stir and cook for 1 more minute. Place over the pasta mixture; coat by tossing. Add in the olive mixture and stir; coat by tossing.

## Nutrition Information

- Calories: 169 calories
- Protein: 7g protein. Diabetic Exchanges: 1-1/2 starch
- Total Fat: 7g fat (2g saturated fat)
- Sodium: 208mg sodium
- Fiber: 2g fiber)
- Total Carbohydrate: 21g carbohydrate (2g sugars
- Cholesterol: 8mg cholesterol

---

### 714. Greek Pasta

*Serving: 4 | Prep: 15mins | Cook: 15mins | Ready in:*

## Ingredients

- 1 pound linguine pasta
- 3 tomatoes
- 1/3 cup olive oil
- 3 cloves garlic, minced
- 1 pound mushrooms, sliced

- 1 teaspoon dried oregano
- 3/4 cup crumbled feta cheese
- 1 (2 ounce) can sliced black olives, drained

## Direction

- Boil a big pot of lightly salted water; briefly plunge whole tomatoes in water till skin begins to peel. Use a slotted spoon to remove; put in cold water. Put pasta in boiling water; cook till al dente or for 8-10 minutes. Drain.
- Peel then chop blanched tomatoes as pasta cooks.
- Heat olive oil in a big skillet on medium heat. Mix in mushrooms and garlic; sauté till mushrooms start to give up their juices. Mix in oregano and tomatoes; cook till tomatoes are tender.
- Serving: Plate pasta then put hot tomato sauce on top; sprinkle olives and feta.

## Nutrition Information

- Calories: 759 calories;
- Protein: 23.3
- Total Fat: 31
- Sodium: 866
- Total Carbohydrate: 102.4
- Cholesterol: 25

### 715. Greek Pasta Salad

*Serving: 8 | Prep: 15mins | Cook: 15mins | Ready in:*

## Ingredients

- 1 (16 ounce) package penne pasta
- 1/4 cup vegetable oil
- 1 teaspoon lemon juice
- 1 teaspoon dried basil
- 1 teaspoon ground black pepper
- 1 teaspoon garlic salt
- 2 tomatoes, chopped
- 1 green bell pepper, chopped
- 1 sweet onion, chopped
- 1 cucumber, coarsely chopped
- 1 cup black olives, chopped

## Direction

- In a big pot of boiling water, add pasta and cook until al dente. Strain and use cold water to rinse.
- Combine black pepper, garlic salt, basil, lemon juice, and oil in a small bowl.
- Mix black olives, cucumber, onion, green pepper, tomatoes, and pasta together in a big bowl. Add the dressing and coat by tossing. Chill in the fridge for 30 minutes.

## Nutrition Information

- Calories: 302 calories;
- Total Carbohydrate: 46.6
- Cholesterol: 0
- Protein: 8.4
- Total Fat: 10.2
- Sodium: 388

### 716. Greek Pinwheels

*Serving: 20 appetizers. | Prep: 20mins | Cook: 10mins | Ready in:*

## Ingredients

- 1 sheet frozen puff pastry, thawed
- 1 tablespoon beaten egg
- 3/4 teaspoon water
- 1/2 cup cream cheese, softened
- 1/3 cup marinated quartered artichoke hearts, drained and finely chopped
- 1/4 cup crumbled feta cheese
- 1 tablespoon finely chopped drained oil-packed sun-dried tomatoes
- 3 Greek olives, finely chopped
- 1 teaspoon Greek seasoning

## Direction

- Roll out puff pastry. Beat together water and egg. Brush pastry with the egg wash mixture. Mix the rest of the ingredients together and spread over pastry to within 1/2 inch of edges. Roll up pastry, jelly-roll style, and cut into twenty slices, about 1/2 inch thick each.
- Arrange on greased baking sheets, 2 inches apart. Bake for 9 to 11 minutes at 425°F until puffed and golden brown. Serve while it's still warm.

## Nutrition Information

- Calories: 92 calories
- Total Fat: 6g fat (2g saturated fat)
- Sodium: 142mg sodium
- Fiber: 1g fiber)
- Total Carbohydrate: 7g carbohydrate (0 sugars
- Cholesterol: 9mg cholesterol
- Protein: 2g protein.

### 717. Greek Potato Salad

*Serving: 10 | Prep: | Cook: 30mins | Ready in:*

## Ingredients

- 2½ pounds yellow or red potatoes, scrubbed and diced (½- to 1-inch)
- ¾ teaspoon salt, divided
- ¼ cup extra-virgin olive oil
- 3 tablespoons white-wine vinegar
- ¼ cup finely chopped shallot
- 1 tablespoon Dijon mustard
- ½ teaspoon ground pepper
- 1 cup halved cherry tomatoes
- ⅓ cup crumbled feta cheese
- ¼ cup quartered Kalamata olives
- 2 tablespoons chopped fresh oregano or 2 teaspoons dried

## Direction

- In a large saucepan (or pot) attached with a steamer basket, bring 1 - 2 inches of water to a boil. Pour potatoes into the basket, cook, covered for 12 to 15 minutes until tender. Single layer the cooked potatoes on a rimmed baking sheet; add 1/4 teaspoon salt to taste, allow to cool for 15 minutes.
- In the meantime, mix the remaining 1/2 teaspoon salt, pepper, mustard, shallot, vinegar and oil together in a large bowl. Add oregano, olives, feta, tomatoes, and potatoes; toss to coat evenly. Place in the fridge until cold or serve at room temperature.

## Nutrition Information

- Calories: 170 calories;
- Saturated Fat: 2
- Fiber: 2
- Protein: 3
- Sodium: 308
- Cholesterol: 4
- Total Carbohydrate: 22
- Sugar: 1
- Total Fat: 8

### 718. Greek Romaine Salad

*Serving: 6-8 servings. | Prep: 10mins | Cook: 0mins | Ready in:*

## Ingredients

- 4 cups torn romaine
- 1 medium sweet red pepper, julienned
- 1 cup chopped cucumber
- 1/4 cup olive oil
- 1 tablespoon lemon juice
- 1 teaspoon sugar
- 1/4 teaspoon garlic salt
- 1/4 teaspoon pepper
- 1 package (4 ounces) crumbled feta cheese

## Direction

- Put together cucumber, red pepper, and romaine in a large salad bowl. Combine pepper, garlic salt, sugar, lemon juice, and oil in an air-tight jar; shake properly. Pour dressing over salad. Add feta cheese into the salad bowl and stir gently.

## Nutrition Information

- Calories: 107 calories
- Protein: 3g protein.
- Total Fat: 9g fat (2g saturated fat)
- Sodium: 196mg sodium
- Fiber: 1g fiber)
- Total Carbohydrate: 3g carbohydrate (1g sugars
- Cholesterol: 8mg cholesterol

## 719. Greek Salad

*Serving: | Prep: | Cook: | Ready in:*

### Ingredients

- 2 cloves garlic
- 1 teaspoon oregano
- 1/2 teaspoon dijon mustard
- 1/4 cup red wine vinegar
- 1/2 teaspoon (kosher) salt
- 1/2 teaspoon ground pepper
- 1/2 cup olive oil

### Direction

- Mince the garlic
- Combine all ingredients.
- You can use any kind of salad, but for a traditional Greek salad, add romaine, feta cheese, tomatoes, peppers, olives, and cucumbers.

## 720. Greek Salad Pitas

*Serving: 2 servings. | Prep: 20mins | Cook: 0mins | Ready in:*

### Ingredients

- 2/3 cup chopped seeded cucumber
- 2/3 cup chopped sweet red pepper
- 2/3 cup chopped tomato
- 2/3 cup chopped zucchini
- 1/4 cup crumbled feta cheese
- 2 tablespoons chopped ripe olives
- 2 teaspoons red wine vinegar
- 2 teaspoons lemon juice
- 3/4 teaspoon dried oregano
- 1/8 teaspoon salt
- 1/8 teaspoon pepper
- 4 lettuce leaves
- 4 pita pocket halves

### Direction

- Mix together the olives, feta cheese, zucchini, tomato, red pepper and cucumber in a small bowl. Whisk the pepper, salt, oregano, lemon juice and vinegar in a separate bowl, then pour it on top of the vegetables and toss until coated. Scoop into pita halves lined with lettuce.

### Nutrition Information

- Calories: 255 calories
- Sodium: 688mg sodium
- Fiber: 5g fiber)
- Total Carbohydrate: 45g carbohydrate (5g sugars
- Cholesterol: 8mg cholesterol
- Protein: 10g protein. Diabetic Exchanges: 2 starch
- Total Fat: 4g fat (2g saturated fat)

## 721. Greek Salad With Bean Spread Pitas

*Serving: 2 servings. | Prep: 20mins | Cook: 0mins | Ready in:*

### Ingredients

- 3/4 cup canned chickpeas, rinsed and drained
- 2 tablespoons lemon juice
- 1 tablespoon sliced green olives with pimientos
- 1 teaspoon olive oil
- 1 garlic clove, minced
- 1 cup fresh baby spinach
- 1/4 cup chopped seeded peeled cucumber
- 1/4 cup crumbled feta cheese
- 2 tablespoons chopped marinated quartered artichoke hearts
- 2 tablespoons sliced Greek olives
- 1/4 teaspoon dried oregano
- 2 whole wheat pita pocket halves

### Direction

- In a food processor, place the initial 5 ingredients, put a cover and process until it has a smooth consistency, then put aside.
- Mix together the oregano, olives, artichokes, cheese, cucumber and spinach in a small bowl.
- On pita halves, spread the bean mixture then add the salad. Serve right away.

### Nutrition Information

- Calories: 292 calories
- Sodium: 687mg sodium
- Fiber: 7g fiber)
- Total Carbohydrate: 38g carbohydrate (3g sugars
- Cholesterol: 8mg cholesterol
- Protein: 10g protein. Diabetic Exchanges: 2 starch
- Total Fat: 12g fat (3g saturated fat)

## 722. Greek Salad With Greek Artisan's Olives

*Serving: 21 servings (3/4 cup each). | Prep: 20mins | Cook: 0mins | Ready in:*

### Ingredients

- 2 packages (5 ounces each) spring mix salad greens
- 3 plum tomatoes, chopped
- 1 small red onion, halved and thinly sliced
- 1 cup Greek olives
- 2/3 cup chopped peeled cucumber
- 1/2 cup olive oil
- 1/4 cup lemon juice
- 1 tablespoon minced fresh oregano or 1 teaspoon dried oregano
- 1 garlic clove, minced
- 1/4 teaspoon salt
- 1/8 teaspoon pepper
- 1 cup (4 ounces) crumbled feta cheese

### Direction

- Combine the first five ingredients in a salad bowl. Combine pepper, salt, garlic, oregano, lemon juice and oil; add to salad mixture and toss until well coated. Add cheese on top.

### Nutrition Information

- Calories: 84 calories
- Protein: 1g protein.
- Total Fat: 8g fat (2g saturated fat)
- Sodium: 190mg sodium
- Fiber: 1g fiber)
- Total Carbohydrate: 2g carbohydrate (1g sugars
- Cholesterol: 3mg cholesterol

## 723. Greek Salad With Green Grapes

*Serving: 9 servings. | Prep: 25mins | Cook: 0mins | Ready in:*

### Ingredients

- 1 package (5 ounces) spring mix salad greens
- 3-1/2 cups torn romaine
- 1 large cucumber, chopped
- 1 cup green grapes
- 1/2 cup cherry tomatoes, halved
- 1/2 cup chopped walnuts
- 1 cup (4 ounces) crumbled feta cheese
- 1 can (3.8 ounces) sliced ripe olives, drained
- GREEK YOGURT VINAIGRETTE:
- 3/4 cup white wine vinegar
- 2 tablespoons plain Greek yogurt
- 2 tablespoons honey
- 2 teaspoons snipped fresh dill
- 1/8 teaspoon salt
- 1/8 teaspoon pepper
- 7 tablespoons olive oil

### Direction

- Mix first 8 ingredients together in a large bowl.
- In a small bowl, combine pepper, salt, dill, honey, yogurt, and vinegar, mix well. Slowly drizzle a steady stream of oil until incorporated. Drizzle over salad and stir until evenly coated.

### Nutrition Information

- Calories: 229 calories
- Protein: 4g protein.
- Total Fat: 19g fat (4g saturated fat)
- Sodium: 268mg sodium
- Fiber: 2g fiber)
- Total Carbohydrate: 13g carbohydrate (8g sugars
- Cholesterol: 8mg cholesterol

## 724. Greek Salad With Lemon Dressing

*Serving: 12 servings (3/4 cup each). | Prep: 30mins | Cook: 0mins | Ready in:*

### Ingredients

- 1/4 cup lemon juice
- 1/4 cup olive oil
- 1 teaspoon sugar
- 1/2 teaspoon Greek seasoning
- 1/2 teaspoon minced fresh oregano
- 1/4 teaspoon minced fresh rosemary
- 1/4 teaspoon pepper
- SALAD:
- 8 cups torn mixed salad greens
- 1 medium cucumber, seeded and chopped
- 1 medium sweet red pepper, thinly sliced
- 1 medium sweet orange or yellow pepper, thinly sliced
- 1 medium tomato, halved and sliced
- 1 package (4 ounces) crumbled tomato and basil feta cheese
- 6 green onions, chopped
- 1 jar (12 ounces) pepperoncini, drained
- 1 cup pitted Greek olives

### Direction

- Whisk the first seven ingredients together in a small bowl until well blended.
- Combine the first seven salad ingredients in a large bowl. Add dressing to salad mixture and toss until well coated. Add olives and pepperoncini on top. Serve right away.

### Nutrition Information

- Calories:
- Total Carbohydrate:
- Cholesterol:
- Protein:
- Total Fat:
- Sodium:
- Fiber:

## 725. Greek Salad With Orzo

*Serving: 4-5 servings. | Prep: 10mins | Cook: 10mins | Ready in:*

### Ingredients

- 4 quarts water
- 1-1/4 cups uncooked orzo pasta
- 1 cup cut fresh green beans, cooked
- 2 large tomatoes, seeded and chopped
- 1/2 teaspoon lemon juice
- 1/4 teaspoon grated lemon peel
- 1/2 cup Greek vinaigrette

### Direction

- Bring water in a Dutch oven to a boil. Pour orzo and cook for 5 minutes. Add beans; cook until both beans and orzo are tender, or for 4 to 5 minutes longer.
- In the meantime, combine peel, lemon juice, and tomatoes in a large salad bowl. Drain beans and orzo; wash with cold water. Combine with tomato mixture. Pour vinaigrette and stir until evenly coated. Refrigerate before serving.

### Nutrition Information

- Calories: 311 calories
- Sodium: 251mg sodium
- Fiber: 3g fiber)
- Total Carbohydrate: 41g carbohydrate (6g sugars
- Cholesterol: 0 cholesterol
- Protein: 7g protein.
- Total Fat: 14g fat (2g saturated fat)

## 726. Greek Salsa

*Serving: Makes 2 cups or 16 servings, 2 Tbsp. each. | Prep: 10mins | Cook: | Ready in:*

### Ingredients

- 1 pkg. (3.5 oz.) ATHENOS Crumbled Reduced Fat Feta Cheese
- 1/2 cup halved Kalamata olives
- 1/2 cup chopped red onion s
- 1/2 cup chopped cucumber s
- 1/2 cup chopped roasted red pepper s
- 2 Tbsp. finely chopped fresh mint
- 1/2 cup KRAFT Greek Vinaigrette with Feta Cheese and Oregano Dressing made with Extra Virgin Olive Oil

### Direction

- 1. Combine all ingredients until well-mixed.
- 2. Serve along with ATHENOS PITA THINS Toasted Chips Original.

### Nutrition Information

- Calories: 35
- Sugar: 1 g
- Protein: 2 g
- Total Fat: 2.5 g
- Saturated Fat: 1 g
- Sodium: 250 mg
- Fiber: 1 g
- Total Carbohydrate: 2 g
- Cholesterol: 5 mg

## 727. Greek Sandwich Bites

*Serving: 16 appetizers. | Prep: 20mins | Cook: 5mins | Ready in:*

### Ingredients

- 1 medium onion, finely chopped
- 1 tablespoon olive oil
- 2 garlic cloves, minced
- 1 pound fresh baby spinach
- 1 cup (4 ounces) crumbled feta cheese
- 1/4 cup pine nuts, toasted
- 1/4 teaspoon salt

- 1/4 teaspoon pepper
- 1/8 teaspoon ground nutmeg
- 8 slices Italian bread (1/2 inch thick)
- 4 teaspoons butter, softened

## Direction

- Sauté the onion in oil in a big nonstick frying pan until it becomes soft, then add garlic. Cook for 1 minute more, then mix in the spinach. Cook and stir until it wilts. Drain and stir in the nutmeg, pepper, salt, pine nuts and feta.
- Spread the mixture on top of the 4 slices of bread, then put leftover bread on top. Use butter to spread the exterior of sandwiches. Over medium heat, grill for 3-4 minutes without a cover or until the cheese melts and bread turns brown, flipping once. Slice each sandwich into four equal portions.

## Nutrition Information

- Calories: 87 calories
- Total Carbohydrate: 8g carbohydrate (1g sugars
- Cholesterol: 6mg cholesterol
- Protein: 4g protein. Diabetic Exchanges: 1 fat
- Total Fat: 5g fat (2g saturated fat)
- Sodium: 200mg sodium
- Fiber: 1g fiber)

## 728. Greek Side Salad

*Serving: 2 servings. | Prep: 15mins | Cook: 0mins | Ready in:*

## Ingredients

- 3 cups torn romaine
- 1/2 cup chopped peeled cucumber
- 1 slice red onion, halved and separated
- 1 small tomato, sliced
- 1/2 cup cubed part-skim mozzarella cheese
- 6 pitted Greek olives
- 4-1/2 teaspoons olive oil
- 1-1/2 teaspoons lemon juice
- 1 teaspoon minced fresh cilantro
- 1 teaspoon minced fresh parsley
- 1 garlic clove, minced
- 1/4 teaspoon salt
- 1/8 teaspoon pepper
- 2 tablespoons crumbled feta cheese
- 1 teaspoon grated Parmesan cheese

## Direction

- Combine the first six ingredients in a serving bowl. In a small bowl, whisk pepper, salt, garlic, parsley, cilantro, lemon juice and oil. Add to salad mixture and toss until well coated. Sprinkle with Parmesan and feta cheeses.

## Nutrition Information

- Calories: 271 calories
- Protein: 12g protein.
- Total Fat: 21g fat (7g saturated fat)
- Sodium: 743mg sodium
- Fiber: 3g fiber)
- Total Carbohydrate: 9g carbohydrate (2g sugars
- Cholesterol: 22mg cholesterol

## 729. Greek Stuffed Mini Potatoes

*Serving: 16 appetizers. | Prep: 25mins | Cook: 45mins | Ready in:*

## Ingredients

- 8 small red potatoes, halved
- 2 tablespoons olive oil
- 1 tablespoon snipped fresh dill
- 1/2 teaspoon salt
- 1/4 teaspoon pepper

- 1/2 medium ripe avocado, peeled
- 16 marinated quartered artichoke hearts, drained
- 16 pitted Greek olives
- 1/3 cup crumbled feta cheese

### Direction

- Set the oven for preheating to 350°. Put the potatoes in a big bowl. Add pepper, salt, dill and oil; toss to coat. Place the mixture in a 15x10x1-in. baking pan that's greased. Roast inside the oven for 40-50 minutes or until softened.
- Halve the avocado making eight slices; slice half crosswise. Allow the potatoes to cool. Once they are cool that it can be handled, scoop out a tablespoon of pulp from each potato half (save for future use). Fill every half with cheese, olive, artichoke and avocado.

### Nutrition Information

- Calories:
- Protein:
- Total Fat:
- Sodium:
- Fiber:
- Total Carbohydrate:
- Cholesterol:

## 730. Greek Three Bean Salad

*Serving: 10 servings. | Prep: 25mins | Cook: 0mins | Ready in:*

### Ingredients

- 2 cups frozen cut green beans, thawed
- 1 can (16 ounces) kidney beans, rinsed and drained
- 1 can (14-1/2 ounces) cut wax beans, drained
- 1 medium red onion, halved and sliced
- 1 can (6 ounces) pitted ripe olives, drained
- 1/2 cup julienned green pepper
- 1/2 cup peeled, seeded and chopped cucumber
- 3/4 cup bottled Greek vinaigrette
- 1 cup (4 ounces) crumbled feta cheese

### Direction

- In a large salad bowl, combine the first seven ingredients. Pour vinaigrette on top and toss until well coated. Refrigerate until serving and add cheese on top. Serve with a slotted spoon.

### Nutrition Information

- Calories:
- Fiber:
- Total Carbohydrate:
- Cholesterol:
- Protein:
- Total Fat:
- Sodium:

## 731. Greek Tomato Salad

*Serving: 8 | Prep: 15mins | Cook: | Ready in:*

### Ingredients

- 4 large tomatoes, cut in wedges
- 1 cucumber, halved lengthwise and sliced
- 1/2 red onion, chopped
- 1/2 cup Greek black olives
- 1/4 teaspoon chopped fresh basil
- 1/4 teaspoon chopped fresh oregano
- 1/3 cup crumbled feta cheese
- 1 (16 fl oz) bottle Greek salad dressing
- 1/8 teaspoon freshly ground black pepper
- 1 sprig fresh basil

### Direction

- In a large bowl, combine oregano, 1/4 teaspoon chopped basil, olives, red onion, cucumber, and tomatoes gently; sprinkle with feta cheese. Drizzle Greek dressing over salad; add black pepper for seasoning. Sprinkle with a fresh basil sprig on top to garnish.

## Nutrition Information

- Calories: 263 calories;
- Total Fat: 25.4
- Sodium: 660
- Total Carbohydrate: 8.5
- Cholesterol: 9
- Protein: 2.7

### 732. Greek Tomatoes

*Serving: 6 servings. | Prep: 30mins | Cook: 0mins | Ready in:*

## Ingredients

- 4 medium tomatoes, cut into 1/4-inch slices
- 1 small red onion, thinly sliced and seprated into rings
- 3/4 cup crumbled feta cheese
- 1/4 cup minced fresh parsley
- 1/2 teaspoon salt
- 1/2 teaspoon coarsely ground pepper
- 1 tablespoon olive oil

## Direction

- On a plate, put slices of onion and tomato then sprinkle with pepper, feta cheese, salt, and parsley. Dribble with oil; cover. Chill for 15 minutes.

## Nutrition Information

- Calories: 91 calories
- Total Fat: 7g fat (3g saturated fat)
- Sodium: 416mg sodium
- Fiber: 1g fiber)
- Total Carbohydrate: 5g carbohydrate (0 sugars
- Cholesterol: 17mg cholesterol

- Protein: 4g protein. Diabetic Exchanges: 1-1/2 fat

### 733. Greek Tortellini Salad

*Serving: 6 | Prep: 20mins | Cook: | Ready in:*

## Ingredients

- 10 ounces refrigerated cheese tortellini (2½ cups)
- ¼ cup crumbled feta cheese
- 3 tablespoons extra-virgin olive oil
- 2 tablespoons red-wine vinegar
- 1 tablespoon chopped fresh oregano
- ½ teaspoon ground pepper
- ¼ teaspoon salt
- 1 cup chopped tomatoes
- 1 cup chopped cucumber
- 1 cup sliced spinach
- ¼ cup chopped red onion

## Direction

- Bring water to a boil in a large pot. Add tortellini and cook for about 4 minutes until just tender. Drain.
- In the meantime, whisk together salt, pepper, oregano, vinegar, oil and feta in a large bowl. Add cooked tortellini, red onion, spinach, cucumber and tomatoes. Toss until well coated.

## Nutrition Information

- Calories: 238 calories;
- Saturated Fat: 4
- Sodium: 353
- Total Carbohydrate: 25
- Sugar: 2
- Total Fat: 12
- Fiber: 2
- Cholesterol: 25
- Protein: 8

## 734. Greek Tossed Salad

*Serving: 4 servings. | Prep: 10mins | Cook: 0mins | Ready in:*

### Ingredients

- 5 cups ready-to-serve salad greens
- 3/4 cup sliced cucumber
- 1 medium tomato, cut into wedges
- 2 tablespoons crumbled feta cheese
- 2 tablespoons sliced ripe olives
- 2/3 cup Greek vinaigrette or salad dressing of your choice

### Direction

- Combine olives, cheese, tomato, cucumber and greens in a salad bowl. Pour dressing over and toss until well coated.

### Nutrition Information

- Calories: 235 calories
- Fiber: 2g fiber)
- Total Carbohydrate: 9g carbohydrate (5g sugars
- Cholesterol: 2mg cholesterol
- Protein: 2g protein.
- Total Fat: 23g fat (4g saturated fat)
- Sodium: 492mg sodium

## 735. Greek Vegetable Salad

*Serving: 4 servings. | Prep: 15mins | Cook: 0mins | Ready in:*

### Ingredients

- 1 medium cucumber, peeled and chopped
- 1 large tomato, seeded and chopped
- 1 medium green pepper, chopped
- 4 green onions, chopped
- 10 pitted Greek olives
- 1/2 cup crumbled feta cheese
- DRESSING:
- 1/3 cup olive oil
- 3 tablespoons cider vinegar
- 1 teaspoon salt
- 1 teaspoon dried oregano
- 1/2 teaspoon sugar

### Direction

- Combine feta cheese, olives, onions, green pepper, tomato and cucumber in a serving bowl. Combine dressing ingredients in a jar that comes with a tight-fitting lid; give it a well shake. Add to salad mixture and toss until well coated. Serve with a slotted spoon.

### Nutrition Information

- Calories: 259 calories
- Total Carbohydrate: 10g carbohydrate (5g sugars
- Cholesterol: 8mg cholesterol
- Protein: 4g protein.
- Total Fat: 23g fat (4g saturated fat)
- Sodium: 885mg sodium
- Fiber: 3g fiber)

## 736. Greek Veggie Omelet

*Serving: 2 servings. | Prep: 10mins | Cook: 10mins | Ready in:*

### Ingredients

- 4 large eggs
- 2 tablespoons fat-free milk
- 1/8 teaspoon salt
- 3 teaspoons olive oil, divided
- 2 cups sliced baby portobello mushrooms
- 1/4 cup finely chopped onion

- 1 cup fresh baby spinach
- 3 tablespoons crumbled feta cheese
- 2 tablespoons sliced ripe olives
- Freshly ground pepper

## Direction

- Put salt, milk, eggs together and whisk. Heat 2 teaspoons oil on medium-high heat in a large nonstick skillet; sauté onion and mushrooms for 5 to 6 minutes till they become golden brown. Put in spinach and stir till it is wilted; get spinach out of pan.
- Heat the remaining oil on medium low heat in the same pan. Add the egg mixture in. When eggs set, move the cooked eggs to the center of the pan, leave the uncooked eggs run underneath. As eggs get thickened and there is no liquid left, use a spoon to place vegetables on one side; use olives and cheese to sprinkle. Fold to close; divide into 2 parts to serve. Use pepper to sprinkle.

## Nutrition Information

- Calories: 271 calories
- Sodium: 475mg sodium
- Fiber: 2g fiber)
- Total Carbohydrate: 7g carbohydrate (3g sugars
- Cholesterol: 378mg cholesterol
- Protein: 18g protein. Diabetic Exchanges: 2 medium-fat meat
- Total Fat: 19g fat (5g saturated fat)

### 737. Greek Veggie Tartlets

*Serving: 45 tartlets. | Prep: 15mins | Cook: 10mins | Ready in:*

## Ingredients

- 3 packages (1.9 ounces each) frozen miniature phyllo tart shells
- 3/4 cup finely chopped seeded peeled cucumber
- 3/4 cup finely chopped red onion
- 3/4 cup finely chopped seeded plum tomatoes
- 3/4 cup finely chopped pitted Greek olives
- 1/2 cup Greek vinaigrette
- 3/4 cup crumbled feta cheese

## Direction

- Set the oven to 350 degrees to preheat. Put shells on 2 15-inch x10-inch x1-inch pans. Bake shells for 7 to 10 minutes, until brown slightly, then allow to cool fully.
- Toss vinaigrette, olives and vegetables together. To serve, scoop into each tart shell with 1 tbsp. of the vegetable mixture and sprinkle cheese over top.

## Nutrition Information

- Calories: 43 calories
- Sodium: 93mg sodium
- Fiber: 0 fiber)
- Total Carbohydrate: 3g carbohydrate (0 sugars
- Cholesterol: 1mg cholesterol
- Protein: 1g protein.
- Total Fat: 3g fat (0 saturated fat)

### 738. Greek Inspired Quinoa Salad

*Serving: 10 servings. | Prep: 15mins | Cook: 15mins | Ready in:*

## Ingredients

- 2 cups water
- 1 cup quinoa, rinsed
- 1 package (10 ounces) frozen chopped spinach, thawed and squeezed dry
- 1-1/2 cups (6 ounces) crumbled feta cheese
- 1 cup grape tomatoes

- 3/4 cup canned black beans, rinsed and drained
- 1/2 cup chopped seeded peeled cucumber
- 1/2 cup sliced pepperoncini
- 1/2 cup Greek olives, pitted and halved
- 3/4 cup reduced-fat Greek or Italian salad dressing, divided

### Direction

- Bring water to a boil in a small saucepan. Add quinoa. Reduce heat, cover and simmer for 12 to 15 minutes or until water is fully absorbed. Remove from the heat.
- Combine olives, pepperoncini, cucumber, beans, tomatoes, cheese, spinach and quinoa in a large bowl. Add 1/2 cup of dressing to quinoa mixture and toss until well coated. Chill, covered, for a minimum of 1 hour.
- Right before serving, add remaining dressing to salad mixture and toss until well coated.

### Nutrition Information

- Calories: 184 calories
- Total Fat: 8g fat (2g saturated fat)
- Sodium: 472mg sodium
- Fiber: 4g fiber)
- Total Carbohydrate: 19g carbohydrate (1g sugars
- Cholesterol: 9mg cholesterol
- Protein: 7g protein.  Diabetic Exchanges: 1-1/2 fat

## 739. Greek Style Green Beans

*Serving: 2 servings. | Prep: 5mins | Cook: 15mins | Ready in:*

### Ingredients

- 2 cups fresh green beans, cut into 2-inch pieces
- 1/2 small sweet onion, cut into thin wedges
- 1 tablespoon olive oil
- 1 small tomato, cut into eighths
- 1/2 teaspoon dried oregano
- 1/4 teaspoon salt
- Dash pepper

### Direction

- In a saucepan, add beans and water to cover, then bring to a boil. Cook until crisp-tender, about 3 to 4 minutes. Drain.
- Sauté onion in a small skillet with oil about 3 minutes. Add in beans and sauté until soft, about 5 minutes. Lower heat and add in pepper, salt, oregano and tomato. Allow to cool until heated through, about 1 minute more.

### Nutrition Information

- Calories: 111 calories
- Cholesterol: 0 cholesterol
- Protein: 3g protein.
- Total Fat: 7g fat (1g saturated fat)
- Sodium: 306mg sodium
- Fiber: 5g fiber)
- Total Carbohydrate: 12g carbohydrate (5g sugars

## 740. Greek Style Pizza

*Serving: 18 servings. | Prep: 25mins | Cook: 25mins | Ready in:*

### Ingredients

- 1/4 cup butter, cubed
- 1/4 cup olive oil
- 1/2 pound sliced fresh mushrooms
- 1 medium onion, sliced
- 3 garlic cloves, minced
- 1 package (10 ounces) fresh spinach, trimmed and coarsely chopped
- 1 tablespoon lemon juice
- 1 teaspoon dried basil

- 1 teaspoon dried oregano
- 1 package (16 ounces, 14x9-inch sheet size) frozen phyllo dough, thawed
- 2 cups shredded part-skim mozzarella cheese
- 1 cup (4 ounces) crumbled feta cheese
- 3 medium ripe tomatoes, sliced
- 1/2 cup seasoned bread crumbs

### Direction

- Put butter in a large skillet to melt. Place into a small bowl; put in oil and put aside. Sauté garlic, onion, and mushrooms in the same skillet until tender. Put in spinach; sauté until wilted. Put in the oregano, basil, and lemon juice; put aside.
- Brush reserved butter mixture onto a 13x9-inch baking dish. Put one sheet of phyllo dough in baking dish; lightly brush with butter mixture. (Use a plastic wrap and a damp towel to cover the rest of the phyllo dough to avoid drying out.) Continue layer with the remaining phyllo, brushing each layer.
- Put spinach mixture on top; sprinkle cheeses over. Use breadcrumbs to coat both sides of tomato slices; arrange over top. Bake for 25 to 30 minutes at 375 degrees or until the crust is golden brown and cheese has melted.

### Nutrition Information

- Calories: 198 calories
- Protein: 8g protein.
- Total Fat: 9g fat (4g saturated fat)
- Sodium: 310mg sodium
- Fiber: 2g fiber)
- Total Carbohydrate: 21g carbohydrate (3g sugars
- Cholesterol: 17mg cholesterol

## 741. Greek Style Squash

*Serving: 4 servings. | Prep: 15mins | Cook: 30mins | Ready in:*

### Ingredients

- 2 small yellow summer squash, thinly sliced
- 2 small zucchini, thinly sliced
- 1 medium tomato, seeded and chopped
- 1/4 cup pitted ripe olives
- 2 tablespoons chopped green onion
- 2 teaspoons olive oil
- 1 teaspoon lemon juice
- 3/4 teaspoon garlic salt
- 1/4 teaspoon dried oregano
- 1/8 teaspoon pepper
- 2 tablespoons grated Parmesan cheese

### Direction

- On a double thickness of heavy-duty foil, 17"x18" in size, add onion, olives, tomato, zucchini and yellow squash. Mix together pepper, oregano, garlic salt, lemon juice and oil, then drizzle over vegetables. Fold foil around mixture, sealing tightly.
- Grill on moderate heat with a cover until vegetables are soft, about 30 to 35 minutes. Carefully open foil to let steam escape.
- Remove vegetables to a serving bowl and sprinkle cheese over top.

### Nutrition Information

- Calories: 80 calories
- Protein: 4g protein. Diabetic Exchanges: 2 vegetable
- Total Fat: 5g fat (1g saturated fat)
- Sodium: 479mg sodium
- Fiber: 3g fiber)
- Total Carbohydrate: 8g carbohydrate (0 sugars
- Cholesterol: 2mg cholesterol

## 742. Green Garden Salad

*Serving: 8-10 servings (1-1/3 cups dressing). | Prep: 25mins | Cook: 0mins | Ready in:*

### Ingredients

- DRESSING:
- 3/4 cup olive oil
- 1/2 cup red wine vinegar
- 2 tablespoons lemon juice, optional
- 2 teaspoons grated Parmesan cheese
- 1 teaspoon dried oregano
- 1/2 teaspoon sugar
- 1/4 teaspoon salt
- 1/4 teaspoon pepper
- SALAD:
- 8 to 10 cups torn salad greens
- 1 red onion, sliced into rings
- 1 cucumber, peeled and sliced
- 2 to 3 tomatoes, cut into wedges
- 1 green pepper, sliced into rings

### Direction

- Combine all dressing ingredients in a bottle or jar with a tight lid. Shake it well then chill. Before serving, mix tomatoes, cucumber, onion, and greens in a big salad bowl. Pour the preferred bulk of dressing you want in the salad; toss to combine. Top using green pepper rings.

### Nutrition Information

- Calories: 173 calories
- Cholesterol: 0 cholesterol
- Protein: 2g protein.
- Total Fat: 17g fat (2g saturated fat)
- Sodium: 80mg sodium
- Fiber: 2g fiber)
- Total Carbohydrate: 6g carbohydrate (3g sugars

## 743. Grilled Dijon Summer Squash

*Serving: 8 servings. | Prep: 20mins | Cook: 10mins | Ready in:*

### Ingredients

- 1/4 cup olive oil
- 2 tablespoons red wine vinegar
- 1-1/2 teaspoons minced fresh oregano or 1/2 teaspoon dried oregano
- 1-1/2 teaspoons Dijon mustard
- 1 garlic clove, minced
- 1/4 teaspoon salt
- 1/8 teaspoon pepper
- 2 medium zucchini, cut into 1/2-inch slices
- 2 medium yellow summer squash, cut into 1/2-inch slices
- 1 medium red onions, quartered
- 1 small sweet red pepper, cut into 2-inch pieces
- 1 small sweet yellow pepper, cut into 2-inch pieces
- 6 to 8 whole fresh mushrooms
- 6 cherry tomatoes

### Direction

- Blend the pepper, salt, garlic, mustard, oregano, vinegar, and oil in a jar covered by a tight-fitting lid. In a shallow baking dish, arrange the vegetables. Put marinade and coat by tossing. Allow to stand for 15 minutes. Let the marinade drain and discard.
- On a vegetable grill rack, arrange the vegetables. Put a cover on and grill on medium heat until tender or 10-12 minutes.

### Nutrition Information

- Calories:
- Fiber:
- Total Carbohydrate:
- Cholesterol:
- Protein:
- Total Fat:

- Sodium:
- Total Carbohydrate: 81g carbohydrate (10g sugars
- Cholesterol: 19mg cholesterol

## 744. Grilled Eggplant Sandwiches

*Serving: 2 servings | Prep: 15mins | Cook: 10mins | Ready in:*

### Ingredients

- 2 tablespoons olive oil
- 1 garlic clove, minced
- 2 ciabatta rolls, split
- 4 slices eggplant (1/2 inch thick)
- 1 medium heirloom tomato, cut into 1/2-inch slices
- 1/4 teaspoon salt
- 1/8 teaspoon pepper
- 2 ounces fresh goat cheese, softened
- 6 fresh basil leaves

### Direction

- Combine garlic and oil, then brush onto both sides of the vegetables and the cut sides of the rolls. Sprinkle pepper and salt over vegetables.
- Grill the eggplant for 4-5 minutes on each side over medium heat with a cover. Grill the tomato for 1 to 2 minutes on each side with cover, until it turns a bit brown. Grill the rolls for 1 to 2 minutes, cut side facing down, until they become toasted.
- Spread goat cheese on roll bottoms and put basil, eggplant and tomato on top, then close the sandwiches.

### Nutrition Information

- Calories: 538 calories
- Protein: 15g protein.
- Total Fat: 21g fat (5g saturated fat)
- Sodium: 958mg sodium
- Fiber: 7g fiber)

## 745. Grilled Eggplant With Feta Relish

*Serving: 8 servings. | Prep: 15mins | Cook: 10mins | Ready in:*

### Ingredients

- 3 tablespoons balsamic vinaigrette
- 1 teaspoon garlic powder
- 1 cup (4 ounces) crumbled feta cheese
- 2/3 cup chopped seeded peeled cucumber
- 1/2 cup chopped seeded plum tomato
- 1/4 cup finely chopped red onion
- 8 slices eggplant (3/4 inch thick)
- 2 tablespoons olive oil
- 1 teaspoon salt
- 1/2 teaspoon pepper
- Minced fresh basil or parsley, optional

### Direction

- Beat garlic powder and vinaigrette in a small bowl until blended. Mix in onion, feta, tomato, and cucumber. Chill with cover until ready to serve.
- Slather oil on the eggplant then season with pepper and salt. Grill on medium heat with cover or broil four inches from heat for 4-5 minutes per side until tender. Add the feta mixture on top of the eggplant. Garnish with basil if desired.

### Nutrition Information

- Calories:
- Sodium:
- Fiber:
- Total Carbohydrate:
- Cholesterol:

- Protein:
- Total Fat:

- Sodium: 198mg sodium
- Fiber: 0 fiber)

## 746. Grilled Feta Quesadillas

*Serving: 12 wedges. | Prep: 15mins | Cook: 5mins | Ready in:*

### Ingredients

- 3 ounces fat-free cream cheese
- 1/2 cup shredded reduced-fat Mexican cheese blend
- 1/3 cup crumbled feta cheese
- 1/2 teaspoon dried oregano
- 4 flour tortillas (6 inches), warmed
- 1/4 cup chopped pitted ripe olives
- 2 tablespoons diced pimientos
- 1 green onion, chopped

### Direction

- Beat the cheeses with oregano in a small bowl until combined. Spread 3 tablespoons of the cheese mixture on top of 1/2 of each tortilla, then put onion, pimientos and olives over. Fold the tortillas over.
- Use cooking oil to moisten a paper towel, then coat the grill rack lightly using long-handled tongs. Grill the quesadillas on medium heat without cover, or let it broil for 1-2 minutes per side, placed 4 inches from the heat source or until it turns golden brown in color. Slice each quesadilla into 3 wedges, then serve it warm.

### Nutrition Information

- Calories: 62 calories
- Total Carbohydrate: 5g carbohydrate (0 sugars
- Cholesterol: 6mg cholesterol
- Protein: 4g protein. Diabetic Exchanges: 1/2 starch
- Total Fat: 3g fat (1g saturated fat)

## 747. Grilled Greek Crostini Topping

*Serving: 8 servings. | Prep: 10mins | Cook: 10mins | Ready in:*

### Ingredients

- 2 large vine-ripe tomatoes, halved and thinly sliced
- 1 package (8 ounces) feta cheese, halved lengthwise
- 3 teaspoons minced fresh oregano
- 3 teaspoons olive oil
- Ground pepper
- Sliced French bread baguette, toasted

### Direction

- On a double thickness of heavy-duty foil approximately 12 in. square, put a third of tomato slices in 1 layer. Put 1/2 of cheese atop tomatoes; scatter a teaspoon oregano over and sprinkle with 1 teaspoon oil. Sprinkle a dash of pepper. Redo layers.
- Atop with leftover slices of tomato. Sprinkle with the rest of the oil and scatter leftover oregano over and sprinkle a dash of pepper. Fold foil around the mixture and secure tightly.
- Let grill with cover over medium heat for 8 to 10 minutes till heated through. Cautiously unseal foil to let steam come out. Put to a serving plate; serve along with toasted baguette.

### Nutrition Information

- Calories: 95 calories
- Total Fat: 8g fat (4g saturated fat)
- Sodium: 318mg sodium

- Fiber: 0 fiber)
- Total Carbohydrate: 2g carbohydrate (2g sugars
- Cholesterol: 25mg cholesterol
- Protein: 4g protein.

## 748. Grilled Greek Potato Salad

*Serving: 16 servings (3/4 cup each). | Prep: 30mins | Cook: 20mins | Ready in:*

### Ingredients

- 3 pounds small red potatoes, halved
- 2 tablespoons olive oil
- 1/2 teaspoon salt
- 1/4 teaspoon pepper
- 1 large sweet yellow pepper, chopped
- 1 large sweet red pepper, chopped
- 1 medium red onion, halved and sliced
- 1 medium cucumber, chopped
- 1-1/4 cups grape tomatoes, halved
- 1/2 pound fresh mozzarella cheese, cubed
- 3/4 cup Greek vinaigrette
- 1/2 cup halved Greek olives
- 1 can (2-1/4 ounces) sliced ripe olives, drained
- 2 tablespoons minced fresh oregano or 1 teaspoon dried oregano

### Direction

- Coat the potatoes with oil and season it with pepper and salt. Coat the potatoes evenly before grilling it. Cook and grill it over medium heat for 20-25 minutes, covered or you can broil it 4-inches away from the heat source until the potatoes are tender.
- Transfer the grilled potatoes in a large bowl and toss it with the remaining ingredients to coat. You can serve it while hot or chilled.

### Nutrition Information

- Calories: 189 calories
- Sodium: 325mg sodium
- Fiber: 2g fiber)
- Total Carbohydrate: 18g carbohydrate (3g sugars
- Cholesterol: 11mg cholesterol
- Protein: 5g protein. Diabetic Exchanges: 1-1/2 fat
- Total Fat: 11g fat (3g saturated fat)

## 749. Grilled Greek Style Zucchini

*Serving: 6 | Prep: 10mins | Cook: 10mins | Ready in:*

### Ingredients

- 4 small zucchini, thinly sliced
- 1 medium tomato, seeded and chopped
- 1/4 cup pitted ripe olives, halved
- 2 tablespoons chopped green onion
- 4 teaspoons olive or canola oil
- 2 teaspoons lemon juice
- 1/2 teaspoon dried oregano
- 1/2 teaspoon garlic salt
- 1/4 teaspoon pepper
- 2 tablespoons grated Parmesan cheese

### Direction

- Mix onion, zucchini, olives, and tomato in a bowl. Mix pepper, oil, garlic salt, oregano, and lemon juice; add on the veggies and toss to coat. Put on a 23x18-inch double-thick heavy-duty foil. Fold the foil surrounding the veggies then tightly seal. On medium heat, grill for 10-15 minutes with cover until the vegetables are tender. Scatter with Parmesan cheese.

## 750. Grilled Lebanese Salad

*Serving: 13 servings (3/4 cup each). | Prep: 30mins | Cook: 10mins | Ready in:*

### Ingredients

- 8 plum tomatoes
- 1/2 pound whole fresh mushrooms
- 2 medium red onions
- 2 medium green peppers
- 6 tablespoons olive oil, divided
- 1/2 teaspoon garlic salt
- 4 cups cubed French bread (3/4-in. cubes)
- 2 teaspoons dried thyme
- 1 teaspoon dried oregano
- 1/2 teaspoon salt
- 1/2 teaspoon pepper
- 1 medium cucumber, peeled, seeded and sliced
- 1/2 cup fresh basil leaves, thinly sliced
- 3 tablespoons balsamic vinegar

### Direction

- Halve the mushrooms and tomatoes and put them in a big bowl. Chop the peppers and onions into 1/2-inch thick slices then put it in the same bowl as the mushrooms. Add in the garlic salt and 4 tablespoons of oil and mix everything together until well-coated.
- In a separate big bowl, put in the cubed breads. Pour in the remaining oil. Season it with salt, thyme, pepper and oregano and mix everything together until well-coated. Insert the seasoned cubed breads onto soaked wooden or metal skewers.
- Place the chopped vegetables in a grill wok or basket. Let the vegetables grill over medium heat for 8-12 minutes without cover until the vegetables have softened, mix it often to cook evenly. Put in the cubed breads and let it grill over medium heat for 1-2 minutes with cover until the breads are toasted, turn the cubed breads from time to time to toast evenly.
- Cut the grilled onions, peppers and tomatoes into coarse pieces and put them in a big bowl. Put in the cucumber, grilled mushrooms, basil and grilled cubed breads; pour in the vinegar and mix everything lightly until well-coated.

### Nutrition Information

- Calories: 113 calories
- Protein: 2g protein. Diabetic Exchanges: 1 starch
- Total Fat: 7g fat (1g saturated fat)
- Sodium: 239mg sodium
- Fiber: 2g fiber)
- Total Carbohydrate: 12g carbohydrate (4g sugars
- Cholesterol: 0 cholesterol

## 751. Grilled Mediterranean Eggplant & Tomato Salad

*Serving: 6 servings. | Prep: 15mins | Cook: 15mins | Ready in:*

### Ingredients

- 1 medium eggplant, cut into 1/2-inch slices
- 1/4 cup olive oil, divided
- 1-1/2 teaspoons minced fresh thyme or 1/2 teaspoon dried thyme
- 1-1/2 teaspoons minced fresh oregano or 1/2 teaspoon dried oregano
- 1/2 pound sliced fresh mushrooms
- 1 large onion, coarsely chopped
- 1 garlic clove, minced
- 1/4 teaspoon salt
- 1/4 teaspoon coarsely ground pepper
- 1/3 cup dry red wine
- 1-1/2 cups cherry tomatoes, halved
- 1/4 cup minced fresh parsley
- 2 tablespoons balsamic vinegar
- 1/2 cup crumbled feta cheese

### Direction

- Use a brush to coat the eggplant with 2 tablespoons of oil then season it with oregano and thyme. Put the seasoned eggplant on a grill over medium heat then cover and let it grill for 3-4 minutes on every side until softened. Slice the grilled eggplant into bite-size pieces once it is cool to the touch.

- While the eggplant is grilling, put the remaining oil in a big skillet and heat it up on medium-high heat. Put in the onion and mushrooms and sauté for 5-7 minutes until soft. Mix in the pepper, garlic and salt and let it cook for 1 more minute. Pour in the wine and let the mixture cook while stirring the browned bits off the skillet. Let it boil and continue cooking for 2-3 minutes until the liquid has reduced.
- Mix the tomatoes, eggplant, vinegar, mushroom mixture and parsley together in a big bowl. Put in the cheese and mix until well-blended.

## Nutrition Information

- Calories:
- Protein:
- Total Fat:
- Sodium:
- Fiber:
- Total Carbohydrate:
- Cholesterol:

## 752. Grilled Pizza With Greens & Tomatoes

*Serving: 2 pizzas (4 slices each). | Prep: 15mins | Cook: 10mins | Ready in:*

## Ingredients

- 1-1/2 cups all-purpose flour
- 1-1/2 cups whole wheat flour
- 2 teaspoons kosher salt
- 1 teaspoon active dry yeast
- 3 tablespoons olive oil, divided
- 1-1/4 to 1-1/2 cups warm water (120° to 130°)
- TOPPING:
- 2 tablespoons olive oil
- 10 cups beet greens, coarsely chopped
- 4 garlic cloves, minced
- 2 tablespoons balsamic vinegar
- 3/4 cup prepared pesto
- 3/4 cup shredded Italian cheese blend
- 1/2 cup crumbled feta cheese
- 2 medium heirloom tomatoes, thinly sliced
- 1/4 cup fresh basil leaves, chopped

## Direction

- Add yeast, salt and flours into a food processor; pulse until incorporated. While motor is running, put in 2 tablespoons of oil and sufficient water in a consistent stream until dough turns into a ball. Transfer dough to a floured area; knead for about 6 to 8 minutes until pliable and smooth.
- Put in an oiled bowl, flipping one time to grease the surface. Put on a cover and allow to rise in a warm area until nearly doubled in size, 1 hour and 30 minutes.
- Deflate dough. Split dough into 2 parts on a slightly floured area. Roll or press every part into a 10-inch round; put each on one greased foil piece, approximately 12-inch square. Brush the rest of the oil on the tops; wrap in plastic and allow to sit for 10 minutes.
- For the topping, heat oil in a 6quart stockpot over moderately-high heat. Put in beet greens; cook, stirring, for 3 to 5 minutes or until softened. Put in the garlic; let cook for an additional of 30 seconds. Take off from heat; mix in the vinegar.
- With cooking oil, dampen one paper towel; coat grill rack lightly by rubbing using tongs with long handle. Cautiously flip the pizza crusts over to a grill rack; take foil off. Grill with a cover for 3 to 5 minutes over moderate heat or until bottoms are browned a little. Flip over; grill until the other side starts to brown, 1 to 2 minutes.
- Take off from grill. Spread pesto over; put tomatoes, cheeses and beet greens on top. Put pizzas back to grill. Cook with a cover for 2 to

4 minutes over moderate heat or until cheese melts. Scatter basil over.

## Nutrition Information

- Calories: 398 calories
- Total Carbohydrate: 42g carbohydrate (3g sugars
- Cholesterol: 11mg cholesterol
- Protein: 12g protein.
- Total Fat: 21g fat (5g saturated fat)
- Sodium: 1007mg sodium
- Fiber: 6g fiber)

## 753. Grilled Vegetable Orzo Salad

*Serving: 8 servings. | Prep: 35mins | Cook: 10mins | Ready in:*

### Ingredients

- 1-1/4 cups uncooked orzo pasta
- 1/2 pound fresh asparagus, trimmed
- 1 medium zucchini, cut lengthwise into 1/2-inch slices
- 1 medium sweet yellow or red pepper, halved
- 1 large portobello mushroom, stem removed
- 1/2 medium red onion, halved
- DRESSING:
- 1/3 cup olive oil
- 1/4 cup balsamic vinegar
- 3 tablespoons lemon juice
- 4 garlic cloves, minced
- 1 teaspoon lemon-pepper seasoning
- SALAD:
- 1 cup grape tomatoes, halved
- 1 tablespoon minced fresh parsley
- 1 tablespoon minced fresh basil
- 1/2 teaspoon salt
- 1/4 teaspoon pepper
- 1 cup (4 ounces) crumbled feta cheese

### Direction

- Follow packaging instructions to cook the orzo. In a big bowl, add vegetables. Beat the dressing ingredients in a small-sized bowl; toss with the vegetables until coated.
- Take out the vegetables and reserve dressing. On medium heat, grill with cover the pepper, mushroom, and onion for 5 to 10 minutes until tender, flipping occasionally. For 3 to 4 minutes, grill with cover the zucchini and asparagus until cooked to the desired doneness, flipping occasionally.
- Let vegetables cool enough to handle; slice into bite-size pieces. Mix together tomatoes, pepper, basil, reserved dressing, parsley, cooked orzo, salt, and grilled vegetables in a big bowl; tossing until blended. Keep in refrigerator until cold or eat at room temperature. Add in cheese just before serving.

## Nutrition Information

- Calories: 260 calories
- Protein: 8g protein. Diabetic Exchanges: 2 fat
- Total Fat: 12g fat (3g saturated fat)
- Sodium: 352mg sodium
- Fiber: 2g fiber)
- Total Carbohydrate: 30g carbohydrate (4g sugars
- Cholesterol: 8mg cholesterol

## 754. Grilled Veggie Sandwiches

*Serving: 4 servings. | Prep: 15mins | Cook: 10mins | Ready in:*

### Ingredients

- 1 small zucchini
- 1 small yellow summer squash
- 1 small eggplant
- Cooking spray
- 1 medium onion, sliced

- 1 large sweet red pepper, cut into rings
- 4 whole wheat hamburger buns, split
- 3 ounces fat-free cream cheese
- 1/4 cup crumbled goat cheese
- 1 garlic clove, minced
- 1/8 teaspoon salt
- 1/8 teaspoon pepper

## Direction

- Slice the eggplant, squash and zucchini into 1/4-inch thick strips, then spray them with cooking spray. Use cooking spray to spritz red pepper and onion.
- Over medium heat, grill the vegetables for 4-5 minutes per side, with a cover or until they becomes crisp-tender. Take out and keep warm. Grill the buns for 30-60 seconds, cut-side facing down, over medium heat until toasted.
- Mix together the pepper, salt, garlic and cheeses in a small bowl, then spread the mixture on top of the bun bottoms. Put vegetables on top, then place back the bun tops.

## Nutrition Information

- Calories: 231 calories
- Fiber: 10g fiber)
- Total Carbohydrate: 39g carbohydrate (12g sugars
- Cholesterol: 10mg cholesterol
- Protein: 11g protein. Diabetic Exchanges: 2-1/2 starch
- Total Fat: 6g fat (2g saturated fat)
- Sodium: 438mg sodium

## 755. Grilled Veggie Wraps

*Serving: 4 servings. | Prep: 15mins | Cook: 15mins | Ready in:*

## Ingredients

- 2 tablespoons balsamic vinegar
- 1-1/2 teaspoons minced fresh basil
- 1-1/2 teaspoons olive oil
- 1-1/2 teaspoons molasses
- 3/4 teaspoon minced fresh thyme
- 1/8 teaspoon salt
- 1/8 teaspoon pepper
- 1 medium zucchini, cut lengthwise into 1/4-inch slices
- 1 medium sweet red pepper, cut into 1-inch pieces
- 1 medium red onion, cut into 1/2-inch slices
- 4 ounces whole fresh mushrooms, cut into 1/2-inch pieces
- 4 ounces fresh sugar snap peas
- 1/2 cup crumbled feta cheese
- 3 tablespoons reduced-fat cream cheese
- 2 tablespoons grated Parmesan cheese
- 1 tablespoon reduced-fat mayonnaise
- 4 flour tortillas (8 inches)
- 4 romaine leaves

## Direction

- Mix together the initial 7 ingredients in a big resealable plastic bag, then add vegetables. Close the bag tightly and flip to coat, then chill in the fridge for 2 hours, flipping once.
- Drain and set aside the marinade. Move the vegetables to a grill basket or wok. Grill for 5 minutes over medium-high heat without a cover, stirring often.
- Reserve 1 tsp of marinade. Flip the vegetables and baste them with the leftover marinade. Grill until they becomes tender, about 5-8 minutes more, stirring often. In the meantime, mix together the mayonnaise and cheeses in a small bowl, then put aside.
- Use the reserved marinade to brush one side of each tortilla. On a grill, put the tortillas, marinade side facing down, for 1 to 3 minutes or until they become slightly toasted.
- Spread 3 tbsp. of cheese mixture on top of the ungrilled side of each tortilla, then put romaine and 1 cup of grilled vegetables on top, then roll up.

## Nutrition Information

- Calories: 332 calories
- Sodium: 632mg sodium
- Fiber: 4g fiber)
- Total Carbohydrate: 39g carbohydrate (9g sugars
- Cholesterol: 26mg cholesterol
- Protein: 13g protein. Diabetic Exchanges: 2 starch
- Total Fat: 14g fat (6g saturated fat)

## 756. Healthy Zucchini Pancakes

*Serving: 8 pancakes. | Prep: 15mins | Cook: 10mins | Ready in:*

### Ingredients

- 1 cup shredded zucchini
- 1/4 cup panko (Japanese) bread crumbs
- 2 green onions, chopped
- 1 egg
- 3 tablespoons minced fresh parsley
- 1 tablespoon snipped fresh dill
- 1 garlic clove, minced
- 1/4 cup crumbled feta cheese
- 3 teaspoons olive oil, divided

### Direction

- Drain zucchini through a colander or sieve, then squeeze to draw out excess liquid. Pat dry. Mix together cheese, garlic, dill, parsley, egg, onions, bread crumbs and zucchini in a small bowl.
- In a big nonstick skillet, heat 1 1/2 tsp. oil on moderately low heat. Drop batter into the oil by heaping tablespoonfuls, then gently press to flatten. Fry, working in batches, until both sides turn golden brown, using leftover oil as necessary.

## Nutrition Information

- Calories: 91 calories
- Cholesterol: 57mg cholesterol
- Protein: 4g protein. Diabetic Exchanges: 1 fat
- Total Fat: 6g fat (2g saturated fat)
- Sodium: 104mg sodium
- Fiber: 1g fiber)
- Total Carbohydrate: 5g carbohydrate (1g sugars

## 757. Hearty Tabbouleh

*Serving: 8 servings. | Prep: 35mins | Cook: 0mins | Ready in:*

### Ingredients

- 1-1/4 cups bulgur
- 1-1/2 cups boiling water
- 1 small cucumber, diced
- 1 large tomato, seeded and diced
- 4 green onions, sliced
- 1 cup (4 ounces) crumbled feta cheese
- 1 can (2-1/4 ounces) sliced ripe olives, drained
- 1/4 cup lemon juice
- 1/4 cup olive oil
- 2 tablespoons minced fresh parsley
- 1 tablespoon minced fresh mint
- 1 tablespoon grated lemon peel
- 2 garlic cloves, minced
- 1 teaspoon salt
- 1/2 teaspoon pepper

### Direction

- In a small bowl, add bulgur and stir in water. Cover and allow to stand until water has been absorbed, about half an hour.
- Drain bulgur and squeeze dry, then allow to cool thoroughly. Remove to a big bowl and stir in leftover ingredients. Place on a cover and chill for a minimum of 1 hour prior to serving.

## Nutrition Information

- Calories: 192 calories
- Fiber: 6g fiber)
- Total Carbohydrate: 21g carbohydrate (1g sugars
- Cholesterol: 8mg cholesterol
- Protein: 6g protein.
- Total Fat: 10g fat (3g saturated fat)
- Sodium: 509mg sodium

## 758. Herbed Feta Dip

*Serving: 8 | Prep: 20mins | Cook: | Ready in:*

### Ingredients

- 3/4 cup nonfat plain yogurt
- 1/2 cup crumbled feta cheese
- 1 (15 ounce) can cannellini beans, drained and rinsed
- 2 cloves garlic
- 1 tablespoon lemon juice
- 2 tablespoons chopped fresh parsley
- 2 tablespoons chopped fresh dill
- 2 tablespoons chopped fresh chives
- 2 tablespoons chopped fresh mint
- 1 teaspoon ground black pepper

### Direction

- In the bowl of a food processor, put lemon juice, garlic, beans, feta, and yogurt and process until smooth. Add pepper, mint, chives, dill, and parsley; pulse until they are thoroughly blended. Move the dip to a serving bowl and refrigerate until ready to enjoy.

### Nutrition Information

- Calories: 81 calories;
- Total Carbohydrate: 10.2
- Cholesterol: 9
- Protein: 4.8
- Total Fat: 2.3
- Sodium: 233

## 759. Herbed Tomato Cucumber Salad

*Serving: 2 servings. | Prep: 25mins | Cook: 0mins | Ready in:*

### Ingredients

- 1 medium tomato, seeded and chopped
- 1/3 cup chopped cucumber
- 1/3 cup crumbled feta cheese
- 1/4 cup chopped red onion
- 2 tablespoons olive oil
- 1 tablespoon minced fresh oregano
- 1-1/2 teaspoons minced fresh basil
- 1/4 teaspoon salt
- 1/4 teaspoon pepper

### Direction

- Mix all ingredients in a small bowl; toss to coat. Before serving, cover and allow to rest for 15 minutes.

### Nutrition Information

- Calories: 194 calories
- Protein: 4g protein.
- Total Fat: 17g fat (4g saturated fat)
- Sodium: 483mg sodium
- Fiber: 2g fiber)
- Total Carbohydrate: 7g carbohydrate (4g sugars
- Cholesterol: 10mg cholesterol

## 760. Italian Tomato Cucumber Salad

*Serving: 4 | Prep: 15mins | Cook: | Ready in:*

### Ingredients

- 4 tomatoes on the vine, cored and chopped
- 1/2 red onion, thinly sliced
- 1/2 seedless English cucumber, chopped
- 3 tablespoons extra-virgin olive oil, or more if needed
- 1 tablespoon chopped fresh oregano
- salt and ground black pepper to taste

### Direction

- In a bowl, combine black pepper, salt, oregano, olive oil, cucumber, red onion, and tomatoes; stir until coated. Put it aside for 30 minutes for the flavors to fully incorporate.

### Nutrition Information

- Calories: 128 calories;
- Total Fat: 10.5
- Sodium: 8
- Total Carbohydrate: 8.1
- Cholesterol: 0
- Protein: 1.6

## 761. Jalapeno Hummus

*Serving: 8 | Prep: 10mins | Cook: | Ready in:*

### Ingredients

- 1 cup garbanzo beans
- 1/3 cup canned jalapeno pepper slices, juice reserved
- 3 tablespoons tahini
- 3 cloves garlic, minced
- 2 tablespoons lemon juice
- 1/2 teaspoon ground cumin
- 1/2 teaspoon curry powder
- crushed red pepper to taste

### Direction

- Mix the lemon juice, garlic, tahini, jalapeno peppers and reserved juice and garbanzo beans in a food processor or blender. Put crushed red pepper, curry powder and cumin to season, then process until it becomes smooth.

### Nutrition Information

- Calories: 75 calories;
- Total Fat: 3.5
- Sodium: 191
- Total Carbohydrate: 9.1
- Cholesterol: 0
- Protein: 2.6

## 762. Kalamata Cheesecake Appetizer

*Serving: 24 servings. | Prep: 30mins | Cook: 25mins | Ready in:*

### Ingredients

- 1-1/4 cups seasoned bread crumbs
- 1/2 cup finely chopped pecans
- 1/3 cup butter, melted
- FILLING:
- 2 packages (one 8 ounces, one 3 ounces) cream cheese, softened
- 1 cup (8 ounces) sour cream
- 1 tablespoon all-purpose flour
- 1/4 teaspoon salt
- 1/4 teaspoon pepper
- 1 large egg, lightly beaten
- 1 large egg yolk
- 1/2 cup pitted kalamata olives, chopped
- 2 teaspoons minced fresh rosemary
- Halved pitted kalamata olives and fresh rosemary sprigs, optional

### Direction

- Mix pecans and bread crumbs in small bowl; mix in butter. Force onto base of an oiled springform pan, 9-inch in size. On baking sheet, put pan. Bake for 12 minutes at 350°. Let cool on wire rack.
- Whip pepper, salt, flour, sour cream and cream cheese in big bowl till smooth. Put egg yolk and egg; on low speed, whip till blended. Fold in minced rosemary and chopped olives. Put on crust. Place pan back to baking sheet.
- Bake till middle is nearly set, for 25 minutes to half an hour. Cool for 10 minutes on wire rack. Detach cheesecake edges using knife from pan. Cool for an additional of 1 hour. Chill overnight.
- Take rim off pan. Put halved olives on top of cheesecake and rosemary sprigs if wished.

## Nutrition Information

- Calories: 142 calories
- Cholesterol: 45mg cholesterol
- Protein: 3g protein.
- Total Fat: 12g fat (6g saturated fat)
- Sodium: 223mg sodium
- Fiber: 0 fiber)
- Total Carbohydrate: 6g carbohydrate (1g sugars

## 763. Lavender & Olive Focaccia

*Serving: 2 loaves (8 wedges each). | Prep: 30mins | Cook: 25mins | Ready in:*

## Ingredients

- 1 package (1/4 ounce) active dry yeast
- 1-2/3 cups warm water (110° to 115°), divided
- 1 tablespoon honey
- 6 tablespoons olive oil, divided
- 2 teaspoons salt
- 4 to 5 cups all-purpose flour
- 15 Greek olives, chopped
- 1 tablespoon dried lavender flowers
- 1 garlic clove, minced
- 1 teaspoon kosher salt

## Direction

- Mix yeast with half a cup of warm water in a big bowl until dissolved. Mix in the honey, let rest for 5 minutes. Add the rest of warm water, salt and 4 tablespoons of oil. Mix in 2 cups of flour until smooth. Mix in enough flour left to get a soft dough.
- Take the dough to a light-floured surface, knead for about 6 to 8 minutes until it gets smooth and elastic. Use oil to grease a big bowl. Put it into the bowl, turn once to grease the top. Cover and let rest in warm place for about 60 minutes, until it rises double in size.
- Press the dough down, cut into two. Cover and let sit for 10 minutes. Form each part into a 9-inch circle. Use cooking spray to coat baking trays. Put the circles on the prepared trays. Cover and let rest until about half an hour, until they rise double in size.
- Make several 1/4-inch deep marks with the end of a wooden spoon handle on top of each. Mix the rest of oil, garlic, lavender and olives together; brush them on the loaves. Dredge kosher salt over. Set oven at 375° and bake until they turn golden brown, for 25 to 30 minutes. Take them out of pans to wire rack. Serve while still warm.

## Nutrition Information

- Calories: 174 calories
- Sodium: 471mg sodium
- Fiber: 1g fiber)
- Total Carbohydrate: 26g carbohydrate (2g sugars
- Cholesterol: 0 cholesterol
- Protein: 3g protein. Diabetic Exchanges: 1-1/2 starch
- Total Fat: 6g fat (1g saturated fat)

## 764. Layered Artichoke Cheese Spread

*Serving: 3 cups. | Prep: 15mins | Cook: 0mins | Ready in:*

### Ingredients

- 1 jar (6-1/2 ounces) marinated quartered artichoke hearts, drained and chopped
- 1/3 cup roasted sweet red peppers, drained and chopped
- 2 packages (8 ounces each) reduced-fat cream cheese
- 1 envelope ranch salad dressing mix
- 3 tablespoons minced fresh parsley
- Assorted crackers

### Direction

- Pat artichokes and peppers dry then set aside. Use plastic wrap to line a 3-cup bowl. Beat dressing mix and cream cheese in a big bowl until smooth. Mix parsley, peppers and artichokes in another bowl.
- Spread into prepared bowl with a third of the cream cheese mixture, then place a half of artichoke mixture on top. Repeat layers and put remaining cream cheese mixture on top. Cover and chill for a minimum of 4 hours. Unmold on a serving plate then serve together with crackers.

### Nutrition Information

- Calories: 63 calories
- Fiber: 0 fiber)
- Total Carbohydrate: 2g carbohydrate (1g sugars
- Cholesterol: 13mg cholesterol
- Protein: 2g protein. Diabetic Exchanges: 1 fat.
- Total Fat: 5g fat (3g saturated fat)
- Sodium: 213mg sodium

## 765. Layered Mediterranean Dip

*Serving: 10 cups. | Prep: 20mins | Cook: 0mins | Ready in:*

### Ingredients

- 2 cans (15 ounces each) pinto beans, rinsed and drained
- 1/3 cup prepared pesto
- 2 cups (16 ounces) reduced-fat sour cream
- 1 package (8 ounces) reduced-fat cream cheese
- 1-1/2 teaspoons Italian seasoning
- 1/2 teaspoon pepper
- 4 plum tomatoes, seeded and finely chopped
- 1 medium green pepper, finely chopped
- 3 green onions, finely chopped
- 2 cups shredded Italian cheese blend
- 1 cup crumbled feta cheese
- 2 cans (2-1/4 ounces each) sliced ripe olives, drained
- Baked pita chips

### Direction

- Put beans in a large bowl; mix in pesto until combined. Transfer to a 13x9-inch dish and spread.
- Whip pepper, Italian seasoning, cream cheese, and sour cream in another bowl until smooth; place over bean mixture and spread. Dust with olives, cheeses, and vegetables. Keep in the refrigerator for at least 30 minutes. Serve with chips.

### Nutrition Information

- Calories: 90 calories
- Sodium: 174mg sodium
- Fiber: 1g fiber)
- Total Carbohydrate: 6g carbohydrate (2g sugars
- Cholesterol: 14mg cholesterol
- Protein: 5g protein.
- Total Fat: 5g fat (3g saturated fat)

## 766. Layered Mediterranean Dip With Pita Chips

*Serving: 5 cups (120 chips). | Prep: 15mins | Cook: 10mins | Ready in:*

### Ingredients

- 1 cup (8 ounces) plain Greek yogurt
- 1 medium seedless cucumber, chopped
- 1 teaspoon white wine vinegar
- 2 teaspoons minced fresh mint or 1 teaspoon dried mint
- 1 carton (10 ounces) hummus
- 1 medium red onion, chopped
- 1 cup chopped roasted sweet red peppers, drained
- 2 packages (4 ounces each) crumbled feta cheese
- 1/2 cup pitted Greek olives, sliced
- 2 plum tomatoes, chopped
- Minced fresh parsley and additional minced fresh mint, optional
- PITA CHIPS:
- 20 pita pocket halves
- 1/4 cup olive oil
- 1/2 teaspoon salt
- 1/4 teaspoon pepper

### Direction

- Line a coffee filter or 4 cheesecloth layers on a strainer then set on top of a bowl. Put yogurt in the lined-strainer; use cheesecloth edges to cover. Chill for 8 hours to overnight. Mix mint, strained yogurt, vinegar, and cucumber in a small bowl.
- Slather hummus at the bottom of a nine-inch deep-dish pie plate. Put peppers, onion, tomatoes, olives, feta cheese, and yogurt mixture in a layer. If desired, add more mint and parsley on top. Refrigerate until serving.
- Slice each pita half to 3 wedges. Split each wedge into 2 portions; arrange on an ungreased baking sheet in one layer. Slather olive oil on each side then season with pepper and salt.
- Bake for 8-10 minutes in 400 degrees oven until crisp, turn one time. Serve it with the dip.

### Nutrition Information

- Calories:
- Protein:
- Total Fat:
- Sodium:
- Fiber:
- Total Carbohydrate:
- Cholesterol:

## 767. Leeks In Mustard Sauce

*Serving: 6-8 servings (3/4 cup sauce). | Prep: 15mins | Cook: 20mins | Ready in:*

### Ingredients

- 10 medium leeks (white portion only)
- 2 green onions with tops, chopped
- 1 garlic clove, minced
- 1 tablespoon olive oil
- MUSTARD SAUCE:
- 3 large egg yolks
- 1/4 cup water
- 2 tablespoons lemon juice
- 6 tablespoons cold butter
- 1 tablespoon Dijon mustard
- Dash white pepper

### Direction

- Slice leeks into 1 1/2-inch portions then julienne. Sauté garlic, onions, and leeks in a big pan with oil until tender.
- In the meantime, beat lemon juice, water, and egg yolks in a small heavy pot. On low heat, cook and stir for 20 minutes until the edges bubble, the mixture starts to thicken, and it reads 160 degrees. Whisk in a tablespoon of

butter at a time, make sure it is melted before adding another. Take off heat; mix in pepper and mustard.
- Move the leek mixture to a serving bowl then add mustard sauce on top.

## Nutrition Information

- Calories: 185 calories
- Protein: 3g protein.
- Total Fat: 13g fat (6g saturated fat)
- Sodium: 160mg sodium
- Fiber: 2g fiber)
- Total Carbohydrate: 17g carbohydrate (5g sugars
- Cholesterol: 103mg cholesterol

## 768. Lemon Dill Couscous

*Serving: 2 servings. | Prep: 5mins | Cook: 5mins | Ready in:*

## Ingredients

- 3/4 cup uncooked plain couscous
- 3-1/4 teaspoons lemon juice
- 1/4 to 1/2 teaspoon dill weed

## Direction

- Cook couscous according to the package instructions, for 2 servings, adding salt to the water and omit the butter or oil from the 1st step. Mix in dill, lemon juice, and couscous. Put a cover on and take away from heat. Let it sit for 5 minutes. Use a fork to fluff.

## Nutrition Information

- Calories: 249 calories
- Fiber: 3g fiber)
- Total Carbohydrate: 53g carbohydrate (2g sugars
- Cholesterol: 0 cholesterol
- Protein: 10g protein.
- Total Fat: 1g fat (0 saturated fat)
- Sodium: 302mg sodium

## 769. Lemon Mint Beans

*Serving: 4 servings. | Prep: 10mins | Cook: 0mins | Ready in:*

## Ingredients

- 1 package (16 ounces) fresh or frozen cut green or wax beans
- 1 tablespoon lemon juice
- 1 tablespoon snipped fresh mint
- 1/4 teaspoon grated lemon peel
- 1/2 teaspoon salt

## Direction

- Cook beans in a saucepan with a little amount of water until softened, then drain. Put in leftover ingredients and toss to coat well.

## Nutrition Information

- Calories: 39 calories
- Total Fat: 0 fat (0 saturated fat)
- Sodium: 297mg sodium
- Fiber: 3g fiber)
- Total Carbohydrate: 9g carbohydrate (0 sugars
- Cholesterol: 0 cholesterol
- Protein: 2g protein. Diabetic Exchanges: 2 vegetable.

## 770. Lemon Parmesan Orzo

*Serving: 4 servings. | Prep: 10mins | Cook: 10mins | Ready in:*

## Ingredients

- 1 cup uncooked whole wheat orzo pasta
- 1 tablespoon olive oil
- 1/4 cup grated Parmesan cheese
- 2 tablespoons minced fresh parsley
- 1/2 teaspoon grated lemon peel
- 1/4 teaspoon salt
- 1/4 teaspoon pepper

### Direction

- Cook orzo following the package instructions; strain. Pour into a small bowl, drizzle with oil. Mix in the rest of the ingredients.

### Nutrition Information

- Calories: 191 calories
- Total Carbohydrate: 28g carbohydrate (0 sugars
- Cholesterol: 4mg cholesterol
- Protein: 7g protein. Diabetic Exchanges: 2 starch
- Total Fat: 6g fat (1g saturated fat)
- Sodium: 225mg sodium
- Fiber: 7g fiber)

## 771. Lemon Feta Angel Hair

*Serving: 4 servings. | Prep: 10mins | Cook: 10mins | Ready in:*

### Ingredients

- 8 ounces uncooked angel hair pasta
- 2 garlic cloves, minced
- 2 tablespoons olive oil
- 1 package (4 ounces) crumbled feta cheese
- 2 teaspoons grated lemon peel
- 1/2 teaspoon dried oregano
- 1/2 teaspoon salt
- 1/2 teaspoon pepper

### Direction

- Cook pasta as directed on package.
- Sauté garlic in oil in a large skillet for 1 minute. Drain cooked pasta; mix into the skillet. Add the rest of ingredients and stir until well coated.

### Nutrition Information

- Calories: 344 calories
- Cholesterol: 15mg cholesterol
- Protein: 13g protein.
- Total Fat: 12g fat (4g saturated fat)
- Sodium: 569mg sodium
- Fiber: 3g fiber)
- Total Carbohydrate: 44g carbohydrate (2g sugars

## 772. Lemon Garlic Spread

*Serving: 1/2 cup. | Prep: 10mins | Cook: 0mins | Ready in:*

### Ingredients

- 1/3 cup mayonnaise
- 2 tablespoons olive oil
- 1 tablespoon red wine vinegar
- 1 garlic clove, minced
- 1 teaspoon grated lemon peel
- 1/4 teaspoon lemon-pepper seasoning

### Direction

- Beat all the ingredients in a small bowl until combined; keep in refrigerate.

### Nutrition Information

- Calories: 195 calories
- Protein: 0 protein.
- Total Fat: 21g fat (3g saturated fat)
- Sodium: 129mg sodium
- Fiber: 0 fiber)
- Total Carbohydrate: 1g carbohydrate (0 sugars
- Cholesterol: 7mg cholesterol

## 773. Lemon Herb Olives With Goat Cheese

*Serving: 6 servings. | Prep: 10mins | Cook: 5mins | Ready in:*

### Ingredients

- 3 tablespoons olive oil
- 2 teaspoons grated lemon peel
- 1 garlic clove, minced
- 1/2 teaspoon minced fresh oregano or rosemary
- 1/4 teaspoon crushed red pepper flakes
- 1/2 cup assorted pitted Greek olives
- 1 package (5.3 ounces) fresh goat cheese
- 1 tablespoon minced fresh basil
- Assorted crackers

### Direction

- In a tiny frying pan, blend the first five ingredients and heat over medium heat for 2-3 minutes, or until just fragrant, stirring infrequently. Mix in olives, heat through to blend flavors. Cool completely.
- Put cheese on a serving plate to serve. Blend olive mixture and basils; spoon over cheese. Use with crackers.

### Nutrition Information

- Calories: 135 calories
- Fiber: 0 fiber)
- Total Carbohydrate: 2g carbohydrate (0 sugars
- Cholesterol: 17mg cholesterol
- Protein: 3g protein.
- Total Fat: 13g fat (3g saturated fat)
- Sodium: 285mg sodium

## 774. Lemony Almond Feta Green Beans

*Serving: 6 servings. | Prep: 15mins | Cook: 15mins | Ready in:*

### Ingredients

- 1 pound fresh green beans, trimmed
- 2 tablespoons butter
- 1 small onion, halved and sliced
- 3 garlic cloves, sliced
- 1/2 cup sliced almonds
- 1 teaspoon grated lemon peel
- 3 tablespoons lemon juice
- 1/4 teaspoon salt
- 1/8 teaspoon pepper
- 1/2 cup crumbled feta cheese

### Direction

- Bring 4 cups water in a large saucepan to a boil. Add green beans into boiling water; cook without a cover until beans are bright green for 4 to 5 minutes. Take beans out of the pan and instantly plunge into ice water. Strain and pat dry.
- Melt butter over medium heat in a large skillet. Sauté onion in melted butter until tender for 6 to 8 minutes. Add garlic; sauté for another minute.
- Mix in almonds and green beans; sauté until beans are crisp-tender for 3 to 4 minutes. Sprinkle with pepper, salt, lemon juice, and lemon peel; stir until incorporated. Sprinkle with cheese.

### Nutrition Information

- Calories: 134 calories
- Total Carbohydrate: 10g carbohydrate (3g sugars
- Cholesterol: 15mg cholesterol
- Protein: 5g protein.
- Total Fat: 9g fat (4g saturated fat)
- Sodium: 224mg sodium
- Fiber: 4g fiber)

## 775. Lemony Fennel Olives

*Serving: 16 servings. | Prep: 15mins | Cook: 5mins | Ready in:*

### Ingredients

- 1 small fennel bulb
- 2 cups pitted ripe olives
- 1 small lemon, cut into wedges
- 1/2 teaspoon whole peppercorns
- 1/2 cup olive oil
- 1/2 cup lemon juice

### Direction

- Trim fennel bulb and slice into wedges. Snip feathery fronds and save 2 teaspoons. Bring salted water in a small saucepan to a boil. Put fennel into the boiling water and boil without a cover until tender-crisp, about one minute. Drain and rinse fennel under cold water.
- Mix together reserved fennel fronds, peppercorns, lemon wedges, olives and fennel in a big bowl. Whisk together lemon juice and oil, then drizzle over olive mixture and toss to coat. Cover and chill overnight.
- Take out of the fridge about one hour before serving. Remove to a serving bowl, then serve together with a slotted spoon.

### Nutrition Information

- Calories: 83 calories
- Total Carbohydrate: 3g carbohydrate (0 sugars
- Cholesterol: 0 cholesterol
- Protein: 0 protein.
- Total Fat: 8g fat (1g saturated fat)
- Sodium: 132mg sodium
- Fiber: 1g fiber)

## 776. Lemony Tossed Salad

*Serving: 4 servings. | Prep: 10mins | Cook: 0mins | Ready in:*

### Ingredients

- 4 cups ready-to-serve salad greens
- 2 medium tomatoes, cut into wedges
- 3/4 cup sliced cucumber
- 1/2 cup olive oil
- 1/4 cup lemon juice
- 1 garlic clove, minced
- 1 teaspoon sugar
- 1 teaspoon dried oregano or mint
- Salt and pepper to taste

### Direction

- Mix cucumbers, tomatoes, and salad greens together in a salad bowl. Mix the rest of the ingredients together in a tightly fitting lidded jar and shake well. Sprinkle over the salad and toss to coat.

### Nutrition Information

- Calories:
- Protein:
- Total Fat:
- Sodium:
- Fiber:
- Total Carbohydrate:
- Cholesterol:

## 777. Lentil Bulgur Salad

*Serving: 10 servings. | Prep: 20mins | Cook: 15mins | Ready in:*

### Ingredients

- 1-1/2 cups boiling water
- 1-1/2 cups bulgur
- 5 cups water

- 1-1/2 cups dried lentils, rinsed
- 1 cup diced green onion
- 1 cup diced sweet red pepper
- 1/2 cup chopped green onions
- 1/2 cup minced fresh parsley
- DRESSING:
- 1/3 cup cider vinegar
- 1/3 cup olive oil
- 1 tablespoon dried basil
- 1 tablespoon dill seed
- 1 teaspoon salt
- 1/4 teaspoon pepper
- 3/4 cup feta cheese

## Direction

- Pour boiling water over bulgur placed into a big bowl and allow to stand for a half hour, until the liquid is absorbed. At the same time, bring water in a saucepan to a boil. Put in lentils, then lower heat. Cover and simmer for 15 minutes until lentils are softened, then drain. Mix together lentils and bulgur in another big bowl, allowing to cool thoroughly.
- Put in parsley, onions and peppers. Mix together pepper, salt, dill, basil, oil and vinegar in a jar with a tight-fitting lid, then drizzle over salad and toss to coat well. Place crumbled feta cheese on top and toss again. Cover and chill about 4 hours, until serving.

## Nutrition Information

- Calories: 271 calories
- Total Carbohydrate: 35g carbohydrate (0 sugars
- Cholesterol: 10mg cholesterol
- Protein: 13g protein. Diabetic Exchanges: 2 lean meat
- Total Fat: 10g fat (3g saturated fat)
- Sodium: 370mg sodium
- Fiber: 13g fiber)

## 778. Lick The Bowl Clean Hummus

*Serving: 2-1/2 cups. | Prep: 10mins | Cook: 35mins | Ready in:*

## Ingredients

- 2 large sweet onions, thinly sliced
- 1/4 cup plus 1/3 cup olive oil, divided
- 1 can (15 ounces) garbanzo beans or chickpeas, rinsed and drained
- 1/4 cup plus 2 tablespoons lemon juice
- 1/4 cup tahini
- 4 garlic cloves, minced
- 1/8 teaspoon salt
- 1/8 teaspoon pepper
- Baked pita chips or assorted fresh vegetables

## Direction

- Sauté onions in 1/4 cup of oil in a big pan, until it becomes soft. Turn down the heat to medium-low, then cook for 30 minutes, stirring once in a while, or until it turns deep golden brown.
- Move to a food processor then stir in the leftover oil, pepper, salt, garlic, tahini, lemon juice and beans. Blend for half a minute, covered, or until it becomes smooth. Serve alongside chips.

## Nutrition Information

- Calories: 218 calories
- Sodium: 91mg sodium
- Fiber: 3g fiber)
- Total Carbohydrate: 14g carbohydrate (5g sugars
- Cholesterol: 0 cholesterol
- Protein: 3g protein.
- Total Fat: 17g fat (2g saturated fat)

## 779. Lime Cilantro Hummus

*Serving: 3 cups. | Prep: 20mins | Cook: 0mins | Ready in:*

### Ingredients

- 2 cans (15 ounces) garbanzo beans or chickpeas, rinsed and drained
- 1 cup coarsely chopped cilantro leaves
- 1/2 cup lime juice
- 1/4 cup water
- 3 tablespoons olive oil
- 4 garlic cloves, halved
- 1-1/2 teaspoons grated lime zest
- 1 teaspoon garlic salt
- 1/2 teaspoon cayenne pepper
- Assorted fresh vegetables or crackers

### Direction

- Process the cayenne, garlic salt, lime zest, garlic, oil, water, lime juice, cilantro and garbanzo beans in a food processor until incorporated. Serve with crackers or vegetables.

### Nutrition Information

- Calories: 100 calories
- Total Carbohydrate: 12g carbohydrate (2g sugars
- Cholesterol: 0 cholesterol
- Protein: 3g protein. Diabetic Exchanges: 1 starch
- Total Fat: 5g fat (0 saturated fat)
- Sodium: 244mg sodium
- Fiber: 3g fiber)

## 780. Mandarin Couscous Salad

*Serving: 7 servings. | Prep: 25mins | Cook: 0mins | Ready in:*

### Ingredients

- 1-1/3 cups water
- 1 cup uncooked couscous
- 1 can (11 ounces) mandarin oranges, drained
- 1 cup frozen peas, thawed
- 1/2 cup slivered almonds, toasted
- 1/3 cup chopped red onion
- 3 tablespoons cider vinegar
- 2 tablespoons olive oil
- 1 tablespoon sugar
- 1/4 teaspoon salt
- 1/4 teaspoon hot pepper sauce

### Direction

- Bring water in a saucepan to boil. Add couscous and stir well. Cover, turn the heat off, and set aside for 5 minutes. Make couscous fluffy with a fork. Cover and chill in the fridge for at least 1 hour.
- Combine couscous, onion, almonds, peas, and oranges in a large bowl. In an air-tight jar, mix pepper sauce, salt, sugar, oil, and vinegar together, shake properly. Drizzle dressing over couscous combination; stir well until evenly coated.

### Nutrition Information

- Calories: 221 calories
- Sodium: 108mg sodium
- Fiber: 4g fiber)
- Total Carbohydrate: 31g carbohydrate (0 sugars
- Cholesterol: 0 cholesterol
- Protein: 6g protein. Diabetic Exchanges: 1-1/2 starch
- Total Fat: 8g fat (1g saturated fat)

## 781. Marinated Cheese Topped Salad

*Serving: 6 servings. | Prep: 25mins | Cook: 0mins | Ready in:*

### Ingredients

- 1/2 cup olive oil
- 2 tablespoons minced fresh Italian parsley
- 2 tablespoons lemon juice
- 1 tablespoon minced fresh oregano
- 1 tablespoon red wine vinegar
- 1 large garlic clove, minced
- 1/4 teaspoon salt
- 1/8 teaspoon pepper
- 1 package (8 ounces) cream cheese, chilled
- 4 cups torn romaine
- 2 cups fresh arugula or baby spinach
- 1-1/2 cups grape tomatoes, halved
- 2 shallots, thinly sliced
- 1/2 cup medium pitted green olives

### Direction

- To make dressing, combine the first eight ingredients in a small bowl. Cut cream cheese to 1/2-inch cubes; toss cream cheese cubes with half of the dressing. Cover and chill for 30 minutes.
- In a large bowl, combine olives, shallots, tomatoes, arugula and romaine. Sprinkle with remaining dressing; mix until well coated. Add marinated cheese on top. Serve right away.

### Nutrition Information

- Calories: 342 calories
- Fiber: 1g fiber)
- Total Carbohydrate: 8g carbohydrate (2g sugars
- Cholesterol: 42mg cholesterol
- Protein: 4g protein.
- Total Fat: 34g fat (11g saturated fat)
- Sodium: 461mg sodium

## 782. Marinated Cucumbers

*Serving: 12 servings. | Prep: 10mins | Cook: 0mins | Ready in:*

### Ingredients

- 6 medium cucumbers, thinly sliced
- 1 medium onion, sliced
- 1 cup white vinegar
- 1/4 to 1/3 cup sugar
- 1/4 cup olive oil
- 1 teaspoon salt
- 1 teaspoon dried oregano
- 1/2 teaspoon garlic powder
- 1/2 teaspoon dried marjoram
- 1/2 teaspoon lemon-pepper seasoning
- 1/2 teaspoon ground mustard

### Direction

- Mix onion and cucumbers together in a big bowl. Mix the rest of the ingredients together in a tightly fitting lidded jar; put the lid on and shake well. Put on the cucumber mixture and mix to combine. Put a cover on and chill for a minimum of 4 hours. Enjoy with a slotted spoon.

### Nutrition Information

- Calories: 85 calories
- Cholesterol: 0 cholesterol
- Protein: 2g protein.
- Total Fat: 5g fat (1g saturated fat)
- Sodium: 216mg sodium
- Fiber: 2g fiber)
- Total Carbohydrate: 10g carbohydrate (8g sugars

### 783. Marvelous Mediterranean Vegetables

*Serving: 9 servings. | Prep: 25mins | Cook: 10mins | Ready in:*

#### Ingredients

- 3 large portobello mushrooms, sliced
- 1 each medium sweet red, orange and yellow peppers, sliced
- 1 medium zucchini, sliced
- 10 fresh asparagus spears, cut into 2-inch lengths
- 1 small onion, sliced and separated into rings
- 3/4 cup grape tomatoes
- 1/2 cup fresh sugar snap peas
- 1/2 cup fresh broccoli florets
- 1/2 cup pitted Greek olives
- 1 bottle (14 ounces) Greek vinaigrette
- 1/2 cup crumbled feta cheese

#### Direction

- Mix zucchini, peppers, and mushrooms together in a large plastic zip bag. Place olives, broccoli, peas, tomatoes, onion, and asparagus in. Pour into bag with vinaigrette; close bag and coat by turning. Let sit for at least 30 minutes in the refrigerator.
- Get rid of marinade. On a grill basket/wok, place vegetables. Allow to grill for 8-12 minutes over medium heat, uncovered, till tender, frequently stirring. Lay on a serving plate; use cheese to dredge on.

#### Nutrition Information

- Calories: 196 calories
- Protein: 4g protein.
- Total Fat: 16g fat (3g saturated fat)
- Sodium: 549mg sodium
- Fiber: 3g fiber)
- Total Carbohydrate: 11g carbohydrate (4g sugars
- Cholesterol: 3mg cholesterol

### 784. Mediterranean Apricot Phyllo Bites

*Serving: 2-1/2 dozen. | Prep: 30mins | Cook: 10mins | Ready in:*

#### Ingredients

- 1/2 cup unblanched almonds
- 1/2 cup chopped dried apricots
- 1 tablespoon plus 1/2 cup butter, melted, divided
- 2 tablespoons honey
- 1/4 teaspoon grated lemon peel
- 1/4 teaspoon almond extract
- 20 sheets phyllo dough (14x9 inches)

#### Direction

- In a food processor, process apricots and almonds with a cover until finely chopped. Mix lemon extract, a tablespoon of butter, lemon peel, and honey in a small bowl; mix in almond mixture until combined.
- Brush the remaining butter lightly on one sheet of phyllo, top with another phyllo sheet then brush again with butter. Cover the remaining phyllo with plastic wrap and a damp towel to prevent from drying. Slice three 14-in by 3-in strips from the 2 layered sheets.
- Put 1 1/2 tsp. of filling in the bottom corner of each strip; fold the dough over the filling to make a triangle. Fold the triangle up then over to make another triangle. Keep on folding resembling a flag until the end of the strip. Brush butter at the end of the dough then press to seal the triangle. Flip then brush melted butter on top of the triangle. Repeat.
- On a greased baking sheet, arrange the triangles then bake for 10-12 minutes in a 375 degrees oven or until golden brown. Place on a wire rack to cool. Dust with confectioners' sugar.

## Nutrition Information

- Calories: 74 calories
- Protein: 1g protein. Diabetic Exchanges: 1/2 starch
- Total Fat: 5g fat (2g saturated fat)
- Sodium: 56mg sodium
- Fiber: 1g fiber)
- Total Carbohydrate: 7g carbohydrate (3g sugars
- Cholesterol: 9mg cholesterol

### 785. Mediterranean Artichoke And Red Pepper Roll Ups

*Serving: 2 dozen. | Prep: 15mins | Cook: 15mins | Ready in:*

## Ingredients

- 1 can (14 ounces) water-packed artichoke hearts, rinsed, drained and finely chopped
- 4 ounces cream cheese, softened
- 1/3 cup grated Parmesan cheese
- 1/4 cup crumbled feta cheese
- 2 green onions, thinly sliced
- 3 tablespoons prepared pesto
- 8 flour tortillas (8 inches), warmed
- 1 jar (7-1/2 ounces) roasted sweet red peppers, drained and cut into strips
- SAUCE:
- 1 cup (8 ounces) sour cream
- 1 tablespoon minced chives

## Direction

- Mix pesto, green onions, feta cheese, parmesan cheese, cream cheese and artichokes till blended in a small bowl. On every tortilla, spread 1/4 cup mixture. Put red peppers on top; tightly roll up.
- Put onto greased baking sheet, 1-in. apart. Bake for 12-15 minutes till heated through at 350°. Slice to thirds. Meanwhile, mix chives and sour crema in a small bowl. Serve with the rolls.

## Nutrition Information

- Calories: 112 calories
- Fiber: 0 fiber)
- Total Carbohydrate: 11g carbohydrate (1g sugars
- Cholesterol: 14mg cholesterol
- Protein: 4g protein.
- Total Fat: 6g fat (3g saturated fat)
- Sodium: 217mg sodium

### 786. Mediterranean Broccoli Slaw

*Serving: 5 servings. | Prep: 10mins | Cook: 0mins | Ready in:*

## Ingredients

- 1 package (12 ounces) broccoli coleslaw mix
- 1 cup (4 ounces) crumbled feta cheese
- 15 Greek olives, sliced
- 3/4 cup Greek vinaigrette

## Direction

- Combine coleslaw mix, olives and cheese in a salad bowl. Add vinaigrette, mix well to coat. Refrigerate until it is ready for serving.

## Nutrition Information

- Calories: 240 calories
- Fiber: 3g fiber)
- Total Carbohydrate: 8g carbohydrate (2g sugars
- Cholesterol: 12mg cholesterol
- Protein: 6g protein.
- Total Fat: 20g fat (5g saturated fat)
- Sodium: 788mg sodium

## 787. Mediterranean Bulgur Bowl

*Serving: 4 servings. | Prep: 15mins | Cook: 15mins | Ready in:*

### Ingredients

- 1 cup bulgur
- 1/2 teaspoon ground cumin
- 1/4 teaspoon salt
- 2 cups water
- 1 can (15 ounces) chickpeas or garbanzo beans, rinsed and drained
- 6 ounces fresh baby spinach (about 8 cups)
- 2 cups cherry tomatoes, halved
- 1 small red onion, halved and thinly sliced
- 1/2 cup crumbled feta cheese
- 1/4 cup hummus
- 2 tablespoons chopped fresh mint
- 2 tablespoons lemon juice

### Direction

- Combine first four ingredients in a 6 quart stockpot; bring to a boil. Lower the heat, cover and simmer for 10 to 12 minutes until soft. Stir in chickpeas; heat through.
- Remove from heat; stir in spinach. Cover and allow to stand for about 5 minutes until spinach is wilted. Stir in remaining ingredients. Serve warm or chill in refrigerator and serve cold.

### Nutrition Information

- Calories: 311 calories
- Total Carbohydrate: 52g carbohydrate (6g sugars
- Cholesterol: 8mg cholesterol
- Protein: 14g protein.
- Total Fat: 7g fat (2g saturated fat)
- Sodium: 521mg sodium
- Fiber: 12g fiber)

## 788. Mediterranean Bulgur Salad

*Serving: 6 | Prep: 15mins | Cook: | Ready in:*

### Ingredients

- 1 1/2 cups boiling water
- 1 cup bulgur wheat
- 1/3 cup chopped cucumber
- salt and ground black pepper to taste
- 2 tablespoons lemon juice
- 2 tablespoons olive oil
- 1 teaspoon minced garlic
- 1/2 teaspoon lemon zest
- 1 (15 ounce) can chickpeas, drained and rinsed
- 1/4 cup chopped green onions

### Direction

- In a bowl, mix bulgur and boiling water. Cover the bowl and allow bulgur to sit for 30 minutes until water is fully absorbed.
- Combine salt and chopped cucumber in a bowl.
- Whisk together ground black pepper, lemon zest, garlic, olive oil and lemon juice in a bowl till well-combined.
- In a bowl, stir together green onions, cucumber, chickpeas and bulgur; drizzle bulgur mixture with dressing and toss until completely coated. Cover the bowl with plastic wrap and chill for at least 1 hour until flavors are well combined.

### Nutrition Information

- Calories: 180 calories;
- Total Carbohydrate: 29.4
- Cholesterol: 0
- Protein: 5.4
- Total Fat: 5.4
- Sodium: 172

### 789. Mediterranean Dip With Garlic Pita Chips

*Serving: 2-1/2 cups dip (30 chips). | Prep: 35mins | Cook: 60mins | Ready in:*

### Ingredients

- 2 medium eggplants, peeled
- 1 large sweet red pepper
- 1 large sweet yellow pepper
- 1 large red onion
- 1/4 cup olive oil
- 1 teaspoon salt
- 1/4 teaspoon pepper
- 2 garlic cloves, minced
- 4 teaspoons tomato paste
- PITA CHIPS:
- 1/4 cup olive oil
- 2 tablespoons grated Parmesan cheese
- 2 garlic cloves, minced
- 1 teaspoon dried basil
- 1 teaspoon dried thyme
- 1/2 teaspoon salt
- 1/2 teaspoon dried tarragon
- 1/4 teaspoon coarsely ground pepper
- 1 package (12 ounces) whole pita breads

### Direction

- Cut onion, peppers and eggplants into pieces with 1-inch size then put into a big bowl. Put in pepper, salt and oil. Toss together to coat well. Remove to 2 greased 15"x10"x1" baking pans.
- Bake about 40 minutes at 400° while stirring one time. Stir in garlic and bake until vegetables are softened, about 5 to 10 minutes more. Allow to cool about 10 minutes. Put in a food processor with tomato paste and vegetables, then cover and process until getting wanted consistency.
- To make pita chips, mix together seasonings, garlic, cheese and oil in a small bowl. Put pita breads on baking sheets and use half of the oil mixture to brush. Bake for 7 minutes at 350°; turn over and brush with the leftover mixture. Bake until crisp, about 7 to 9 minutes more. Slice each pita into 6 wedges, then serve together with dip.

### Nutrition Information

- Calories: 236 calories
- Protein: 5g protein.
- Total Fat: 12g fat (2g saturated fat)
- Sodium: 533mg sodium
- Fiber: 5g fiber)
- Total Carbohydrate: 29g carbohydrate (5g sugars
- Cholesterol: 1mg cholesterol

### 790. Mediterranean Dip With Pita Chips

*Serving: 3-1/2 cups (6 dozen chips). | Prep: 20mins | Cook: 10mins | Ready in:*

### Ingredients

- 12 pita pocket halves
- Cooking spray
- 1-3/4 teaspoons garlic powder, divided
- 12 ounces cream cheese, softened
- 1 cup (8 ounces) plain yogurt
- 1 teaspoon dried oregano
- 3/4 teaspoon ground coriander
- 1/4 teaspoon pepper
- 1 large tomato, seeded and chopped
- 5 pepperoncini, sliced
- 1/2 cup pitted Greek olives, sliced
- 1 medium cucumber, seeded and diced
- 1/3 cup crumbled feta cheese
- 2 tablespoons minced fresh parsley

### Direction

- Cut every pita half to 3 wedges. Separate every wedge to 2 pieces. Put it on a baking

sheet without grease. Spray both wedge sides using cooking spray. Place 1 teaspoon of garlic powder on by sprinkling it.
- Bake for 5 to 6 minutes on both sides at 350 degrees Fahrenheit until it's golden brown. Cool it on a wire rack.
- While it bakes, beat remaining garlic powder, pepper, coriander, oregano, yogurt, and cream cheese in a small bowl. Spread on a 9-inch pie plate. Place parsley, feta cheese, cucumber, olives, pepperoncini, and tomato on top. Serve with the pita chips.

## Nutrition Information

- Calories:
- Cholesterol:
- Protein:
- Total Fat:
- Sodium:
- Fiber:
- Total Carbohydrate:

## 791. Mediterranean Green Salad

*Serving: 10 servings. | Prep: 15mins | Cook: 0mins | Ready in:*

## Ingredients

- 1 package (16 ounces) ready-to-serve salad greens
- 2 cups grape tomatoes
- 6 green onions, thinly sliced
- 1 jar (7-1/2 ounces) marinated quartered artichoke hearts, drained and coarsely chopped
- 1 cup (4 ounces) crumbled feta cheese
- 1 medium sweet yellow pepper, cut into thin strips
- 3/4 cup pitted Greek olives, halved
- 1/2 cup sunflower kernels
- 1/2 cup Italian salad dressing

## Direction

- Mix the first eight ingredients together in a large salad bowl. Just before serving, pour salad dressing on top and toss until well coated.

## Nutrition Information

- Calories: 194 calories
- Cholesterol: 6mg cholesterol
- Protein: 5g protein.
- Total Fat: 16g fat (3g saturated fat)
- Sodium: 594mg sodium
- Fiber: 3g fiber)
- Total Carbohydrate: 9g carbohydrate (2g sugars

## 792. Mediterranean Layered Dip

*Serving: 20 servings. | Prep: 15mins | Cook: 0mins | Ready in:*

## Ingredients

- 2-1/2 cups roasted garlic hummus
- 3/4 cup chopped roasted sweet red peppers
- 1 cup fresh baby spinach, coarsely chopped
- 3 tablespoons lemon juice
- 2 tablespoons olive oil
- 2 tablespoons coarsely chopped fresh basil
- 1 tablespoon coarsely chopped fresh mint
- 1/2 cup crumbled feta cheese
- 1/2 cup Greek olives, sliced
- 1/4 cup chopped red onion
- Assorted fresh vegetables or baked pita chips

## Direction

- In a round serving platter with 12-inch size, spread the hummus and put roasted peppers on top.

- Mix the mint, basil, oil, lemon juice and spinach in a small bowl, then scoop the spinach mixture on the peppers with a slotted spoon. Sprinkle onion, olives and cheese on top, then serve alongside pita chips and vegetables.

## Nutrition Information

- Calories: 83 calories
- Fiber: 1g fiber)
- Total Carbohydrate: 6g carbohydrate (1g sugars
- Cholesterol: 2mg cholesterol
- Protein: 2g protein.
- Total Fat: 6g fat (1g saturated fat)
- Sodium: 347mg sodium

## 793. Mediterranean Lentil Salad

*Serving: 8 | Prep: 10mins | Cook: 20mins | Ready in:*

### Ingredients

- 1 cup dry brown lentils
- 1 cup diced carrots
- 1 cup red onion, diced
- 2 cloves garlic, minced
- 1 bay leaf
- 1/2 teaspoon dried thyme
- 2 tablespoons lemon juice
- 1/2 cup diced celery
- 1/4 cup chopped parsley
- 1 teaspoon salt
- 1/4 teaspoon ground black pepper
- 1/4 cup olive oil

### Direction

- Mix thyme, bay leaf, garlic, onion, carrots, and lentils together in a saucepan. Add sufficient water to submerge by 1 inch. Boil it, decrease heat and simmer without a cover until lentils are softened but not mushy, about 15-20 minutes.
- Strain vegetables and lentils and take out bay leaf. Add pepper, salt, parsley, celery, lemon juice, and olive oil. Mix and toss and enjoy at room temperature.

## Nutrition Information

- Calories: 147 calories;
- Cholesterol: 0
- Protein: 6
- Total Fat: 7.1
- Sodium: 453
- Total Carbohydrate: 16.2

## 794. Mediterranean Mashed Potatoes

*Serving: 16 servings (3/4 cup each). | Prep: 25mins | Cook: 15mins | Ready in:*

### Ingredients

- 8 large potatoes (about 6-1/2 pounds), peeled and cubed
- 3 garlic cloves
- 1 teaspoon plus 3/4 teaspoon salt, divided
- 1/2 cup olive oil
- 1/4 cup lemon juice
- 1/2 cup pine nuts, toasted

### Direction

- Put potatoes in a stockpot; pour in water to cover. Heat to a boil. Lower the heat; cook, without covering, for 10 to 15 minutes until softened.
- In the meantime, mince the garlic; scatter 1 teaspoon of salt over. Use the flat side of the knife blade to mash garlic, forming into a smooth paste. In a small bowl, blend the leftover salt, garlic mixture, lemon juice, and oil until well-blended.

- Drain potatoes; bring back to pan. Mash potatoes, slowly put in oil mixture. Place to a serving dish; scatter pine nuts on top.

## Nutrition Information

- Calories: 192 calories
- Cholesterol: 0 cholesterol
- Protein: 3g protein. Diabetic Exchanges: 1-1/2 starch
- Total Fat: 9g fat (1g saturated fat)
- Sodium: 262mg sodium
- Fiber: 2g fiber)
- Total Carbohydrate: 26g carbohydrate (2g sugars

## 795. Mediterranean Omelet

*Serving: Makes 2 servings. | Prep: 5mins | Cook: | Ready in:*

## Ingredients

- 4 egg s
- 1 cup sliced fresh mushrooms
- 1-1/2 tsp. finely chopped fresh parsley
- 1 Tbsp. finely chopped fresh basil
- 2 Tbsp. ATHENOS Crumbled Reduced Fat Feta Cheese
- 2 OSCAR MAYER Wieners, cut lengthwise in half

## Direction

- In a medium bowl, beat eggs. In a medium nonstick skillet greased with cooking spray, cook mushrooms 2 minutes over medium-high heat, mixing from time to time, until tender. Put into eggs with basil and parsley; blend nicely.
- Place 1/2 egg mixture in skillet; cook for 2 minutes until set, using a spatula to lift the edge and tiling the skillet to let the uncooked portion flow underneath. Once egg mixture is set yet the top is still lightly moist, put 2 wiener halves and 1 tablespoon cheese on top of 1/2 the omelet. Slip spatula beneath the omelet, tip skillet to loosen then gradually fold omelet in half. Cook for 2 minutes until cheese melts and the wieners are heated through. Flip or slide the omelet onto a serving plate.
- Use paper towel to wipe the skillet clean then grease with cooking spray. Continue to make the 2nd omelet with the rest of ingredients.

## Nutrition Information

- Calories: 360
- Protein: 22 g
- Saturated Fat: 11 g
- Sodium: 800 mg
- Fiber: 1 g
- Cholesterol: 475 mg
- Total Fat: 28 g
- Sugar: 1 g
- Total Carbohydrate: 4 g

## 796. Mediterranean Orange Salad

*Serving: 2 servings. | Prep: 10mins | Cook: 0mins | Ready in:*

## Ingredients

- 2 medium navel oranges, peeled and sliced
- 2 slices red onion, separated into rings
- 2 tablespoons olive oil
- 1/4 teaspoon salt
- 1/8 teaspoon pepper
- 2 lettuce leaves

## Direction

- Combine pepper, salt, oil, onion and oranges in a large bowl; toss gently until well coated. Cover and keep cold in refrigerator for 2 hours.

- Transfer orange mixture to lettuce-lined plates with a slotted spoon.

## Nutrition Information

- Calories: 189 calories
- Protein: 2g protein. Diabetic Exchanges: 2 fat
- Total Fat: 14g fat (2g saturated fat)
- Sodium: 298mg sodium
- Fiber: 4g fiber)
- Total Carbohydrate: 17g carbohydrate (14g sugars
- Cholesterol: 0 cholesterol

## 797. Mediterranean Palmiers

*Serving: 40 appetizers. | Prep: 10mins | Cook: 10mins | Ready in:*

### Ingredients

- 1 package (17.3 ounces) frozen puff pastry, thawed
- 1/4 cup prepared pesto
- 1/2 cup crumbled feta cheese
- 1/4 cup chopped oil-packed sun-dried tomatoes, patted dry
- 1/4 cup finely chopped walnuts

### Direction

- Take one sheet of puff pastry and roll it out. Spread 2 T. pesto to within 1/2 in. of the edges then top with walnuts, tomatoes and half of the cheese.
- Starting from the left and right sides, roll the pastry's edges toward the center, like a jelly roll. Roll at 1-in. intervals so that the sides meet in the center. Do the same with the rest of the ingredients then slice each pastry rolls into 20 pieces.
- Arrange on baking tray lined with parchment paper, cut side down and 2 inches apart. Bake for 10 to 12 minutes at 400°F or until golden brown. Serve while it's still warm.

## Nutrition Information

- Calories: 77 calories
- Protein: 2g protein. Diabetic Exchanges: 1 fat
- Total Fat: 5g fat (1g saturated fat)
- Sodium: 68mg sodium
- Fiber: 1g fiber)
- Total Carbohydrate: 7g carbohydrate (0 sugars
- Cholesterol: 1mg cholesterol

## 798. Mediterranean Pasta Salad

*Serving: 2 | Prep: 10mins | Cook: 15mins | Ready in:*

### Ingredients

- 1 cup macaroni
- 2 ounces roasted red bell peppers, diced
- 1/4 cup sliced black olives
- 1/4 cup crumbled feta cheese
- 1 tablespoon olive oil
- 1 tablespoon minced garlic
- 1 teaspoon lemon juice
- salt and pepper to taste

### Direction

- In a cup or small bowl, whisk sliced garlic and olive oil. Reserve.
- Cook pasta until al dente in a big pot of boiling water. Drain off the water.
- Place pasta into a medium mixing bowl, and put in feta cheese, olives and roasted red peppers. Toss with lemon juice and olive oil mixture. Sprinkle pepper and salt to season. Serve right away.

### Nutrition Information

- Calories: 340 calories;
- Sodium: 472
- Total Carbohydrate: 44.2

- Cholesterol: 17
- Protein: 10.3
- Total Fat: 13.6

## 799. Mediterranean Pastry Pinwheels

*Serving: 16 appetizers. | Prep: 20mins | Cook: 15mins | Ready in:*

### Ingredients

- 1 sheet frozen puff pastry, thawed
- 1 package (8 ounces) cream cheese, softened
- 1/4 cup prepared pesto
- 3/4 cup shredded provolone cheese
- 1/2 cup chopped oil-packed sun-dried tomatoes
- 1/2 cup chopped ripe olives
- 1/4 teaspoon pepper

### Direction

- Preheat oven to 400 degrees F. Roll out the puff pastry and form into a 10-inch square.
- Whisk the pesto and cheese until smooth and add in the rest of the ingredients. Place the cheese mixture onto the pastry within 1/2 inch edges, then in jelly-roll style, roll up the pastry. Keep in freezer for 30 minutes. Slice into 16 pieces, crosswise.
- Prepare a baking sheet by lining with a parchment paper and place pastry seam side down; bake for 12 to 15 minutes. For freezing option: Cover the unbaked pastry pieces and freeze on a baking sheet lined with waxed paper until pastry is firm. Place into a resealable plastic freezer bags, then put back in the freezer. To use: Preheat oven to 400 degrees F. Bake the pastries for 15 to 20 minutes until golden brown.

### Nutrition Information

- Calories: 170 calories
- Sodium: 227mg sodium
- Fiber: 2g fiber)
- Total Carbohydrate: 11g carbohydrate (1g sugars
- Cholesterol: 18mg cholesterol
- Protein: 4g protein.
- Total Fat: 13g fat (5g saturated fat)

## 800. Mediterranean Polenta Cups

*Serving: 2 dozen. | Prep: 40mins | Cook: 5mins | Ready in:*

### Ingredients

- 4 cups water
- 1/2 teaspoon salt
- 1 cup yellow cornmeal
- 1/2 teaspoon minced fresh thyme or 1/4 teaspoon dried thyme
- 1/4 teaspoon pepper
- 4 plum tomatoes, finely chopped
- 1/4 cup crumbled feta cheese
- 2 tablespoons chopped fresh basil
- 1 garlic clove, minced

### Direction

- Boil the salt and water in a heavy, big saucepan. Lower the heat to gentle boil and gradually whisk in the cornmeal. Let it cook and, using a wooden spoon, stir for 15 to 20 minutes or until the polenta pulls away cleanly from the sides of the pan and becomes thick. Take it out of the heat and mix in pepper and thyme.
- Scoop heaping tablespoonfuls into the cooking spray coated miniature muffin cups. Make an indentation in the middle of each using the back of a spoon. Put cover and let it chill until it becomes set. In the meantime, mix together the garlic, basil, feta cheese and tomatoes in a small bowl.

- Take off the polenta cups from the mold and put it on ungreased baking tray. Put 1 heaping tablespoon of tomato mixture on top of each and let it broil for 5 to 7 minutes, placed 4 inches from the heat source or till heated completely.

## Nutrition Information

- Calories: 26 calories
- Protein: 1g protein. Diabetic Exchanges: 1/2 starch.
- Total Fat: 0 fat (0 saturated fat)
- Sodium: 62mg sodium
- Fiber: 1g fiber)
- Total Carbohydrate: 5g carbohydrate (0 sugars
- Cholesterol: 1mg cholesterol

## 801. Mediterranean Romaine Salad

*Serving: 6 servings. | Prep: 20mins | Cook: 10mins | Ready in:*

## Ingredients

- 2-1/2 cups cubed French bread
- 1 tablespoon olive oil
- 1 garlic clove, minced
- 1 jar (7-1/2 ounces) marinated quartered artichoke hearts, drained
- 1 cup roasted sweet red peppers, thinly sliced
- 1 medium cucumber, peeled and thinly sliced
- 1 celery rib, sliced
- 1 can (2-1/4 ounces) sliced ripe olives, drained
- 1/3 cup thinly sliced red onion
- 1/2 cup balsamic vinaigrette
- 1 bunch romaine, torn
- 1/4 teaspoon coarsely ground pepper
- Shaved Parmesan cheese, optional

## Direction

- Prepare an ungreased 15x10x1-inch baking pan and put cubed bread onto it. Mix garlic with oil; drizzle over bread cubes and stir until evenly coated. Bring to bake until golden brown, or for 6 to 8 minutes at 400°, stirring 1 time. Put to the side.
- Mix onion, olives, celery, cucumber, red peppers, and artichokes together in a big bowl; pour vinaigrette and stir well to coat. Prepare romaine lettuce in another bowl just before serving. Add croutons and artichoke combination, stir until evenly coated. Add pepper to taste. Garnish with cheese on top if desired.

## Nutrition Information

- Calories: 196 calories
- Fiber: 2g fiber)
- Total Carbohydrate: 18g carbohydrate (6g sugars
- Cholesterol: 0 cholesterol
- Protein: 2g protein.
- Total Fat: 13g fat (2g saturated fat)
- Sodium: 637mg sodium

## 802. Mediterranean Salad Sandwiches

*Serving: 4 servings. | Prep: 15mins | Cook: 15mins | Ready in:*

## Ingredients

- 2 tablespoons olive oil, divided
- 1 garlic clove, minced
- 1/4 teaspoon salt
- 4 large portobello mushrooms, stems removed
- 2 cups spring mix salad greens
- 1 medium tomato, chopped
- 1/2 cup chopped roasted sweet red peppers
- 1/4 cup crumbled reduced-fat feta cheese
- 2 tablespoons chopped pitted Greek olives
- 1 tablespoon red wine vinegar

- 1/2 teaspoon dried oregano
- 4 slices sourdough bread, toasted and halved

## Direction

- Mix together the salt, garlic and 1 tbsp. oil in a small bowl, then brush the mixture on top of the mushrooms.
- Use cooking oil to moisten a paper towel, then coat the grill rack lightly using long-handled tongs. Grill the mushrooms for 6-8 minutes per side over medium heat with a cover until they become soft.
- Mix together the olives, cheese, peppers, tomato and salad greens in a big bowl. Whisk the leftover oil, oregano and vinegar in a small bowl. Pour the mixture on top of the salad mixture, then toss until coated.
- Layer a mushroom and 3/4 cup salad mixture on each of the 4 half slices of toast, then put leftover toast on top.

## Nutrition Information

- Calories: 225 calories
- Protein: 8g protein. Diabetic Exchanges: 2 vegetable
- Total Fat: 9g fat (2g saturated fat)
- Sodium: 495mg sodium
- Fiber: 3g fiber)
- Total Carbohydrate: 26g carbohydrate (4g sugars
- Cholesterol: 3mg cholesterol

### 803. Mediterranean Salsa

*Serving: about 2-1/2 cups. | Prep: 15mins | Cook: 15mins | Ready in:*

## Ingredients

- 2 cups cubed peeled eggplant (1/2-inch cubes)
- 1 cup cubed sweet red pepper (1/2-inch cubes)
- 1 cup cubed green pepper (1/2-inch cubes)
- 1 cup cubed zucchini (1/2-inch cubes)
- 3 garlic cloves, minced
- 2 tablespoons olive oil
- 1 large tomato, cut into 1/2-inch cubes
- 2 tablespoons cider vinegar
- 1 tablespoon dried basil
- 1 teaspoon dried thyme
- 1/2 teaspoon sugar
- 1/2 teaspoon salt
- 1/4 to 1/2 teaspoon coarsely ground pepper
- Toasted bread rounds

## Direction

- Sauté together garlic, zucchini, peppers and eggplant with oil in a big nonstick skillet about 8 minutes. Put in pepper, salt, sugar, thyme, basil, vinegar and tomato, then cook for more 4 to 5 minutes until vegetables are softened. Cover and chill for a minimum of 4 hours, then serve along with toasted bread.

## Nutrition Information

- Calories: 45 calories
- Sodium: 121mg sodium
- Fiber: 1g fiber)
- Total Carbohydrate: 5g carbohydrate (0 sugars
- Cholesterol: 0 cholesterol
- Protein: 1g protein. Diabetic Exchanges: 1 vegetable
- Total Fat: 3g fat (0 saturated fat)

### 804. Mediterranean Vegetable Pitas

*Serving: 4 servings. | Prep: 20mins | Cook: 0mins | Ready in:*

## Ingredients

- 1/4 cup olive oil
- 2 tablespoons balsamic vinegar
- 2 teaspoons grated lemon peel

- 2 teaspoons minced fresh oregano or 1/2 teaspoon dried oregano
- 1/2 teaspoon garlic powder
- 1/2 teaspoon pepper
- 1/8 teaspoon cayenne pepper, optional
- 1 large tomato, chopped
- 1 cup chopped seeded cucumber
- 1/2 cup chopped red onion
- 1 can (2-1/4 ounces) sliced ripe olives, drained
- 2 cups torn romaine
- 8 whole wheat pita pocket halves
- 1/2 cup crumbled feta cheese

### Direction

- Whisk the initial 6 ingredients in a big bowl until combined; mix in cayenne if preferred. Add olives, onion, cucumber and tomato, then toss until coated. Let it chill in the fridge until ready to serve.
- Add the lettuce to the vegetables and toss to blend. Spoon into pita halves and sprinkle cheese on top, then serve.

### Nutrition Information

- Calories: 354 calories
- Cholesterol: 8mg cholesterol
- Protein: 9g protein.
- Total Fat: 19g fat (4g saturated fat)
- Sodium: 580mg sodium
- Fiber: 7g fiber)
- Total Carbohydrate: 39g carbohydrate (5g sugars

### 805. Mexican Salsa Dip

*Serving: 3 cups. | Prep: 10mins | Cook: 5mins | Ready in:*

### Ingredients

- 2 cups fat-free sour cream
- 1 cup salsa
- 4 pita breads (6 inches)

### Direction

- Combine salsa and sour cream in a bowl. Let chill, covered, for at least 2 hours.
- Cut 6 wedges from each pita and divide each wedges into 2 pieces. Transfer into an ungreased baking sheet. Bake for 5-10 minutes at 275° till crisp. Serve with dip.

### Nutrition Information

- Calories: 72 calories
- Fiber: 1g fiber)
- Total Carbohydrate: 13g carbohydrate (3g sugars
- Cholesterol: 6mg cholesterol
- Protein: 3g protein. Diabetic Exchanges: 1 vegetable
- Total Fat: 0 fat (0 saturated fat)
- Sodium: 130mg sodium

### 806. Millet Stuffed Red Peppers

*Serving: 4 servings. | Prep: 40mins | Cook: 55mins | Ready in:*

### Ingredients

- 1/2 cup uncooked millet, rinsed and drained
- 1-1/2 cups vegetable broth
- 4 medium sweet red peppers
- 3/4 cup frozen corn, thawed
- 1 medium onion, finely chopped
- 1/3 cup finely chopped celery
- 1/4 cup chopped walnuts
- 1 green onion, finely chopped
- 1 tablespoon chopped fresh mint or 1 teaspoon dried mint flakes
- 2 teaspoons shredded lemon peel
- 1-1/2 teaspoons fresh chooped oregano or 1/2 teaspoon dried oregano
- 1 garlic clove, minced
- 1/2 teaspoon salt

- 1/4 teaspoon pepper
- 2 tablespoons olive oil

## Direction

- Boil broth and millet in a saucepan. Lower the heat, put a cover on and simmer for 30-35 minutes until the millet has absorbed the broth and is soft. Remove into a big bowl to cool.
- In the meantime, chop the tops off peppers and take out the seeds. Cook peppers in boiling water in a big kettle, about 3-5 minutes. Strain and use cold water to rinse; put aside.
- Fluff the cooled millet using a fork. Add seasonings, green onion, nuts, celery, onion, and corn; stir thoroughly. Put in the sweet peppers using spoon. Drizzle oil over. Put on an oil-coated 11x7-in. baking dish. Put a cover on and bake at 350° until soft, about 55-60 minutes.

## Nutrition Information

- Calories: 281 calories
- Cholesterol: 0 cholesterol
- Protein: 8g protein. Diabetic Exchanges: 2 starch
- Total Fat: 13g fat (1g saturated fat)
- Sodium: 684mg sodium
- Fiber: 6g fiber)
- Total Carbohydrate: 37g carbohydrate (0 sugars

### 807. Mimi's Lentil Medley

*Serving: 8 servings. | Prep: 15mins | Cook: 25mins | Ready in:*

## Ingredients

- 1 cup dried lentils, rinsed
- 2 cups water
- 2 cups sliced fresh mushrooms
- 1 medium cucumber, cubed
- 1 medium zucchini, cubed
- 1 small red onion, chopped
- 1/2 cup chopped soft sun-dried tomato halves (not packed in oil)
- 1/2 cup rice vinegar
- 1/4 cup minced fresh mint
- 3 tablespoons olive oil
- 2 teaspoons honey
- 1 teaspoon dried basil
- 1 teaspoon dried oregano
- 4 cups fresh baby spinach, chopped
- 1 cup (4 ounces) crumbled feta cheese
- 4 bacon strips, cooked and crumbled, optional

## Direction

- Put lentils in a small saucepan. Pour in water; boil. Lower heat; let it simmer while covered till soft or for 20 to 25 minutes. Drain off and wash under cold water.
- Place in a big bowl. Put in tomatoes, onion, zucchini, cucumber and mushrooms. Combine oregano, basil, honey, oil, mint, and vinegar in a small bowl. Sprinkle on top of lentil mixture; coat by tossing. Put in cheese, spinach and bacon if you want; combine by tossing.

## Nutrition Information

- Calories: 225 calories
- Fiber: 5g fiber)
- Total Carbohydrate: 29g carbohydrate (11g sugars
- Cholesterol: 8mg cholesterol
- Protein: 10g protein. Diabetic Exchanges: 1-1/2 fat
- Total Fat: 8g fat (2g saturated fat)
- Sodium: 404mg sodium

### 808. Mini Feta Pizzas

*Serving: 4 servings. | Prep: 10mins | Cook: 10mins | Ready in:*

### Ingredients

- 2 whole wheat English muffins, split and toasted
- 2 tablespoons reduced-fat cream cheese
- 4 teaspoons prepared pesto
- 1/2 cup thinly sliced red onion
- 1/4 cup crumbled feta cheese

### Direction

- Preheat the oven to 425 degrees. Put muffins in a baking sheet.
- Combine pesto and cream cheese; slather over the muffins then top with feta cheese and onion. Bake for 6-8 minutes until pale brown.

### Nutrition Information

- Calories: 136 calories
- Sodium: 294mg sodium
- Fiber: 3g fiber)
- Total Carbohydrate: 16g carbohydrate (4g sugars
- Cholesterol: 11mg cholesterol
- Protein: 6g protein. Diabetic Exchanges: 1 starch
- Total Fat: 6g fat (3g saturated fat)

## 809. Mint Dressing For Fruit

*Serving: about 1 cup. | Prep: 10mins | Cook: 0mins | Ready in:*

### Ingredients

- 1/2 cup sour cream
- 2 tablespoons minced fresh mint
- 2 tablespoons minced fresh cilantro
- 2 tablespoons olive oil
- 2 tablespoons cider vinegar
- 1 teaspoon sugar
- 1 teaspoon lemon juice
- 1/2 teaspoon ground cumin
- Assorted fresh fruit

### Direction

- Combine cumin, lemon juice, sugar, vinegar, oil, cilantro, mint and sour cream in a small bowl. Serve with fruit.

### Nutrition Information

- Calories: 107 calories
- Total Fat: 9g fat (3g saturated fat)
- Sodium: 21mg sodium
- Fiber: 0 fiber)
- Total Carbohydrate: 4g carbohydrate (0 sugars
- Cholesterol: 10mg cholesterol
- Protein: 2g protein. Diabetic Exchanges: 2 fat.

## 810. Minted Cucumber Salad

*Serving: 6 servings. | Prep: 20mins | Cook: 0mins | Ready in:*

### Ingredients

- 2 large cucumbers, chopped
- 2 cups seeded chopped tomatoes
- 1/2 cup chopped fresh mint
- 1/2 cup chopped fresh parsley
- 1/2 cup thinly sliced green onions
- 1/4 cup lemon juice
- 1/4 cup olive oil
- 1 teaspoon salt
- 1/4 teaspoon pepper

### Direction

- Mix the first 5 ingredients together in a big bowl. In a small bowl, combine pepper, salt, oil, and lemon juice. Put on the cucumber mixture; mix to combine.

### Nutrition Information

- Calories: 113 calories
- Fiber: 2g fiber)

- Total Carbohydrate: 7g carbohydrate (4g sugars
- Cholesterol: 0 cholesterol
- Protein: 2g protein. Diabetic Exchanges: 2 fat
- Total Fat: 9g fat (1g saturated fat)
- Sodium: 403mg sodium

## 811. Minted Potato Salad

*Serving: 6 servings. | Prep: 10mins | Cook: 20mins | Ready in:*

### Ingredients

- 4 medium potatoes (about 1 pound)
- 1/2 cup chopped fresh parsley
- 3 tablespoons olive oil
- 2 tablespoons lemon juice
- 1 tablespoon chopped fresh mint
- 1 garlic clove, minced
- 1/2 teaspoon salt, optional
- Pinch pepper

### Direction

- Cook potatoes in boiling water in a saucepan until very soft. Remove skins and cut into cubes. Put in a medium bowl. In a small bowl, mix remaining ingredients together. Pour potatoes in and mix gently. Freeze in the fridge for at least 1 hour before enjoying.

### Nutrition Information

- Calories: 113 calories
- Total Carbohydrate: 12g carbohydrate (0 sugars
- Cholesterol: 0 cholesterol
- Protein: 2g protein. Diabetic Exchanges: 1 starch
- Total Fat: 7g fat (0 saturated fat)
- Sodium: 5mg sodium
- Fiber: 0 fiber)

## 812. Minty Beet Carrot Salad

*Serving: 6 servings. | Prep: 20mins | Cook: 40mins | Ready in:*

### Ingredients

- 12 fresh beets (2 inches each), trimmed
- 6 large carrots, thinly sliced
- 1 cup crumbled goat cheese
- 2 tablespoons minced shallot
- 1/3 cup tarragon vinegar
- 1/3 cup chopped fresh mint
- 1/4 cup olive oil
- 1-1/2 teaspoons sugar
- 1/2 teaspoon salt
- 1/4 teaspoon pepper
- 1/4 cup minced chives

### Direction

- Use a foil to line a baking sheet. Put beets on the foil and use water to drizzle lightly. Wrap the foil securely around the beets. Bake until soft at 350°, or for about 40-45 minutes and let it cool down. Peel the skin and slice the beets into thin pieces.
- In a steamer basket,] put the carrots; put in a saucepan above 1-inch of water. Boil it with a cover on and steam until soft and crunchy, or for about 6-8 minutes.
- Move the beet and carrot slices onto salad plates, piling the slices on each other. Use shallot and cheese to drizzle. Combine pepper, salt, sugar, oil, mint, and vinegar in a small bowl; drizzle over the vegetables. Use chives to sprinkle.

### Nutrition Information

- Calories: 266 calories
- Total Carbohydrate: 20g carbohydrate (14g sugars
- Cholesterol: 22mg cholesterol
- Protein: 9g protein.

- Total Fat: 18g fat (7g saturated fat)
- Sodium: 446mg sodium
- Fiber: 4g fiber)

## 813. Minty Orzo And Peas

*Serving: 6 servings. | Prep: 10mins | Cook: 10mins | Ready in:*

### Ingredients

- 1 cup uncooked orzo pasta
- 1 small onion, finely chopped
- 1 garlic clove, minced
- 2 tablespoons butter
- 2 cups frozen peas
- 1 teaspoon grated lemon peel
- 1/4 teaspoon salt
- 1/8 teaspoon pepper
- 2 tablespoons finely chopped fresh mint

### Direction

- Cook orzo following package directions. Drain and set aside.
- Sauté garlic and onion in butter in a large skillet until soft. Add peas. Cook for 2 minutes or until soft. Add orzo, pepper, salt and lemon peel; heat through. Stir in mint.

### Nutrition Information

- Calories: 200 calories
- Sodium: 194mg sodium
- Fiber: 3g fiber)
- Total Carbohydrate: 33g carbohydrate (0 sugars
- Cholesterol: 10mg cholesterol
- Protein: 7g protein. Diabetic Exchanges: 2 starch
- Total Fat: 5g fat (3g saturated fat)

## 814. Minty Rice Salad

*Serving: 6 servings. | Prep: 10mins | Cook: 0mins | Ready in:*

### Ingredients

- 2 cups cooked brown or wild rice
- 3 medium tomatoes, seeded and finely chopped
- 1 cup fresh or frozen peas
- 1 cucumber, seeded and finely chopped
- 1 green pepper, finely chopped
- 1/2 cup sliced green onions
- 1/2 cup sliced radishes
- 1/3 cup olive oil
- 3 tablespoons lemon juice
- 1/2 teaspoon salt, optional
- 2 tablespoons chopped fresh mint
- 1/4 teaspoon pepper

### Direction

- Mix radishes, green onions, green pepper, cucumber, peas, tomatoes and rice in a large bowl and set aside. Blend the rest of ingredients in a small bowl. Add to veggies and rice and mix well. Refrigerate for a minimum of 1 hour. Serve cool.

### Nutrition Information

- Calories: 231 calories
- Total Fat: 12g fat (0 saturated fat)
- Sodium: 225mg sodium
- Fiber: 0 fiber)
- Total Carbohydrate: 27g carbohydrate (0 sugars
- Cholesterol: 0 cholesterol
- Protein: 5g protein. Diabetic Exchanges: 2 fat

## 815. Mixed Greens And Apple Salad

*Serving: 4 servings. | Prep: 10mins | Cook: 0mins | Ready in:*

### Ingredients

- 5-1/3 cups mixed salad greens
- 2 medium apples, cut into 3/4-inch pieces
- 2 tablespoons crumbled feta cheese
- LEMON HONEY SALAD DRESSING:
- 4 teaspoons lemon juice
- 2-1/2 teaspoons honey
- 3/4 teaspoon fat-free reduced-sugar vanilla yogurt
- 1 teaspoon canola oil
- 1/4 teaspoon minced fresh garlic
- Dash salt
- Dash white pepper
- Dash ground nutmeg

### Direction

- Mix feta cheese, apple, and salad greens together in a big salad bowl. Mix salad dressing ingredients together in a tightly covered jar. Shake well. Sprinkle on the salad, mix to coat.

### Nutrition Information

- Calories: 82 calories
- Total Carbohydrate: 15g carbohydrate (0 sugars
- Cholesterol: 4mg cholesterol
- Protein: 2g protein. Diabetic Exchanges: 1 vegetable
- Total Fat: 3g fat (1g saturated fat)
- Sodium: 107mg sodium
- Fiber: 3g fiber)

## 816. Moroccan Chickpea Stew

*Serving: 4 | Prep: 15mins | Cook: 25mins | Ready in:*

### Ingredients

- 1 tablespoon olive oil
- 1 small onion, chopped
- 2 cloves garlic, minced
- 2 teaspoons ground cumin
- 2 teaspoons ground coriander
- 1/2 teaspoon cayenne pepper, or to taste
- 1 teaspoon garam masala
- 1/2 teaspoon curry powder
- 1 pinch salt
- 3 potatoes, cut into 1/2-inch cubes
- 1 (14.5 ounce) can diced tomatoes, undrained
- 1 cup tomato sauce
- 1 cup golden raisins
- water, or enough to cover
- 1 (14.5 ounce) can chickpeas, drained and rinsed
- 1 bunch kale, ribs removed, chopped
- 1/2 cup chopped fresh cilantro

### Direction

- Heat olive oil in a big pot on medium heat; cook garlic and onion in hot oil for 5-7 minutes till onions are translucent. Mix salt, curry powder, garam masala, cayenne pepper, coriander and cumin into the garlic and onion; cook together for 1 minute till fragrant. Add raisins, tomato sauce, diced tomatoes and potatoes into the pot. Put enough water on mixture to cover; simmer. Cook for 10-15 minutes till potatoes are soft.
- Put kale and chickpeas into the pot; simmer for 3 minutes till kale wilts. Sprinkle cilantro on the stew; take pot off the heat immediately.

### Nutrition Information

- Calories: 476 calories;
- Total Fat: 6.5
- Sodium: 1263
- Total Carbohydrate: 96.1

- Cholesterol: 0
- Protein: 15.7

### 817. Moroccan Stuffed Mushrooms

*Serving: 2 dozen. | Prep: 45mins | Cook: 10mins | Ready in:*

#### Ingredients

- 24 medium fresh mushrooms
- 1/2 cup chopped onion
- 1/3 cup finely shredded carrot
- 1 teaspoon canola oil
- 1 garlic clove, minced
- 1/2 teaspoon salt
- 1/2 teaspoon ground cumin
- 1/4 teaspoon ground coriander
- 3/4 cup vegetable broth
- 2 tablespoons dried currants
- 1/2 cup uncooked couscous
- 2 tablespoons minced fresh parsley
- 2 tablespoons minced fresh mint

#### Direction

- Take the stems from the mushrooms and chop the stems finely; put the caps aside. In a big non-stick skillet, sauté chopped stems, carrot and onion in oil till tender-crisp.
- Put in coriander, cumin, salt and garlic. Cook and whisk for 60 seconds. Put in the currants and broth; boil. Whisk in the couscous. Take out of heat; cover and allow it to rest till the broth has been absorbed or for 5 to 10 minutes. Fluff using the fork. Whisk in the mint and parsley. Stuff to the mushroom caps.
- Arrange onto the baking sheet. Bake at 400 degrees till the mushrooms soften or for 10 to 15 minutes.

#### Nutrition Information

- Calories: 25 calories
- Total Fat: 0 fat (0 saturated fat)
- Sodium: 81mg sodium
- Fiber: 1g fiber)
- Total Carbohydrate: 5g carbohydrate (1g sugars
- Cholesterol: 0 cholesterol
- Protein: 1g protein.

### 818. Moroccan Tapenade

*Serving: 4 cups. | Prep: 25mins | Cook: 0mins | Ready in:*

#### Ingredients

- 10 ounces dried figs
- 3/4 cup tequila
- 2 cups pimiento-stuffed olives
- 1 cup pitted Greek olives
- 1/2 cup pickled hot cherry peppers, seeded and quartered
- 2 shallots, finely chopped
- 3 tablespoons fresh lime juice
- 2 tablespoons olive oil
- 2 tablespoons minced fresh basil
- 2 teaspoons ground cumin
- 2 teaspoons ground coriander
- 1-1/2 teaspoons grated lime zest
- Assorted crackers

#### Direction

- In a food processor, pulse figs until chopped coarsely; move to small bow. Pour in tequila then let it sit for 10 minutes.
- In the meantime, mix shallots, peppers, and olives in a food processor and pulse with cover until chopped coarsely; move to a big bowl. Mix in lime zest, lime juice, coriander, olive oil, cumin, and basil. Drain and press the figs to release any liquid; put figs in the olive mixture. Serve along with crackers.

#### Nutrition Information

- Calories: 67 calories
- Sodium: 293mg sodium
- Fiber: 1g fiber)
- Total Carbohydrate: 8g carbohydrate (5g sugars
- Cholesterol: 0 cholesterol
- Protein: 1g protein.
- Total Fat: 4g fat (0 saturated fat)

## 819. Mushroom Caponata

*Serving: 6 cups. | Prep: 40mins | Cook: 10mins | Ready in:*

### Ingredients

- 2 large green peppers, chopped
- 1 large onion, chopped
- 2 tablespoons butter, divided
- 2 tablespoons olive oil, divided
- 2 pounds fresh mushrooms, coarsely chopped
- 1/2 cup pitted Greek olives, chopped
- 1/4 cup balsamic vinegar
- 1/4 cup tomato paste
- 1 tablespoon sugar
- 1 teaspoon dried oregano
- 1/2 teaspoon salt
- 1/4 teaspoon coarsely ground pepper
- Bagel chips or lightly toasted French bread baguette slices

### Direction

- Sauté onion and green peppers with 1 tbsp. of each oil and butter in a big skillet until turning golden brown, about 10 minutes.
- Put in leftover oil and butter and 1/2 of the mushrooms, then sauté until softened. Take the onion mixture out and set aside. Sauté the leftover mushrooms until softened, then put all back to the pan. Cover and simmer about 2 minutes on medium high heat.
- Put in pepper, salt, oregano, sugar, tomato paste, vinegar and olives. Lower heat, then simmer without a cover until thickened, about 10 minutes.
- Serve at room temperature or warm together with baguette slices or bagel chips.

### Nutrition Information

- Calories: 53 calories
- Cholesterol: 3mg cholesterol
- Protein: 2g protein. Diabetic Exchanges: 1/2 starch
- Total Fat: 3g fat (1g saturated fat)
- Sodium: 107mg sodium
- Fiber: 1g fiber
- Total Carbohydrate: 6g carbohydrate (3g sugars

## 820. Mushroom Polenta Appetizers

*Serving: 2 dozen. | Prep: 20mins | Cook: 15mins | Ready in:*

### Ingredients

- 2 tubes (1 pound each) polenta, cut into 1/2-inch slices
- 3 tablespoons olive oil
- 1/2 pound sliced baby portobello mushrooms
- 1/2 pound sliced fresh shiitake mushrooms
- 1 tablespoon chopped shallot
- 1 tablespoon butter
- 1 garlic clove, minced
- 1/4 cup white wine
- 1 tablespoon minced fresh parsley
- 1/2 teaspoon minced fresh thyme
- 1/2 cup heavy whipping cream
- 1/4 cup grated Parmesan cheese

### Direction

- Arrange polenta on buttered baking sheets. Brush oil over polenta. Bake for 15 to 20

minutes at 425° or until edges turn golden brown.
- In the meantime, stir-fry shallot and mushrooms in butter in a large skillet until tender. Add garlic; stir-fry for another minute. Add thyme, parsley, and wine; stir-fry until liquid has evaporated. Stream in cream. Cook, stirring, until thickened. Add cheese and mix to combine.
- Spread a rounded tablespoon of mushroom mixture on top of each slice of polenta to serve.

## Nutrition Information

- Calories: 75 calories
- Total Fat: 4g fat (2g saturated fat)
- Sodium: 146mg sodium
- Fiber: 1g fiber)
- Total Carbohydrate: 8g carbohydrate (1g sugars
- Cholesterol: 9mg cholesterol
- Protein: 1g protein.

## 821. Navy Bean Tossed Salad

*Serving: 7 servings. | Prep: 10mins | Cook: 0mins | Ready in:*

## Ingredients

- 4 cups torn romaine
- 1 can (15 ounces) navy beans, rinsed and drained
- 1 cup cherry tomatoes, halved
- 1 cup (4 ounces) crumbled reduced-fat feta cheese
- 3/4 cup sliced cucumber
- 1/2 cup red onion rings, halved
- 1/2 cup roasted sweet red peppers, chopped and patted dry
- 2 tablespoons sliced ripe olives, drained
- 1/2 cup fat-free creamy Caesar salad dressing

## Direction

- Mix the first 8 ingredients together in a big salad bowl. Use the dressing to drizzle, toss to coat.

## Nutrition Information

- Calories: 146 calories
- Protein: 10g protein.
- Total Fat: 2g fat (1g saturated fat)
- Sodium: 774mg sodium
- Fiber: 5g fiber)
- Total Carbohydrate: 23g carbohydrate (4g sugars
- Cholesterol: 6mg cholesterol

## 822. Onion Bulgur Salad

*Serving: 8 servings. | Prep: 10mins | Cook: 0mins | Ready in:*

## Ingredients

- 3/4 cup bulgur
- 2 cups boiling water
- 3/4 cup finely chopped red onion
- 1 teaspoon salt
- 1/2 teaspoon ground allspice
- 1 cup diced seeded cucumber
- 1 cup diced seeded tomato
- 1/2 cup minced fresh basil
- 1/2 cup minced fresh parsley
- 1/2 cup chopped green onions
- 1/4 cup minced fresh mint
- 1/4 cup lemon juice

## Direction

- In a bowl, place bulgur; stir in the boiling water. Cover and allow to stand for 1 hour or until liquid is fully absorbed. In the meantime, combine allspice, salt and onion in a large bowl; allow to stand for 30 minutes.

- Drain bulgur, squeeze until dry; add remaining ingredients and bulgur to onion mixture. Gently toss until well combined. Serve or chill in refrigerator.

## Nutrition Information

- Calories: 64 calories
- Protein: 2g protein. Diabetic Exchanges: 1 vegetable
- Total Fat: 0 fat (0 saturated fat)
- Sodium: 302mg sodium
- Fiber: 4g fiber)
- Total Carbohydrate: 14g carbohydrate (0 sugars
- Cholesterol: 0 cholesterol

## 823. Onion Tart

*Serving: 8 | Prep: | Cook: | Ready in:*

### Ingredients

- 1/4 cup butter
- 1 1/2 pounds onions, sliced
- 2 eggs, beaten
- 1 (9 inch) pie crust, baked
- 4 slices bacon

### Direction

- Preheat oven to 350° F (175° C).
- In a big frying pan, melt butter then saute onions till soft. Take away from heat. In a large and deep frying pan, place the bacon. Cook over medium high heat till equally brown. Drain, crumble then leave aside.
- Stir in eggs.
- Spread into the prepared shell then bake at 350° F (175° C) for around 20 minutes. Top with bacon. Can be used cold or warm.

## Nutrition Information

- Calories: 248 calories;
- Sodium: 280
- Total Carbohydrate: 16
- Cholesterol: 71
- Protein: 4.9
- Total Fat: 18.6

## 824. Onion Trio Salad

*Serving: 2 servings. | Prep: 20mins | Cook: 5mins | Ready in:*

### Ingredients

- 6 fresh pearl onions
- 1 tablespoon water
- 1/4 cup chopped red onion
- 1/4 cup chopped cucumber
- 1/4 cup chopped sweet red pepper
- 4 cherry tomatoes, quartered
- 3 green onions, cut into 1-inch pieces
- GREEK VINAIGRETTE:
- 1 tablespoon olive oil
- 1 tablespoon red wine vinegar
- 1 garlic clove, minced
- 3/4 teaspoon dried oregano
- 1/4 teaspoon salt
- 1/8 teaspoon pepper
- 1/4 cup crumbled feta cheese

### Direction

- In a microwave-safe bowl, place pearl onions and water. Cover and microwave on high for 1 to 2 minutes or until onions become crisp-tender; drain and peel.
- Combine pearl onions, green onions, tomatoes, red pepper, cucumber and red onion in a serving bowl. In a small bowl, whisk together pepper, salt, oregano, garlic, vinegar and oil.
- Add dressing to vegetable mixture and toss until well coated. Add feta cheese on top just before serving.

### Nutrition Information

- Calories: 150 calories
- Protein: 4g protein. Diabetic Exchanges: 2 vegetable
- Total Fat: 9g fat (2g saturated fat)
- Sodium: 440mg sodium
- Fiber: 3g fiber)
- Total Carbohydrate: 13g carbohydrate (5g sugars
- Cholesterol: 8mg cholesterol

### 825. Onions And Spice, Parsley And Rice

*Serving: 6 servings. | Prep: 15mins | Cook: 30mins | Ready in:*

#### Ingredients

- 1-3/4 cups thinly sliced green onion
- 1-1/2 cups coarsely chopped onion
- 2/3 cup uncooked long grain rice
- 1/2 cup minced fresh parsley
- 2 tablespoons butter
- 1 teaspoon salt
- 1 teaspoon dill weed
- 1/2 teaspoon dried mint
- 1/4 teaspoon white pepper
- 1-1/2 cups water
- 3 tablespoons lemon juice
- 1/2 teaspoon grated lemon peel

#### Direction

- Cook parsley, green onions, rice, and onions for 3 minutes in a big non-stick pan until evenly coated in butter. Mix in pepper, salt, mint, dill, lemon peel, lemon juice, and water; boil. Lower heat; let it simmer for 16-18 minutes with cover until the rice is tender. Use a fork to fluff the rice.

### Nutrition Information

- Calories: 144 calories
- Total Carbohydrate: 24g carbohydrate (0 sugars
- Cholesterol: 10mg cholesterol
- Protein: 3g protein. Diabetic Exchanges: 1 starch
- Total Fat: 4g fat (2g saturated fat)
- Sodium: 442mg sodium
- Fiber: 2g fiber)

### 826. Orange 'n' Red Onion Salad

*Serving: 4 servings. | Prep: 15mins | Cook: 0mins | Ready in:*

#### Ingredients

- 4 cups torn romaine
- 2 medium navel oranges, peeled and sectioned
- 1 small red onion, sliced and separated into rings
- 1/4 cup olive oil
- 3 tablespoons red wine vinegar
- 1 teaspoon sugar
- 1/4 teaspoon salt
- 1/8 teaspoon pepper

#### Direction

- Distribute onion, oranges, and romaine over a serving platter. Combine remaining ingredients in a small bowl and pour over the salad.

### Nutrition Information

- Calories: 173 calories
- Total Carbohydrate: 13g carbohydrate (9g sugars
- Cholesterol: 0 cholesterol
- Protein: 2g protein.
- Total Fat: 14g fat (2g saturated fat)
- Sodium: 153mg sodium

- Fiber: 3g fiber)

### 827. Orange Couscous

*Serving: 8 servings. | Prep: 15mins | Cook: 0mins | Ready in:*

### Ingredients

- 1 cup orange juice
- 1 cup water
- 1 teaspoon ground cumin
- 1 package (10 ounces) couscous
- 2 tablespoons olive oil
- 2 tablespoons lime juice
- 2 tablespoons reduced-sodium soy sauce
- 1/4 cup minced fresh cilantro
- 2 tablespoons minced fresh basil or 2 teaspoons dried basil
- 2 tablespoons minced chives
- 1 teaspoon minced fresh gingerroot
- 1/4 teaspoon salt
- 1 can (11 ounces) mandarin oranges, drained
- 1/4 cup slivered almonds, toasted

### Direction

- Bring cumin, water, and orange juice to a boil in a large saucepan. Mix in couscous; put off the heat. Put the lid on and allow to stand until liquid is absorbed, or for 5 minutes; fluff using a fork. Pour into a large bowl; allow to cool.
- Stir soy sauce, lime juice, and oil together in a small bowl. Mix in salt, ginger, chives, basil, and cilantro. Pour mixture over the couscous and stir until evenly coated. Add almonds and oranges; stir gently to combine. Place in the fridge until serving.

### Nutrition Information

- Calories: 206 calories
- Total Carbohydrate: 34g carbohydrate (8g sugars
- Cholesterol: 0 cholesterol
- Protein: 6g protein. Diabetic Exchanges: 1-1/2 starch
- Total Fat: 6g fat (1g saturated fat)
- Sodium: 231mg sodium
- Fiber: 2g fiber)

### 828. Orange Streusel Muffins

*Serving: 8 muffins. | Prep: 20mins | Cook: 20mins | Ready in:*

### Ingredients

- 1-3/4 cups all-purpose flour
- 1/4 cup sugar
- 2-1/2 teaspoons baking powder
- 1/2 teaspoon salt
- 1 egg
- 3/4 cup milk
- 1/3 cup vegetable oil
- 1/4 cup orange marmalade
- STREUSEL:
- 2 tablespoons all-purpose flour
- 2 tablespoons brown sugar
- 1 teaspoon ground cinnamon
- 1 tablespoon cold butter

### Direction

- Mix together the salt, sugar, baking powder and flour in a bowl. In a different bowl, beat the egg; add milk and oil into the beaten egg. Stir this mixture into the dry mix till everything is just moistened. Fill the batter up to 1/2 full into eight muffin cups that are greased or lined with paper. Add 1 teaspoon marmalade on top of each one. Put the remaining batter on top. To make the streusel, mix together the cinnamon, brown sugar and flour in a small bowl. Cut butter into the mix till crumbly; sprinkle it on top of batter. Bake until muffins test done, at 400° for about 20-25 minutes.

## Nutrition Information

- Calories: 285 calories
- Sodium: 314mg sodium
- Fiber: 1g fiber)
- Total Carbohydrate: 40g carbohydrate (18g sugars
- Cholesterol: 34mg cholesterol
- Protein: 5g protein.
- Total Fat: 12g fat (3g saturated fat)

## 829. Orzo Vegetable Salad

*Serving: 6 servings. | Prep: 20mins | Cook: 10mins | Ready in:*

## Ingredients

- 1/2 cup uncooked orzo pasta
- 3 plum tomatoes, chopped
- 1 cup marinated quartered artichoke hearts, chopped
- 1 cup coarsely chopped fresh spinach
- 2 green onions, chopped
- 1/2 cup crumbled feta cheese
- 1 tablespoon capers, drained
- DRESSING:
- 1/3 cup olive oil
- 4 teaspoons lemon juice
- 1 tablespoon minced fresh tarragon or 1 teaspoon dried tarragon
- 2 teaspoons grated lemon peel
- 2 teaspoons rice vinegar
- 1/2 teaspoon salt
- 1/4 teaspoon pepper

## Direction

- Cook orzo following package directions.
- In the meantime, combine capers, cheese, onions, spinach, artichokes and tomatoes in a large bowl. Whisk together the dressing ingredients in a small bowl.
- Drain orzo and wash under cold water. Add to vegetable mixture.
- Drizzle dressing on top of salad; toss until well coated. Refrigerate until ready to serve.

## Nutrition Information

- Calories: 259 calories
- Sodium: 460mg sodium
- Fiber: 2g fiber)
- Total Carbohydrate: 18g carbohydrate (2g sugars
- Cholesterol: 5mg cholesterol
- Protein: 4g protein.
- Total Fat: 19g fat (4g saturated fat)

## 830. Orzo With Feta And Almonds

*Serving: 12 servings. | Prep: 20mins | Cook: 15mins | Ready in:*

## Ingredients

- 1 package (16 ounces) orzo pasta
- 1 large onion, chopped
- 8 tablespoons olive oil, divided
- 2 cups (8 ounces) crumbled feta cheese
- 1 cup sliced almonds, toasted
- 1/2 cup dried currants
- 3 tablespoons minced fresh parsley
- 2 tablespoons minced fresh oregano or 2 teaspoons dried oregano
- 2 tablespoons lemon juice
- 2 teaspoons grated lemon peel
- 1/4 teaspoon salt
- 1/4 teaspoon pepper

## Direction

- Following the package directions, cook the orzo. At the same time, sauté onion in a

tablespoon of oil in a large skillet until getting tender. Let drain the orzo; bring into a large bowl. Add in the onion, oregano, parsley, currants, almonds, and cheese.
- Whisk the remaining olive oil, pepper, salt, lemon juice, and peel in a small bowl. Lightly sprinkle on the orzo mixture; coat by tossing.

## Nutrition Information

- Calories: 336 calories
- Protein: 10g protein.
- Total Fat: 17g fat (4g saturated fat)
- Sodium: 234mg sodium
- Fiber: 3g fiber)
- Total Carbohydrate: 37g carbohydrate (6g sugars
- Cholesterol: 10mg cholesterol

## 831. Orzo With Spinach And Pine Nuts

*Serving: 12 servings (3/4 cup each). | Prep: 10mins | Cook: 25mins | Ready in:*

## Ingredients

- 1 package (16 ounces) orzo pasta
- 1 cup pine nuts
- 1 garlic clove, minced
- 1/2 teaspoon dried basil
- 1/2 teaspoon crushed red pepper flakes
- 1/4 cup olive oil
- 1 tablespoon butter
- 2 packages (6 ounces each) fresh baby spinach
- 1 teaspoon salt
- 1/4 teaspoon pepper
- 1/4 cup balsamic vinegar
- 2 cups (8 ounces) crumbled feta cheese
- 1 large tomato, finely chopped

## Direction

- Cook pasta following package directions in a large saucepan.
- In the meantime, cook pepper flakes, basil, garlic and pine nuts in butter and oil in a Dutch oven over medium heat just until nuts turn to light brown color.
- Add pepper, salt and spinach; cook, stirring frequently, for 4 to 5 minutes or just until spinach is wilted. Move to a large bowl.
- Drain pasta. Stir into spinach mixture. Pour dressing on top; sprinkle with tomato and cheese.

## Nutrition Information

- Calories: 313 calories
- Protein: 12g protein.
- Total Fat: 15g fat (4g saturated fat)
- Sodium: 411mg sodium
- Fiber: 3g fiber)
- Total Carbohydrate: 33g carbohydrate (3g sugars
- Cholesterol: 13mg cholesterol

## 832. Orzo With Zucchini And Feta

*Serving: 5 servings. | Prep: 5mins | Cook: 15mins | Ready in:*

## Ingredients

- 1 cup uncooked orzo pasta
- 1 medium zucchini, cut into 1/4-inch pieces
- 2 tablespoons water
- 3/4 cup crumbled feta cheese
- 4 teaspoons olive oil
- 2 teaspoons dried oregano
- Salt and pepper to taste

## Direction

- Cook orzo as directed on the package. As orzo cooks, combine water and zucchini in a small

- microwaveable bowl. Cook, covered, on high power until crisp-tender for 1 minute; drain off water.
- Drain off water; transfer to a large bowl. Add pepper, salt, oregano, oil, feta cheese, and zucchini; stir to coat. Serve pasta warm or chilled.

## Nutrition Information

- Calories: 216 calories
- Total Carbohydrate: 32g carbohydrate (2g sugars
- Cholesterol: 6mg cholesterol
- Protein: 9g protein. Diabetic Exchanges: 2 starch
- Total Fat: 6g fat (2g saturated fat)
- Sodium: 226mg sodium
- Fiber: 2g fiber)

## 833. Oven Roasted Veggies

*Serving: 8 servings. | Prep: 15mins | Cook: 45mins | Ready in:*

## Ingredients

- 10 small unpeeled potatoes (about 1-3/4 pounds), quartered
- 2 cups whole baby carrots
- 1 small onion, cut into wedges
- 1/4 cup olive oil
- 2 tablespoons lemon juice
- 3 garlic cloves, minced
- 1 teaspoon dried rosemary, crushed
- 1 teaspoon dried oregano
- 1/2 teaspoon salt
- 1/2 teaspoon cayenne pepper
- 1 medium green pepper, cut into 1/2-inch strips
- 1 medium sweet red pepper, cut into 1/2-inch strips

## Direction

- In an ungreased 13x9-inch baking dish, put onion, carrots, and potatoes. Mix cayenne, oil, salt, lemon juice, oregano, rosemary, and garlic in a small bowl; sprinkle on veggies and gently toss to coat.
- Bake for half an hour in 450 degrees oven without cover. Add pepper strips on top. Bake for another 15 minutes until the veggies are tender.

## Nutrition Information

- Calories: 196 calories
- Total Carbohydrate: 32g carbohydrate (5g sugars
- Cholesterol: 0 cholesterol
- Protein: 3g protein.
- Total Fat: 7g fat (1g saturated fat)
- Sodium: 184mg sodium
- Fiber: 4g fiber)

## 834. Parsley Tabbouleh

*Serving: 4 | Prep: | Cook: 35mins | Ready in:*

## Ingredients

- 1 small cucumber, peeled, seeded and diced
- 4 scallions, thinly sliced
- 1 cup water
- ½ cup bulgur
- ¼ cup lemon juice
- 2 tablespoons extra-virgin olive oil
- ½ teaspoon minced garlic
- ¼ teaspoon salt
- ¼ cup chopped fresh mint
- 2 tomatoes, diced
- Freshly ground pepper, to taste
- 2 cups finely chopped flat-leaf parsley, (about 2 bunches)

## Direction

- In a small saucepan, mix bulgur with water. Boil it completely, take away from the heat and put a cover on, let it sit for 25 minutes or as the package directs until the bulgur is soft and has soaked up the water. If there is any liquid left, use a fine-mesh sieve to strain the bulgur.
- In a small bowl, mix together pepper, salt, garlic, oil, and lemon juice. Add scallions, cucumber, tomatoes, mint, and parsley into the bulgur. Add the dressing and toss. Refrigerate for a minimum of 1 hour to enjoy cold or you can enjoy at room temperature.

## Nutrition Information

- Calories: 162 calories;
- Saturated Fat: 1
- Sodium: 175
- Cholesterol: 0
- Total Carbohydrate: 21
- Sugar: 3
- Total Fat: 8
- Fiber: 5
- Protein: 4

### 835. Pasta With Tomatoes And White Beans

*Serving: 4 servings. | Prep: 5mins | Cook: 15mins | Ready in:*

## Ingredients

- 3 cups uncooked penne pasta
- 2 cans (14-1/2 ounces each) Italian diced tomatoes
- 1 can (15 ounces) white kidney or cannellini beans, rinsed and drained
- 1 package (10 ounces) fresh spinach, chopped
- 1/2 cup finely crumbled feta cheese

## Direction

- Following the package instructions, cook the pasta. At the same time, boil the beans and tomatoes in a large skillet. Turn down the heat; uncover and allow to simmer for 10 minutes.
- Add the spinach; allow to simmer and stir occasionally until wilted for 2 minutes. Drain the pasta; put cheese and the tomato mixture on top.

## Nutrition Information

- Calories: 364 calories
- Sodium: 722mg sodium
- Fiber: 9g fiber)
- Total Carbohydrate: 65g carbohydrate (8g sugars
- Cholesterol: 8mg cholesterol
- Protein: 17g protein.
- Total Fat: 4g fat (2g saturated fat)

### 836. Peachy Tossed Salad With Poppy Seed Dressing

*Serving: 8 servings. | Prep: 20mins | Cook: 0mins | Ready in:*

## Ingredients

- 1 package (10 ounces) ready-to-serve salad greens
- 1 to 2 medium peaches, cut into wedges
- 1/2 cup thinly sliced cucumber
- 1/2 cup crumbled feta cheese
- 1/4 cup thinly sliced red onion, separated into rings
- CREAMY POPPY SEED DRESSING:
- 2/3 cup canola oil
- 1/4 cup sugar
- 1/4 cup white vinegar
- 1/4 cup sour cream
- 2 teaspoons poppy seeds
- 1/2 teaspoon salt

### Direction

- Combine onion, feta cheese, cucumber, peaches and greens in a large salad bowl. Whisk the dressing ingredients in a small bowl. Serve dressing with salad.

### Nutrition Information

- Calories:
- Total Fat:
- Sodium:
- Fiber:
- Total Carbohydrate:
- Cholesterol:
- Protein:

## 837. Pecan Pear Tossed Salad

*Serving: 8 servings. | Prep: 20mins | Cook: 0mins | Ready in:*

### Ingredients

- 2 tablespoons fresh raspberries
- 3/4 cup olive oil
- 3 tablespoons cider vinegar
- 2 tablespoons plus 1 teaspoon sugar
- 1/4 to 1/2 teaspoon pepper
- SALAD:
- 4 medium ripe pears, thinly sliced
- 2 teaspoons lemon juice
- 8 cups torn salad greens
- 2/3 cup pecan halves, toasted
- 1/2 cup fresh raspberries
- 1/3 cup crumbled feta cheese

### Direction

- Press raspberries through a sieve to drain off all the juice, saving the juice. Throw away the seeds. In a bowl, whisk together saved raspberries juice, pepper, sugar, vinegar and oil. Toss lemon juice and pear slices together; drain. Combine raspberries, pecans, pears and salad greens in a salad bowl. Add cheese on top and drizzle with dressing.

### Nutrition Information

- Calories: 337 calories
- Sodium: 82mg sodium
- Fiber: 5g fiber)
- Total Carbohydrate: 21g carbohydrate (14g sugars
- Cholesterol: 4mg cholesterol
- Protein: 3g protein.
- Total Fat: 28g fat (4g saturated fat)

## 838. Penne From Heaven

*Serving: 5 servings. | Prep: 10mins | Cook: 15mins | Ready in:*

### Ingredients

- 6 ounces uncooked penne pasta
- 1/2 pound fresh mushrooms, sliced
- 1 tablespoon olive oil
- 1 can (14-1/2 ounces) diced tomatoes, undrained
- 1 tablespoon minced fresh basil or 1 teaspoon dried basil
- 1/4 teaspoon salt
- 1/3 cup crumbled feta cheese

### Direction

- Following the package instructions, cook the pasta. At the same time, sauté the mushrooms in oil in a large skillet for 5 minutes. Add the salt, basil, and tomatoes; stir and cook for 5 minutes. Let the pasta drain, then transfer into the skillet. Add cheese and stir; cook thoroughly.

### Nutrition Information

- Calories: 188 calories

- Cholesterol: 9mg cholesterol
- Protein: 7g protein. Diabetic Exchanges: 2 starch
- Total Fat: 5g fat (2g saturated fat)
- Sodium: 335mg sodium
- Fiber: 3g fiber)
- Total Carbohydrate: 28g carbohydrate (0 sugars

## 839. Penne With Caramelized Onions

*Serving: 4 servings. | Prep: 5mins | Cook: 25mins | Ready in:*

### Ingredients

- 2 cups uncooked penne pasta
- 1/4 cup pine nuts
- 2 garlic cloves, minced
- 1 tablespoon butter
- 1 large onion, chopped
- 2 tablespoons olive oil
- 16 pitted Greek olives, coarsely chopped
- 1/4 teaspoon salt
- 1/4 teaspoon dried basil
- 1/4 teaspoon dried oregano
- 1/4 teaspoon pepper
- 3/4 cup crumbled feta cheese

### Direction

- Cook pasta as directed on the package. While pasta is cooking, sauté garlic and pine nuts in butter in a small skillet until golden brown; put to one side.
- Sauté onion in oil over medium heat in a large skillet, stirring constantly, until golden brown for 10 to 15 minutes. Turn heat to low. Mix in pepper, oregano, basil, salt, and olives. Drain pasta; put into onion mixture. Mix in pine nut mixture and feta cheese.

### Nutrition Information

- Calories: 374 calories
- Total Carbohydrate: 33g carbohydrate (4g sugars
- Cholesterol: 19mg cholesterol
- Protein: 11g protein.
- Total Fat: 22g fat (6g saturated fat)
- Sodium: 627mg sodium
- Fiber: 3g fiber)

## 840. Pepperoncini Pasta Salad

*Serving: 6 servings. | Prep: 15mins | Cook: 0mins | Ready in:*

### Ingredients

- 3 cups cooked small shell pasta
- 1 cup halved cherry tomatoes
- 1 cup whole pitted ripe olives
- 1 cup pepperoncini, thinly sliced
- 3 tablespoons olive oil
- 3 tablespoons lemon juice
- 1 garlic clove, minced
- 1 teaspoon minced fresh oregano or 1/4 teaspoon dried oregano
- 1 teaspoon salt
- 1/4 teaspoon pepper

### Direction

- Combine pepperoncini, olives, tomatoes and pasta in a bowl. In a small bowl, combine pepper, salt, oregano, garlic, lemon juice and oil. Add to pasta mixture and toss until evenly coated. Cover and chill for a minimum of 3 hours.

### Nutrition Information

- Calories: 184 calories
- Cholesterol: 0 cholesterol
- Protein: 3g protein. Diabetic Exchanges: 2 fat
- Total Fat: 10g fat (1g saturated fat)
- Sodium: 936mg sodium

- Fiber: 1g fiber)
- Total Carbohydrate: 20g carbohydrate (0 sugars

### 841. Persimmon Breakfast Parfaits

*Serving: 4 servings. | Prep: 20mins | Cook: 0mins | Ready in:*

#### Ingredients

- 2 cups plain yogurt
- 1 cup mashed ripe persimmon pulp
- 4 teaspoons honey
- 1/4 teaspoon ground ginger
- 1/4 teaspoon ground cardamom
- 1 medium Asian pear, chopped
- 2 cups granola
- 1 ripe persimmon, peeled and sliced
- 1/4 cup pomegranate seeds
- 1/4 cup chopped pistachios

#### Direction

- Mix persimmon pulp, yogurt, honey, cardamom and ginger. Scoop quarter cup into each four parfait glasses. Top each glass with quarter cup granola and pear. Make layer starting with quarter cup yogurt mixture, persimmon slices and end with the rest of the granola. Garnish with the remaining yogurt mixture sprinkled with pistachios and pomegranate seeds.

#### Nutrition Information

- Calories: 445 calories
- Total Carbohydrate: 72g carbohydrate (33g sugars
- Cholesterol: 16mg cholesterol
- Protein: 17g protein.
- Total Fat: 16g fat (3g saturated fat)
- Sodium: 111mg sodium

- Fiber: 15g fiber)

### 842. Pesto Buttermilk Dressing

*Serving: 1-3/4 cups. | Prep: 10mins | Cook: 0mins | Ready in:*

#### Ingredients

- 2/3 cup buttermilk
- 1/2 cup fat-free plain Greek yogurt
- 1/2 cup prepared pesto
- 1/4 cup shredded Parmesan cheese
- 1 tablespoon white wine vinegar
- 1 tablespoon grated lemon peel
- 1 garlic clove, minced
- 1/2 teaspoon coarsely ground pepper
- 1/8 teaspoon salt

#### Direction

- Find a jar with a tight-fitting lid and put all ingredients inside the jar then shake it well. Put in the fridge for an hour. Shake the dressing when you are ready to serve.

#### Nutrition Information

- Calories: 50 calories
- Cholesterol: 2mg cholesterol
- Protein: 2g protein. Diabetic Exchanges: 1 fat.
- Total Fat: 4g fat (1g saturated fat)
- Sodium: 165mg sodium
- Fiber: 0 fiber)
- Total Carbohydrate: 2g carbohydrate (1g sugars

### 843. Pesto Egg Wraps

*Serving: 2 servings. | Prep: 10mins | Cook: 5mins | Ready in:*

### Ingredients

- 1/4 cup oil-packed sun-dried tomatoes, chopped
- 4 large eggs, lightly beaten
- 2 tablespoons crumbled feta cheese
- 2 tablespoons prepared pesto
- 2 whole wheat tortillas (8 inches), warmed

### Direction

- On moderate heat, heat a big skillet. Put in tomatoes, then cook and stir until heated through. Add in eggs, then cook and stir until no liquid egg remains and eggs are thickened. Take away from the heat, then sprinkle over with cheese.
- Spread across center of each tortilla with 1 tbsp. of pesto, then put egg mixture on top. Fold bottom, as well as sides of tortilla over the filling and roll up.

### Nutrition Information

- Calories: 407 calories
- Total Carbohydrate: 27g carbohydrate (2g sugars
- Cholesterol: 432mg cholesterol
- Protein: 21g protein.
- Total Fat: 23g fat (6g saturated fat)
- Sodium: 533mg sodium
- Fiber: 3g fiber)

## 844. Pesto Pita Appetizers

*Serving: 2 servings. | Prep: 5mins | Cook: 10mins | Ready in:*

### Ingredients

- 1 whole pita bread (6 inches)
- 3 tablespoons prepared pesto
- 3 tablespoons grated Parmesan cheese

### Direction

- Divide the pita bread into 2 rounds. Spread pesto all over then scatter cheese on top. Slice each circle to 6 wedges then arrange on an ungreased baking sheet. Bake for 10-12 mins in a 350 degrees F oven or until crisp. Serve warm.

### Nutrition Information

- Calories: 233 calories
- Total Fat: 13g fat (4g saturated fat)
- Sodium: 479mg sodium
- Fiber: 1g fiber)
- Total Carbohydrate: 19g carbohydrate (1g sugars
- Cholesterol: 13mg cholesterol
- Protein: 10g protein.

## 845. Picnic Salad Skewers

*Serving: 8 servings. | Prep: 15mins | Cook: 15mins | Ready in:*

### Ingredients

- 8 unpeeled small red potatoes
- 8 fresh pearl onions
- 1 tablespoon water
- 1 medium sweet red pepper, cut into 1-inch pieces
- 1 medium green pepper, cut into 1-inch pieces
- 16 cherry tomatoes
- 1 small zucchini, cut into 1/4-inch slices
- VINAIGRETTE:
- 2/3 cup olive oil
- 1/3 cup red wine vinegar
- 2 garlic cloves, minced
- 1 tablespoon dried oregano
- 1 teaspoon salt
- 1/4 teaspoon pepper
- 4 ounces crumbled feta cheese, optional

### Direction

- Put potatoes with water to cover in a saucepan; boil. Cook till softened or for 10 to 13 minutes; drain off. Transfer water and onions into a microwave-safe bowl. Cover up and microwave till tender-crisp or for one to one and a half minutes on high heat; drain off.
- Alternately thread zucchini, tomatoes, pepper, onions and potatoes on wooden/metal skewers. Add into a big resealable plastic bag or big shallow plastic container.
- Combine pepper, salt, oregano, garlic, vinegar and oil in a bowl. Put on top of vegetable skewers. Let it marinate for at least 60 minutes, flipping often. Drizzle with feta cheese if you want.

## Nutrition Information

- Calories:
- Sodium:
- Fiber:
- Total Carbohydrate:
- Cholesterol:
- Protein:
- Total Fat:

### 846. Picnic Vegetable Salad

*Serving: 18 servings. | Prep: 30mins | Cook: 0mins | Ready in:*

## Ingredients

- 3 cups fresh broccoli florets
- 3 cups fresh cauliflowerets
- 2 cups cherry tomatoes, halved
- 2 medium cucumbers, cut into chunks
- 1 each medium green, sweet yellow and red pepper, cut into chunks
- 6 green onions, thinly sliced
- 1 can (6 ounces) pitted ripe olives, drained and halved
- 1 bottle (16 ounces) Greek vinaigrette
- 1 cup (4 ounces) crumbled feta cheese

## Direction

- Combine olives, green onions, peppers, cucumbers, tomatoes, cauliflowers and broccoli in a large bowl. Pour dressing over salad mixture and toss until well coated. Refrigerate until serving. Add cheese on top just before serving.

## Nutrition Information

- Calories: 147 calories
- Cholesterol: 3mg cholesterol
- Protein: 3g protein.
- Total Fat: 12g fat (2g saturated fat)
- Sodium: 438mg sodium
- Fiber: 2g fiber)
- Total Carbohydrate: 7g carbohydrate (3g sugars

### 847. Portobello Pockets

*Serving: 8 servings. | Prep: 30mins | Cook: 10mins | Ready in:*

## Ingredients

- 1/4 cup water
- 3 tablespoons lime juice
- 2 tablespoons canola oil
- 1 tablespoon Italian seasoning
- 1 teaspoon dried minced garlic
- 1/2 teaspoon dried celery flakes
- 1/4 teaspoon salt
- 1/4 teaspoon ground cumin
- 1/4 teaspoon ground nutmeg
- 1/4 teaspoon pepper
- 1/8 teaspoon cayenne pepper
- 1 pound sliced baby portobello mushrooms
- 1 each medium sweet yellow and red pepper, thinly sliced
- 1 medium red onion, thinly sliced
- 2 small zucchini, cut into 1/4-inch slices

- 1 cup shredded reduced-fat Mexican cheese blend
- 8 pita breads (6 inches), cut in half

### Direction

- Mix together the initial 11 ingredients in a big resealable bag, then add the zucchini, onion, peppers and mushrooms. Seal the bag and turn to coat and let it chill in the fridge overnight.
- Use cooking spray to coat a big nonstick frying pan, then cook and stir the vegetable mixture for 6 to 8 minutes on medium high heat or until it becomes crisp-tender. Mix in cheese, then cook for 2 to 3 minutes more or until the cheese melts. Use 1/2 cup vegetable cheese mixture to stuff each pita half.

### Nutrition Information

- Calories: 272 calories
- Protein: 12g protein. Diabetic Exchanges: 2 starch
- Total Fat: 8g fat (2g saturated fat)
- Sodium: 500mg sodium
- Fiber: 3g fiber)
- Total Carbohydrate: 41g carbohydrate (4g sugars
- Cholesterol: 10mg cholesterol

## 848. Potato Tossed Salad

*Serving: 8 servings. | Prep: 15mins | Cook: 0mins | Ready in:*

### Ingredients

- 1/2 cup olive oil
- 2 tablespoons lemon juice
- 2 teaspoons dried oregano
- 1 garlic clove, minced
- 1/4 teaspoon salt
- 1/2 pound small red potatoes, cooked, peeled and sliced
- 6 cups torn mixed salad greens
- 2 small tomatoes, cut into wedges
- 1 small cucumber, thinly sliced
- 1 small red onion, thinly sliced into rings
- 1/2 cup crumbled feta cheese

### Direction

- Whisk together the first five ingredients in a small bowl. Add potatoes; toss gently. Cover and chill for 1 hour. Drain, saving the dressing.
- In a large bowl, place salad greens. Add potatoes, cheese, onion, cucumber and tomatoes on top. Drizzle with the saved dressing.

### Nutrition Information

- Calories: 177 calories
- Total Carbohydrate: 9g carbohydrate (2g sugars
- Cholesterol: 4mg cholesterol
- Protein: 3g protein.
- Total Fat: 15g fat (3g saturated fat)
- Sodium: 156mg sodium
- Fiber: 2g fiber)

## 849. Pressure Cooker Frittata Provencal

*Serving: 6 servings. | Prep: 30mins | Cook: 35mins | Ready in:*

### Ingredients

- 1 tablespoon olive oil
- 1 medium Yukon Gold potato, peeled and sliced
- 1 small onion, thinly sliced
- 1/2 teaspoon smoked paprika
- 1 cup water
- 12 large eggs

- 1 teaspoon minced fresh thyme or 1/4 teaspoon dried thyme
- 1 teaspoon hot pepper sauce
- 1/2 teaspoon salt
- 1/4 teaspoon pepper
- 1 log (4 ounces) crumbled fresh goat cheese, divided
- 1/2 cup chopped sun-dried tomatoes (not packed in oil)

### Direction

- On a 6-quart electric pressure cooker, choose the sauté mode then turn to high heat; heat oil. Cook and stir onion and potato for 5-7mins until the potato is slightly brown. Mix in paprika; move the mixture to a lightly oiled 1 1/2-quart soufflé or round baking dish. Clean the pressure cooker then add water.
- Beat the next 5 ingredients in a big bowl; mix in 2 oz. of cheese then add on top of the potato mixture. Put the remaining goat cheese and tomatoes on top. Use foil to cover the dish then put on a trivet with handles. Lower into the pressure cooker then lock the lid; close the vent.
- Choose manual setting then turn to high; put the timer on 35 mins. Once done, naturally release the pressure for 10 mins. Allow the remaining pressure to release using quick-release following the manufacturer's instructions.

### Nutrition Information

- Calories: 245 calories
- Fiber: 2g fiber)
- Total Carbohydrate: 12g carbohydrate (4g sugars
- Cholesterol: 385mg cholesterol
- Protein: 15g protein.
- Total Fat: 14g fat (5g saturated fat)
- Sodium: 12mg sodium

## 850. Pumpkin Hummus

*Serving: 20 | Prep: 15mins | Cook: 1hours35mins | Ready in:*

### Ingredients

- 1 3/4 cups dry garbanzo beans
- 1 (15 ounce) can pumpkin puree
- 5 fluid ounces lemon juice
- 1/3 cup extra-virgin olive oil
- 1/2 cup tahini paste
- 3 cloves garlic, minced
- 1/2 teaspoon ground cinnamon
- 1/2 teaspoon ground nutmeg
- 1/2 teaspoon ground allspice
- salt to taste

### Direction

- In a large container, put the garbanzo beans then cover with a few inches of cold water; let it soak for 8 hours or overnight. Or, make it boil in a large pot over high heat. Turn off heat once boiling, then cover and let it soak for 1 hour. Strain and wash before using.
- Get a large saucepan and put the soaked garbanzo beans in it then pour water a few inches enough to cover the beans. Make it boil over high heat, then turn the heat to medium-low, then cover, and gently boil for 1 1/2 to 2 hours until beans are softened.
- Then place the cooked beans and liquid inside the refrigerator until chilled.
- Strain the garbanzo beans, preserve the cooking liquid for later use. Get a blender and put a 1/2 cup of preserved cooking liquid and beans in it, mix well until forms a smooth paste. Stir in the allspice, nutmeg, cinnamon, garlic, tahini, olive oil, lemon juice and pumpkin puree. Blend well until becomes smooth. To reach a smooth consistency, add cooking liquid as necessary. Add salt to taste.

### Nutrition Information

- Calories: 143 calories;

- Sodium: 70
- Total Carbohydrate: 14.5
- Cholesterol: 0
- Protein: 4.7
- Total Fat: 8.1

## 851. Quick Colorful Tossed Salad

*Serving: 2 servings. | Prep: 15mins | Cook: 0mins | Ready in:*

### Ingredients

- 2 cups torn romaine
- 1 small tomato, coarsely chopped
- 3 tablespoons coarsely chopped walnuts, toasted
- 3 tablespoons crumbled Gorgonzola cheese
- 1 tablespoon raisins
- 1 tablespoon finely chopped red onion
- 4 teaspoons olive oil
- 2 teaspoons balsamic vinegar
- 1/4 teaspoon sugar
- 1/4 teaspoon grated Parmesan cheese
- 1/8 to 1/4 teaspoon lemon-pepper seasoning
- 1/8 teaspoon garlic salt
- Dash coarsely ground pepper

### Direction

- Combine onion, raisins, cheese, walnuts, tomato and romaine in a salad bowl.
- Combine remaining ingredients in a jar that comes with a tight-fitting lid; cover and shake properly. Add to salad mixture and toss until well coated.

### Nutrition Information

- Calories: 228 calories
- Protein: 7g protein.
- Total Fat: 19g fat (4g saturated fat)
- Sodium: 299mg sodium

- Fiber: 3g fiber)
- Total Carbohydrate: 11g carbohydrate (6g sugars
- Cholesterol: 10mg cholesterol

## 852. Quick Couscous Salad

*Serving: 6 servings. | Prep: 20mins | Cook: 0mins | Ready in:*

### Ingredients

- 1-1/4 cups water
- 1 cup uncooked couscous
- 1/2 teaspoon salt
- 1/2 cup fat-free Italian salad dressing
- 3/4 cup chopped fresh mushrooms
- 1 can (2-1/4 ounces) sliced ripe olives, drained
- 1/2 cup diced cucumber
- 1/3 cup each diced onion, green pepper and sweet red pepper

### Direction

- Boil water in a small saucepan. Mix in salt and couscous. Cover it up and take off from the heat source; let it rest for 5 minutes. Use a fork to fluff it. Mix peppers, onion, cucumber, olives, mushrooms, salad dressing and couscous in a big bowl. Keep it covered and let chill in the refrigerator for 20 minutes.

### Nutrition Information

- Calories: 147 calories
- Total Carbohydrate: 29g carbohydrate (4g sugars
- Cholesterol: 1mg cholesterol
- Protein: 5g protein. Diabetic Exchanges: 1-1/2 starch
- Total Fat: 2g fat (0 saturated fat)
- Sodium: 580mg sodium
- Fiber: 2g fiber)

## 853. Quick Garlic Bean Dip

*Serving: 6 servings. | Prep: 10mins | Cook: 0mins | Ready in:*

### Ingredients

- 1 can (15 ounces) garbanzo beans or chickpeas, rinsed and drained
- 1/3 cup reduced-fat mayonnaise
- 2 tablespoons minced fresh parsley
- 4-1/2 teaspoons lemon juice
- 1 garlic clove, peeled
- 1/4 teaspoon salt
- Pita bread wedges

### Direction

- Mix together salt, garlic, lemon juice, parsley, mayonnaise and beans in a food processor, then cover and process until smooth.
- Turn to a serving dish then cover and chill about 1 hour. Serve with pita bread.

### Nutrition Information

- Calories: 112 calories
- Sodium: 297mg sodium
- Fiber: 3g fiber)
- Total Carbohydrate: 13g carbohydrate (2g sugars
- Cholesterol: 5mg cholesterol
- Protein: 3g protein. Diabetic Exchanges: 1 starch
- Total Fat: 6g fat (1g saturated fat)

## 854. Quick Greek Pasta Salad

*Serving: 2 servings. | Prep: 15mins | Cook: 0mins | Ready in:*

### Ingredients

- 1 cup cooked spiral pasta
- 2 plum tomatoes, chopped
- 1/4 cup pitted Greek olives, sliced
- 1 tablespoon capers, drained
- 2 tablespoons Greek vinaigrette
- 1 garlic clove, minced
- 1-1/2 teaspoons minced fresh parsley
- 1/4 cup crumbled feta cheese

### Direction

- Combine capers, olives, tomatoes and pasta in a small bowl. In another bowl, whisk together parsley, garlic and vinaigrette. Add dressing to salad mixture and toss until well coated. Add feta cheese on top, serve right away.

### Nutrition Information

- Calories: 262 calories
- Fiber: 2g fiber)
- Total Carbohydrate: 25g carbohydrate (3g sugars
- Cholesterol: 8mg cholesterol
- Protein: 6g protein.
- Total Fat: 15g fat (3g saturated fat)
- Sodium: 694mg sodium

## 855. Quinoa Tabbouleh

*Serving: 4 | Prep: 15mins | Cook: 15mins | Ready in:*

### Ingredients

- 2 cups water
- 1 cup quinoa
- 1 pinch salt
- 1/4 cup olive oil
- 1/2 teaspoon sea salt
- 1/4 cup lemon juice
- 3 tomatoes, diced
- 1 cucumber, diced
- 2 bunches green onions, diced
- 2 carrots, grated

- 1 cup fresh parsley, chopped

### Direction

- Place water in a saucepan and make it boil. Then put a pinch of salt and quinoa. Minimize heat to low, and simmer for 15 minutes, covered. Let it cool at room temperature; use fork to fluff.
- In the meantime, mix together in a large bowl the parsley, carrots, green onions, cucumber, tomatoes, lemon juice, sea salt, and olive oil. Mix in cooled quinoa.

### Nutrition Information

- Calories: 354 calories;
- Sodium: 286
- Total Carbohydrate: 45.7
- Cholesterol: 0
- Protein: 9.6
- Total Fat: 16.6

## 856. Quinoa Tabbouleh Salad

*Serving: 12 | Prep: 25mins | Cook: 15mins | Ready in:*

### Ingredients

- 2 cups vegetable broth
- 1 cup quinoa
- 1 cucumber, chopped
- 2 tomatoes, chopped
- 1/2 cup fresh parsley, chopped
- 2 green onions, chopped
- 2 tablespoons chopped fresh mint
- 2 cloves garlic, minced
- 1/4 cup olive oil
- 1/4 cup lemon juice
- 1/2 teaspoon salt, or to taste

### Direction

- Please quinoa and broth in a sauce pan then make it boil. Minimize heat to medium low, and simmer for about 15 minutes, covered, until the water has been absorbed and quinoa is soft.
- In a large bowl, mix together the garlic, mint, green onions, parsley, tomatoes and cucumber. Then add salt, lemon juice, olive oil and quinoa to cucumber mixture; then combine well by tossing.
- Use plastic wrap to cover the bowl and place inside the refrigerator for at least one hour until flavors are combined.

### Nutrition Information

- Calories: 107 calories;
- Total Carbohydrate: 12.3
- Cholesterol: 0
- Protein: 2.6
- Total Fat: 5.5
- Sodium: 178

## 857. Red Pepper & Feta Dip

*Serving: 1-1/2 cups. | Prep: 5mins | Cook: 0mins | Ready in:*

### Ingredients

- 1 package (8 ounces) cream cheese, softened
- 1 tablespoon 2% milk
- 1/2 cup chopped roasted sweet red peppers
- 1/2 cup crumbled feta cheese
- Baked pita chips

### Direction

- Beat milk and cream cheese in a large bowl till smooth. Stir in feta cheese and red peppers gently. Serve the dip with pita chips.

### Nutrition Information

- Calories: 163 calories
- Sodium: 277mg sodium

- Fiber: 0 fiber)
- Total Carbohydrate: 2g carbohydrate (1g sugars
- Cholesterol: 47mg cholesterol
- Protein: 5g protein.
- Total Fat: 15g fat (9g saturated fat)

## 858. Red Potato Salad With Lemony Vinaigrette

*Serving: 12 servings (3/4 cup each). | Prep: 15mins | Cook: 20mins | Ready in:*

### Ingredients

- 3 pounds red potatoes, cubed (about 10 cups)
- 1/3 cup olive oil
- 2 tablespoons lemon juice
- 2 tablespoons red wine vinegar
- 1-1/2 teaspoons salt
- 1/4 teaspoon pepper
- 2 tablespoons minced fresh parsley
- 1 garlic clove, minced
- 1/2 teaspoon dried oregano
- 1/2 cup pitted Greek olives, chopped
- 1/3 cup chopped red onion
- 1/2 cup shredded Parmesan cheese

### Direction

- In a 6-qt. stockpot, put potatoes and fill with water. Boil it. Decrease the heat, cook without the cover until softened, or for 10-15 minutes. Strain, move to a big bowl.
- Mix pepper, salt, vinegar, lemon juice, and oil together in a small bowl until combined, mix in oregano, garlic, and parsley. Sprinkle on potatoes, mix to coat. Lightly mix in onion and olives. Put in the fridge and cover for 2 hours at least prior to serving.
- Mix in cheese before serving.

### Nutrition Information

- Calories: 168 calories
- Sodium: 451mg sodium
- Fiber: 2g fiber)
- Total Carbohydrate: 20g carbohydrate (1g sugars
- Cholesterol: 2mg cholesterol
- Protein: 4g protein. Diabetic Exchanges: 2 fat
- Total Fat: 9g fat (2g saturated fat)

## 859. Rice And Mushrooms

*Serving: 8 servings. | Prep: 10mins | Cook: 15mins | Ready in:*

### Ingredients

- 1 small onion, finely chopped
- 1 celery rib, chopped
- 1/2 cup chopped celery leaves
- 2 tablespoons butter
- 1 pound sliced fresh mushrooms
- 3 cups uncooked instant rice
- 3 cups water
- 4 teaspoons Greek seasoning
- 1/2 cup chopped pecans, toasted

### Direction

- Sauté together celery leaves, celery and onion with butter in a big nonstick skillet sprayed with cooking spray about 4 minutes. Put in mushrooms and cook for another 4 minutes.
- Put in rice and cook until browned slightly, about 4 to 5 minutes. Stir in Greek seasoning and water, then bring the mixture to a boil. Take away from the heat and allow to stand, covered, about 5 minutes. Use a fork to fluff and sprinkle over with pecans.

### Nutrition Information

- Calories: 232 calories
- Protein: 5g protein. Diabetic Exchanges: 2 starch

- Total Fat: 9g fat (2g saturated fat)
- Sodium: 529mg sodium
- Fiber: 2g fiber)
- Total Carbohydrate: 35g carbohydrate (2g sugars
- Cholesterol: 8mg cholesterol

## 860. Rice With Lemon And Spinach

*Serving: 6 servings. | Prep: 20mins | Cook: 30mins | Ready in:*

### Ingredients

- 1 small onion, chopped
- 1 cup sliced fresh mushrooms
- 2 garlic cloves, minced
- 1 tablespoon olive oil
- 3 cups cooked long grain rice
- 1 package (10 ounces) frozen chopped spinach, thawed and squeezed dry
- 3 tablespoons lemon juice
- 1/2 teaspoon salt
- 1/4 teaspoon dill weed
- 1/8 teaspoon pepper
- 1/3 cup crumbled feta cheese, divided

### Direction

- Sauté together garlic, mushrooms and onion in a skillet with oil until softened. Stir in pepper, dill, salt, lemon juice, spinach and rice. Save 1 tbsp. of cheese, then stir into skillet with the rest of cheese and blend well.
- Remove to an 8-inch square baking dish sprayed with cooking spray and use reserved cheese to sprinkle over. Bake at 350 degrees, covered, about 25 minutes. Take off the cover and bake until heated through and cheese has melted, about 5 to 10 more minutes.

### Nutrition Information

- Calories: 167 calories
- Protein: 5g protein. Diabetic Exchanges: 1-1/2 starch
- Total Fat: 4g fat (2g saturated fat)
- Sodium: 324mg sodium
- Fiber: 2g fiber)
- Total Carbohydrate: 27g carbohydrate (2g sugars
- Cholesterol: 7mg cholesterol

## 861. Roasted Asparagus With Feta

*Serving: Makes 6 servings | Prep: | Cook: | Ready in:*

### Ingredients

- 2 1/2 pound medium asparagus, trimmed
- 2 tablespoons extra-virgin olive oil
- 1/2 teaspoon salt
- 1/4 teaspoon black pepper
- 2 ounce feta (preferably French), crumbled (1/2 cup)

### Direction

- Place the oven rack on the lower third of the oven then preheat to 500 degrees F.
- In a big shallow baking pan, mix pepper, asparagus, salt, and oil; arrange in one layer. Roast for a total of 8-14 mins until the asparagus is just fork-tender, while shaking the pan one time halfway through cooking. Scatter cheese on top to serve.

### Nutrition Information

- Calories: 111
- Cholesterol: 11 mg(4%)
- Protein: 6 g(12%)
- Total Fat: 7 g(11%)
- Saturated Fat: 3 g(13%)
- Sodium: 312 mg(13%)
- Fiber: 4 g(16%)

- Total Carbohydrate: 8 g(3%)
- Fiber: 4g fiber)
- Total Carbohydrate: 15g carbohydrate (0 sugars
- Cholesterol: 0 cholesterol

## 862. Roasted Garlic White Bean Dip

*Serving: 2-1/4 cups. | Prep: 20mins | Cook: 30mins | Ready in:*

### Ingredients

- 1 whole garlic bulb
- 1 teaspoon plus 3 tablespoons olive oil, divided
- 2 cans (15 ounces each) white kidney or cannellini beans, rinsed and drained
- 1 to 1-1/2 teaspoons grated lemon peel
- 2 tablespoons lemon juice
- 1-1/2 teaspoons Italian seasoning
- 3/4 teaspoon salt
- Assorted fresh vegetables

### Direction

- Set the oven to 425°. Get rid of papery outer skin from garlic bulb without peeling or separating the cloves. Cut off top of garlic bulb to expose individual cloves. Brush with 1 tsp. oil and use foil to wrap bulb. Bake until cloves are soft, about 30 to 35 minutes. Unwrap and cool for 10 minutes.
- Mix together remaining oil, salt, Italian seasoning, lemon juice, lemon peel and beans in a food processor. Squeeze garlic from skins into food processor then process until smooth. Cover and chill until cold, then serve together with vegetables.

### Nutrition Information

- Calories: 124 calories
- Protein: 4g protein. Diabetic Exchanges: 1 starch
- Total Fat: 5g fat (1g saturated fat)
- Sodium: 315mg sodium

## 863. Roasted Goat Cheese With Garlic

*Serving: about 1-1/4 cups. | Prep: 45mins | Cook: 15mins | Ready in:*

### Ingredients

- 6 to 8 garlic cloves, peeled
- 1 tablespoon canola oil
- 1 medium red onion, thinly sliced
- 2 tablespoons butter
- 1 tablespoon brown sugar
- 8 ounces crumbled goat or feta cheese
- 1 tablespoon white balsamic vinegar
- Salt and pepper to taste
- 1/4 cup thinly sliced fresh basil
- Thinly sliced French bread or assorted crackers

### Direction

- In a pie plate, arrange garlic and oil. Cover, bake for 30 minutes at 350°.
- In the meantime, sauté onion in butter in a small skillet until it turns light brown and becomes tender. Stir in and cook brown sugar until dissolved. Take away from the heat.
- Take away garlic from the pie plate. Pour onion mixture into the pie plate and put cheese on top. Put garlic over cheese. Uncover and bake until cheese melts, or for 15-20 minutes.
- Use a fork to mash garlic mixture. Combine pepper, salt, and the vinegar. Then move to a serving bowl; use basil to dust. Serve warm with crackers or French bread.

### Nutrition Information

- Calories: 213 calories
- Cholesterol: 40mg cholesterol
- Protein: 9g protein.
- Total Fat: 17g fat (10g saturated fat)
- Sodium: 236mg sodium
- Fiber: 0 fiber)
- Total Carbohydrate: 6g carbohydrate (5g sugars

## 864. Roasted Parmesan Green Beans

*Serving: 6 servings | Prep: 10mins | Cook: | Ready in:*

### Ingredients

- 1 lb. fresh green beans, trimmed
- 2 Tbsp. olive oil
- 1/2 cup KRAFT Seasoned Grated Parmesan Cheese Classic Italian

### Direction

- In the shallow casserole, toss the beans with oil.
- Bake until the beans become tender-crisp, for 10 minutes.
- Scatter cheese on top.

### Nutrition Information

- Calories: 110
- Total Fat: 8 g
- Saturated Fat: 2.5 g
- Fiber: 3 g
- Sugar: 2 g
- Total Carbohydrate: 6 g
- Protein: 5 g
- Sodium: 170 mg
- Cholesterol: 10 mg

## 865. Roasted Potato Salad With Feta

*Serving: 4 servings. | Prep: 15mins | Cook: 20mins | Ready in:*

### Ingredients

- 1 pound small red potatoes, quartered
- 3 tablespoons olive oil, divided
- 1/2 teaspoon salt
- 1/2 teaspoon pepper
- 2 tablespoons sherry vinegar
- 1 teaspoon Dijon mustard
- 2/3 cup julienned roasted sweet red peppers
- 4 green onions, sliced
- 1/3 cup crumbled feta cheese

### Direction

- Shake potatoes with pepper, salt, and 1 tablespoon oil in a large bowl. Deliver to oily 15x10x1-inch baking pan. Bake for 20 to 25 minutes at 400° or until tender.
- Instantly drip 1 tablespoon vinegar over potato mixture, set aside for 5 minutes.
- In the meantime, mix vinegar, the remaining oil, and mustard in a small bowl. Put cheese, onions, red peppers, and potato mixture together and mix in a large bowl. Pour dressing and slightly shake to coat.

### Nutrition Information

- Calories: 217 calories
- Fiber: 3g fiber)
- Total Carbohydrate: 21g carbohydrate (3g sugars
- Cholesterol: 5mg cholesterol
- Protein: 4g protein.
- Total Fat: 12g fat (2g saturated fat)
- Sodium: 574mg sodium

## 866. Roasted Red Pepper Bread

*Serving: 2 loaves (12 slices each). | Prep: 45mins | Cook: 20mins | Ready in:*

### Ingredients

- 1-1/2 cups roasted sweet red peppers, drained
- 1 package (1/4 ounce) active dry yeast
- 2 tablespoons warm water (110° to 115°)
- 1-1/4 cups grated Parmesan cheese, divided
- 1/3 cup warm 2% milk (110° to 115°)
- 2 tablespoons butter, softened
- 1-1/4 teaspoons salt
- 3-1/4 to 3-3/4 cups all-purpose flour
- 1 large egg
- 1 tablespoon water
- 1-1/2 teaspoons coarsely ground pepper

### Direction

- In a food processor, process red peppers until pureed while covering. Dissolve yeast in a big bowl with warm water. Beat in 1 1/2 cup flour, the red peppers, salt, a cup of cheese, butter, and milk until smooth. Mix in enough of the remaining flour until a firm dough forms.
- Transfer the dough onto a floured surface and knead for around 6-8 mins until elastic and smooth. Move to a greased bowl then turn to grease the surface one time; cover. Let it sit in a warm area for approximately an hour until it doubles.
- Punch the dough down then place on a lightly floured surface; split into 6 portions. Form each portion into an 18-inch rope. On a greased baking sheet, braid the 3 ropes; pinch and seal the ends then tuck beneath. Repeat with the rest of the dough. Cover then set aside to rise for around an hour until it doubles.
- Mix water and egg in a small bowl; brush on top of the braids. Scatter the remaining cheese and pepper on top. Bake for 18-22 mins in a 350 degrees F oven or until golden brown.

### Nutrition Information

- Calories: 99 calories
- Sodium: 254mg sodium
- Fiber: 1g fiber)
- Total Carbohydrate: 14g carbohydrate (1g sugars
- Cholesterol: 15mg cholesterol
- Protein: 4g protein. Diabetic Exchanges: 1 starch.
- Total Fat: 3g fat (1g saturated fat)

## 867. Roasted Red Pepper Hummus

*Serving: 8 | Prep: 10mins | Cook: | Ready in:*

### Ingredients

- 1 (15 ounce) can no-salt-added chickpeas, rinsed
- 1 (7 ounce) jar roasted red peppers, drained and blotted dry
- ¼ cup tahini
- ¼ cup extra-virgin olive oil
- ¼ cup lemon juice
- 1 clove garlic
- 1 teaspoon ground cumin
- ½ teaspoon salt

### Direction

- Mix tahini, oil, salt, cumin, garlic, lemon juice, chickpeas, cumin, peppers and chickpeas together in a food processor. Put it on puree until it gets really smooth. Eat it with crudités, veggie chips, or pita chips.

### Nutrition Information

- Calories: 180 calories;
- Fiber: 2
- Cholesterol: 0

- Total Carbohydrate: 13
- Protein: 4
- Total Fat: 12
- Sodium: 362
- Sugar: 0
- Saturated Fat: 2

## 868. Roasted Red Pepper Spread

*Serving: 30 | Prep: | Cook: | Ready in:*

### Ingredients

- 6 pounds red bell peppers
- 1 pound Italian plum tomatoes
- 2 cloves garlic, unpeeled
- 1 small white onion
- 1/2 cup red wine vinegar
- 2 tablespoons finely chopped fresh basil
- 1 tablespoon sugar
- 1 teaspoon salt
- 5 Ball® or Kerr® Half-pint (8 oz) Jars with lids and bands

### Direction

- Roast the onion, garlic, tomatoes and red peppers on a grill or under a broiler at 425°F, then flip to roast all sides, until the peppers and tomatoes become soft, blackened and blistered and the onion and garlic becomes black in spots. Take it out of the heat.
- In paper bags, put the tomatoes and pepper, then secure the opening and allow it to cool for around 15 minutes. Let the onion and garlic cool. Peel the onion and garlic. Chop the garlic finely, then put aside. Chop the onion finely and measure 1/4 cup, then put aside. Peel and take out the seeds of tomatoes and peppers. In a blender or food processor, put the tomatoes and peppers, work in batches, and process it until it has a smooth consistency.
- Prepare the boiling water canner. Heat the lids and jars in simmering water until ready to use, but don't boil. Put the bands aside.
- In a big saucepan, mix together the salt, sugar, basil, vinegar, onion, garlic, tomato and pepper puree, then boil. Lower the heat and let it simmer for about 20 minutes until the mixture mounds on a spoon and becomes thick.
- Ladle the hot spread into hot jars and leave a 1/2-inch headspace, then wipe the rim. Put the hot lid on the center of the jar, apply the band and adjust until fit is fingertip tight.
- Process it for 10 minutes in a boiling water canner, then adjust the altitude. Take out the jars and let it cool. After 24 hours, check the lids for seal. The lid must not flex down and up once pressed in the center.

### Nutrition Information

- Calories: 35 calories;
- Protein: 1.1
- Total Fat: 0.3
- Sodium: 82
- Total Carbohydrate: 7.1
- Cholesterol: 0

## 869. Roasted Sweet Potato & Chickpea Pitas

*Serving: 6 servings. | Prep: 15mins | Cook: 15mins | Ready in:*

### Ingredients

- 2 medium sweet potatoes (about 1-1/4 pounds), peeled and cubed
- 2 cans (15 ounces each) chickpeas or garbanzo beans, rinsed and drained
- 1 medium red onion, chopped
- 3 tablespoons canola oil, divided
- 2 teaspoons garam masala
- 1/2 teaspoon salt, divided

- 2 garlic cloves, minced
- 1 cup plain Greek yogurt
- 1 tablespoon lemon juice
- 1 teaspoon ground cumin
- 2 cups arugula or baby spinach
- 12 whole wheat pita pocket halves, warmed
- 1/4 cup minced fresh cilantro

### Direction

- Set an oven to preheat to 400 degrees. In a big microwavable bowl, place the potatoes then microwave for 5 minutes on high with a cover. Mix in onion and chickpeas, then toss it with 1/4 tsp. salt, garam masala and 2 tbsp. oil.
- Spread into a 15x10x1-inch pan. Roast for approximately 15 minutes, until the potatoes becomes soft. Allow it to cool a bit.
- In a small microwavable bowl, put the leftover oil and garlic, then microwave on high for 1-1 1/2 minutes or until the garlic turns light brown. Mix in leftover salt, cumin, lemon juice and yogurt.
- Toss arugula with potato mixture, then spoon into pitas. Put cilantro and sauce on top.

### Nutrition Information

- Calories: 462 calories
- Protein: 14g protein.
- Total Fat: 15g fat (3g saturated fat)
- Sodium: 662mg sodium
- Fiber: 12g fiber)
- Total Carbohydrate: 72g carbohydrate (13g sugars
- Cholesterol: 10mg cholesterol

## 870. Roasted Veggie Orzo

*Serving: 8 servings. | Prep: 25mins | Cook: 20mins | Ready in:*

### Ingredients

- 1-1/2 cups fresh mushrooms, halved
- 1 medium zucchini, chopped
- 1 medium sweet yellow pepper, chopped
- 1 medium sweet red pepper, chopped
- 1 small red onion, cut into wedges
- 1 cup cut fresh asparagus (1-inch pieces)
- 1 tablespoon olive oil
- 1 teaspoon each dried oregano, thyme and rosemary, crushed
- 1/2 teaspoon salt
- 1-1/4 cups uncooked orzo pasta
- 1/4 cup crumbled feta cheese

### Direction

- In a cooking spray-coated 15x10x1-inch baking pan, put vegetables. Use oil to drizzle and seasonings to sprinkle; stir to coat. Bake at 400° until soft, or for 20-25 minutes, tossing from time to time.
- In the meantime, cook orzo following the package instructions. Strain, remove into a serving bowl. Mix in the roasted vegetables. Use cheese to sprinkle.

### Nutrition Information

- Calories: 164 calories
- Total Carbohydrate: 28g carbohydrate (3g sugars
- Cholesterol: 2mg cholesterol
- Protein: 6g protein. Diabetic Exchanges: 1-1/2 starch
- Total Fat: 3g fat (1g saturated fat)
- Sodium: 188mg sodium
- Fiber: 3g fiber)

## 871. Rosemary Beet Phyllo Bites

*Serving: 6 dozen. | Prep: 25mins | Cook: 0mins | Ready in:*

### Ingredients

- 1 jar (16 ounces) pickled whole beets, drained and chopped
- 1 tablespoon olive oil
- 2 teaspoons minced fresh rosemary
- 1 teaspoon grated orange zest
- 2 cups fresh arugula, torn
- 72 frozen miniature phyllo tart shells
- 3/4 cup crumbled feta cheese

## Direction

- Use paper towels to pat dry beets; move to a small bowl. Toss in orange zest, rosemary, and olive oil to combine.
- Split arugula between tart shells then add the beet mixture on top. Top with feta cheese.

## Nutrition Information

- Calories: 31 calories
- Total Fat: 1g fat (0 saturated fat)
- Sodium: 33mg sodium
- Fiber: 0 fiber)
- Total Carbohydrate: 3g carbohydrate (1g sugars
- Cholesterol: 1mg cholesterol
- Protein: 1g protein.

## 872. Rosemary Goat Cheese Bites

*Serving: 1 dozen. | Prep: 25mins | Cook: 0mins | Ready in:*

## Ingredients

- 1/4 cup finely chopped pecans
- 1/4 teaspoon ground cinnamon
- 1 log (4 ounces) fresh goat cheese
- 1-1/2 teaspoons minced fresh rosemary, divided
- Toasted French bread baguette slices, optional
- 1 tablespoon honey

## Direction

- Toss cinnamon and pecans in a shallow bowl. In a small bowl, stir 3/4 teaspoon of rosemary and cheese until mixed. Form mixture into 12 balls; then coat them by rolling in pecan mixture. Slightly flatten into patties.
- Serve patties with toasted baguette slices as desired. Drizzle with honey and sprinkle with remaining rosemary.

## Nutrition Information

- Calories: 39 calories
- Total Carbohydrate: 2g carbohydrate (2g sugars
- Cholesterol: 6mg cholesterol
- Protein: 1g protein.
- Total Fat: 3g fat (1g saturated fat)
- Sodium: 38mg sodium
- Fiber: 0 fiber)

## 873. Salsa Bean Dip

*Serving: 1-1/2 cups. | Prep: 10mins | Cook: 0mins | Ready in:*

## Ingredients

- 1/2 cup pineapple salsa
- 1 tablespoon lemon juice
- 1 can (15 ounces) garbanzo beans or chickpeas, rinsed and drained
- 1/4 cup minced fresh parsley
- 1/4 teaspoon pepper
- Tortilla chips

## Direction

- Mix together pepper, parsley, beans, lemon juice and salsa in a food processor, then cover and process until smooth. Turn to a serving dish, then serve together with tortilla chips and chill the leftovers.

## Nutrition Information

- Calories: 39 calories
- Protein: 1g protein. Diabetic Exchanges: 1/2 starch.
- Total Fat: 1g fat (0 saturated fat)
- Sodium: 77mg sodium
- Fiber: 2g fiber)
- Total Carbohydrate: 7g carbohydrate (2g sugars
- Cholesterol: 0 cholesterol

### 874. Saucy Portobello Pitas

*Serving: 4 servings. | Prep: 25mins | Cook: 10mins | Ready in:*

## Ingredients

- CUCUMBER SAUCE:
- 1 cup (8 ounces) reduced-fat plain yogurt
- 1/2 cup chopped peeled cucumber
- 1/4 to 1/3 cup minced fresh mint
- 1 tablespoon grated lemon peel
- 1 tablespoon lemon juice
- 1 teaspoon garlic powder
- PITAS:
- 4 large portobello mushrooms, stems removed
- 1/2 teaspoon pepper
- 1/4 teaspoon onion powder
- 1/4 teaspoon garlic powder
- 1/4 teaspoon Greek seasoning
- 2 tablespoons canola oil
- 8 pita pocket halves, warmed
- 8 thin slices red onion, separated into rings
- 8 slices tomato

## Direction

- Mix together the cucumber sauce ingredients in a small bowl. Put a cover and let it chill in the fridge until ready to serve.
- Sprinkle Greek seasoning, garlic powder, onion powder and pepper on mushrooms. Cook the mushrooms in oil in a big frying pan for 3-5 minutes per side or until it becomes soft.
- Halve the pita breads then line each with tomato and onion slice. Halve the mushrooms then put it in pitas. Serve it with cucumber sauce.

## Nutrition Information

- Calories: 303 calories
- Protein: 11g protein. Diabetic Exchanges: 3 starch
- Total Fat: 9g fat (1g saturated fat)
- Sodium: 411mg sodium
- Fiber: 4g fiber)
- Total Carbohydrate: 45g carbohydrate (9g sugars
- Cholesterol: 3mg cholesterol

### 875. Savory Marinated Mushroom Salad

*Serving: 6-8 servings. | Prep: 25mins | Cook: 0mins | Ready in:*

## Ingredients

- 2-1/2 quarts water
- 3 tablespoons lemon juice
- 3 pounds small fresh mushrooms
- 2 medium carrots, sliced
- 2 celery ribs, sliced
- 1/2 medium green pepper, chopped
- 1 small onion, chopped
- 1 tablespoon minced fresh parsley
- 1/2 cup sliced pimiento-stuffed olives
- 1 can (2-1/4 ounces) sliced ripe olives, drained
- DRESSING:
- 1/2 cup prepared Italian salad dressing
- 1/2 cup red or white wine vinegar
- 1 garlic clove, minced
- 1/2 teaspoon salt
- 1/2 teaspoon dried oregano

### Direction

- Boil lemon juice and water in a big saucepan. Add and cook mushrooms for 3 minutes, stirring once in a while. Drain it off; let it cool down.
- In a big bowl, add mushrooms with olives, parsley, onion, green pepper, celery and carrots. Combine the dressing ingredients in a small bowl. Put on top of the salad. Keep it covered and chilled in the fridge overnight.

### Nutrition Information

- Calories: 142 calories
- Total Fat: 9g fat (1g saturated fat)
- Sodium: 671mg sodium
- Fiber: 3g fiber)
- Total Carbohydrate: 14g carbohydrate (5g sugars
- Cholesterol: 0 cholesterol
- Protein: 6g protein.

## 876. Savory Omelet Cups

*Serving: 4 servings. | Prep: 35mins | Cook: 10mins | Ready in:*

### Ingredients

- 1/4 cup sun-dried tomatoes (not packed in oil)
- 1/2 cup water, divided
- 3 eggs
- 6 egg whites
- 2 tablespoons minced fresh cilantro
- 4 teaspoons butter, melted
- 1/2 teaspoon salt
- 1/4 teaspoon pepper
- 1/3 cup shredded provolone cheese
- 1 cup chopped leeks (white portion only)
- 2 green onions, chopped
- 1 tablespoon olive oil
- 2 tablespoons chopped Greek olives
- 2 teaspoons minced fresh oregano or 1/2 teaspoon dried oregano
- 1/4 cup grated Parmesan cheese
- 1 tablespoon honey

### Direction

- In a small bowl, put tomatoes. Fill with 1/4 cup of water; let sit for 30 minutes.
- In the meantime, beat pepper, the rest of the water, salt, butter, cilantro, egg whites, and eggs in a big bowl.
- Heat an oiled (use cooking spray) 8-in. nonstick frying pan, add about 1/2 cup of the egg mixture to the middle of the frying pan. Swirl the pan so that the mixture coats the bottom of the pan evenly. Cook until the top looks dry, about 1 1/2 -2 minutes, flip and cook until set, about another 30-45 seconds.
- Take out from the pan and push into a grease-coated ramekin or 1-cup baking dish. Do the same with the rest of the egg mixture, preparing another 3 omelet cups (grease the frying pan with cooking spray if necessary). Use provolone cheese to drizzle into the cups.
- Start preheating the oven to 350°. Strain the tomatoes, cut and put aside. Sauté onions and leeks in oil in a big nonstick skillet until soft. Mix in oregano, olives, and tomatoes, cook over medium heat for 2-3 minutes. Put in the omelet cups. Use Parmesan cheese to drizzle then top with honey.
- Put in the preheated oven to bake until cooked through, about 10-12 minutes.

### Nutrition Information

- Calories: 246 calories
- Sodium: 764mg sodium
- Fiber: 1g fiber)
- Total Carbohydrate: 12g carbohydrate (7g sugars
- Cholesterol: 178mg cholesterol
- Protein: 15g protein. Diabetic Exchanges: 2 lean meat
- Total Fat: 16g fat (6g saturated fat)

## 877. Seasoned Asparagus

*Serving: 4 | Prep: 5mins | Cook: 15mins | Ready in:*

### Ingredients

- 1 bunch asparagus, trimmed
- 1/4 cup olive oil
- 1/4 cup seasoned bread crumbs
- 3 tablespoons grated Parmesan cheese
- 2 tablespoons garlic powder
- 1/4 tablespoon sea salt (optional)

### Direction

- In a saucepan, heat olive oil on moderately high heat for about one minute. Cook in the hot oil with asparagus while turning frequently for 5 minutes, until tender a bit. Put in garlic powder, Parmesan cheese and bread crumbs. Use a spatula to turn asparagus to coat with the mixture evenly. Lower heat to medium and keep on cooking for 8 minutes, until asparagus is totally tender. Use sea salt to season.

### Nutrition Information

- Calories: 201 calories;
- Total Fat: 15.2
- Sodium: 523
- Total Carbohydrate: 12.7
- Cholesterol: 3
- Protein: 5.7

## 878. Seasoned Couscous

*Serving: 6 servings. | Prep: 5mins | Cook: 10mins | Ready in:*

### Ingredients

- 2 cups water
- 1 tablespoon butter
- 1 tablespoon dried parsley flakes
- 2 teaspoons chicken bouillon granules
- 1/2 teaspoon dried minced onion
- 1/2 teaspoon dried basil
- 1/4 teaspoon pepper
- 1/8 teaspoon garlic powder
- 1 package (10 ounces) couscous

### Direction

- Mix the first 8 ingredients together in a big saucepan, boil it. Take away from heat, mix in couscous. Put a cover on and let sit until the liquid is absorbed, about 5 minutes. Use a fork to fluff.

### Nutrition Information

- Calories: 185 calories
- Sodium: 299mg sodium
- Fiber: 2g fiber)
- Total Carbohydrate: 36g carbohydrate (1g sugars
- Cholesterol: 5mg cholesterol
- Protein: 7g protein.
- Total Fat: 3g fat (1g saturated fat)

## 879. Seven Layer Mediterranean Dip

*Serving: 2-1/2 cups. | Prep: 15mins | Cook: 0mins | Ready in:*

### Ingredients

- 1 carton (8 ounces) hummus
- 1 cup (8 ounces) reduced-fat sour cream
- 1 jar (8 ounces) roasted sweet red peppers, drained and chopped
- 1/4 cup crumbled feta cheese
- 1/4 cup chopped red onion
- 12 Greek olives, pitted and chopped
- 2 tablespoons chopped fresh parsley

- Baked pita chips

### Direction

- In a 9-inch pie plate, place the hummus then spread. Put olives, onion, cheese, red peppers and sour cream on top, then sprinkle with parsley. Let it chill in the fridge until serving time. Serve alongside pita chips.

### Nutrition Information

- Calories:
- Protein:
- Total Fat:
- Sodium:
- Fiber:
- Total Carbohydrate:
- Cholesterol:

## 880. Slim Greek Deviled Eggs

*Serving: 1 dozen. | Prep: 20mins | Cook: 0mins | Ready in:*

### Ingredients

- 6 hard-boiled large eggs
- 3 tablespoons reduced-fat mayonnaise
- 2 tablespoons crumbled feta cheese
- 1 teaspoon dried oregano
- 1/2 teaspoon grated lemon peel
- 1/2 teaspoon lemon juice
- 1/8 teaspoon salt
- 1/8 teaspoon pepper
- Greek olives, optional

### Direction

- Slice the eggs into two lengthwise. Scoop out the yolks, put four yolks and egg whites aside (get rid of the rest of the yolks or save or later use).
- Crush the saved yolks in a big bowl. Mix in pepper, salt, lemon juice, lemon peel, oregano, feta, and mayonnaise. Use the mixture to pipe or stuff into each egg white. Use olives to garnish if you want. Refrigerate until eating.

### Nutrition Information

- Calories: 42 calories
- Protein: 3g protein.
- Total Fat: 3g fat (1g saturated fat)
- Sodium: 96mg sodium
- Fiber: 0 fiber)
- Total Carbohydrate: 1g carbohydrate (0 sugars
- Cholesterol: 70mg cholesterol

## 881. Smoky Cauliflower

*Serving: 8 servings. | Prep: 10mins | Cook: 20mins | Ready in:*

### Ingredients

- 1 large head cauliflower, broken into 1-inch florets (about 9 cups)
- 2 tablespoons olive oil
- 1 teaspoon smoked paprika
- 3/4 teaspoon salt
- 2 garlic cloves, minced
- 2 tablespoons minced fresh parsley

### Direction

- Put cauliflower in a big bow. Mix salt, paprika, and oil; sprinkle on cauliflower and toss to coat then move to a 15-in by 10-in by 1-in baking pan. Bake for 10 minutes in 450 degrees oven without cover.
- Mix in garlic. Bake for another 10-15 minutes until the cauliflower is pale brown and tender, mix from time to time. Top with parsley.

### Nutrition Information

- Calories: 58 calories

- Protein: 2g protein. Diabetic Exchanges: 1 vegetable
- Total Fat: 4g fat (0 saturated fat)
- Sodium: 254mg sodium
- Fiber: 3g fiber)
- Total Carbohydrate: 6g carbohydrate (3g sugars
- Cholesterol: 0 cholesterol

## 882. Spanakopita Bites

*Serving: 10-1/2 dozen. | Prep: 20mins | Cook: 35mins | Ready in:*

### Ingredients

- 1 large egg, lightly beaten
- 1 package (10 ounces) frozen chopped spinach, thawed and squeezed dry
- 2 cups (8 ounces) crumbled feta cheese
- 1 cup (8 ounces) 4% small-curd cottage cheese
- 3/4 cup butter, melted
- 16 sheets phyllo dough (14x9-inch size)

### Direction

- Start preheating the oven to 350°. Combine cheeses, spinach, and egg in a big bowl. Brush some of the butter over a 15x10x1-inch baking pan.
- In the prepared pan, put 1 phyllo dough sheet, brush butter over. Lay on 7 more phyllo sheets, brushing each layer. (Cover the leftover phyllo with a damp towel and plastic wrap to avoid drying). Spread the spinach mixture over the top. Put the leftover phyllo dough on top, brush butter over each sheet.
- Put a cover on and freeze for 30 minutes. Slice into 1-inch squares with a sharp knife. Bake until turning golden brown, about 35-45 minutes. Chill the leftovers.

### Nutrition Information

- Calories: 21 calories
- Sodium: 40mg sodium
- Fiber: 0 fiber)
- Total Carbohydrate: 1g carbohydrate (0 sugars
- Cholesterol: 6mg cholesterol
- Protein: 1g protein.
- Total Fat: 2g fat (1g saturated fat)

## 883. Spanakopita Pinwheels

*Serving: 2 dozen. | Prep: 30mins | Cook: 20mins | Ready in:*

### Ingredients

- 1 medium onion, finely chopped
- 2 tablespoons olive oil
- 1 teaspoon dried oregano
- 1 garlic clove, minced
- 2 packages (10 ounces each) frozen chopped spinach, thawed and squeezed dry
- 2 cups (8 ounces) crumbled feta cheese
- 2 eggs, lightly beaten
- 1 package (17.3 ounces) frozen puff pastry, thawed

### Direction

- Stir-fry the onions in oil on a small pan until tender. Toss in the garlic and oregano and cook for another minute. Stir in spinach and cook for 3 minutes more until liquid has evaporated. Place into a large bowl and allow to cool.
- Add eggs and feta cheese into the spinach mixture until well blended. Roll out puff pastry. Place half of the spinach mixture on the surface to within 1/2 inch of edges. In jelly-roll style, roll up the sheets. Slice each of the sheets into 12 pieces, 3/4 inch in size. Transfer into the greased baking sheets, seam side down.
- Bake for about 18 to 22 minutes at 400 degrees F, until golden brown. Serve while warm.

### Nutrition Information

- Calories: 197 calories
- Cholesterol: 39mg cholesterol
- Protein: 7g protein.
- Total Fat: 13g fat (5g saturated fat)
- Sodium: 392mg sodium
- Fiber: 3g fiber)
- Total Carbohydrate: 14g carbohydrate (1g sugars

## 884. Spicy Hummus

*Serving: 16 | Prep: 10mins | Cook: |Ready in:*

### Ingredients

- 1 (15 ounce) can garbanzo beans (chickpeas), drained and liquid reserved
- 1/4 cup minced garlic
- 2 serrano chile peppers, chopped
- 2 tablespoons sun-dried tomatoes
- 1/2 teaspoon ground cumin

### Direction

- In a blender on low, blend sun-dried tomatoes, garbanzo beans, garlic, cumin and serrano peppers for 30 seconds to 1 minute until the resulting mix is smooth.

### Nutrition Information

- Calories: 26 calories;
- Protein: 1.1
- Total Fat: 0.2
- Sodium: 62
- Total Carbohydrate: 5
- Cholesterol: 0

## 885. Spinach Feta Croissants

*Serving: 6 servings. | Prep: 20mins | Cook: 0mins | Ready in:*

### Ingredients

- 1/2 cup Italian salad dressing
- 6 croissants, split
- 3 cups fresh baby spinach
- 4 plum tomatoes, thinly sliced
- 1 cup (4 ounces) crumbled feta cheese

### Direction

- Brush the salad dressing on top of the cut sides of the croissants. Layer the spinach, tomatoes and feta cheese on the bottom halves, then place back the tops.

### Nutrition Information

- Calories: 363 calories
- Fiber: 3g fiber)
- Total Carbohydrate: 30g carbohydrate (4g sugars
- Cholesterol: 48mg cholesterol
- Protein: 9g protein.
- Total Fat: 23g fat (10g saturated fat)
- Sodium: 959mg sodium

## 886. Spinach Feta Croissants For 2

*Serving: 2 servings. | Prep: 10mins | Cook: 0mins | Ready in:*

### Ingredients

- 3 tablespoons Italian salad dressing
- 2 croissants, split
- 1 cup fresh baby spinach
- 1 plum tomato, thinly sliced
- 1/3 cup crumbled feta cheese

### Direction

- On the cut sides of the croissants, brush the salad dressing, then layer the spinach, tomato and feta cheese on the bottom halves and place back the tops.

## Nutrition Information

- Calories: 302 calories
- Protein: 9g protein.
- Total Fat: 15g fat (9g saturated fat)
- Sodium: 940mg sodium
- Fiber: 3g fiber)
- Total Carbohydrate: 31g carbohydrate (9g sugars
- Cholesterol: 49mg cholesterol

## 887. Spinach Flatbreads

*Serving: 4 servings. | Prep: 10mins | Cook: 10mins | Ready in:*

### Ingredients

- 2/3 cup sliced onion
- 4 teaspoons olive oil, divided
- 4 whole pita breads
- 2 cups fresh baby spinach
- 1-1/2 cups shredded part-skim mozzarella cheese
- 1/4 teaspoon pepper

### Direction

- Put 2 teaspoons oil and onion in a small frying pan, sauté until tender then put aside.
- Put pitas on an ungreased baking tray, brush the remaining oil over surface. Make a layer of spinach, onion, and cheese. Season with pepper. Bake at 425 degrees until cheese melts, about 6-8 minutes.

### Nutrition Information

- Calories: 322 calories
- Total Fat: 12g fat (5g saturated fat)
- Sodium: 528mg sodium
- Fiber: 2g fiber)
- Total Carbohydrate: 37g carbohydrate (3g sugars
- Cholesterol: 24mg cholesterol
- Protein: 16g protein. Diabetic Exchanges: 2 starch

## 888. Spinach Mushroom Salad

*Serving: 6 servings. | Prep: 15mins | Cook: 0mins | Ready in:*

### Ingredients

- 5 tablespoons olive oil
- 1 tablespoon lemon juice
- 1 tablespoon lime juice
- 1-1/2 teaspoons white wine vinegar
- 1 garlic clove, minced
- 3/4 teaspoon minced fresh parsley
- 1/4 teaspoon salt
- 1/4 teaspoon ground mustard
- 1/8 teaspoon dried basil
- 1/8 teaspoon dried oregano
- 1/8 teaspoon rubbed sage
- Dash to 1/8 teaspoon coarsely ground pepper
- 8 medium fresh mushrooms, sliced
- 7 cups torn fresh spinach

### Direction

- Mix well the initial twelve ingredients in a small bowl. Add in mushrooms and coat by tossing. Keep it covered and let chill in the refrigerator for at least half an hour. Just prior to serving, in a salad bowl, mix the mushroom mixture and spinach.

### Nutrition Information

- Calories:
- Cholesterol:
- Protein:
- Total Fat:

- Sodium:
- Fiber:
- Total Carbohydrate:

### 889. Spinach Orzo Salad

*Serving: 10 servings. | Prep: 20mins | Cook: 10mins | Ready in:*

**Ingredients**

- 1 package (16 ounces) orzo pasta
- 6 ounces fresh baby spinach (about 8 cups), finely chopped
- 3/4 cup finely chopped red onion
- 3/4 cup crumbled feta cheese
- 3/4 cup reduced-fat balsamic vinaigrette
- 1/2 teaspoon dried basil
- 1/4 teaspoon white pepper
- 1/4 cup pine nuts, toasted

**Direction**

- Follow the package directions to cook the orzo, then drain. Rinse under cold water and drain well.
- Mix together the orzo, cheese, onion and spinach in a big bowl. Combine the pepper, basil and vinaigrette, then gently toss with the spinach mixture. Chill until serving. Right before serving, stir in pine nuts.

**Nutrition Information**

- Calories: 255 calories
- Protein: 8g protein.
- Total Fat: 8g fat (2g saturated fat)
- Sodium: 279mg sodium
- Fiber: 2g fiber)
- Total Carbohydrate: 38g carbohydrate (3g sugars
- Cholesterol: 5mg cholesterol

### 890. Spinach Penne Salad

*Serving: 10 servings. | Prep: 20mins | Cook: 10mins | Ready in:*

**Ingredients**

- 1 package (16 ounces) uncooked whole wheat penne pasta
- VINAIGRETTE:
- 1/2 cup olive oil
- 1/2 cup white wine vinegar
- 1/3 cup grated Parmesan cheese
- 1 tablespoon Dijon mustard
- 2 garlic cloves, minced
- 1 teaspoon dried oregano
- 1/4 teaspoon salt
- 1/4 teaspoon pepper
- SALAD:
- 1 package (6 ounces) fresh baby spinach
- 3 medium tomatoes, seeded and chopped
- 3/4 cup (6 ounces) crumbled feta cheese
- 4 green onions, thinly sliced
- 1/2 cup sliced ripe or Greek olives

**Direction**

- Follow the package directions to cook pasta in a Dutch oven. Drain and rinse under cold water, then drain again.
- At the same time, whisk the vinaigrette ingredients in a small bowl. Mix together olives, onions, feta cheese, tomatoes, spinach and pasta in a big bowl. Pour the vinaigrette over and toss together to coat evenly, then serve promptly.

**Nutrition Information**

- Calories: 327 calories
- Total Fat: 15g fat (3g saturated fat)
- Sodium: 233mg sodium
- Fiber: 7g fiber)
- Total Carbohydrate: 38g carbohydrate (2g sugars

- Cholesterol: 7mg cholesterol
- Protein: 11g protein.

### 891. Spinach Phyllo Bundles

*Serving: 28 appetizers. | Prep: 35mins | Cook: 15mins | Ready in:*

## Ingredients

- 1 medium onion, chopped
- 2 tablespoons plus 1/2 cup butter, divided
- 1 package (10 ounces) frozen chopped spinach, thawed and squeezed dry
- 1 cup (4 ounces) crumbled feta cheese
- 3/4 cup 4% cottage cheese
- 3 eggs, lightly beaten
- 1/4 cup dry bread crumbs
- 3/4 teaspoon salt
- 1/2 teaspoon dill weed
- Pepper to taste
- 20 sheets phyllo dough (14-inch x 9-inch sheet size)

## Direction

- Sauté onion in a big pan with 2 tablespoon butter until tender; take off from heat. Mix in pepper, spinach, dill, feta cheese, bread crumbs, eggs, and cottage cheese.
- Melt the rest of the butter. Layer and slather five sheets of phyllo with melted butter. Use plastic wrap and a moist towel to cover the remaining dough to avoid drying. Slice the buttered sheets into 2-inch strips lengthwise. Put filling by 1 heaping tablespoonful on one end of every strip then fold like a flag into a triangle. Arrange on an ungreased baking dish then slather with butter. Repeat three times more with five phyllo sheets each time.
- Bake for 15-20 minutes in 400 degrees oven until golden brown. Serve warm.

## Nutrition Information

- Calories: 280 calories
- Protein: 10g protein.
- Total Fat: 18g fat (10g saturated fat)
- Sodium: 683mg sodium
- Fiber: 2g fiber)
- Total Carbohydrate: 20g carbohydrate (3g sugars
- Cholesterol: 116mg cholesterol

### 892. Spinach Phyllo Triangles

*Serving: 2 dozen. | Prep: 30mins | Cook: 15mins | Ready in:*

## Ingredients

- 1/2 cup chopped onion
- 1 garlic clove, minced
- 1 package (10 ounces) frozen chopped spinach, thawed and squeezed dry
- 1/2 teaspoon dried oregano
- 1-1/2 cups (6 ounces) crumbled feta cheese
- 12 sheets phyllo dough (14 inches x 9 inches)
- Butter-flavored cooking spray

## Direction

- Cook the onion in a nonstick frying pan coated with cooking spray until it becomes tender, then add garlic and let it cook for 1 minute more. Mix in oregano and spinach and let it cook on medium-low heat just until the spinach becomes warm. Let it drain. Take it out of the heat and mix in feta cheese, then put aside.
- Use butter-flavored cooking spray to spritz 1 sheet of phyllo dough. (Keep the leftover phyllo covered using plastic wrap and a moist towel to avoid it from drying.) Fold the dough in 1/2 lengthwise and spritz it with butter-flavored cooking spray. Halve the dough lengthwise to create 2 strips.
- On the lower corner of each strip, put 1 tablespoon of the spinach mixture, then fold the dough on top of the filling to create a

triangle. Keep folding like a flag until you reach the end of each strip. Spritz it using butter-flavored cooking spray and make sure that all the edges are sealed and sprayed. Redo the process with the leftover filling and phyllo.
- Put the triangles on a cooking spray coated baking tray. Let it bake for 15 to 20 minutes at 375 degrees or until it turns golden brown in color. Transfer to a wire rack. Serve it warm.

## Nutrition Information

- Calories: 74 calories
- Sodium: 199mg sodium
- Fiber: 2g fiber)
- Total Carbohydrate: 8g carbohydrate (1g sugars
- Cholesterol: 8mg cholesterol
- Protein: 4g protein. Diabetic Exchanges: 1/2 starch
- Total Fat: 3g fat (2g saturated fat)

## 893. Spring Greek Pasta Salad

*Serving: 16 servings (3/4 cup each). | Prep: 15mins | Cook: 15mins | Ready in:*

## Ingredients

- 4 cups veggie rotini or other spiral pasta (about 12 ounces)
- VINAIGRETTE:
- 1/4 cup olive oil
- 3 tablespoons lemon juice
- 2 tablespoons balsamic vinegar
- 1 tablespoon water
- 3 garlic cloves, minced
- 1 teaspoon salt
- 1/4 teaspoon pepper
- 3 tablespoons minced fresh oregano or 1 tablespoon dried oregano
- SALAD:
- 3 large tomatoes, seeded and chopped
- 1 medium sweet red pepper, chopped
- 1 small cucumber, seeded and chopped
- 1 small zucchini, chopped
- 1 small red onion, halved and thinly sliced
- 1/3 cup sliced pitted Greek olives, optional
- 1 cup (4 ounces) crumbled feta cheese

## Direction

- Cook pasta following the directions on package. Drain well; use cold water to rinse. Drain thoroughly.
- Mix pepper, salt, garlic, water, vinegar, lemon juice and oil together in a small bowl until combined. Add oregano and stir.
- Mix together vegetables, pasta and olive oil if desired in a large bowl. Add cheese and vinaigrette, stir well to combine. Put it into the refrigerator with cover until serving.

## Nutrition Information

- Calories: 142 calories
- Sodium: 219mg sodium
- Fiber: 2g fiber)
- Total Carbohydrate: 20g carbohydrate (3g sugars
- Cholesterol: 4mg cholesterol
- Protein: 5g protein. Diabetic Exchanges: 1 starch
- Total Fat: 5g fat (1g saturated fat)

## 894. Stovetop Orzo Medley

*Serving: 8 servings. | Prep: 15mins | Cook: 15mins | Ready in:*

## Ingredients

- 1-1/4 cups uncooked orzo pasta
- 2 shallots, finely chopped
- 1 tablespoon olive oil
- 3/4 pound fresh snow peas

- 1/2 pound assorted fresh mushrooms (such as portobello, button and/or shiitake), thinly sliced
- 1/4 cup pine nuts
- 2 tablespoons butter
- 1 teaspoon salt
- 1/2 teaspoon coarsely ground pepper
- 1/4 cup finely chopped sweet red pepper

## Direction

- Cook orzo as directed on the package. In the meantime, sauté shallots in oil in a large skillet, about 2 minutes. Add mushrooms and peas; sauté for 3 more minutes. Add pine nuts; sauté until vegetables are softened.
- Drain orzo; mix in pepper, salt, butter, and shallot mixture until well combined. Sprinkle red pepper over the pasta.

## Nutrition Information

- Calories: 203 calories
- Protein: 7g protein. Diabetic Exchanges: 2 starch
- Total Fat: 7g fat (2g saturated fat)
- Sodium: 322mg sodium
- Fiber: 3g fiber)
- Total Carbohydrate: 28g carbohydrate (4g sugars
- Cholesterol: 8mg cholesterol

## 895. Strawberry Orange Phyllo Cups

*Serving: 2 servings. | Prep: 25mins | Cook: 0mins | Ready in:*

## Ingredients

- 2 sheets phyllo dough (14 inches x 9 inches)
- Butter-flavored cooking spray
- 3/4 cup sliced unsweetened strawberries, divided
- 3-1/2 teaspoons confectioners' sugar, divided
- 1/8 teaspoon grated orange zest
- 2 tablespoons fat-free vanilla yogurt
- 1 medium navel orange, peeled and sectioned

## Direction

- Place sheets of phyllo dough on top of each other. Longitudinally halve the stack, then halve widthwise. Use cooking spray to spritz top sheet of each, then press one stack lightly into a 6-oz. custard cup coated with cooking spray. Press a second stack on top lightly, then repeat with the leftover stacks in another custard cup. Bake for 10 to 12 minutes at 375°, until golden brown. Allow to cool about 5 minutes, then carefully turn phyllo cups to a wire rack to cool thoroughly.
- At the same time, in a blender, add orange zest, 3 tsp. confectioners' sugar and 1/2 cup of strawberries, then cover and process until smooth. Mix in yogurt and place phyllo cups on serving plates. Fill cups with remaining strawberries and orange segments. Put yogurt sauce on top and sprinkle with leftover confectioners' sugar.

## Nutrition Information

- Calories: 136 calories
- Total Carbohydrate: 29g carbohydrate (0 sugars
- Cholesterol: 0 cholesterol
- Protein: 3g protein. Diabetic Exchanges: 1 starch
- Total Fat: 1g fat (0 saturated fat)
- Sodium: 104mg sodium
- Fiber: 3g fiber)

## 896. Stuffed Phyllo Pastries

*Serving: about 60 pastries. | Prep: 30mins | Cook: 10mins | Ready in:*

## Ingredients

- FILLING:
- 1 package (10 ounces) frozen chopped spinach, thawed
- 1 pound feta cheese, crumbled
- 3 ounces grated Parmesan cheese
- 2 large eggs, beaten
- 1 teaspoon nutmeg
- 1/2 teaspoon pepper
- 1 package (16 ounces, 14-inch x 9-inch sheet size) frozen phyllo dough, thawed
- 1 to 1-1/2 cups unsalted butter, melted

## Direction

- In a fine strainer, push the spinach to get rid of the excess moisture; mix with pepper, cheeses, nutmeg, and eggs to make the filling. Set aside.
- Prep a big work surface, a baking sheet, melted butter, the filling, pastry brush, a clean and slightly moist towel, and knife to put the pastries together. Unbox the dough; unfold sheets cautiously, take 2 sheets, place two sheets on a work surface then spread butter lightly. Take another sheet and put another sheet directly on top then spread butter. Repeat until you have five layered sheets. Use a damp towel to cover the remaining dough.
- Slice the layers in half lengthwise then slice the halves into six strips lengthwise. Put 1 1/2 teaspoons of filling at the upper part of each strip. Fold each strip like a flag into triangles beginning at the base close to filling. Repeat with more phyllo dough layers until all the filling is used. Arrange on an ungreased baking sheet then slather with butter.
- Bake for 10-15 minutes in 400 degrees oven until golden brown. You can freeze the uncooked pastries for future use. You can directly bake the frozen pastries, just increase the baking time.

## Nutrition Information

- Calories: 234 calories
- Protein: 9g protein.
- Total Fat: 15g fat (9g saturated fat)
- Sodium: 416mg sodium
- Fiber: 2g fiber)
- Total Carbohydrate: 16g carbohydrate (1g sugars
- Cholesterol: 61mg cholesterol

## 897. Stuffed Red Peppers

*Serving: 6 | Prep: 15mins | Cook: 1hours30mins | Ready in:*

## Ingredients

- 2 cups brown rice
- 4 cups water
- 1 pound ground beef
- 1 onion, diced
- 1/4 cup chopped mushrooms, or to taste
- 3 cloves garlic, chopped
- 1 (26 ounce) jar tomato sauce
- 1 (16 ounce) can diced tomatoes
- 1 (6 ounce) can tomato paste
- 1 teaspoon Italian seasoning
- salt and ground black pepper to taste
- 6 red bell peppers, tops and seeds removed
- 1/4 cup grated Parmesan cheese, or to taste

## Direction

- In a saucepan, bring to a boil the brown rice and water. Lower down heat to medium low, put on lid of the saucepan, and simmer for about 40 minutes, until rice is tender; take out brown rice from saucepan and place it in a large mixing bowl.
- Set oven to 350°F (175 degrees C) for preheating.
- Over medium-high heat, warm a large skillet. Crumble ground beef and put in the skillet. Sauté with onion, garlic and mushroom for 7 to 10 minutes, until beef turns completely brown. Pour beef mixture over brown rice then mix.

- Combine diced tomatoes, tomato sauce and tomato paste, and Italian seasoning with the rice mixture; sprinkle salt and black pepper to season.
- In a baking dish, lay out bell peppers. Fill the bell peppers with a spoon of filling.
- Bake filled peppers in the preheated oven for about 1 hour, until peppers are tender. Top with Parmesan cheese and serve.

## Nutrition Information

- Calories: 504 calories;
- Cholesterol: 50
- Protein: 24
- Total Fat: 12.6
- Sodium: 1095
- Total Carbohydrate: 74.3

## 898. Summer Garden Couscous Salad

*Serving: 9 servings. | Prep: 15mins | Cook: 15mins | Ready in:*

## Ingredients

- 3 medium ears sweet corn, husks removed
- 1 cup reduced-sodium chicken broth or vegetable broth
- 1 cup uncooked couscous
- 1 medium cucumber, halved and sliced
- 1-1/2 cups cherry tomatoes, halved
- 1/2 cup crumbled feta cheese
- 1/4 cup chopped red onion
- 3 tablespoons minced fresh parsley
- 3 tablespoons olive oil
- 3 tablespoons lemon juice
- 1 teaspoon dried oregano
- 3/4 teaspoon ground cumin
- 1/2 teaspoon salt
- 1/2 teaspoon pepper

## Direction

- In a Dutch oven, place the corn covered with water; boil. Cover and cook until tender for 6-9 minutes. As it cooks, boil broth in a small saucepan. Mix in couscous. Take off heat and let stand, covered, until water is absorbed for 5-10 minutes. Fluff using a fork then put aside to slightly cool.
- Mix parsley, onion, cheese, tomatoes, and cucumber in a big bowl. Drain corn then quickly put in ice water. Drain then pat dry. Cut kernels off the cobs. Add into cucumber mixture. Mix in couscous.
- Whisk seasonings, lemon juice, and oil in a small bowl. Pour on couscous mixture while tossing until coated.
- Immediately serve or keep in the fridge, covered, until chilled.

## Nutrition Information

- Calories: 171 calories
- Total Carbohydrate: 25g carbohydrate (3g sugars
- Cholesterol: 3mg cholesterol
- Protein: 6g protein.  Diabetic Exchanges: 1-1/2 starch
- Total Fat: 6g fat (1g saturated fat)
- Sodium: 265mg sodium
- Fiber: 3g fiber)

## 899. Summer Garden Salad

*Serving: 2 servings. | Prep: 20mins | Cook: 0mins | Ready in:*

## Ingredients

- 1 medium tomato, thinly sliced
- 1/2 small cucumber, thinly sliced
- 3 tablespoons chopped celery
- 2 tablespoons sliced ripe olives
- 2 tablespoons chopped sweet onion
- 1 tablespoon minced fresh mint
- 2 teaspoons minced fresh parsley

- 2 teaspoons olive oil
- 2 teaspoons balsamic vinegar
- 1 small garlic clove, minced
- Dash salt
- Dash pepper
- 1 tablespoon crumbled feta cheese
- Fresh mint leaves, optional

## Direction

- Put cucumber and tomato in a small bowl. Add parsley, mint, onion, olives, and celery. Combine by tossing.
- Whisk pepper, salt, garlic, vinegar, and oil in a separate small bowl. Pour on tomato mixture then toss until coated. Distribute vegetables between 2 plates. Top with cheese. Garnish using mint leaves, if preferred.

## Nutrition Information

- Calories: 89 calories
- Protein: 2g protein. Diabetic Exchanges: 1 vegetable
- Total Fat: 6g fat (1g saturated fat)
- Sodium: 197mg sodium
- Fiber: 2g fiber)
- Total Carbohydrate: 7g carbohydrate (3g sugars
- Cholesterol: 2mg cholesterol

### 900. Summer Orzo

*Serving: 16 servings (3/4 cup each). | Prep: 30mins | Cook: 0mins | Ready in:*

## Ingredients

- 1 package (16 ounces) orzo pasta
- 1/4 cup water
- 1-1/2 cups fresh or frozen corn
- 24 cherry tomatoes, halved
- 2 cups (8 ounces) crumbled feta cheese
- 1 medium cucumber, seeded and chopped
- 1 small red onion, finely chopped
- 1/4 cup minced fresh mint
- 2 tablespoons capers, drained and chopped, optional
- 1/2 cup olive oil
- 1/4 cup lemon juice
- 1 tablespoon grated lemon peel
- 1-1/2 teaspoons salt
- 1 teaspoon pepper
- 1 cup sliced almonds, toasted

## Direction

- Cook orzo until al dente following the directions on the package. Drain pasta; wash with cold water and drain again. Remove pasta to a large bowl. Cook water over medium heat in a large nonstick skillet. Add corn; cook until 3 to 4 minutes, stirring, or until crisp-tender. Add corn to the bowl of orzo; mix in mint, onion, cucumber, feta cheese, tomatoes, and capers (if desired). Stir pepper, salt, lemon peel, lemon juice, and oil together in a small bowl until well combined. Drizzle over orzo mixture; stir until evenly coated. Chill in the fridge for half an hour.
- Mix in almond just before serving.

## Nutrition Information

- Calories:
- Protein:
- Total Fat:
- Sodium:
- Fiber:
- Total Carbohydrate:
- Cholesterol:

### 901. Summer Squash & Tomato Medley

*Serving: 6 servings. | Prep: 15mins | Cook: 5mins | Ready in:*

### Ingredients

- 3 medium yellow summer squash, thinly sliced
- 3 tablespoons lemon juice
- 3 tablespoons olive oil
- 2 tablespoons snipped fresh dill or 1-1/2 teaspoons dill weed
- 1 garlic clove, minced
- 1-1/2 teaspoons Dijon mustard
- 3/4 teaspoon sugar
- 1/2 teaspoon salt
- 1/4 teaspoon pepper
- 3/4 cup crumbled feta cheese
- 2 medium tomatoes, diced
- 1/2 cup finely chopped sweet onion

### Direction

- Boil an inch of water in a small saucepan; put in squash. Boil for 3-4 mins while covering or until the squash is tender. Drain.
- Mix pepper, lemon juice, salt, oil, sugar, dill, mustard, and garlic in a big bowl. Mix in cheese and squash gently; move to a serving platter. Mix onion and tomato; scoop on top of the squash mixture. Serve right away.

### Nutrition Information

- Calories: 393 calories
- Cholesterol: 23mg cholesterol
- Protein: 13g protein.
- Total Fat: 28g fat (7g saturated fat)
- Sodium: 1101mg sodium
- Fiber: 7g fiber)
- Total Carbohydrate: 26g carbohydrate (14g sugars

---

## 902. Summer Squash And Tomato Side Dish With Feta

*Serving: 2 servings. | Prep: 15mins | Cook: 5mins | Ready in:*

### Ingredients

- 1 medium yellow summer squash, thinly sliced
- 1 tablespoon lemon juice
- 1 tablespoon olive oil
- 2 teaspoons snipped fresh dill or 1/2 teaspoon dill weed
- 1 small garlic clove, minced
- 1/2 teaspoon Dijon mustard
- 1/4 teaspoon sugar
- 1/4 teaspoon salt
- 1/8 teaspoon pepper
- 1/4 cup crumbled feta cheese
- 1 medium tomato, diced
- 1/4 cup finely chopped sweet onion

### Direction

- Bring 1/2 inch of water in a small saucepan to a boil, then put in squash and boil with a cover until soft, about 3 to 4 minutes. Drain.
- Mix together pepper, salt, sugar, mustard, garlic, dill, oil and lemon juice in a big bowl, then stir in cheese as well as squash gently. Move the mixture to a serving platter. Mix onion and tomato, then pour over squash mixture. Serve at once.

### Nutrition Information

- Calories: 140 calories
- Fiber: 3g fiber)
- Total Carbohydrate: 11g carbohydrate (6g sugars
- Cholesterol: 8mg cholesterol
- Protein: 5g protein.
- Total Fat: 9g fat (3g saturated fat)
- Sodium: 467mg sodium

### 903. Summer Fresh Quinoa Salad

*Serving: 14 servings. | Prep: 15mins | Cook: 10mins | Ready in:*

### Ingredients

- 2 cups quinoa, rinsed
- 1 cup boiling water
- 1/2 cup sun-dried tomatoes (not packed in oil)
- 1 medium cucumber, peeled, seeded and chopped
- 1 each medium green, sweet red and yellow peppers, chopped
- 6 green onions, thinly sliced
- 1 package (4 ounces) crumbled garlic and herb feta cheese
- 1/2 cup reduced-fat sun-dried tomato salad dressing, divided

### Direction

- Prepare the quinoa following the package instructions; move to a big bowl then completely cool.
- Put tomatoes and water in a small bowl; set aside for 5 minutes then drain. Chop the tomatoes then put into the quinoa. Mix in a quarter cup of salad dressing, cucumber, cheese, onions, and peppers.
- Cover then chill for 2 hours. Mix in the remaining salad dressing barely before serving.

### Nutrition Information

- Calories: 148 calories
- Total Carbohydrate: 22g carbohydrate (3g sugars
- Cholesterol: 6mg cholesterol
- Protein: 5g protein. Diabetic Exchanges: 1-1/2 starch
- Total Fat: 4g fat (1g saturated fat)
- Sodium: 248mg sodium
- Fiber: 2g fiber)

### 904. Sun Dried Tomato Goat Cheese Spread

*Serving: 4 | Prep: 10mins | Cook: | Ready in:*

### Ingredients

- 1 cup soft goat cheese
- 1/3 cup chopped sun-dried tomatoes
- 3 cloves garlic, minced
- 1 tablespoon chopped fresh parsley

### Direction

- In a food processor, add parsley, garlic, tomatoes, and goat cheese and mix until blended properly.

### Nutrition Information

- Calories: 222 calories;
- Protein: 13
- Total Fat: 17.1
- Sodium: 387
- Total Carbohydrate: 4.8
- Cholesterol: 45

### 905. Sun Dried Tomato Hummus

*Serving: 16 | Prep: 15mins | Cook: | Ready in:*

### Ingredients

- 4 cloves garlic
- 1 teaspoon salt
- 3 tablespoons tahini paste
- 1/4 cup fresh lemon juice
- 2 (15.5 ounce) cans garbanzo beans, drained
- 1/2 cup olive oil
- 1/2 cup oil-packed sun-dried tomatoes, drained
- 1/4 cup finely shredded fresh basil

- 2 tablespoons olive oil
- 1/8 teaspoon paprika (optional)

## Direction

- In a food processor, process the lemon juice, tahini, salt and garlic until it becomes smooth. Stir in 1/2 cup of olive oil and garbanzo beans then blend until it becomes smooth again; occasionally scrape the bowl's side. Stir in the sun-dried tomatoes when the mixture is already smooth, then process until chopped to very fine pieces and combined well into the hummus. Lastly, put the basil and process several times until incorporated.
- In a shallow serving dish, spread the hummus and form several decorative grooves on the top. Let it chill in the fridge for a minimum of 1 hour, then trickle with 2 tablespoons of olive oil and sprinkle paprika on top prior to serving.

## Nutrition Information

- Calories: 163 calories;
- Sodium: 349
- Total Carbohydrate: 14.6
- Cholesterol: 0
- Protein: 3.5
- Total Fat: 10.6

## 906. Sweet Onion, Tomato & Cuke Salad

*Serving: 10 servings. | Prep: 15mins | Cook: 0mins | Ready in:*

## Ingredients

- 3 large tomatoes, chopped
- 3 large cucumbers, peeled, halved, seeded and sliced
- 1 large sweet onion, halved and thinly sliced
- 1/2 cup olive oil
- 3 tablespoons mayonnaise
- 2 tablespoons rice vinegar
- 1 tablespoon Dijon mustard
- 1 garlic clove, minced
- 1/2 teaspoon salt
- 1/4 teaspoon pepper
- 1/4 cup crumbled feta cheese

## Direction

- Mix onion, cucumbers, and tomatoes together in a large bowl. Combine pepper, salt, garlic, mustard, vinegar, mayonnaise, and oil in a small bowl, stir properly. Pour over the tomato mixture and toss until evenly coated. Top with cheese.

## Nutrition Information

- Calories: 164 calories
- Cholesterol: 3mg cholesterol
- Protein: 2g protein.
- Total Fat: 15g fat (2g saturated fat)
- Sodium: 209mg sodium
- Fiber: 2g fiber)
- Total Carbohydrate: 7g carbohydrate (4g sugars

## 907. Sweet Potato Hummus

*Serving: 20 | Prep: 20mins | Cook: 45mins | Ready in:*

## Ingredients

- 3 sweet potatoes
- 1 (15 ounce) can garbanzo beans, drained (reserve liquid) and rinsed
- 2 tablespoons extra-virgin olive oil
- 2 tablespoons tahini
- 2 tablespoons lemon juice
- 1/2 teaspoon lemon zest
- 1/4 teaspoon ground cumin
- 1/4 teaspoon ground coriander
- 1/4 teaspoon ground white pepper

- sea salt to taste

### Direction

- Set an oven to preheat at 200°C (400°F).
- Using a fork, prick the sweet potatoes all over to make holes.
- In the preheated oven, roast the sweet potatoes for about 45 minutes until tender and let it cool. Halve the sweet potatoes lengthwise.
- In a blender, mix olive oil and garbanzo beans then pulse a few times to puree. Scoop out the flesh of sweet potato peels and put it in the blender, then process to blend. Stir into mixture the sea salt, white pepper, coriander, cumin, lemon zest, lemon juice and tahini, then process until it becomes smooth. If necessary, add reserved garbanzo bean liquid to create a creamy and smooth hummus.

### Nutrition Information

- Calories: 75 calories;
- Total Carbohydrate: 12.2
- Cholesterol: 0
- Protein: 1.6
- Total Fat: 2.3
- Sodium: 83

### 908. Tabbouleh Salad

*Serving: 10 servings. | Prep: 30mins | Cook: 0mins | Ready in:*

### Ingredients

- 1 cup bulgur
- 2 cups boiling water
- 4 medium tomatoes, chopped
- 2 medium cucumbers, peeled and sliced
- 1 cup minced fresh parsley
- 1 cup minced fresh mint
- 4 green onions, finely chopped
- 1/3 cup lemon juice
- 1/3 cup olive oil
- 1 tablespoon chopped seeded jalapeno pepper
- 2 garlic cloves, minced
- 1/2 teaspoon salt
- 1/2 teaspoon ground allspice
- 1/4 teaspoon pepper
- Bibb or Boston lettuce leaves

### Direction

- In a small bowl, put bulgur and mix in boiling water. Put a cover on and let it sit until the bulgur has soaked up nearly all of the water, or for about 30 minutes. Strain thoroughly.
- Put in a big bowl. Add onions, mint, parsley, cucumbers, and tomatoes. Combine pepper, allspice, salt, garlic, jalapeno, oil, and lemon juice in a small bowl. Put on the bulgur mixture and toss to coat.
- Put a cover on and chill for a minimum of 2 hours. Enjoy on lettuce leaves.

### Nutrition Information

- Calories: 142 calories
- Protein: 3g protein. Diabetic Exchanges: 1-1/2 fat
- Total Fat: 8g fat (1g saturated fat)
- Sodium: 129mg sodium
- Fiber: 5g fiber)
- Total Carbohydrate: 17g carbohydrate (3g sugars
- Cholesterol: 0 cholesterol

### 909. Tabouli Primavera

*Serving: 10 servings. | Prep: 20mins | Cook: 0mins | Ready in:*

### Ingredients

- 1 cup bulgur
- 3 cups boiling water
- 1 cup chopped tomatoes

- 1 cup shredded carrots
- 1 package (4 ounces) crumbled feta cheese
- 2 cans (2-1/4 ounces each) sliced ripe olives, drained
- 1/4 cup minced fresh basil
- 2 tablespoons lemon juice
- 1 tablespoon olive oil
- 1/2 teaspoon salt

### Direction

- Add the bulgur into the big bowl; whisk in the boiling water. Keep covered and allow it to rest for half an hour or till most of liquid has been absorbed. Drain and squeeze them to dry.
- In a separate big bowl, mix the salt, oil, lemon juice, basil, olives, feta cheese, carrots and tomatoes. Put in the bulgur and coat by tossing.

### Nutrition Information

- Calories: 105 calories
- Sodium: 291mg sodium
- Fiber: 4g fiber)
- Total Carbohydrate: 14g carbohydrate (2g sugars
- Cholesterol: 6mg cholesterol
- Protein: 4g protein.
- Total Fat: 4g fat (2g saturated fat)

## 910. Tahini Roasted Vegetables

*Serving: 6 servings. | Prep: 25mins | Cook: 25mins | Ready in:*

### Ingredients

- 1 medium eggplant, peeled
- 2 medium sweet red peppers
- 1 medium zucchini
- 1 medium onion
- 1 tablespoon olive oil
- 1 tablespoon tahini
- 2 teaspoons rice vinegar
- 2 teaspoons honey
- 1/2 teaspoon salt
- 1/4 teaspoon pepper
- 2 tablespoons minced fresh parsley

### Direction

- Cut onion, zucchini, red peppers and eggplant into pieces with 1 inch size. Put in a 15"x10"x1" baking pan coated with cooking spray. Mix together pepper, salt, honey, vinegar, tahini and oil in a small bowl, then pour over vegetables and toss to coat well.
- Bake at 450° without a cover until softened, about 25 to 30 minutes while stirring sometimes. Whisk in parsley before serving.

### Nutrition Information

- Calories: 91 calories
- Protein: 2g protein. Diabetic Exchanges: 2 vegetable
- Total Fat: 4g fat (1g saturated fat)
- Sodium: 203mg sodium
- Fiber: 4g fiber)
- Total Carbohydrate: 13g carbohydrate (8g sugars
- Cholesterol: 0 cholesterol

## 911. Tangerine Tabbouleh

*Serving: 8 servings. | Prep: 35mins | Cook: 0mins | Ready in:*

### Ingredients

- 1 cup bulgur
- 1 cup boiling water
- 1 can (15 ounces) garbanzo beans or chickpeas, rinsed and drained
- 2 tangerines, peeled, sectioned and chopped

- 2/3 cup chopped dates
- 1/2 cup pistachios, coarsely chopped
- 1/3 cup dried cranberries
- 1/2 cup tangerine juice
- 2 tablespoons olive oil
- 1 teaspoon grated tangerine peel
- 1/4 teaspoon ground ginger
- 1/8 teaspoon salt

### Direction

- Combine bulgur and water in a large bowl. Cover and allow to stand for 30 minutes or until the liquid is mostly absorbed. Drain properly.
- Stir in cranberries, pistachios, dates, tangerines and garbanzo beans. In a small bowl, combine salt, ginger, tangerine peel, oil and tangerine juice. Add to bulgur mixture and toss until well coated. Cover and chill for a minimum of 1 hour. Stir before serving.

### Nutrition Information

- Calories: 261 calories
- Protein: 7g protein.
- Total Fat: 8g fat (1g saturated fat)
- Sodium: 142mg sodium
- Fiber: 8g fiber)
- Total Carbohydrate: 44g carbohydrate (19g sugars
- Cholesterol: 0 cholesterol

## 912. Tangy Caesar Salad

*Serving: 6-8 servings. | Prep: 15mins | Cook: 0mins | Ready in:*

### Ingredients

- 8 cups torn romaine
- 1/4 cup creamy Caesar salad dressing
- 1 tablespoon lemon juice
- 1/2 teaspoon pepper
- 1 cup Caesar salad croutons
- 1/3 cup grated Parmesan cheese

### Direction

- In a big salad bowl, insert the romaine. Beat pepper, lemon juice and salad dressing together in a small bowl. Pour this mixture into the bowl with the romaine in a drizzling motion, tossing until coated. Put the cheese and croutons over the top.

### Nutrition Information

- Calories:
- Total Carbohydrate:
- Cholesterol:
- Protein:
- Total Fat:
- Sodium:
- Fiber:

## 913. Tangy Feta Herb Dip

*Serving: 1 cup. | Prep: 15mins | Cook: 0mins | Ready in:*

### Ingredients

- 2 cups (16 ounces) plain yogurt
- 1/2 cup crumbled feta cheese
- 1-1/2 teaspoons olive oil
- 1 small garlic clove, minced
- 1 teaspoon minced fresh parsley
- 1/2 teaspoon dried oregano
- 1/4 teaspoon salt
- 1/8 teaspoon pepper
- Baked pita chips and/or assorted fresh vegetables

### Direction

- Line 1 coffee filter or 4 cheesecloth layers on a strainer and set over a bowl. In the prepped strainer, place the yogurt and use cheesecloth's edges to cover the yogurt. Store

for 8 hours to overnight in the fridge. Take the yogurt out of the cheesecloth and remove the liquid from the bowl.
- Combine pepper, salt, oregano, parsley, garlic, oil, cheese and yogurt in a large bowl. Let chill till serving. Serve with vegetables or/and pita chips.

## Nutrition Information

- Calories: 127 calories
- Total Fat: 8g fat (4g saturated fat)
- Sodium: 339mg sodium
- Fiber: 1g fiber)
- Total Carbohydrate: 7g carbohydrate (6g sugars
- Cholesterol: 23mg cholesterol
- Protein: 7g protein.

## 914. Tangy Marinated Vegetables

*Serving: 12 servings. | Prep: 25mins | Cook: 0mins | Ready in:*

## Ingredients

- 3/4 cup lemon juice
- 3/4 cup canola oil
- 3 tablespoons sugar
- 1 tablespoon salt
- 1-1/2 teaspoons dried oregano
- 1/2 teaspoon pepper
- 1 can (15 ounces) whole baby corn, rinsed and drained
- 1 cup halved brussels sprouts, cooked
- 1 cup halved fresh mushrooms
- 1 cup fresh cauliflowerets
- 1 cup fresh snow peas, halved
- 1 cup cherry tomatoes
- 1 cup sliced sweet yellow pepper
- 1 cup sliced sweet red pepper

## Direction

- Beat the pepper, oregano, salt, sugar, oil and lemon juice together in a small bowl then empty this bowl out into a big resealable plastic bag. Insert vegetables. After sealing the bag up, coat everything by turning. Keep the bag in the fridge for 6 hours or through the night.

## Nutrition Information

- Calories:
- Protein:
- Total Fat:
- Sodium:
- Fiber:
- Total Carbohydrate:
- Cholesterol:

## 915. Terrific Tomato Tart

*Serving: 8 servings. | Prep: 15mins | Cook: 20mins | Ready in:*

## Ingredients

- 12 sheets phyllo dough (14 inches x 9 inches)
- 2 tablespoons olive oil
- 2 tablespoons dry bread crumbs
- 2 tablespoons prepared pesto
- 3/4 cup crumbled feta cheese, divided
- 1 medium tomato, cut into 1/4-inch slices
- 1 large yellow tomato, cut into 1/4-inch slices
- 1/4 teaspoon pepper
- 5 to 6 fresh basil leaves, thinly sliced

## Direction

- Put 1 sheet of phyllo dough on a parchment paper-lined baking tray, then brush it using 1/2 teaspoon oil and sprinkle 1/2 teaspoon breadcrumbs on top. (Keep the leftover phyllo covered with a plastic wrap and moist towel to avoid it from drying out.) Redo the layers and

- be careful to brush the oil all the way to the edges.
- To form a rim, fold each side 3/4-inch towards the middle. Spread pesto and sprinkle 1/2 of the feta cheese on top. Lay out the yellow and red slices of tomato alternately on top of the cheese. Sprinkle leftover feta and pepper on top.
- Let it bake for 20 to 25 minutes at 400 degrees or until the crust becomes crispy and turns golden brown in color. Allow it to cool for 5 minutes on a wire rack. Take off the parchment paper prior to cutting. Put basil on top to garnish.

## Nutrition Information

- Calories: 135 calories
- Protein: 5g protein. Diabetic Exchanges: 1-1/2 fat
- Total Fat: 7g fat (2g saturated fat)
- Sodium: 221mg sodium
- Fiber: 1g fiber)
- Total Carbohydrate: 13g carbohydrate (1g sugars
- Cholesterol: 7mg cholesterol

## 916. Three Cheese Tomato Garlic Bread

*Serving: 16 appetizer servings. | Prep: 20mins | Cook: 15mins | Ready in:*

## Ingredients

- 1 loaf (1 pound) unsliced French bread
- 1/4 cup butter, melted
- 3 garlic cloves, minced
- 1/3 cup prepared pesto
- 3/4 cup spaghetti sauce
- 1 cup shredded part-skim mozzarella cheese
- 1/3 cup water-packed artichoke hearts, rinsed, drained and chopped
- 1/2 cup chopped ripe olives
- 1/4 cup oil-packed sun-dried tomatoes, finely chopped
- 4 medium tomatoes, sliced
- 1/2 cup crumbled feta cheese
- 1/4 cup grated Parmesan cheese

## Direction

- Halve the bread lengthwise, then cut in half widthwise. Mix garlic and butter; brush over the cut sides of the bread. Arrange on 2 ungreased baking sheets.
- Next, spread with spaghetti sauce and pesto; dust with mozzarella. Lay the remaining ingredients on top.
- Bake for 14-16 minutes at 400°, or until golden brown. Then cut into slices.

## Nutrition Information

- Calories: 192 calories
- Total Carbohydrate: 20g carbohydrate (3g sugars
- Cholesterol: 17mg cholesterol
- Protein: 8g protein.
- Total Fat: 9g fat (4g saturated fat)
- Sodium: 442mg sodium
- Fiber: 2g fiber)

## 917. Thyme 'n' Thyme Again Salad Dressing

*Serving: 1 cup. | Prep: 5mins | Cook: 0mins | Ready in:*

## Ingredients

- 1/3 cup olive oil
- 1/4 cup red wine vinegar
- 1/4 cup crumbled feta cheese
- 2 tablespoons minced fresh thyme
- 1 tablespoon minced fresh oregano
- 1 tablespoon minced fresh marjoram
- 1 tablespoon Dijon mustard
- 1 garlic clove, minced

- 1-1/2 to 2 teaspoons sugar
- 1/4 teaspoon white pepper
- 1/8 teaspoon salt
- Mixed salad greens

### Direction

- Combine the first 11 ingredients in a jar that comes with a tight-fitting lid. Shake properly just before serving; pour over salad greens. Store in the refrigerator.

### Nutrition Information

- Calories: 196 calories
- Total Carbohydrate: 4g carbohydrate (2g sugars
- Cholesterol: 4mg cholesterol
- Protein: 2g protein.
- Total Fat: 20g fat (3g saturated fat)
- Sodium: 236mg sodium
- Fiber: 1g fiber)

## 918. Tomato Artichoke Salad

*Serving: 4 servings. | Prep: 15mins | Cook: 0mins | Ready in:*

### Ingredients

- 1/4 cup lemon juice
- 1/4 cup chopped seeded peeled cucumber
- 2 tablespoons fat-free plain yogurt
- 1/2 teaspoon dried oregano
- 1/4 teaspoon salt
- 1/4 teaspoon pepper
- 1 can (14 ounces) water-packed artichoke hearts, rinsed, drained and halved
- 1 can (2-1/4 ounces) sliced ripe olives, drained
- 2 medium tomatoes, seeded and chopped
- 1/2 cup julienned silken firm tofu
- 1/2 cup chopped red onion

### Direction

- To make dressing, combine pepper, salt, oregano, yogurt, cucumber and lemon juice in a food processor or a food blender; cover and process until well blended.
- Combine onion, tofu, tomatoes, olives and artichokes in a bowl. Drizzle with dressing and toss until well coated. Chill, covered, for a minimum of 30 minutes before serving.

### Nutrition Information

- Calories: 102 calories
- Protein: 6g protein. Diabetic Exchanges: 2 vegetable
- Total Fat: 3g fat (0 saturated fat)
- Sodium: 555mg sodium
- Fiber: 2g fiber)
- Total Carbohydrate: 15g carbohydrate (5g sugars
- Cholesterol: 0 cholesterol

## 919. Tomato Couscous Soup

*Serving: 2 servings. | Prep: 10mins | Cook: 30mins | Ready in:*

### Ingredients

- 1/4 cup chopped onion
- 1 garlic clove, minced
- 2 teaspoons olive oil
- 1-1/2 cups reduced-sodium chicken or vegetable broth
- 2 medium tomatoes, peeled, seeded and chopped
- 1 teaspoon fresh oregano or 1/4 teaspoon dried oregano
- 3 tablespoons uncooked couscous
- 1/8 teaspoon salt

### Direction

- Sauté garlic and onion in oil in a large saucepan until softened. Add oregano,

tomatoes, and the broth. Bring to a boil. Lower heat; simmer, covered until tomatoes are tender, or for 20 to 25 minutes.
- Turn off the heat; mix in couscous, and season with salt. Allow to sit for 5 minutes before serving.

## Nutrition Information

- Calories: 152 calories
- Protein: 6g protein. Diabetic Exchanges: 1 starch
- Total Fat: 5g fat (1g saturated fat)
- Sodium: 625mg sodium
- Fiber: 3g fiber)
- Total Carbohydrate: 22g carbohydrate (0 sugars
- Cholesterol: 0 cholesterol

## 920. Tomato Feta Salad

*Serving: 4 servings. | Prep: 20mins | Cook: 0mins | Ready in:*

## Ingredients

- 2 tablespoons balsamic vinegar
- 1-1/2 teaspoons minced fresh basil or 1/2 teaspoon dried basil
- 1/2 teaspoon salt
- 1/2 cup coarsely chopped sweet onion
- 1 pound grape or cherry tomatoes, halved
- 2 tablespoons olive oil
- 1/4 cup crumbled feta cheese

## Direction

- In a large bowl, mix salt, basil and vinegar. Put onion in the bowl; toss to coat. Allow to sit for 5 minutes. Then put feta cheese, oil and tomatoes in the bowl; toss to coat. Use a slotted spoon to serve.

## Nutrition Information

- Calories: 121 calories
- Cholesterol: 8mg cholesterol
- Protein: 3g protein.
- Total Fat: 9g fat (2g saturated fat)
- Sodium: 412mg sodium
- Fiber: 2g fiber)
- Total Carbohydrate: 9g carbohydrate (3g sugars

## 921. Tomato Pea Couscous

*Serving: 4 servings. | Prep: 10mins | Cook: 10mins | Ready in:*

## Ingredients

- 1/2 cup chopped onion
- 2 garlic cloves, minced
- 1 tablespoon olive oil
- 1/2 teaspoon ground cumin
- 1 cup reduced-sodium chicken broth or vegetable broth
- 1 cup frozen peas
- 1/2 cup coarsely chopped seeded tomato
- 3/4 cup uncooked couscous

## Direction

- Sauté garlic and onion in oil in a big saucepan until tender. Mix in cumin, cook while stirring for 30 seconds. Mix in tomato, peas, and broth. Cook until the peas are almost soft, about 1-2 minutes. Mix in couscous and put a cover on. Take away from heat, let sit for 5 minutes. Use a fork to fluff.

## Nutrition Information

- Calories: 184 calories
- Sodium: 182mg sodium
- Fiber: 3g fiber)
- Total Carbohydrate: 31g carbohydrate (0 sugars
- Cholesterol: 0 cholesterol

- Protein: 6g protein.  Diabetic Exchanges: 2 starch
- Total Fat: 4g fat (1g saturated fat)

## 922. Tomato Rosemary Hummus

*Serving: 3 cups. | Prep: 15mins | Cook: 20mins | Ready in:*

### Ingredients

- 1 medium onion, chopped
- 3 tablespoons olive oil
- 4 garlic cloves, minced
- 2 cans (15 ounces each) garbanzo beans or chickpeas, rinsed and drained
- 1 can (6 ounces) tomato paste
- 1 tablespoon minced fresh rosemary or 1 teaspoon dried rosemary, crushed
- 1/2 teaspoon salt
- 1/4 teaspoon pepper
- Baked pita chips

### Direction

- Sauté onion in a large pan with oil until it becomes soft. Turn down the heat to medium-low and cook and stir for 20-30 minutes, stirring from time to time, or until it turns light golden brown in color. Add garlic. Cook for an additional 2 minutes.
- Let it cool slightly, then move the onion mixture into the food processor. Process the pepper, salt, rosemary, tomato paste and beans, covered, until it become smooth. Serve alongside chips.

### Nutrition Information

- Calories: 115 calories
- Sodium: 199mg sodium
- Fiber: 3g fiber)
- Total Carbohydrate: 15g carbohydrate (4g sugars
- Cholesterol: 0 cholesterol
- Protein: 4g protein.  Diabetic Exchanges: 1 starch
- Total Fat: 5g fat (0 saturated fat)

## 923. Tomato Zucchini Platter

*Serving: 6 servings. | Prep: 20mins | Cook: 5mins | Ready in:*

### Ingredients

- 4 medium zucchini, cut into 1/4-inch slices
- 3 medium tomatoes, cut into 1/4-inch slices
- 1/3 cup vegetable oil
- 3 tablespoons white vinegar
- 1-1/2 teaspoons lemon juice
- 1 teaspoon sugar
- 1/2 teaspoon salt
- 1/2 teaspoon ground mustard
- 1/2 teaspoon dried oregano
- 1/4 teaspoon coarsely ground pepper
- Pitted ripe olives

### Direction

- In a big skillet, pour in 1 in. of water and zucchini; boil. Lower heat; keep it covered and let it simmer till tender-crisp or for 2 to 3 minutes. Drain off and pat dry. Arrange tomatoes and zucchini in alternating circles on a serving platter.
- Mix pepper, oregano, mustard, salt, sugar, lemon juice, vinegar and oil in tight-fitting lidded jar; shake the mixture well. Sprinkle on top of tomatoes and zucchini. Keep it covered and let chill in the fridge for no less than 2 hours. Add olives in middle of veggies.

### Nutrition Information

- Calories: 146 calories

- Total Carbohydrate: 8g carbohydrate (5g sugars
- Cholesterol: 0 cholesterol
- Protein: 2g protein.
- Total Fat: 13g fat (2g saturated fat)
- Sodium: 207mg sodium
- Fiber: 2g fiber)

## 924. Tomato Green Bean Salad

*Serving: 4 servings. | Prep: 10mins | Cook: 10mins | Ready in:*

### Ingredients

- 1/2 pound fresh green beans, trimmed
- 1-1/2 cups cherry tomatoes, halved
- 3/4 cup pitted ripe olives, halved
- 1/4 cup Italian salad dressing
- 2/3 cup crumbled feta cheese

### Direction

- In a big saucepan, put beans and fill with water. Boil it. Cook without a cover on until soft and crunchy, or for about 8 – 10 minutes. Strain and put the beans in ice water immediately. Strain and tap dry.
- Mix olives, tomatoes, and beans together in a big bowl. Use the dressing to sprinkle and toss to coat. Refrigerate until serving. Use cheese to drizzle right before eating.

### Nutrition Information

- Calories: 153 calories
- Sodium: 626mg sodium
- Fiber: 4g fiber)
- Total Carbohydrate: 9g carbohydrate (4g sugars
- Cholesterol: 10mg cholesterol
- Protein: 5g protein.
- Total Fat: 11g fat (3g saturated fat)

## 925. Tomatoes With Feta Cheese

*Serving: 4 servings. | Prep: 5mins | Cook: 0mins | Ready in:*

### Ingredients

- 8 slices tomato
- 2 tablespoons crumbled feta cheese
- 1 tablespoon balsamic vinegar
- 2 tablespoons minced fresh basil
- Pepper to taste

### Direction

- Place slices of tomatoes onto a serving plate. Use feta cheese to sprinkle. Pour drizzles of vinegar, use pepper and basil to sprinkle.

### Nutrition Information

- Calories: 20 calories
- Total Carbohydrate: 3g carbohydrate (2g sugars
- Cholesterol: 2mg cholesterol
- Protein: 1g protein.
- Total Fat: 1g fat (0 saturated fat)
- Sodium: 38mg sodium
- Fiber: 1g fiber)

## 926. Tossed Greek Salad

*Serving: 12 servings. | Prep: 15mins | Cook: 0mins | Ready in:*

### Ingredients

- 12 cups torn romaine
- 2 medium tomatoes, cut into wedges

- 1 medium cucumber, peeled, halved and sliced
- 1/2 medium green pepper, thinly sliced
- 1/2 medium red onion, cut into rings
- 1/2 cup sliced ripe olives
- 1/2 cup crumbled feta cheese
- LEMON DRESSING:
- 1/4 cup olive oil
- 2 tablespoons lemon juice
- 2 teaspoons Dijon mustard
- 2 garlic cloves, minced
- 1/2 teaspoon sugar
- 1/2 teaspoon dried oregano
- 1/4 teaspoon salt
- 1/4 teaspoon dried thyme
- 1/8 teaspoon pepper

## Direction

- Combine the first seven ingredients in a salad bowl. Whisk dressing ingredients together. Add dressing to salad mixture and toss until well coated. Serve right away.

## Nutrition Information

- Calories: 87 calories
- Total Carbohydrate: 6g carbohydrate (0 sugars
- Cholesterol: 6mg cholesterol
- Protein: 2g protein. Diabetic Exchanges: 1-1/2 fat
- Total Fat: 7g fat (2g saturated fat)
- Sodium: 196mg sodium
- Fiber: 2g fiber)

### 927. Traditional Greek Salad

Serving: 4 | Prep: 20mins | Cook: | Ready in:

## Ingredients

- 3 tablespoons extra-virgin olive oil
- 1 tablespoon lemon juice
- 1 tablespoon red-wine vinegar
- 1 teaspoon dried oregano
- ¼ teaspoon salt
- ¼ teaspoon ground pepper
- 2 ripe medium tomatoes, cut into ¾-inch dice
- 1½ cups diced cucumber (¾-inch)
- 1 cup diced green bell pepper (¾-inch)
- ⅓ cup thinly sliced red onion
- ¼ cup quartered pitted Kalamata olives
- ½ cup diced feta cheese (2½ ounces)

## Direction

- Put salt, pepper, oregano, vinegar, lemon juice, and oil in a large bowl; whisk. Put in feta, olives, onion, bell pepper, cucumber and tomatoes. Toss to coat.

## Nutrition Information

- Calories: 189 calories;
- Cholesterol: 17
- Total Carbohydrate: 8
- Sugar: 4
- Protein: 4
- Total Fat: 16
- Saturated Fat: 4
- Sodium: 422
- Fiber: 2

### 928. Tuscan Bean And Olive Spread

Serving: 1-1/2 cups. | Prep: 20mins | Cook: 0mins | Ready in:

## Ingredients

- 6 sun-dried tomato halves (not packed in oil), finely chopped
- 1/2 cup boiling water
- 1 can (15 ounces) white kidney or cannellini beans, rinsed and drained
- 2 tablespoons water
- 1 tablespoon olive oil

- 1-1/2 teaspoons dried basil
- 1 garlic clove, halved
- 1/2 teaspoon dried rosemary, crushed
- 1/4 teaspoon pepper
- 1/8 teaspoon crushed red pepper flakes
- 1/4 cup Greek olives, chopped
- Bagel chips

### Direction

- Mix boiling water and tomatoes in a small bowl. Allow to stand about 5 minutes, then drain and set tomatoes aside.
- Put pepper flakes, pepper, rosemary, garlic, basil, oil, water and beans in a food processor, then cover and process until blended. Mix in tomatoes. Remove the mixture to a serving bowl, then sprinkle olives over.
- Serve together with bagel chips.

### Nutrition Information

- Calories: 99 calories
- Cholesterol: 0 cholesterol
- Protein: 3g protein.
- Total Fat: 4g fat (1g saturated fat)
- Sodium: 231mg sodium
- Fiber: 3g fiber)
- Total Carbohydrate: 12g carbohydrate (1g sugars

## 929. Tzatziki Potato Salad

*Serving: 12 servings (3/4 cup each). | Prep: 15mins | Cook: 10mins | Ready in:*

### Ingredients

- 3 pounds small red potatoes, halved
- 1 carton (12 ounces) refrigerated tzatziki sauce
- 2 celery ribs, thinly sliced
- 1/2 cup plain Greek yogurt
- 2 green onions, chopped
- 2 tablespoons snipped fresh dill
- 2 tablespoons minced fresh parsley
- 1/2 teaspoon salt
- 1/4 teaspoon celery salt
- 1/4 teaspoon pepper
- 1 tablespoon minced fresh mint, optional

### Direction

- Put potatoes in a Dutch oven, add water until submerged. Boil it. Decrease the heat, cook, take away the cover until softened, about 10-15 minutes. Strain and put in a big bowl. Put in the fridge, put a cover on until chilled.
- Whisk pepper, celery salt, salt, parsley, dill, green onions, yogurt, celery, and tzatziki sauce in a small bowl. You can add mint if you want. Place on the potatoes, mix to coat.

### Nutrition Information

- Calories: 128 calories
- Cholesterol: 7mg cholesterol
- Protein: 4g protein. Diabetic Exchanges: 1-1/2 starch
- Total Fat: 3g fat (2g saturated fat)
- Sodium: 190mg sodium
- Fiber: 2g fiber)
- Total Carbohydrate: 21g carbohydrate (3g sugars

## 930. Vegetarian Spinach Curry

*Serving: 4 servings. | Prep: 5mins | Cook: 20mins | Ready in:*

### Ingredients

- 1 cup chopped onion
- 2 garlic cloves, minced
- 1 tablespoon curry powder
- 1 tablespoon canola oil
- 1 can (8 ounces) tomato sauce
- 1 package (10 ounces) frozen chopped spinach, thawed and squeezed dry

- 1 can (15 ounces) garbanzo beans or chickpeas, rinsed and drained, divided
- 1 cup reduced-sodium chicken broth or vegetable broth
- 1/4 teaspoon salt
- 1/4 teaspoon pepper
- Hot cooked couscous, optional

## Direction

- In the non-stick skillet, cook curry powder, garlic and onion in the oil till the onion softens, about 3 to 4 minutes. Whisk in 1 cup of the garbanzo beans, spinach and tomato sauce. In the blender, mix the leftover garbanzo beans and broth; keep covered and blend for roughly 2 minutes or till smooth. Whisk to the skillet. Drizzle with the pepper and salt. Cook while stirring the mixture till thoroughly heated. Serve on top of the couscous if you want.

## Nutrition Information

- Calories: 193 calories
- Fiber: 8g fiber)
- Total Carbohydrate: 28g carbohydrate (0 sugars
- Cholesterol: 0 cholesterol
- Protein: 9g protein. Diabetic Exchanges: 2 vegetable
- Total Fat: 6g fat (0 saturated fat)
- Sodium: 764mg sodium

### 931. Veggie Couscous Quiche

*Serving: 6 servings. | Prep: 25mins | Cook: 50mins | Ready in:*

## Ingredients

- 1 large egg
- 1/2 teaspoon onion salt
- 2 cups cooked couscous, cooled
- 1/4 cup shredded Swiss cheese
- FILLING:
- 4 large eggs
- 1 cup half-and-half cream
- 4 cups frozen broccoli florets, thawed
- 1 can (6 ounces) sliced mushrooms, drained
- 1 cup shredded Swiss cheese, divided
- 1/4 teaspoon ground nutmeg
- 1 plum tomato, finely chopped
- 2 green onions, chopped

## Direction

- Combine onion salt and egg in a big bowl. Add cheese and couscous, whisk until mixed. Press up the sides and onto the bottom of a 9-inch deep-dish pie plate coated with oil. Bake for 5 minutes at 350°.
- To prepare the filling, stir together cream and eggs in a big bowl. Mix in nutmeg, 1/2 cup cheese, mushrooms, and broccoli. Add to the crust. Bake until a knife will come out clean when you insert it into the middle, about 45-55 minutes.
- Sprinkle onions and tomato, then the leftover cheese over. Bake until the cheese melts, about another 3-5 minutes. Allow to sit before slicing, about 10 minutes.

## Nutrition Information

- Calories: 281 calories
- Protein: 17g protein.
- Total Fat: 15g fat (8g saturated fat)
- Sodium: 423mg sodium
- Fiber: 3g fiber)
- Total Carbohydrate: 19g carbohydrate (4g sugars
- Cholesterol: 217mg cholesterol

### 932. Viva Panzanella

*Serving: 6 servings. | Prep: 30mins | Cook: 10mins | Ready in:*

## Ingredients

- 3/4 pound sourdough bread, cubed (about 8 cups)
- 2 tablespoons olive oil
- 2-1/2 pounds tomatoes (about 8 medium), chopped
- 1 can (15 ounces) white kidney or cannellini beans, rinsed and drained
- 1 can (14 ounces) water-packed artichoke hearts, rinsed, drained and quartered
- 1 cup thinly sliced roasted sweet red peppers
- 1/2 cup fresh basil leaves, thinly sliced
- 1/3 cup thinly sliced red onion
- 1/4 cup Greek olives, quartered
- 3 tablespoons capers, drained
- DRESSING:
- 1/4 cup balsamic vinegar
- 3 tablespoons minced fresh parsley
- 3 tablespoons olive oil
- 3 tablespoons lemon juice
- 2 tablespoons white wine vinegar
- 3 teaspoons minced fresh thyme or 1 teaspoon dried thyme
- 1-1/2 teaspoons minced fresh marjoram or 1/2 teaspoon dried marjoram
- 1-1/2 teaspoons minced fresh oregano or 1/2 teaspoon dried oregano
- 1 garlic clove, minced

## Direction

- Set the oven to preheat to 450°. Toss oil and bread together in a large bowl and place on a baking sheet. Bake for 8 to 10 minutes or until bread turns golden brown. Cool to room temperature.
- In a large bowl, combine bread, capers, olives, onion, basil, peppers, artichokes, beans and tomatoes.
- Whisk dressing ingredients in a small bowl. Add to salad and toss until well coated. Serve right away.

## Nutrition Information

- Calories: 424 calories
- Fiber: 7g fiber)
- Total Carbohydrate: 59g carbohydrate (10g sugars
- Cholesterol: 0 cholesterol
- Protein: 13g protein.
- Total Fat: 15g fat (2g saturated fat)
- Sodium: 1004mg sodium

## 933. Walnut Balls

*Serving: 12 | Prep: | Cook: |Ready in:*

## Ingredients

- 1/2 cup butter, softened
- 1 1/8 cups all-purpose flour
- 1 cup chopped walnuts
- 1/8 teaspoon salt
- 1 teaspoon vanilla extract
- 2 tablespoons white sugar
- 1/2 cup super fine sugar

## Direction

- Set an oven to preheat to 180°C (350°F).
- Cream the butter and sugar and add vanilla, salt, nuts and flour, then stir well. The batter will get very crumbly.
- Form it into 1-inch balls and let it bake for 15 minutes. Take it out of the oven and Let it cool for 3 minutes. Roll it in superfine sugar. Roll it again once cooled, if preferred.

## Nutrition Information

- Calories: 216 calories;
- Protein: 2.8
- Total Fat: 14.1
- Sodium: 79
- Total Carbohydrate: 20.7
- Cholesterol: 20

## 934. Walnut Cheese Spinach Salad

*Serving: 8 servings. | Prep: 15mins | Cook: 0mins | Ready in:*

### Ingredients

- 2 cups fresh raspberries
- 1/3 cup sugar
- 1/3 cup canola oil
- 2 tablespoons white vinegar
- 1/4 teaspoon Worcestershire sauce, optional
- 1 package (6 ounces) fresh baby spinach
- 1 small red onion, thinly sliced and separated into rings
- 1/2 to 1 cup crumbled feta cheese
- 1/2 cup chopped walnuts

### Direction

- Combine raspberries and sugar in a saucepan; Bring to a boil on medium heat. Cook for 1 minute. Strain and throw away the pulp.
- Combine Worcestershire sauce (optional), vinegar, oil and raspberry juice in a blender; cover and process until mixture is smooth.
- Combine walnuts, cheese, onion and spinach in a large salad bowl. Sprinkle with preferred amount of dressing; toss until well coated. Keep remaining dressing in refrigerate.

### Nutrition Information

- Calories: 202 calories
- Total Carbohydrate: 15g carbohydrate (10g sugars
- Cholesterol: 4mg cholesterol
- Protein: 4g protein.
- Total Fat: 15g fat (2g saturated fat)
- Sodium: 85mg sodium
- Fiber: 3g fiber)

## 935. Warm Feta Cheese Dip

*Serving: 2 cups. | Prep: 5mins | Cook: 25mins | Ready in:*

### Ingredients

- 1 package (8 ounces) cream cheese, softened
- 1-1/2 cups (6 ounces) crumbled feta cheese
- 1/2 cup chopped roasted sweet red peppers
- 3 tablespoons minced fresh basil or 2 teaspoons dried basil
- Sliced French bread baguette or tortilla chips

### Direction

- Set the oven to 400 degrees F. Beat basil, cream cheese, peppers, and feta cheese in a small bowl until well combined. Move to an oiled three-cup baking dish then bake for 25-30mins until bubbling. Serve the dip with chips or baguette slices.
- You can make this in a slow cooker. Combine the ingredients as directed then move to greased 1 1/2- quart slow cooker. Cook with a cover on for 2-3hrs on low until completely heated.

### Nutrition Information

- Calories: 155 calories
- Sodium: 362mg sodium
- Fiber: 1g fiber)
- Total Carbohydrate: 2g carbohydrate (1g sugars
- Cholesterol: 42mg cholesterol
- Protein: 5g protein.
- Total Fat: 13g fat (8g saturated fat)

## 936. Warm Mushroom Salad

*Serving: 4 | Prep: 15mins | Cook: 10mins | Ready in:*

### Ingredients

- 1 tablespoon olive oil

- 1 1/2 cups sliced fresh mushrooms
- 1 clove garlic, chopped (optional)
- 2 1/2 tablespoons olive oil
- 2 1/2 tablespoons balsamic vinegar
- salt and pepper to taste
- 1 (10 ounce) package baby greens mix

## Direction

- Over medium heat, heat 1 tbsp. of olive oil in a pan. Put in mushrooms, and cook while stirring until tender. Keep on cooking until the juices from the mushrooms have decreased to roughly two tbsps. Mix in the pepper, salt, balsamic vinegar and the leftover olive oil until equally blended. Turn the heat off, and let the mushrooms rest in the pan till just warm but not hot anymore – or else the greens will be overly wilted.
- Transfer the baby greens to a serving bowl, and put the warm mushroom mixture on top of them. Blend by tossing, and serve right away.

## Nutrition Information

- Calories: 130 calories;
- Total Fat: 12.1
- Sodium: 24
- Total Carbohydrate: 4.9
- Cholesterol: 0
- Protein: 2.2

## 937. Watermelon Cups

*Serving: 16 appetizers. | Prep: 25mins | Cook: 0mins | Ready in:*

## Ingredients

- 16 seedless watermelon cubes (1 inch)
- 1/3 cup finely chopped cucumber
- 5 teaspoons finely chopped red onion
- 2 teaspoons minced fresh mint
- 2 teaspoons minced fresh cilantro
- 1/2 to 1 teaspoon lime juice

## Direction

- Scoop out the middle of each watermelon cube with a measuring spoon or a small melon baller, keeping a quarter-inch shell. Set the pulp aside for another use.
- Mix the remaining ingredients in a small bowl; scoop into watermelon cubes.

## Nutrition Information

- Calories: 7 calories
- Protein: 0 protein.
- Total Fat: 0 fat (0 saturated fat)
- Sodium: 1mg sodium
- Fiber: 0 fiber)
- Total Carbohydrate: 2g carbohydrate (2g sugars
- Cholesterol: 0 cholesterol

## 938. White Bean 'n' Olive Toasts

*Serving: 1-1/2 dozen. | Prep: 20mins | Cook: 5mins | Ready in:*

## Ingredients

- 1 can (15 ounces) white kidney or cannellini beans, rinsed and drained, divided
- 10 pitted Greek olives, chopped
- 2 tablespoons minced fresh parsley, divided
- 1 tablespoon lemon juice
- 1/4 teaspoon salt
- 1/8 teaspoon pepper
- 18 slices French bread (1/2 inch thick)
- 1/2 cup chopped seeded tomatoes

## Direction

- Mash 1 cup beans in a small bowl. Add pepper, salt, lemon juice, 1 tablespoon parsley, and olives.
- Arrange bread slices on an unoiled baking sheet. Broil about 3 to 4 inches away from the heat source until lightly browned, 1 to 2 minutes. Spread mashed bean mixture over bread slices. Top with tomatoes, remainder of beans, and parsley.

## Nutrition Information

- Calories: 56 calories
- Sodium: 166mg sodium
- Fiber: 1g fiber)
- Total Carbohydrate: 10g carbohydrate (0 sugars
- Cholesterol: 0 cholesterol
- Protein: 2g protein. Diabetic Exchanges: 1/2 starch.
- Total Fat: 1g fat (0 saturated fat)

## 939. Whole Wheat Orzo Salad

*Serving: 8 servings. | Prep: 20mins | Cook: 10mins | Ready in:*

## Ingredients

- 2-1/2 cups uncooked whole wheat orzo pasta (about 1 pound)
- 1 can (15 ounces) cannellini beans, rinsed and drained
- 3 medium tomatoes, finely chopped
- 1 English cucumber, finely chopped
- 2 cups (8 ounces) crumbled feta cheese
- 1-1/4 cups pitted Greek olives (about 6 ounces), chopped
- 1 medium sweet yellow pepper, finely chopped
- 1 medium green pepper, finely chopped
- 1 cup fresh mint leaves, chopped
- 1/2 medium red onion, finely chopped
- 1/4 cup lemon juice
- 2 tablespoons olive oil
- 1 tablespoon grated lemon peel
- 3 garlic cloves, minced
- 1/2 teaspoon pepper

## Direction

- Cook ozro as directed on package. Drain; use cold water to rinse orzo. In the meantime, mix together remaining ingredients in a large bowl. Add drained orzo and stir until incorporated. Chill before serving.

## Nutrition Information

- Calories: 411 calories
- Sodium: 740mg sodium
- Fiber: 13g fiber)
- Total Carbohydrate: 51g carbohydrate (3g sugars
- Cholesterol: 15mg cholesterol
- Protein: 14g protein.
- Total Fat: 17g fat (4g saturated fat)

## 940. Whole Wheat Pita Bread

*Serving: 12 | Prep: 30mins | Cook: 6mins | Ready in:*

## Ingredients

- 1 cup warm water
- 1 (.25 ounce) package active dry yeast
- 1 tablespoon molasses
- 1 teaspoon salt
- 1 1/2 cups whole wheat flour
- 1 1/2 cups soy flour
- cooking spray
- cornmeal for dusting

## Direction

- Combine water, molasses, salt and yeast in a bowl. Let it stand for 5 to 10 minutes and slowly stir in the whole wheat flour and soy flour. On a floured surface, place the dough

and knead until becomes smooth. Move the dough in a lightly greased large bowl. Cover with towel and set aside for 1 hour at room temperature.
- Deflate dough and knead for about 5 to 10 minutes. Cut the dough into 6 portions. Roll out each portion to about 1/8 inch in thickness on a floured surface using a rolling pin. Cover with towel and set aside for 30 minutes.
- Set the oven to 230 degrees C (450 degrees F) for preheating. Place a baking sheet inside the oven for 2 minutes to make it warm then take out the baking sheet and put on cornmeal.
- Position the dough rounds on the baking sheet prepared earlier and bake in the preheated oven for 6 minutes. Remove from the oven and cover using a moist towel to soften the bread. Slice the bread in half when cooled and make bread pockets using a knife.

## Nutrition Information

- Calories: 101 calories;
- Total Fat: 1.1
- Sodium: 197
- Total Carbohydrate: 17.1
- Cholesterol: 0
- Protein: 7.4

### 941. Witch's Caviar

*Serving: 4 cups. | Prep: 10mins | Cook: 0mins | Ready in:*

## Ingredients

- 2 cans (4-1/4 ounces each) chopped ripe olives, undrained
- 2 cans (4 ounces each) chopped green chilies, undrained
- 2 medium tomatoes, seeded and chopped
- 3 green onions, chopped
- 2 garlic cloves, minced
- 1 tablespoon red wine vinegar
- 1 tablespoon olive oil
- 1/2 teaspoon pepper
- Dash seasoned salt
- Tortilla chips

## Direction

- Mix together the first 9 ingredients in a big bowl, then cover and chill overnight. Serve together with tortilla chips.

## Nutrition Information

- Calories: 17 calories
- Total Fat: 1g fat (0 saturated fat)
- Sodium: 98mg sodium
- Fiber: 1g fiber)
- Total Carbohydrate: 1g carbohydrate (1g sugars
- Cholesterol: 0 cholesterol
- Protein: 0 protein.

### 942. Witches' Hats

*Serving: 32 | Prep: 1hours | Cook: | Ready in:*

## Ingredients

- 2 (16 ounce) packages fudge stripe cookies
- 1/4 cup honey, or as needed
- 1 (9 ounce) bag milk chocolate candy kisses, unwrapped
- 1 (4.5 ounce) tube decorating gel

## Direction

- On a work surface, lay a fudge stripe cookie with the bottom-side up. Slather about 1/8 tsp of honey onto the base of a chocolate kiss; place the candy piece into the middle of the cookie and secure, covering the hole. Pipe a small bow at the bottom of the candy piece on the cookie using decorating gel. Repeat with the rest of the ingredients.

## Nutrition Information

- Calories: 204 calories;
- Sodium: 170
- Total Carbohydrate: 28.5
- Cholesterol: 2
- Protein: 2.4
- Total Fat: 8.7

## 943. Zesty Greek Salad

*Serving: 2 servings. | Prep: 25mins | Cook: 0mins | Ready in:*

### Ingredients

- 2 cups torn red leaf lettuce
- 1 small tomato, cut into wedges
- 4 cucumber slices, halved
- 2 radishes, sliced
- 1 red onion slice, quartered
- 2 tablespoons sliced ripe olives
- 1 tablespoon crumbled feta cheese
- DRESSING:
- 1 tablespoon red wine vinegar
- 2 teaspoons water
- 2 teaspoons olive oil
- 1 garlic clove, minced
- 1/4 teaspoon sugar
- 1/8 teaspoon salt
- Dash pepper

### Direction

- Combine feta cheese, olives, onion, radishes, cucumber, tomato and lettuce in a small bowl. In separate small bowl, whisk together dressing ingredients. Add to salad mixture and toss until well coated.

### Nutrition Information

- Calories: 89 calories
- Sodium: 265mg sodium
- Fiber: 2g fiber)
- Total Carbohydrate: 7g carbohydrate (3g sugars
- Cholesterol: 2mg cholesterol
- Protein: 2g protein. Diabetic Exchanges: 1 vegetable
- Total Fat: 6g fat (1g saturated fat)

## 944. Zesty Veggie Pitas

*Serving: 4 servings. | Prep: 20mins | Cook: 0mins | Ready in:*

### Ingredients

- 1/2 cup hummus
- 4 whole pocketless pita breads or flatbreads, warmed
- 4 slices pepper jack cheese
- 1 cup thinly sliced cucumber
- 1 large tomato, cut into wedges
- 1/4 cup sliced pepperoncini
- 1/4 cup sliced ripe olives
- 1/4 cup fresh cilantro leaves

### Direction

- Spread the hummus atop pita breads. Put leftover ingredients on top and fold the pitas, then serve.

### Nutrition Information

- Calories: 323 calories
- Protein: 14g protein. Diabetic Exchanges: 3 starch
- Total Fat: 11g fat (4g saturated fat)
- Sodium: 758mg sodium
- Fiber: 4g fiber)
- Total Carbohydrate: 42g carbohydrate (2g sugars
- Cholesterol: 23mg cholesterol

## 945. Zucchini & Cheese Roulades

*Serving: 2 dozen. | Prep: 15mins | Cook: 10mins | Ready in:*

### Ingredients

- 1 cup part-skim ricotta cheese
- 1/4 cup grated Parmesan cheese
- 2 tablespoons minced fresh basil or 2 teaspoons dried basil
- 1 tablespoon capers, drained
- 1 tablespoon chopped Greek olives
- 1 teaspoon grated lemon peel
- 1 tablespoon lemon juice
- 1/8 teaspoon salt
- 1/8 teaspoon pepper
- 4 medium zucchini

### Direction

- Combine the first 9 ingredients in a small bowl.
- Cut the zucchini into 24, 1/8-inch-thick slices lengthwise. On medium heat, grill zucchini in batches for 2-3 minutes per side on a greased grill rack, with cover, until tender.
- Put 1 tablespoon of the ricotta mixture on each of the zucchini slice's end. Roll up then secure each one with a toothpick.

### Nutrition Information

- Calories: 24 calories
- Total Carbohydrate: 2g carbohydrate (1g sugars
- Cholesterol: 4mg cholesterol
- Protein: 2g protein.
- Total Fat: 1g fat (1g saturated fat)
- Sodium: 58mg sodium
- Fiber: 0 fiber)

## 946. Zucchini Carrrot Couscous

*Serving: 2 servings. | Prep: 5mins | Cook: 15mins | Ready in:*

### Ingredients

- 3/4 cup water
- 1/2 cup uncooked couscous
- 1/2 cup chopped carrot
- 1/2 cup chopped onion
- 1 tablespoon butter
- 1/2 cup chopped zucchini
- 1 green onion, thinly sliced
- 1/2 teaspoon salt
- Dash to 1/8 teaspoon white pepper

### Direction

- Bring water to a boil in a saucepan. Stir in couscous, then cover and remove from the heat. Allow to stand for 5 minutes.
- Sauté onion and carrot in butter in a small skillet until crisp-tender for about 3-4 minutes. Add green onion and zucchini; continue to sauté until tender for 2-3 minutes more. Dust with pepper and salt. Use a fork to fluff the couscous, then add the vegetable mixture and toss to combine.

### Nutrition Information

- Calories: 249 calories
- Fiber: 4g fiber)
- Total Carbohydrate: 43g carbohydrate (0 sugars
- Cholesterol: 15mg cholesterol
- Protein: 8g protein.
- Total Fat: 7g fat (4g saturated fat)
- Sodium: 666mg sodium

# Chapter 8: Awesome Greek Cuisine Recipes

***

## 947. Ali's Greek Tortellini Salad

*Serving: 8 | Prep: 15mins | Cook: 15mins | Ready in:*

### Ingredients

- 2 (9 ounce) packages cheese tortellini
- 1/2 cup extra virgin olive oil
- 1/4 cup lemon juice
- 1/4 cup red wine vinegar
- 2 tablespoons chopped fresh parsley
- 1 teaspoon dried oregano
- 1/2 teaspoon salt
- 6 eggs
- 1 pound baby spinach leaves
- 1 cup crumbled feta cheese
- 1/2 cup slivered red onion

### Direction

- Boil lightly salted water in a large pot. Add tortellini and cook until al dente or for about 7 minutes. Drain.
- Mix the salt, oregano, parsley, red wine vinegar, lemon juice and olive oil in a large bowl. Transfer the cooked tortellini to the bowl and toss together to coat. Cover and place in the refrigerator to chill for at least 2 hours.
- Put eggs in a saucepan with enough amount of water to cover and boil. Remove from heat and for about 10 to 12 minutes, let the eggs sit in hot water. Drain, allow the eggs to cool, peel, and then quarter.
- Slowly mix the onion, feta cheese and spinach with the pasta in the bowl. Arrange quartered eggs around the salad and serve.

### Nutrition Information

- Calories: 486 calories;
- Sodium: 836
- Total Carbohydrate: 35.7
- Cholesterol: 196
- Protein: 19.8
- Total Fat: 30.3

## 948. Amazing Greek Pasta

*Serving: 4 | Prep: 15mins | Cook: 2hours | Ready in:*

### Ingredients

- 1 small yellow onion, diced
- 1 tablespoon olive oil
- 5 cloves garlic, minced
- 1 (16 ounce) can organic Italian diced tomatoes
- 1 (6.5 ounce) can tomato sauce
- 1 tablespoon capers, chopped
- 15 kalamata olives, pitted and sliced
- 2 tablespoons balsamic vinegar
- salt and pepper to taste
- crushed red pepper to taste (optional)
- crumbled Feta or grated Parmesan Cheese

### Direction

- Cook onion in olive oil in a skillet over medium high heat until translucent and softened. Add garlic; cook and stir for 1 minute. Put in crushed red pepper (optional), pepper, salt, vinegar, olives, capers, tomato sauce and tomatoes.
- Lower the heat; let it simmer with cover up to 2 hours or for at least 30 minutes (if time will permit). Place over chicken, fish or pasta to serve. Use grated Parmesan or crumbled feta cheese to top.

## Nutrition Information

- Calories: 205 calories;
- Total Carbohydrate: 12.8
- Cholesterol: 28
- Protein: 6.8
- Total Fat: 14
- Sodium: 1442

### 949. Avgolemono Soup

*Serving: 6 | Prep: 25mins | Cook: 2hours | Ready in:*

## Ingredients

- 1 (3 pound) whole chicken
- 2 teaspoons salt, or more to taste
- 1 onion, chopped
- 2 ribs celery, chopped
- 1 carrot, chopped
- 2 bay leaves
- 1/4 teaspoon dried oregano leaves
- 3 quarts cold water
- 2 cups finely diced onion
- 2 tablespoons extra-virgin olive oil
- 2/3 cup arborio rice, or more to taste
- 2 large eggs
- 1/2 teaspoon ground black pepper
- 1 pinch cayenne pepper
- 1/2 cup fresh lemon juice

## Direction

- In a large pot, arrange oregano, bay leaves, carrot, celery, chopped onion, and chicken. Pour water on the top; boil, turn down the heat to medium-low and simmer for 1-1 1/2 hours until the chicken falls off the bone, removing foam as needed. An instant-read thermometer must register 74°C (165°F) when inserted in the thickest part of the thigh, near the bone. Place the chicken into a bowl to cool, filter all the vegetables from the simmering broth, get rid of the vegetables and place the broth back into the pot. Then chop the cooked chicken meat.
- In a large skillet, mix a pinch of salt, olive oil, and 2 cups of diced onion. Stir and cook the onion mixture on medium heat for 7-10 minutes until the onion is golden, sweet, and soft.
- In the pot, add the onion mixture into the chicken broth and stir, then place on medium-low heat; add a pinch of salt and Arborio rice. Simmer; cook and stir from time to time for 45 minutes until the broth flavors blend and rice becomes very tender.
- In a bowl, beat together black pepper, cayenne pepper, and eggs; beat in the lemon juice. Pour a cup of the broth mixture slowly into the egg mixture and beat continuously. Add another cup of the broth into the egg mixture, then beat. In the pot, pour the egg mixture into the broth and add the chopped chicken, cook for 5 more minutes until completely heated.

## Nutrition Information

- Calories: 485 calories;
- Protein: 36.6
- Total Fat: 22.3
- Sodium: 926
- Total Carbohydrate: 32.7
- Cholesterol: 161

### 950. Avocado Tzatziki

*Serving: 8 | Prep: 5mins | Cook: | Ready in:*

## Ingredients

- 1 large avocado, peeled and pitted
- 2 cloves garlic, minced
- 1 lemons, juiced
- 1/4 cup sour cream (optional)
- 1/2 cup chopped seeded cucumber
- 1/2 teaspoon red pepper flakes, or to taste

- 1 tablespoon chopped fresh cilantro
- 1 tablespoon chopped fresh mint
- salt and pepper to taste

## Direction

- Mix the cucumber, sour cream, lemon juice, garlic, and avocado in a medium bowl. Use a fork to mash until smooth. Use a food processor if avocado is not that ripe. Add pepper, salt, mint, cilantro and red pepper flakes to season. Cover and place inside the refrigerator for 1 hour before serving.

## Nutrition Information

- Calories: 78 calories;
- Sodium: 7
- Total Carbohydrate: 5.5
- Cholesterol: 3
- Protein: 1.2
- Total Fat: 6.8

## 951. Cephalonian Meat Pie

*Serving: 12 | Prep: 1hours | Cook: 2hours | Ready in:*

## Ingredients

- 8 cups all-purpose flour
- 1/3 cup olive oil
- 1/2 cup dry white wine
- 2 cups water
- 1/2 teaspoon salt
- 1/4 cup olive oil
- 1 onion, finely chopped
- 2 cloves garlic, minced
- 1 pound boneless lamb shoulder, cut into 1-inch cubes
- 1 pound boneless pork shoulder, cut into 1-inch cubes
- 1/4 cup tomato paste
- 1/4 cup dry white wine
- 3/4 cup water
- 1 cup grated Greek Kefalotiri or Parmesan cheese
- 1 potato, peeled and cut into 1/2-inch cubes
- 1/2 cup long grain rice
- 1 teaspoon minced parsley
- 1 teaspoon chopped fresh mint or spearmint
- 1/2 teaspoon dried marjoram
- salt and pepper to taste
- 1 egg, beaten

## Direction

- In a large bowl, prepare the dough placing flour. Create a well in the center and put in salt, water, white wine, and 1/3 cup of olive oil. Use your hands to mix together for a few minutes to shape a smooth dough. Wrap in plastic wrap and put in the refrigerator while you move on with the recipe.
- Over medium heat, in a large saucepan, heat olive oil. Stir in garlic and onion, then cook for a few minutes until the onion is tender and turns transparent. Stir in pork and lamb; increase the heat to medium-high and keep cooking for about 5 minutes until the onion starts to brown.
- Blend in tomato paste until the meat is covered. Mix in white wine and simmer for 1 minute. Add water and heat to a simmer. Lower the heat to medium-low and simmer, covered, for about 45 minutes until softened.
- Once the meat is done, turn off the heat and let cool while making the crust.
- Start preheating the oven to 450°F (230°C). Lightly grease olive oil onto a 9x13-inch glass baking dish.
- Cut the dough into 2 pieces, with one piece larger than the other. On a floured surface, roll out the large piece until it is large enough to fit the base of the baking dish and come up the sides of the pan; press into the baking dish. Form the smaller piece of dough into a rectangle to use as the top crust; put aside.
- Stir rice, potato, and Kefalotiri cheese into the meat mixture. Flavor with pepper, salt, marjoram, mint, and parsley. Add egg and beat until well-blended. Transfer this mixture

into the baking dish and top with the leftover piece of dough. Brush the top with olive oil and a little water.
- Bake pie in the prepared oven for 1 hour until deep golden brown.

## Nutrition Information

- Calories: 691 calories;
- Sodium: 398
- Total Carbohydrate: 75.8
- Cholesterol: 76
- Protein: 28.6
- Total Fat: 28.1

## 952. Chef John's Tzatziki Sauce

*Serving: 12 | Prep: 15mins | Cook: | Ready in:*

### Ingredients

- 1 large English cucumber, peeled and grated
- 1/2 teaspoon salt
- 2 cups Greek yogurt
- 4 cloves garlic, minced
- 1 pinch cayenne pepper, or to taste
- 1/2 lemon, juiced
- 2 tablespoons chopped fresh dill
- 1 tablespoon chopped fresh mint
- salt and ground black pepper to taste
- 1 sprig fresh dill for garnish
- 1 pinch cayenne pepper for garnish

### Direction

- In a bowl with grated cucumber, sprinkle over with 1/2 tsp. salt and allow to stand about 10-15 minutes to extract the juice.
- In a separate bowl, add yogurt. On a sturdy and dry cloth towel or paper, dump cucumber and its juice to squeeze as much moisture from the cucumber as possible. Combine cucumber into the yogurt, then put in lemon juice, cayenne pepper and garlic, blend thoroughly.
- Stir into the yogurt-cucumber mixture with mint and dill, then season with black pepper and salt. Adjust to taste with all seasonings.
- Use plastic wrap to cover the bowl and chill about 3-4 hours or overnight. Turn to a serving bowl and decorate with a sprinkle of cayenne pepper and a sprig of dill for color.

## Nutrition Information

- Calories: 49 calories;
- Total Carbohydrate: 2.5
- Cholesterol: 8
- Protein: 2.2
- Total Fat: 3.4
- Sodium: 120

## 953. Cucumber Gyro Sauce

*Serving: 6 | Prep: 15mins | Cook: | Ready in:*

### Ingredients

- 1 cup sour cream
- 2/3 cup peeled and grated cucumber
- 1/2 teaspoon minced garlic
- 1/2 teaspoon chopped fresh dill
- 1/4 teaspoon prepared mustard
- 1/4 teaspoon garlic powder

### Direction

- Mix in bowl the garlic powder, mustard, dill, garlic, cucumber and sour cream; mix to incorporate. Refrigerate to chill for not less than an hour prior to serving.

## Nutrition Information

- Calories: 85 calories;
- Total Fat: 8.1
- Sodium: 21

- Total Carbohydrate: 2.4
- Cholesterol: 17
- Protein: 1.4

- Sodium: 198
- Total Carbohydrate: 26.8
- Cholesterol: 0
- Protein: 9
- Total Fat: 18.4

## 954. Fasolatha

*Serving: 6 | Prep: | Cook: |Ready in:*

### Ingredients

- 1 cup white kidney beans
- 1 onion, thinly sliced
- 2 small carrots, sliced
- 1 stalk celery, chopped
- 1 (14.5 ounce) can diced tomatoes
- 1 tablespoon tomato paste
- 1 teaspoon dried oregano
- 1 teaspoon dried thyme
- 1/2 cup olive oil
- 3 cups water
- 2 tablespoons chopped fresh parsley
- salt to taste
- ground black pepper to taste

### Direction

- Wash and strain soaked beans before placing them in a large saucepan. Cover the beans with water and allow it to boil for 2-3 minutes. Drain and discard the water.
- Cover the beans with 3 cups of water. Allow it to boil before stirring in tomato paste, celery, carrots, olive oil, pepper, onions, tomatoes, thyme, salt, and oregano. Place a cover and let it cook for 50-60 minutes until the beans are tender. Add parsley.
- In case your cooking this in a pressure cooker, mix and cook all the ingredients except the parsley for 3-4 minutes under 15 pounds pressure. Add in the parsley.

### Nutrition Information

- Calories: 304 calories;

## 955. Fijian Dhal Soup

*Serving: 12 | Prep: | Cook: |Ready in:*

### Ingredients

- 4 cups water
- 2 cups dry lentils
- 1/2 teaspoon fenugreek seeds
- 1/2 teaspoon mustard seed
- 10 cups water
- 2 tablespoons olive oil
- 6 cloves garlic, chopped
- 2 cups chopped onion
- 1/2 teaspoon crushed dried chile pepper
- 4 carrots, chopped
- 3 large stalks celery, chopped
- 1 teaspoon salt
- 1/2 teaspoon ground turmeric
- 1 teaspoon curry powder
- 2 tablespoons chicken bouillon powder
- 3 tablespoons soy sauce

### Direction

- Put mustard seeds, fenugreek seeds, dhal peas, and 4 cups water in a medium-sized stockpot and soak for approximately 60 minutes. Once tender, strain and thoroughly rinse.
- Boil the strained dhal pea mixture and 10 cups water in a big stockpot. Lower the heat and simmer until the peas are tender, approximately 30 minutes.
- Cook onions and garlic in olive oil in a sauté pan until turning light brown.
- Add celery, carrots, crushed chili pepper, and onion mixture to the big stockpot. Cook until the carrots are soft, 15 minutes.

- In a food processor or a blender, puree the soup in batches. Put back into the stockpot and add soy sauce, chicken soup base, curry powder, turmeric, and salt. Simmer for 5 minutes longer and then enjoy.

## Nutrition Information

- Calories: 168 calories;
- Total Fat: 3
- Sodium: 811
- Total Carbohydrate: 26.1
- Cholesterol: < 1
- Protein: 9.7

## 956. French Greek Salad Dressing

*Serving: 6 | Prep: 10mins | Cook: |Ready in:*

## Ingredients

- 1 tablespoon Greek seasoning
- 1 tablespoon water
- 1 clove garlic
- 1/4 teaspoon kosher salt
- 1/3 cup olive oil
- 1/4 cup wine vinegar
- 2 tablespoons lemon juice
- 1 teaspoon grated lemon zest
- 1/4 teaspoon Dijon mustard
- 1/4 teaspoon ground black pepper
- 1/4 teaspoon white sugar

## Direction

- In a small bowl, mix water and Greek seasoning together; allow it to stand for about 5mins until the seasoning is moist.
- Pound the garlic clove using the flat side of a knife; add kosher salt. With the knife's edge, crush salt and garlic together to form a paste.
- Combine the Greek seasoning mixture, garlic mixture, sugar, olive oil, pepper, wine vinegar,

Dijon mustard, lemon juice, and lemon zest until well blended.

## Nutrition Information

- Calories: 113 calories;
- Sodium: 324
- Total Carbohydrate: 1.6
- Cholesterol: 0
- Protein: 0.2
- Total Fat: 12.1

## 957. Greek Avgolemono Chicken Soup

*Serving: 6 | Prep: 15mins | Cook: 1hours |Ready in:*

## Ingredients

- 1 (3 pound) whole chicken
- 1/2 cup uncooked white rice
- salt and freshly ground black pepper to taste
- 3 egg, beaten
- 2 lemons, juiced

## Direction

- Wash chicken, take out organs inside. Place in a big pot that is just sufficient to move chicken around (the broth will be watery if the pot is too big). Put in chicken neck if there is one. Pour in sufficient water to cover by 1 inch. Put on cover and heat to a boil. When boiling, decrease to low heat and let simmer 45-60 minutes; once fat collects on the surface, skim off.
- If chicken is done, meat will pull from bones easily. Remove to a big bowl, put aside to cool down. Add in rice, season the broth with pepper and salt. Allow to simmer 20 minutes longer over low heat, or until rice is tender.
- In a bowl, whisk lemon juice and eggs. Turn of the heat once the rice is done. Slowly blend a ladle full of hot broth into eggs so that eggs

won't curdle. Gradually blend in additional broth till egg mixture is heated. Return egg mixture to the pot, mixing briskly. The soup should look cloudy and creamy. If wished, season with lemon juice or additional pepper and salt.
- Serve soup alongside with salted chicken or serve with pieces of chicken added to the soup.

## Nutrition Information

- Calories: 321 calories;
- Total Fat: 17.4
- Sodium: 94
- Total Carbohydrate: 16.4
- Cholesterol: 154
- Protein: 25.6

## 958. Greek Brown Rice Salad

*Serving: 6 | Prep: 25mins | Cook: | Ready in:*

## Ingredients

- 1 cucumber, diced
- 1 cup chickpeas, drained and rinsed
- 1 cup cooked gluten-free brown rice
- 1 (4 ounce) package crumbled feta cheese
- 1 cup sun-dried tomatoes
- 1/2 cup chopped red onion
- 1/2 cup sliced Kalamata olives
- 1/2 cup chopped fresh parsley
- 2 tablespoons freshly squeezed lemon juice
- 2 cloves garlic, minced
- 2 tablespoons chopped fresh basil
- 1 tablespoon extra-virgin olive oil
- salt and ground black pepper to taste

## Direction

- In a bowl, combine olives, onion, tomatoes, feta, rice, chickpeas and cucumber.
- In another bowl, whisk together olive oil, basil, garlic, lemon juice, and parsley. Stir the mixture into the rice mixture. Use salt and pepper to season. Before serving, allow the salad to stand for an hour so that the rice absorbs the flavors.

## Nutrition Information

- Calories: 226 calories;
- Total Fat: 10.4
- Sodium: 734
- Total Carbohydrate: 27.5
- Cholesterol: 17
- Protein: 7.7

## 959. Greek Chicken Stew (Stifado)

*Serving: 8 | Prep: 15mins | Cook: 1hours15mins | Ready in:*

## Ingredients

- 10 small shallots, peeled
- 1 cup olive oil
- 2 teaspoons butter
- 1 (4 pound) whole chicken, cut into pieces
- 2 cloves garlic, finely chopped
- 1/2 cup red wine
- 1 cup tomato sauce
- 2 tablespoons chopped fresh parsley
- salt and ground black pepper to taste
- 1 pinch dried oregano, or to taste
- 2 bay leaves
- 1 1/2 cups chicken stock, or more if needed

## Direction

- Pour lightly salted water in a big pot, heat to a boil. Add shallots and cook without a cover until just tender, about 3 minutes. Place in a colander to drain, then immerse in ice water immediately, or wash with cold water for a few minutes until cold to stop the cooking process. When the shallots become cold, drain well then put aside.

- In a big pot or a Dutch oven, heat butter and olive oil over medium heat, until butter melts and is bubbling, and oil is hot. In the skillet, put chicken pieces and the whole, blanched shallots; cook, flipping chicken pieces till they are not pink inside anymore and shallots have turned translucent and softened, about 15 minutes. Mix in chopped garlic then cook until garlic begins to turn golden, about 3 more minutes.
- Pour tomato sauce and red wine over the mixture then put in bay leaves, oregano, salt and pepper, and parsley. Cover chicken pieces with chicken stock, and stir to blend.
- Simmer the stew over medium-low heat with a cover until chicken is tender and shallots are soft, about 50 minutes.

## Nutrition Information

- Calories: 574 calories;
- Cholesterol: 100
- Protein: 31.8
- Total Fat: 45.3
- Sodium: 394
- Total Carbohydrate: 6.8

## 960. Greek Cream Cheese Stuffed Chicken

*Serving: 6 | Prep: 15mins | Cook: 15mins | Ready in:*

## Ingredients

- 6 skinless, boneless chicken breast halves, or more to taste
- 1 (8 ounce) container whipped cream cheese
- 3/4 cup crumbled feta cheese
- 1 tomato, diced
- 1 (6 ounce) can chopped black olives
- 1/4 onion, chopped
- 1/4 cup chopped fresh spinach

## Direction

- Set an outdoor grill to medium-high heat to preheat and grease the grate lightly.
- From 1 side of each chicken breast, slice horizontally through the middle to within a 1/2 inch of the other side. Open 2 sides and spread them out like an open book.
- In a large bowl, mix spinach, onion, olives, tomato, feta cheese, and cream cheese. Scoop mixture onto 1 side of each opened chicken breast. Fold each chicken closed and arrange on a piece of aluminum foil.
- On the preheated grill, cook the chicken breasts for 15-20 minutes or until the center is no longer pink and the juices run clear. An instant-read thermometer should read at least 74°C (165°F) when inserted into the center.

## Nutrition Information

- Calories: 356 calories;
- Sodium: 818
- Total Carbohydrate: 6.6
- Cholesterol: 128
- Protein: 30.4
- Total Fat: 23.2

## 961. Greek Lamb Stew

*Serving: 4 | Prep: 15mins | Cook: 2hours20mins | Ready in:*

## Ingredients

- 2 tablespoons olive oil
- 1 pound lamb shoulder blade chops
- salt and pepper to taste
- 1 large onion, chopped
- 3 cloves garlic, minced
- 1/2 cup dry red wine
- 2 cups chopped tomatoes

- 1 (15 ounce) can tomato sauce
- 1 cup lamb stock
- 1/2 lemon, zested and juiced
- 1/2 teaspoon dried oregano
- 1/2 teaspoon ground cinnamon
- 1 bay leaf
- 1 pound fresh green beans, trimmed
- 1/4 cup chopped fresh parsley

## Direction

- In a big, heavy bottomed pot, heat olive oil over medium-high heat. Put pepper and salt to season the lamb, put to pot, and let cook for 5 minutes per side till browned deeply. Mix in garlic and onions, and let cook for 2 minutes till browned slightly.
- Into the pot, put the wine, and boil while scratching up browned bits of food off from base of pan using a wooden spoon. Mix in bay leaf, cinnamon, oregano, lemon zest and juice, lamb stock, tomato sauce and tomatoes. Over high heat, return to a boil, then turn heat to medium-low, put cover, and allow to simmer for 1 1/2 hours till lamb is really soft. Mix in green beans and cook for 20 minutes longer till soft.
- Take off any bones and bay leaf from stew. Garnish with chopped fresh parsley.

## Nutrition Information

- Calories: 365 calories;
- Total Fat: 20.3
- Sodium: 606
- Total Carbohydrate: 24.4
- Cholesterol: 61
- Protein: 20

## 962. Greek Lamb Feta Burgers With Cucumber Sauce

*Serving: 4 | Prep: | Cook: | Ready in:*

## Ingredients

- 4 large unpeeled garlic cloves
- 1 1/4 pounds ground lamb
- 1/2 cup crumbled feta cheese
- 3/4 teaspoon dried oregano
- 1/2 teaspoon salt
- 1/2 teaspoon black pepper
- 1/2 large cucumber, peeled, grated and squeezed very dry in a clean towel
- 3/4 cup sour cream
- 1 tablespoon minced fresh mint leaves
- 1 teaspoon red or rice wine vinegar
- 1 clove garlic, minced
- 4 large, thin red onion slices
- 4 large, thin tomato slices
- 4 small (4 inch) pita breads

## Direction

- Place a small skillet on the stove and turn on medium high heat then add 4 whole garlic cloves; toast for about five minutes until spotty brown in color. Peel, mince, and reserve.
- In a medium bowl, break up lamb. Sprinkle on pepper, salt, oregano, feta and roasted garlic over the meat; use a fork to mix until well combined. Split into four pieces. Form a ball by tossing meat back and forth between cupped hands. Use fingertips to Pat and flatten to 4 inches wide. Then place inside the refrigerator.
- In a small bowl, combine to taste pepper, salt, 1 minced clove of garlic, vinegar, mint, sour cream and cucumber. Place the sauce inside the refrigerator until ready to serve.
- On one side of grill, build a hot fire. Then put the rack back on. Once coals are covered with white ash, put on burgers. Cook and cover, flipping only once, until done, for 4 to 5 minutes each side for medium to medium well burgers.
- Place the pitas on grill for about one minute or so each side becomes spotty brown in color and hot. Divide crosswise. Over for pita halves, spread a couple of tablespoons of the

sauce. Place an Onion slice, tomato slice and a burger on top. Drizzle some of the left sauce over each burger. Then place left pita halves on top.

## Nutrition Information

- Calories: 650 calories;
- Total Carbohydrate: 25.2
- Cholesterol: 139
- Protein: 31.2
- Total Fat: 46.8
- Sodium: 761

## 963. Greek Lemon Chicken Soup

*Serving: 16 | Prep: 25mins | Cook: 40mins | Ready in:*

## Ingredients

- 8 cups chicken broth
- 1/2 cup fresh lemon juice
- 1/2 cup shredded carrots
- 1/2 cup chopped onion
- 1/2 cup chopped celery
- 6 tablespoons chicken soup base
- 1/4 teaspoon ground white pepper
- 1/4 cup margarine
- 1/4 cup all-purpose flour
- 1 cup cooked white rice
- 1 cup diced, cooked chicken meat
- 16 slices lemon
- 8 egg yolks

## Direction

- Mix together the white pepper, soup base, celery, onions, carrots, lemon juice and chicken broth in a big pot. Let the mixture boil on high, and then make it simmer for 20 minutes.
- Blend the butter and the flour together. Slowly add it to the soup mixture. Make the mixture simmer for 10 minutes more while stirring often.
- For the meantime, beat the egg yolks until it turns light in color. Slowly add some hot soup to the yolks while continuously stirring. Place the egg mixture back to the soup pot and heat completely. Add the rice and chicken. Put the hot soup into bowls using a ladle and garnish with the lemon slices.

## Nutrition Information

- Calories: 124 calories;
- Total Fat: 6.6
- Sodium: 1237
- Total Carbohydrate: 9.1
- Cholesterol: 110
- Protein: 7.8

## 964. Greek Lentil Soup (Fakes)

*Serving: 4 | Prep: 20mins | Cook: 1hours | Ready in:*

## Ingredients

- 8 ounces brown lentils
- 1/4 cup olive oil
- 1 tablespoon minced garlic
- 1 onion, minced
- 1 large carrot, chopped
- 1 quart water
- 1 pinch dried oregano
- 1 pinch crushed dried rosemary
- 2 bay leaves
- 1 tablespoon tomato paste
- salt and ground black pepper to taste
- 1 teaspoon olive oil, or to taste
- 1 teaspoon red wine vinegar, or to taste (optional)

## Direction

- In a large saucepan, put lentils; cover with water by 1 inch. Allow the water to boil and cook for about 10 minutes until tender; strain.
- Place a saucepan on medium heat and heat olive oil. Put in carrot, onion and garlic; cook while stirring for 5 minutes, till the onions are translucent and soft. Transfer in bay leaves, rosemary, oregano, 1 quart of water and lentils. Bring to a boil. Lower the heat to medium-low; simmer with a cover for 10 minutes.
- Mix in tomato paste; season with pepper and salt. Simmer with a cover for 30-40 minutes; stir occasionally until the lentils are well softened. If the soup turns too thick, put in additional water. Taste with red wine vinegar and a teaspoon of olive oil.

## Nutrition Information

- Calories: 357 calories;
- Total Carbohydrate: 40.3
- Cholesterol: 0
- Protein: 15.5
- Total Fat: 15.5
- Sodium: 57

## 965. Greek Saganaki

*Serving: 4 | Prep: 10mins | Cook: 5mins | Ready in:*

## Ingredients

- 8 ounces feta cheese
- 1 egg
- 1 teaspoon finely chopped fresh oregano
- 1/2 cup all-purpose flour
- 2 tablespoons olive oil
- freshly ground black pepper
- 2 large ripe tomatoes, sliced
- 1 lemon, cut into wedges

## Direction

- Slice feta into 2x3/8-in. square, around 8 slices. Beat oregano and egg in a small bowl. Dip each slice of the feta into the egg; shake off any excess; coat in flour.
- Place a frying pan on medium heat; heat olive oil. Cook cheese quickly, turning once, till golden. Using paper towels, pat dry.
- Spread the feta on a plate with thick tomato slices; season with black pepper; use lemon wedges to garnish.

## Nutrition Information

- Calories: 302 calories;
- Protein: 12.1
- Total Fat: 20.4
- Sodium: 656
- Total Carbohydrate: 18.5
- Cholesterol: 97

## 966. Greek Sausage: Sheftalia

*Serving: 3 | Prep: 1hours | Cook: 1hours | Ready in:*

## Ingredients

- 1 pound ground pork
- 1 large onion, finely chopped
- 1/2 cup finely chopped fresh parsley
- 1 pinch salt and pepper to taste
- 1 tablespoon vinegar
- 1/2 pound caul fat
- 10 skewers

## Direction

- Mix the ground pork, pepper, salt, onion, and parsley in a medium-sized bowl.
- Pour warm water into the bowl to fill, and then add vinegar. Dunk the caul fat into the water and soak for 1 minute. Wash it with cold water. Lay the caul fat onto the clean work surface and open it up carefully. Cut the caul fat into 4-inch or 10-centimeter squares.

- Place a small compressed handful of sausage close to the edge of one square. Fold the sides of the square over and roll it up firmly. Do the same with the remaining fat and meat until you can form a total of 10 sausages.
- Start preheating the charcoal grill for high heat. Arrange the sausages onto the skewers.
- Grill the sausages for 20 minutes while occasionally flipping it until the inside is not anymore pinkish and the outside is dark and crispy.

## Nutrition Information

- Calories: 1070 calories;
- Total Fat: 103.4
- Sodium: 97
- Total Carbohydrate: 5.7
- Cholesterol: 160
- Protein: 27.7

### 967. Greek Seasoning

*Serving: 12 | Prep: 5mins | Cook: | Ready in:*

## Ingredients

- 1 1/2 teaspoons dried oregano
- 1 teaspoon dried thyme
- 1/2 teaspoon dried basil
- 1/2 teaspoon dried marjoram
- 1/2 teaspoon dried minced onion
- 1/4 teaspoon dried minced garlic

## Direction

- In a small bowl, mix together garlic, onion, marjoram, basil, thyme and oregano. Store in an airtight container in dry and cool area for up to 6 months.

## Nutrition Information

- Calories: 1 calorie;
- Sodium: < 1
- Total Carbohydrate: 0.3
- Cholesterol: 0
- Protein: 0.1
- Total Fat: 0

### 968. Greek Seasoning Blend

*Serving: 8 | Prep: 5mins | Cook: | Ready in:*

## Ingredients

- 2 teaspoons salt
- 2 teaspoons garlic powder
- 2 teaspoons dried basil
- 2 teaspoons dried Greek oregano
- 1 teaspoon ground cinnamon
- 1 teaspoon ground black pepper
- 1 teaspoon dried parsley
- 1 teaspoon dried rosemary, minced
- 1 teaspoon dried dill weed
- 1 teaspoon dried marjoram
- 1 teaspoon cornstarch
- 1/2 teaspoon ground thyme
- 1/2 teaspoon ground nutmeg

## Direction

- In a bowl, combine nutmeg, thyme, cornstarch, marjoram, dill, rosemary, parsley, black pepper, cinnamon, oregano, basil, garlic powder and salt. Keep in an airtight container for storage. For a finer mixture, blend spices in a spice grinder alternately.

## Nutrition Information

- Calories: 9 calories;
- Total Fat: 0.2
- Sodium: 583
- Total Carbohydrate: 1.9
- Cholesterol: 0
- Protein: 0.3

## 969. Greek Shrimp Dish From Santorini

*Serving: 6 | Prep: 20mins | Cook: 1hours45mins | Ready in:*

### Ingredients

- 1/4 cup butter
- 2 tablespoons garlic, minced
- 1 bunch flat-leaf parsley, chopped
- 2 pints grape tomatoes, halved
- 1/2 (750 milliliter) bottle dry white wine
- 2 pounds peeled and deveined medium shrimp
- 1 (4 ounce) container crumbled feta cheese
- 2 lemons, halved
- 2 sprigs fresh flat-leaf parsley

### Direction

- In a saucepan, melt the butter over medium heat. Mix in wine, tomatoes, chopped parsley and the garlic. Bring the mixture to a simmer, then lower the heat to medium-low and cook while stirring a few times until the sauce has slightly thickened, about 1 hour.
- Set oven to 250 0 F (120 0 C) and preheat.
- Mix the shrimp into the tomato sauce and cook for 2 minutes; take away from heat. In a shallow baking dish, pour the shrimp mixture; top with crumbled feta cheese. Put in the prepared oven and bake for 45 minutes to an hour until the shrimp are not transparent anymore and the feta has softened. Juice the lemon halves and pour over the shrimp; decorate with the parsley sprigs to serve.

### Nutrition Information

- Calories: 369 calories;
- Cholesterol: 267
- Protein: 35.6
- Total Fat: 14.9
- Sodium: 513
- Total Carbohydrate: 14.5

## 970. Greek Spice Rub

*Serving: 11 | Prep: 5mins | Cook: | Ready in:*

### Ingredients

- 1/2 teaspoon sea salt
- 1 teaspoon cracked black pepper
- 1 1/2 teaspoons onion powder
- 1 1/2 teaspoons garlic powder
- 1 teaspoon chicken bouillon granules
- 1/2 teaspoon ground cinnamon
- 1/2 teaspoon ground nutmeg
- 1/2 teaspoon dried marjoram
- 2 teaspoons dried oregano
- 1 teaspoon dried parsley
- 1 teaspoon dried thyme

### Direction

- In a small bowl, mix completely. Save unused rub in a sealed airtight jar.

### Nutrition Information

- Calories: 6 calories;
- Total Fat: 0.1
- Sodium: 114
- Total Carbohydrate: 1.1
- Cholesterol: < 1
- Protein: 0.2

## 971. Greek Squid (Soupies)

*Serving: 4 | Prep: 15mins | Cook: 1hours15mins | Ready in:*

### Ingredients

- 2 pounds squid - tentacles and tubes, cleaned and cut into chunks
- 2 medium onions, finely chopped
- 2 bay leaves
- 5 whole cloves
- 1 (3 inch) cinnamon stick
- 2 cups dry red wine
- 1/3 cup olive oil
- 1/3 cup malt vinegar
- 1/4 teaspoon ground black pepper

### Direction

- In a big saucepan, put bay leaves, cloves, cinnamon stick, onions, and squid. Cover then simmer for about 10 minutes on low heat. As it simmers, squid will release its juices. Uncover the pan. Simmer until juices mostly evaporated. Take out bay leaves, cloves, and cinnamon stick.
- Mix in pepper, malt vinegar, wine, and olive oil. Cover then cook for about 1 hour on low heat, occasionally stirring. If needed, take out lid shortly prior to the end of cooking to let the sauce thicken. Place in bowls. Serve.

### Nutrition Information

- Calories: 446 calories;
- Total Fat: 20.3
- Sodium: 17
- Total Carbohydrate: 11.9
- Cholesterol: 0
- Protein: 31.7

## 972. Greek Stew

*Serving: 6 | Prep: 15mins | Cook: 1hours25mins | Ready in:*

### Ingredients

- 1 cooking spray (such as Pam®)
- 2 tablespoons olive oil, divided
- 2 large onions, cut into 1/2-inch dice
- 4 cloves garlic, or more to taste, minced
- 8 chicken thighs, or more to taste, trimmed
- 2 cups dry white wine
- 2 (6.5 ounce) cans tomato sauce
- 1/2 teaspoon ground black pepper
- 1 lemon, juiced
- 1 drop hot pepper sauce (such as Tabasco®)
- 1 pinch ground cinnamon

### Direction

- Prepare a big pot or a Dutch oven with cooking spray. In the Dutch oven, heat 1 tablespoon oil over medium heat. In hot oil, cook and stir garlic and onion about 5 minutes until onion is translucent and soft. Transfer onion mixture to a bowl.
- In the pot, heat remaining olive oil over medium heat. Place chicken in hot oil and cook for 5 minutes or until browned, turning several times.
- Pour wine on the chicken; bring to a simmer and cook about 15 minutes until chicken is not pink inside anymore.
- Mix cinnamon, hot pepper sauce, lemon juice, black pepper, tomato sauce, and onion mixture into the simmering chicken. Heat to a boil, decrease heat to low, cover the pot and cook at a simmer for 1 hour till the chicken can be pulled apart easily.

### Nutrition Information

- Calories: 383 calories;
- Sodium: 402
- Total Carbohydrate: 11.1
- Cholesterol: 86
- Protein: 25.3
- Total Fat: 19.7

## 973. Greek Style Beef Stew

*Serving: 6 | Prep: 35mins | Cook: 15mins | Ready in:*

### Ingredients

- 1 tablespoon olive oil
- 1 pound cubed beef stew meat
- 1 onion, peeled and chopped
- 1 large clove garlic, minced
- 1/4 cup red wine
- 2 tablespoons red wine vinegar
- 1/2 cup fat-free reduced-sodium beef broth
- 1 tablespoon tomato paste
- 1/2 teaspoon dried rosemary
- 1/2 teaspoon dried oregano
- 6 whole black peppercorns
- 2 bay leaves
- 1 teaspoon ground cumin
- 1/8 teaspoon ground cinnamon
- 1 pinch ground cloves
- 1/4 teaspoon ground black pepper
- 1 1/2 teaspoons light brown sugar
- 1 (28 ounce) can whole plum tomatoes, undrained and quartered
- 1/2 cup water
- 2 potatoes, peeled and cut into 2-inch pieces
- 2 carrots, peeled and sliced
- salt to taste (optional)

### Direction

- In a 5-qt pressure cooker, heat olive on medium-high heat. Cook and stir half of the beef until all sides are well browned. Use a slotted spoon to remove the beef; set aside. Cook the remaining beef, set aside.
- Sauté chopped onion in the pressure cooker for a minute. Stir in garlic and cook for another minute. Add tomato paste, beef broth, red wine vinegar, and red wine; stir well.
- Use a spice grinder or mortar and pestle to crush peppercorns, oregano, and rosemary. Put the crushed spice with brown sugar, bay leaves, black pepper, cumin, cloves, and cinnamon in the cooker.
- Add the tomatoes and their juice; swish half cup water on the can and add water in the cooker. Place carrots, potatoes, and return the browned meat to the pressure cooker. The 5-quart pot should be half full and a bit soupy. The potato will dissolve a bit and will thicken it after cooking. Cover the pot and secure the lid.
- On high heat, bring the pot and set the pressure to high. Turn heat to low to maintain the full pressure, cook for 15 minutes. Turn off heat and naturally release the pressure. Season stew with salt to taste.

### Nutrition Information

- Calories: 289 calories;
- Total Fat: 13
- Sodium: 367
- Total Carbohydrate: 26.8
- Cholesterol: 42
- Protein: 15.9

| 974. | Greek Tzatziki |
|---|---|

*Serving: 40 | Prep: 20mins | Cook: | Ready in:*

### Ingredients

- 1 (32 ounce) container plain low-fat yogurt
- 1/2 English cucumber with peel, grated
- 1 clove garlic, pressed
- 2 tablespoons fresh lemon juice
- 2 tablespoons extra-virgin olive oil
- 2 teaspoons grated lemon zest
- 3 tablespoons chopped fresh dill
- 1 tablespoon salt, or to taste
- 1 tablespoon freshly ground black pepper, or to taste

### Direction

- In a bowl, stir olive oil, lemon juice, garlic, grated cucumber and yogurt together. Put in pepper, salt, dill and lemon zest, then whisk until smooth. Transfer into a serving dish and chill about 8 hours before serving, covered tightly.

## Nutrition Information

- Calories: 22 calories;
- Sodium: 191
- Total Carbohydrate: 1.9
- Cholesterol: 1
- Protein: 1.3
- Total Fat: 1

### 975. Greek Inspired Lemon Chicken Soup

*Serving: 8 | Prep: 15mins | Cook: 20mins | Ready in:*

## Ingredients

- 3 tablespoons olive oil
- 1 sweet onion, quartered and sliced into thin strips
- 8 cloves garlic, minced
- 10 cups chicken broth
- 2 skinless, boneless chicken breasts
- 1 lemon, zested
- 1/2 teaspoon red pepper flakes
- 1 cup Israeli (large pearl) couscous
- 1 teaspoon salt
- ground black pepper to taste
- 1/2 (4 ounce) package crumbled feta cheese
- 1/3 cup chopped fresh chives

## Direction

- In a big sauce pot over medium-low heat, add olive oil. Sauté garlic and onion in the heated oil for 3-4 minutes until tender.
- Add red pepper flakes, lemon zest, chicken breasts, and chicken broth to the pot. Raise the heat to high, put a cover on the pot and boil. Lower the heat to medium and simmer for 5 minutes. Mix in pepper, salt, and pearl couscous. Simmer for another 5 minutes. Take away from heat.
- Using tongs, take the chicken breasts out of the pot. Shred the chicken using tongs and a fork. Put back into the pot. Mix chives and feta cheese into the soup. Taste and season as necessary. Enjoy warm.

## Nutrition Information

- Calories: 229 calories;
- Total Fat: 9.1
- Sodium: 1340
- Total Carbohydrate: 20
- Cholesterol: 21
- Protein: 15.8

### 976. Homemade Spanakopita

*Serving: 8 | Prep: 30mins | Cook: 1hours | Ready in:*

## Ingredients

- 5 (10 ounce) packages frozen chopped spinach - thawed, drained and squeezed dry
- 6 eggs
- 1 cup chopped fresh dill leaves
- 1 large onion, chopped
- 1 pound crumbled feta cheese
- 1/2 pound cottage cheese
- 1 teaspoon ground black pepper, or to taste
- 8 sheets phyllo dough, thawed
- 3 tablespoons olive oil, divided
- sour cream for garnish (optional)

## Direction

- Prepare oven and preheat at 190 degrees C (375 degrees F).
- Combine eggs, onion, cottage cheese, feta cheese, spinach, black pepper and dill in a large bowl; mix to well blend.
- Prepare a 9x13-inch baking dish and put 2 sheets of phyllo dough. Add approximately 1 tablespoon of olive oil and place 2 more sheets of phyllo dough on top. Pour evenly spinach filling on top of the phyllo sheets then gently press it down. Put 2 more phyllo sheets on top. Add again 1 tablespoon of olive oil and place

the remaining 2 phyllo sheets on top. Pour the remaining 1 tablespoon of olive oil.
- Place in the preheated oven then bake for 1 hour until top turns brown and filling sets. Slice into squares and add a dollop of sour cream on top. Serve.

### Nutrition Information

- Calories: 415 calories;
- Total Fat: 26.3
- Sodium: 1027
- Total Carbohydrate: 23.4
- Cholesterol: 198
- Protein: 24.7

## 977. Instant Pot® Greek Chicken

*Serving: 8 | Prep: 10mins | Cook: 35mins | Ready in:*

### Ingredients

- 2 tablespoons avocado oil
- 6 cloves roasted garlic, mashed
- 2 pounds skinless, boneless chicken breasts
- 1 tablespoon garlic and herb seasoning, or more to taste
- 1/2 teaspoon garlic salt
- 1/4 teaspoon ground black pepper
- 1 (8 ounce) jar marinated artichoke hearts, drained
- 1 cup sliced Kalamata olives
- 1/2 medium red onion, sliced
- 1/2 (16 fl oz) bottle Greek salad dressing
- 1 tablespoon arrowroot starch, or as needed
- 1 (4 ounce) package crumbled feta cheese (optional)

### Direction

- Set the multi-functional electric pressure cooker (like Instant Pot®) into Sauté function.
- Pour oil and add roasted garlic to the pot, stir and let it cook for 60 seconds until fragrant.
- Flavor one side of the chicken breast with garlic salt, black pepper, and half of the garlic and herb seasoning. Transfer the chicken into the pot, flavored side down. Let it cook for 2 minutes until all browned. Top it again with the remaining garlic salt, black pepper, and remaining garlic and herb seasoning. Turn it over and cook the other side for another 2 minutes until browned.
- Position the olives and artichoke hearts around the chicken. Make sure that you place it in any gaps on the top and bottom of the chicken. Place red onion on top and pour the dressing on top of the chicken.
- Close and secure the lid tightly. Follow the manufacturer's guide on setting the pressure to high and set timer to 15 minutes. Let the pressure build inside for 10-15 minutes.
- Use the quick-release method in releasing the pressure for about 5 minutes. Slowly unlock and remove its lid.
- Take the chicken out from the pot. Whisk arrowroot starch to the liquid inside the pot until combine. Place the chicken back to the pot. Wait for at least 3 minutes to allow the sauce to thick. Add pepper and salt and sprinkle feta cheese on top.

### Nutrition Information

- Calories: 376 calories;
- Total Fat: 26.2
- Sodium: 939
- Total Carbohydrate: 8.5
- Cholesterol: 77
- Protein: 27.1

## 978. Kagianas (Greek Eggs And Tomato)

*Serving: 3 | Prep: 15mins | Cook: 17mins | Ready in:*

### Ingredients

- 3 large ripe tomatoes, quartered
- 3 tablespoons olive oil
- salt and freshly ground black pepper to taste
- 6 eggs, beaten

### Direction

- In a food processor, add tomatoes; blend until smooth.
- In a skillet, heat olive oil on medium-high. Mix in pepper, salt, and tomatoes; cook while stirring for 10-15 minutes until all liquid has evaporated from the tomatoes.
- Lower the heat to medium. Put in eggs; cook and stir constantly for 7-10 minutes, until mixture is evenly dry, and no large chunks left.

### Nutrition Information

- Calories: 295 calories;
- Sodium: 201
- Total Carbohydrate: 7.9
- Cholesterol: 372
- Protein: 14.2
- Total Fat: 23.8

## 979. Kreatopita Argostoli

*Serving: 12 | Prep: | Cook: | Ready in:*

### Ingredients

- 24 sheets phyllo dough
- 4 cups cooked white rice
- 1 clove garlic, minced
- 3 cups cubed cooked lamb
- 1 lemon, juiced
- 2 potatoes, peeled and quartered
- 4 hard-cooked eggs, quartered
- 2 tablespoons lemon zest
- 2 tablespoons chopped fresh parsley
- 2 tablespoons chopped fresh mint leaves
- 1 1/2 cups crumbled feta cheese
- 1/2 cup olive oil
- 1 cup beef broth
- 1 tablespoon chopped fresh oregano
- 1/2 teaspoon ground black pepper
- 1 egg, beaten
- 1/2 cup butter, melted

### Direction

- Preheat an oven to 165°C/325°F. Boil a big pot of salted water. Add potatoes; cook for 15 minutes till tender yet firm. Drain and cool; chop.
- Brush melted butter on 9x13-in. pan lightly. Put 1 phyllo sheet into pan; brush butter lightly. Add phyllo sheets, lightly brushing butter on each (doesn't need to fully cover every phyllo sheet in butter), till you get 12 in total.
- Spread cooked rice on phyllo; sprinkle minced garlic. In an even layer, add lamb; sprinkle lemon juice. Put 1 cup diced potatoes on lamb.
- Arrange 1/4 eggs; sprinkle lemon zest, mint and parsley. Add the crumbled feta cheese.
- Add beef broth and olive oil; sprinkle pepper and oregano then add beaten egg.
- Put leftover 12 phyllo sheets over, lightly brushed in melted butter.
- Bake at 165°C/325°F for 40-50 minutes. Put temperature on 175°C/350°F at final 10 minutes. Remove from oven; cool for 15 minutes on a rack. Cut to squares or diamonds; serve warm.

### Nutrition Information

- Calories: 543 calories;
- Total Fat: 29.4
- Sodium: 575
- Total Carbohydrate: 43.4
- Cholesterol: 172
- Protein: 25.8

## 980. Lamb Stew With Green Beans

*Serving: 12 | Prep: 30mins | Cook: 1hours30mins | Ready in:*

### Ingredients

- 3 tablespoons olive oil
- 1 large onion, chopped
- 1 stalk celery, chopped
- 3 pounds boneless lamb shoulder, cut into 2 inch pieces
- 1 (8 ounce) can tomato sauce
- 3 cups hot water
- 2 pounds fresh green beans, trimmed
- 1 tablespoon chopped fresh parsley
- 1/2 teaspoon dried mint
- 1/2 teaspoon dried dill weed
- 1 pinch ground cinnamon
- 1 pinch white sugar
- salt and pepper to taste

### Direction

- In a large pot over medium heat, heat oil. Add celery and onion and sauté in hot oil until golden in color. Stir in lamb and cook until browned evenly. Stir in water and tomato sauce. Lower the heat and simmer for about 60 minutes.
- Stir in green beans. Add pepper, salt, sugar, cinnamon, dill, mint and parsley to season. Continue to cook until beans are softened.

### Nutrition Information

- Calories: 363 calories;
- Protein: 20.6
- Total Fat: 27.9
- Sodium: 272
- Total Carbohydrate: 7.8
- Cholesterol: 82

## 981. Lemon Chicken Orzo Soup

*Serving: 12 | Prep: 20mins | Cook: 1hours | Ready in:*

### Ingredients

- 8 ounces orzo pasta
- 1 teaspoon olive oil
- 3 carrots, chopped, or more to taste
- 3 ribs celery, chopped
- 1 onion, chopped
- 2 cloves garlic, minced
- 1/2 teaspoon dried thyme
- 1/2 teaspoon dried oregano
- salt and ground black pepper to taste
- 1 bay leaf
- 3 (32 ounce) cartons fat-free, low-sodium chicken broth
- 1/2 cup fresh lemon juice
- 1 lemon, zested
- 8 ounces cooked chicken breast, chopped
- 1 (8 ounce) package baby spinach leaves
- 1 lemon, sliced for garnish (optional)
- 1/4 cup grated Parmesan cheese (optional)

### Direction

- Boil a big pot of lightly salted water. Let the orzo cook in the boiling water for about 5 minutes, until partly cooked through but not yet soft; drain. Rinse it in cold water until completely cooled.
- Heat the oil in a big pot on medium heat. Cook and stir the onion, celery and carrots in the hot oil for 5-7 minutes, until the onion is translucent, and the veggies start to soften. Add the garlic and cook and stir for about 1 more minute until aromatic. Sprinkle bay leaf, black pepper, salt, oregano and thyme to season the mixture. Keep on cooking for additional 30 seconds prior to pouring the chicken broth into the pot.
- Boil the broth, then partly cover the pot. Lower the heat to medium-low. Let it simmer for about 10 minutes, until the veggies are just tender.

- Mix lemon zest, lemon juice and orzo into the broth, then add chicken. Cook for around 5 minutes, until the orzo and chicken are thoroughly heated. Add the baby spinach and cook for 2-3 minutes, until the orzo is tender and the spinach wilts into the broth. Ladle the soup into the bowls and put Parmesan cheese and slices of lemon on top to garnish.

## Nutrition Information

- Calories: 167 calories;
- Cholesterol: 20
- Protein: 12.1
- Total Fat: 4.1
- Sodium: 187
- Total Carbohydrate: 21.7

## 982. Lemon And Potato Soup

*Serving: 12 | Prep: 10mins | Cook: 35mins | Ready in:*

## Ingredients

- 8 potatoes, cubed
- 4 cloves garlic - peeled and sliced
- 6 stalks celery with leaves, chopped
- 1/2 teaspoon ground turmeric
- 2 lemons, juiced
- 1 cube chicken bouillon
- salt and pepper to taste

## Direction

- In a large stockpot, place celery, garlic, and potatoes and cover with water. Put lid on and bring to a boil. Cook for about 25 minutes until potatoes are tender.
- Season with chicken bouillon cube, lemon juice, and turmeric, and pepper and salt to taste. Stew for another 10 minutes. Crush some of the potato chunks to get a thicker consistency.

## Nutrition Information

- Calories: 119 calories;
- Total Carbohydrate: 27.8
- Cholesterol: < 1
- Protein: 3.4
- Total Fat: 0.2
- Sodium: 121

## 983. Mediterranean Orzo Spinach Salad

*Serving: 6 | Prep: 15mins | Cook: 20mins | Ready in:*

## Ingredients

- 1 cup uncooked orzo pasta
- 2 tablespoons extra virgin olive oil, divided
- 1 pound ground lamb
- 2 cloves garlic, chopped
- 1 tablespoon ground coriander
- salt and pepper to taste
- 4 cups fresh spinach leaves, chopped
- 3 tomatoes, seeded and chopped
- 1 lemon, zested and juiced
- 1/4 cup chopped fresh mint leaves
- 1/4 cup chopped fresh parsley
- 5 green onions, chopped
- 1 cup crumbled feta cheese

## Direction

- Boil a big pot of lightly salted water. Cook orzo pasta in boiling water for 5mins or until al dente; drain.
- On medium heat, heat a tablespoon of olive oil in a pan; add in garlic and lamb. Sprinkle pepper, salt, and coriander over the lamb to season. Cook the lamb until evenly brown. Take off from heat, then drain.
- Combine the remaining olive oil, green onions, parsley, mint, lemon zest and juice, tomatoes and spinach in a big bowl. Toss with the feta cheese, lamb and orzo. Serve.

### Nutrition Information

- Calories: 461 calories;
- Sodium: 535
- Total Carbohydrate: 34.5
- Cholesterol: 88
- Protein: 25.6
- Total Fat: 25

## 984. Molly's Mouthwatering Tzatziki Cucumber Sauce

*Serving: 22 | Prep: 15mins | Cook: | Ready in:*

### Ingredients

- 1 large cucumber, peeled and cut into chunks
- 1 1/2 cups plain Greek yogurt
- 2 cloves garlic, minced
- 1/2 cup sour cream
- 1/4 cup mayonnaise
- salt and pepper to taste

### Direction

- In a food processor, chop cucumber until nearly liquefied, then use a piece of cheesecloth to strain cucumber to remove excess moisture. Be careful to not over-drain and lose too much the fresh flavor.
- In a bowl, combine together mayonnaise, sour cream, garlic, yogurt and cucumber, then season with pepper and salt.

### Nutrition Information

- Calories: 49 calories;
- Total Carbohydrate: 1.4
- Cholesterol: 6
- Protein: 1.1
- Total Fat: 4.5
- Sodium: 26

## 985. Orzo Pasta Salad

*Serving: 4 | Prep: 15mins | Cook: 10mins | Ready in:*

### Ingredients

- 1 cup uncooked orzo pasta
- 1/4 cup chopped sun-dried tomatoes
- 1/2 cup boiling water
- 1 tablespoon extra-virgin olive oil
- 1 lemon, juiced and zested
- 1/2 cup kalamata olives
- 1/4 cup finely chopped fresh parsley
- 1/4 cup crumbled feta cheese
- salt and pepper to taste

### Direction

- Pour lightly salted water to fill a pot, then bring to rolling boil on high heat. Cook the pasta for about 11minutes without cover, while mixing from time to time, until the pasta is completely cooked but still firm to chew. Drain it well in a colander over the sink.
- In a bowl with boiling water, put the sun-dried tomatoes. Allow to stand for 10 minutes to let it plump up; drain the extra water.
- In a bowl, toss the feta cheese, parsley, olives, lemon zest, lemon juice, olive oil, sun-dried tomatoes and cooked orzo together. Sprinkle pepper and salt to taste.

### Nutrition Information

- Calories: 316 calories;
- Cholesterol: 8
- Protein: 9.8
- Total Fat: 11.2
- Sodium: 455
- Total Carbohydrate: 45.7

## 986. Orzo And Tomato Salad With Feta Cheese

*Serving: 6 | Prep: 15mins | Cook: 10mins | Ready in:*

### Ingredients

- 1 cup uncooked orzo pasta
- 1/4 cup pitted green olives
- 1 cup diced feta cheese
- 3 tablespoons chopped fresh parsley
- 3 tablespoons chopped fresh dill
- 1 ripe tomato, chopped
- 1/4 cup virgin olive oil
- 1/8 cup lemon juice
- salt and pepper to taste

### Direction

- Boil a big pot of lightly salted water; add orzo. Cook for 8-10mins or until al dente; drain the orzo and rinse under cold water.
- Once cooled, transfer the cooled orzo to a medium bowl; mix in tomato, dill, parsley, feta cheese and olives. Whisk the lemon juice and oil together in a small bowl. Pour on top of the pasta, then mix well. Sprinkle pepper and salt to taste. Refrigerate the pasta prior to serving.

### Nutrition Information

- Calories: 329 calories;
- Total Fat: 19.6
- Sodium: 614
- Total Carbohydrate: 28.1
- Cholesterol: 37
- Protein: 10.9

## 987. Peppy's Pita Bread

*Serving: 8 | Prep: 30mins | Cook: 15mins | Ready in:*

### Ingredients

- 1 1/8 cups warm water (110 degrees F/45 degrees C)
- 3 cups all-purpose flour
- 1 teaspoon salt
- 1 tablespoon vegetable oil
- 1 1/2 teaspoons white sugar
- 1 1/2 teaspoons active dry yeast

### Direction

- In the bread pan of your bread machine, combine all ingredients and set to Dough cycle and press Start. A beep from machine will indicate that dough has risen long enough.
- Place dough on surface dusted with flour. Roll and stretch gently the dough to make a 12inch rope. Cut the dough into 8 pieces using a sharp knife. Shape each dough into a smooth ball. Flatten each ball into a 6 to 7-inch circle using a rolling pin. Set aside on a countertop slightly floured. Cover with towel. Let the pitas rise until slightly puffy, 30 minutes.
- Set oven to 260 degrees C (500 degrees F) to preheat. Transfer 2 or 3 pitas to a wire cake rack. Put the cake rack on the oven rack directly. Bake for 4 to 5 minutes or until pitas are puffy and beginning to brown. Take out of the oven and transfer pitas to a sealed brown paper bag immediately or use a damp towel to cover them to soften. When pitas become soft, cut in half or split top edge of whole or half pitas. Shelf life of pitas in a plastic bag inside the refrigerator is several days but 1 to 2 months inside the freezer.

### Nutrition Information

- Calories: 191 calories;
- Sodium: 293
- Total Carbohydrate: 36.8
- Cholesterol: 0
- Protein: 5.1
- Total Fat: 2.2

## 988. Raw Hummus

*Serving: 20 | Prep: 15mins | Cook: 2mins | Ready in:*

### Ingredients

- 1 1/2 cups dry garbanzo beans
- 2 tablespoons tahini
- 1 teaspoon sea salt
- 2 lemons, juiced
- 4 cloves garlic, crushed or to taste
- 1 cup filtered or spring water
- 1 pinch paprika

### Direction

- Leave the beans to soak for 24 hours. Strain; allow to sit for 2-3 days, till the sprouts are around 1/2-inch long. Wash once or twice a day.
- Pour water into a large saucepan; allow to boil. Take away from the heat; allow to sit for 1 minute. Put the beans into the hot water; allow to stand for 1 minute. Strain. The hummus will turns out awful if you skip this step.
- Put the beans into a large food processor or a container. Include in garlic, lemon juice, sea salt and tahini. Blend till smooth, 3-5 minutes; include in water if needed. Allow to sit for 5 minutes in the container to let the beans absorb as much water as possible. Include in more water and whisk again if it turns too thick. Season with seasonings if necessary. Using a spoon, transfer into a plate. Serve with paprika on top.

### Nutrition Information

- Calories: 67 calories;
- Sodium: 94
- Total Carbohydrate: 10.8
- Cholesterol: 0
- Protein: 3.3
- Total Fat: 1.8

## 989. Real Hummus

*Serving: 20 | Prep: 15mins | Cook: | Ready in:*

### Ingredients

- 1 clove garlic
- 1 (19 ounce) can garbanzo beans, half the liquid reserved
- 4 tablespoons lemon juice
- 2 tablespoons tahini
- 1 clove garlic, chopped
- 1 teaspoon salt
- black pepper to taste
- 2 tablespoons olive oil

### Direction

- Chop the garlic in a blender and pour in garbanzo beans; set aside about 1 tablespoon for decoration. Stir in salt, tahini, lemon juice and reserved liquid then blend until well incorporated and creamy.
- Move the mixture to a medium-sized serving bowl. Drizzle olive oil on top and sprinkle with pepper. Decorate with garbanzo beans that you reserved.

### Nutrition Information

- Calories: 54 calories;
- Sodium: 199
- Total Carbohydrate: 6.8
- Cholesterol: 0
- Protein: 1.6
- Total Fat: 2.5

## 990. Roasted Garlic Tzatziki

*Serving: 8 | Prep: 15mins | Cook: | Ready in:*

### Ingredients

- 1 (16 ounce) container Greek yogurt
- 1/2 English cucumber

- 2 tablespoons roasted garlic puree
- 2 tablespoons lemon juice
- 10 fresh mint leaves, chopped
- 2 tablespoons olive oil
- salt to taste

### Direction

- Put the yogurt in four layers of cheesecloth, paper towel, or paper coffee filter placed in a colander or strainer; set it on top of a bowl to hold the liquid. Let the yogurt strain for 24hrs inside the fridge.
- Skin and grate the cucumber; press the excess water out. Put in a bowl; mix in olive oil, strained yogurt, mint, lemon juice, and garlic puree until blended. Sprinkle salt to taste. Refrigerate until chilled then serve.

### Nutrition Information

- Calories: 108 calories;
- Sodium: 37
- Total Carbohydrate: 3.4
- Cholesterol: 13
- Protein: 3.6
- Total Fat: 9.1

## 991. Saffron Mussel Bisque

*Serving: 6 | Prep: 35mins | Cook: 35mins | Ready in:*

### Ingredients

- 2 pounds mussels, cleaned and debearded
- 1 1/4 cups white wine
- 1 1/2 cups water
- 3 tablespoons margarine
- 1 tablespoon olive oil
- 1 onion, chopped
- 1 clove garlic, crushed
- 1 leek, bulb only, chopped
- 1/2 teaspoon fenugreek seeds, finely crushed
- 1 1/2 tablespoons all-purpose flour
- 6 saffron threads
- 1 1/4 cups chicken broth
- 1 tablespoon chopped fresh parsley
- salt and pepper to taste
- 2 tablespoons whipping cream

### Direction

- In small bowl, cover saffron threads in 1 tbsp. boiling water; put aside.
- In a few changes of fresh water, scrub mussels clean; pull bears off. Discard mussels that don't tightly close when tapped and are cracker. Place mussels in saucepan with water and wine. Cover. Cook, frequently shaking pan, for 6-7 minutes till shells open on high heat. Remove mussels; discard unopened ones. Through fine sieve, strain liquid; put aside.
- Heat oil and butter in saucepan; add fenugreek, leek, garlic and onion. Gently cook for 5 minutes. Mix flour in; cook for a minute. Add chicken broth, 2 1/2 cups reserved cooking liquid and saffron mixture; boil. Gently simmer for 15 minutes, covered.
- Meanwhile, retain 8 mussels in shells; remove leftover mussels from shells. Put all mussels in soup; mix cream, pepper, salt and chopped parsley in. Heat through for 2-3 minutes. Use parsley sprigs to garnish if desired. Serve hot.

### Nutrition Information

- Calories: 205 calories;
- Sodium: 343
- Total Carbohydrate: 9
- Cholesterol: 27
- Protein: 9.7
- Total Fat: 10.4

## 992. Traditional Pita Breads

*Serving: 12 | Prep: 30mins | Cook: 10mins | Ready in:*

## Ingredients

- 1 package active dry yeast
- 1 1/4 cups warm water (100 to 110 degrees F/40 to 45 degrees C)
- 3 1/2 cups all-purpose flour, or as needed - divided
- 1 1/2 teaspoons salt
- 1/4 cup vegetable shortening

## Direction

- In a mixing bowl with warm water, dredge yeast over and let it stand until creamy foam created, about 5 minutes. Combine shortening, salt and 2 cups of flour, using a fork to beat the mixture for 2 minutes. If necessary, stir in as much of the leftover 1 1/2 cup flour.
- Place dough on a surface spread with flour and knead until flexible and smooth. If dough is sticky, knead in more flour. Shape into a ball and set aside in a warm area to let it rest for 15 minutes, covered with a kitchen towel.
- Set oven to 260°C or 500°F.
- Split dough to 12 commensurate parts. Get your hands floured and shape each dough part into a ball. Let it rest for 10 minutes using a kitchen towel to cover balls. Flatten the balls into rounds on a surface spread with flour and let it rest for 10 more minutes, cover them by using kitchen towel. On a surface with dredged flour, gradually form each dough ball into a circle about 6" in diameter. On a baking sheet with no coated oil, put pita breads in a single layer.
- In a preheated oven, bake for 3 to 4 minutes until the pita breads were inflated. Use a spatula to turn bread over, put it back to oven and bake for 2 more minutes. Take out of oven and place on wire racks to cool, then halve pita breads and make pockets for filing by slowly separating bottoms and tops.

## Nutrition Information

- Calories: 172 calories;
- Sodium: 292
- Total Carbohydrate: 28
- Cholesterol: 0
- Protein: 4
- Total Fat: 4.7

### 993. Tzatziki A Greek Mother's Sauce

*Serving: 8 | Prep: 10mins | Cook: | Ready in:*

## Ingredients

- 2 small cucumbers, peeled and grated
- 1 (12 ounce) package silken tofu
- 1 tablespoon chopped fresh dill
- 1 teaspoon minced garlic
- Himalayan pink salt to taste
- 1 pinch ground black pepper to taste

## Direction

- Use paper towel to draw out excess water from cucumber.
- In a food processor, blend together black pepper, pink salt, garlic, dill, tofu and cucumber until combined evenly.

## Nutrition Information

- Calories: 38 calories;
- Sodium: 10
- Total Carbohydrate: 2
- Cholesterol: 0
- Protein: 3.7
- Total Fat: 2.1

### 994. Tzatziki II

*Serving: 4 | Prep: 10mins | Cook: | Ready in:*

## Ingredients

- 1 cucumber
- 1 cup plain yogurt
- 2 cloves garlic, finely chopped
- 1/4 teaspoon salt
- 1 teaspoon chopped fresh mint leaves

### Direction

- Peel the cucumber and halve it longitudinally. Use a spoon to remove the seeds, then grate cucumber into a small bowl. Fold in chopped mint, salt, garlic and yogurt. Refrigerate for a minimum of a half hour before serving to let the flavor develop.

### Nutrition Information

- Calories: 48 calories;
- Total Fat: 1
- Sodium: 189
- Total Carbohydrate: 6.6
- Cholesterol: 4
- Protein: 3.6

## 995. Tzatziki Sauce

*Serving: 8 | Prep: 20mins | Cook: | Ready in:*

### Ingredients

- 2 (8 ounce) containers plain yogurt
- 2 cucumbers - peeled, seeded and diced
- 2 tablespoons olive oil
- 1/2 lemon, juiced
- salt and pepper to taste
- 1 tablespoon chopped fresh dill
- 3 cloves garlic, peeled

### Direction

- Mix garlic, yogurt, dill, cucumber, pepper, olive oil, salt, and lemon juice in a blender or food processor until well blended. Pour dressing in a separate container; cover. Chill for a minimum of 1 hour to bring out the flavor.

### Nutrition Information

- Calories: 75 calories;
- Cholesterol: 3
- Protein: 3.4
- Total Fat: 4.4
- Sodium: 41
- Total Carbohydrate: 6.4

## 996. Tzatziki Sauce (Yogurt And Cucumber Dip)

*Serving: 16 | Prep: 25mins | Cook: | Ready in:*

### Ingredients

- 1 (16 ounce) container low-fat plain yogurt
- 1 cucumber, peeled, seeded, and grated
- 1 clove garlic, minced
- 1 tablespoon chopped fresh parsley
- 1 tablespoon chopped fresh mint
- 1 tablespoon fresh lemon juice
- salt and pepper to taste

### Direction

- In a colander, line two layers of cheesecloth and put it over a medium bowl. Pour the yogurt on the cheesecloth and use plastic wrap to cover the colander. Let yogurt drain overnight.
- On a plate lined with paper towel, place grated cucumber; let drain 1-2 hours.
- In a bowl, combine pepper, salt, lemon juice, mint, parsley, garlic, cucumber, and drained yogurt. Before serving, refrigerate at least 2 hours.

### Nutrition Information

- Calories: 21 calories;

- Total Fat: 0.5
- Sodium: 45
- Total Carbohydrate: 2.8
- Cholesterol: 2
- Protein: 1.6

## 997. Tzatziki Sauce I

*Serving: 12 | Prep: 5mins | Cook: | Ready in:*

### Ingredients

- 8 ounces plain yogurt
- 2 tablespoons olive oil
- 1 tablespoon lemon juice
- 1/2 teaspoon salt
- 1/2 teaspoon ground black pepper
- 1 tablespoon chopped fresh dill
- 3 cloves pressed garlic

### Direction

- Mix together garlic, dill, pepper, salt, lemon juice, olive oil and yogurt in a mixing bowl. Blend the mixture thoroughly and serve.

### Nutrition Information

- Calories: 33 calories;
- Total Fat: 2.5
- Sodium: 110
- Total Carbohydrate: 1.7
- Cholesterol: 1
- Protein: 1.1

## 998. Tzatziki Sauce II

*Serving: 24 | Prep: 6hours | Cook: | Ready in:*

### Ingredients

- 2 cups plain yogurt
- 2 cloves crushed garlic
- 1/2 teaspoon salt
- 1/4 teaspoon ground black pepper
- 1/4 cup chopped fresh mint leaves
- 1 large cucumber - peeled, seeded and shredded

### Direction

- Strain the yogurt into a bowl through a cheese cloth about 3-4 hours, until most of water has drained.
- Press excess liquid out of the shredded cucumber. Stir strained yogurt and cucumber together in a medium bowl, then blend in mint, pepper, salt and garlic. Refrigerate the mixture about 1-2 hours.

### Nutrition Information

- Calories: 15 calories;
- Protein: 1.2
- Total Fat: 0.3
- Sodium: 63
- Total Carbohydrate: 1.8
- Cholesterol: 1

## 999. Tzatziki VII

*Serving: 7 | Prep: 15mins | Cook: | Ready in:*

### Ingredients

- 1 (32 ounce) container plain yogurt
- 2 cucumbers
- 1 medium head garlic
- 1/4 cup extra virgin olive oil
- 3 tablespoons lemon juice
- 1 teaspoon chopped fresh dill weed
- salt and pepper to taste

### Direction

- In a big square of double cheesecloth, add yogurt. Tie the cheesecloth at the top and

allow any excess liquid to drain, about 4 hours.
- Peel cucumbers and use a spoon to remove seeds. Shred the cucumbers, then squeeze to drain excess liquid.
- Peel and chop garlic.
- Whisk together pepper, salt, dill, lemon juice and olive oil in a moderate-sized bowl, then put in garlic, cucumbers and yogurt and stir until blended evenly. Chill until serving.

## Nutrition Information

- Calories: 171 calories;
- Total Fat: 12.3
- Sodium: 62
- Total Carbohydrate: 10.6
- Cholesterol: 17
- Protein: 5.3

## 1000. Vasilopita (Orange Sweet Bread)

*Serving: 12 | Prep: 30mins | Cook: 31mins | Ready in:*

## Ingredients

- 1/2 cup orange juice
- 1/2 cup water
- 1 tablespoon ground cinnamon
- 3 (.25 ounce) packages rapid-rise yeast
- 2 cups white sugar
- 1 cup unsalted margarine (such as Fleischmann's®), melted
- 4 eggs
- 1 orange, zested
- 7 cups bread flour, or more as needed
- 1 tablespoon salt
- 1 tablespoon baking powder
- 2 coins wrapped in aluminum foil
- 1 egg white
- 1 teaspoon vanilla extract

## Direction

- In a microwave-safe bowl, stir cinnamon, water and orange juice. In microwave, heat for 1 to 2 minutes till mixture reads 43 °C or 110 °F on an instant-read thermometer.
- Into the mixture of orange juice, mix the yeast. Allow to sit for 45 minutes till yeast is foamy and creamy.
- In a stand mixer bowl, mix together margarine and sugar. Whip till creamy. Put in the eggs; whip for 30 seconds on high speed. Blend in orange zest and yeast mixture till well incorporated.
- In a bowl, sift together baking powder, salt and flour. Put in gradually to mixture in stand mixer for 5 minutes, stirring using a bread hook till a sticky, soft dough creates.
- Turn dough onto a big glass bowl. Put on plastic wrap to cover; allow to rise in warm area for 2 to 4 hours till doubled in volume.
- Preheat an oven to 175 °C or 350 °F. Lightly oil 2 round cake pans.
- Split dough into 2 even portions. In each portion, place a wrapped coin; knead for 2 to 3 minutes and form into a ball. Transfer dough balls in each of the cake pan. Put on plastic wrap to cover; allow to rise for an additional of 2 to 4 hours till puffy.
- In a small bowl, beat together vanilla and egg white. Brush on the dough surface.
- In the prepped oven, bake for 30 to 55 minutes till an inserted knife into the middle gets out with several crumbs attached.

## Nutrition Information

- Calories: 303 calories;
- Sodium: 695
- Total Carbohydrate: 36.1
- Cholesterol: 62
- Protein: 3.2
- Total Fat: 16.6

## 1001. Whole Wheat Rigatoni And Cauliflower, Wilted Arugula, Feta & Olives

*Serving: 6 | Prep: | Cook: | Ready in:*

### Ingredients

- 1 pound bite-size whole wheat pasta, such as rigatoni or penne
- 1 tablespoon Salt
- 1 medium head cauliflower, trimmed and cut into bite-size florets
- 3 tablespoons olive oil
- 1/2 red bell pepper, cut into medium dice
- 1/2 yellow bell pepper, cut into medium dice
- 3 cloves garlic, minced
- 1 cup canned crushed tomatoes
- 1 teaspoon Italian seasoning
- 1/4 cup coarsely chopped pitted kalamata olives
- 4 cups factory-washed arugula or spinach
- 3/4 cup crumbled feta cheese, divided
- 1 pinch Freshly ground black pepper

### Direction

- In a large soup kettle, boil a generous 2 quarts of water and salt; add in pasta and cook, partially covered, for 4 minutes. Add in cauliflower and cook, covered partially, for an addition of 6 minutes till pasta and cauliflower are tender. Reserve 1 cup of cooking liquid, let the pasta drain and return top pot.
- In the meantime, in a 10-inch skillet, heat oil. Add in peppers, and sauté for around 4 minutes till soften. Add in garlic; continue to sauté for 1 minute more till fragrant and golden. Add olives, seasoning and tomatoes; simmer sauce for about 5 minutes. Add sauce to pasta, along with the reserved cooking liquid, a half cup feta and arugula. Toss, add pepper for seasoning to taste. Serve with additional feta.
- For lunch, in leak-proof containers, pack pasta and extra feta. Warm pasta in microwave and add feta on top.

### Nutrition Information

- Calories: 404 calories;
- Protein: 15.7
- Total Fat: 13.6
- Sodium: 1550
- Total Carbohydrate: 60.9
- Cholesterol: 17

# Index

## A

Ale 3,20

Almond 3,10,12,40,330,354,421,449

Apple 6,8,10,12,161,268,331,442

Apricot 6,8,9,12,161,180,236,305,426

Arborio rice 508

Artichoke 6,7,8,9,10,11,12,13,162,173,214,274,288,332,362,374,376,417,427,493

Asparagus 4,9,10,13,74,292,333,334,367,464,473

Avocado 3,14,29,508

## B

Bagel 11,377,444,498

Barley 6,7,10,165,186,372

Basil 6,7,10,166,190,338,356

Beans 3,4,8,10,11,12,13,14,36,41,75,246,372,387,403,419,421,452,466,525

Beef 4,6,7,8,9,14,84,163,166,167,171,184,202,235,251,268,278,308,323,520

Biscuits 5,120

Black pepper 97,143,233

Blackberry 9,299

Bran 4,54

Bread 6,11,13,14,171,342,389,390,467,492,503,528,530,534

Brie 10,19,355

Broccoli 11,12,391,427

Burger 4,6,7,11,14,56,63,65,66,79,83,87,92,93,175,176,190,211,232,383,515

Butter 3,5,6,10,12,38,116,119,175,290,313,340,455,479,481

## C

Cabbage 6,166

Cake 5,10,115,120,128,129,131,340

Caramel 8,12,249,454

Carrot 12,440

Cashew 10,341

Catfish 4,6,7,9,53,175,198,320

Cauliflower 13,14,474,535

Caviar 13,504

Champ 6,175,176

Cheddar 23,70,74,75

Cheese 3,4,5,7,9,10,11,12,13,14,19,22,26,35,46,63,70,74,106,199,220,252,259,309,331,333,341,342,343,355,363,374,378,379,381,383,386,397,415,417,421,424,432,465,466,470,486,492,496,501,506,507,514,528

Cherry 10,343

Chestnut 4,82

Chicken 4,5,6,7,8,9,14,51,58,59,60,61,64,66,67,70,72,73,76,78,82,84,86,87,95,96,110,149,169,170,172,174,178,179,180,181,182,183,190,191,192,193,194,195,196,197,199,201,209,212,213,239,240,243,245,246,247,250,251,252,253,254,255,265,269,271,272,273,274,276,277,281,288,298,300,301,302,305,308,313,315,317,320,321,323,325,512,513,514,516,522,523,525

Chickpea 6,8,10,11,12,13,181,256,345,346,383,442,468

Chips 11,12,378,397,418,429

Chocolate 5,129

Chorizo 7,169,221

Chutney 6,174

Clams 4,61

Cod 8,9,242,256,315

Coffee 10,340

Couscous 4,5,6,7,8,9,10,11,12,13,67,68,135,151,152,155,174,179,183,193,241,247,250,273,291,296,341,346,349,350,351,352,353,354,357,385,419,424,448,460,473,483,493,494,499,506

Crab 6,156

Crackers 10,335

Cranberry 7,10,183,341,354,355

Cream 3,5,7,8,10,14,16,107,116,117,119,124,125,127,129,131,221,254,340,356,500,514

Crisps 3,28

Croissant 13,476

Crostini 11,385,407

Crumble 177,199,252,327,363,386,397,432,482

Cucumber 3,5,6,9,10,11,12,14,17,137,154,291,292,335,345,357,363,369,373,375,414,425,439,510,515,527,532

Cumin 211

Curry 7,13,187,498

# D

Dab 199,227,278

Dijon mustard 95,136,137,143,148,169,171,188,216,222,249,260,270,273,282,286,288,289,290,291,297,299,319,324,335,341,393,405,418,466,478,485,487,492,497,512

Dill 3,7,9,10,12,36,190,216,222,292,324,358,359,419

# E

Egg 3,4,5,6,7,8,10,11,12,13,14,40,68,78,86,102,120,154,215,255,344,360,365,386,406,409,455,474,523

English muffin 259,439

# F

Falafel 4,88

Fat 5,15,16,17,18,19,20,21,22,23,24,25,26,27,28,29,30,31,32,33,34,35,36,37,38,39,40,41,42,43,44,45,46,47,48,49,50,51,52,53,54,55,56,57,58,59,60,61,62,63,64,65,66,67,68,69,70,71,72,73,74,75,76,77,78,79,80,81,82,83,84,85,86,87,88,89,90,91,92,93,94,95,96,97,98,99,100,101,102,103,104,105,106,107,108,109,110,111,112,113,114,115,116,117,118,119,120,121,122,123,124,125,126,127,128,129,130,131,132,133,134,135,136,137,138,139,140,141,142,143,144,145,146,147,148,149,150,151,152,153,154,155,156,157,158,159,160,161,162,163,164,165,166,167,168,169,170,171,172,173,174,175,176,177,178,179,180,181,182,183,184,185,186,187,188,189,190,191,192,193,194,195,196,197,198,199,200,201,202,203,204,205,206,207,208,209,210,211,212,213,214,215,216,217,218,219,220,221,222,223,224,225,226,227,228,229,230,231,232,233,234,235,236,237,238,239,240,241,242,243,244,245,246,247,248,249,250,251,252,253,254,255,256,257,258,259,260,261,262,263,264,265,266,267,268,269,270,271,272,273,274,275,276,277,278,279,280,281,282,283,284,285,286,287,288,289,290,291,292,293,294,295,296,297,298,299,300,301,302,303,304,305,306,307,308,309,310,311,312,313,314,315,316,317,318,319,320,321,322,323,324,325,326,327,328,329,330,331,332,333,334,335,336,337,338,339,340,341,342,343,344,345,346,347,348,349,350,351,352,353,354,355,356,357,358,359,360,361,362,363,364,365,366,367,368,369,370,371,372,373,374,375,376,377,378,379,380,381,382,383,384,385,386,387,388,389,390,391,392,393,394,395,396,397,398,399,400,401,402,403,404,405,406,407,408,409,410,411,412,413,414,415,416,417,418,419,420,421,422,423,424,425,426,427,428,429,430,431,432,433,434,435,436,437,438,439,440,441,442,443,444,445,446,447,448,449,450,451,452,453,454,455,456,457,458,459,460,461,462,463,464,465,466,467,468,469,470,471,472,473,474,475,476,477,478,479,480,481,482,483,484,485,486,487,488,489,490,491,492,493,494,495,496,497,498,499,500,501,502,5

03,504,505,506,507,508,509,510,511,512,513,514,515,516,517,518,519,520,521,522,523,524,525,526,527,528,529,530,531,532,533,534,535

Fennel 5,8,9,10,12,107,249,250,318,334,422

Fenugreek 5,96

Feta 3,4,5,6,7,8,9,10,11,12,13,14,19,21,22,31,35,36,39,46,49,57,63,66,74,75,76,91,107,135,136,140,142,143,154,157,172,181,189,190,191,196,199,212,240,252,293,296,297,310,311,330,341,345,352,355,356,358,359,362,363,364,365,366,367,370,375,386,397,406,407,414,420,421,432,438,449,450,462,464,466,476,485,490,494,496,501,507,515,528,535

Fettuccine 8,9,257,307

Fig 3,7,9,19,192,283

Fish 4,6,7,8,62,166,190,215,258

Flank 9,282,295,311

Flatbread 6,7,13,177,197,477

Flour 120

Focaccia 11,416

French bread 331,385,388,407,409,435,444,465,470,492,501,502

Fruit 10,12,370,439

# G

Garlic 3,4,6,7,8,11,12,13,14,19,27,42,82,180,197,213,240,242,283,374,375,376,377,378,420,429,461,465,492,529

Gorgonzola 3,20,79,460

Grain 7,186

Grapes 11,396

Gravy 229

# H

Halibut 6,7,8,9,161,216,222,223,277,324

Hazelnut 5,128

Heart 7,8,11,223,274,413

Honey 5,7,121,228

Hummus 3,9,10,11,12,13,14,15,16,18,23,24,28,30,35,304,347,383,415,423,424,459,467,476,486,487,495,529

# J

Jus 194,430,477

# K

Kale 5,11,140,378

# L

Lamb 3,4,6,7,8,9,14,24,56,71,90,91,92,93,164,165,169,170,175,176,177,184,185,186,187,188,199,217,218,219,225,226,231,232,233,234,235,236,237,238,241,243,248,260,267,271,274,279,280,282,283,284,285,286,287,288,289,299,300,301,303,305,306,312,314,319,322,325,329,514,515,525

Leek 12,418

Lemon 3,4,5,6,7,8,9,10,11,12,13,14,42,44,72,73,120,136,162,175,181,191,199,200,201,213,231,239,240,241,242,243,272,273,296,301,313,320,332,339,376,380,396,419,420,421,422,463,464,516,522,525,526

Lettuce 11,388

Lime 9,12,190,325,424

Ling 7,8,9,189,244,262,263,297,311

# M

Macaroni 11,389

Mandarin 12,424

Mayonnaise 354,374

Meat 4,5,7,8,9,14,74,94,101,102,110,111,187,200,267,327,509

Meringue 129

Millet 12,437

Mince 194,293,328,360,394,406,418

Mint 4,6,8,9,10,12,71,181,232,267,322,332,352,419,439,440,441

Mozzarella 259

Muffins 10,12,362,448

Mushroom 7,8,10,12,13,214,247,353,443,444,463,471,477,501

Mussels 5,107

Mustard 7,8,12,216,270,354,418

# N

Nut 4,9,12,15,16,17,18,19,20,21,22,23,24,25,26,27,28,29,30,31,32,33,34,35,36,37,38,39,40,41,42,43,44,45,46,47,48,49,50,51,52,53,54,55,56,57,58,59,60,61,62,63,64,65,66,67,68,69,70,71,72,73,74,75,76,77,78,79,80,81,82,83,84,85,86,87,88,89,90,91,92,93,94,95,96,97,98,99,100,101,102,103,104,105,106,107,108,109,110,111,112,113,114,115,116,117,118,119,120,121,122,123,124,125,126,127,128,129,130,131,132,133,134,135,136,137,138,139,140,141,142,143,144,145,146,147,148,149,150,151,152,153,154,155,156,157,158,159,160,161,162,163,164,165,166,167,168,169,170,171,172,173,174,175,176,177,178,179,180,181,182,183,184,185,186,187,188,189,190,191,192,193,194,195,196,197,198,199,200,201,202,203,204,205,206,207,208,209,210,211,212,213,214,215,216,217,218,219,220,221,222,223,224,225,226,227,228,229,230,231,232,233,234,235,236,237,238,239,240,241,242,243,244,245,246,247,248,249,250,251,252,253,254,255,256,257,258,259,260,261,262,263,264,265,266,267,268,269,270,271,272,273,274,275,276,277,278,279,280,281,282,283,284,285,286,287,288,289,290,291,292,293,294,295,296,297,298,299,300,301,302,303,304,305,306,307,308,309,310,311,312,313,314,315,316,317,318,319,320,321,322,323,324,325,326,327,328,329,330,331,332,333,334,335,336,337,338,339,340,341,342,343,344,345,346,347,348,349,350,351,352,353,354,355,356,357,358,359,360,361,362,363,364,365,366,367,368,369,370,371,372,373,374,375,376,377,378,379,380,381,382,383,384,385,386,387,388,389,390,391,392,393,394,395,396,397,398,399,400,401,402,403,404,405,406,407,408,409,410,411,412,413,414,415,416,417,418,419,420,421,422,423,424,425,426,427,428,429,430,431,432,433,434,435,436,437,438,439,440,441,442,443,444,445,446,447,448,449,450,451,452,453,454,455,456,457,458,459,460,461,462,463,464,465,466,467,468,469,470,471,472,473,474,475,476,477,478,479,480,481,482,483,484,485,486,487,488,489,490,491,492,493,494,495,496,497,498,499,500,501,502,503,504,505,506,507,508,509,510,511,512,513,514,515,516,517,518,519,520,521,522,523,524,525,526,527,528,529,530,531,532,533,534,535

# O

Octopus 5,98

Oil 5,10,19,43,65,73,106,114,115,116,120,121,122,125,129,166,175,306,330,363,379,397

Olive 3,4,5,7,8,9,10,11,12,13,14,20,21,27,76,115,149,221,223,238,272,315,341,347,351,360,363,364,366,390,395,397,416,421,422,497,502,535

Onion 8,10,11,12,13,237,328,343,379,445,446,447,454,487,516

Orange 5,8,12,13,14,128,271,432,447,448,481,534

Oregano 8,211,240,272,397

Ouzo 5,27,107,178

# P

Paella 6,7,9,169,223,316

Pancakes 11,413

Paprika 169

Parfait 12,455

Parmesan 8,12,13,21,23,51,56,57,71,99,100,106,107,112,147,162,168,193,197,202,203,205,209,210,227,230,246,252,255,259,270,271,273,274,276,294,304,309,321,333,337,344,345,362,374,391,398,404,405,408,412,419,420,427,429,435,444,455,456,460,463,466,467,472,473,478,482,483,490,492,506,507,509,525,526

Parsley 12,447,451

Pasta 4,5,6,7,8,9,10,11,12,13,14,69,74,75,98,136,139,141,142,143,150,155,158,159,162,168,192,195,201,202,226,252,261,263,274,294,304,334,374,391,392,433,452,454,461,480,507,527

Pastry 5,8,12,104,118,275,434

Peach 12,452

Pear 6,11,12,151,379,453

Peas 3,12,36,441

Pecan 6,12,175,453

Peel 50,102,133,154,218,263,289,306,377,392,440,468,515,532,534

Penne 3,4,7,8,9,12,13,48,76,195,245,322,453,454,478

Pepper 3,4,5,6,7,9,12,13,18,19,30,80,85,91,95,108,110,143,164,168,177,211,218,314,329,383,427,437,454,462,467,468,479,482,496

Pesto 8,12,276,455,456

Pickle 3,26

Pie 4,5,7,9,14,51,57,94,104,105,106,121,122,172,207,290,308,509

Pineapple 8,10,278,279,337

Pistachio 5,128

Pizza 4,6,7,8,9,10,11,12,76,84,182,188,197,198,203,204,205,206,210,214,215,216,229,232,259,276,282,304,327,366,379,403,410,438

Plum 8,9,279,284

Polenta 12,434,444

Pork 4,6,7,8,9,55,65,77,89,160,171,193,242,249,259,279,280,285,328

Port 5,7,9,12,13,90,128,226,227,280,457,471

Potato 3,4,6,8,10,11,12,13,14,42,43,44,46,47,55,72,73,152,153,167,179,236,344,358,359,363,376,380,382,393,398,408,431,440,458,463,466,468,487,498,526

Prawn 3,27

Pulse 23,110

Pumpkin 5,6,12,121,180,459

# Q

Quinoa 5,6,11,12,13,134,136,144,156,157,173,402,461,462,486

# R

Rabbit 5,102

Raisins 10,351

Raspberry 8,10,237,361

Ratatouille 8,235

Rice 3,4,6,8,10,11,12,13,14,24,38,39,48,49,50,60,145,271,338,368,372,373,441,447,463,464,513

Ricotta 9,310

Rigatoni 14,535

Roast lamb 284

Rosemary 4,6,9,13,89,170,285,287,288,289,313,469,470,495

# S

Saffron 14,530

Sage 9,289

Salad 3,5,6,7,9,10,11,12,13,14,22,133,134,135,136,137,138,139,140,141,142,143,144,145,146,147,148,149,150,151,152,153,154,155,156,157,158,159,206,252,326,332,334,335,337,338,339,341,343,345,346,348,349,350,351,354,357,358,359,361,363,365,366,368,369,370,371,372,373,374,381,384,385,386,387,388,389,390,392,393,394,395,396,397,398,399,400,401,402,405,408,409,411,414,422,424,428,430,431,432,433,435,439,440,441,442,445,446,447,449,452,453,454,456,

457,458,460,461,462,463,466,471,477,478,480,483,486,487,488,490,492,493,494,496,497,498,501,503,505,507,512,513,526,527,528

Salmon 6,7,8,9,173,217,220,221,222,232,247,260,275,291,292

Salsa 4,7,9,11,12,13,71,183,322,397,436,437,470

Salt 149,164,211,233,236,238,244,279,299,309,321,322,337,343,359,367,373,422,450,465,535

Sausage 6,7,9,14,178,206,293,294,316,517

Savory 9,13,295,471,472

Seafood 7,8,227,244,261

Seasoning 14,252,518

Sirloin 6,9,172,298

Snapper 8,266

Soup 10,13,14,350,493,508,511,512,516,519,522,525,526

Spaghetti 3,4,5,7,8,9,43,49,92,100,208,209,246,255,303

Spinach 3,4,5,6,7,8,9,10,12,13,14,31,38,39,50,51,57,76,94,104,105,106,107,149,210,237,243,308,309,310,311,312,327,338,356,366,367,450,464,476,477,478,479,498,501,526

Squash 3,6,7,8,9,10,11,13,49,167,177,209,255,298,303,340,404,405,484,485

Squid 14,519

Steak 6,7,9,155,189,214,218,222,282,295,311

Stew 3,6,7,8,9,12,14,42,165,179,185,230,236,244,253,261,268,297,305,323,324,325,328,329,442,513,514,520,525,526

Strawberry 7,13,193,481

Stuffing 4,8,82,232,241

Sugar 4,6,55,149,180,192,200,253,259,264,283,348,355,363,374,383,386,393,397,400,432,452,466,468,497

Swordfish 5,9,96,317,318,319

Syrup 113,118,128,129,132

# T

Tabasco 520

Taco 7,189,211,224

Tahini 3,5,13,48,98,489

Tangerine 13,489

Tapenade 9,10,12,320,331,443

Tarragon 7,9,221,321

Tea 116,123

Thyme 9,13,211,289,492

Tilapia 6,8,162,264

Tomato 3,4,5,6,7,9,10,11,12,13,14,27,36,37,41,49,75,80,98,104,107,140,143,151,154,173,190,293,295,311,312,315,318,324,332,338,343,345,350,352,359,360,369,377,381,399,400,409,410,414,452,484,485,486,487,491,492,493,494,495,496,523,528

Tortellini 10,11,14,343,400,507

Turkey 4,5,6,7,8,9,52,63,82,83,110,161,200,211,241,264,327

# V

Vegan 5,111,115

Vegetables 3,4,6,9,10,12,13,37,40,44,60,142,303,319,353,426,489,491

Vegetarian 3,5,13,45,111,329,498

Venison 5,112

Vinegar 166

# W

Walnut 5,6,11,13,115,157,383,500,501

Watermelon 5,13,122,502

Wine 7,192

Worcestershire sauce 134,177,217,233,237,249,273,279,282,293,295,307,316,329,501

Wraps 10,11,12,365,412,455

# Z
Zest 9,13,85,252,317,354,505
# L
lasagna 83,84

# Conclusion

Thank you again for downloading this book!

I hope you enjoyed reading about my book!

If you enjoyed this book, please take the time to share your thoughts and post a review on Amazon. It'd be greatly appreciated!

Write me an honest review about the book – I truly value your opinion and thoughts and I will incorporate them into my next book, which is already underway.

Thank you!

If you have any questions, **feel free to contact at:** *author@parsniprecipes.com*

Lisa Morales

parsniprecipes.com

Printed in Poland
by Amazon Fulfillment
Poland Sp. z o.o., Wrocław

64822220R00304